Foundation Game Design
with ActionScript 3.0
Second Edition

Rex van der Spuy

friendsof

DESIGNER TO DESIGNER™

an Apress company*

Foundation Game Design with ActionScript 3.0, Second Edition

ISBN-13 (pbk): 978-1-4302-3993-2
ISBN-13 (electronic): 978-1-4302-3994-9

Distributed to the book trade worldwide by Springer Science+Business Media New York, 233 Spring Street, 6th Floor, New York, NY 10013. Phone 1-800-SPRINGER, fax (201) 348-4505, e-mail orders-ny@springer-sbm.com, or visit www.springeronline.com.

For information on translations, please e-mail rights@apress.com or visit www.apress.com.

Apress and friends of ED books may be purchased in bulk for academic, corporate, or promotional use. eBook versions and licenses are also available for most titles. For more information, reference our Special Bulk Sales–eBook Licensing web page at www.apress.com/bulk-sales.

Any source code or other supplementary materials referenced by the author in this text is available to readers at www.apress.com. For detailed information about how to locate your book's source code, go to www.apress.com/source-code/.

Credits

President and Publisher: Paul Manning	**Copy Editor:** Mary Behr
Lead Editor: Ben Renow-Clarke	**Compositor:** Apress (Brigid Duffy)
Technical Reviewers: Joshua Freeney	**Production Editor:** Brigid Duffy
Editorial Board: Steve Anglin, Mark Beckner, Ewan Buckingham, Gary Cornell, Morgan Ertel, Jonathan Gennick, Jonathan Hassell, Robert Hutchinson, Michelle Lowman, James Markham, Matthew Moodie, Jeff Olson, Jeffrey Pepper, Douglas Pundick, Ben Renow-Clarke, Dominic Shakeshaft, Gwenan Spearing, Matt Wade, Tom Welsh	**Indexer:** BIM Indexing & Proofreading Services **Artist:** SPi Global **Cover Image Artist:** Corné van Dooren
Coordinating Editor: Kelly Moritz	**Cover Designer:** Anna Ishchenko

Dedicated to my father, Mani van der Spuy,
without whom this book would not have been written.
Thanks, Dad, for always believing in me.

Contents

ABOUT THE AUTHOR

Rex van der Spuy is a freelance interactive media designer specializing in Flash/AS3.0 game design, interface design, and ActionScript programming. He currently divides his time between Canada, India, and South Africa. When not coding video games, he wanders around the world playing the sitar.

ABOUT THE TECHNICAL REVIEWER

Josh Freeney is currently an instructor for the Digital Animation and Game Design program at Ferris State University in Grand Rapids, Michigan. He teaches Flash game development classes focused on rapid agile production with maximum reusability, and he has spoken at the Michigan Flash Festival. He likes board games, hiking, sleeping in, and anything Lego. He continues to consult with anyone anywhere who has a Flash problem that needs fixing.

ABOUT THE COVER IMAGE DESIGNER

 **Corné van Dooren** designed the front cover image for this book. After taking a break from friends of ED to create a new design for the Foundation series, he worked at combining technological and organic forms, with the results now appearing on the cover of this and other books.

Corné spent his childhood drawing on everything at hand and then began exploring the infinite world of multimedia—and his journey of discovery hasn't stopped since. His mantra has always been "the only limit to multimedia is the imagination," a saying that keeps him moving forward constantly.

Corné works for many international clients, writes features for multimedia magazines, reviews and tests software, authors multimedia studies, and works on many other friends of ED books. If you like Corné's work, be sure to check out his chapter in *New Masters of Photoshop: Volume 2* (friends of ED, 2004). You can see more of his work (and contact him) at his web site, www.cornevandooren.com.

ACKNOWLEDGMENTS

My unending gratitude to Ben, Josh, and Kelly for the vision, dedication, hard work, and encouragement that made this book a reality.

Thanks to Preston and Rahle at the world's most innovative interactive media company, PixelProject, for hosting my sojourn in Cape Town, and for all your inspiration and friendship.

This book was written in remote areas of the Himalayas with scant access to the Internet (or even electricity). I wish to send out a big thank you to the people of Ladakh, India and Nepal for their incredible generosity and graciousness while I was working on this project.

(And, for the one person out there who might find this noteworthy: Yes, it is possible to walk 9 days to the Annapurna glacier in flip-flops and program a video game 1500 meters above your laptop's 3000 meter maximum specified operating altitude.)

INTRODUCTION

So you want to make a video game. Where do you start? What do you need to learn? To whom can you look for help?

If you've ever asked any of these questions, you know how difficult it is to find the answers. I asked myself these same questions many years ago in a little village outside of Bangalore, India, where I was teaching programming and interactive media at an international school. All my students were playing games and they all wanted to create games, but there were no comprehensive books or online resources available on how to do this.

A little bit of research turned up something surprising: not only did basic game design require relatively little programming knowledge but the same set of techniques could also be used over and over again in different contexts to create completely different kinds of games. It was fun to do, the results were immediate, and it was a great creative outlet. The result of this research was an in-house textbook on game design that formed the basis of three high school–level courses and inspired the writing of this book.

That was back in the now almost prehistoric days of Flash 4 and 5, when the ActionScript programming language was still in version 1.0 and Flash had some wonderful built-in interactive tutorials that guided new users every step of the way. It seemed as if everyone was a beginner in those days, so it was relatively easy to find books and tutorials that assumed the reader had no background knowledge.

ActionScript is now in version 3.0, and things are not so easy. The ActionScript language has become much more powerful but also much more complex. Many of the resources that you'll find for AS3.0 are focused on that complexity, and it's harder and harder for beginners with little previous programming experience to get a comprehensive foothold to start learning. The irony of all this is that AS3.0 actually makes it much *easier* to build games than in the days of AS1.0. This book strips away the apparent complexity of AS3.0 and gets to the core of what you need to know to make games. It's fun and easy, and anyone can do it.

Game design is a fantastic thing, and what you're about to learn is as close to creating magic as the real world allows. Hang on for a wild ride—you'll be amazed by what you'll start producing very quickly.

About the second edition

The first edition of this book, *Foundation Game Design with Flash*, was all about how to make games using Flash Professional software. It used to be that using Flash Professional was the only way to make Flash games, and even when other technologies gradually became available, it was still the best way. In the almost three years since that first edition was published, AS3.0 has taken on a life of its own—it's become the best cross-platform development tool for making games for the Web and for desktop and mobile devices. It's also the easiest to learn for beginners, and it has most comprehensive and best integrated set of tools for making games than any other single technology. This edition shows you how to build games using pure AS3.0 code and whole host of complementary technologies for the greatest flexibility in the development process. Making games with AS3.0 has never been more fun, and the potential audience that you can reach with your games has never been wider.

Layout conventions

To keep this book as clear and easy to follow as possible, the following text conventions are used throughout:

Important words or concepts are normally highlighted on the first appearance in *italic type*.

Code is presented in `fixed-width font`.

New or changed code is normally presented in **`bold fixed-width font`**.

Pseudo-code and variable input are written in *`italic fixed-width font`*.

Menu commands are written in the form Menu ➤ Submenu ➤ Submenu.

When I want to draw your attention to something, I've highlighted it like this:

Ahem, don't say I didn't warn you.

Sometimes code won't fit on a single line in a book. When this happens, I use an arrow like this: ➥.

```
This is a very, very long section of code that should be written on ➥
the same line without a break.
```

Chapter 1

Programming Foundations: How To Make A Video Game

Congratulations on picking up this book! Video game design is one of the most interesting and creative things you can do with a computer. You're about to embark on a remarkable journey, and this book will guide you every step of the way.

So how do you make a video game? Although there are probably as many ways to make games as there are readers of this book, a good place to start is with a technology called **Flash and ActionScript**. Not only is it easy to learn how to make games with these technologies, but you can also use them to produce games of great complexity and professional quality if you have the time and imagination. You can also publish your games for desktop computers, laptops, the Internet, mobile phones, and tablets without having to learn any additional skills. And all the skills you'll acquire while making games with Flash and ActionScript can be directly applied to game design using other technologies if you want to take your learning further.

Learning game design with Flash and ActionScript is really a two- step process.

- You need to learn how to make graphics and illustrations for your games. This is commonly done with graphic design software such as Adobe Photoshop, Illustrator, Flash Professional, or open source software such as GIMP (GNU Image Manipulation Program).

- You also need to learn a **programming language** called **ActionScript**. A programming language is a kind of language, similar to English, that we humans use to communicate with computers.

1

When you've created you graphics and programmed your game, the underlying technology, which you will learn all about in this book, then puts it all together to make your game work.

There are two common ways to make games with Flash and ActionScript.

- You can use software called Flash Professional, which is made by Adobe. This software allows you to create all the visual graphics for your game and perform all the computer programming using only one piece of software.

- The second approach is to create the graphics for your game using any graphic design or illustration software you like, and then use a **computer programming code editor**, such as Flash Builder or Flash Develop to program the ActionScript code to make your game work.

This book takes the second approach. It's much more flexible because it allows you to choose any graphic design or programming software you're comfortable using. It also means that the skills you learn won't be tied to any particular version of Adobe's Flash Professional software, which is subject to frequent change, and it frees you from the considerable cost of buying or upgrading it, which can be a significant barrier for someone just starting out in game design. It used to be that the only way to make Flash games was with Adobe's Flash Professional software, but this is fortunately no longer the case. There are now far more flexible tools available for making Flash games, and this book will show you how to use them.

Tens of thousands of people around the world have made a career out of designing games with Flash. With this book and a little bit of practice, you could become one of them.

Basic requirements

Surprisingly, video game design can be a relatively low-tech affair. Here's the basic equipment you'll need to make use of this book.

1. A computer

You need a reasonably up-to-date computer, either running Windows or the latest version of Mac OS X.

2. Graphic design software

You need graphic design software, such as Photoshop, Photoshop Elements, Illustrator, or the free, open source GIMP. Photoshop is the most widely used graphic design software on the planet, so it's extremely useful to learn how to use it; however, it's very expensive. You can download **Photoshop** from Adobe's website at

www.adobe.com/products/photoshop.html

You could also make all your game graphics using **Adobe Illustrator**, and indeed most of the game graphics in this book were created using it. It's unfortunately also quite expensive, but it's definitely worth making the long term investment of purchasing it and learning how to use it if you're serious about game design because it's probably the overall best illustration software available. You can find Adobe Illustrator at `www.adobe.com/products/photoshop.html`

A much cheaper alternative to Illustrator or Photoshop is **Photoshop Elements**. Elements has all the functionality of the full version of Photoshop without some of the high-end professional features. For creating game graphics, you probably won't need any of those high-end features, most of which are specialized for photography and print production. Photoshop Elements may be a very good choice. You can download and purchase it from

`www.adobe.com/products/photoshopel/`

Or you could save your money and download a free copy of **GIMP**. GIMP does almost everything that Photoshop does for the purposes of making game graphics. The one big disadvantage is that the menus and windows are very different to Photoshop's, so you'll find it very difficult to follow the instructions in this book. Happily, there's a good solution to this problem. You can install a software plug-in for GIMP called **GIMPshop**. GIMPshop makes GIMP look and function exactly like Photoshop. That means that you can follow all the instructions in this book—and in any other Photoshop tutorials—without having to spend a penny on the somewhat prohibitive cost of Photoshop.

You'll find a free copy of GIMP at

`www.gimp.org/`

And you'll find GIMPshop at

`www.gimpshop.com/`

Another option is that you can create your game graphics using free web-based software, such as Aviary.

`www.aviary.com/`

Aviary has many of the same basic features as Photoshop and Illustrator, and it doesn't require you to purchase or install anything. If you don't have any other graphics design or illustration software installed on your computer, and aren't yet sure about purchasing any, Aviary may be an excellent place to start.

3. Computer programming software

You'll also need computer programming software, either **Flash Builder** or **Flash Develop**. These pieces of software are known as **IDEs** (integrated development environments). Don't let that term scare you! They are just text editors or word processors that are specialized to help you write and edit computer programming code. They will also put all the pieces of your finished game together for you, usually at the click of a button.

At the time of writing, Flash Builder is free if you're a student or an unemployed developer. But if you're not either of those, it may worth paying full price for it because it will save you a great deal of time and trouble. Flash Builder currently comes in three versions: Educational, Standard, and Premium. The Standard version is all you'll need to make use of this book. You can find out if you qualify for the free Educational version of Flash Builder by visiting Adobe's educational web site and following the links.

www.adobe.com/devnet/edu.html

You can download and buy the Standard version of Flash Builder from

www.adobe.com/products/flash-builder-standard.html

If you're running Windows, consider using the completely free and superb Flash Develop. It will not be difficult for you to use the techniques in this book with Flash Develop, if that's what you prefer to use. All the game design techniques and programming code in this book are compatible with both Flash Builder and Flash Develop. However, if you do decide to use Flash Develop, you'll need to make a little more effort to install and use it. Some aspects of the installation and configuration can be a little tricky, so don't consider starting with it unless you're highly computer literate. You can download Flash Develop from

www.flashdevelop.org

If you decide to use Flash Develop, you'll also need to download and install two additional software components. First, you need Adobe's free **Flex SDK** (software development kit). The Flex SDK is actually the brains behind what makes all your Flash games work. You can download the latest version from Adobe's web site at

http://opensource.adobe.com/wiki/display/flexsdk/Flex+SDK

You will also need the **debug version** of Adobe's Flash Player software. You'll find it at

http://www.adobe.com/support/flashplayer/downloads.html

Download the Flash Player version for your system that's called a **content debugger**. The Flash Player is the software that actually runs your games. You need the special debug version so that Flash Develop can tell you if you've made any mistakes in your programming code.

However, if you already have another version Adobe's Flash Player on your computer, it's wise to first uninstall it before installing the new debug version. Doing so can prevent some quirky bugs from occurring. You can download a Flash Player uninstaller for Windows from

http://kb2.adobe.com/cps/141/tn_14157.html

If you need a Flash Player uninstaller for Mac OSX, you'll find it at

http://kb2.adobe.com/cps/909/cpsid_90906.html

After you've uninstalled your current version of the Flash Player, install the new debug version.

There are very many other IDEs besides Flash Builder and Flash Develop that you could use to write your ActionScript programs, such as **Eclipse** (for Windows and Mac OSX), **TextMate,** or **XCode** (only for Mac OSX). Or, with a bit of effort you could also use the humble **Notepad** (Windows) or **TextEdit** (Mac OSX) applications. All of these will require a bit of research on your part to set up and use to make Flash games, but many professional Flash game designers use them exclusively. I don't recommend any of them if you're just learning to program, but you might want to look into them once you have a bit more experience.

Adobe Flash Professional

Optionally, you could also use also use Adobe's **Flash Professional** to make both the graphics for your games and write the programming code in a single piece of software. The book's bonus download chapter, "Flash Animation and Publishing Your Games" will show you how to do this. Download Flash Professional from

`www.adobe.com/cfusion/tdrc/index.cfm?product=flash`

Making games exclusively with Flash Professional was the subject of the first edition of this book, *Foundation Game Design with Flash*. Using Flash Professional is still a great way to make Flash games, and it's still possibly the quickest and easiest. But learning how to make games without it gives you a number of advantages. It means your skills won't be tied to one particular pieces of software or one version of a piece of software. It means that you're free to choose whichever software you like to program your game and make your graphics in. It also means that you'll be developing skills and work styles that will be easy to transfer to other game design or programming technologies when you're ready to take that step. This is the more flexible approach I'll be taking in this edition of the book.

The software used in this book

The examples and instructions in this book use Flash Builder, Photoshop (or Photoshop Elements), and Illustrator. These programs were picked because they're widely available, easy to use, don't require any complicated installation or configuration, and are common to both Windows and Macintosh. As a bare minimum, these are the only pieces of software you'll need to make good use of this book.

Chapter 2 includes an introduction on to how to use Photoshop. You'll learn how to make game graphics using Illustrator in Chapter 7.

If you choose to use any other graphic design or programming software, make sure you read its documentation carefully and are comfortable using it before you start working through the projects in this book.

Things you need to know

This book assumes that you haven't had any experience making graphics for games or any experience with computer programming. You'll go on a step-by- step journey through these fascinating worlds. If you want to learn to design games from scratch and know absolutely nothing about it, this book is all you need to get started.

That said, game development and the ActionScript programming language are huge topics that you could easily spend a lifetime studying. No one book can provide all the answers to all the questions you might have while you're learning. If you've never had any experience with professional graphic design software, I highly recommend that you spend a bit of extra time learning how to use Photoshop, GIMP, or Illustrator before you proceed much further in this book. You're going to be making lots and lots of graphics and illustrations for your games, and you'll have much more confidence when tackling the programming side of game design if you're comfortable making graphics. Spend a weekend tinkering around with Photoshop or

GIMP, and you'll have your head well above water when you get to game programming. Here are some resources to help get you started.

If you're using Photoshop, read through the documentation and work through some of the exercises and sample projects in Adobe's online help system. (To access them, select Help ↗ Photoshop Help from Photoshop's menu.)

If you're using GIMP with the GIMPshop plug-in, you can follow any tutorials intended for Photoshop. A good place to start is Adobe's "Getting Started" tutorial site, which contains many helpful videos on basic Photoshop use. Go to

www.adobe.com/support/photoshop/gettingstarted/

A web search for "Photoshop tutorials for beginners" will also turn up a voluminous trove of tutorial sites, too numerous to mention here, but many of which are excellent.

But, hey, if you want to dive into the deep end right away, I'm with you! This book is a great a place to start and is the only resource you need.

And the things you don't need to know

Perhaps even more enlightening is what you *don't* have to know to be able to make use of this book.

- Math (not much, anyway!)
- Computer programming
- Web site design
- Graphic design
- Practically anything else!

In fact, I'll even allow you to say, "I hate computers," or let you indulge in a fantasy of hurtling a particularly heavy blunt object at your monitor. Rest assured that I have shared exactly those same feelings at some point or another!

It's all about programming

Most of the content of this book is about how to write computer programs. Apart from a brief introduction on how to make simple game graphics using Photoshop and Illustrator, I'm going to leave it to you to explore the graphics and illustration side of game design, which is well covered in other resources.

So what is a computer program?

A computer program is like a movie script that tells the characters and objects in your games what they should do and how to behave under certain conditions. For example, suppose that you designed a game in which the player must use the arrow keys on the keyboard to guide a duck through a pond infested with hungry snapping turtles. How will the duck know that it must move when the arrow keys are pressed? You need to write a program to tell the duck to do this.

ActionScript is the name of the computer programming language that you'll be using to write the programs for your games. It's a very sophisticated and powerful language, closely related to Java. ActionScript is currently in version 3 and is known as AS3.0 for short. It's a wonderful language for learning to program because of the following:

- It is completely integrated into Flash Builder and Flash Develop, which means you can often see the results of your code on the screen right away. This makes the experience of programming very concrete, very satisfying, and far less abstract than learning to program in many other programming languages.

- Adobe, the creator of AS3.0, has done a lot of work to make the experience of programming with AS3.0 extremely user friendly. It has simplified the technical hurdles to getting programs up and running as a one-click process.

- AS3.0 is a "real" programming language, like Java or C++. The great thing about learning to program with AS3.0 is that the skills you learn will be directly applicable to the study of other programming languages, and you'll be able to build on these skills for years to come. ActionScript is here to stay, and you can grow with it.

- Games and programs created with AS3.0 are *cross-platform*, which means that they run on any computer operating system (Windows, Mac OSX, or Linux), as well as mobile platforms like iOS and Android, as long as that system has Adobe's free Flash Player software installed. This is a huge benefit because it means you only need to learn one technology, Flash, rather than several. Flash and AS3.0 are currently the only technologies that allows you to publish to all these platforms without requiring you to learn anything new. The Flash Player is one of most widely installed pieces of software in history, so you're guaranteed a potentially huge audience for your games without having to rewrite the programming code from scratch for each system.

- There is a huge community of friendly AS3.0 developers on the Internet who have devoted vast amounts of time to writing tutorials and helping others in online forums and discussion boards. If you get stuck while writing a program, just ask a question on one of the many Flash and ActionScript discussion boards, and you'll surely get a helpful reply.

Programming? But I'm terrible at math!

So is the author of this book! One of the biggest misunderstandings that nonprogrammers have about computer programming is that programming is some kind of math. It's not. It might look the same on the surface, and some of its style has been borrowed from mathematics for matters of convenience, but the whole underlying system is completely different.

That's not to say you won't be using any math in these lessons—you will. How much? You'll use addition, subtraction, multiplication, division, and some very basic algebra (the kind you might remember from fifth grade). That's as complex as the math gets, and you don't have to any of that math yourself. You just need to know how to tell AS3.0 to do it for you. It's just like using a calculator.

But it certainly can get more complicated if you want it to. In later chapters you'll use a bit of trigonometry to achieve some specific motion effects. However, you won't need to necessarily understand the mechanics of how trigonometry is achieving those effects—just how to use it in the context of your game. This book is written largely from a non-math point of view, so mathophobes of the world are welcome!

> Note: Although you certainly don't need to use much math to start building great games right away, acquiring a deeper understanding of the mathematical possibilities of programming with AS3.0 will definitely give you many more options as a game developer. Two very comprehensive and highly readable books that cover this area in much more detail than the scope of this book allows are Foundation ActionScript Animation: Making Things Move! by Keith Peters and Flash Math Creativity by various authors. Both books are published by friends of ED and are perfect companions to Foundation Game Design with Flash. You can apply all the techniques they discuss directly to the game projects in this book.

I already know how to program!

This book has been written to be as accessible as possible for beginners and doesn't assume any programming background. However, many of you might be experienced programmers who are reading this book to find out how you can use your existing AS3.0 skills to create games. Don't worry; although the earlier chapters are definitely geared toward people new to Flash and ActionScript, later chapters deal with fairly advanced areas of object-oriented programming that provide quite a bit of meat for you to sink your programming teeth into.

If you are already a programmer, I recommend that you flip ahead to Chapter 4, which is the first chapter that uses programming techniques to build a complete game from beginning to end. If it seems a bit complex or if there are some terms and concepts you don't understand, step back by a chapter or two until you find your comfort level. Otherwise, if Chapter 4 seems like a good level for you, go for it! From a programming point of view, things get quite a bit more interesting from that chapter onward.

Many of the techniques involved in game design are quite specialized. Even though you might know quite a lot about ActionScript or programming, it's not always obvious how to use those skills to build games. The focus of this book is on the architecture of game design instead of the specific nuts and bolts of programming. If you have a lot of programming experience, this book will show you how you can use those skills within the context of completely developed games.

What kind of games can I make?

This book is about how to make two-dimensional action, adventure, and arcade games; it also touches on puzzle and logic games. Flash is a fantastic medium for creating these types of games. Each chapter guides you through every step of the design process, but the projects are very open-ended and encourage you to come up with your own original ways of using the techniques in your own games.

This book excludes 3D games because 3D is a large topic that deserves a whole book in its own right. The great thing is that most of the game design techniques you learn in the context of 2D, particularly how games are structured, can be applied directly to 3D games with little or no modification. To simplify the learning process and make sure the material is as focused and clear as it can be, however, I decided to stick to 2D games.

Learning new terms

Like any large specialized field, programming comes with a lot of new terminology to learn. This book will try to sidestep as much of the jargon as possible in favor of slightly longer and concrete descriptions. However, some terminology is so widely used that you should make an effort learn it because it may inhibit your further learning from other sources if you don't. This book will explain all new terms in the text.

Laying the foundation

As a game developer, you can think of yourself as an architect. All buildings of any size or shape have some fundamental things in common: they all have a foundation, walls, and a roof. No matter how big or small, humble or grand your house is, you need to dig a foundation, erect some walls, and put up a roof. After that you can start the really fun stuff: designing the interior layout, doing the landscaping, buying the furniture, and throwing a housewarming party.

Over the course of the rest of this chapter, you'll write a very simple program that will lay the foundation for all the games and programs you'll be creating in the rest of the book. If you haven't done any programming before or are just starting to get a grip on AS3.0, this chapter is for you.

If you have prior programming experience, you might want to jump ahead to the end of the chapter to see how much of the technical and conceptual material looks familiar. Make sure that you become acquainted with the structure you'll be using to build your games and programs, but feel free to skip this chapter if it all looks pretty straightforward.

In a tip-of-the hat to the history of computer programming, you'll write a program called a **Hello World program**. It is traditionally the first program that novice programmers write when learning a new programming language because it's the simplest complete program that can be written. It does something very simple; it just outputs the words "Hello World! Can you read this?" That's all!

The program might seem modest, but you will achieve two very important things by learning to write it.

- You'll build a robust and flexible system for programming that will become the core of all the projects in this book and probably hold you in good stead with your own projects for years to come.

- You'll complete a crash course in programming with AS3.0 that will lay the foundation for some of the very important concepts and techniques covered in later chapters.

Scared of programming? Ha! Not you! In this chapter, you'll grab the programming beast by the horns and wrestle it to the ground!

Using Flash Builder

Flash Builder is a comprehensive piece of software for writing AS3.0 programs and making Flash games. The next few sections will walk you through some of the basics of how to set it up and use it so that you have a solid basis for programming your games for the rest of the book.

If you are using a version of Flash Builder that came bundled with Adobe's Creative Suite 5.5, be aware that it's afflicted with a quirky bug. Flash Builder needs the debug version of the Flash Player software to show you whether there are any problems with your programs and to display special messages called **trace output**. The debug version of the Flash Player is installed automatically when you install Adobe Creative Suite, but some for strange reason, Flash Builder sometimes can't find it when you try to run your programs. Instead you'll get a message saying, "Installed Flash Player is not a debugger."

The solution to this is to uninstall the current version of the Flash Player, and then re-install the special debug version. To uninstall the current version, you need a special Flash Player uninstaller that you can download from Adobe's web site.

You can find Flash Player uninstaller for Windows at

`http://kb2.adobe.com/cps/141/tn_14157.html`

You can find Flash Player uninstaller for Mac OSX at

`http://kb2.adobe.com/cps/909/cpsid_90906.html`

Once you've uninstalled the current Flash Player, quit Flash Builder and your web browser if they are running, and then download and install the latest debug version of the Flash Player, which you'll find at

`www.adobe.com/support/flashplayer/downloads.html`

If you encountered this problem while working on a project, copy all your code from Flash Builder's code editing window, and paste it into a new ActionScript project with a new name. Everything should then work just fine.

Adobe publishes a comprehensive online manual on how to use Flash Builder. You can find it at

`http://help.adobe.com/en_US/flashbuilder/using/`

Make sure you refer to it if you have other questions about how to use it that are not covered in this chapter.

Setting up the work environment in Flash Builder

Before you start writing your Hello World program, let's make a few changes to the way Flash Builder is set up so that it's a bit easier to work with.

1. Launch Flash Builder. You'll see a start page that will look something like that in Figure 1-1.

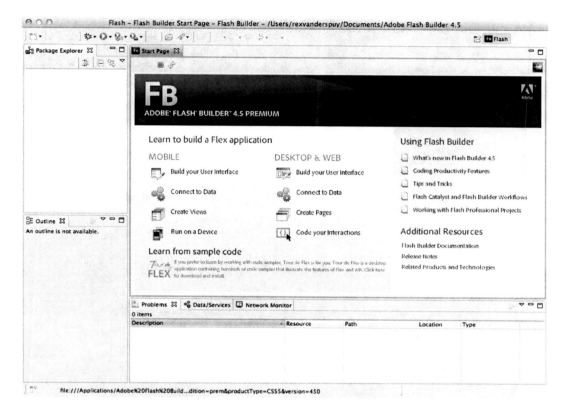

Figure 1-1. Flash Builder home page

Figure 1-1 shows what Flash Builder 4.5 looks like, which was the current version when this book was written.

> *If you're using a different, future version of Flash Builder, such as 5 or 6, some of the specifics described here might be slightly different, although the general concepts will be the same. If there's anything you can't figure out, make sure that you refer to Adobe's most recent documentation for the version you are using. You'll find it at* `http://help.adobe.com/en_US/flashbuilder/using/`.

If this is your first look at Flash Builder, don't let it intimidate you! You won't understand anything on this screen, but that's not important. You'll only need to use and understand about 5% of what Flash Builder is capable of to start making Flash games. That 5%, and more, will be covered in this chapter. The other 95% is specialized functionality that in all likelihood you may never need to worry about in your entire career as a game programmer.

Create a new, blank ActionScript project

You're now going to create your very first AS3.0 **project**. A project in Flash Builder is a collection of AS3.0 folders and files that contain all the programming code for your games. Flash Builder creates all the initial files and folders for you automatically. Here's how:

2. With Flash Builder still open, select File ↗ New, and choose ActionScript Project. Figure 1-2 illustrates what this looks like on Flash Builder running in Mac OSX.

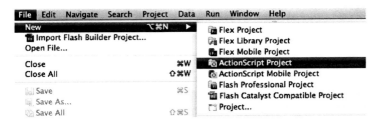

Figure 1-2. Create an ActionScript project

A New ActionScript Project dialog box opens, as shown in Figure 1-3.

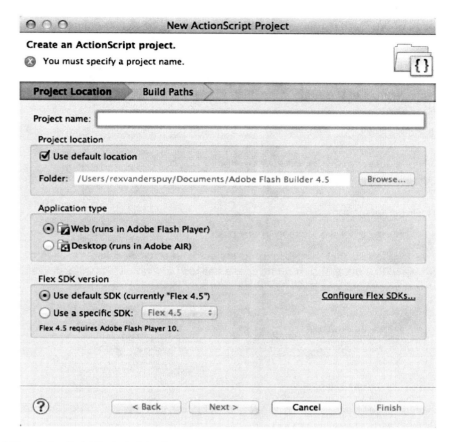

Figure 1-3. A New ActionScript Project dialog box

The first thing you need to do is give your project a name. You're going to call it "HelloWorld."

In the Project Name field, type "HelloWorld" (Figure 1-4). Notice that there is no space between the words "Hello" and "World." This is important and I'll explain why later.

Project name: HelloWorld

Figure 1-4. Name the project

If this is the first time you're running Flash Builder, you'll notice that the Use default location tick box is checked, and under it you will see something that looks like this:

```
/Users/rexvanderspuy/Documents/Adobe Flash Builder 4.5/HelloWorld
```

This is the location where Flash Builder will save your work. It will be slightly different on your computer, of course, but the main thing is that Flash Builder will save the HelloWorld project in a folder called Adobe Flash Builder 4.5 in your Documents folder.

Flash Builder automatically chooses this location for you, which may not be the most convenient place for you to save your work. Let's change it so that it saves the HelloWorld project in a folder called FlashGames.

Uncheck the Use default tick box if it's checked, as shown in Figure 1-5.

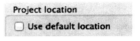

Figure 1-5. Don't use the default location.

You're now free to change the save location to any place in your computer that you choose.

Change the save location so that the HelloWorld project is in a folder called FlashGames, as shown in Figure 1-6. Note again that there should be no space between the words "Flash" and "Games." Figure 1-6 shows what the text field might look like.

Figure 1-6. A location of your own choosing

You can optionally use the Browse button to browse to any location on your hard drive where you would like your work to be saved.

3. Click the Finish button near the bottom right of the dialogue box (Figure 1-7).

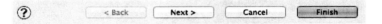

Figure 1-7. Click the Finish button.

As soon as you click the Finish button, Flash builder generates a new screen which will look something like Figure 1-8.

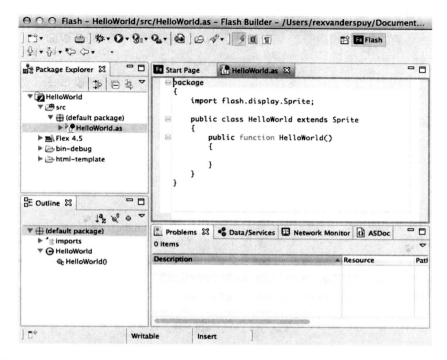

Figure 1-8. Project screen

This will look like a chaotic jumble of technical confusion if you are new to programming or Flash Builder. Think of it this way: you are really looking at a word processor for writing computer code. There are just lots of little buttons to help make your work easier, and I'll gradually introduce the how most of these work over the course of this book. By the end of this chapter, you'll understand almost everything about this screen.

The main thing that you need to focus on is the area where you'll be writing your code, which I've highlighted in Figure 1-9.

```
Start Page    HelloWorld.as  ✕

package
{
    import flash.display.Sprite;

    public class HelloWorld extends Sprite
    {
        public function HelloWorld()
        {

        }
    }
}
```

Figure 1-9. Area for writing code

This is where you will be writing all you computer code. Flash Builder has automatically filled this box with some computer code that it thinks might be a useful place for you to start. It actually is, but for the purposes of learning, I'm going to ask you to delete all of it so that you can start with a completely blank slate.

Select all the text in the code editing window, as shown in Figure 1-10.

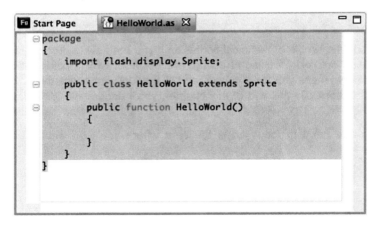

Figure 1-10. Select the canned code

Delete all of it so that the window is completely empty, as shown in Figure 1-11.

Figure 1-11. Completely blank code editing window

You now have a completely blank code editing window. This is where you will write your first computer program.

Next, you need to make a small change to Flash Builder's configuration to tell it to run your program directly in the Flash Player window, not the web browser.

Telling Flash Builder to run your programs in the Flash Player

When you create games with Flash Builder, it takes the programming code that you write in the editor window and plays it in the Flash Player software. The Flash Player software was installed on your computer automatically when you installed Flash Builder. However, when you first install Flash Builder, it's set up so that it runs the Flash Player inside a web browser. This is a slow and inefficient because every time you test your game you'll have wait for a browser window to pop open. It's much better if Flash Builder runs your game directly inside the Flash Player window. Fortunately, this is very easy to set up by making a small change to Flash Builder's configuration.

1. Select Project ↗ Properties from Flash Builder's main menu at the top of the screen, as shown in Figure 1-12.

Figure 1-12. Select the Properties option

    2.   A new Project Properties window will open. Select ActionScript Compiler from the menu on the left, and you should see the options appear on the right, as shown in Figure 1-13.

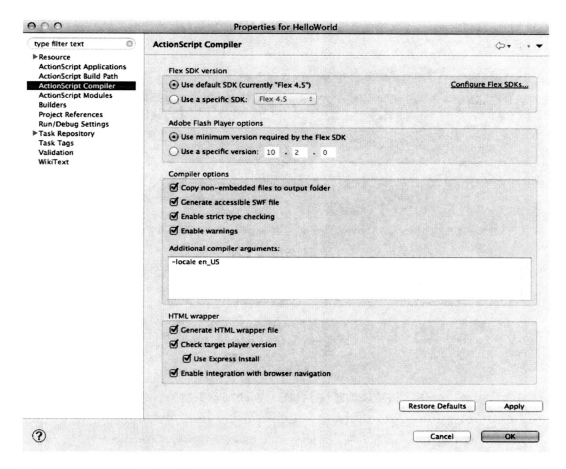

Figure 1-13. ActionScript Complier options

3.   Find the HTML wrapper section near the bottom of this screen. Uncheck the option called Generate HTML wrapper file. It should now look like Figure 1-14.

Figure 1-14. Don't generate a HTML wrapper file

This is the option that automatically opens your game in a web browser. By unchecking it, Flash Builder will open your game directly in the Flash Player.

4.   Select the OK button to save this change.

19

You're now ready to write your first AS3.0 computer program!

Writing your first program

You now have most of the pieces in place to begin writing your first program. In the next few steps, you'll do the following:

1. Learn how to make ActionScript files with the .as file extension.
2. Create a package that groups all the code neatly together.
3. Import graphics capabilities that you'll need to display text and images.
4. Create a class that is the first building block of your program.
5. Create a constructor method that triggers the first actions in your program to run.
6. Create a directive that is the actual action that you want your program to perform.
7. Import Flash's built-in Sprite class to help your program display its output.
8. Publish the finished Flash file to see the actual output of all your hard work.

This process might seem like a lot of work, but at the end of it you'll have a complete system in place that will form the basis for all the projects in the rest of the book and a flexible foundation for you to build your own programs and games.

ActionScript files and the .as file extension

An ActionScript computer program is what controls your entire game. It tells all the game characters and elements exactly how they should behave. ActionScript programs are the most important components of a game, and most of this book is devoted to explaining how to write and understand them.

An ActionScript program is nothing more than a text file containing special words and characters. When you write an ActionScript computer program, you're just creating a simple text file on your computer with a **.as** extension. Files with a .as extension are known as ActionScript files or AS files.

You can see this in Flash Builder by looking at the top of the code editing window. If you've followed the instructions in this chapter, the highlighted tab bar at the top of the code editing window will read HelloWorld.as. Figure 1-15 shows what this looks like.

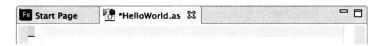

Figure 1-15. The highlighted tab bar at the top of the code editing window in Flash Builder tells you that you are creating an ActionScript file with a .as extension.

Look to the left of the code editing window and you'll find the Package Explorer, as shown in Figure 1-16. The HelloWorld.as file will be highlighted.

Figure 1-16. The Package Explorer shows you which files and folders are being used in your project.

The Package Explorer shows you all the files and folders that are being used in your ActionScript project. You don't need to worry about any of them for the moment except the HelloWorld.as file. It's important to know that the Package Explorer is actually showing you real files and folders that Flash Builder created automatically for you on your computer. The Package Explorer is telling you that the HelloWorld.as file is in a folder called src which in turn is in a folder called FlashGames.

Where are these folders and files on your computer?

You may recall that when you created the HelloWorld project in Flash Builder, you told it to save the project here:

`/Users/rexvanderspuy/Documents/FlashGames/HelloWorld`

That means that the HelloWorld project should be in a folder called FlashGames which, in turn, should be in the computer's Documents folder.

Is it really? Let's check.

Figure 1-17 shows you what I see when I open up the Documents folder in my computer.

Figure 1-17. The HelloWorld.as file and all the other ActionScript project files that Flash Builder needs were created for you automatically in the location that you specified.

Yes, it is!

The HelloWorld.as file is in a folder called src, which is short for **source files**. These are files that contain computer programming code. Traditionally, computer programmers keep their computer programs in a folder called src. All of your ActionScript programs will be stored in folders called src. Flash Builder does this for you automatically.

The src folder is, in turn, stored in a parent folder called HelloWorld, which is the name of your project. The HelloWorld folder is, in turn, stored in a folder called FlashGames.

So that means that the Package Explorer is showing you real files and folders that are stored on your computer. It's important to remember that whenever you make any changes to an AS file in Flash Builder's code editing window, you're making real changes to a real file that you can find in your computer.

I'll take that to go!

The previous section introduced the Package Explorer in Flash Builder. It helps you find all the files and folders you're using in your game project. But what is a package?

A package is the first fundamental building block of an AS3.0 program. It ties together all the bits of AS3.0 programming code and wraps all the code in a **package**. A package consists of three parts.

- **Keyword**: This keyword is called, conveniently enough, package. Keywords are special words that AS3.0 understands and that do a special job (such as creating a package!). When you type keywords in your program, Flash Builder colors them purple and blue so you can spot them in the code.

- **Identifier**: An identifier can any be any name you want to give the package. (It is optional, and you won't be using package identifiers in this book.)

- **Curly braces**: Curly braces look like this:

```
{
}
```

They are used to keep whatever is inside them together. You can think of them as the string that ties the package together. Here's a simple example:

```
{
  Anything between the two curly braces is being kept together
}
```

Let's create the package for your Hello World program.

1. Open the AS3.0 editing window that contains the blank HelloWorld.as file that you created in the previous steps.

2. Enter the following text into the editor window:

```
package
{

}
```

Your ActionScript editor window should now look like Figure 1-18.

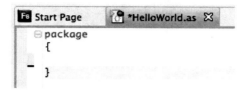

Figure 1-18. Create a package in the HelloWorld.as file.

> *Notice that you've left one blank line between the opening brace and the closing brace. This is because you're going to insert something into that line in the steps ahead.*

What you just created is something programmers call a **block statement**. Block statements define a particular section of the program and are used to group together all the code between the curly braces. In this case, the package block statement is completely empty because there's nothing between the curly braces except a blank line. But don't worry; it won't remain empty for long!

Before continuing, however, it's worth taking a closer look at exactly what you created.

As you started typing the code in the ActionScript editor window, you noticed that the word "package" was automatically colored purple by the editor. This is the editor's helpful way of telling you that what you've just typed is a keyword—a word it understands. Keywords are also known as *reserved words*. This means that those words belong to ActionScript and ActionScript alone; you can't use them as names for your packages, classes, variables, or methods (more on those soon). The package keyword simply tells Flash, "Hey, I'm creating a package!" Not too hard, is it?

After the package keyword come our dear little friends, the curly braces:
```
{
}
```

Cute, aren't they? At the moment, they're completely empty, they don't contain anything. But that's about to change very quickly. Soon you'll put something inside them {like this!}.

A little magic with sprites

Sprites are supernatural creatures—like elves, fairies, or nymphs—that dwell in woodland glens near the banks of forest streams and wizened old oak and willow trees. Strangely enough, they also live inside Flash and ActionScript. If you want to make text or graphics appear on the screen, you have to evoke AS3.0's sprites.

AS3.0's sprites live in something called the library. The library is a vast repository of computer code that was installed for you automatically when you installed Flash Builder. This library contains hundreds of bits of pre-written computer code that you can freely use in your own programs. The sprites are made out of bits of computer code in the library, and it's their job is to display text and graphics.

The library is actually part of something called the Flex SDK, which is the brains behind all your AS3.0 programs. When you request some code from the library, Flash Builder goes into the SDK, pokes around the stacks, and brings you what you're looking for so that you can use it in your programs. It contains the core computer code that makes your Flash games work. You'll find the SDK in your Flash Builder installation directory in a folder called sdks.

It's also important to know that Flash Builder is really just an interface for interacting with the SDK. All you really need to make Flash games is the SDK and the debug version of the Flash Player. As long as you've got those two components, you can use Flash Develop, TextMate, Eclipse, Xcode, or any other IDE to make Flash games.

A great thing about the SDK is that if Adobe brings out a new version of the SDK with some cool new features you want to use in your game, you just need to download and install that new SDK in Flash Builder. The SDK is free, and you won't need to spend any money to upgrade to a new version of Flash Builder.

The library is a big place, and it's divided into many different sections. Where do the sprites live? They live in a section of the library called **display**, and that in turn is in a bigger section of the library called **flash**. You can find them using these directions:

```
flash.display.Sprite
```

The dots between each word indicate a new section of the library. This shows that the display section is part of the flash section, and the Sprite section is part of the display section. This is like saying, "Start at the flash section, then follow the signs to the display section. In the display section you'll find the sprites." But that's not enough. You have to tell your program to explicitly invoke the sprites using a special keyword called import. The import keyword is used to bring code out of the library so that you can use it in your program.

Here's how to import a sprite:

```
import flash.display.Sprite;
```

This instructs the program to go and get a Sprite from the library in the flash.display section. This line of code is called an **import statement**. You'll be using many import statements in your AS3.0 programs and games when you want to use specialized code from the library.

Notice that at the very end of the import statement is a semicolon (;). This is a bit of programming punctuation that means "Do what I've just told you to!" You'll see much more of the semicolon in the examples ahead.

Also, very importantly, notice that the "S" in Sprite is capitalized. I'll explain exactly why later in the book, but for now just know that when you use the word Sprite in your AS3.0 programs, it must be capitalized.

Now that you know what a Sprite is, where to find it, and the line of code that you need to write to use it in your program, go and get yourself a Sprite!

1. Enter the following text in bold in the code editing window. Make sure that you enter it *between* the two curly braces.

```
package
{
  import flash.display.Sprite;
}
```

Notice that this new text is indented from the left margin. The code editor does this for you automatically when you add the new text. The code examples in this book use indent levels of two spaces, but the ActionScript editor window indents your code by four spaces, which is just fine.

The indentation shows that the new code you just added is *inside* the package's curly braces. Very soon you'll see how important it is to indent your code like this.

You can force the indentation of any line of code by pressing the Tab key.

You now have the magic of AS30's Sprites at your disposal to display text and graphics!

Your code editing window should now look like Figure 1-19.

Figure 1-19. Import a Sprite from the library to help you display text and images.

Don't skip class!

Now that you've created a package and imported a Sprite, the next step is to create a **class** inside that package. You can think of a class as a basic building block for creating an ActionScript program.

2. With your ActionScript editor window still open, add the following text in bold directly inside the package's curly braces:

```
package
{
  import flash.display.Sprite;

  public class HelloWorld extends Sprite
  {
  }
}
```

There's one blank line after the import statement and before the new code. This is optional, but as you'll see in later examples, it will make your program a little easier to read.

As with the import statement, the new code is indented from the left margin to show that it's inside the package's curly braces.

Figure 1-20 shows what your code editing window should now look like.

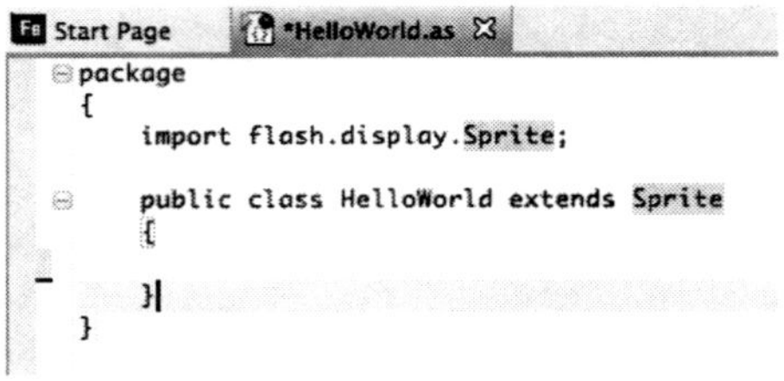

Figure 1-20. Create a class inside the package.

So what have you just done?

You've created a class called HelloWorld. You've created it inside the package. The words `public`, `class`, and `extends` will be colored blue and purple to show you that they're reserved keywords that AS3.0 understands.

Any ActionScript program you write must have at least one class, but most of the programs and games you'll be building in this book will have many. Take a quick look at the new code.

```
public class HelloWorld extends Sprite
{
}
```

This code is called a **class definition**. Just like the package, a class definition has a pair of empty braces hanging there in space. This shows you that, like the package, it's also a block statement. Those braces are empty at the moment, so the class can't do anything yet. That will change very soon.

A class definition does three main things.

- It creates the class. The keyword `class` tells Flash that you are creating a class. Simple enough!

- It gives the class some rules to follow. This should be obvious: how many of you have been in a class without rules? This code tells Flash that the class you're creating is **public**. This means that the information it contains can be shared by any other classes that are part of the same package or part of any other packages your program might be using. The information the class contains is freely available to all. (Although most of this book uses public classes, sometimes you'll want to prevent classes from sharing information, much like a school football team wouldn't want to share its strategy with a competing school. In such cases, you would define a class as **internal**. Internal classes share their information only with other classes that reside in the same package.)

- It gives the class an identifier, a name, which can be any name you choose. In this case, the class is called HelloWorld.

You're not experiencing déjà vu! You have seen the phrase "HelloWorld" before. It's the name of the AS file that you're working on: HelloWorld.as. This is no coincidence. When you create a class, it has to be saved in a file that has an identical name to the class name. For every new class you create, you must create a new AS file that shares the same class name.

- Finally it **extends** another class. This means that it's using some other class to help it do its work. In this case, it's using the magic of your infamous Sprite that you imported in the previous line of code. The keyword extends is telling the HelloWorld class to use the magic of Sprite to make text and images visible.

There's a lot going on here, so let's look at this new line of code and simplify it in plain English so you can better grasp what it is saying.

```
public class HelloWorld extends Sprite
{
}
```

It's saying this: "Make a public class that other code you write can easily access. The name of this new class is HelloWorld. It extends another class called Sprite, which gives it the magical ability to display text and images."

Figure 1-21 illustrates what this new code means.

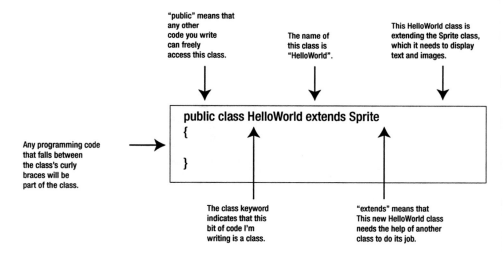

Figure 1-21. The class will contain most of your program's code, the core of your games and programs, between its two curly braces.

The class definition's poor little curly braces are still empty. Let's put them to use!

Using the constructor method

The **constructor method** is the section of the program that makes things happen. Specifically, it throws the class into action as soon as the class is told to start working. Any programming code it contains is run instantly. If the class definition alone is just an empty shell, the constructor method is like its heart and lungs.

3. Let's create the constructor method for the HelloWorld class. Add the code in bold to the code you already wrote.

```
package
{
  import flash.display.Sprite;

  public class HelloWorld extends Sprite
  {
    public function HelloWorld()
    {

    }
  }
}
```

Your ActionScript editing window should now look like Figure 1-22.

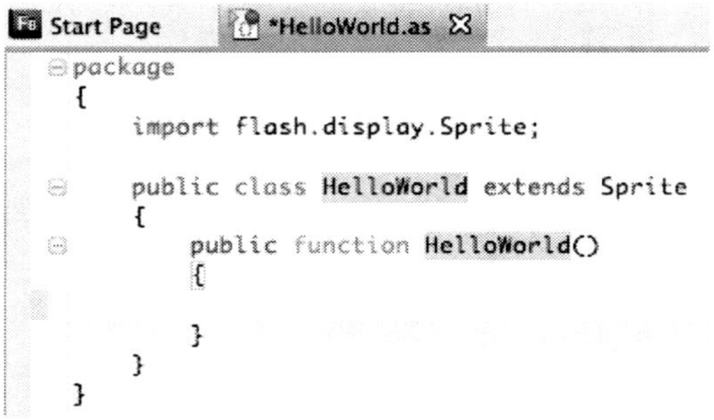

Figure 1-22. Add the constructor method inside the class.

As you can see, the constructor method is simply another block statement with empty curly braces that looks an awful lot like the class definition. In fact, it has the same name: HelloWorld. This is no accident: all classes need to have constructor methods that are named exactly the same as the class name.

The other thing you'll recognize is the keyword public.

```
public function HelloWorld()
{
}
```

As with the class definition, using the word public tells Flash that the constructor method is freely available to be used by different classes from different packages. (A strange quirk of the AS3.0 language, however, is that constructor methods can only ever be public.)

One new thing here is the function keyword.

```
public function HelloWorld()
{
}
```

It tells Flash that you're creating a **function definition**. Function definitions are simply block statements that perform actions. They do all the work in your program. You can think of function definitions as dutiful servants who snap to attention with a prearranged set of chores as soon as you call on them. The constructor method, which will always be the first function definition you write when you create a class, has the special job of running any actions it contains immediately—as soon as the class is called upon and before any other methods you might be using are put to work. The constructor method is a bit like the head servant who's up at the crack of dawn, gets all the other servants out of bed, and greets you with a fresh pot of tea and the morning paper before you've even found your slippers.

The last thing you should notice about the constructor method are the parentheses after the method name, which are highlighted here in bold:

```
HelloWorld()
```

Those empty parentheses allow you to provide the method with extra information, known as **parameters**, if the method needs it. You'll look at method parameters in detail fairly soon, but for now you just need to know that you must provide a set of parentheses when creating a function definition, even if those parentheses are empty.

Aligning code

You might have noticed an interesting pattern developing in the format of the code. Like a set of hollow wooden Russian dolls, the HelloWorld constructor method is inside the HelloWorld class, which is inside the package block statement. Each item sits inside the outer item's pair of curly braces, and you now have three levels of block statements. The only way that you can tell where one ends and the other begins is by whether the block statement's curly brace is open or closed.

As you can see, this could easily result in a confusing tangle of curly braces. If you weren't absolutely sure which pair of braces belonged to which block statement, you could start adding new code in the wrong place, and you'd get all sorts of errors when you tried to run the program.

The code formatting that Flash Builder does for you automatically helps solve this potential confusion somewhat. I recommend you use this style of formatting for the projects in this book. Figure 1-23 shows that you can draw an imaginary line between a block statement's opening brace and its closing brace. It very clearly shows you at which indentation level you should be adding code.

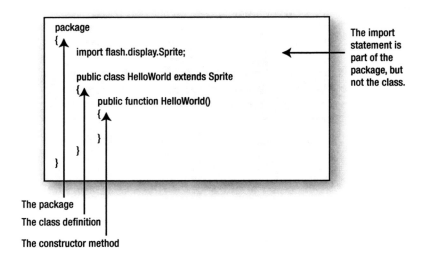

Figure 1-23. You can make sure that you're adding code in the right place by keeping each block statement's opening and closing braces aligned along an imaginary line.

You can clearly see from Figure 1-23 that the import statement is part of the package, not the class. And you can also see that the constructor method is part of the class because it's contained within the class's curly braces. That's thanks to the indentation.

There's another way of visualizing how the code is being organized. I've been throwing around the term "block statement" quite a bit. This term is actually a very concrete description of how indentation and curly braces are used to structure the code. You can think of each pair of curly braces as an empty box or block. Every time you create another statement with its own set of curly braces, you create a new block inside the first one. Figure 1-24 illustrates how you've created three blocks of code in your program so far. Each block sits inside the other.

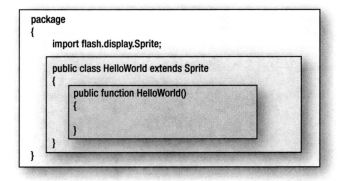

Figure 1-24. Each pair of curly braces contains a block of code. Blocks can contain other blocks.

A frequent confusion when programming code is not being certain where one block statement ends and another begins. If you use this suggested format and can see these imaginary divisions while you write, it will really help you to prevent accidentally adding a line of code in the wrong place.

If you're using Flash Builder, you can use its Outline window to see all the code blocks in your program and in which of those blocks you're currently working in. You'll find the Outline window to the bottom left of the code editing window. Figure 1-25 shows what your Outline window will look like if you've followed the instructions in this chapter so far.

Figure 1-25. The Outline window shows you all the code blocks in your program.

The Outline window clearly shows that you've got three blocks: the package, the class definition, and the constructor method. It even throws in a few cute little icons to illustrate them. The import statement is part of the package block because it's at the same level of indentation.

The Outline window and the code editing window are linked. If you click on a block in the Outline window, the code editing window will highlight the same block, and vice versa. For example, if you click the constructor method block in the Outline window, the constructor method in the code editing window is also highlighted, as shown in Figure 1-26.

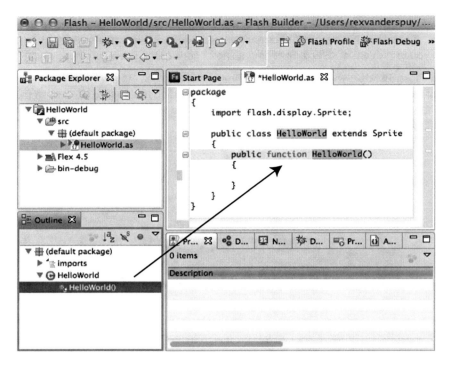

Figure 1-26. If you select a code block in the Outline window, the same block of code is highlighted in the editing window, and vice versa.

In long or complex programs, you can use the Outline window to quickly find the blocks of code that you want to work on.

What's your directive?

The next bit of code that your program needs is a **directive**. One of the great pleasures of computer programming is being able to bandy about terms like "constructor method" and "directive" as though you were the captain of your own personal galactic cruise liner. Very simply, a directive is a single action that you want the program to perform. It tells your program, "Do this now!" Methods are made up of one or more directives, and with them the program springs to life.

4. The directive you'll add to the constructor method will tell the program to display the words "Hello World!" in its Console window when the program runs. Add the following bold text to your program:

```
package
{
  import flash.display.Sprite;

  public class HelloWorld extends Sprite
```

```
{
   public function HelloWorld()
   {
      trace("Hello World! Can you read this?");
   }
 }
}
```

Your code editing window should now look like Figure 1-27.

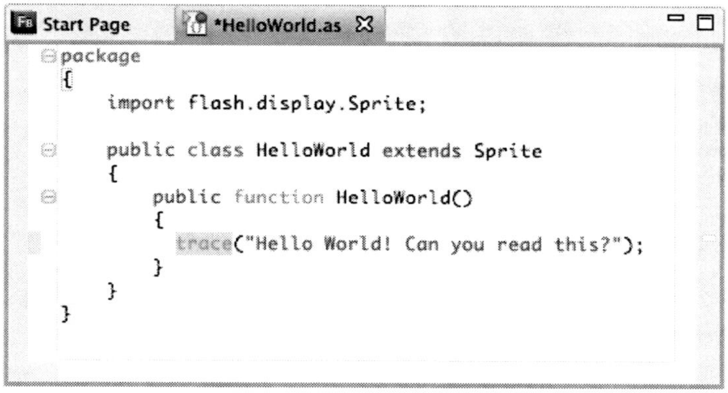

Figure 1-27. Add the new trace method to your code. It will display any text in quotation marks that is between its parentheses.

This is the new line of code that you wrote:

```
trace("Hello World! Can you read this?");
```

This is called a **trace method**. It's a special directive that tells your program to send whatever is in parentheses to Flash Builder's Console window when you debug your program. You haven't seen the Console window yet, but you will very soon! In this case, the trace method will send the words, "Hello World! Can you read this?" to the Console window. The important keyword here is trace.

If you want to send the Console window some text using trace, that text needs to be surrounded by quotation marks. AS3.0 has lots of built-in methods, such as trace, that you can use to do all kinds of interesting things, and you'll be looking at many of them in detail over the course of this book.

Directives end in a semicolon (;). The semicolon is a basic piece of punctuation that lets the program know that "The directive is finished! Do this work!" It's like a period at the end of a sentence. Whenever you see a semicolon at the end of a line of code, you know it's a directive. It's telling the program to perform a specific action. You used a semicolon earlier in the line of code that imported the Sprite from the library. That line of code was also a directive.

If you forget to add a semicolon at the end of a directive, Flash Builder will give you the benefit of the doubt and assume that you intended to add one. Your program will still run flawlessly without it. Thanks, Flash Builder! But in the interest of good programming style, you should always add a semicolon. If you go on to learn other programming languages that aren't as lenient (and most aren't), you'll have already developed an excellent habit.

Figure 1-28 illustrates how trace works to display text in the Console window when you run and debug the program, which you'll be doing in the steps ahead.

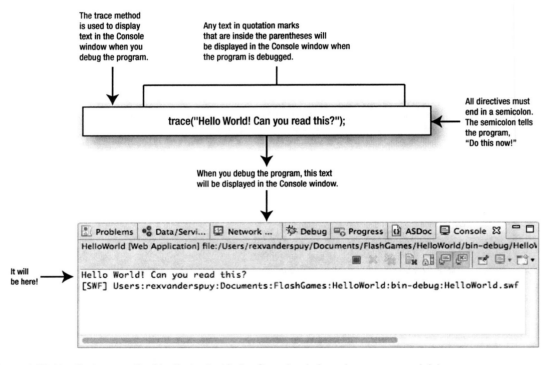

Figure 1-28. Use the trace method to display text in the Console window when you run and debug your program.

But don't go looking for that text in the Console widow yet! You won't see it until you debug the program. You're going to do that in the steps ahead.

Adding comments to your code

Let's add one more feature to your program before you see what it actually does: a **comment**. When you're writing a computer program, it is often useful to write a short note about what a particular section of code does. This is especially helpful if you've solved a complex programming problem that you're not certain you'll actually understand the next time you look at your code. It also helps other people who might be looking at your code to understand it better.

There are two ways to add comments to your code. The first is by using two forward slashes (//). Any text you add on the same line after these forward slashes will not be interpreted by AS3.0 as programming code. You can write anything you like; it will be ignored it when your program runs. Here's an example:

```
//Hi mom!! This is a comment. You can write whatever you like here.
```

Sometimes you might want to write a comment that contains more text than you can easily fit on one line. You can do this by creating a **multiline comment**. Multiline comments look like this:

```
/*
Anything between the opening and
closing multiline comment characters
will not be interpreted as
programming code.
*/
```

Multiline comments start with the character sequence /* and end with the character sequence */. You can write anything you like between them over any number of lines.

In addition to leaving notes to yourself, comments are especially useful for disabling sections of code if you want to test how your program behaves without them.

1. To get used to using comments, add one to your program. Modify your code with the following line in bold:

```
package
{
  import flash.display.Sprite;

  public class HelloWorld extends Sprite
  {
    public function HelloWorld()
    {
      //The next line displays some text
      trace("Hello World! Can you read this?");
    }
  }
}
```

Before you go any further, ensure that your program looks like Figure 1-29.

Figure 1-29. Add a comment to your code.

The ActionScript editor window colors comments green so that you can easily differentiate them from your programming code.

    2.   Finally, if everything looks good, save the HelloWorld.as file.

You're now ready to see result of the program in action.

Running your program and compiling the SWF file

So far you've only been working on one file, the HelloWorld.as file. This is your ActionScript program, and it's known as an AS file. It's the file that you do all your work in, but it's not your finished product.

Your finished product will be an SWF file. This is a file with a .swf extension. It's the file that will run in the Flash Player in a web browser and it's the file that you can upload to the Internet or share with others. The act of creating a SWF file is known as *compiling* it. (It's also known as *building* it, which is where Flash Builder gets its name from.)

There are two ways you can compile an SWF file in Flash Builder.

- You can select Run ↗ Run from Flash Builder's main menu, or click the green play icon in toolbar. When you do this, Flash Builder builds the SWF file for you in the bin-debug folder in your project directory. It then launches it in the Flash Player.

- You can select Run ↗ Debug from the main menu, or click the little beetle icon in the toolbar. This is a better option. This does the same thing as the ordinary Run command, but it also opens the Console window. The Console window will display any `trace` directives you used in your program. It will also give you error messages in the Problems window that tell you if you've made some mistakes in your program. When you choose the Debug option, it actually runs the program *and* launches the debugger. Two for the price of one!

You'll be using the Debug option almost exclusively when you make your games because the information it gives you in the Console and Problems window is extremely useful. Let's find out how by debugging your program and seeing what happens!

> *From now on, I'm going to refer to the debug option as **compiling**. Whenever I ask you to compile your program in this book, hit that little beetle button.*

1. Select Run ␓ Debug from the main menu or click the little beetle icon in the toolbar, as shown in Figure 1-30. Flash Builder may ask you if you want to save your work before continuing. If you've run the debugger for this program before, it may ask you if you wish to terminate any existing debugging session. In both cases, click the OK button. It may also ask if you want to open Flash Builder's **debugging perspective.** If it does, select No. (You'll find out what the debugging perspective is and how to switch to it if you want to near the end of this chapter.)

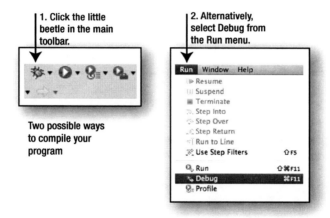

Figure 1-30. Choose one of these two possible ways to compile your program.

If Flash Builder is installed properly and you've followed all the instructions in this chapter to the letter, here's what will happen:

- Flash Builder will launch a Flash Player window. It will be blank. That's just fine; it should be! (If you didn't deselect the "Generate HTML wrapper file" option in the Project Properties panel, a blank web page will open instead. Refer to the section "Tell Flash Builder to Run Your Programs in the Flash Player" near the beginning of this chapter to prevent this from happening.)

- Flash Builder will also open the Console window. You should see the words, "Hello World! Can you read this?" in the Console window. Figure 1-31 illustrates what you should see. The Console window will also display some technical information that confirms that it has created the SWF file, which is your finished work.

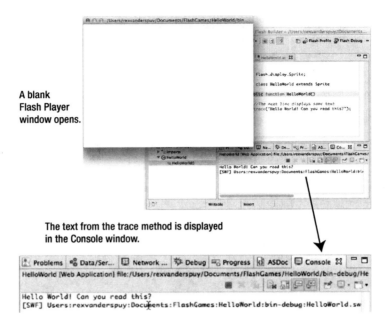

A blank
Flash Player
window opens.

The text from the trace method is displayed
in the Console window.

Figure 1-31. Compile your program and see the result in the Console window.

If this is what happened when you compiled the program, congratulations, you've programmed and run your first computer program! If this didn't happen and you got some sort of strange error messages that you didn't understand, continue reading to see if you can figure out where the problem might lie.

What happened when you compiled the program

Let's assume for a moment that your program worked perfectly, you saw the result I described in the previous section, and you didn't get any error messages. Here's what happened:

When you clicked the Debug button, Flash Builder sent your program to something called the **compiler**. The compiler is a piece of software that is part of the Flex SDK. Its job is to take AS3.0 code and turn it into an SWF file that you can view in the Flash Player. It also checks your code to see if there are any errors. If there are, it warns you, or prevents the code from running if they're serious.

But if the code ran fine, then the compiler displayed your trace message in the Console window and created an SWF file for you in the bin-debug folder of the HelloWorld project directory. Let's see if it actually did this. Open your bin-debug folder and take a look. Your HelloWorld project directory should look something like Figure 1-32.

Figure 1-32. When you compile the program, the AS3.0 compiler creates an SWF file for you in the project folder.

You're interested in the HelloWorld.swf file. SWF files with the same name as your project are what will contain your finished games, which you'll make in later chapters.

But there are also a few more files and folders in that directory. They're not necessary for any of the projects in this book. They're all part of what's known as the **HTML wrapper**. These are the files that you need if you want to upload any of your projects to the Internet. These files will still be created even if you've told Flash Builder not to generate an HTML wrapper, but it won't use them to launch your program in a web browser Let's take a look at what they do—they might be useful to you at some point.

- **HelloWorld.html**: This is an HTML file (a web page) that the compiler generated for you automatically when you ran and debugged the program. It contains code that plays the SWF file. You can use this HTML file, along with the other files in this directory, as the basis for creating a web page you can publish to the Internet so that others can play your game.

- **swfObject.js**: This is a JavaScript (JS) file that embeds the SWF file into the HTML page and checks whether the user viewing your game over the Internet has the Flash Player installed.

- **playerProdcutinstall.swf**: This is a Flash application that prompts users to download the latest version of the Flash Player if the current version isn't compatible with your game.

- **History**: This folder contains specialized code that lets users navigate your game or web application using the browser's forward and back buttons.

It's beyond the scope of this book to go into the details of publishing HTML files for the web, but all you would need to do in theory is upload these five files and the history folder to a web address (URL) and anyone in the world will be able to play your game. You can find out more about the Flash Builder's HTML wrapper at Adobe's web site at

http://help.adobe.com/en_US/flashbuilder/using/index.html

So that's what you see if everything worked as it should have. But what if....

It didn't work?

There might be an unlucky few of you who did not see the output shown in Figure 1-31. In fact, if this is the first time you've ever done any computer programming, it's almost certain that you made a small mistake somewhere that would have prevented the program from running properly. Don't feel bad! There are many things that could have gone wrong and being able to figure out what they are is an essential part of the learning process.

If this is the first time that you've compiled a program with Flash Builder, there's a good chance that Flash Builder wasn't installed properly or you don't have the debug version of the Flash Player installed. If you see an error message saying "Installed Flash Player is not a debugger" then this is the likely cause. Follow the instructions in the section "Using Flash Builder" near the beginning of this chapter to solve this problem.

If Flash Builder was installed properly, your problems will be easy to solve with a bit of careful checking of the code you've written. First, when you hit the Debug button, you might have seen a dialog box called Errors in Workspace, as shown in Figure 1-33.

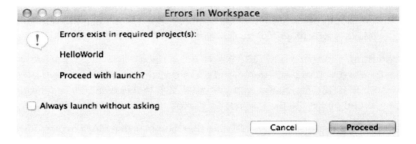

Figure 1-33. Flash Builder will tell you if you have any problems with your code when you compile the program.

If you see this dialog box, click Cancel. This is important because if you click Proceed, Flash Builder will still try to create the SWF anyway, even though there are errors in your code. This could lead you to the false belief that your program is working properly, when it actually isn't. In a complex game project, with hundreds of lines of code, this could blind you to the fact that there are errors in your code that will manifest as complex bugs that could be difficult to solve or detect.

After cancelling the launch of the SWF, look for the Problems widow at the bottom of Flash Builder's workspace. The Problems window tells you how many errors it thinks you have in your code. Click the small triangle next to where it says Errors, and you'll see a list of exactly what Flash Builder thinks the problems are. Figure 1-34 shows an example.

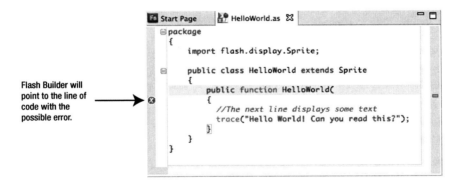

Figure 1-34. Click the triangle next to Errors in the Problems window to see the possible errors in your program.

I can guarantee that whatever it tells you will be completely meaningless to you! It's will take you a lot of time working with Flash Builder to gradually make sense of what these error messages are trying to tell you. However, the term "syntax error" is important. It means that you wrote some code that the AS3.0 language doesn't understand. It's AS3.0's way of saying, "Huh?" This usually indicates that you mistyped or misspelled something. It could also mean that you forgot to open or close one of the curly braces or a parenthesis. Or you just accidentally left something out somewhere. The other confusing thing about these messages is that Flash Builder doesn't really know what's wrong. The error messages are vague. They often don't point to what the real problem is so you'll have to use your powers of deduction to figure out what could be wrong.

But Flash Builder doesn't just leave you with vague error messages; it points to where in your code it thinks the problem is. If you look at the left side of your editor window, you'll see a small red circle with an X through it. Flash Builder thinks the problem lies in that line of code. Figure 1-35 shows an example.

Flash Builder will point to the line of code with the possible error. →

```
Start Page    HelloWorld.as

package
{
    import flash.display.Sprite;

    public class HelloWorld extends Sprite
    {
        public function HelloWorld(
        {
            //The next line displays some text
            trace("Hello World! Can you read this?");
        }
    }
}
```

Figure 1-35. Flash Builder will point to the line of code with the possible error.

> Note: If you have a small problem that isn't too serious but you should probably fix, Flash Builder with let you know with a triangular, yellow warning sign. This won't prevent the program from running properly, but it could lead to bigger problems later down the line if you don't fix it.

The line that Flash Builder highlights is an important clue! However, it can be very misleading because Flash Builder only tells you the point at which it stopped being able to understand your code. Usually the real the problem is at a point which is *just before this spot*.

This can be confusing! Here's a more concrete example: imagine you're walking through the woods, trip on the root of a tree, and bump your head on a rock. Flash Builder will point to the rock as the problem. But you know that the real problem is the root of the tree.

Take a good look at Figure 1-35 and compare it with the final code you wrote in the previous section. Does it look like there's anything wrong with the line that Flash Builder is pointing to? No, it's perfectly fine.

But take a look at the line just before it. This is what it looks like:

```
public function HelloWorld(
```

Do you notice something wrong? Yes! The closing parenthesis is missing. The line should look like this:

```
public function HelloWorld()
```

These kinds of simple mistakes are very easy to make, especially when you're just learning how to program and all of this is completely unfamiliar to you.

But Flash Builder didn't tell you that this was the problem. It pointed you to the rock that it bumped its head on, not the tree root that tripped it up. But it did give you an idea of where to look. If you fixed this code and debugged the program again, it would run perfectly and all the error messages would disappear.

Unfortunately, the compiler doesn't know what you intend your code to do; it can only tell you what it expects and what it doesn't understand. If you're lucky, it precisely pinpoints the problem. But more often than not, it will just be able to give you a general idea of where to look and what to look for. It's a bit like a two-year-old yelping with pain and pointing to his big toe. You know where the problem is, but whether it's a thumbtack, a bee sting, or just another way of saying, "The last time I did this you gave me some chocolate," the remedy will depend on experience, skeptical investigation, and a thoughtful diagnosis. It's up to you to intelligently analyze what you think the error is telling you and what you might have to fix or change to get your program running properly.

If you're not sure where the problem with your program lies, ask yourself whether one or more of these might be the issue:

- Did you spell everything correctly and use the correct case?

- Did you save the files in the correct location, and do the spelling and case of your folders and files match the package and class names? (This generally isn't a problem if you're using Flash Builder, which does these things for you automatically, but it could be with another IDE.)

- Are all the AS3.0 keywords (such as `import`, `package`, and `function`) a blue or purple color? If one of them isn't, that's a clear indication that you might have spelled or capitalized it incorrectly.

- Have you closed all your curly braces and parentheses?

- Did your cat jump on the keyboard while you were in the kitchen getting another cup of coffee?

And here are some more general pointers that you should always keep in mind while debugging your programs:

- If you receive more than one error message, always fix the first one first. Subsequent errors are usually the result of bits of code that depend on the earlier bits of code working correctly. Fix the first one, and the correction will cascade through the code and often magically correct the rest.

- Check the line of code that's *just above the line that Flash thinks is the problem.* Often, small mistakes in the line above, which might not be big enough in themselves to generate a compile error, could be enough to trip up the code in the next line down.

- *Always save the AS file you're working on before you compile it again!* I can't stress enough how common an oversight this is. A programmer will find an error and fix it, but then gets exactly the same error message when the SWF is republished. This is because the file wasn't saved after the fix was made, so the earlier saved version of the file is the one that Flash is actually compiling. This is not a problem if you're using Flash Builder, because it will automatically save the AS file for you before it attempts to run your code, but most other IDEs won't do this.

- Make only one single change before you compile the program to test it again. If your program worked and then suddenly stopped working after you made that change, you know exactly what is causing the problem. If you run and debug it only after making five changes and it doesn't work, you won't know which of those five things is tripping you up.

- Finally, the programmer's universal mantra: test early, test often. Do lots of testing and solve lots of tiny manageable problems early on to avoid having to deal with hulking intractable problems that can grind your project to a halt later.

Except for a few exceptional cases, this is the last discussion of debugging issues in any detail in this book. You'll be on your own from here on out, but the sooner you gain practice debugging your own code, the better. Experience counts for everything in this realm, and there is no better whetstone upon which to sharpen your skills as a programmer than a tricky debugging problem.

Also, get used to the Problems window—you'll be seeing a lot of it! It will become your closest ally in finding and tracking down problems.

Some common error messages

This section lists some common error messages that you might see in your first attempts at debugging, with suggestions as to what the problem could be.

- `1087: Syntax error: extra characters found after end of program.`

  You probably forgot to open or close one of the curly braces.

- `1116: A user-defined namespace attribute can only be used at the top level of a class definition.`

  You misspelled a keyword in the class definition. Maybe you spelled "public" as "pulbic."

- 1071: Syntax error: expected a definition keyword (such as function) after attribute public, not clas.

  You spelled the word "class" as "clas." This error will often be displayed when you misspell a keyword.

- 1084: Syntax error: expecting leftbrace before exteds.

  You misspelled the word "extends."

- 1017: The definition of base class Sprie was not found.

  You misspelled the word "Sprite."

- 1017: The definition of base class Sprite was not found.

  You misspelled one of the words, such as "flash" or "display" in this line of code:

  import flash.display.Sprite;

  You might also have left out one of the dots between the words.

- 1114: The public attribute can only be used inside a package.

  You probably misspelled the word "package."

- 1153: A constructor can only be declared public.

  You misspelled the word "public" in the constructor method.

- 1071: Syntax error: expected a definition keyword (such as function) after attribute public, not functon.

  You misspelled the word "function."

- A file found in a source-path 'HelloWorld' must have the same name as the class definition inside the file 'HeloWorld'.

  You misspelled "HelloWorld" as "HeloWorld" in the class definition.

- 1008: return value for function 'HeloWorld' has no type declaration.

  You misspelled "HelloWorld" as "HeloWorld" in the constructor method.

- 1084: Syntax error: expecting identifier before leftbrace.

  You forgot to close a parenthesis.

- 1180: Call to a possibly undefined method trae.

  You misspelled "trace" as "trae."

- 1084: Syntax error: expecting rightparen before semicolon.

  You forgot to close a parenthesis.

Don't let these error messages scare you! You'll soon get a feeling for what they're trying to tell you, and by carefully checking your code you'll always be able to find the source of the problem.

Confirm your program with the original source files

If you're unsure about any of the code in this book, you can download the original source files that I wrote and check your work against mine. You can download them from the book's download page at www.apress.com. Open the folder for the chapter you are working on, and you'll find the folders and files organized exactly as I've described them in this book. You can open any of the individual files directly in Flash Builder or open the whole folder as a Flash Builder project.

To open the source files as a project, select File ↗ Import Flash Builder project from the main menu. A new dialogue box will open, asking whether you want to import a file or a project folder. Select project folder and click Finish. The project will be imported into Flash Builder, and you can then run and debug it, just as you can run and debug your own programs.

If the project folder you're trying to import has the same name as a project currently open in Flash Builder, rename the project folder before you import it.

More about Flash Builder

Flash Builder is a complex bit of software that contains many more features than you'll probably ever need. Let's take quick look at some of the most useful.

Editing window quirks and features

The ActionScript editing window has a few advanced features which, unfortunately for beginners, can result in some frustrating quirks if you're not aware of them. They could cause your work to seem to disappear or not run properly. However, with a bit more experience, you'll actually find these features extremely helpful.

Collapsing code

First, the Editing window allows you to *collapse* your code. Look at the very left side of the window and you'll see small minus signs. There's a minus sign next to each block of code. If you click one of those minus signs, the block of code collapses into a single line. It looks like your code has disappeared completely, but it hasn't. Click the new plus sign next to the code block, and your code appears again. This is useful if you're working on a very long program and want to temporarily hide bits of code so that they don't distract you from other bits you're working on. Figure 1-36 illustrates this.

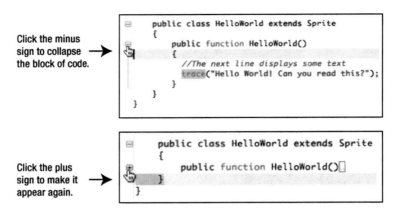

Click the minus sign to collapse the block of code.

Click the plus sign to make it appear again.

Figure 1-36. Collapse blocks of code you're not currently working on if you want to de-clutter your editing window.

Breakpoints

If you're working on a complex program and want to test only part of it, not the whole thing, you can add a **breakpoint** to your code. When you add a breakpoint, the code will stop running at that point. This is very useful if you know you have an error further down the line, but just want to test your code up to the point where you know it's working.

Unfortunately, it's also very easy to accidentally add breakpoints to your code if you double click on the left margin without thinking about it. As a beginner, you won't know the breakpoints are there. You'll just notice that your program won't run properly. You won't get any errors, but the program will just seem to stop part way. If this happens to you, check to make sure that you haven't added any accidental breakpoints, and delete them if you have.

You add a breakpoint to your code by double-clicking on the left margin of the editing window. You'll see a tiny blue circle appear, as shown in Figure 1-37

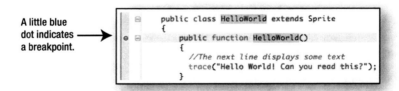

A little blue dot indicates a breakpoint.

Figure 1-37. Adding breakpoints to your code will stop it from running after this point. This is useful for checking to see which parts of your code are working and which aren't.

When you've added that breakpoint, your code will stop at that point when you run and debug it. That means that it won't run the trace statement that follows, and you'll see nothing in the Console window except a message that the SWF file was created.

You can remove the breakpoint by double-clicking on it again. After you do this, run and debug your program again, and the program should run to completion just fine.

However, sometimes you'll want to use breakpoints to check which sections of your code are working and which aren't. In that case, leave a breakpoint in place, and open the Breakpoint view window. You can make the Breakpoint view visible by selecting Run ↗ Debug ↗ Other. A new Show View window will open. Open the Debug folder and select Breakpoints, and click the OK button, as shown in Figure 1-38.

Figure 1-38. Display the Breakpoint view window to help manage your breakpoints.

You'll now see a new Breakpoints window at the bottom of Flash Builder's workspace, as shown in Figure 1-39. It will show you all the breakpoints in your code.

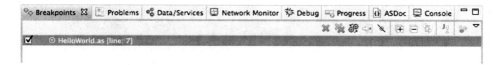

Figure 1-39. Display the Breakpoints window to see where the breakpoints are in your code.

The Breakpoints window comes with its own menu bar at the top right. You can deactivate a breakpoint by unchecking it. If you double-click on a breakpoint, the cursor in the code editing window will jump to the spot where you added it. You can remove breakpoints by selecting them and clicking the X button in the menu bar. Many of these same options are available from Flash Builder's Run menu.

If you run and debug your code with a breakpoint and want to see what will happen if your code continues from that point, you can select Resume from the Project menu, as shown in Figure 1-40.

Figure 1-40. Resuming from a breakpoint shows you what will happen if your code runs from that point onward.

From the same Run menu, you can also *step over* a breakpoint. This is useful if you set a breakpoint on a line that you think contains an error and want to test your program without having that line run. It omits the suspect line from your program and shows you how your program will run without it.

There are some more advanced features of breakpoints, such as setting them to run conditionally, and you can find out more about them in the chapter "Debugging Tools in Flash Builder" in Adobe's Flash Builder documentation at

```
http://help.adobe.com/en_US/flashbuilder/using/index.html
```

When you start writing long, complex programs, you'll gradually appreciate how useful breakpoints can be to help you test and to isolate the parts of your code that are working from the parts that aren't. Breakpoints are an essential debugging tool.

Perspectives

Flash Builder has a feature called **Perspectives** that changes the way that windows are organized in the workspace. If you've just installed and started working with Flash Builder, you're probably using the perspective called **Flash**. The Flash perspective arranges the workspace in the way that I've described it in this book, with the Package Explorer and Outline window to the left of the editing window and the Console and Problems windows at the bottom.

There's no reason to change this perspective, but it's important to know that you can if you want to. And there's also a chance that in your exploration of Flash Builder you may have accidentally switched the perspective and you can't get back to the standard Flash perspective I've been describing.

The top right corner of Flash Builder's toolbar has buttons that let you switch perspective, as shown in Figure 1-41.

Figure 1-41. Change the way windows are organized in Flash Builder's workspace by switching the perspective.

The perspective that is currently selected will be indicated by the depressed button. Figure 1-40 shows that the Flash workspace is currently selected. What happens if you select the Flash Debug perspective? Figure 1-42 shows what it looks like.

Figure 1-42. The Flash Debug perspective

All the windows that are used for solving problems and debugging your program are in a useful arrangement and easily accessible. The Breakpoints window is at the top right, in addition to two new windows, Variables and Expressions.

There are many other perspectives included with Flash Builder, and you can find them all by clicking on the Open Perspective button and the clicking Other, as shown in Figure 1-43.

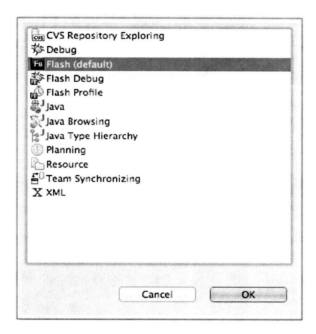

Figure 1-43. There are many perspectives to choose from, if you need them.

You should know that these perspectives exist, but you probably won't need to use any for the projects in this book.

Another issue to keep in mind is that if you double-click the title bar of any window, it will expand to fill the whole workspace. Just double-click it again to make it shrink back.

Creating a clean compile of your program

Occasionally you'll compile a program and even though there are no error messages, the program won't seem to behave the way you expect it to. Recent changes you'd made to the program won't seem to have taken effect, and you can't find anything wrong with your code at all.

If this happens, you'll need to reset the compiler by doing a clean compile of your program. To do this, select Project ↗ Clean. Select the project you want to clean and click the OK button. The compiler will now recompile your program from scratch.

Creating a release build of your SWF file

When your program or game is completely finished, it's a good idea to create a **release build** of it. This is an SWF file that is slightly smaller in size than the SWF file that's created when you run and debug your programs. The reason it's smaller is because it doesn't contain any debugging information or trace statements. The release build SWF should be your final product.

To create a release build SWF file, select Project ↗ Export Release Build from Flash Builder's main menu. A new window will open with options that you will probably never have to change. Click the Finish button, and Flash Builder will make the SWF file for you.

When it's done, you'll find the release SWF in a folder called bin-release in your project folder, as shown in Figure 1-44.

Figure 1-44. Create a release build SWF, which is smaller in size that the SWF files that are created during debugging.

A little more about AS3.0 and the Flash Player

At the end of this process, you have a SWF file that you can take to any computer and run, as long as the Flash Player is also installed on that same computer. The fact that the SWF file needs the help of the Flash Player to run is very important. As a game designer, you need to know why this is and the kinds of limitations it might impose on you. Let's take a closer look at what's going on behind the scenes when you publish a SWF file.

AS3.0 is a type of **high-level programming language**. High-level programming languages, such as Java, C++, and Visual Basic, are designed so that humans can easily read, write, and understand them. They use real English words such as "function" and "class," and use elements of English grammar such as quotation marks and semicolons. But computers don't understand English. Try asking your computer for help with the dishes this evening, and I expect you'll get nothing but a stony silence. (If not, let someone, hopefully a professional, know about it!)

At their most basic level, computers understand only a binary language of 1s and 0s. All the AS3.0 code has to be translated into binary code so the computer can understand it. Fortunately, you don't have to do that manually, so you can put away the pencil and paper. Flash has a built-in compiler (a software component that translates code) to do the job for you.

Keep in mind that, unlike writing a program in a language such as C++ or Visual Basic, Flash's compiler doesn't compile your code so it's directly readable by your computer's central processing unit (CPU), which is your computer's main brain. It compiles it only so that it can be read by the Flash Player software.

Before you can run any of your AS3.0 programs, the Flash Player software has to be installed on your system because it's the job of the Flash Player to interpret your code to the CPU. Because of this, AS3.0, like Java, is known as an **interpreted programming language**. Interpreted languages use a piece of software known as a **virtual machine**, which acts as an interpreter between the CPU and your program. The Flash Player is AS3.0's virtual machine.

Interpreted languages have a number of advantages over languages that compile directly to the CPU. Most importantly, it means that your programs will run flawlessly and exactly the same way on any operating system (Windows, Linux, or Mac OS X) that has the Flash Player installed. You only need to write your code once, and the Flash Player, which is written for each operating system that it's available for, will take care of the job of making sure your code runs properly. The other advantage is that the Flash Player protects the computer it's running on from any code that you might have written that could accidentally freeze or crash your system. All this tends to make interpreted languages very convenient and reliable languages in which to program.

One major disadvantage with interpreted languages, however, is in the area of performance. *Performance* is a bit of computer jargon that basically means how efficiently or quickly your program runs. Imagine visiting a foreign country where you don't speak the language, but instead are accompanied by a translator who painstakingly translates every word you say and then translates each reply back into English. It would be a very slow and tedious process. Unfortunately, this is exactly what's happening between the Flash Player and the CPU when you run your AS3.0 programs. How slow is it? Exact numbers are hard to come by, but a reasonable estimate might be 10 to 20 times slower than if the code were compiled as binary machine language and running directly on the CPU. (By "slow," I mean exactly how quickly the CPU can process each instruction or calculation your program asks it to perform.)

Adobe has done a great deal with each successive generation of the Flash Player to improve performance, but this is a major handicap for game developers who depend on squeezing every iota of processing power out of a system to maximize performance in their games. This is why 3D Flash games, which require a vast amount of processing power to calculate geometry, struggle to compete with the rich graphic splendor of 3D on the game consoles (such as the Xbox, PlayStation, and Wii.) The consoles use custom compilers that optimize all the game code to run directly as machine language on their specific processors.

If you're thinking of eventually getting into game design for consoles, however, you're still in pretty good shape with Flash: the skills you'll learn by programming in AS3.0 can be directly applied to programming for consoles when you're ready to take that step. The AS3.0 programming environment is also probably the most user-friendly programming environment you can learn in. And, hey, make a game with Flash, post it on the Web, and you've got a potential worldwide audience for it—that's power!

Naming conventions

Before this chapter closes, let's take a quick look at an aspect of programming practice called **naming conventions**. You might have noticed something peculiar about the kinds of names that you gave the file, class, and method names. Look at the choice of file name for the AS file:

HelloWorld

Does it look a little strange to you? It should. You'll notice that the *H* and *W* are uppercase, and there's no space between the two words. This is a style of giving things names that programmers affectionately call **camel case** (also known as **humpBackNotation**). Can you guess why it's called that? I'm sure you can!

With camel case, you can write a compound phrase using more than one word. The words are not separated with blank spaces, and the phrase is still easily readable by you and by AS3.0. Blank spaces in the middle of compound names are the programming equivalent to foxes in a chicken coop—avoid them at all cost! The AS3.0 code compiler throws its hands in the air when it encounters a blank space where there shouldn't be one, so camel case was developed by programmers as an efficient way of writing compound words or phrases without spaces. You should also avoid blank spaces in any of your folder names, because if you're using an IDE other than Flash Builder, the underlying Flex SDK that compiles your code can't process paths to files that include spaces.

Camel case is an important feature of naming conventions, which are rules that programmers decide on before they start a project about the style they'll use for creating package, variable, class, object, method, and file names. By strictly sticking to these naming conventions, programmers are better able to dodge the easy-to-make errors that come from misspelling or incorrectly capitalizing any elements in their code. They can also easily see what kind of programming object they're dealing with simply by the way it's been capitalized.

There are two types of camel case that you'll be using throughout this book.

- **Lower camel case**: startsWithLowerCaseLetter. You'll be using this case for package names, variables, methods, and instances.

- **Upper camel case**: StartsWithUpperCaseLetter. You'll use this case for class names and constructor method names. You'll also use it for the names of AS class files such as HelloWorld.as and Main.as, which must be named exactly like the class they define in the file.

Because ActionScript is a case sensitive programming language, keep in mind that helloWorld is different from HelloWorld, which is different still from helloworld. Make sure that you follow all the capitalization as it appears in the text; otherwise, your programs won't work. If you write a program that seems perfect in every way but just doesn't run, check your spelling and capitalization! This is one of the most common mistakes that novice programmers make, and many a programmer will tell you tales of woe about debugging sessions running till 4 a.m. where the culprit, when eventually smoked out, was revealed to be a single misspelled or incorrectly capitalized word. The author of this book refuses comment!

Summary

Well done! You've written and published your first AS3.0 program! It wasn't so hard, was it? In fact, congratulate yourself for getting through one of the most difficult chapters in the book. I've laid the programming foundations for all the games and projects to come, and you'll find that you'll use this same format for setting up your programs over and over again in your career as a game designer.

This chapter has covered a lot of theory, and if you are new to programming, you might have found some of it a bit heavy. I sympathize with you! But you don't necessarily need to completely understand all the theory to create games. The most important thing is that you know what programming code you need to use to get the results you want. A deeper understanding will come with time, a lot of trial and error, and doing as much experimenting with your own projects as you can.

A deep dark secret that most programmers often don't like to share with the rest of the world is that a great deal of the world's software is built with a little bit of understanding and an awful lot of copy/paste. That's all part of the learning process. Of course, you need to know exactly what bits of code you need to copy and paste, and how to change them to get the results you want, which is something only experience (and this book!) can teach you. But as time goes on, you'll soon recognize the usual suspects and be copying and pasting along with the best of them.

I encourage you to go back to parts of this chapter that might have been little fuzzy the first time through to try to get a solid understanding of them before continuing much further. If you don't get it all just yet, don't worry! If you managed to get the little Hello World program running and you generally understand what made it work, you're in the game!

In the next chapter, you'll take a bit of break from programming and learn how to use Photoshop to make graphics for your games. In Chapter 3, you'll see how you can use those graphics with the skills you learned in this chapter to start programming your first interactive game world.

Chapter 2

Making Game Graphics

Over the next two chapters you're going to learn the two most essential skills of video game design: how to make game graphics, and then how to program them. All of the most important core techniques of game design are in these two chapters. It's these techniques that you're going to build on to make the rest of the game projects in this book.

Flash Builder is just for writing programming code, not for making the graphics that your games will use. So you need to use some graphics software to make those graphics. This chapter is about making game graphics using Photoshop. In the next chapter I'll show you how to program these graphics using AS3.0 programming code so that they become completely interactive.

This chapter assumes you've had no or very little experience using Photoshop or any other graphic design software. It starts right from the beginning and covers all the basics. If you have a lot of experience making computer graphics, flip through this chapter just to see what kind of graphics to make, the file names they should have, and where and how they should be saved. Although this chapter focuses on the use of Photoshop, which is the most widely used graphic design software, you can use any software you like that produces PNG files: Fireworks, GIMP, Illustrator, or any other software you're comfortable using.

By the end of the chapter, you will have created the background game world shown in Figure 2-1.

Figure 2-1. A background game world

You will also have created a game character made out of basic shapes, shown in Figure 2-2.

Figure 2-2. A game character

And you'll have made some button graphics that you're going to use to control this character, shown in Figure 2-3.

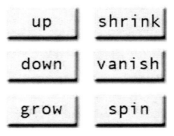

Figure 2-3. Buttons to control your game character

All these graphics will be made with Photoshop and saved in a file format called PNG (Portable Network Graphics). PNG image files are generally the best for Flash games.

Here's what you'll learn in this chapter:

- How to open a new file in Photoshop.

- How to use Photoshop tools to create basic shapes.

- How to use layers to organize shapes.

- How to apply special effects to your graphics.

- How to save your graphics as PNG files that you can then program with AS3.0.

So let's get started building a game world!

Photoshop is complex software with thousands of different settings that you can change and customize. It's also frightfully easy to accidentally "customize" the layout with a few unwitting clicks that will make windows, panels, and tools disappear—apparently for good. This is especially a problem if you're new to Photoshop and are exploring the software. You might drag or click a window into apparent oblivion.

*Fortunately it's quite easy to make all these windows reappear in their proper positions. Photoshop uses a concept called **workspaces** which are collections of windows and Tools panels that are grouped in different arrangements, depending on the kind of work you're doing. When you first install and launch Photoshop, it loads a workspace called **Essentials**. There's no reason to change this workspace, and it's the one that I recommend you use while you're learning, therefore it's the one on which I've based the instructions in this book.*

Here's how to confirm that you're working in the Essentials workspace. You can also confirm this by selecting Window ↗ Workspace from Photoshop's main menu. You should see a checkmark next to Essentials. Further down the same menu you'll see an option called Reset Essentials. This is the magic option! If you ever lose any of your windows or Tools panels and can't find them anywhere, select Reset Essentials, and they'll all pop back into the places they were in when you started Photoshop for the first time. You'll also see a big button called Essentials near the top left corner of the workspace. If it looks pressed down, you're working in the Essentials workspace.

You can also selectively hide and display windows and Tools panels from the Windows menu in the main menu bar at the top of Photoshop's workspace. All the windows and panels that are visible in the workspace will have a checkmark next to them. If there's a window you're looking for and can't find it on the screen, select it from the Windows menu.

Create a game world background

In this first section you're going to create a background game environment that your character will inhabit. I'll walk you through every step of the process, and at the end of it you'll have produced an image that looks like Figure 2-4.

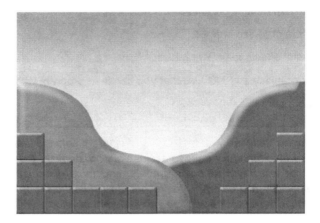

Figure 2-4. The game world

Create a new file in Photoshop

First, launch Photoshop and set up a new file that you can use to draw your background scene.

1. Launch Photoshop.

2. Select File ↗ New from the main menu. A dialog window will open that will ask you for the name of the new file that you're creating and what size you want to make your image. Here are the options that you should change:

   ▪ Name: background

   ▪ Width: 550 pixels

   ▪ Height: 400 pixels

You can leave all the other settings as is. When you're done, the New file dialog window should look like Figure 2-5.

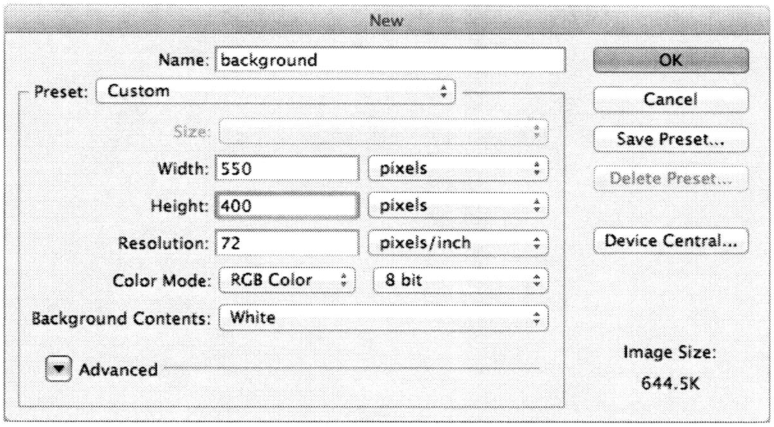

Figure 2-5. The New file dialogue window should look like this.

If the New file dialogue box that you see doesn't look exactly like this, there's a good chance that you're using a slightly different version of Photoshop than I am. This book was written using Photoshop CS 5.1, which was the latest at time of publication. If you're using an earlier or later version, it's likely that some of the options you see won't be exactly the same or may be in slightly different places. However, I can assure you they'll all be there somewhere! Use your judgment and intelligence and look for them.

Adobe makes tiny little tweaks to the layout and placement of tools and menu items from version to version, but it rarely makes radical changes. In fact, in the 20 years that I've been using Photoshop, the basic features that I'll describe in this chapter really haven't changed much at all. That's a good thing because it means the time you put into learning Photoshop tends to be a good long term investment. It also means that if you're using a much older version of Photoshop, even one that's 10 years old, such as Photoshop 5, you'll still be able to follow most of the instructions in this chapter and produce great game graphics.

Click the OK button and a new blank window will open, which is the window in which you'll draw your background. This is called the **canvas**. Figure 2-6 shows what you'll see.

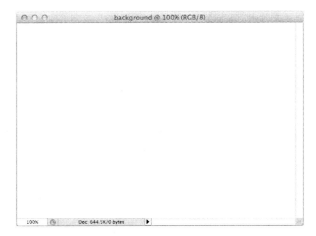

Figure 2-6. The blank canvas where you will draw the background scene

What are pixels?

When you created your new blank canvas, you gave it a width of 550 pixels and a height of 400 pixels. What are pixels?

Pixels are tiny squares that make up a computer graphic. They're the smallest thing you can see on your screen. Nothing can be smaller than a pixel. If you zoom into a computer graphic, you'll see that it's made up of tiny little squares. Those are the pixels. Figure 2-7 shows an example.

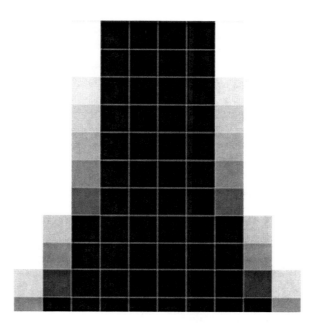

Figure 2-7. Pixels are the tiny squares that make up computer graphics.

It's important to know that the new blank canvas you created is really just a grid of these tiny little squares. You can't see them yet because they're all colored white, but they're there. This new blank canvas, so plain and innocent looking to the untrained eye, is really composed of 220,000 tiny white pixels. Figure 2-8 Illustrates this.

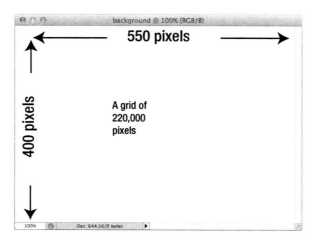

Figure 2-8. The deceptively blank canvas is really a grid of tiny white squares called pixels.

It's important to start thinking of this canvas as a grid of pixels. In the next chapter you'll see how you access and control the position of all your game elements on every point in this invisible grid.

> *Note: Pixels are the basic building blocks of computer graphics, but they're not the only ones. There is another way you can make computer graphics using* **vectors***. Graphics made using vectors have lines as their most basic element, not squares. Photoshop is specialized for creating graphics using pixels, but software such as Illustrator and Flash Professional use vectors. In the chapters ahead you'll learn how you can use vectors to make sophisticated illustrations for your games.*
>
> *Photoshop's Shape tools also use vectors as their primary building blocks.*

Draw the sky

To the left of the Photoshop workspace you'll find the Tools panel. You'll find most of Photoshop's drawing tools here. The Tools panel has one potentially confusing feature, which is that many of the tools are hidden until you hold your left mouse down over one of its buttons. Doing so reveals a list of all the tools that are grouped together as part of that button set. You can then select the tool you're looking for from that list. It will take you a bit of practice and experience to find and remember which tools are grouped with which button sets, but you'll gradually get the hang of it. Figure 2-9 shows where most of the important drawing tools are hidden. Refer back to this illustration if you're struggling to find any of the tools I ask you to use in the instructions ahead.

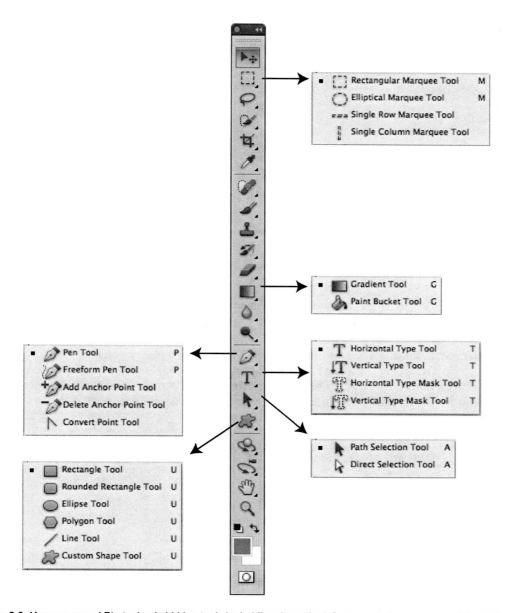

Figure 2-9. You can reveal Photoshop's hidden tools by holding down the left mouse button over any of the button sets.

The first thing you're going to draw is a blue sky that will form the background for the rest of your scene. In these next steps you'll learn how to draw a square using the Rectangle Tool, fill it with color, and use a gradient to give it a natural sense of depth.

Select the Rectangle Tool from the Tools panel. You'll know that it's been properly selected when you see its icon appear as a depressed button in the Tools panel, as in Figure 2-10.

Figure 2-10. Select the Rectangle Tool.

Next you're going to select a color for the rectangle. There are two places you can do this. At the very bottom left of the Tools panel you'll see two overlapping squares. Selecting the top square allows you choose an object's foreground color. Selecting the square behind it lets you choose its background color. If you ever need to, you can swap these colors by clicking the curved arrows icon. Figure 2-11 illustrates this.

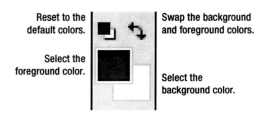

Figure 2-11. Select an object's foreground or background color.

Photoshop also has something called the **Options bar** that runs along the top of the workspace. It's *context sensitive*, which means that the buttons and settings you'll find here will change depending on which tools you've selected. With a bit of experience, you'll start to learn which tools and options you can select here when different tools are active. When the Rectangle Tool is active, you can change its color in the Options bar, as shown in Figure 2-12.

Change the
rectangle's
foreground
color here

Figure 2-12. The context-sensitive Options bar allows you change many tool options, including the color.

> *Note: If for some reason you can't seem to find the Options bar, it might be hidden. To reveal it, select Window ↗ Options from Photoshop's main menu. There should be a checkmark next to Options.*
>
> *Just above the Options bar is the Application bar. You can use it to make changes to the canvas's zoom percentage and also modify how Photoshop displays its panels and windows.*

Click the foreground color selection box in either the Tools panel or Options bar, as described previously.

The Color Picker window opens to allows you to choose a color. Use the slider in the middle of the window to choose a color, and then choose the shade (lightness) of that color in the large square box to the left of it. The box labeled "new" shows you what your new color will look like and compares it to the currently selected color. If you feel there's just too much choice, click the Color Library button and load a pre-selected collection of colors you can choose from. Figure 2-13 shows what the Color Picker looks like.

Here's the new
color you've chosen

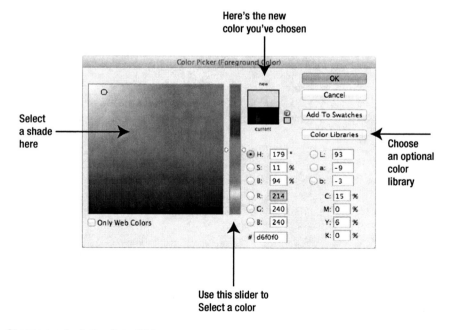

Select
a shade
here

Choose
an optional
color
library

Use this slider to
Select a color

Figure 2-13. Choose a color in the Color Picker.

Instead of using the Color Picker you can also choose a color from the Color or Swatches panel on the right side of the workspace. Click on the Swatches tab and little squares of colors (called swatches) appear that you can select. When you move your mouse over a swatch, the mouse pointer arrow turns into an eyedropper, which is a cute way of telling you that you can slurp up a bit of color to use in your drawing. When you select a color with the eyedropper, it appears in the New box of the Color Picker window. Figure 2-14 illustrates this.

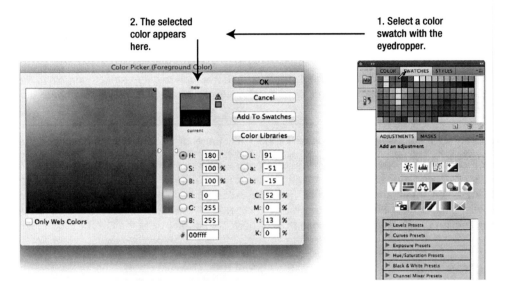

Figure 2-14. Optionally select a color from the Swatches panel.

> You can also click on a color swatch directly without having to open the Color Picker. The color will be directly applied to the rectangle or any other shape you're working with.
>
> The swatches that you see in the Swatches panel by default are a good selection of colors to start with, but there are many more. Click the small button to the extreme right of the panel that looks like a list with a downward pointing arrow next to it. This will open a list of color collections you can choose from. Find a collection you like. You can return to the original swatch collection by choosing Reset Swatches from this same list.

You're going to be drawing a sky background, so select a bright blue color. Click the OK button in the Color Picker window when you're done. The new color you've chosen will become visible in the Foreground color box at the bottom of the Tools panel.

Return to the blank canvas. Hold the left mouse button down over it and drag to draw a square or rectangle shape, as shown in Figure 2-15. It should be the same as the color you selected in the previous steps.

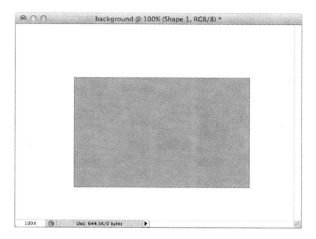

Figure 2-15. Draw a rectangle in the new workspace.

This isn't bad, but you really want the blue rectangle to fill the whole screen. Let's fix this in the next step.

Select the Move tool at the top of the Tools panel. The Move tool lets you move objects around the canvas and resize or rotate them. As soon as you select it, the Options bar gives you some options you should change. One of these is extremely important: a checkbox called Show Transform Controls.

Make sure that the Show Transform Controls is selected with a checkmark. Without this option selected, you won't be able to easily resize or rotate objects. Figure 2-16 shows what the Move Tool button and the Options bar should look like.

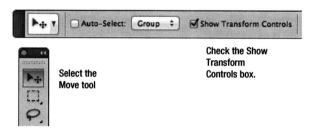

Figure 2-16. Select the Move Tool and make sure that the Show Transform Controls checkbox is selected in the Options bar.

As soon as you select the Move Tool with Show Transform Controls, you'll notice that small squares appear on the corners, sides, and middle of the rectangle you drew. These are called **drag handles**. While the Move Tool is selected, you can drag these handles with the mouse to resize and rotate the rectangle.

When you move the mouse over one of these handles, you'll see one of two icons appear. Diagonally pointing arrows mean that you can resize the rectangle (this is also called **scaling** it). A curved arrow means that you can rotate it. Figure 2-17 illustrates how you can use these drag handles to change the size or orientation of the rectangle.

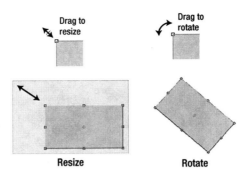

Figure 2-17. Use the Move Tool to resize or rotate an object.

Changing the size and orientation of a drawing object like this is called *transforming* it in Photoshop's terminology. You can choose more transform options by selecting Edit ↗ Transform Path or Edit ↗ Transform from Photoshop's main menu. The options you'll find there are Scale (resize), Rotate, Skew, Distort, Perspective, and Warp. You'll also find options to flip and rotate an object by fixed amounts.

Use the Move Tool and drag handles to resize the rectangle so that it fills the whole canvas, as in Figure 2-18. The canvas should now be completely blue.

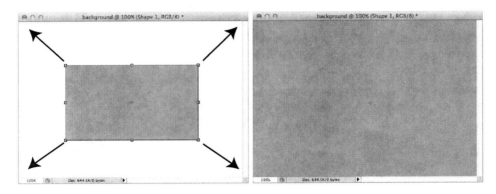

Figure 2-18. Resize the rectangle so that it fills the whole canvas.

When you've finished resizing, press the Enter key. This applies the transformation, and you need to do this before many of Photoshop's options become active again. You can also apply the transformation by selecting the Move tool again. Photoshop will open a dialog box asking whether you wish to apply the transformation. Click OK to accept it.

While you're resizing or rotating a shape or selection, Photoshop disables most of the options from its main menu and also many of the buttons in the panels on the right. If you ever find yourself struggling with apparently frozen buttons or inexplicably dimmed-out menu options, you probably forgot to apply the transformation on the shape you were working on. Press Enter to apply it immediately, or select the Move tool to open a confirmation window. Everything will work fine after that!

You now have a blue background that will be the basis of your sky. It could be fine as it is, but let's make it better by adding a gradient to give it a sense of depth.

Add a gradient

A **gradient** is a color that gradually changes, either from light to dark or from one color to another. In this next step you'll add a gradient to the rectangle so that it's dark blue near the top and light blue near the bottom. This will create the illusion of the sky disappearing into the horizon.

When you work with Photoshop's shapes, like circles and rectangles, you apply gradients to them with the Layer Style menu. Select Layer ↗ Layer Styles ↗ Gradient Overlay (Figure 2-19).

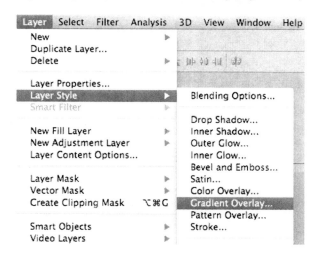

Figure 2-19. Select the Gradient Overlay Layer style.

As soon as you select Gradient Overlay, the rectangle will be filled with a simple gradient, and the Layer Style window will open with the Gradient Overlay option selected, as you can see in Figure 2-20.

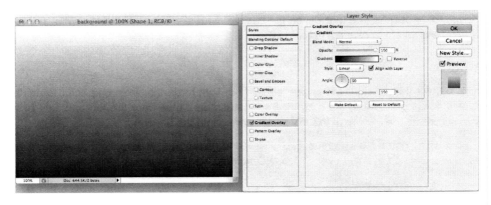

Figure 2-20. The Layer Style window lets you create and edit a gradient on a shape.

To edit the gradient, click the Gradient box in the Layer Style window. When you do this the Gradient Editor window will open, as shown in Figure 2-21.

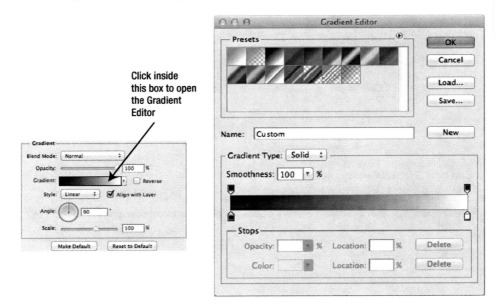

Figure 2-21. Click inside the Gradient box.

You can change the color and transparency of a gradient by selecting and moving the **stops**. The stops are the four little squares that you can see on the corners of the gradient preview, which is the long gradient strip at the bottom half of the window. The bottom stops determine the color of the gradient. The top stops determine its transparency, which is known as *opacity*. Figure 2-22 illustrates this.

Figure 2-22. Use the stops in the Gradient preview to customize the gradient

The stops are quirky little things. It's going to take a bit of playing around with them until you get the hang of how to use them. You can slide them back and forth to change where the gradient starts and ends. You can add new stops by clicking anywhere along the top or bottom of the gradient preview. You can delete them by dragging them off.

The stops along the top control the gradient's opacity. When you click an opacity stop, the Opacity option in the Gradient Editor becomes active and you can control the transparency of that section of the gradient. An opacity of 0% means that it's completely transparent and 100% means that it's completely opaque (solid), so 50% will make the gradient semi-transparent at the position of the stop. Figure 2-23 illustrates this.

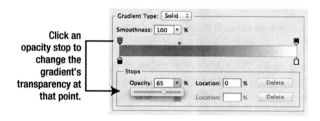

Figure 2-23. If you select an opacity stop, you can control the transparency at that point in the gradient by changing its opacity percentage.

You'll notice that if you change the Opacity value, you'll see a checkerboard pattern appear under the gradient. This is Photoshop's way of telling you that the color is transparent.

The Location option determines at which percentage position along the gradient the stop should be placed. It's just an alternative to sliding the stop with the mouse.

The bottom stops control the colors in the gradient. If you double-click a color stop, the Color Picker window will open, which lets you choose a color for that section of the gradient. Let's do that in the next step.

Double-click the color stop on the left side of the Gradient preview. The Color Picker window will open. (Photoshop calls it the Select stop color window.) Choose a nice light blue color, either from the Color Picker window or from the Swatches panel, as shown in Figure 2-24.

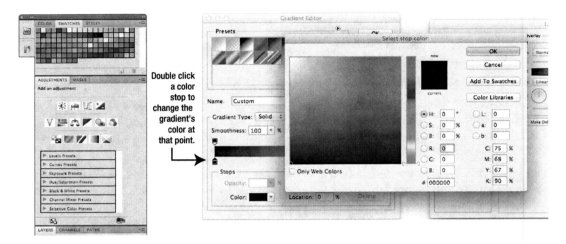

Figure 2-24. Change the gradient's color.

Click OK in the Select stop color window. The new color you chose will be applied to gradient at the point of the stop.

The next thing you're going to do is change the **color midpoint**, which determines the center of the gradient. The color midpoint is a tiny circle along the bottom of the gradient preview. For a natural looking sky gradient, slide the color midpoint circle to the left until the Location option reads about 25%, as shown in Figure 2-25.

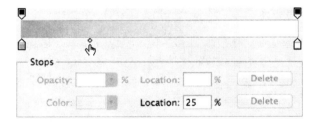

Figure 2-25. Change the gradient's midpoint.

Click OK in the Gradient Editor window when you're happy with the way the gradient looks. You should now have a gradient that looks something like Figure 2-26.

Figure 2-26. Your gradient so far

There's something wrong with this picture! Your sky is actually upside down. So you need to flip the direction of the gradient by 90 degrees so that the dark part is at the top and the light part is at the bottom.

The Layer Style window should still be open. Find the Angle option and set the gradient's angle to -90, either by entering that into the text field or by turning the Angle wheel with the mouse, as shown in Figure 2-27. The rectangle's gradient will match this rotation and the sky will now appear right side up.

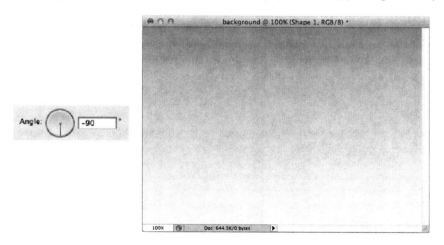

Figure 2-27. Rotate the gradient's angle by 90 degrees.

Click the OK button in the Layer Style window to apply the gradient to the rectangle.

> *As an alternative to rotating the gradient, you could also have rotated the rectangle shape with the Move Tool.*

The Layer Style window also lets you change the gradient from Linear, which is what you used in this example, to Radial, Angle, Reflected, or Diamond. Radial gradients are particularly useful for creating a pseudo 3D effect for circle shapes. Figure 2-28 shows what these different gradient types look like.

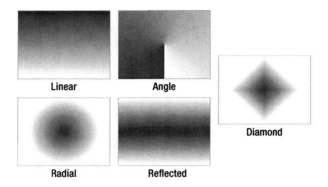

Figure 2-28. Photoshop's different gradient styles

Gradients are a complex topic in Photoshop and the best way to learn about them is to create some shapes and experiment with the settings in the Gradient Editor to see what kinds of effects you can produce. If you've created a gradient that you particularly like, the Gradient Editor lets you save it so that you can later load it into another shape.

Drawing hills

With your sky finished, it's time to add some green background hills to the scene. You're going to draw the hills in front of the sky. But before you can do that, you must look at an important Photoshop technique: how to use **layers** to organize the depth position of objects on the canvas.

Understanding layers

Layers allow you to organize your graphics so that they sit above or below other graphics. The Layers panel is at the bottom right of Photoshop's workspace. If you've followed the directions in this chapter so far, you should have two layers: a blank background layer and the rectangle shape that you drew in the earlier steps.

Next to each layer are icons that look like eyes. If you click on these, they can temporarily make the layer invisible on the canvas, letting you see the layer underneath. (Click the eye icon again to make the layer visible again.)

If there is a lock icon next to any layer, it means that the layer can't be edited. The background layer will always be locked. You can lock any layer by selecting the layer and clicking the Lock button near the top of the Layers panel. It's useful to lock layers if you've done a lot of work on graphics on that layer and want to prevent yourself from accidentally messing it up.

You can change the opacity (transparency) of each layer individually by selecting the layer and adjusting the opacity slider. If you give a layer an opacity of less that 100%, you'll be able to see the layers below it.

You can create and delete layers with the buttons at the bottom of the Layers panel. Figure 2-29 illustrates these basic features and where to find them.

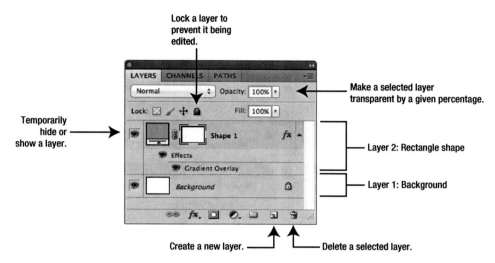

Figure 2-29. The Layers panel lets you organize your graphics so that they're above or below other graphics.

Each layer also tells you quite a bit of information about the kinds of things that are on that layer. You can see that on the second layer there's a shape; that's your sky rectangle. You can see that it's had a special layer effect applied to it, which is what the fx icon tells you. You can also see that it's a gradient overlay effect. In fact, if you want to edit the gradient effect, just double-click on Gradient Overlay in the Layers panel and the Layer Style window will open, letting you make any changes to the gradient that you like. You can temporarily hide an effect that you've created by clicking the eye icon next to the effect name. You can hide all the effects on a layer by clicking the eye icon next to Effects.

If you want add any other special effects to your layers, you can click the little FX button at the bottom of the panel and choose an effect from the list. Figure 2-30 illustrates these features of the Layers panel.

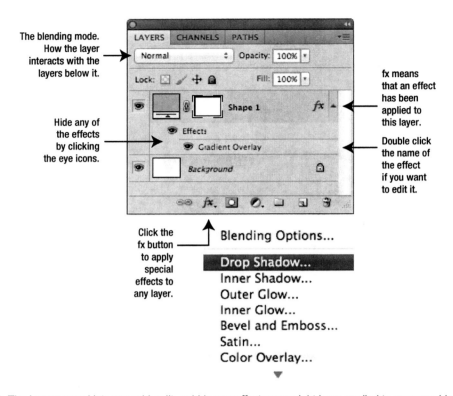

The blending mode. How the layer interacts with the layers below it.

Hide any of the effects by clicking the eye icons.

fx means that an effect has been applied to this layer.

Double click the name of the effect if you want to edit it.

Click the fx button to apply special effects to any layer.

Blending Options...

Drop Shadow...

Inner Shadow...

Outer Glow...

Inner Glow...

Bevel and Emboss...

Satin...

Color Overlay...

Figure 2-30. The Layers panel lets you add, edit, or hide any effects you might have applied to your graphics.

While you're working, keep a particular eye on the blending mode that you can select from the option menu at the top left of the Layers panel. The blending mode determines how a layer interacts with the layers below it. If you work in a blending mode other than normal, you can produce some interesting and often beautiful layer effects. However, you probably won't need any of these for simple game graphics, so you'll probably always want to keep the blending mode set to normal.

There's always a chance, however, that you might accidentally change the blending mode while you're working. If you notice that your game graphics suddenly become, dim, transparent, strangely outlined, or wildly psychedelic, there's a good chance that you might have switched a layer's blending mode.

As you can see, the Layers panel gives you an awful lot of control over your work. However, although you'll possibly use all of these features when creating your own game graphics, you don't need to worry about most of them for now. The most important thing to know is this: *anything on a layer above will hide things on layers below.*

Before you start work drawing on a new layer, give the sky layer a name and lock it so that you don't accidentally select or change it.

Double-click the words "Shape 1" in the Layers panel. This makes the text editable. Change it so that it reads "Sky." (Press the Enter key to apply the name change.) It's a good habit to give your layers names so that you can easily find them. You'll appreciate this when you're working on complex graphics with 20 or 30 layers.

Click the padlock button to lock the layer. Again, it's a good habit to lock layers after you've finished working on them so that you don't accidentally select and change them while working on new layers above. (You can easily unlock layers again to work them by again selecting the locked layer and clicking the padlock button.) Your Sky layer should now look like Figure 2-31.

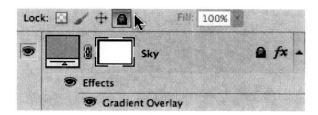

Figure 2-31. Give the layer a name and lock it to prevent accidental changes.

There are plenty of very advanced layer features that I haven't mentioned here. You won't need to use any of them to create the game graphics in this book because many are specialized for photo editing, but for a comprehensive explanation of what they all do, refer to Adobe's most recent online documentation at

http://help.adobe.com/en_US/photoshop/cs/using/index.html

Browse to the chapter called "Layers."

Let's create some hills for your game world scene so you can see this concept in action.

Drawing with the pen tool

Photoshop's Pen Tool lets you make complex shapes. Even though it's called a pen, it doesn't work like any pen that exists in the known universe. It's better to think of the Pen Tool as a way of making dots, and then connecting those dots with straight lines. Connect enough dots together, and you have a shape. You can then bend the lines in the shape to make really complex shapes with curves. Learning to use the Pen Tool properly is one of the most powerful and flexible graphic design techniques you can acquire.

Anchor points and paths

You're going to create two hills for your game world. Each of them will be on a different layer. For the first hill, click the "Create new layer" button at the bottom of the Layer's panel. (It looks like a new page with a corner turned over.) A new layer will appear above the Sky layer. Double-click the name of this new layer and give it the name "Hill 1." Figure 2-32 shows what your new layer should look like.

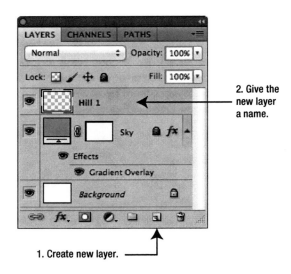

2. Give the new layer a name.

1. Create new layer.

Figure 2-32. Create a new layer to draw a hill.

You now have three layers, and it's on this new layer, "Hill 1," where you're going to do your next drawing.

Select the Pen Tool from the Tools panel (Figure 2-33).

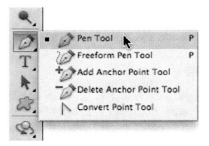

Figure 2-33. The Pen Tool

You're going to use the Pen Tool to roughly draw the general shape of the hill by creating a series of dots and connect them with straight lines. In further steps, you'll refine it by adding curves.

With the Pen Tool selected, click once anywhere in the canvas. (You're now drawing on the Hill layer.) A black square will appear. This is called an **anchor point**; it's the starting point of your shape.

Figure 2-34. Click with the Pen Tool to add an anchor point

Click to add a few more anchor points in a zigzag fashion, down and to the left of the first point, as in Figure 2-35. You'll notice that each time you add a point it's connected by a line to the previous point. This is called a **path**.

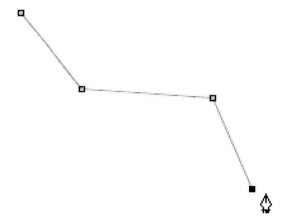

Figure 2-35. Create a path by clicking to add more anchor points.

If you make a mistake in Photoshop and want to undo an action, the good old Edit ↗ Undo or CRTL+Z (Windows) or Command+Z (Mac OS X) will undo the last thing you did.

However, Photoshop is only set up to undo the very last thing you did, and no more. If you did a few actions and then realize you need to go back and undo five or six steps, open Photoshop's History panel (Window ↗ History). The History panel records the previous 20 actions you did, as shown in Figure 2-36. It lets you revert back to a previous state by clicking any of these previous actions.

You can use the camera button at the bottom of the History panel to take a snapshot of your work. This is a good idea if you're just about to start a complex or experimental phase of your project and don't want to risk losing what you've done up till now. When you take a snapshot, Photoshop saves a version of your work in its current state, and you can get back to that state by clicking the snapshot at the top of the History panel. Snapshots aren't saved with the image file, however, so if you want to revert to snapshot, you need to do so before you close the file you're working on.

Figure 2-36. Undo previous actions by moving back in time with the History panel.

Continue the path so that it looks like Figure 2-37. You can complete the shape by clicking on the very first anchor point you added. When you do this, you'll notice a small "O" icon appear next to the Pen Tool. This shows you that you're going to **close the path**. When you close a path, you make a shape.

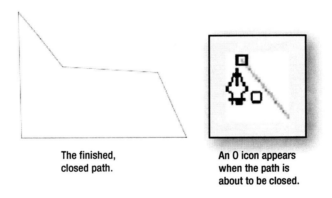

The finished,
closed path.

An 0 icon appears
when the path is
about to be closed.

Figure 2-37. Close the path to create the rough shape for the hill graphic.

Hold down the Shift key when you click to add anchor points and you can draw perfectly straight lines at fixed 90 and 45 degree angles between points.

Anchor points determine what your shape will look like. If you're not happy with where you've placed them, they're easy to move. Choose the Direct Selection Tool from the Tools panel. Everyone calls this the **white arrow**, which is exactly what it is. Click any of your anchor points with the white arrow and drag it to a new location, as shown in Figure 2-38. You can use this tool to move any of your anchor points and change the shape.

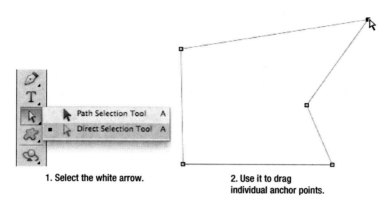

1. Select the white arrow.

2. Use it to drag individual anchor points.

Figure 2-38. Use the Direct Selection Tool (the white arrow) to move anchor points.

The Pen Tool and the white arrow are always used together like this. In fact, it's so common to switch between the Pen and the white arrow that's it's worth learning the keyboard shortcut to do it. With the Pen Tool selected, hold down the Ctrl key (Windows) or the Command Key (Mac OS X) and the Pen will temporarily change into the white arrow. This is a handy shortcut because if you're making lots of game graphics with the Pen Tool in Photoshop, you'll be switching back and forth between these two tools thousands of times.

You can move an entire shape path around the canvas by dragging it with the **black arrow** (the Path Selection Tool). Figure 2-39 illustrates this.

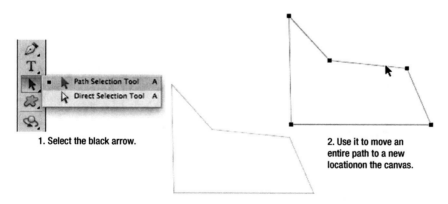

1. Select the black arrow.

2. Use it to move an entire path to a new locationon the canvas.

Figure 2-39. Use the Path Selection Tool (the black arrow) to move and entire path around the canvas.

It's easy to add and delete anchor points. To add a point, select the Pen Tool and move it over any line on the path. You'll see a little plus sign icon appear next to the Pen. Click on that spot on the path, and a new anchor point will be added. (It will add this new anchor point with a new feature called **direction handles**, and you'll be looking at how those work in the next section ahead.)

You can remove anchor points in a similar way. Move the Pen Tool over an existing anchor point and you'll see a minus sign icon appear next to it. Click the anchor point and it will disappear. Figure 2-40 shows how to add and delete anchor points.

If you're using an older version of Photoshop, you might not be able to add and remove anchor points so easily. It's likely you'll have to choose the Add Anchor Point or Delete Anchor Point Pen Tools from the Tools panel to achieve the same effect.

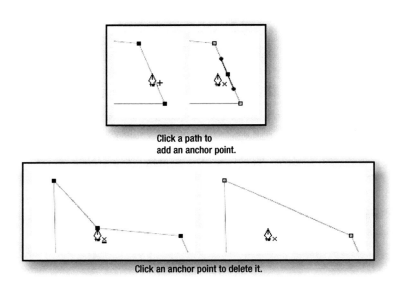

Figure 2-40. Use the Pen Tool to add and delete anchor points.

If you know how to create paths by adding and deleting anchor points with the Pen Tool, and you know how to move them with the white arrow, you have the essential skills for creating complex shapes with Photoshop. So far, however, you've been just been working with a shape that has straight lines. In the next section I'll show you how to make shapes with curves.

Make curves with direction handles

To curve your shape, you need to add direction handles to the anchor points.

Choose the Convert Point Tool from the Tools panel. Click on one of the anchor points. Then, while holding down the left mouse button, drag it across the canvas. Two direction handles appear; you can use them to bend the path at that point. The longer you make the directions handles by dragging and rotating them, the bigger the curve will be. Figure 2-41 illustrates this.

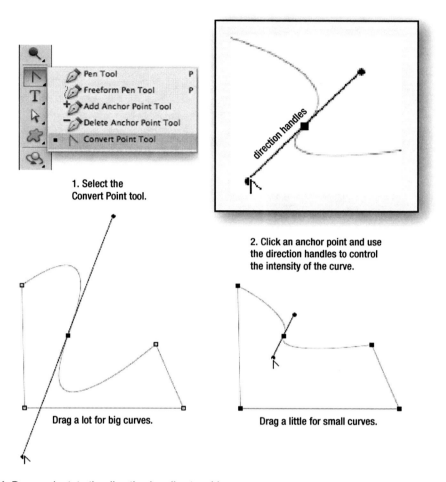

1. Select the
Convert Point tool.

2. Click an anchor point and use
the direction handles to control
the intensity of the curve.

Drag a lot for big curves.

Drag a little for small curves.

Figure 2-41. Drag and rotate the direction handles to add curves

The first time you use the Convert Point Tool, you'll be able to move both direction handles at the same time. They stay connected together and move in the same direction. But the second time you click and drag a direction handle, you'll notice that you'll only be moving one of them. The second click with the Convert Point Tool breaks the connection between the two handles. This is actually fine because being able to move the direction handles independently is very useful in fine-tuning the curve, as you can see in Figure 2-42.

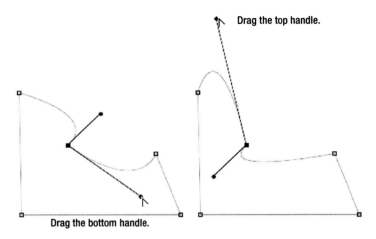

Figure 2-42. Use the Convert Point Tool to drag and rotate the direction handles independently. This lets you fine tune the curve.

But what if you want to move both the direction handles at the same time again? You can do this with the Direct Selection Tool—the white arrow.

Select the white arrow from the Tools panel. Hold down the Alt key (Windows) or the Option key (OS X) and drag one of the direction handles. You'll see they both start moving together again. Release Alt/Option and you can use the white arrow to move the direction handles independently again (see Figure 2-43).

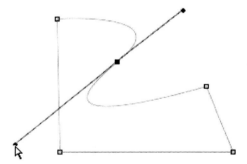

Figure 2-43. Use the white arrow and hold down Alt (Windows) or Option (OS X) to move both direction handles together.

By using these techniques together, you can have very fine control over the curves of your shapes. Let's put them to use in this next step.

Use the techniques to make your shape look as close as possible to Figure 2-44. You want it to look a bit like a ski slope, as seen from the side.

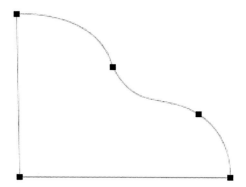

Figure 2-44. The finished shape path

If you're new to using the Pen Tool and direction handles, you probably won't get this right on your first attempt. In fact, you almost certainly won't. That's nothing to worry about! There's no magic formula for making shapes with curves; you just have to keep playing around with the tools until you're happy with the result. Use the History panel to undo any mistakes. But you can't really go wrong—just keep trying. Be disciplined about following these directions, and you'll soon get the hang of it. It takes a lot of practice to use the Pen Tool properly, but it's one of the most useful and powerful graphic design skills you can learn.

Resizing paths

If you've made a path and want to make it bigger or smaller, select the black arrow from the Tools panel. Select the Show Bounding Box in the option bar at the top of Photoshop's workspace. Click on the finished path you've drawn with the black arrow. You'll see that it's surrounded by a bounding box with handles on the corners. Drag these handles to resize the path so that your shape is as large or small as you want it to be. Figure 2-45 illustrates this.

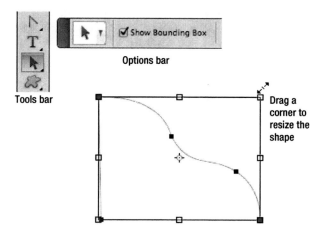

Figure 2-45. Use the black arrow to resize the path.

For the purpose of this project, make this path you've drawn quite big.

Resize the path and position it so that it fills the left size of the canvas. Remember to press the Enter key to apply the transformation after you've finished resizing and positioning it. Your canvas should now look similar to Figure 2-46.

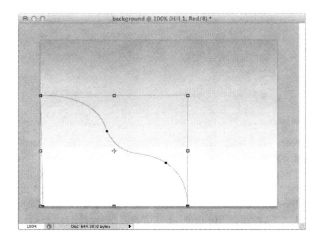

Figure 2-46. Resize and position the path.

Fill the path with color

The path you've just drawn represents the outline of the shape you want to make, but it's not going to be useful to you as a game graphic until you fill it with color. The Paths panel to the right of the Photoshop workspace lets you do this.

For this next trick to work, the path you drew in the previous section needs to be selected with the black arrow tool. Click on it once with the black arrow to select it. You can tell it's selected because the shape path will be surrounded by a black bounding box with drag handles on the corners, as shown in Figure 2-47.

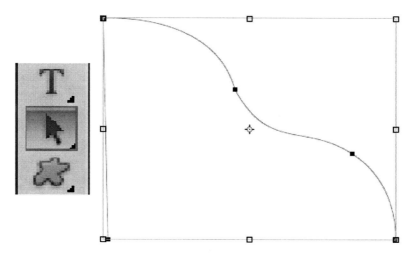

Figure 2-47. Make sure the shape path is still selected with the black arrow tool.

Before you can successfully apply a color to the path, there's one more important setting you need to make. With the black arrow tool still selected, click the "Add shape to area (+)" button in the Options bar at the top of Photoshop's workspace. Figure 2-48 shows you where to find it. If this button isn't selected, the following steps won't work properly. It's this button that will allow you to fill the inside area of the shape path with color. (If the button is dimmed and you can't click it, it means that you didn't first select the path with the black arrow. Click the path with the arrow so that it's selected and try again.)

Figure 2-48. Click the "Add shape to area (+)" button in the black arrow options.

Next, choose a color for your shape. Select a nice bright green color in the foreground color box in the Tools panel (Figure 2-49), using the techniques you learned earlier in this chapter.

Figure 2-49. Select a green foreground color.

Open the Paths panel, which you'll find as a tab option in the same window that contains the Layers panel. As you can see in Figure 2-50, you'll find a small thumbnail image of the path that you just drew with some buttons along the bottom. Those buttons let you fill the path with color, outline it with a brush stroke, turn it into a selection, or delete it. If you give the path a unique name, Photoshop automatically saves the path with the document so that you can reuse it somewhere else if you ever need to. I've named my path "Hill."

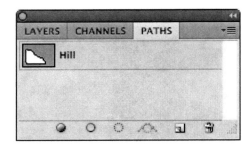

Figure 2-50. The Paths panel lets you fill a path with color.

Click the Fill path with foreground color button at the bottom of the Paths panel. The shape path will be filled with the green foreground color, as shown in Figure 2-51.

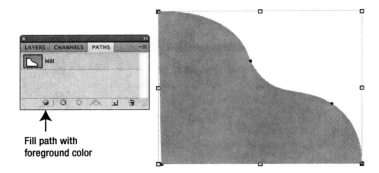

Fill path with
foreground color

Figure 2-51. Fill the path with the foreground color.

If necessary, you can reverse this effect by clicking the "Subtract from shape area (-)" button in the black arrow's Options bar. This will fill the surrounding area with color and keep the shape empty.

Your canvas should now look similar to Figure 2-52.

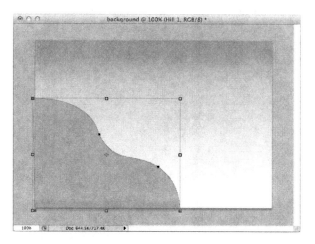

Figure 2-52. The hill is now filled with color.

What actually happened here? The path you drew in the previous sections was just a stencil. What you've done now is poured color into that stencil. The color has been poured onto the transparent surface of the Layer. It's like using a stencil to color in a shape on a transparent sheet of plastic.

All you care about is the color you've just poured onto the layer. You can get rid of the path completely because it's served its purpose and you don't need to use it again. Let's delete it.

The path should still be selected with the black arrow tool. (You can confirm this by the bounding box that will be around the path.) If it isn't selected, click the path once with the black arrow. Press the Delete key on your keyboard and the path will disappear.

What you're left with is a nice green hill. In the next section you're going to make another copy of this hill, change its color, and reposition it on the right side of the canvas behind this first hill.

When you're comfortable working with the Pen Tool and its related tools and techniques, try using the Freeform Pen Tool. You'll like it; it works like a real pen! You can draw a shape freehand, and then use the Convert Point Tool and white arrow to fine-tune your shape.

Duplicating, modifying, and arranging layers

You need two hills in your scene. But rather than going to all the trouble of making another hill, just duplicate the one you've already got and make a few changes to it.

With the Hill 1 layer selected in the Layers panel, select Layers ↗ Duplicate from the main menu. (You can also right-click on the Hill 1 layer and select Duplicate.) The Duplicate Layer dialog box will open and ask you for the name of the new Layer. Give it the name "Hill 2," as shown in Figure 5-53. Click the OK button.

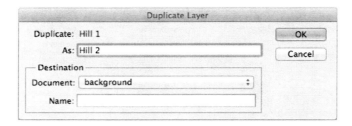

Figure 2-53. Duplicate the layer.

As soon as you do this, you'll see a new layer called Hill 2 appear above the Hill 1 layer (Figure 2-54). The layers look identical.

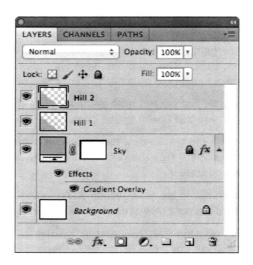

Figure 2-54. The new layer is duplicated and is floating above the first one.

You now have two hills on the canvas, even though it just looks like you have one. That's because the new layer you just created is in exactly the same place as the first one. The new hill is sitting directly on top of the first hill. Move it out of the way so that you can see both hills

Select the Move Tool. In the Options bar, check Auto-Select and choose Layers from the option menu. The Auto-Select option allows the Move Tool to automatically select objects on the correct layers when you click on them, which is very convenient. If you don't change this setting, you'll have to first click the layer you want to work on in the Layers panel before you can move that layer around the canvas. While you're at it, make sure that Show Transform Controls is also selected. Figure 2-55 shows what the Move Tool options should look like.

Figure 2-55. Auto-selecting layers lets the Move Tool automatically select objects on the correct layer when you click on them.

With the Move Tool still selected, move the hill on the canvas. Doing so will magically reveal the first hill on the layer below, as shown in Figure 2-56.

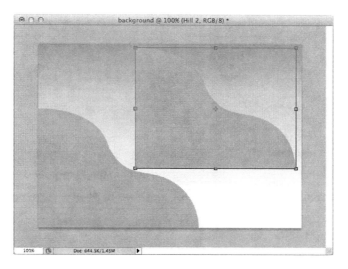

Figure 2-56. Move the new duplicated hill to reveal the original on the layer below.

Flip it horizontally so it's facing the opposite direction to the first hill. Select Edit ↗ Transform ↗ Flip Horizontal from Photoshop's main menu. The hill will flip around to face the other way, as you can see in Figure 2-57.

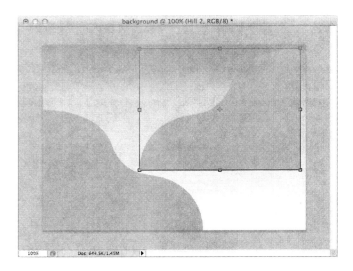

Figure 2-57. Flip the new hill horizontally.

Now let's change the new hill's color. Select a dark green color in the Foreground color box.

Select the Paint Bucket Tool. Click inside the new hill, and it will be filled with the new color (Figure 2-58).

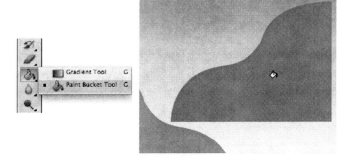

Figure 2-58. Select the Paint Bucket Tool and click inside the new hill to change its color.

Select the Move Tool and move the hill to the bottom left corner of the canvas, as shown in Figure 2-59.

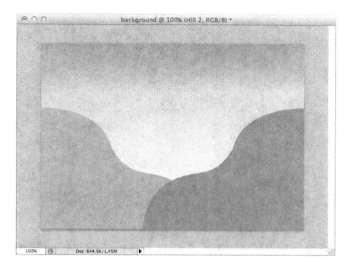

Figure 2-59. Move the new hill into its position.

The new, darker hill that you've created should be behind the first so that it looks like it's a bit further away in the distance. Let's move its layer so that it's below the first hill's layer.

In the Layers palette, drag the Hill 2 layer so that it's below the Hill 1 layer. Release the mouse and you should now see the darker green hill behind the light green hill, as shown in Figure 2-60.

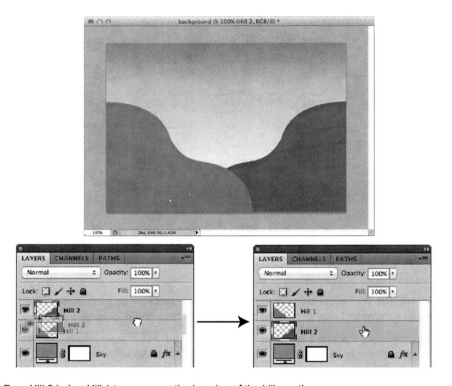

Figure 2-60. Drag Hill 2 below Hill 1 to rearrange the layering of the hills on the canvas.

Being able to rearrange layers like this is one of the most basic, but most powerful, Photoshop techniques.

Your hills are looking better, but let's go one step further and give them a slight 3D effect with a technique called *beveling*.

Bevel and emboss

The complementary effects of bevel and emboss allow you to give objects an appearance of shallow depth. Embossing makes an object appear imprinted into a surface. Beveling makes it look slightly raised from the surface. Figure 2-61 illustrates bevel and emboss effects.

Figure 2-61. Bevel and emboss effects

An important concept to keep in mind when you apply effects like this in Photoshop is that you don't apply effects to the actual image you've drawn; you apply them to the layer that contains the object. That's why they're called layer effects. Any graphics on that layer will be affected by whatever effects you've applied to that layer. This is different from many other graphics and drawing applications where you apply effects directly to graphic objects.

So, apply a bevel effect to your hills. Select the Hill 1 layer and choose Bevel and Emboss from the FX menu, as shown in Figure 2-62.

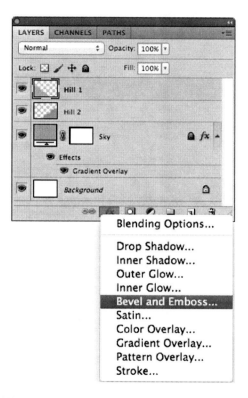

Figure 2-62. Select the Bevel and Emboss from the FX menu.

The Layer Style window opens. You saw this window before when you were working with gradients. But now the Bevel and Emboss option has been selected, which allows you to apply either of those effects

Select Inner Bevel from the Style menu. Make sure that the Preview option is checked so that you can see how your changes affect the graphics on the canvas. Play around with the settings until you achieve an effect you like. You'll have a more dramatic effect if you uncheck the "Use global light" option. Figure 2-63 shows what my Layer Styles window looks like, and Figure 2-64 shows the result of the bevel effect on the hill. But whatever you do, don't click the OK button just yet!

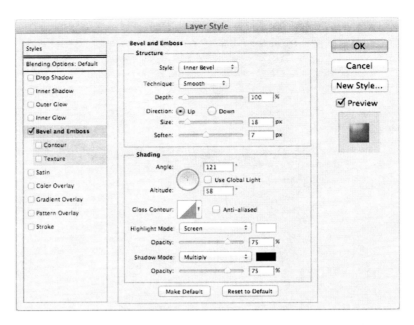

Figure 2-63. The Layer Style window lets you set up and apply Bevel and Emboss effects to selected layers.

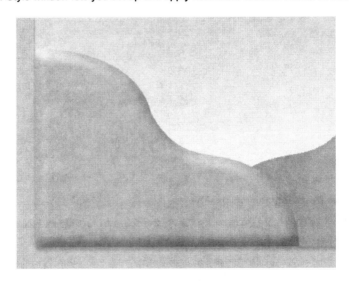

Figure 2-64. The finished bevel effect

Creating bevel and emboss effects is very much a question of just playing around with the settings until you find something you like.

Save this layer style so that you can apply the same effect on the second hill. Click the New Style button in the Layer Effects window. A New Style window will open. Enter the name Hill and click the OK button (Figure 2-65).

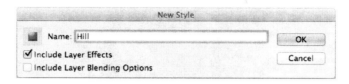

Figure 2-65. Save this style so you can use it later.

Click OK in the Layer Style window to apply the bevel effect to the hill.

You're now going to apply the same effect to the second hill.

Select the Hill 2 layer.

Open the Styles panel, which you'll find in the same window group as the Colors panel. The Styles panel shows you a thumbnail list of some preset styles that can be applied to layers. The very last one will be the Hill style that you created and saved in the previous section. Click on it, and you'll see the style immediately applied to the second hill. Figure 2-66 shows what you'll see.

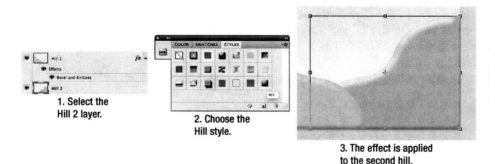

1. Select the Hill 2 layer.

2. Choose the Hill style.

3. The effect is applied to the second hill.

Figure 2-66. Click the Hill style in the Styles panel to apply the saved style to the second hill.

You've finished working on the hills, so lock both the Hill 1 and Hill 2 layers to prevent accidentally editing them in the next steps. Select the layer you want to lock, and click the padlock buttons. Padlock icons will appear on the layer (Figure 2-67).

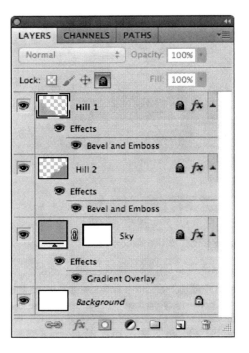

Figure 2-67. Lock the layers to prevent further editing.

You now have a nice background scene with a sky and some hills. In the next section, you're going to add some boxes to the foreground and learn how to make shapes using selection areas.

Making boxes with the rectangular selection tool

So far I've shown you two ways to make shapes with Photoshop. The first was how to use the Rectangle shape tool to make the sky. The second was how to create a path with the Pen Tool and fill the path with color. In this section, you'll look at a third way: how to create a selection area and fill it with color.

You'll find Photoshop's Selection tools at the top of the Tools panel. They're usually used to select areas of a photograph for editing, such as to copy, paste, or delete sections, but they're also a quick and easy way to make shapes. You're going to use the Rectangular selection tool to make some boxes for the foreground of your game world scene.

Click the new layer button in the Layers panel to create a new layer above the hill layers. Give it the name "Box" (Figure 2-68).

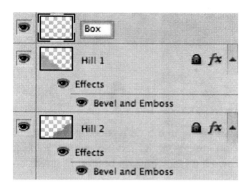

Figure 2-68. Create a new layer above the previous layers.

Select the Rectangular Marquee Tool from the Tools panel. You're going to use it to make square boxes with the exact dimensions of 50 by 50 pixels. The Option bar lets you create fixed size selection areas. Look for the Style option and select Fixed Size from the menu. Enter a Width of "50 px" and a Height of "50 px." Adding the "px" (for pixels) is important; otherwise Photoshop might think that you're using dimensions in centimeters if you haven't changed its default units in Photoshop's preferences. Confirm that your Options bar looks like Figure 2-69.

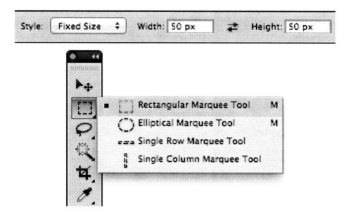

Figure 2-69. Select the Rectangular Marquee Tool and set it to a fixed size of 50 by 50 pixels.

Photoshop calls these "marquee" selection tools because when you select something with them, the selection area is surrounded by an animation of moving lines that looks a bit like the lights of a flashing movie or theatre marquee sign. Another whimsical name for them is "marching ants."

Click the canvas. A square, defined by a border of dashed moving lines, will appear on the canvas, as shown in Figure 2-70. It's exactly 50 by 50 pixels in size.

Figure 2-70. Click the canvas to add a 50 by 50 pixel selection square.

This is a selection area. If you were using it in a conventional way, you could use it to copy anything that was under it or you could paste an image into it. Instead, you're going to use it to make a square game box. In the next few steps, you'll give it a black outside border, fill it with color, and give it a bevel effect.

Right-click and choose Stroke from the option menu. When you're making graphics, you can think of "stroke" as Photoshop's term for "the outline." (In other contexts, however, strokes can be used for much more than just outlining shapes.) A new window will open that allows you to set the border option. Give it a width of 5 px and choose a nice black color. Click OK when you're done and you'll see that the selection area now has a black border. Figure 2-71 shows what this will look like.

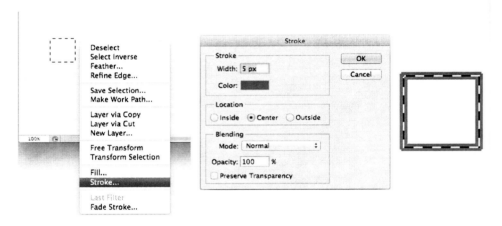

Figure 2-71. Add a border to the selection area.

Next, add a fill color. Right-click and choose Fill from the option menu. A Fill window will open. Select Color from the menu in the Contents section. The standard Color Picker window will open so that you can choose a color. Choose a bright red, and click OK in the Fill window when you're done. The square selection area is now filled with the color you choose. Figure 2-72 shows what your square should now look like.

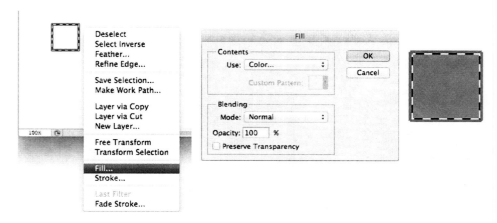

Figure 2-72. Add a fill color to the selection.

You can also fill a selection by choosing a foreground color and clicking inside the selection with the Paint Bucket Tool.

If you want to fill a selection area with a gradient, use the Gradient Tool. (You'll find it in the same button set as the Paint Bucket.) To use it, click and drag in the selection area, and the selection will be filled with a gradient that uses the foreground and background color. You can edit the gradient by double-clicking the gradient preview in the Options bar.

You've now got a red square with a black border. But notice that the selection is still active. You don't need it anymore, so deselect it. Choose Select ↗ Deselect from the main menu or press Ctrl+D (Windows) or Command+D (Mac OS X) to deselect it. The marquee, the animated black lines, will disappear.

Next, give your red square a bevel effect. Click the FX button at the bottom of the Layers panel, and use the techniques you learned in the previous section to apply a bevel to the square. Your square might now look something like Figure 2-73.

Figure 2-73. Add a bevel.

You now have a nice, all-purpose game square. Make a few more copies of it to decorate the foreground of your scene.

Select the square with the Move Tool. Hover the mouse over the square and hold down the Alt (Windows) or Option (Mac OS X) Key. You'll see the mouse icon change so that it looks like a double arrow. Hold down the left mouse button and drag. Photoshop will make an exact duplicate of the square on its own new layer. (You could also duplicate the layer like you did in the previous step, but it's not as much fun!) Figure 2-74 illustrates this technique.

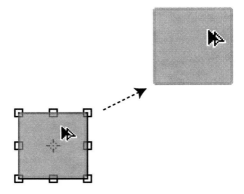

Figure 2-74. Hold down Alt (Windows) or Option (Mac OS X) and drag to duplicate the square.

Use this same technique to make 10 or 15 more squares like this. Use the Move Tool to organize them along the bottom of the canvas like a stack of children's building blocks. (Make sure that the Move Tool's Auto-Select Layers option is selected in the Options bar. That makes it easy to select each square's layer just by clicking the square on the canvas.) Your final scene will look something like Figure 2-75 when you're done.

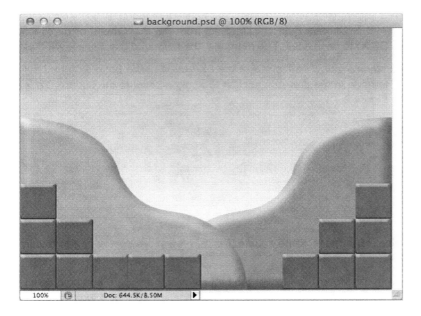

Figure 2-75. The final background scene

When you're duplicating and moving these little squares around the canvas, be careful not to click the little crosshair section in the squares' very centers. This is what determines the center of the square for rotation. You can actually move this center point if you want to rotate an object off-axis, which is something that's often very useful to do. However, if you accidentally drag from the center crosshair while trying to duplicate a square, the duplicate action will be disabled and instead you'll find yourself dragging this little center crosshair all over the canvas. To reset this so that you can start duplicating again, double-click the square. It's best to start dragging from the inner corners of the squares so that you avoid accidentally resizing them or repositioning their centers.

Now save your work in a format that's good for using in Flash games.

Saving the image

To use the image you've just created in an AS3.0 game or program (which you'll do in the next chapter) you have to save it in PNG format. PNG is a *compressed file format. Compressed files* have a very small file size, which means that they load quickly over the Internet and don't take up much space on a hard drive. PNG is a high-quality image file format that has a small file size but preserves any areas of the image that are transparent. (Other compressed file formats like JPEG or GIF don't preserve transparency, although GIF has limited 1-bit transparency that doesn't preserve any gradual changes in opacity, like those in shadows or semi-transparent gradient effects.)

The only problem with PNG files is that you can't edit them. This means that if you decide you want to make changes to an image, all the layers, styles, or other settings you might have saved while working in Photoshop will be gone.

For that reason, you need to save two versions of the image file. The first should be in PSD (Photoshop Document) format. PSD files are big, but you can make changes to them. The second file should be the compressed PNG file. You won't be able to edit this file, but it's the one that you'll use in your games. If you need to make any changes to an image, first make the changes in the PSD file and then create the PNG file from that PSD file.

Here's how to save your work and make the PNG file that you'll use in the next chapter:

Select File ↗ Save As from Photoshop's main menu. If this is the first time you've saved your work, give it the name "background", and make sure that "Photoshop" is selected from the Format menu. Choose a location on your computer to save your work and click the Save button. (If a Maximize Compatibility window opens while you do this, just ignore it by clicking OK.)

Let's next save the image as a PNG file. Select File ↗ Save for Web and Devices from the main menu. A new window will open, showing many different settings to optimize the quality and file size of the image. In the Preset menu at the top right of this window, select PNG-24. Figure 2-76 shows what this should look like. Click the Save button. A new window will open to allow you to change the file name, if you need to, and choose a save location. Pick a location for the file and then click the Save button.

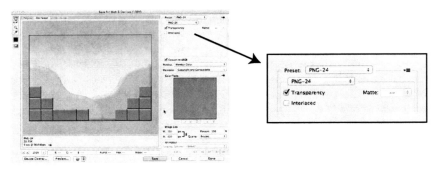

Figure 2-76. The Save for Web and Devices window lets you save your work as a compressed PNG file.

You now have two versions of the image file saved: a PSD version that you can edit and a PNG version that you can use in your AS3.0 games and programs.

Check the location(s) where you saved these images. You should see these two files:

- background.psd
- background.png

You've got a background image for your game world; now you can put all your new Photoshop skills to work and make a game character.

Making a game character

If you've worked through all the exercises and instructions in this chapter, you now have a comprehensive set of skills for making game graphics with Photoshop. Photoshop is capable of much more but, for the purposes of drawing and making graphics, I've just about covered everything. The rest is mostly just a question of practicing what you've learned, refining your skills, and tweaking some settings.

Let's use these techniques to make a game character. I'll get you started on creating a new file and give you a few pointers along the way, but I'm going to leave you on your own for most of this one. Hey, you've got the skills, imagination, and the all-important History panel, so don't be scared. Go for it!

Create a new file

Before you start drawing, open a new Photoshop document file.

Select File ↗ New from Photoshop's main menu.

Give this new file the name "character." Set both the width and height to 100 pixels.

Very importantly, set the Background Contents to transparent. This allows any transparent or unfilled areas of your drawing to let the background show through. You'll be able to tell you're drawing on a transparent background because the background will be filled with a checkerboard pattern.

Figure 2-77 shows what the new window should look like.

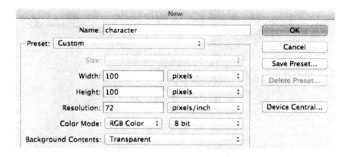

Figure 2-77. Create a new file with the dimensions 100 by 100. Set the Background Contents to Transparent.

Click the OK button to open a new blank canvas.

It's going to be a little small, so select View ⁊ Zoom In from the main menu until you find a size you like. More conveniently, hold down Ctrl (Windows) or Command (Mac OS X) and press the plus (+) and minus (-) keys on your keyboard to zoom in and out.

There are many more magnification options in Photoshop. You can use the magnifying glass from the Tools panel to draw an area around part of your image you want to zoom into. Double-click on the magnifying glass to make your image return to normal magnification. At the very bottom left of the canvas you'll find a number with a percentage next to it—that's the amount that you're zoomed in. You can enter any zoom percentage here that you like. You can also change the zoom percentage from the Application bar, which is directly above the Options bar.

You're now ready to start drawing!

Draw your character

Your new canvas is 100 by 100 pixels square. When you draw your game character, try to fill all the space right up to the borders of the canvas. This is especially important in later chapters in this book so that the edges of your game characters will appear to touch the edges of the game world.

Using only the techniques in this chapter, Figure 2-78 shows the game character I created.

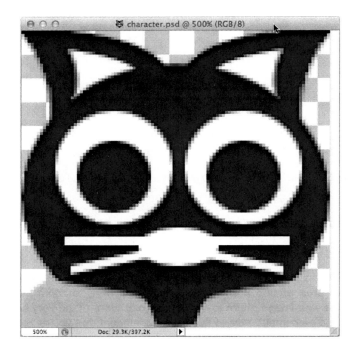

Figure 2-78. A game character

Notice that the background is filled with a grey and white checkerboard pattern. This shows that the background is transparent, which is what you need for the game world show through the character's edges. Your Photoshop canvas will look like this if you selected Background Contents Transparent when you created the new file. If you forgot to do this, you can make it transparent by clicking the eye icon in the Background layer.

You're going to learn a lot about Photoshop while you work on this character, and you'll probably have quite a few more questions by the time you finish. Let's look at a few more techniques that might help you with this project.

Making circles

Circles? Yes, of course! You haven't made any circle shapes in this chapter so far, but they're extremely easy to make. Just choose either the Circle Tool (which is part of the same button set as the Rectangle Tool) or the Elliptical Marquee Tool (from the same button set as the Rectangular Marquee Tool.) Then just follow the same techniques you followed for making rectangular shapes. You can force your circular shapes to be perfect circles by holding down the Shift key while dragging with the mouse. You can start a drawing a circle from its center point by holding down the Alt (Windows) or Option (OSX) key while dragging.

Linking and grouping layers

Sometimes your graphics will have complex features that involve shapes that span multiple layers. In those cases, it's useful to work on all those layers together as a single group. Photoshop has two features to help you do this: linking and grouping layers.

By linking layers you can select all the graphics on those layers just by selecting one of them. You can then move, resize, or rotate all those layers as a group. When I was working on my cat character, I linked the white and black shapes that make up the cat's eyes. That made it easy to move the eyes around the canvas because I didn't need to select the black and white parts separately.

To link layers together, hold down the Shift key and click on all the layers that you want to link. (Holding down Shift lets you select multiple items.) Then click the chain button at the bottom of the Layers panel. Figure 2-79 illustrates this.

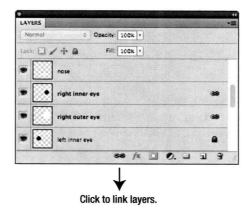

Click to link layers.

Figure 2-79. Link layers to work with them as a single unit.

Another option is to group layers together. By grouping layers you can create a folder in the Layers panel and organize related layers into them. You can then open and close the folder to reduce clutter in the Layers panel.

To group two or more layers, select the layers by holding down the Shift key and clicking with the left mouse button. Select Layer ↗ Group Layers from Photoshop's main menu. You'll then see that your selected layers are organized into a folder in the Layers panel. Click the small triangle next to the folder name to open and close it. Give the folder a name to remind you which layers are inside. Figure 2-80 shows how I've organized the feet layers of my cat character into their own folder.

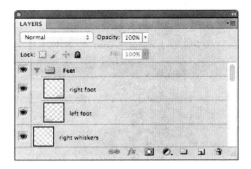

Figure 2-80. Group related layers to reduce clutter in the **Layers** panel.

After you've created a group, you can move layers into it by holding down Alt (Windows) or Option (Mac OS X) and dragging the layer into the group.

Ungroup layers by selecting the name of the group and choosing Layer ↗ Ungroup Layers from Photoshop's main menu.

Save your game character

When you're finished working on your character, save it following the same steps you used to save the background image. Make sure that you save two versions of the file: the PSD file and the PNG file. Make sure these two files are named character.psd and character.png.

Making buttons

In Chapter 3, you're going to build an interactive toy that lets you control your game character by clicking on buttons. You need some buttons to click, so you're going to make those buttons next. In Chapter 3, you're going to attach some AS3.0 programming code to these buttons to make them work.

You need six buttons that will look like those in Figure 2-81.

Figure 2-81. Six buttons

They'll be easy to make because you can make them all in one Photoshop file. Let's see how.

Create a new file

You should be getting pretty good at this by now, but let's go over the basics of creating a new Photoshop document again just to make sure you don't miss something important.

Select File ↗ New from Photoshop's main menu.

Give this new file the name "buttons."

Set the width to 100 px and the height to 50 px

Set the Background Contents to Transparent.

Click the OK button to open a new blank canvas.

Draw the button

There are two ways that you can make square or circular shapes in Photoshop: using the Shape tools or the Selection tools. You've used both in this chapter.

But there's one important difference between them. When you create shapes with the Selection tools, Photoshop makes the shapes by drawing pixels on the canvas—tiny little squares. When you use the Shape tools, it doesn't do this. The shapes created by the Shape tools are made using **vectors**, which are mathematical formulas based on lines. Zoom into the shapes as much as you like, and you'll never see any pixels. Shapes made with vectors are a little easier to edit because Photoshop doesn't have to recalculate the positions of all the pixels, and possibly distort them slightly, if you resize a shape.

But there is one disadvantage to vector shapes. Out of the box, you can't use them in combination with layer effects, like bevel, emboss, or drop shadows. That's because those layer effects only work on pixels, not vector shapes. You need to make a slight change to the Shape Tool options so that those layer effects will work. You need to force the Shape Tools to use pixels instead of vectors. I'll show you how to do this while you make your buttons in the steps that follow.

1.   Select the Rectangle Shape from the Tools panel.

2.   Choose a nice bright yellow color in the Foreground color box in the Tools panel.

3.   In the Options bar, click the Fill pixels button. This is the magic button that lets you use the Shape tools to draw pixels.

4.   Draw a yellow rectangle on the canvas. Leave a bit of space, about 4 or 5 pixels, on the right and bottom of the canvas. That's so you have room for the drop shadow effect that you'll add in the steps ahead. Figure 2-82 shows what this process should look like.

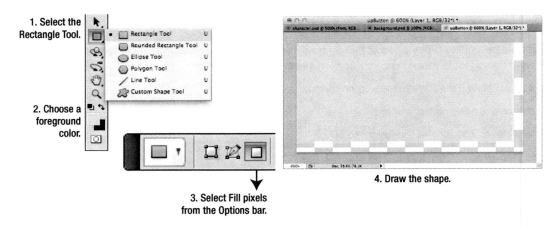

1. Select the Rectangle Tool.

2. Choose a foreground color.

3. Select Fill pixels from the Options bar.

4. Draw the shape.

Figure 2-82. Use the Fill pixels option to make the Shape tools use pixels.

The shape is now filled with pixels, which means you can use any of the layer effects. In the next steps, you're going to add bevel and drop shadow effects.

5.   Click the FX button at the bottom of the Layers panel and choose Bevel and Emboss. Make any changes you like in the Layer Style window for a nice bevel effect.

6.   With the Layer Style window still open, click Drop Shadow in the left hand option menu. The Drop Shadow options will open. A **drop shadow** gives an image a slight shadow effect, which enhances its 3D appearance.

Set the following Drop shadow options:

o   Opacity: 75

o   Angle: 120

o   Distance: 4

o   Size: 4

Figure 2-83 shows what the Drop Shadow options look like.

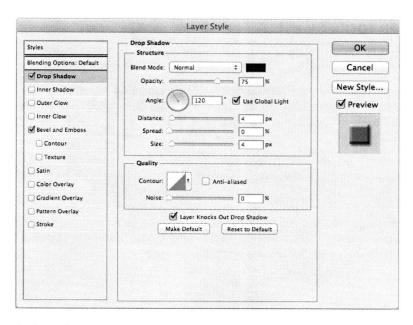

Figure 2-83. Drop shadow options

Remember, you can edit these effects at any time by double-clicking the effect name in the Layers panel.

7. Click OK in the Layer Style window when you're happy with the way the bevel and drop shadow effects look. When you're finished, your canvas and layers might now look something like Figure 2-84.

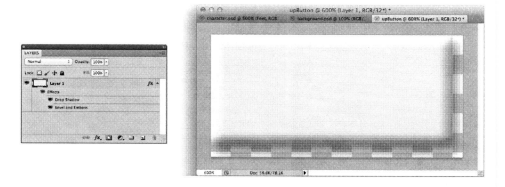

Figure 2-84. The button so far with the bevel and drop shadow effect

8. Finally, give the layer a name, perhaps "button background," and lock the layer to prevent further editing.

Your button is almost finished; all you need to do next is add some text.

Using the type tool

Photoshop's Type tools are extremely easy to use. You're going to use the Horizontal Type Tool to add the word "up" to the button.

Select the Horizontal Type Tool from the Tools panel. The Options bar lets you choose the font, size, and color. Choose a nice large font and make sure it's black. (The default color will be the same foreground color that you just used, so you'll need to change it if you want to see the text against the button background.)

> *If you ever need to add text that runs vertically down the canvas, select the Vertical Type Tool.*

Click the canvas and type the word "up." As soon as you click the canvas to add text, Photoshop creates a new layer for you automatically. Use the Move Tool to position the text to the centre of the button. Figure 2-85 shows what my button looks like and the text options I used.

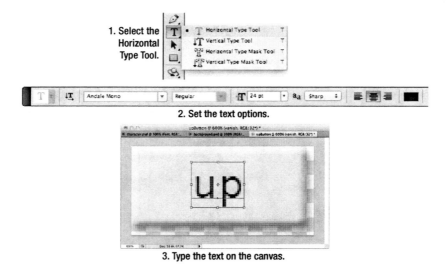

Figure 2-85. Set the Type Tool options and add some text to the button.

When you add text to the canvas, Photoshop automatically creates a new layer for it with the same name as the text you wrote. However, this will only happen if you switch tools, like selecting the Move Tool, before adding some more text. If you don't switch tools, Photoshop will add the new text to the same layer. In that case, create the new layer manually by selecting the Create new layer button at the bottom of the Layers panel.

That's one button finished. Now let's make the rest of them.

Making more buttons

You need to make six buttons in total. You need buttons with the labels "up," "down," "grow," "shrink," "vanish," and "spin." They'll all look exactly the same; the only change will be the text. You could make all these buttons as individual PSD files. That's fine, but you'll then end up with six different Photoshop files to manage, as well as the six accompanying PNG files. There's a way to simplify this a bit.

I'm going to show you a well worn trick to keeping all the buttons in one PSD file. You'll then use that one PSD file to make the six different PNG files that you'll need—one for each button.

It works like this: The button background will be on the bottom layer. You'll then have six text layers above the background, each with different button label text. All the text layers will be hidden using the eye icon, except for one of them. That means only one button label will be visible at any one time. You'll then create that button's PNG file using the button background and the single visible text label. After that PNG file has been made, you'll hide the visible text and display the next label on the layer above. You'll then use that state to make the next button PNG file.

It's easier to understand this when it's put in practice, so let's get to work!

First, make sure that your layers looks similar to mine in Figure 2-86. You should have one text layer above the button background and the button background should be locked.

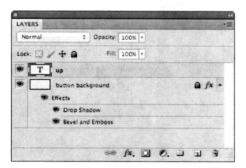

Figure 2-86. Your button layers so far

Click the eye icon next to the "up" layer to hide it. The text will disappear from the canvas.

Select the Horizontal Type Tool and type the word "down" on the Canvas. Your canvas and layers should now look similar to Figure 2-87.

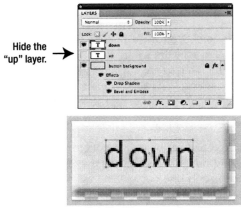

Hide the
"up" layer.

Only the "down" layer is visible.

Figure 2-87. Add new next above the hidden layer.

If you want to make sure that you align the new text correctly, temporarily make the "up" layer visible and position the "down" text directly above it. Make the up layer invisible again when you're done.

Next, hide the "down" layer that you just created so that the text disappears from the canvas.

Select the Horizontal Text Tool again and type the word "grow" on the canvas. Your canvas and layers should now look similar to Figure 2-88.

Hide both
the "up"
and "down"
layers.

Only the "grow" text is visible.

Figure 2-88. Add another layer of button text, which should be the only one visible.

Do you see a pattern developing? All the button labels will be added like this, but only one will be visible at any given time. Keep doing this till you've added the text for all the buttons you need.

Add more text layers for the words "shrink," "vanish," and "spin." When you're done, make all the layers invisible except the "up" layer and the "button background" layer. Your finished layers and canvas should now look like Figure 2-89.

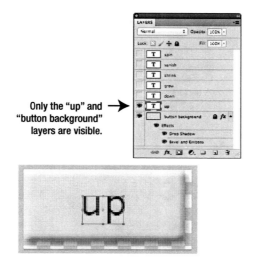

Only the "up" and → "button background" layers are visible.

Figure 2-89. Your finished buttons

Save your work and make the PNG files

You now have one Photoshop document that contains all the graphics you need to make your buttons. First, save it in PSD format so you don't accidentally lose all your hard work. Select File ↗ Save As from the main menu. Find a convenient location to save this file.

You can now use this file to make six PNG files, one for each button. Start with the "up" button.

Select File ↗ Save for Web and Devices. Set the Preset option to PNG-24.

If for some reason the "Save for Web and Devices" option is dimmed and you can't select it, you might be accidentally working in 32-bit color mode. Select Image ↗ Mode and choose either the 16bits/channel option or 8bits/channel. Photoshop will then ask you if you wish to merge the layers—don't do this! Merging layers compresses all your layers into one, which makes it impossible to selectively hide and display them. Click the Don't Merge button. The "Save for Web and Devices" option will now be available again.

Click the Save button and name the PNG file "upButton." Make sure the "u" is lowercase, the "B" is upper case, and that there is no space between the words. This is an example of the lowerCamelCase naming convention that you looked at in Chapter 1. From now on, you're going to use this naming convention for all the images you make in this book.

Photoshop's main workspace will now be visible again. Hide the "up" layer by clicking the eye icon next to it.

Make the "down" layer visible by clicking its eye icon. You should now just see the text "down" over the button background, as shown in Figure 2-90.

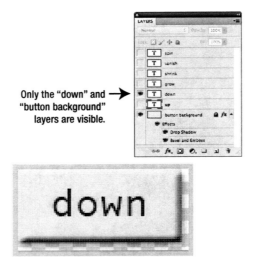

Only the "down" and "button background" layers are visible.

Figure 2-90. Hide all the text except for "down."

Select File ↗ Save for Web and Devices. The PNG-24 option should already be set. Click the Save button.

Choose a save location and give the new file the name "downButton." Follow the same lowerCamelCase naming convention. Click the Save button to create the PNG file.

Do you see a pattern developing here? You should! Follow the same system for creating button PNG files for the four remaining button labels. Save the PNG files with the names "grow.png," "shrink.png," "vanish.png," and "spin.png."

When you're finished, you should have the "buttons.psd" file and the six PNG files saved somewhere on your computer.

Checking your work

You did a lot of work in this chapter! Before you go any further, double check to make sure that you've got the following files saved somewhere on your computer:

- A file called background.psd and its accompanying PNG file called background.png.

- A file called character.psd and its accompanying PNG file called character.png.

- A file called buttons.psd and its six accompanying PNG files called up.png, down.png, grow.png, shrink.png, vanish.png, and spin.png.

The PNG files are the most important of these because you're going to use them in the next chapter to make an interactive game world with AS3.0 programming code. Figure 2-91 shows what the PNG files should look like and what their file names should be.

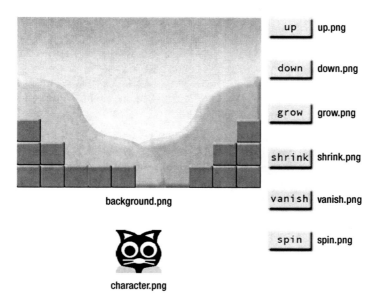

background.png

character.png

Figure 2-91. The PNG files you produced by the end of this chapter

If your files match this, you're all set to go to start programming in Chapter 3!

More about Photoshop

There's much more to learn about Photoshop; what you've covered in this chapter really just scratches the surface. You've looked at most of the important techniques you need to know to start making professional-looking game graphics, and these skills may be all you need. But there's more to learn if you're curious—which you should be! The best place to start is probably Adobe's excellent document, *Using Photoshop*. You can download it as a PDF file from

`http://help.adobe.com/en_US/photoshop/cs/using/photoshop_cs5_help.pdf`

(The latest version, at time of publication, was for Photoshop CS5. Search Adobe's site if you're looking a version of the document that matches the version of Photoshop you're using.)

Using Photoshop goes into exhaustive detail about all of Photoshop's many features, including painting and image editing which I don't have space to cover in this book. If you have any detailed questions about any aspect of how Photoshop works or what it can do, you'll find it in this document.

You'll also find many more help resources at Adobe's Photoshop's help site, including an HTML version of the same document, at http://help.adobe.com/en_US/photoshop/cs/using/index.html

If you've worked through this chapter, you'll be able to make good use of all these resources and be well on your way to becoming a Photoshop expert.

Summary

If you're new to making computer graphics, I hope you enjoyed this chapter on how to draw basic game objects and characters. Photoshop's drawing and design tools give you a great deal of control and are very easy to use with a bit of practice. For designing game characters and environments, they're ideal.

I covered quite a lot of new material very quickly, so if this is your first time using Photoshop, you might want to take a short break and experiment further. Create a new blank PSD file and create a few objects and characters. You'll soon become comfortable with it and, if you're like me, Photoshop will soon become your favorite drawing application. Chapter 7 will introduce an alternative graphics and illustration application, Adobe Illustrator, which is just as much fun to use.

In this chapter, you made some basic game graphics. In the next chapter, you'll bring these graphics to life with a bit of simple programming magic.

Chapter 3

Programming Objects

In Chapter 2, you created a game character, a game world background, and some buttons. This chapter shows you how to use AS3.0 programming code to start programming those images. Make them do something useful!

This chapter covers some very important AS3.0 programming concepts and techniques:

- How to load image files into the Flash Player
- How to position objects on the stage
- What variables are and how to use them
- Variable types
- How to make objects that you can target with programming code
- Dot notation
- Method calls and function definitions
- Method arguments and parameters
- Event listeners
- How to program buttons to control objects on the stage.

After you finish the chapter, you'll have a completely interactive game character that you control by clicking buttons. Figure 3-1 shows what you'll be able to make.

Figure 3-1. Control a game character with buttons.

But I'm a bit scared of programming!

Although I'll introduce a lot of important programming theory in this chapter, the most important thing you should come away with is how the programming code you type in the ActionScript editor window changes the behavior of the objects on the stage. The theory is important, but if you don't understand it all right away, don't worry. It takes a lot of practice for this stuff to sink in. We're going to look at many practical examples and you'll have ample opportunity to try out your new skills. Just take it slowly, and don't jump ahead until you feel ready.

Just as having a general idea of how the engine of a car works is a good idea for any driver, you don't have to become a mechanical engineer if all you want to do is drive a car. You can always come back to this theory later if you have some specific questions about how some detail of the code works. If you generally understand how the code you type affects the objects on the stage and can use that code with confidence in your projects, you're more than in the game.

Always remember that programming is a creative tool to help you express yourself, just as a paintbrush is a creative tool for an artist. It can help create the painting, but is of no use at all without the imagination of the artist—you!

This is really a two-part chapter. In the first part, I'm going to show you how to load images from a file and display them in the Flash Player. In the second part I'm going to show you how to program your objects to bring them to life.

So how do we get our images that we created in Chapter 2 and display them in the Flash Player?

Loading and displaying images

Before we start any programming, let's look at the problem we have to solve.

Somewhere on your computer you've got some PNG files that you want to display in the Flash Player window. How do we get them from the folder where they're sitting into the Flash Player? Figure 3-2 illustrates our conundrum.

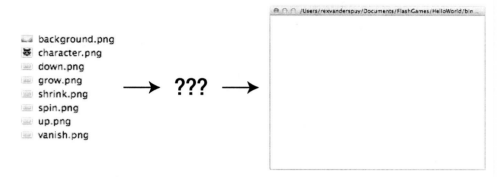

Figure 3-2. How do you load image files into the Flash Player?

It turns out to be a four-part problem:

First, we need to know the location on your computer where the image is stored, and get its address.

Next, you need to send the image's location address to something called a **loader**. A loader is a temporary container that uses the address to load files from anywhere on your computer into your program.

After an image is in the loader, the next step is to copy it into a Sprite. Remember sprites? We talked a bit about them in Chapter 1. Sprites make game magic, and they're going to be at the heart of your games. You can think of a sprite as a box that contains your image and knows how to talk to the rest of the game. When an image is copied into a Sprite, you can attach AS3.0 programming code to it so that you can completely control its behavior in the Flash Player.

The last step is to add the Sprite to the **stage**. The stage is what you've seen as the blank Flash Player window. The stage is where all the action happens. You won't be able to see any of your game sprites until you add them to the stage.

So first you need to get the image's address, retrieve the image with a loader, copy it into a Sprite, and finally add it to the stage. We're going to do all this next with AS3.0 code. Figure 3-3 illustrates this basic concept.

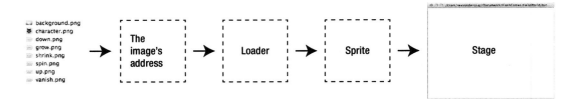

Figure 3-3. The general process of loading and displaying images in the Flash Player

> *Sprites are what you'll be using for most of the projects of this book, but you should also know that there are two other options. After an image is loaded, you can also copy it into a MovieClip or a Bitmap. We won't be looking at Bitmap objects in this book, but you can find out all about MovieClip objects in the download chapter "Using Flash Professional and Publishing Your Games." MovieClip objects are identical to Sprites, with the one addition that they can contain pre-planned scenes of animation.*

Setting up a new AS3.0 project

Before we start programming, we're going to create a new AS3.0 project and copy the image files we created in chapter 2 into its project directory.

Create a new ActionScript project in your IDE, either Flash Builder or Flash Develop, and give it the name "GameWorld" Refer back to Chapter 1 if you're a bit hazy about how to create AS3.0 projects. If you're using Flash Builder, you'll have a project directory that looks similar to Figure 3-4.

> *Note: Alternatively, if you're using Flash Builder, you can import the GameWorldSetup folder from this chapter's source files. This contains the basic setup files that we're going to use to start this project, including all the example images. To import a project into Flash Builder, select File ↗ Import Flash Builder Project from Flash Builder's main menu. Select Project folder from the new window that opens. Browse to the folder, select it, and click the Open button. Click Finish in the import window to load the project.*
>
> *However, resist the temptation to do this! At this stage of your learning, you need the practice of methodically typing out code by hand. It's the best way to get under the skin of the code and start developing a relationship with it. You'll also certainly make a few small mistakes while you type it out, and you're going to need to learn what those mistakes are and how to fix them.*

Figure 3-4. Your default project directory when you create a new ActionScript project with Flash Builder

In the GameWorld folder, create a new subfolder called images. Copy all the PNG files that you made in Chapter 2 into this new images folder. Your GameWorld project folder should now look like Figure 3-5. Take care that your PNG image files have exactly the same names as you see them here, otherwise the steps ahead won't work.

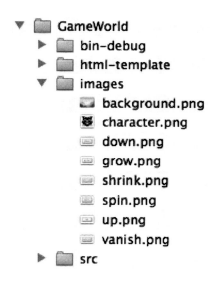

Figure 3-5. Create an images folder and copy the PNG files into it.

We're now ready to start adding some programming code. The job of this first bit of code is just to set up the program with some basic settings so that we're ready to start working. You won't understand any of it yet, but you will in just a few short pages from now. Type out the code blindly for the moment, and I'll explain everything ahead.

Copy the following code into the ActionScript editor widow.

```
package
{
  import flash.net.URLRequest;
  import flash.display.Loader;
  import flash.display.Sprite;
  import flash.events.MouseEvent;

  [SWF(width="550", height="400",
```

```
      backgroundColor="#FFFFFF", frameRate="60")]

   public class GameWorld extends Sprite
   {
     public function GameWorld()
     {
       trace("This is the game world!");
     }
   }
}
```

Confirm that your editor window looks like Figure 3-6

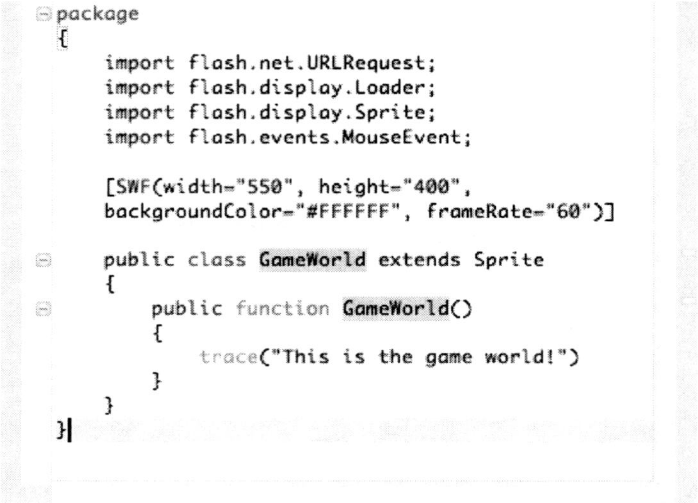

```
package
{
    import flash.net.URLRequest;
    import flash.display.Loader;
    import flash.display.Sprite;
    import flash.events.MouseEvent;

    [SWF(width="550", height="400",
    backgroundColor="#FFFFFF", frameRate="60")]

    public class GameWorld extends Sprite
    {
        public function GameWorld()
        {
            trace("This is the game world!")
        }
    }
}
```

Figure 3-6. The start of the program

Compile the program. In Flash Builder, that means hit the debug button. (If you're using Flash Develop, select Project ↗ Test Movie.) You should see a blank Flash Player window and the trace message "This is the game world!". If you didn't see this or received some error messages, double check that you haven't mistyped anything and compare your work against the file in the GameWorldSetup project folder in the chapter's source files.

We're now ready to add the meat of our program. But before we do, let's find out what all these new pieces of code to.

Understanding the setup file

You'll notice that the code we wrote is very similar to the code in the HelloWorld program from Chapter 1. You should recognize all the main sections: The package, the import statement that loaded the Sprite, the class definition and constructor method. The structure is identical. The only difference is that I've slipped a bit of new code into the package block. It's important, and it's code you're going to be using for many of the projects in this book, so let's see what it does.

The import statements

You'll recall from Chapter 1 that the `import` statement is used to load code from the Library. The Library is a vast, cavernous storehouse of pre-written code that's part of the Flex SDK. You can import any of these bits of code to use in your programs if there are particular tasks that you need your program to do. These "bits of code" are called **classes**. You can always spot a class because its name starts with a capital letter. The HelloWorld program we wrote in Chapter 1 is a class, and the GameWorld program we're writing in this chapter is also a class.

Our program imports four classes.
```
import flash.net.URLRequest;
import flash.display.Loader;
import flash.display.Sprite;
import flash.events.MouseEvent;
```

The last items, `Sprite`, `Loader`, `URLRequest,` and `MouseEvent` are the names of the classes. You'll never see the actual classes themselves, nor do you need to. They're invisibly imported into your program and run in the background. All you need to know are the names of the classes you want to use. Don't worry, I'll keep you posted about exactly what they are and when you'll need them. You'll soon start to recognize the usual suspects.

Preceding the class names are words with dots between them, like `flash.display` and `flash.events`. These are the folders in the Library where the classes can be found.

These import statements can be in any order you like.

We can see that our program is going to import four classes. Here's what they do:

- **Sprite**: Containers that help you control and display your images on the stage.

- **Loader**: A temporary container that loads your image from your project directory into your AS3.0 program.

- **URLRequest**: Understands a directory location on your computer, such as ../images/background.png.

- **MouseEvent**: Code that lets you interact with game objects using the mouse.

All the code that we're going to write in this chapter is going to require the help of these classes.

Set up the Flash Player with a metadata tag

You'll have noticed that when you compile your programs a blank Flash Player window opens. The Flash Player window has certain properties that you can control. For example, how big you do you want to make it? What should its background color be? How often should it update its display for animations? All of these properties, and quite a few more, are controlled with a **metadata tag**. In our program, this is what it looks like:

```
[SWF(width="550", height="400",
  backgroundColor="#FFFFFF", frameRate="60")]
```

It creates a Flash Player window that's 550 pixels wide and 400 pixels high. It fills the Flash Player window with a white background color, and updates it at the rate of 60 frames per second.

Metadata tags are framed with square brackets, like this:

[Anything inside these square brackets is metadata]

In this case, the metadata tag is describing properties of the SWF file that your program will create when you compile it. All the SWF properties, and the values you give them, are contained in the inner parenthesis.

```
[SWF(set all the swf file properties here)]
```

Take a good look at the metadata tag. Can you see the four properties it's setting? Here they are:

- **width:** How wide the Flash player window should be, in pixels.

- **height:** The height of the Flash Player window, in pixels

- **backgroundColor:** The background color of the Flash Player window. The strange string of characters you see here, #FFFFFF, is a **hexadecimal** color code. Hexadecimal codes are a standardized way of describing colors using a combination of letters and numbers. #FFFFFF is the code for white. It's telling the SWF file to display a white background when the Flash Player launches.

A web search for "hexadecimal color chart" will bring up a comprehensive list of colors and their respective hexadecimal codes, and you can also find them in Photoshop's color palette, that we looked at in chapter 2.Here are the codes for a few common colors:

Black: #000000

White: #FFFFFF

Red: #FF0000

Blue:#0000FF

Green: #00FF00

Yellow: #FFFF00

Orange: #FF9900

Violet: #CC33FF

> *Note: You can shorten black to #000 and White to #FFF. If all 6 characters in the hexadecimal code are the same, you only need to use the first 3 characters.*

- **frameRate:** How often the SWF display is updated. "60" means that it's updated 60 times per second, or **frames per second** (fps). This determines how smoothly animation is displayed. Any number between 30 and 60 will give you smooth animation for your games. A higher frame rate will make your computer's processor work a little harder to display game animations, but they'll look better. 60 frames per second looks great for Flash games, and it's not too taxing on the CPU.

Try making a few changes to the metadata tag, and you'll immediately see the effect it has on the Flash player. Try changing the values of the properties, shown in bold text, in the metadata tag:

```
[SWF(width="100", height="200",
backgroundColor="#000", frameRate="60")]
```

Compile the program again, and you'll see that the Flash Player is now just 100 pixels wide, 200 pixels high, and filled with a black background color, as shown in Figure 3-7. Make sure you change it back to its original values when you're done.

Figure 3-7. Use a metadata tag to change the properties of the SWF that runs in the Flash Player.

Why did we set the width and height properties to 550 by 400? Because those are exactly the same dimensions as the background.png image file that we created in Chapter 2. You could of course use any width and height that you like for your games.

Metadata tags can also be used to embed images, sounds and fonts into your game, and we'll look at some of these uses of metadata tags later in the book. However, this SWF metadata tag, that we've just looked at, will be a standard fixture of all the programs we'll write, and you probably won't need to change any of its properties.

> *Always make sure that the SWF metadata tag comes directly after the import statements and just before the class definition. This is the only place in the program where it will work properly.*

Loading and displaying the background.png image

We're now ready to load our first image, background.png, into our program. Let's add the new code to our program to see if it works. I'll explain each detail of the code in the pages ahead.

Add the following in bold text to the GameWorld.as file (your ActionScript editor window will look like Figure 3-8 when you're done. Note that the original `trace` directive has been removed.):

```
package
{
  import flash.net.URLRequest;
  import flash.display.Loader;
  import flash.display.Sprite;
  import flash.events.MouseEvent;

  [SWF(width="550", height="400",
    backgroundColor="#FFFFFF", frameRate="60")]

  public class GameWorld extends Sprite
  {
    //Declare the variables we need
    public var backgroundURL:URLRequest;
    public var backgroundLoader:Loader;
    public var background:Sprite;

    public function GameWorld()
    {
      //Add the background to the stage
      backgroundURL = new URLRequest();
      backgroundLoader = new Loader();
      background = new Sprite();

      backgroundURL.url = "../images/background.png";
      backgroundLoader.load(backgroundURL);
      background.addChild(backgroundLoader);
      stage.addChild(background);
    }
  }
}
```

```
package
{
    import flash.net.URLRequest;
    import flash.display.Loader;
    import flash.display.Sprite;
    import flash.events.MouseEvent;

    [SWF(width="550", height="400",
    backgroundColor="#FFFFFF", frameRate="60")]

    public class GameWorld extends Sprite
    {
        //Declare the variables we need
        public var backgroundURL:URLRequest;
        public var backgroundLoader:Loader;
        public var background:Sprite;

        public function GameWorld()
        {
            //Add the background to the stage
            backgroundURL = new URLRequest();
            backgroundLoader = new Loader();
            background = new Sprite();

            backgroundURL.url = "../images/background.png";
            backgroundLoader.load(backgroundURL);
            background.addChild(backgroundLoader);
            stage.addChild(background);
        }
    }
}
```

Figure 3-8. Add new code to the program.

Remember that any lines of code that begin with a double forward slash, //, are comments. They aren't part of the program, they're just notes about what the code does. You don't have to include the comments in the program – they won't affect how it runs at all.

Compile the program. If background.png file is in the correct folder in the project directory, and you've copied the code exactly as it appears here, you'll see the Flash Player open and display the background image, as shown in Figure 3-9.

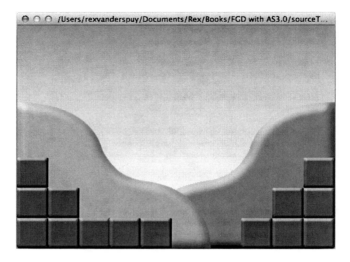

Figure 3-9. The program loads and displays the background image.

> *If you get any error messages when you compile this code, refer back to chapter 1 and the section on debugging your code to get some ideas as to what might be wrong. There's a particularly odd error message that you might receive in this project:*
>
> *"SecurityError: Error #2000: No active security context."*
>
> *This is not a helpful error message at all! But I can tell you exactly what it means: you've misspelled the filename or mistyped the path to the background.png file or one of your other image files.*

How did that work?

The format that we've used for the program so far is exactly the same as the format we used for the HelloWorld program in Chapter 1. Refer to that chapter if there's anything about the basic structure of this code that you think you don't quite understand. There are many new lines of code that you haven't seen before, and I'll go into detail about how they work.

Create the Sprite and Loader objects

At the beginning of this chapter I explained that in order to load the image from the folder on your computer into the program, we need three things:

- We need to know the location of the image file.

- We need a Loader to load it into the program.

- We need a Sprite to control the image with programming code.

That's exactly what the first lines of our new code prepare the program to do.

The first line creates something called a **variable**. That's what this line does. The variable's name is backgroundURL

```
public var backgroundURL:URLRequest;
```

backgroundURL will have the special job of telling the program where to look on your computer to find the background.png file.

> *URL stands for Uniform Resource Locator. Yes, I know, that's an absolutely meaningless phrase, but you'll see it used everywhere, so you'll need to learn it. All it means is "where to look to find a file". It could be a path to file on a hard drive, or it could be a website address. You'll often see website addresses referred to as a URL.*

The code next creates another variable called backgroundLoader.

```
public var backgroundLoader:Loader;
```

backgroundLoader will be our Loader object. It will load the image from its location in the folder in your computer into the program

The code then creates a third variable called background.

```
public var background:Sprite;
```

background will be our Sprite object. All of the fun we're going to have in this program will be with this object.

We haven't created these objects just yet, we're just telling our program that we've created variables that will store them.

Look at these three lines carefully, and you'll notice that their structure is the same. Notice also that all three lines end with semicolons. That means they *do something*. Programming code that does something is called a directive (we discussed directives in Chapter 1.) You can always spot a directive because it ends in a semicolon.

In programming terms, these directives are known as **variable declarations.** We've created three **variables**:

```
backgroundLoader
background
backgroundURL
```

Figure 3-10 illustrates the structure of a variable declaration in detail.

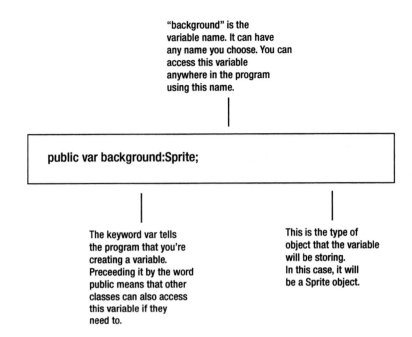

"background" is the
variable name. It can have
any name you choose. You can
access this variable
anywhere in the program
using this name.

public var background:Sprite;

The keyword var tells
the program that you're
creating a variable.
Preceeding it by the word
public means that other
classes can also access
this variable if they
need to.

This is the type of
object that the variable
will be storing.
In this case, it will
be a Sprite object.

Figure 3-10. The variable declaration

Whoa, that's suddenly a lot to absorb very quickly! And what are variables, anyway?

Let's take a break for a moment and find out what variables are and how to use them.

Variables

You can think of **variables** as little boxes that store information. Every box has its own name and stores different kinds of information.

Figure 3-11 illustrates three imaginary variables called score, name, and enemy. Each variable name is associated with a box that contains information.

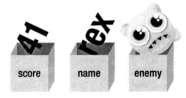

Figure 3-11. Variables are like boxes that store information.

If you need to use the information inside the box, you just need to refer to the box's name anywhere in the program. For example, if you want to find out what the current score is, use the variable name `score`; the program will interpret it as 41. If you want to reference the enemy Sprite, use the word enemy.

You can also empty the box at any time and put new information into it. It's variable!

That's all variables are: storage containers with names.

Variable types

If you're organizing lots of little boxes filled with different types of things, it's sometimes useful to know what **type** of information each box should contain. Imagine that you have a sugar container and you accidentally pour a bag of salt into it. That could be a problem when the aunties come to visit for tea! You need to know that the container you fill is the sugar container.

In AS3.0, you can tell a variable what type of information it should store. To do this, use a colon and the name of the type, like this:

`:Sugar`

If your kitchen existed in an AS3.0 universe, you could label the containers in the cupboards like this:

`smallBluePlasticTub:Sugar; glassJar:Salt;`

That labeling would prevent you from putting the wrong substance in the wrong container and spoiling the tea parties. Mom would be proud!

Figure 3-12 shows what the imaginary variables might look if like you assigned them types. This will prevent you from putting the wrong type of thing into the wrong container. (In AS3.0, any information made up of letters is referred to as a **string**, as in "string of letters or words.")

Typing variables prevents you from putting the wrong type of information into the wrong container.

You can't store a Sprite object in a variable made to store numbers.

Figure 3-12. Assign types to variables so that you don't put the wrong type of information or object into the wrong container.

Creating empty boxes

Let's have a quick look at our first three new lines of code:

```
public var backgroundLoader:Loader;
public var background:Sprite;
public var backgroundURL:URLRequest;
```

Are they making a little more sense to you now?

These directives are creating empty storage containers called backgroundLoader, background, and backgroundURL.

Where are these storage containers? They're sitting empty in the program, waiting for us to fill them with something. If you could see them, they would look a little bit like Figure 3-13

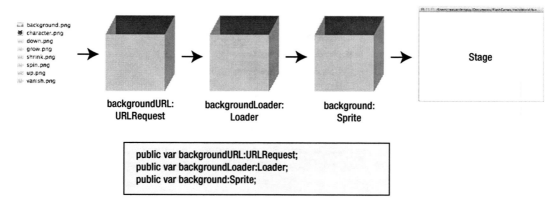

Figure 3-13. Three empty boxes waiting to be filled with content

Let's put something in these boxes!

Creating instances and objects

So far, our code has created three empty variables. The next step is to fill those boxes with something useful. We're going to fill them with objects. That's what the next three new directives do:

```
backgroundURL = new URLRequest();
backgroundLoader = new Loader();
background = new Sprite();
```

Our empty variables are now no longer empty; they're filled with programming code from three of the classes that we imported. They've become useful objects. Objects are programming elements that are copies of classes we can control with programming code.

Wait, before you get confused, let's step back a moment!

Remember that a class is the name of pre-written programming code from the library. You can't see that programming code, nor would you want to, you just need to know its class name if you want to use it. Our program imported four classes: URLRequest, Loader, Sprite, and MouseEvent. All these four classes contain specialized code that we need to use in our program.

Also, remember that you can always spot a class because the first letter of its name is capitalized. Can you see the names of three of the classes we imported in the lines of code above? You should be able to! The classes are on the right side of the equal sign, and the variables are on the left. Figure 3-14 illustrates this.

The variables   The classes

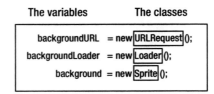

Figure 3-14. Creating new objects from classes

Here's what's happening: *the classes are being copied from the library, and their code is being put into the variables.* The variables are being filled with all the specialized code that the classes contain, giving them all the power of the classes they're being copied from. Another way of saying "making a copy" is "making an **instance**". AS3.0's terminology uses the term *instance* for any variable that contains a copy of a class.

The three variables are now *instances* of the classes they've been made from. For example, The `background` variable is now a Sprite instance, and the `backgroundLoader` variable is now a `Loader` instance.

All three lines of code contain the keyword new. The job of the new keyword is to "make a *new* instance of a class."

Directly after the variable name is an equal sign. The job of the equal sign is to assign the new instance of the class to the variable.

> *Before you go much further, let's take a closer look at exactly what the purpose of that equal sign is. In AS3.0, an equal sign is known as an* **assignment operator** *because it is used to assign a value from whatever is to the right of it to a variable on its left. This is very different from how an equal sign is used in mathematics, and this difference often trips up novice programmers. In math, an equal sign means "is equal to." In programming, an equal sign means "gets the value of."*
>
> *Here's a really simple example. Let's say you have a variable that you want to use in a game to keep track of the player's score. Let's call it playersScore. Suppose that one player in the game gets a score of 12 points, and you want the game to remember this number so you can figure out how well the player is doing. You can use the equal sign to copy the number 12 into the playersScore variable, the same way you would write an important number into a notebook for future reference. The code might look something like this:*
>
> *playersScore = 12;*
>
> *AS3.0 literally interprets this as follows: "The playersScore variable gets the value of 12." Now whenever the program sees the playersScore variable, a little light goes on and it thinks, "Aha! That means 12!"*

Figure 3-15 illustrates exactly how this process is working.

Make a new instance of the
Sprite class and copy it
into the background variable

Figure 3-15. Use the new keyword to make an instance of a class.

The bottom line is that our three empty variables are no longer empty. They're full of programming code that we can access in our program.

- backgroundURL is filled with a copy of the URLRequest class.

- backgroundLoader is filled with a copy of the Loader class.

- background is filled with a copy of the Sprite class.

Figure 3-16 shows what these variables have now been filled with.

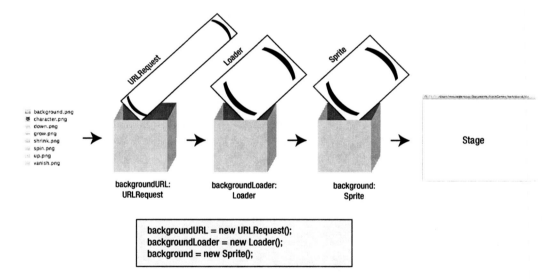

Figure 3-16. The variables are now instances of classes. They've become objects.

The result of this process is that our variables have been transformed into objects. An object is an instance (copy) of a class that you can target with programming code. Objects are at the very heart of programming with AS3.0

Objects or variables?

Remember that a variable is just an empty box. It becomes an object when an instance of a class is copied into it. It's like a caterpillar turning into a butterfly.

*All objects start out as humble variables, but not all variables become objects. In this book, I'm going to use the name **variable** to refer to anything that contains one item of plain data. Here are some examples:*

playersScore = 14;

name = "Player's name";

These are simple storage containers for single pieces of information.

*I'm going to use the name **object** to refer to any complex thing that's created with the **new** keyword. Here are some examples:*

background = new Sprite();

button = new SimpleButton();

When you see the new keyword, you know that I'm making an object.

(From a purely technical point of view, everything in an AS3.0 program is an object. Conceptually that's important to know when you get into much more advanced programming, but while you're still learning, don't worry about this discrepancy, it will confuse you more than anything else.)

You might be wondering what the empty parentheses are after the class names. They're there for adding any extra details that the class needs to do its work when it makes the instance. You can see from Figure 3-16 that they're completely empty. We'll see how we can fill parentheses with useful information next.

Displaying the image on the stage

So far our code has created three empty variables and turned them into objects. We can now put these objects to use to display the background image on the stage. The next three lines of code do all this work.

```
backgroundURL.url = "../images/background.png";
backgroundLoader.load(backgroundURL);
background.addChild(backgroundLoader);
```

The first new line tells the backgroundURL object where to look in the project directory to find the background.png file. You can see that the name of the object is followed by ".url" (highlighted below)

```
backgroundURL.url = "../images/background.png";
```

The dot shows that url is a **property** of backgroundURL. The job of url is to store the location of the file. In this case, where on your computer to look for the background.png file. The text in quotation marks, "../images/background.png", is being copied into this url property by the equal sign. We're going to discuss exactly what a *property* is in detail in the pages ahead. But for now think of it as a storage container inside an object for specific information. The url property is a storage cupboard inside the backgroundURL object that know the location address of the image.

Figure 3-17 illustrates exactly how this line of code works and how our program is starting to fill up with useful information.

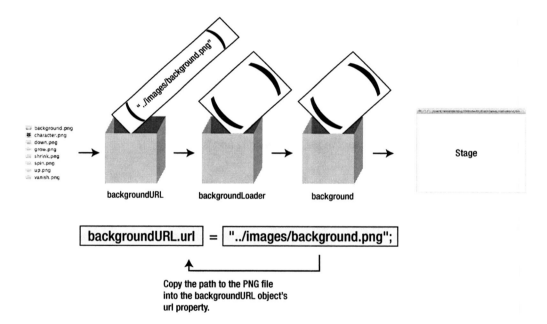

Figure 3-17. Tell the program where to find the image file.

If you're new to working with file path names, this bit of text might be confusing to you:

../images/background.png

It's the location of your file; the URL

It's easier to understand if you break it up into pieces. The last thing is the name of the image file – it's the image we want to load:

background.png

Easy enough!

Just before that is the name of the folder where it lives:

images/

The forward slash shows that this is a folder.

Our program also needs to know where to find the images folder. That's what these characters do:

../

Two dots and a forward slash tell the program to look for the images folder in the directory just outside the current directory. What does that mean?

Images are loaded by the SWF file that's created when you compile the program. In this case, it's the GameWorld.swf file which is in the bin-debug folder. If we tried to use the following path name to look for the file, we wouldn't find it.

images/background.png

That's because the program would look for the images folder inside the folder where the SWF file is running: in the bin-debug folder. The images folder isn't inside the bin-debug folder, it's just outside it. So we have to tell the program to it to look outside the current directory for the images folder. That's what the ../ means: "check the directory just outside this one."

Figure 3-18 shows how this works.

It's important to keep in mind that if you ever change the location of the SWF file, you'll have to also move the images folder relative to it, otherwise your images won't load and you'll get an error message telling you, "No active Security context". This just means that the SWF can't find the images.

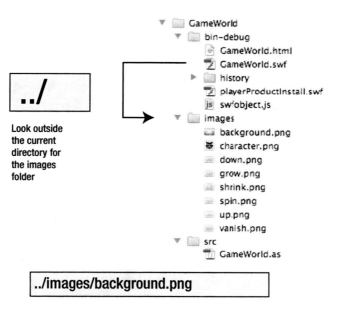

Look outside the current directory for the images folder

../images/background.png

Figure 3-18. "../" tells the program to look for the images folder outside the folder where the SWF file is running

The next line of code uses the location of the file contained by backgroundURL and sends it to the Loader object.

```
backgroundLoader.load(backgroundURL);
```

Remember that backgroundLoader is a type of Loader. It's a Loader object. The job of Loader objects is to load things. It does this with the help of the word load, which appears right after the dot (highlighted below.):

```
backgroundLoader.load(backgroundURL);
```

load is what's known as a **method**. Methods are actions that help objects do things. In this case, the load method is loading the image we specified in backgroundURL into the backgroundLoader. Methods are usually followed by parentheses, and they act upon whatever information is insider those parentheses. Anything inside those parentheses is called the method's **argument**. We're going to take a detailed look at what methods are and how they work very soon. For now, all you need to know is that the load method has loaded the backgroundURL into the backgroundLoader. Figure 3-19 illustrates what this line of code does.

143

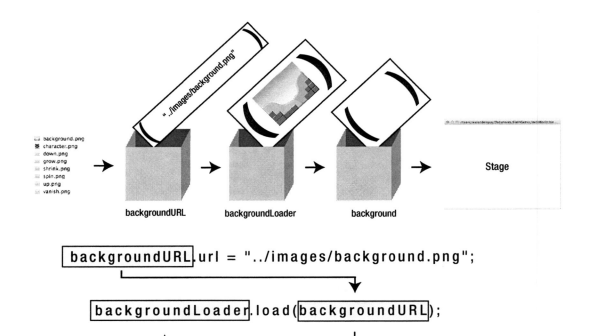

```
backgroundURL.url = "../images/background.png";
```

```
backgroundLoader.load(backgroundURL);
```

Load the backgroundURL object
into the backgroundLoader.

Figure 3-19. Load the image path into the backgroundLoader.

We've seen a method before in this book. Do you remember this line of code from Chapter 1?

trace("Hello World! Can you read this?");

trace is a method. It used the words in the parentheses that followed it to display that text in the Console window. Look for lower case words followed by parentheses and you'll have spotted a method!

The backgroundLoader is a temporary storage container for files you want to load into your program. It's a necessary step for loading files, but it's not really much use as is. Let's make the image file more useful by adding it to our background Sprite.

```
background.addChild(backgroundLoader);
```

background is a Sprite object. Sprite objects are things that you can actually see on the stage. Most of the programming you'll do in your games will be about controlling Sprite objects. You can think of a Sprite as a box than contains an image and moves around the stage.

Sprite objects have a method called addChild. If you think of the Sprite as a protective parent, whenever you use addChild you're giving the Sprite something to take care of. In this case addChild is adding the contents of backgroundLoader to the background Sprite. What is the content of backgroundLoader? It's our image. Figure 3-20 illustrates how this line of code works.

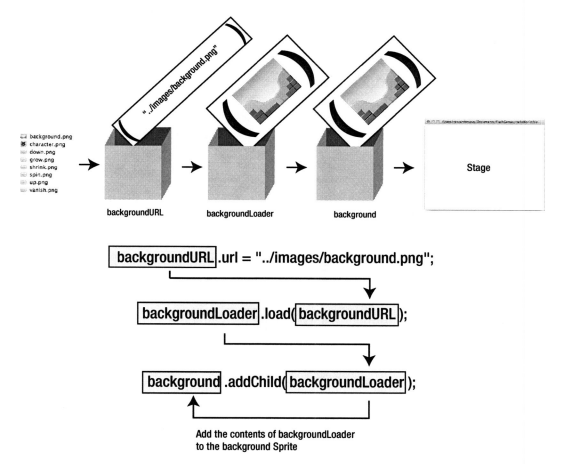

Figure 3-20. Use the addChild method to add the image from the Loader to the background Sprite.

The image is now safely under the parental care of the background Sprite object, but we can't see it on the stage yet. That's the job of the last new line of code we wrote:
stage.addChild(background);

AS3.0 has a built in object called stage. Whenever you use the stage.addChild() method, whatever is inside the parentheses will be displayed on the stage (as longs as it's a Sprite, MovieClip, or Bitmap object.)

What `addChild` has done in this line of code is take the `background` Sprite object and add it to something called the **display list**. Any instances that are on the display list are visible on the stage. We can now see our background image... yay! Figure 3-21 shows how this final hurdle in our little game of leapfrog results in a visible image.

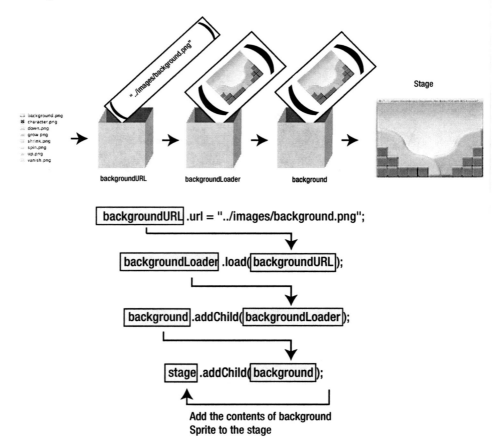

Figure 3-21. In the final step, use addChild to add the image from the background Sprite to the stage.

You can see from Figure 3-21 that it's really just a question of shuffling the image from one object to the next until it ends up on the stage. A little later in this chapter I'm going to show you some shortcuts to combine some of these steps together so you have much less typing to do. But for now, get to grips with this system because it clearly exposes the underlying mechanics of how variables become objects, and how objects are used to make things happen.

Understanding the code structure

The structure that we've been using to write this code is identical to the structure we used in the HelloWorld project from chapter one. All of our code blocks are there: the package, the class definition, and the constructor method. We've been writing our code into this structure. Take a good look at the code you've written so far and see if you can spot the structure.

We've written certain bits of code into certain blocks. If you understand why, the program will start to make much more sense to you. Here's what code should appear in which block:

- **The package block**: import statements and the SWF metatag. This is basic configuration that the program needs to run.

- **The class definition block**: Here's where you declare your variables and objects. These are all the things that you're going to make that you want to use in your program.

- **The constructor method block**: Here's where you make and do things to set up your game. All the fun starts here!

We're going to be adding many more blocks of code to our program, but they'll all be built on this basic structure. In fact, every AS3.0 game and program you ever write will use this basic structure. Figure 3-22 illustrates this.

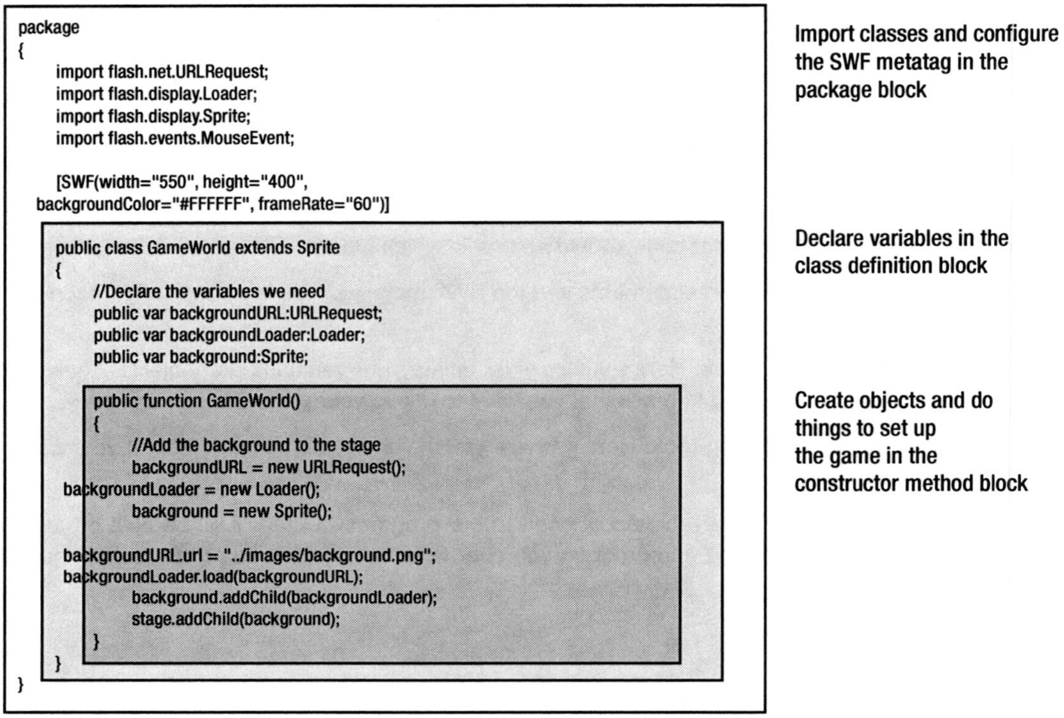

```
package
{
    import flash.net.URLRequest;
    import flash.display.Loader;
    import flash.display.Sprite;
    import flash.events.MouseEvent;

    [SWF(width="550", height="400",
    backgroundColor="#FFFFFF", frameRate="60")]

    public class GameWorld extends Sprite
    {
        //Declare the variables we need
        public var backgroundURL:URLRequest;
        public var backgroundLoader:Loader;
        public var background:Sprite;

        public function GameWorld()
        {
            //Add the background to the stage
            backgroundURL = new URLRequest();
            backgroundLoader = new Loader();
            background = new Sprite();

            backgroundURL.url = "../images/background.png";
            backgroundLoader.load(backgroundURL);
            background.addChild(backgroundLoader);
            stage.addChild(background);
        }
    }
}
```

Import classes and configure the SWF metatag in the package block

Declare variables in the class definition block

Create objects and do things to set up the game in the constructor method block

Figure 3-22. The basic structure of an AS3.0 program

Positioning Sprites on the stage

We have a total of seven images that we need to add to the stage. We're going to use exactly this same model to add the rest of them. Let's add the game character next.

Carefully add the following lines of code in bold to the class definition, just after the previous code we wrote:

```
public class GameWorld extends Sprite
{
    //Declare the variables we need
    public var backgroundURL:URLRequest;
    public var backgroundLoader:Loader;
    public var background:Sprite;

    //Character
    public var characterURL:URLRequest;
    public var characterLoader:Loader;
    public var character:Sprite;
```

```
public function GameWorld()
{...
```

Now add these new lines of code in bold to the constructor method, just after the code you added in the last section.

```
public function GameWorld()
{
    //Add the background to the stage
    backgroundURL = new URLRequest();
    backgroundLoader = new Loader();
    background = new Sprite();

    backgroundURL.url = "../images/background.png";
    backgroundLoader.load(backgroundURL);
    background.addChild(backgroundLoader);
    stage.addChild(background);

    //Add the character to the stage
    characterURL = new URLRequest();
    characterLoader = new Loader();
    character = new Sprite();

    characterURL.url = "../images/character.png";
    characterLoader.load(characterURL);
    character.addChild(characterLoader);
    stage.addChild(character);
}
```

You should see that this code is exactly the same as the code that we used to display the background. Its function is identical. The only differences are the variable names and the file path to the image. I've just replaced "background" with "character" for all the names.

Compile the program and you should see that your game character now appears at the top left corner of the Flash Player window, as you can see in Figure 3-23.

Figure 3-23. Add the game character to the stage.

> *When you add objects to the stage, the objects you added last always appear above the objects you added first. This is called the* **stacking order***, and you'll learn much more about how to control it in Chapter 9*

My cat character looks pretty cute sitting up there, but let's use some AS3.0 code to move it down to the center of the stage.

Understanding x and y positions of objects

The stage is 550 pixels high and 400 pixels wide. We know that because those are the values we entered in the SWF metatag.

```
[SWF(width="550", height="400",
backgroundColor="#FFFFFF", frameRate="60")]
```

What this means is that the stage is really just a 550 by 400 grid of pixels. The top left corner is position 0. When you add a Sprite to the stage, it always adds it at position zero, as you can see from Figure 3-24.

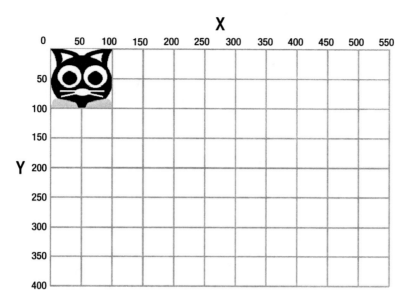

Figure 3-24. The stage is a grid of pixels.

The horizontal position on the grid is referred to as X, and the vertical position is referred to as Y. You can refer to any position on the grid by referring to its x and y coordinates. For example, if you want to refer to the very center of the grid, you can describe it like this:

```
x = 275
y = 200
```

Figure 3-25 illustrates this.

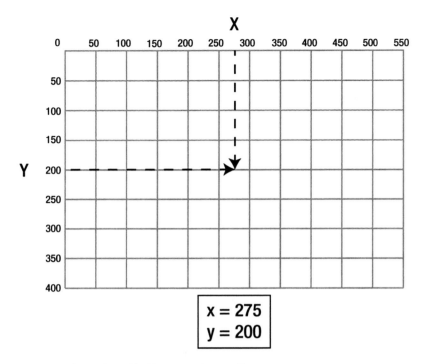

Figure 3-25. Describe any point on the grid with an x and y coordinate.

We can move the character to the center of the stage by writing code that looks like this:

```
character.x = 275;
character.y = 200;
```

Sprites have properties called x and y. Any number you assign to those properties will move the Sprite to that coordinate on the stage. Figure 3-26 shows how our character would be positioned on the stage if we used the code above.

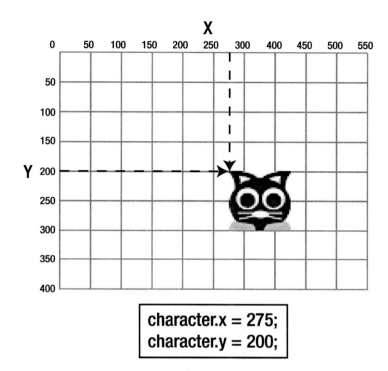

Figure 3-26. Use the x and y properties to position a Sprite object.

But is the character centered? It definitely isn't! That's because the Sprite object is moved from its top left corner. This is called the **registration point**.

If you want to center a sprite, you have to subtract half its width and half its height from the x and y coordinates.

We know that the character Sprite is 100 pixels high and 100 pixels wide (that's how large we made the image in Chapter 2.) That means we have to subtract 50 from the x position and 50 from the y position if we want the character to be completely centered in the middle of the stage. The code we'd use would look like this:

```
character.x = 225;
character.y = 150;
```

Figure 3-27 shows that these x and y positions will exactly center the character on the stage.

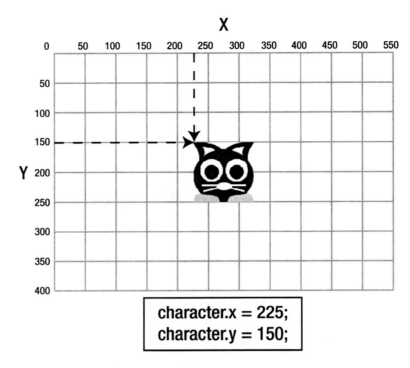

Figure 3-27. Use the x and y properties to position a Sprite object.

Let's now use this code to actually center the character on the stage in our GameWorld program.

Enter the following code in bold text, directly after the new code you've written

```
characterURL.url = "../images/character.png";
characterLoader.load(characterURL);
character.addChild(characterLoader);
stage.addChild(character);

character.x = 225;
character.y = 150;
```

Compile the code, and you'll now see that the character is exactly centered on the stage, as shown in Figure 3-28

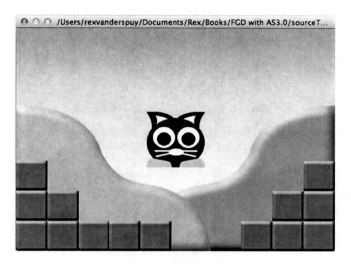

Figure 3-28. The character is centered on the stage.

Let's now use these new techniques to load, display, and position the buttons along the left side of the stage.

Displaying and positioning the buttons

We next need to load our six buttons and position them. This is simply a matter of repeating this same code model, but replacing "background" and "character" with these button names: "upButton", "downButton", "growButton", "shrinkButton", "vanishButton," and "spinButton".

Let's add the up button together, and I'll then leave you on your own to add the rest of them.

Add the following new code in bold text just after the existing code in the class definition.

```
public class GameWorld extends Sprite
{
  //Declare the variables we need
  public var backgroundURL:URLRequest;
  public var backgroundLoader:Loader;
  public var background:Sprite;

  //Character
  public var characterURL:URLRequest;
  public var characterLoader:Loader;
  public var character:Sprite;

  //upButton
  public var upButtonURL:URLRequest;
  public var upButtonLoader:Loader;
  public var upButton:Sprite;

  public function GameWorld()
  {...
```

Next, add the following new code in bold text to the constructor method. Add it directly after the code you wrote that set the character's x and y properties. I've included the entire constructor method block so that you can see all this code in its proper context.

```
public function GameWorld()
{
    //Add the background to the stage
    backgroundURL = new URLRequest();
    backgroundLoader = new Loader();
    background = new Sprite();

    backgroundURL.url = "../images/background.png";
    backgroundLoader.load(backgroundURL);
    background.addChild(backgroundLoader);
    stage.addChild(background);

    //Add the character to the stage
    characterURL = new URLRequest();
    characterLoader = new Loader();
    character = new Sprite();
    characterURL.url = "../images/character.png";
    characterLoader.load(characterURL);
    character.addChild(characterLoader);
    stage.addChild(character);
    character.x = 225;
    character.y = 150;

    //Add the upButton
    upButtonURL = new URLRequest();
    upButtonLoader = new Loader();
    upButton = new Sprite();
    upButtonURL.url = "../images/up.png";
    upButtonLoader.load(upButtonURL);
    upButton.addChild(upButtonLoader);
    stage.addChild(upButton);
    upButton.x = 25;
    upButton.y = 25;
}
```

Compile the program and you'll see that the up button is positioned near the top left corner of the stage, as shown in Figure 3-29.

Figure 3-29. Add the up button to the stage.

Follow this exact same format to add the remaining 5 buttons to the stage. Figure 3-30 shows what you your final work will look like.

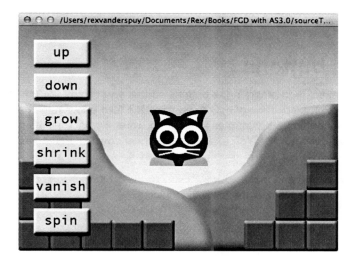

Figure 3-30. Add all the buttons to the stage.

Here are the x and y positions that you'll need to align the buttons correctly:

```
downButton.x = 25;
downButton.y = 85;

growButton.x = 25;
```

```
growButton.y = 145;

shrinkButton.x = 25;
shrinkButton.y = 205;

vanishButton.x = 25;
vanishButton.y = 265;

spinButton.x = 25;
spinButton.y = 325;
```

You're going to be doing a lot typing, but that's an important part of the learning process. You need to develop an intuitive sense of what it feels like to type out AS3.0 code, character by character, so that you cultivate an innate familiarity with it. You also need to learn about what kinds of mistakes you're making while you're writing code. Every time you add code for a new button, compile your program to make sure that everything is working properly. It's important to catch mistakes early.

Over the next two chapters you're going to learn some shortcuts and new techniques that will drastically reduce the amount of code you need to enter to load images- by a fraction of what we've used here. But by doing it the long way, as we've done in this chapter, we're exposing the very fundamentals of how to make variables, use classes, and create objects. You need to know these things to make games.

If you have any doubts about the code you're writing, there's a complete listing of the code at end of the chapter. You can also download a project folder called GameWorldLoadedImages from the chapter's source files. You'll find all the code, up to this point, in that folder.

Programming buttons

The next step in our project is to program the buttons so that you control the game character by clicking them. But before I go into the specifics of how to do this, let's take a few steps back and look at some of the underlying principles behind the code you're going to write. It's not difficult, but there will be a lot of new concepts to absorb quite quickly. You need to break them down into manageable chunks and look at them one at a time.

So grab a cup of masala chai and make yourself comfortable on the sofa. You'll take a short break from programming to have a detailed look at the following topics:

- Dot notation

- Methods

- Event listeners

These three elements will be working together in the new code you're going to write.

> *There's a lot of theory in this next section, but it's all optional. You may find you'll actually understanding it better by just rolling up your sleeves and seeing how these concepts work in the context of some practical programming. Consider jumping ahead to*

> *the section "Making your buttons work" where all this theory is put into practice. You can always come back to this section later if you feel you need greater detail about how the code is working.*
>
> *Learning to program is about writing a bit of code and watching what happens. Don't let yourself get bogged down or confused by theory or technical terms! If you feel that happening, just start working on the next practical project in this book, and carefully observe the effect your code is having. That's the best way to learn.*

Understanding dot notation

You may be wondering about the exact purpose of all those dots you've noticed between the bits of code we've written. The dots have three main functions.

First, they can tell you about the hierarchy of any given object. For example, take a look at this `import` statement that you've seen many times:

```
import flash.display.Sprite;
```

The dots tell you that `Sprite` is part of `display`, and `display`, in turn, is part of `flash`. That's the hierarchy that describes how to find the `Sprite` class in the Library.

The dots can also help you access **properties** of objects. A property is specific information about an object, such as its size, color, or position. We've just seen that the `character` object can be positioned on the stage by changing its x and y properties. You can refer to the x and y properties like this:

```
character.x
character.y
```

The dot is used to show that x and y *belong* to the `character` object. We'll take a detailed look at properties later in this chapter.

Finally, dots can show you that an object is using a method to perform a specific task. Here's a good example from the code we've just written:

```
stage.addChild(character);
```

The dot shows the `addChild` method is being used by the `stage` object to make the character appear.

This system of using dots to access objects and their properties and methods is called **dot notation.** It's a key feature of AS3.0 and its related programming languages such as C++ and Java.

Methods

I've written a lot about methods so far in this book, but before we go much further we should take a detailed look at exactly what they are and how they work.

Methods perform some kind of useful action in the program. They're made up of two parts:

- **Function definition**: This part is a block statement that includes directives that do the tasks you want the method to perform.
- **Method call**: This part is a word that activates the directives in the function definition.

Let's have a closer look at these two elements.

Using method calls

You've seen three method calls already in this book so far: `trace`, `addChild`, and `load`. Here's how they were used:

```
trace("Hello World!");
stage.addChild(background);
backgroundLoader.load(backgroundURL);
```

Anything interesting that's happened in our programs so far has been thanks to a method call.

The nice thing about method calls is that you can use them without having to know how they actually work. Do you know how `trace` actually displays text, or how `addChild` puts a Sprite on the stage? Of course not – you just need to know how to use it to get the result you want. How the method actually does this work is part of its **function definition**, and we'll be looking at function definitions in a moment.

You can always spot a method call because its name is always followed by parentheses. Whatever is inside those parentheses is extra information that methods need to do their job. In programming terminology, this extra information is called an **argument**. Arguments are the stuff in the parentheses.

Here's an example of a `trace` method call:

```
trace("Wow! This is an argument!");
```

The text in quotation marks inside the parentheses is the method call's argument. Here's another example:

```
stage.addChild(character);
```

No surprise. You saw this one before! `addChild()` is the method call, and `character` is the method's argument. Any Sprite object name supplied as the argument of the `addChild` method is displayed on the stage.

The keyword `stage` and the dot that precedes the method name tell us that this is a method that belongs to the `stage`. The stage is using this method to get its work done.

Some methods don't need arguments to do their job. Method calls without arguments simply use empty parentheses. Here's an example:

```
simpleMethod();
```

Even though this method call has no arguments, you still need to provide empty parentheses.

Using function definitions

With one exception, all the methods used in this book so far have been built into the AS3.0 language. (The one exception is the constructor methods you've created in the HelloWorld and GameWorld projects. Constructor methods are a special kind of function definition used to initialize classes.) You've been lucky because these built-in methods have been very useful and have saved you some work. however, as a programmer you can create your own methods. If there's any specific task that you need your program to perform, you can create a method that is specialized to do that job.

To create your own method, you need to define it. here's the basic format for defining a method:

```
public function methodName():void
{
  //add directives here
}
```

This is called a **function definition**. Function definitions are block statements, which you can tell because they're formed by a pair of curly braces. As we learnt in Chapter 1, the braces form a "block" of code. Any code that is inside the braces is part of that block. Programs are structured by using many of these blocks together.

Function definitions start with the keyword `function`, followed by the name of the method and then the parentheses. If the method call doesn't use any arguments (extra information), the parentheses are empty. If the method call uses arguments, the parentheses have to include a **parameter** (you'll be looking at how to use method parameters in a moment).

After the parentheses comes the **type declaration**, which is a colon followed by a word that describes the type of information the method might return to the rest of the program. You've seen types before. remember these?

```
:Sugar
:Salt
:Sprite
```

Methods need to include types, too. However, many methods don't need to return any information back to the rest of the program, so their type is irrelevant. To specify that a method doesn't return any information, you can specify a return type of `void`. It looks like this:
```
:void
```

Before you become overwhelmed by all this new information, spend a bit of time looking over Figures 3-31 and 3-32 and get comfortable with what method calls look like and how function definitions are structured.

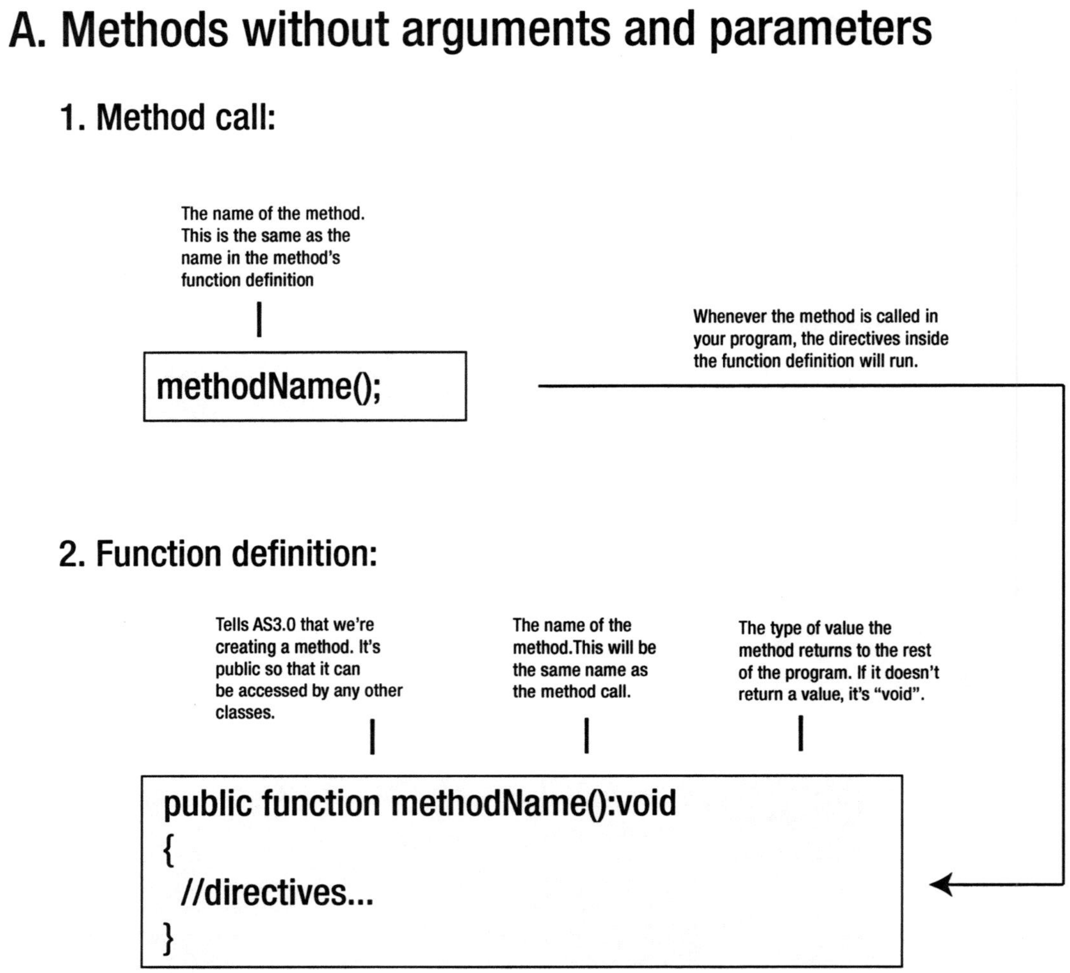

A. Methods without arguments and parameters

1. Method call:

The name of the method. This is the same as the name in the method's function definition

Whenever the method is called in your program, the directives inside the function definition will run.

```
methodName();
```

2. Function definition:

Tells AS3.0 that we're creating a method. It's public so that it can be accessed by any other classes.

The name of the method. This will be the same name as the method call.

The type of value the method returns to the rest of the program. If it doesn't return a value, it's "void".

```
public function methodName():void
{
  //directives...
}
```

Figure 3-31. Format for a basic method

A. Methods with arguments and parameters

1. Method call:

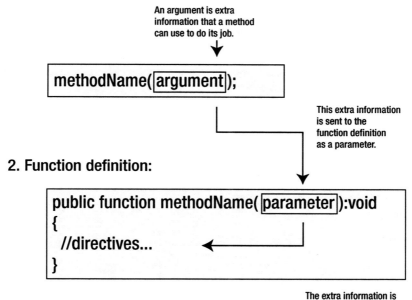

An argument is extra information that a method can use to do its job.

methodName(argument);

This extra information is sent to the function definition as a parameter.

2. Function definition:

```
public function methodName( parameter ):void
{
  //directives...
}
```

The extra information is used in the directives.

Figure 3-32. Format for methods that use extra information supplied by arguments

Using a basic method

Let's look at how to use a very simple method in a program.

Create a new AS3.0 project and type out the code that follows into the editor window:

```
package
{
  import flash.display.Sprite;

  public class MethodWithoutParameters extends Sprite
  {
    public function MethodWithoutParameters()
    {
      displayText();
    }

    public function displayText():void
    {
```

```
    trace("This is text from the function definition");
  }
 }
}
```

Compile the program, and you'll see the following trace message displayed:

This is text from the function definition

The structure of this program is quite important. The method call, displayText(), is inside the program's constructor block. The reason for this is that whatever is inside the constructor method is run immediately when the program first starts. The displayText function definition comes directly after the constructor block. This is much easier to see as an illustration, so take a look at Figure 3-33 which shows how the program blocks are organized.

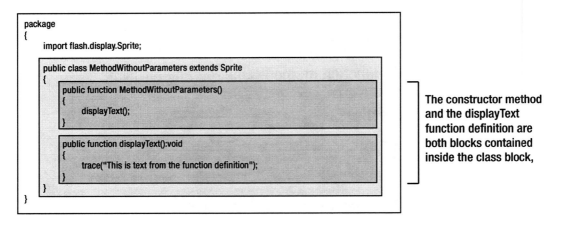

The constructor method and the displayText function definition are both blocks contained inside the class block,

Figure 3-33. The displayText function definition is part of the class block.

Figure 3-34 illustrates how the method call and the function definition work together to display the text.

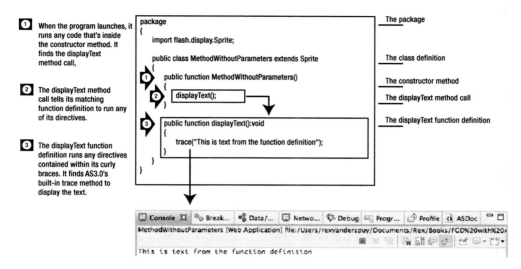

1 When the program launches, it runs any code that's inside the constructor method. It finds the displayText method call,

2 The displayText method call tells its matching function definition to run any of its directives.

3 The displayText function definition runs any directives contained within its curly braces. It finds AS3.0's built-in trace method to display the text.

The package

The class definition

The constructor method

The displayText method call

The displayText function definition

Figure 3-34. How the displayText method works

Always keep in mind that methods are a two-part system: you have to create a function definition to define the method and then you need a method call to use it. You'll find a working example of this program in the MethodWithoutParameters project folder in the chapter's source files.

Creating method arguments and parameters

The simple `displayText` method works pretty well, but it has a limitation. The text it displays always stays the same. Wouldn't it be nice if you could write the method so that you could supply it with new text to display every time it's called?

Of course it would be! Here's what the new method call might look like:

`displayText("You can write any text you like here!");`

The method call now includes an argument. The argument is the text that you want to display.

To display this text, you need to rewrite the function definition using a parameter. The parameter is just a variable that is used to store this new information. That variable can then be used anywhere in the function definition to access the information that was sent by the method call.

It's really easy to do. Have a look:

```
public function displayText(textYouWantToDisplay:String):void
{
  trace(textYouWantToDisplay);
}
```

If you use this method in a program and ran it, you'd see this message `"You can write any text you like here!"`

165

Let's test this with a simple program.

Create a new AS3.0 project called MethodWithParameters

Enter the following code into the editor window:

```
package
{
  import flash.display.Sprite;

  public class MethodWithParameters extends Sprite
  {
    public function MethodWithParameters()
    {
      displayText("You can write any text you like here!");
    }

    public function displayText(textYouWantToDisplay:String):void
    {
      trace(textYouWantToDisplay);
    }
  }
}
```

Compile the program, and you'll see the following trace message:

`You can write any text you like here!`

Now watch how flexible our method has become. Change the `displayText` method call to the following:

`displayText("This is some new text");`

Compile the program again, and you'll see the following:

`This is some new text`

The beauty of this system is that you need to write the function definition only once. You can change the text that the method displays just by changing the text in the method call's argument. For example, you can use any of these method calls, and the trace output will change to match it:

```
displayText("All this text");
displayText("can change whenever you want it to");
displayText("without changing the function definition");
```

This makes the method very versatile. Here's the key to understanding it:

- The text in the method call's argument is sent to the function definition.

- The function definition stores that text in a variable. The name of the variable that it stores it in is supplied in the parameter. In this case, the name of the variable is `textYouWantToDisplay`.

Whenever you use `textYouWantToDisplay` in the function definition, it's replaced by the text that was supplied in the method call's argument. Figure 3-35 illustrates how all this works.

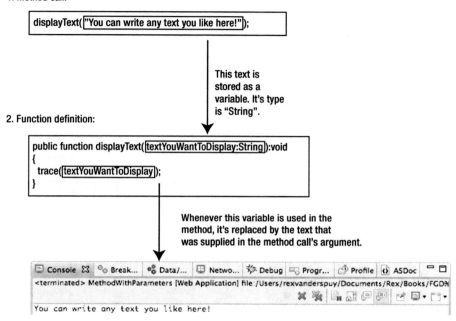

1. Method call:

displayText("You can write any text you like here!");

This text is stored as a variable. It's type is "String".

2. Function definition:

public function displayText(textYouWantToDisplay:String):void
{
  trace(textYouWantToDisplay);
}

Whenever this variable is used in the method, it's replaced by the text that was supplied in the method call's argument.

You can write any text you like here!

Figure 3-35. Format for a basic method

> *Note: You'll notice that the variable textYouWantToDisplay was given the type String. String variables are variables that contain text. We'll be discussing them in detail in chapter 4*

You'll find this working example program in the folder MethodWithParameters in the chapter source files.

Using multiple arguments and parameters

Methods can use more than one argument or parameter. A function definition that uses more than one parameter looks like this:

```
public function methodName (valueOne:Type,  valueTwo:Type):void
{
  //directives...
}
```

The parameters are simply separated by a comma inside the parentheses.

If the function definition uses more than one parameter, the method call also needs to send it the same number of arguments. Here's what a method call with two arguments might look like:

```
methodName(argumentOne,  argumentTwo);
```

All you need to do is separate the arguments with a comma. You can create methods with any number of parameters in this same way.

> *At some point in your programming career you might need to use a method, but you won't know how many parameters you'll need. Suppose that you have a method that needs to track items from trips to the grocery store and you never know how many items you're going to buy. Today you might have three items, like this:*
>
> *methodName (itemOne, itemTwo, itemThree);*
>
> *Tomorrow you might have five items, like this:*
>
> *methodName (itemOne, itemTwo, itemThree, itemFour, itemFive);*
>
> *To avoid having to write two different function definitions, you can create one that stores the arguments it receives in an array. I'll be introducing arrays in Chapter 9, so you'll probably just want to file this information away for reference later. The function definition will look like this:*
>
> *function methodName (...itemArray):void*
>
> *{*
>
> *   //directives…*
>
> *}*
>
> *All the arguments are stored as elements in an array called itemArray. The three dots in front of the parameter name indicate that the parameter is an array, not a variable. (For now, you can think of arrays as big filing cabinets that can store lots and lots of variables.)*

If you're new to programming, you'll need a bit of practice using methods and looking at different examples before you really start to get any of this. Don't worry! I'm going to give you plenty of practice to do this in the pages and chapters ahead. No one completely understands methods at first. Just keep this chapter at hand and experiment with some of the sample programs included in this chapter's source files. You'll see many concrete examples of methods at work in this book and you'll gradually feel comfortable using them.

Understanding events and event listeners

Events are things in a program that happen. You'll be happy to let most things that happen in your program take care of themselves without needing to be bothered with the details. But you'll want to know about some events, such as button clicks, so that you can specify certain things to happen when they occur.

AS3.0 allows you to attach **event listeners** to objects. An event listener "listens" for things that happen in the program. When an event occurs, the listener triggers instructions for what to do. You can think of an event listener as an extremely clever little dog that loves to bark. You've trained your little dog not only to bark madly at burglars but also to dial the number of the police station while doing so and then bark the address of your house to the officer on the other end of the phone. Clever little dog! And that's the kind of dog you have at your disposal with event listeners in AS3.0.

Creating event listeners is a three-step process. You need to do the following to set them up and use them in the program:

1. Import an event class from Flash's events package.

2. Add an event listener to an object using a method call to AS3.0's built-in `addEventListener` method. The method call includes a number of arguments, such as the kind of event to listen for and what to do when the event occurs.

3. Create an **event handler**, which is a specialized function definition that tells the program what to do when the event occurs. It "handles" the event. The event handler includes a special parameter that allows it to accept an event object, which provides quite a bit of information about the event that took place. You can use this information in your program.

The best way to understand how event listeners work is to see one in action. Let's write a simple program that shows you one of the most basic event listeners you can make

Create a new AS3.0 project called EventListener.

Type the following program into the code editor:

```
package
{
  import flash.display.Sprite;
  import flash.events.MouseEvent;

  public class EventListener extends Sprite
  {
    public function EventListener()
    {
      stage.addEventListener(MouseEvent.CLICK, clickHandler);
    }
    public function clickHandler(event:MouseEvent):void
    {
      trace("You clicked on the stage");
    }
  }
}
```

Compile the program. Click on the blank Flash Player window with the mouse. You'll see the phrase "You clicked on the stage" displayed as a trace message each time you click.

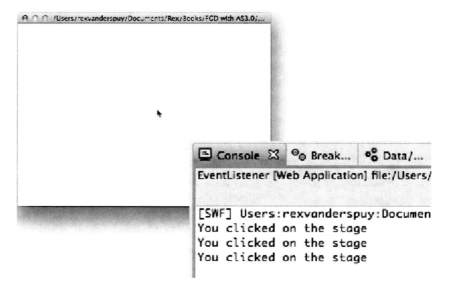

Figure 3-36. Every time you click the stage you'll see the trace message displayed.

Let's look at how this program works

Importing an event class

To use an event listener, first import one of AS3.0's event classes. In this book you'll be using the MouseEvent and KeyboardEvent classes most frequently, although there are many others. The import statement for the MouseEvent class looks like this:

```
import flash.events.MouseEvent;
```

Once it's imported, you can use it to find out what the mouse is doing, such as clicking things or moving around the stage.

Adding an event listener

The next step is to add an event listener, which detects when the mouse is clicked.

```
stage.addEventListener(MouseEvent.CLICK, clickHandler);
```

Event listeners are usually added to objects. The dot between "stage" and "addEventListener" shows that the listener is connected to the stage.

Let's break this directive down into smaller pieces. The most important thing is this method call:

```
addEventListener
```

It's a method call to one of AS3.0's built-in methods. It's used to register the event so that the listener can start its job.

At its most basic, the `addEventListener` method call takes two parameters:

`(MouseEvent.CLICK, clickHandler)`

The first parameter is the kind of event you're listening for. In this case, you're listening for mouse clicks. The format for describing the kind of event to listen for is to use the imported event class name, followed by a dot and then the event you're interested in:

`MouseEvent.CLICK`

The kind of event you want to listen for is the CLICK event. As I'm sure you can guess, it listens for mouse clicks. (Events names are always written in uppercase.)

> *The reason events names are written in uppercase is because they're actually a programming element called a **constant**. Constants are always written in uppercase, which is the naming convention they follow. (You'll see how to use constants in Chapter 9.) The CLICK constant is built in to the AS3.0 MouseEvent class.*

The second parameter is the function definition that you want to call when the event occurs. Our example program uses this one:

`clickHandler`

This is the name of the event handler. Its name must exactly match the name of the function definition that contains the directives you want to run when the mouse button is clicked.

Using the event handler

This is what the event handler looks like in the example program:

```
public function clickHandler(event:MouseEvent):void
{
  trace("You clicked on the stage");
}
```

It's exactly like the function definitions that you looked at earlier in the section on methods. however, there are two unique things about event handlers that distinguish them from ordinary function definitions.

The first difference is the name. By convention, the names for event handlers always end with the word *handler*. Programmers choose to give event handlers names like `clickHandler`, `moveHandler`, or `someOtherKindOfEvnetHandler` so that they're easy to spot among the other function definitions. You're free to give the event handler any name you like, but you'll make your life a little easier if you stick to this convention. I'll be doing so for the rest of this book.

The second difference is the function definition's parameter:

`(event:MouseEvent)`

Event handlers have to declare a special **event variable**, which also has to be the same type as the event that occurred, such as `MouseEvent`.

What is this event variable? It's actually an object that is automatically created by AS3.0 when the event takes place. Here's how it works:

Imagine clicking the stage with the mouse. As soon as that happens, a CLICK event is triggered. The CLICK event is sent by AS3.0 to something called the **event dispatcher**. (You don't need to know much about the event dispatcher except that it's a bit like a little software robot hanging around your program listening for things. But you'll never see it or interact with it directly.) As soon as it hears an event that you've told it to listen for, it takes out a notebook and scribbles down quite a bit of information about the event. For example, if you click a button, it can tell you the name of the button you clicked and where on the stage the click took place. All this information is packaged together into an event object, which is sent to the event handler (the function definition you programmed to run when the event occurs). however, the event handler has to create a variable as one of its parameters to contain the event object. Even though you may not actually need to use this event object in the function definition, AS3.0 requires that you create a variable as a parameter to contain it.

So what kind of information does this event object contain? You can find out by using `trace` to display its contents. You can change the example function definition so that it looks something like this:

```
public function clickHandler(event:MouseEvent):void
{
  trace(event);
}
```

Now if you compile the program again, and then click the stage, you'll see a trace message that looks like this:

```
[MouseEvent type="click" bubbles=true cancelable=false eventPhase=2 localX=360 localY=139
stageX=360 stageY=139 relatedObject=null ctrlKey=false altKey=false shiftKey=false
buttonDown=false delta=0]
```

That's a lot of information! Some of it might actually be very useful, although certainly not for anything we need to do right now. Later in the book you'll look at how you can access this information and use it in your games.

You can access all this information using dot notation. All you need to do is use the name of the event object, followed by a dot, and then followed by the property of the event object that you need to access. Based on the preceding example, you could use the following code to find out the x position of where the mouse clicked the stage:

```
function onClick(event:MouseEvent):void

{

  trace(event.stageX);
```

> *}*
>
> *If there are other objects on the stage, you can find out the name of the object that was clicked by using the target property. Using event.target will give you the name of the object you clicked:*
>
> ```
> function onClick(event:MouseEvent):void
> ```
>
> ```
> {
> ```
>
> ```
>   trace(event.target);
> ```
>
> ```
> }
> ```
>
> *If you use this in the example code, it will output the following:*
>
> ```
> [object Stage]
> ```
>
> *That's the stage.*

Soon you'll see how we're going to use event listeners to program the buttons that will control our game character.

Figure 3-37 gives you a general overview of how this example program works.

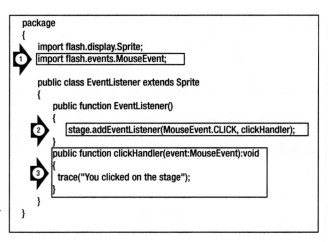

① Import the MouseEvent class. You need to import one of AS3.0's event classes before you can listen for events in your program.

② Register an event listener for mouse clicks. The event listener is attached to the stage. When the mouse is clicked, the clickHandler is called.

③ The code inside the clickHandler function definition runs when the stage is clicked. Its name matches the second parameter in the the addEventListener method call.

A function definition that handles events is called an "event handler".

Figure 3-37. A simple program that demonstrates event listeners

Understanding other events

This example showed you how to use the CLICK event from the MouseEvent class. The MouseEvent class contains many other events that you're sure to find some use for. Table 3-1 shows the event names and what they do.

Table 3-1. Event Names

Event name	Triggers an event when . . .
CLICK	The left mouse button is pressed down and released
DOUBLE_CLICK	The left mouse button is double-clicked
MOUSE_DOWN	The left mouse button is pressed down
MOUSE_MOVE	The mouse moves
MOUSE_OUT	The mouse leaves the area of an object
MOUSE_OVER	The mouse moves over an object
MOUSE_UP	The left mouse button is released
MOUSE_WHEEL	The mouse wheel is moved
ROLL_OVER	The mouse moves over an object (or any of its sub-objects)

ROLL_OUT	The mouse moves away from an object (or any of its sub-objects)

Many of these events don't work with the stage object that you used in the example, but they all work with Sprite objects. here are some examples of how you might register these events using addEventListener:

```
addEventListener(MouseEvent.ROLL_OVER, onRollOver);
addEventListener(MouseEvent.ROLL_OUT, onRollOut);
addEventListener(MouseEvent.MOUSE_MOVE, onMouseMove);
```

Figure 3-38 illustrates the basic model for creating an event listener and what happens when the event occurs.

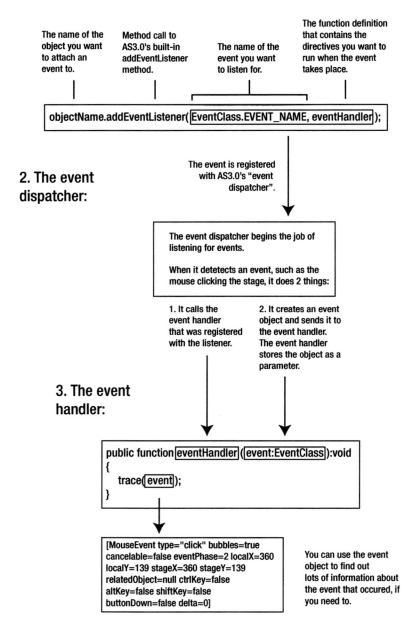

Figure 3-38. How event listeners work

As you did with methods, you'll need a bit of practice and a few more practical examples before you fully grasp how event listeners work. You'll see lots of examples of event listeners in action over the course of this book, so you'll have plenty of opportunity to experiment with them and see their effects in different contexts. The nice thing about event listeners is that they all use exactly this same format. You don't have to absolutely understand every detail about how they work yet; you just need to know how to use them to get the results you want for your game.

Making your buttons work

Now that we know about dot notation, methods, and event listeners, we can use these techniques to help us program the buttons in our GameWorld project. Let's program the up button to display a message when we click on it.

1. Make sure that the GameWorld project is open.

2. Add the following code in bold directly after the previous code you wrote.

> *To save space in this book, I've left out all the variable declarations you wrote in the class definition, and also all the code we used to create, display and position objects in the constructor method. I've replaced all that code with comments, so you'll need to be careful to insert this new code in the correct place in your own work. If you have any doubts about where to add this new code, have a look at the file GameWorldButtonTest in the chapter's source file. It contains the completed working code of this next step. You'll also find a complete listing of the finished project at the end of this chapter.*

```
package
{
  import flash.display.Loader;
  import flash.display.Sprite;
  import flash.events.MouseEvent;
  import flash.net.URLRequest;

  [SWF(width="550", height="400",
    backgroundColor="#FFFFFF", frameRate="60")]

  public class GameWorld extends Sprite
  {
    //All the variable declarations...

    public function GameWorld()
    {
      //All the code that creates, displays
      //and positions the objects...

      //Add the button listeners
      upButton.addEventListener(MouseEvent.CLICK, upButtonHandler);
    }
    public function upButtonHandler(event:MouseEvent):void
```

```
    {
      trace("You clicked the up button");
    }
  }
}
```

3. Compile the program. When it runs, click the up button on the stage. You'll see the trace message "You clicked the up button." Figure 3-39 shows what you'll see.

Figure 3-39. Click the up button to test your button event.

So far, this very simple little program is a great example of how objects, dot notation, methods, and event listeners all work together. But it doesn't do anything really fun yet. To make it really interactive, and the basis of something we can use to make a game, we need to learn more about Sprite objects and how to control them.

Controlling Sprite objects with properties

A large part of game design with AS3.0 is all about learning how to control Sprite objects. This is usually done by changing a Sprite's properties. We've already encountered two Sprite properties so far in this chapter: the x and y properties. We learnt how to change those properties to position objects on the stage. Let's take a closer look at what Sprite properties are and what you can do with them.

Properties are the features of an object that you can control with code. What are these features? they can be variables that are attached to objects that you create. Or they can be any of the built-in properties that are part of the Sprite class. These built-in properties are of particular use to game designers.

The Sprite class has a huge number of properties that you can access, use, and sometimes modify. But for the kind of interactivity that you'll need for most of the games in this book, there are a just few properties that you'll be using very frequently. As a bonus, they're the really fun-to- use properties, too! Table 3-1 shows what these are.

Table 3-1. Sprite Class Properties

Property	What it represents
alpha	Refers to the transparency of an object. You can assign it any value between zero (0) and 1. Zero means that the object is completely transparent; 1 means that it's completely opaque. the values in between, such as 0.5, make the object translucent. All objects start out with a default value of 1.
height	The height of an object in pixels. If you assign it a value of 100, the object becomes 100 pixels tall. A **pixel** is an illuminated dot on the screen. One pixel is the smallest possible size that a graphic can be. however, you can assign a fractional value (a value with a decimal) if you need to, such as 7.8.
width	The width of an object in pixels.
rotation	The rotation of the object in degrees. A value from 0 to 180 represents a clockwise rotation. Values from 0 to -180 represent a counterclockwise rotation.
scaleX	The horizontal scale of an object. All objects start out with a scaleX value of 1. If you change it to 2, the object will become twice as wide (200%). A value of 0.5 will make the object 50% narrower. A value of 1.1 will make the object 10% wider. scaleX is similar to the width property, except that it deals with percentages of scale instead of fixed pixels.
scaleY	Similar to scaleX, except that it refers to the vertical scale of the object.
visible	Determines whether the object is visible. the visible property can take two values: true or false. true/false values are known in computer programming terminology as **Boolean** values. the word *Boolean* refers to George Boole, the founder of Boolean algebra, which is the basis of computer mathematics.
x	The horizontal position of an object on the stage in pixels. The leftmost position of the stage is 0. If the stage is 550 pixels wide, and you want to position an object in the center, you'd give the x property a value of 275. to move it to a position 100 pixels from the right side, you'd give it a value of 450.
y	The vertical position of an object on the stage. This is also a value in pixels. the very top of the stage is position 0. As you work your way down, the numbers increase. this means that if the stage is 400 pixels high, and you want to position an object 100 pixels from the top, you'd give its y property a value of 100. to position it 100 pixels from the bottom of the stage, you'd give the y property a value of 300.

Several additional properties are used for transforming an object in 3D space. You won't be using them in this book, but you should know that they exist and experiment with them when you have the chance. Although their primary purpose is to be used as building blocks for creating 3D objects and spaces, you might find uses for these properties for special effects in some of your games. Table 3-2 shows 3D properties you might want to get to know.

Table 3-2. Sprite Class's 3D properties

3D property	What it represents
z	The depth of the object in 3D space. Higher numbers make the object appear farther away; lower numbers make it appear closer.
scaleZ	The scale (ratio of its original size) of the object in 3D space. the object is scaled from its center registration point.
rotationX	The rotation of the object around the x axis.
rotationY	The rotation of the object around the y axis.
rotationZ	The rotation of the object around the z axis.

You can have a lot of fun with all these properties, and they're very easy to use. In the next few sections, we'll use them in our GameWorld project to turn the character object into an interactive toy.

Going up and down

The first thing we'll do is program our up and down buttons to move the character up and down the stage. there are a few ways to program these buttons. To demonstrate exactly how the x and y properties work, and how to change them, we'll start with the simplest way and then modify the program a little so that the effect is a bit more realistic.

Add or change the following code in bold to the GameWorld.as file (we'll be taking a look at exactly how it works in the next section):

```
package
{
  import flash.display.Loader;
  import flash.display.Sprite;
  import flash.events.MouseEvent;
  import flash.net.URLRequest;

  [SWF(width="550", height="400",
    backgroundColor="#FFFFFF", frameRate="60")]

  public class GameWorld extends Sprite
  {
    //All the variable declarations...

    public function GameWorld()
    {
      //All the code that creates, displays
      //and positions the objects...

      //Add the button listeners
      upButton.addEventListener(MouseEvent.CLICK, upButtonHandler);
      downButton.addEventListener
        (MouseEvent.CLICK, downButtonHandler);
```

```
  }
  public function upButtonHandler(event:MouseEvent):void
  {
    character.y = 100;
  }
  public function downButtonHandler(event:MouseEvent):void
  {
    character.y = 200;
  }
 }
}
```

The maximum line width for code examples in this book is 70 characters. However many lines of AS3.0 code you will write will be much, much longer than that. To make these code examples easily readable, without having to use a confusing line break character, I've implemented a simple formatting system for long lines of code.

I'm going to break long lines of code at an **operator**. Operators can mean any of these characters: ( ) = + - * / || !

I'll then indent by two spaces and continue the line of code at that point.

Here's an example from the program you just wrote. The following bit of code was too long to fit onto a single line:

```
downButton.addEventListener(MouseEvent.CLICK, downButtonHandler);
```

So I broke the line at the left parenthesis, started a new line, indented it by two spaces, and continued the code at that point:

```
downButton.addEventListener

  (MouseEvent.CLICK, downButtonHandler);
```

How you space or indent your code won't make a difference to the way the program runs. Just remember that the semicolon will always tell you where the directive ends.

We're going to be writing some very long single lines of code in this book. I'll show you some strategies for formatting them so that they're easier to read as we encounter them.

Compile the program. Click the up and down buttons, and watch the character move up and down the stage. Figure 3-40 shows you what you'll see.

Figure 3-40. Click the buttons to move the character up and down the stage.

That's amazing, isn't it? Funny how such a simple little effect can be so satisfying to watch, especially after all the effort you've put into the program so far.

You should recognize much of the new code. You've created an event listener and a handler for the down button. And you've added two directives to the button event handlers to change the character's y position property when the buttons are clicked.

Moving incrementally

The buttons work: they move my cat character up and down the stage. But the jump is quite big, and you can only move it back and forth between two positions. Wouldn't it be nice if you could move the character with small, gradual increments, and not be limited to two points? That would be a much more realistic effect and make the cat toy a little more fun to play with. Fortunately, this is very easy to do:

1. Update the directives in the upButtonHandler and downButtonHandler with the following new text in bold:

```
public function upButtonHandler(event:MouseEvent):void
{
  character.y = character.y - 15;
}
public function downButtonHandler(event:MouseEvent):void
{
  character.y = character.y + 15;
}
```

2. Compile the program. Click the up and down buttons again, and now the cat moves 15 pixels in either direction. Much better!

But how did this work? The logic behind it is very simple once you get your head around it. Let's have a look at the `downButtonHandler`'s directive:

```
character.y = character.y + 15;
```

This directive takes the current y position of the cat, adds 15 pixels to it, and then reassigns the new total back to the cat's current y position. Think of it this way: the cat's new position is a combination of its position before the button was clicked, plus 15 pixels. You want to move the cat down the stage, so you need to *increase* its y position.

I know, this is a bit of a brain- twister! Let's break it down a little more. The starting position of the character in my program is 150 pixels. Whenever the program sees `character.y`, it interprets that to mean "150 pixels." You've set up the program so that every time the down button is clicked, 15 pixels are added to the character's y position. That's what this part of the directive in bold does:

```
character.y = character.y + 15;
```

It just adds 15 to the cat's y position, so the cat's new y position is 165. So you could actually write the directive this way:

```
character.y = 165;
```

Pretty simple, really, isn't it?

The next time the button is clicked, exactly the same thing happens, except that `character.y` now starts with a value of 165 pixels. Fifteen pixels are added again, so the new value becomes 180. Each new button click adds another 15 pixels to the position, and the result is that the cat looks like it's gradually moving down the stage.

Tracing the output

To help you come to grips with how this is working, add a `trace` directive to the event handlers in the program:

    1.   Add the following code in bold to the `upButtonHandler` and `downButtonHandler` :

```
public function upButtonHandler(event:MouseEvent):void
{
  character.y = character.y - 15;
  trace(character.y);
}
public function downButtonHandler(event:MouseEvent):void
{
  character.y = character.y + 15;
  trace(character.y);
}
```

    2.   Compile the program again.

Click the down button a few times. Each time you click it, you'll see the new value of the `character.y` property displayed as a `trace` message. Although your numbers will be different, the effect will be similar to what you can see in Figure 3-41. The values increase by 15 with each click.

Clicking the up button produces numbers in the opposite direction as the character moves up the stage.

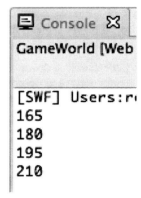

Figure 4-41. The character's y position increases by 15 pixels with each click of the down button.

Using a `trace` directive is a great way to help you figure out what your code is doing, and you'll be using it a lot to help test and debug the projects in this book.

Using increment and decrement operators

There's a slightly more efficient way to write this code. Updating values incrementally, as you've just done, is such a common and useful thing that AS3.0 has specialized operators that do the work for you.

> **Operators** *are symbols such as =, -, + and *, which perform specialized tricks with values, such as assigning, adding, or subtracting them.*

The two new operators that you'll use are called the **increment** and **decrement** operators. Let's update the `upButtonHandler` and `downButtonHandler` so that they use these operators:

1. Change `upButtonHandler` and `downButtonHandler` so that they match the code below. (I haven't included the trace directives, and you can remove them if you want to. Leaving them in is just fine too, it won't affect how the program runs.)

```
public function upButtonHandler(event:MouseEvent):void
{
  character.y-= 15;
}
public function downButtonHandler(event:MouseEvent):void
{
  character.y+= 15;
```

}

    2.   Compile the program and click the up and down buttons again.

The functionality of the program is exactly the same, but I simplified the code a bit by using the decrement operator:

`-=`

and the increment operator:

`+=`

These operators work by assigning the new value back into the original property. The -= operator subtracts the value, and the += operator adds it.

Incrementing and decrementing are a game designer's staple, so get used to using them because you'll be seeing them a lot from now on.

Limiting movement

You might have noticed that there's no limit to how high or low the cat can go on the stage. In fact, you can make the character go all the way to the top of the stage and continue going beyond it endlessly. There is a kind of existential appeal to being able to model such an abstract concept as infinity in such a concrete way, but it doesn't help your game!

You have to limit the character's range by using a **conditional statement**. You can create a conditional statement using the `if` keyword. The conditional statement checks to see whether the character's y position is in an allowable range; if not, it prevents the directive in the event handler from running.

An if statement is very easy to implement. It's a block statement that you can drop anywhere in the program to check whether a certain condition is true. If the condition is true, the directives inside the block run. If they're false, they don't run.

Here's a plain English example of how an if statement works:

```
if (whatever is inside these parentheses is true)
{
    ...   then run the directives inside these braces.
}
```

Let's use a real-world if statement in the methods you've just written to test it. We'll prevent our game character from moving beyond the top or bottom of the stage,

    1.   Add the following code in bold to the program:

```
public function upButtonHandler(event:MouseEvent):void
{
  if(character.y> 0)
  {
    character.y -= 15;
```

```
    }
  }
  public function downButtonHandler(event:MouseEvent):void
  {
    if(character.y< 300)
    {
      character.y += 15;
    }
  }
}
```

2. Compile the program and try clicking the up and down buttons again. The character is now prevented from moving beyond the top and bottom of the stage. Exactly the effect we want to achieve!

Let's look at how the if statement works in the upButtonHandler:

```
if(character.y> 0)
{
  character.y -= 15;
}
```

The key to making it work is the conditional statement inside the parentheses:

```
if(character.y> 0)
```

Conditional statements are used to check whether a certain condition is true or false. The preceding conditional statement is checking to see whether the y position of the cat is greater than 0.If the condition resolves as true, the directive it contains inside the curly braces is executed. Remember that 0 is the y value of the very top of the stage, and that the character's y position is measured from its top left corner.

Conditional statements use **conditional operators** to do their checking for them. The conditional operator used in the if statement is the **greater-than** operator. It looks like this:

```
>
```

This operator checks whether the value on its left (the character's y position) is greater than the value on its right. there are many conditional operators available to use with AS3.0, and table 4-3 shows the most common ones.

Table 3-3. Conditional Operators

Symbol	Name	What it does
==	equality operator.	Literally means "is equal to." Checks to see whether two values are equal to one another.
		10 == 10 returns a value of `true`.
		10 == 3 returns a value of `false`.
		Make sure that you don't confuse the equality operator(==) with the assignment operator (=). This is a common confusion! Remember that = means "gets the value of" and is used to assign values to variables or properties. == is used to compare values. There is a strict version of the equality operator that makes sure that the two values are of the same type before the comparison is made. This can help avoid certain kinds or errors that happen when trying to compare incompatible value types, such as trying to compare apples and oranges. The strict equality operator looks like this:===You should know that this strict version exists, but you won't need to use it in this book.
!=	Inequality operator.	Literally means "is not equal to." (the ! sign represents the word *not*.) Checks to see whether two values are not equal to one another.
		10 != 15 returns a value of `true`.
		10 != 10 returns a value of `false`.
		You might be surprised at how useful the inequality operator is. In many cases, it's more useful to know if a condition isn't true instead of whether it is. You'll be using this operator a lot in your game design projects. The strict version of the inequality operator, which prevents you from comparing incompatible types of objects, looks like this:
		!==
		Again, we won't be using the strict version in this book.
<	Less-than operator.	Checks to see whether the value on the left is less than the value on the right.
		10 < 15 returns a value of `true`.
		15 < 10 returns a value of `false`.
>	Greater-than operator.	Checks to see whether the value on the left is greater than the value on the right.
		10 > 15 returns a value of `false`.
		15 > 10 returns a value of `true`.

<=	Less-than-or-equal-to operator.	Similar to the less-than operator, but it also resolves as `true` if the values are equal to one another, which is a very useful thing to test for in many cases.
		10 <= 15 returns a value of `true`.
		15 <= 10 returns a value of `false`.
		10 <= 10 returns a value of `true`.
>=	Greater-than-or-equal-to operator.	Similar to the greater-than operator, but, like its sister operator, it also resolves as `true` if the values are equal to one another.
		10 >= 15 returns a value of `false`.
		15 >= 10 returns a value of `true`.
		10 >= 10 returns a value of `true`.

Keep this chart nearby because you'll be using many of these operators very frequently in the projects to come.

The code that checks whether the character has moved too far down the stage may be a little trickier to comprehend:

```
if(character.y< 300)
{
  character.y += 15;
}
```

It's basically saying, "Let the character move 15 pixels down the stage, while its y position is less than 300". That means that if the character's y position is equal to or greater than 300, the character won't move.

But where did the number 300 come from? We know that the top of the stage has a y position of 0, and the bottom of the stage has a y position of 400. If we want to stop the character from moving beyond the bottom of the stage, shouldn't we use 400?

Not in this case, we have to use 300 and here's why:

Here are two important facts to remember about our game character:

- Its y position is measured from its top left corner,
- It's 100 pixels tall.

That means when its feet reach the bottom of the stage, its top left corner will still be 100 pixels above the bottom of the stage. To accurately stop its feet from crossing the bottom of the stage, we have to stop moving it when its top left corner is at a y position of 300. That's the stage height, subtracted by the character's height. If we stop it at 400, the character's entire body will already have disappeared. Test this in your program and see!

When we look at setting stage boundaries in chapter 5, we'll examine this issue in much more detail.

Making it bigger and smaller

There's so much fun you can have playing around with Sprite properties. The next thing we'll do is tear a page out of *Alice in Wonderland* and use the scaleX and scaleY properties to make the character grow and shrink in size:

1. Carefully add the following new code in bold to the GameWorld.as file:

```
package
{
  import flash.net.URLRequest;
  import flash.display.Loader;
  import flash.display.Sprite;
  import flash.events.MouseEvent;

  [SWF(width="550", height="400",
    backgroundColor="#FFFFFF", frameRate="60")]

  public class GameWorld extends Sprite
  {
    //All the variable declarations...

    public function GameWorld()
    {
      //All the code that creates, displays
      //and positions the objects...

      //Add the button listeners
      upButton.addEventListener(MouseEvent.CLICK, upButtonHandler);
      downButton.addEventListener
        (MouseEvent.CLICK, downButtonHandler);
      growButton.addEventListener
        (MouseEvent.CLICK, growButtonHandler);
      shrinkButton.addEventListener
        (MouseEvent.CLICK, shrinkButtonHandler);
    }
    public function upButtonHandler(event:MouseEvent):void
    {
      if(character.y> 0)
      {
        character.y -= 15;
      }
    }
    public function downButtonHandler(event:MouseEvent):void
    {
      if(character.y< 300)
      {
        character.y += 15;
      }
    }
    public function growButtonHandler(event:MouseEvent):void
    {
      character.scaleX += 0.1;
```

```
    character.scaleY += 0.1;
  }
  public function shrinkButtonHandler(event:MouseEvent):void
  {
    character.scaleX -= 0.1;
    character.scaleY -= 0.1;
  }
 }
}
```

2. Compile the program, then click the grow and shrink buttons. You can now change the size of the character, as shown in Figure 3-42.

Figure 3-42. Click the grow and shrink buttons to change the size of the cat.

> You'll notice that the character changes size from its top left corner. That's because the top left corner is where its registration point is. It would look more natural if the character grew and shrank evenly from its center. At the end of this chapter, I'll show you how to center a Sprite's registration point to achieve just such an effect.

The basic functionality of growButtonHandler and shrinkButtonHandler is identical to that used for the up and down buttons. But instead of using the y property, you're using the scaleX and scaleY properties to scale the character horizontally and vertically. You need to use both these properties together to scale it evenly. If you use only one, say scaleX, the character will become very fat around the middle without growing in height at all. (try it and see!)

> In fact, now that you know you can change two properties simultaneously, you can also try this with the x and y properties. To move the character up and down the stage diagonally, you can change the event handlers for the up and down buttons so that they look like this:
>
> public function upButtonHandler(event:MouseEvent):void

```
{

    if(character.y> 0)

    {

        character.y -= 15;

        character.x += 10;

    }

}

public function downButtonHandler(event:MouseEvent):void

{

    if(character.y< 300)

    {

        character.y += 15;

        character.x -= 10;

    }

}
Try it!
```

The scaleX and scaleY properties use values that refer to a ratio of the object's scale. That means that all objects have a value of 1 at their original size. If you want to double the size of the object, you need to give it a scaleX and scaleY value of 2. In the new code you've added, you're increasing or decreasing the cat's scale by 0.1 each time the button is clicked, and that's a change of 10% of its original size.

It's interesting to contrast the scaleX and scaleY properties with the height and width properties. They both modify the size of an object, but the height and width properties use pixel values. Let's make a few small changes to growButtonHandler and shrinkButtonHandler to test it. We'll make it more interesting by using different numbers for height and width, so that the character doesn't change size evenly on all sides.

1. Make the following changes to growButtonHandler and shrinkButtonHandler by replacing the original code with the code in bold:

```
public function growButtonHandler(event:MouseEvent):void
{
  character.height += 25;
  character.width += 15;
}
public function shrinkButtonHandler(event:MouseEvent):void
{
  character.height -= 25;
  character.width -= 15;
}
```

2. Compile the program.

Click both the grow and shrink buttons a few times, and you'll notice that they gradually stretch and flatten the character, as you can see in Figure 3-43.This is because, although the character is exactly 100 pixels high and 100 pixels wide, the directives are adding a different number of pixels for both the height and width. If you supply exactly the same values for height and width, it will grow and shrink evenly in both dimensions.

Figure 3-43. Change height and width by different increments to flatten and stretch a square object.

Vanishing!

The next little trick uses the visible property to make the character disappear. The visible property is a little different from the others you've looked at so far because it uses **Boolean** values. Boolean values are values that can be only true or false. This allows you to use a bit of programming sleight-of-hand to make a **toggle button**. You'll be able to switch (or **toggle**) the cat's visibility on and off with only one button.

1. Add the following new code in bold to the GameWorld.as file:

```
package
{
  import flash.net.URLRequest;
```

```
import flash.display.Loader;
import flash.display.Sprite;
import flash.events.MouseEvent;

[SWF(width="550", height="400",
  backgroundColor="#FFFFFF", frameRate="60")]

public class GameWorld extends Sprite
{
  //All the variable declarations...

  public function GameWorld()
  {
    //All the code that creates, displays
    //and positions the objects...

    //Add the button listeners
    upButton.addEventListener(MouseEvent.CLICK, upButtonHandler);
    downButton.addEventListener
      (MouseEvent.CLICK, downButtonHandler);
    growButton.addEventListener
      (MouseEvent.CLICK, growButtonHandler);
    shrinkButton.addEventListener
      (MouseEvent.CLICK, shrinkButtonHandler);
    vanishButton.addEventListener
      (MouseEvent.CLICK, vanishButtonHandler);
  }
  public function upButtonHandler(event:MouseEvent):void
  {
    if(character.y> 0)
    {
      character.y -= 15;
    }
  }
  public function downButtonHandler(event:MouseEvent):void
  {
    if(character.y< 300)
    {
      character.y += 15;
    }
  }
  public function growButtonHandler(event:MouseEvent):void
  {
    character.height += 15;
    character.width += 15;
  }
  public function shrinkButtonHandler(event:MouseEvent):void
  {
    character.height -= 15;
    character.width -= 15;
  }
  public function vanishButtonHandler(event:MouseEvent):void
```

```
    {
        character.visible = false;
    }
  }
}
```

2. Compile the program and click the vanish button. The cat will disappear. Figure 3-44 shows what you... won't see!

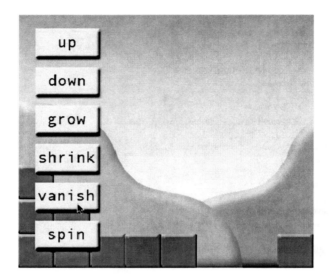

Figure 3-44. Make an object disappear by setting its visible property to false.

The directive that accomplished this disappearing act was this line in the vanishButtonHandler:

character.visible = false;

Like the other properties you've seen, the visible property is simply attached to the object using dot notation. Unlike them, however, this is the first property you've seen that uses the false Boolean value. This directive just means, "No, the character is not visible."

After you clicked the vanish button, the little cat was not only gone, but gone for good. No amount of clicking the button could bring it back. The cat is still actually on the stage as an object you can program; you just can't see it. How can you make the cat visible again?

There are two ways. One way is to create another button and program it with exactly the same code as the visibility button, except that you give the visible property a value of true, like this:

character.visible = true;

The second way is a bit more fun: use a single button to make the cat both disappear and reappear.

If the two states that you're toggling between can be defined with true and false values, AS3.0 has a very easy way to make a toggle button using the **not operator**. The not operator is simply an exclamation mark, like this:

!

It literally means "not." When used with Boolean values, it means "the opposite value of." You can put the not operator in front of any Boolean value to read it as its opposite value. Let's use the not operator in the vanishButtonHandler to turn the vanish button into a toggle button:

1. Modify the directive in the vanishButtonHandler so that it looks like the following:

```
public function vanishButtonHandler(event:MouseEvent):void
{
    character.visible = !character.visible;
}
```

2. Compile the program and click the vanish button a few times. You should see the cat appear and disappear each time you click it.

This is the new value you gave the visible property:

```
!character.visible;
```

It literally means "the opposite of the character's current visibility state." If the cat's current visibility state is true, the opposite state will be false. And if it's false, the state will be read as true.

When the program first runs, the character is (obviously) visible. Its visible property is true. When the vanish button is clicked, the program therefore reads !character.visible as false. The character disappears! The second time the button is clicked, the character's visible property is now false, so the program reads !character.visible as true. The character reappears!

The beauty of using the not operator in this way is that you never need to know whether the visible property is true or false. The program keeps track of this for you. And you need only one button to toggle between these two states.

You can use this feature of the not operator to toggle between two states with any variables or properties that accept Boolean values (true or false). Boolean values are extremely useful in game design for keeping track of things such as whether enemies are dead or alive, whether items have been picked up or not, and whether doors are locked or unlocked. Wherever you use Boolean values, you'll probably find a clever use for the not operator, like you've used it here.

Spinning around

The next thing we'll do is program the spin button to make the character rotate around its registration point. This will show you how to use the rotation property.

1. Add the following new code in bold text to the code you've already written:

```
package
{
  import flash.net.URLRequest;
  import flash.display.Loader;
  import flash.display.Sprite;
  import flash.events.MouseEvent;

  [SWF(width="550", height="400",
    backgroundColor="#FFFFFF", frameRate="60")]

  public class GameWorld extends Sprite
  {
    //All the variable declarations...

    public function GameWorld()
    {
      //All the code that creates, displays
      //and positions the objects...

      //Add the button listeners
      upButton.addEventListener(MouseEvent.CLICK, upButtonHandler);
      downButton.addEventListener
        (MouseEvent.CLICK, downButtonHandler);
      growButton.addEventListener
        (MouseEvent.CLICK, growButtonHandler);
      shrinkButton.addEventListener
        (MouseEvent.CLICK, shrinkButtonHandler);
      vanishButton.addEventListener
        (MouseEvent.CLICK, vanishButtonHandler);
      spinButton.addEventListener
        (MouseEvent.CLICK, spinButtonHandler);
    }
    public function upButtonHandler(event:MouseEvent):void
    {
      if(character.y> 0)
      {
        character.y -= 15;
      }
    }
    public function downButtonHandler(event:MouseEvent):void
    {
      if(character.y< 300)
      {
        character.y += 15;
      }
    }
    public function growButtonHandler(event:MouseEvent):void
    {
      character.height += 15;
      character.width += 15;
    }
    public function shrinkButtonHandler(event:MouseEvent):void
```

```
    {
      character.height -= 15;
      character.width -= 15;
    }
    public function vanishButtonHandler(event:MouseEvent):void
    {
      character.visible = false;
    }
    public function spinButtonHandler(event:MouseEvent):void
    {
      character.rotation += 20;
    }
  }
}
```

2. Click the spin button. The character now spins around the axis of its top left corner, as shown in Figure 3-45.

Figure 3-45. Click to spin the character.

The `rotation` property works much like the other properties that you've looked at so far:

`character.rotation += 20;`

The `rotation` property accepts values in degrees of a circle, so you have 360 values that you can work with. Positive values rotate the object clockwise, and negative values rotate it counterclockwise. The center of the rotation is the object's own center registration point. In this case, it's my cat's left ear. In the next section I'll show you how you can create Sprite objects with a registration point at their very center.

More properties?

There are two other important properties from the table at the beginning of this chapter that you haven't yet used in this little interactive toy:

- `alpha`: controls the transparency of an object and accepts values from 0 (completely transparent) to 1 (completely opaque, or solid)

- `x`: controls the horizontal position of an object, and like its partner-in- crime, the `y` property, accepts values in pixels

The functionality of these properties is very similar to the properties you already used. So, here's a little assignment for you. How about building a pair of buttons that move the cat left and right, and another pair that gradually makes the cat disappear and reappear? I'm sure you can figure it out! Also experiment with the 3D properties: z, rotationX, rotationY, rotationZ, and scaleZ.

Have fun, and I'll meet you at the next section when you're done.

Centering Sprites

As you've just seen, the spin button works fine, but wouldn't it be nice if you could spin your character around its center point? The grow and shrink buttons also work, but your character grows and shrinks starting from its top left corner. For most games you'd want these effects to happen from the object's actual center point.

As we discussed earlier in the chapter, this has to do with the character's registration point being its top left corner. When you load a PNG image file into a `Sprite`, AS3.0 automatically aligns it in this way.

But why? Let's take a few steps back and remind ourselves about what happens when you load an image into a program and display it on the stage.

You'll recall that the image is loaded into `Loader` object. The `Loader` is then added to a `Sprite` object. Finally, the `Sprite` is added to the stage. Figure 3-46 illustrates this.

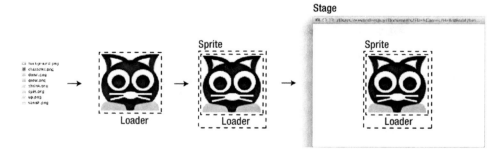

Figure 3-46. Images are contained by three objects: The Loader, the Sprite, and the Stage.

So although you can only see the image of your character on the stage, it's actually surrounded by an invisible Sprite that contains an invisible Loader. It's our set of wooden Russian dolls again! Keep this in mind.

You know that the stage is a grid, and that you can position the Sprite object anywhere on that grid using x and y properties. But what you don't know is that the Sprite that contains the image is *also* a grid. When you add an image to a Sprite, the image loader's left corner is positioned at an x and y position of 0,0 *inside the Sprite's own grid*. 0,0 is the Sprite's registration point. Figure 3-47 shows what this looks like.

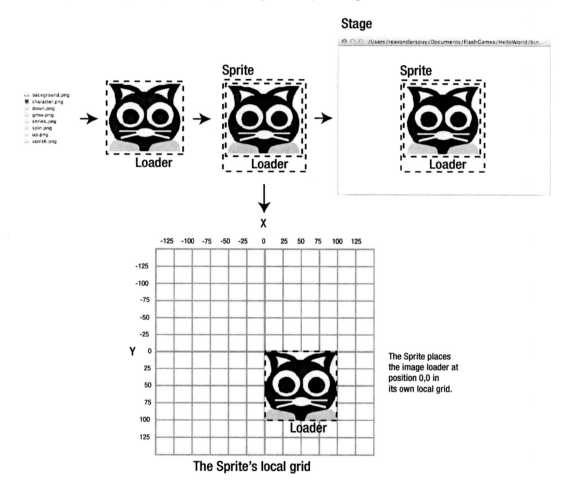

Figure 3-47. Sprites place the image loaders at position 0,0 in their own local grid.

This highlights a very important concept. An image actually has two coordinates: its **stage coordinates** and its **local coordinates** inside the Sprite that contains it. Keep this in mind, because you'll often need to be aware of both these coordinates to fine tune the positioning of objects in your game.

Position 0,0 in the Sprite's local grid is its registration point. You can see this clearly in Figure 3-47. The cat's left ear is at the 0,0 point. If we want the registration point to be at the center of the cat image, we have to move the image loader inside the Sprite's grid so that it's centered over position 0,0. Figure 3-48 illustrates what we have to achieve.

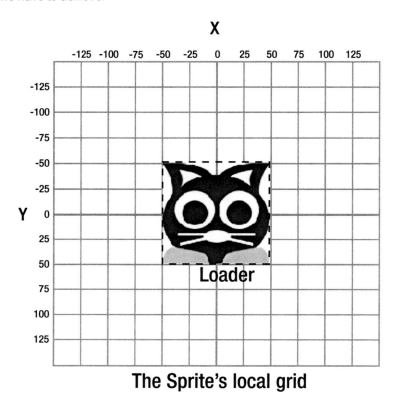

Figure 3-48. Center the image loader over the Sprite's 0,0 point to center its registration point.

If we can do this, the character will grow, shrink, and spin from its center. All this can be done with two simple lines of code. Let's see how.

1. Find the section of code in the GameWorld.as file where you added the character to the stage. Carefully add the following new code in bold text below.

```
//Add the character to the stage
characterURL = new URLRequest();
characterLoader = new Loader();
character = new Sprite();
characterURL.url = "../images/character.png";
characterLoader.load(characterURL);
characterLoader.x = -50;
characterLoader.y = -50;
character.addChild(characterLoader);
```

```
stage.addChild(character);
character.x = 225;
character.y = 150;
```

2. Compile the program.

The first thing you'll notice is that the character is no longer centered on the stage. It has shifted 50 pixels up and to the left, as you can see in Figure 3-49

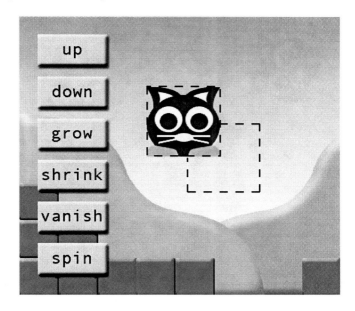

Figure 3-49. The character is now offset by 50 pixels.

If you've paid attention during this chapter it should now be obvious why this is happening. The new code you just added shifted the image loader object 50 pixels to the left, and 50 pixels up.

```
characterLoader.x = -50;
characterLoader.y = -50;
```

You've positioned it *inside the Sprite*. Because the character is exactly 100 pixels square, the image loader is now centered directly over the Sprite's registration point.

This is great, but it also means that you'll need to compensate for this by adjusting all of the character's x and y property values by 50 pixels. If you want to center the character on the stage, add 50 pixels to the previous values you used to center it, like this:

```
character.x = 275;
character.y = 200;
```

If you modify these properties and compile the program again, the very center of the character will now be at the very center of the stage.

Hey, now go ahead and try the grow, shrink and spin buttons! We now have exactly the effects we're looking for - they all happen from the center of the character, as you can see in Figure 3-50. We've successfully centered the image over the Sprite's registration point.

Figure 3-50. Grow, shrink, and spin from the center.

To keep things simple, most of the code in this book keeps the registration point of Sprites at the top left corner. But as you can see, there are many occasions where centering the registration point is essential to achieve certain effects.

Code summary

We've written a lot of AS3.0 code in this chapter! Just in case you have any doubts about what you've written, here's the complete, finished code for the GameWorld project. I've used bold highlighted comments to act as headings for major sections of code so that you can easily see how the sections are organized. You'll also find the working example of this project in the GameWorldFinished folder in the chapter's source files.

```
package
{
  import flash.display.Loader;
  import flash.display.Sprite;
  import flash.events.MouseEvent;
  import flash.net.URLRequest;
```

```
[SWF(width="550", height="400",
  backgroundColor="#FFFFFF", frameRate="60")]

public class GameWorld extends Sprite
{
  //Declare the variables we need
  public var backgroundURL:URLRequest;
  public var backgroundLoader:Loader;
  public var background:Sprite;

  //Character
  public var characterURL:URLRequest;
  public var characterLoader:Loader;
  public var character:Sprite;

  //upButton
  public var upButtonURL:URLRequest;
  public var upButtonLoader:Loader;
  public var upButton:Sprite;

  //downButton
  public var downButtonURL:URLRequest;
  public var downButtonLoader:Loader;
  public var downButton:Sprite;

   //growButton
  public var growButtonURL:URLRequest;
  public var growButtonLoader:Loader;
  public var growButton:Sprite;

  //shrinkButton
  public var shrinkButtonURL:URLRequest;
  public var shrinkButtonLoader:Loader;
  public var shrinkButton:Sprite;

  //vanishButton
  public var vanishButtonURL:URLRequest;
  public var vanishButtonLoader:Loader;
  public var vanishButton:Sprite;

  //spinButton
  public var spinButtonURL:URLRequest;
  public var spinButtonLoader:Loader;
  public var spinButton:Sprite;

  public function GameWorld()
  {
    //Add the background to the stage
    backgroundURL = new URLRequest();
    backgroundLoader = new Loader();
    background = new Sprite();
```

203

```
backgroundURL.url = "../images/background.png";
backgroundLoader.load(backgroundURL);
background.addChild(backgroundLoader);
stage.addChild(background);

//Add the character to the stage
characterURL = new URLRequest();
characterLoader = new Loader();
character = new Sprite();
characterURL.url = "../images/character.png";
characterLoader.load(characterURL);
character.addChild(characterLoader);
stage.addChild(character);
character.x = 225;
character.y = 150;

//Add the upButton
upButtonURL = new URLRequest();
upButtonLoader = new Loader();
upButton = new Sprite();
upButtonURL.url = "../images/up.png";
upButtonLoader.load(upButtonURL);
upButton.addChild(upButtonLoader);
stage.addChild(upButton);
upButton.x = 25;
upButton.y = 25;

//Add the downButton
downButtonURL = new URLRequest();
downButtonLoader = new Loader();
downButton = new Sprite();
downButtonURL.url = "../images/down.png";
downButtonLoader.load(downButtonURL);
downButton.addChild(downButtonLoader);
stage.addChild(downButton);
downButton.x = 25;
downButton.y = 85;

//Add the growButton
growButtonURL = new URLRequest();
growButtonLoader = new Loader();
growButton = new Sprite();
growButtonURL.url = "../images/grow.png";
growButtonLoader.load(growButtonURL);
growButton.addChild(growButtonLoader);
stage.addChild(growButton);
growButton.x = 25;
growButton.y = 145;

//Add the shrinkButton
shrinkButtonURL = new URLRequest();
```

```
    shrinkButtonLoader = new Loader();
    shrinkButton = new Sprite();
    shrinkButtonURL.url = "../images/shrink.png";
    shrinkButtonLoader.load(shrinkButtonURL);
    shrinkButton.addChild(shrinkButtonLoader);
    stage.addChild(shrinkButton);
    shrinkButton.x = 25;
    shrinkButton.y = 205;

    //Add the vanishButton
    vanishButtonURL = new URLRequest();
    vanishButtonLoader = new Loader();
    vanishButton = new Sprite();
    vanishButtonURL.url = "../images/vanish.png";
    vanishButtonLoader.load(vanishButtonURL);
    vanishButton.addChild(vanishButtonLoader);
    stage.addChild(vanishButton);
    vanishButton.x = 25;
    vanishButton.y = 265;

    //Add the spinButton
    spinButtonURL = new URLRequest();
    spinButtonLoader = new Loader();
    spinButton = new Sprite();
    spinButtonURL.url = "../images/spin.png";
    spinButtonLoader.load(spinButtonURL);
    spinButton.addChild(spinButtonLoader);
    stage.addChild(spinButton);
    spinButton.x = 25;
    spinButton.y = 325;

    //Add the button listeners
    upButton.addEventListener
      (MouseEvent.CLICK, upButtonHandler);
    downButton.addEventListener
      (MouseEvent.CLICK, downButtonHandler);
    growButton.addEventListener
      (MouseEvent.CLICK, growButtonHandler);
    shrinkButton.addEventListener
      (MouseEvent.CLICK,shrinkButtonHandler);
    vanishButton.addEventListener
      (MouseEvent.CLICK, vanishButtonHandler);
    spinButton.addEventListener
      (MouseEvent.CLICK, spinButtonHandler);
}

//The event handlers
public function upButtonHandler(event:MouseEvent):void
{
  if(character.y> 0)
  {
    character.y -= 15;
```

```
        //Optional:
        //character.x += 10;
      }
    }
    public function downButtonHandler(event:MouseEvent):void
    {
      if(character.y< 300)
      {
        character.y += 15;

        //Optional:
        //character.x -= 10;
      }
    }
    public function growButtonHandler(event:MouseEvent):void
    {
      character.scaleX += 0.1;
      character.scaleY += 0.1;

      //Optional:
      //character.height += 25;
      //character.width += 15;
    }
    public function shrinkButtonHandler(event:MouseEvent):void
    {
      character.scaleX -= 0.1;
      character.scaleY -= 0.1;

      //Optional:
      //character.height -= 25;
      //character.width -= 15;
    }
    public function vanishButtonHandler(event:MouseEvent):void
    {
      character.visible = !character.visible;
    }
    public function spinButtonHandler(event:MouseEvent):void
    {
      character.rotation += 20;
    }
  }
}
```

Summary

Whether you know it yet or not, you now have a considerable arsenal of skills at your disposal to build very rich interactive game worlds. In this chapter we looked at the very basic techniques necessary to build these worlds—and you really don't need many more. If you understand how to make, display, and control Sprite objects and how to use event listeners to make actions happen in your game, you have the basics that will make up rest of the projects of this book.

In Chapter 4, we're going to build our first complete game. It's a number guessing game, which will expand your programming skills considerably. You'll learn how to analyze a player's input to create a basic artificial intelligence system, modularize your program using methods, add interactive text, and keep players guessing (literally!) using random numbers.

Chapter 4

Decision Making

This chapter will be your first real look at designing a complete game. It's a short, simple game, but it contains all the basic structural elements of game design that you'll be returning to again and again. Input and output, decision making, keeping score, figuring out whether the player has won or lost, random numbers, and giving the player a chance to play again—it's all here. You'll also be taking a much closer look at variables and if statements. Furthermore, you'll learn how to modularize your program by breaking down long segments of code into bite-sized methods. By the end of the chapter, you'll have all the skills necessary to build complex logic games based on this simple model.

The game you'll build is a simple number guessing game. The game asks you to guess a number between 0 and 99. If you guess too high or too low, the game tells you this until you're able to figure out what the mystery number is by deduction. Figure 4-1 shows what the game will look like when it's done.

Figure 4-1. The number guessing game

You'll actually build this game in a few phases. You'll start with the most basic version of the game and then gradually add more features such as limiting the number of guesses, giving the player more detailed information about the status of the game, randomizing the mystery number, and adding an option to play the game again. You'll also learn how to make game buttons that change how they look depending on how you interact with them.

Sound like a lot? Each phase of the game is self-contained, so you can give yourself a bit of a break to absorb and experiment with the new techniques before moving on to the next phase. You'll be surprised at how easy and simple it is when you put all the pieces together.

Using text

In the previous chapter you learned how to load, display, and position images. In most games, however, you'll combine images with text. And the text will usually change depending on how the game changes. The first thing you're going to look at in this chapter is how to make and use interactive text using `TextField` and `TextFormat` objects.

Setting up the project

I'm going to start you with a basic program that sets up two text fields on the stage and displays a trace message that says "Game started". You won't understand much of this new code, but I'll explain all of it in the pages ahead. If you don't feel like typing all this out, you'll find this setup file in the chapter's source files in a project folder called NumberGuessingGameSetup.

1. Create a new AS3.0 project and enter the following program into the editor window:

```
package
{
  import flash.net.URLRequest;
  import flash.display.Loader;
  import flash.display.Sprite;
  import flash.events.MouseEvent;
  import flash.events.KeyboardEvent;
  import flash.ui.Keyboard;
  import flash.text.*;

  [SWF(width="550", height="400",
  backgroundColor="#FFFFFF", frameRate="60")]

  public class NumberGuessingGame extends Sprite
  {
    //Create the text objects
    public var format:TextFormat = new TextFormat();
    public var output:TextField = new TextField();
    public var input:TextField = new TextField();

    public function NumberGuessingGame()
    {
      setupTextfields();
      startGame();
    }
    public function setupTextfields():void
```

```
{
  //Set the text format object
  format.font = "Helvetica";
  format.size = 32;
  format.color = 0xFF0000;
  format.align = TextFormatAlign.LEFT;

  //Configure the output text field
  output.defaultTextFormat = format;
  output.width = 400;
  output.height = 70;
  output.border = true;
  output.wordWrap = true;
  output.text = "This is the output text field";

  //Display and position the output text field
  stage.addChild(output);
  output.x = 70;
  output.y = 65;

  //Configure the input text field
  format.size = 60;
  input.defaultTextFormat = format;
  input.width = 80;
  input.height = 60;
  input.border = true;
  input.type = "input";
  input.maxChars = 2;
  input.restrict = "0-9";
  input.background = true;
  input.backgroundColor = 0xCCCCCC;
  input.text = "";

  //Display and position the input text field
  stage.addChild(input);
  input.x = 70;
  input.y = 150;
  stage.focus = input;
  }
  public function startGame():void
  {
    trace("Game started")
  }
  }
}
```

2. Compile the program. You'll get a trace message saying "Game started". The Flash Player window will open, showing you two text fields. The larger one will display the words "This is the output text field" in red text. The smaller one, with a gray background, will have a flashing cursor in it; this is where you can type your guess. Figure 4-2 shows what you'll see.

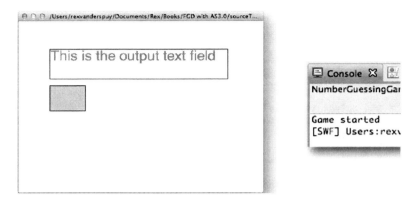

Figure 4-2. What happens when you compile the setup program

Don't let the code intimidate you. It doesn't contain any concepts that you haven't covered in the previous chapter—it's just dressed up a little differently. Let's see how it works.

The classes you have to import

You'll notice that this program is importing all the same classes from the previous chapter, but with the addition of a few new ones. Here's the new import code:

```
import flash.events.KeyboardEvent;
import flash.ui.Keyboard;
import flash.text.*;
```

The first two new lines import the **KeyboardEvent** and **Keyboard** classes. These are two special classes that you need to use if you want make games where the player interacts with the keyboard. You'll be using keyboard interactivity in this project, and you'll see how these two classes are put to use as the program develops.

The third line is interesting, because there's no class specified, just an asterisk:

```
import flash.text.*;
```

The asterisk means "give me all the text classes you've got." The AS3.0 library has a section called `flash.text` that contains all the classes that are used to display and manipulate text. There are many of them, and whenever you need display text in a game, you'll need most of them. Rather than going to all the trouble of importing each class individually, you can simply use an asterisk in place of a class name. The program will then load *all* the classes from `flash.text`. If you were to import each class individually, you'd have to write four import statements that look like this:

```
import flash.text.TextFormat;
import flash.text.TextField;
import flash.text.TextFormatAlign;
import flash.text.TextFieldAutoSize;
```

There's no technical advantage to using an asterisk to import all these classes over importing them individually, as long as you know you're going to use all the classes in your program. If you definitely know you're not going to use a class, it's best to import the classes individually so that you can exclude the one you don't need. If you import a class you don't use, it will take longer for your code to compile because the AS3.0 compiler will still have to browse through the class you didn't use when it makes your SWF file. Importing unnecessary classes won't affect how your game runs, however.

You can use an asterisk to import all the classes from any of the AS3.0 code packages. For example, if you want to import all the classes from the display package, you could do it like this:

```
import flash.display.*;
```

You're going to use all these classes in this project.

Creating TextFormat and TextField objects

You'll recall from Chapter 3 that making an object, like a Sprite, is a two-step process.

First, you have to declare a variable to contain the Sprite object, like this:

```
public var gameCharacter:Sprite;
```

Next, you need to turn that variable into a Sprite object with the new keyword.

```
gameCharacter = new Sprite();
```

You wrote a lot of code like this in the previous chapter. But what you probably didn't know is that you can combine both lines of code into one, like this:

```
public var gameCharacter:Sprite = new Sprite();
```

This line of code declares the variable and creates the object in one step. The result is the same: you end up with a Sprite object, but you've saved yourself a line of code.

Sometimes you'll write a program where you won't know, when the program starts, exactly what kind of object a variable will contain. That's because in some complex programs the objects you want to create don't exist until the program starts running. In those cases, you'll need to declare the variable first and then create the object later in the program. You'll see examples of why this is important in the later chapters of this book.

However, you'll often know exactly what type of object to create when the program first initializes. In those cases, declare the variable and create the object in one step. That's what the first three new lines of code do in the class definition:

```
public class NumberGuessingGame extends Sprite
{
  public var format:TextFormat = new TextFormat();
  public var output:TextField = new TextField();
  public var input:TextField = new TextField();
```

They create one TextFormat object and two TextField objects.

The TextFormat object is called format. Its job is to determine how text should look on the stage: such as its font, color, size, and the text alignment.

The TextField objects care called input and output. These objects are the actual text you see on the stage. You saw them both on the stage when you compiled this program: the output field is along the top and the input field is the small one with the gray background just below it.

Let's find out how these TextFormat and TextField properties work.

Setting the format of text

Look in the setupTextfields function definition and you'll see these four lines of code:

```
format.font = "Helvetica";
format.size = 32;
format.color = 0xFF0000;
format.align = TextFormatAlign.LEFT;
```

This code is setting four properties of the format object. You'll recall from Chapter 3 that all objects have properties that you can change to achieve different effects. You'll remember that Sprite objects have properties like x, y, visible, scaleX, and scaleY.

format is a TextFormat object, and its properties determine what text looks like on the stage. Here are the four properties that it's setting:

- **font** is the font that you want your text to display in. This example uses Helvetica. You can use the name of any font that's installed on your computer. Surround the exact name of the font with quotation marks.

  The font property works fine while you're testing your game, but if it plays on another computer that doesn't have exactly the same font installed as you've specified, the font obviously can't load. It will instead be replaced by another font that the Flash Player thinks might be close. If you want the fonts in your game to look exactly the same on all computers, no matter whether or not the font is installed, you have to use a technique called **font embedding**. Embedding fonts can sometimes produce quirky results, but you'll find out how to do this at the end of this chapter in the "A quick guide to embedding fonts" section.

- **color** is the hexadecimal code for the font. You can use any hex code you like; just precede it with 0x. This example uses 0xFF0000, which is the hex code for red.

- **size** is the font size.

- **Align** is the alignment of the text: left, right, or centered. Here are the property values you can use if you want to change the alignment:

  - TextFormatAlign.LEFT

  - TextFormatAlign.RIGHT

  - TextFormatAlign.CENTER

> *You may wonder why the values for setting the align property look so strange.*
>
> *TextFormatAlign.LEFT*
>
> *TextFormatAlign is a special built-in class that just contains properties for aligning text. (You can tell it's a class because it starts with an uppercase letter.) After the class name is a dot. You know that whatever follows a dot will be either a property or a method. In this case, the dot is followed by properties, like LEFT and RIGHT.*
>
> *These properties are all written in full uppercase characters because they're programming elements called **constants**. You'll be looking at what constants are and how to use them in Chapter 9. But one feature of constants is that they're always written in full uppercase letters.*

In Figure 4-3 you can see the result of all these text properties.

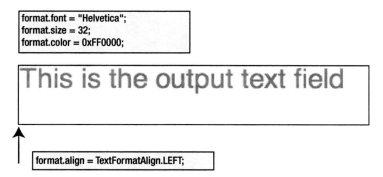

```
format.font = "Helvetica";
format.size = 32;
format.color = 0xFF0000;
```

This is the output text field

```
format.align = TextFormatAlign.LEFT;
```

Figure 4-3. How the format properties affect the text

These are the four most useful TextFormat properties, but there are many others. Table 4-1 shows you other properties that are available.

Table 4-1. TextFormat Properties

Property	Description	Possible values
bold	Makes text bold	True or false

blockindent	Text indent amount	Any number in pixels
bullet	Indents the text and adds a bullet to show that it's part of a list	True or false
indent	The number of pixels by which to indent the first line of text	Any number in pixels
italic	Whether or not the text is italic	True or false
leading	How much space to put between lines of text	Any number in pixels
leftMargin	How wide to make the left margin	Any number in pixels
letterSpacing	How much extra space should be between letters	Any number in pixels.
rightMargin	How wide to make the right margin	Any number in pixels
underline	Whether or not to underline the text	True or false

In addition, there are a few more rarely used text properties: kerning, tabStops, target, and url. You can find out more about these properties in the TextFormat chapter in Adobe's AS3.0 documentation at `http://help.adobe.com/en_US/ActionScript/3.0_ProgrammingAS3/`.

TextFormat objects determine what the text will look like, but not what the text actually is. Displaying the actual text is the job of TextField objects.

Configuring and displaying the output text

TextField objects have the very simple job of displaying text. Your program has two TextField objects: `output` and `input`. In this program, it's going to be the job of the `output` TextField to tell you what's happening in the game. Here's all the code that configures it and displays it on the stage:

```
//Configure the output text field
output.defaultTextFormat = format;
output.width = 400;
output.height = 70;
output.border = true;
output.wordWrap = true;
output.text = "This is the output text field";

//Display and position the output text field
stage.addChild(output);
output.x = 70;
output.y = 65;
```

Let's see how this code works.

The `output` TextField needs to know how it should be formatted.

```
output.defaultTextFormat = format;
```

defaultTextFormat is a TextField property that determines how the text should be formatted. What's the value that you're supplying it on the right side of the equal sign? That's your **format** object! You're telling the output TextField that it should use the format object that you just configured. Now any text that's displayed by the output TextField will take on all of the format object's qualities.

The next five lines set some very important properties.

```
output.width = 400;
output.height = 70;
output.border = true;
output.wordWrap = true;
output.text = "This is the output text field";
```

The width and height properties determine how large the text field should be. You can use any number in pixels. Figure 4-4 shows that the width of 400 and height of 70 match the dimensions of the border that surrounds the text.

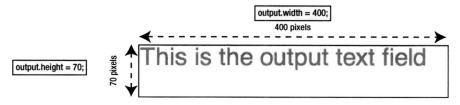

Figure 4-4. Width and height properties determine the size of the text field.

> *Often you'll find it convenient to have the text field height and width set automatically based on the size of the text it contains. In that case, don't set the height and width properties. Use this line of code instead:*
>
> ```
> output.autoSize = TextFieldAutoSize.LEFT;
> ```
>
> *The autoSize property uses the special TextFieldAutoSize class to automatically size the text field, no matter how large or small the text. LEFT indicates that the text is aligned to the left side of the field. Other values you can use here are RIGHT and CENTER.*

The border property determines whether there's a border around the text. If it's set to true, the border is visible, as you can see in Figure 4-4. If you don't set the border property at all or set its value to false, the border won't be visible.

Wrapping is what happens when text is automatically carried over to a new line when it reaches the right-hand margin. The wordWrap property is important because it's used to tell the text field whether or not to force text from the first line onto the second line if the text from the first line is too long.

Figure 4-5 illustrates the different effect that setting the wordWrap property to true of false has on a long line of text.

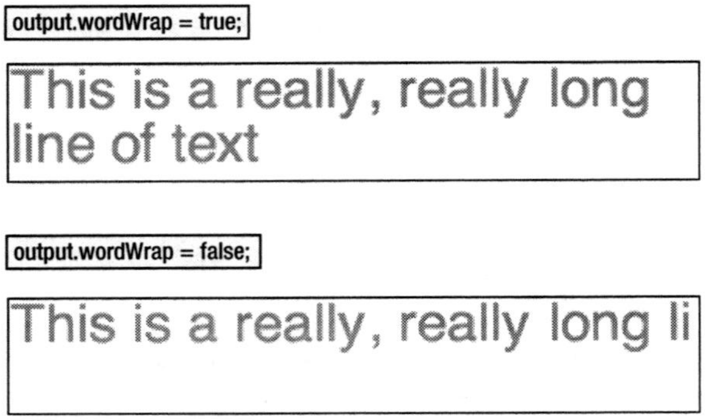

```
output.wordWrap = true;
```

This is a really, really long
line of text

```
output.wordWrap = false;
```

This is a really, really long li

Figure 4-5. Text field wrapping styles

When wordWrap is set to true, the text creates a new line when it bumps into the text field's right margin. When it's set to false, it doesn't, so it could get cut off if the text field isn't long enough to contain it.

The last property that's set on the output TextField is the most important. It's the text property. It determines what words will actually be displayed in the text field.
```
output.text = "This is the output text field";
```

You can change these words to anything you like, and whatever you type will be displayed in the text field, as you can see in Figure 4-6.

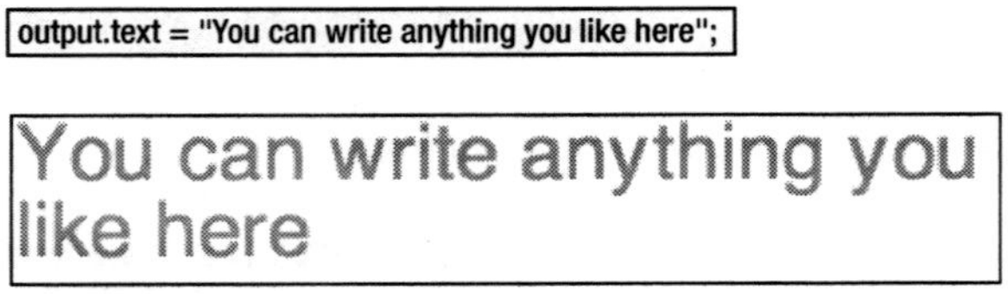

```
output.text = "You can write anything you like here";
```

You can write anything you
like here

Figure 4-6. The text property determines which words are displayed in the text field.

You're going to be changing the output TextField's text property a lot when you write your game, and you'll see what an important effect this will have.

With all the properties set, the last thing to do is add and position the output TextField on the stage.

```
stage.addChild(output);
output.x = 70;
output.y = 65;
```

This is exactly the same way you added and positioned Sprite objects in the previous chapter.

Configuring and displaying the input field

Here's the code that configures and displays the input text field:

```
//Configure the input text field
format.size = 60;
input.defaultTextFormat = format;
input.width = 80;
input.height = 60;
input.border = true;
input.type = "input";
input.maxChars = 2;
input.restrict = "0-9";
input.background = true;
input.backgroundColor = 0xCCCCCC;
input.text = "";
```

//Display and position the input text field
```
stage.addChild(input);
input.x = 70;
input.y = 150;
stage.focus = input;
```

The job of the input TextField is to accept user input. You can actually type things into it, and, when your game is programmed, all that information will go into the game. When you write your number guessing game, you're going to be using the input TextField to enter guesses.

The input TextField uses all the same properties as the output field, such as height, width, and border, but it also uses a few specialized new ones.

Where they're similar is that both text fields use the same format object to determine the font style, size, color, and alignment. But look at the line just above that applies the formatting:

format.size = 60;
```
input.defaultTextFormat = format;
```

Before the formatting is applied to the input field, the format object's size property is set to 60. That's because I wanted the input TextField to have exactly the same formatting as the output TextField, with the simple change that its font size should be bigger. So, before I assigned the format object to the input field, I first changed the format object's size property to 60. This makes the font size bigger, but keeps the style, color, and alignment the same. You can see this in Figure 4-7.

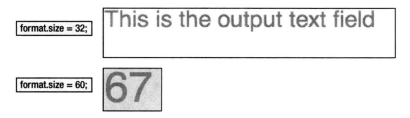

Figure 4-7. The text formatting is the same for both text fields, except that the font size of the input field is larger.

This saved me the trouble of having to create a completely new TextFormat object, although I probably would have done so if I needed to change more than just the font size.

After setting the height, width, and border, the next few lines are particularly important.

```
input.type = "input";
```

Setting the type property to "input" allows you to enter text into the field. That means you can type right into it. (The other value you can give it is "dynamic", which prevents users from typing into it. All newly created TextField objects are automatically set to "dynamic" by default.)

maxChars prevents you from typing in more than two characters.

```
input.maxChars = 2;
```

That's important in this number guessing game because you'll want the player to guess a number from 0 to 99. You won't want the player to enter numbers greater than two characters, such as 134 or 746.

The next property, restrict, prevents the player from entering anything but numbers.

```
input.restrict = "0-9";
```

Try entering letters into the input field. You can't. You can only enter the numbers 0 through 9. That's also important for your game. It's a number guessing game, so what would happen to your poor game if a player entered the word "bicycle" as one of the guesses? Restricting player input like this means that your game doesn't have to deal with unexpected information like that.

If you want to restrict the text field to only the uppercase letters A, B, and C, you could set the restrict property like this:

```
input.restrict = "ABC";
```

You can restrict a range of numbers or letters by separating the first character in the range from the last character with a dash. Here are some examples:

- To allow only the uppercase letters from M to O, use "M-O".
- To allow all uppercase letters, use "A-Z".
- To restrict input to just lowercase letters, use "a-z".
- To allow only uppercase and lowercase letters, use "A-Za-z".

Your life as a programmer will often be improved by restricting certain types of input because if a user enters something that your program doesn't know how to deal with, the whole program could stop working.

You'll notice that the input field has a light gray background color. This is thanks to the next two lines of code:

```
input.background = true;
input.backgroundColor = 0xCCCCCC;
```

Before you can assign a background color, you first have to set the background property to true. You can then assign any hexadecimal color code you like to the backgroundColor property.

The input field is displayed and positioned on the stage in exactly the same way as the output field, but the very last line of code is important:

```
stage.focus = input;
```

This creates a blinking cursor in the input text field.

When an object on the stage, such as a button or a text field, has been selected by the user, it's said to have **focus**. When input text fields have focus, a blinking cursor appears, and whatever the user types is automatically entered into it. Note that focus is a property of the built-in Stage class, which is at the root of the hierarchy for all display objects (all objects you can see on the stage). When the SWF file runs the program, an instance of the Stage class is automatically created (called, conveniently enough, stage). To assign focus to a text field, all you need to do is assign the name of the text field object to the stage.focus property, as you did here.

If you need to remove focus from a text field, you can give it a null value, such as the following:

```
stage.focus = null;
```

There are many more properties that you can set for TextField objects, and Table 4-2 lists the most useful of these.

Table 4-2. TextField Properties

Property	Description	Possible values
borderColor	The color of the border	Any hexadecimal color code value
displayAsPassword	Replaces any text with asterisk (star) characters. This is useful for making password input fields.	True or false
htmlText	Text that allows limited formatting using HTML tags.	HTML code
length	Number of characters in a text field	You can't change the value, but you can read it.
mouseWheelEnabled	Whether or not the user can scroll the text field with the mouse wheel. This is true by default.	True or false
Multiline	Whether or not the text field can span more than one line.	True or false
numLines	Defines the number of lines in a multiline text field.	Any whole number
Selectable	Whether or not the text can be selected.	True or false.

Property	Description	Possible values
textColor	The color of the text. Use this, and the next two properties, if your text hasn't set a TextFormat object.	Any hexadecimal color code value
textHeight	The height of the text	Any number in pixels
textWidth	The width of the text	Any number in pixels

There are many more specialized TextField properties; you can find out more about all them in Adobe's reference at http://help.adobe.com/en_US/FlashPlatform/reference/actionscript/3/flash/text/TextField.html.

And you'll be happy to know that this is pretty much all you'll need to know for working with text in Flash games. Now let's use this setup file as a basis for writing your very first game.

Building a simple guessing game

You'll build the number guessing game in three separate phases so that you can get a solid grasp of the techniques before you add more complexity. The first phase is the most basic version, but it's the most important because it contains the very heart of the game.

The game starts by asking the player to guess a number from 0 to 99. It will tell the player whether the guess is too high or too low until eventually the correct number is found. In this version of the game, the player gets an unlimited number of guesses, but you'll fix that and add a few more interesting features in phase 2.

Understanding the program structure

There's something a little fishy happening in your program so far that you have take a closer look at before you start writing the game. You'll recall from Chapter 1 that any code you put inside the constructor method will run immediately when the program is launched. Let's look at the constructor method for your game so far:

```
public function NumberGuessingGame()
{
  setupTextfields();
  startGame();
}
```

This is very different from the constructor methods you used in earlier chapters, which were packed full of lots of code. You now have only two simple directives:

```
setupTextfields();
startGame();
```

What are those? They're **method calls**. Method calls trigger a method's function definition to run its directives. The methods being "called" here are the setupTextfields and startGame methods. This means that as soon as the constructor runs, it immediately tells these two methods to perform whatever tasks you've assigned to them.

First, the setupTextfields method is run. You just looked at it in detail; it sets up and displays the two text fields. Here's an abridged version with a comment replacing the actual code:

```
public function setupTextfields():void
{
  //Setup and display the input and output fields...
}
```

After this, the constructor runs the startGame method.

```
public function startGame():void
{
  trace("Game started")
}
```

It doesn't do much at the moment. It just displays a simple trace message to let you know that everything is working properly, but you're going to start writing into it soon.

By splitting the constructor method's work into two separate methods, you're starting to **modularize** your program. Program modularization is a way of keeping related code together as a single unit so that it's easier to work with. Instead of having to rummage through a big listing of jumbled code, modularized code is broken into small, related units. This helps you to focus on specific areas of your program without having to be distracted by unrelated code.

In your program, the code you wrote to set up the text fields has nothing to do with the mechanics of the game. In fact, you'll never need to touch the code that sets up the text fields again. It therefore makes sense to keep it separate from the rest of the program so that you don't need to be bothered by it. I've done this by keeping all the code that displays the text fields in its own method: setupTextFields.

Likewise, all the code that initializes the game is in its own method: startGame. This means when you write this code, you can ignore every other part of the program except the startGame method. This will really help you to focus and organize your work.

It also means that after you play the game, you just need to run the startGame method again if you want to play a second time. This would not be possible unless you've moved all game initialization code into its own method, like you've done here. You'll see how convenient this will be when you create a Play again button at the end of the chapter.

Figure 4-8 illustrates how the constructor launches the setupTextFields and startGame methods.

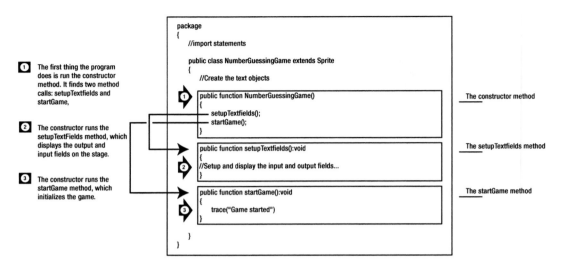

Figure 4-8. The constructor method shares the work of setting up the program between two different methods.

You're going to see many more examples of how to write modular code in pages ahead.

Learning more about variables

Your first job is to initialize some of the basic variables that you need in the game. The most important is the mystery number that the player has to guess. You'll also initialize the first message that the player receives in the output text field. Both of these values are assigned using variables. To see this in action, follow these steps:

1. Add the following text in bold to the class definition:

```
public class NumberGuessingGame extends Sprite
{
  //Create the text objects
  public var format:TextFormat = new TextFormat();
  public var output:TextField = new TextField();
  public var input:TextField = new TextField();

  //Game variables
  public var startMessage:String;
  public var mysteryNumber:uint;
```

2. Add this text to the `startGame` method (delete the existing trace directive):

```
public function startGame():void
{
```

```
//Initialize variables
startMessage = "I am thinking of a number between 0 and 99";
mysteryNumber = 50;

//Initialize text fields
output.text = startMessage
input.text = "";
}
```

3. Compile the program. You should see the words "I am thinking of a number between 0 and 99" appear in the output text field, and the input text field should be blank, as shown in Figure 4-9.

I am thinking of a number between 0 and 99

Figure 4-9. The game is now initialized.

The first thing you did was to declare two new variables in the class definition. You've used variables in earlier chapters, but there's something new here—the variable types (which follow the colon).

```
public var startMessage:String;
public var mysteryNumber:uint;
```

What are these variable types, String and uint?

You might recall from the previous chapter that when you created variables to hold Sprite objects, you declared their type to be the class from which they were made. What did this line of code mean?

```
public var character:Sprite;
```

It meant that the character variable was a type of Sprite. The new code you've just written does something very similar. This line means that startMessage is a type of String:

```
public var startMessage:String;
```

And this line means that mysteryNumber is a type of uint (which stands for **unsigned integer**):

```
public var mysteryNumber:uint;
```

Okay, that's pretty meaningless, isn't it? Don't worry; it will become clear soon!

Let's a take a step back. When you declare a variable, you need to tell the program what type of information that variable will be holding. Will you be using the variable to store numbers or words? If you're using it to store numbers, what kind of numbers will they be? Hey, it might seem like more detail than you need, but AS3.0 wants this information to make sure that you don't start trying to mix variables that contain

225

words with variables that contain numbers or any of the other kinds of possibly incompatible data types that variables can contain.

So what kind of variable types are there? Here are all the data types that can be used by variables in AS3.0:

- **Boolean** can take one of two values: true or false; its default value is false.

- **Number** is any number, such as whole numbers (also known as **integers**) and numbers that include decimal places (also known as **floating point** numbers).

- **int** stands for **integer**, which is a whole number without a decimal place. It can be positive or negative. Because the CPU doesn't have to calculate any decimal places, using it speeds up the program's performance. It's usually better to use the int type over the Number type if you know you won't need to use decimals. The default value for the int type is 0.

- **uint** stands for **unsigned integer**. uint is an integer that is only positive. This is an even leaner version of the int type, so it's the fastest of them all. Use it whenever you can for the best performance. uint has a default value of 0.

- **String** can be letters, words, or phrases—any text at all. You can even use the String type to store numbers, but if you do, the numbers will be interpreted as text and you won't be able to manipulate them mathematically. The default value for the String type is null, which means "no data of any kind."

- **Object** is a general type. The Object class in AS3.0 is the base class for all other objects. The Object class also has a default value of null.

- **void** is a very specialized type that is used only for methods that don't return values. It's not used for variables. It can contain only one value: undefined. The undefined value is very similar to the null value, except that it is used when the variable hasn't yet been assigned a data type, or if it contains numbers or Boolean values. All the methods so far have been declared with a data type of void.

- *** (asterisk)** is used when you want to create a variable that has no specific type or you need it to be really flexible to be able to contain different data types at different times, replace the type name with an asterisk. For example, you might use a line of code like this:

```
variableName:*;
```

- This variable now can hold any type of data. One suggestion regarding the use of the asterisk is this: don't use it! Unless you have an extremely good reason why you want your variables to be able to contain more than one type of data, you're opening up your program to a potential can of worms. Forcing variables to a particular type is one of the great strengths of AS3.0 because it prevents bugs and errors that are the result of the wrong type of data being stored in the wrong type of variable. These kinds of errors can often be very difficult to debug.

> *Note: The int, uint, and void data types start with a lowercase letter; the others all start with uppercase letters.*

You can file these data types away for later, but you'll be using all of them over the course of this book. From today's menu, you have two of them on the plate: `startMessage` is a String, and `mysteryNumber` is a uint type.

The first thing the `startGame` method does is to assign values to these variables.

```
startMessage = "I am thinking of a number between 0 and 99";
mysteryNumber = 50;
```

The next thing that happens is that the text from the `startMessage` variable is copied into the output text field's `text` property.

```
output.text = startMessage;
```

`output`, of course, is the text field on the stage. You could have easily written this same line of code as follows and the result would have been identical:

```
output.text =  "I am thinking of a number between 0 and 99";
```

Why did you go to all that extra trouble of creating the extra `startMessage` variable when you could have assigned the text directly?

First, you got some practice in creating String variables—that's not such a bad reason, is it? Second, it's sometimes useful to store all the text you'll be using in your program in variables that you can access in one spot. If you know that all the text in your program is assigned to variables in your `startGame` method, you don't need to go hunting through your code to find them if you need to make changes. This isn't an important issue in small programs like this number guessing game, but it could become a real chore in bigger programs. Finally, you want to make sure that the `input` text field is completely blank so that players are free to type whatever they want into it. To clear a text field of any characters, assign it a pair of empty quotation marks, like so:

```
input.text =  "";
```

Empty quotation marks are to string variables what 0 is to number variables: it just means that there's no text there yet.

Listening for key presses

In Chapter 3 you made things happen in your game world by clicking buttons. In this game you're going to make things happen by pressing the Enter key on the keyboard. The code you'll need to write follows the same format as the code you wrote for buttons.

- You need to create an event listener that listens for key presses.

- You need to create an event handler that tells your program what should happen when a key is pressed.

Let's add an event listener and handler to your program to capture key presses.

1. Add this new code in bold directly below the previous code you wrote:

```
public function startGame():void
{
  //Initialize variables
  startMessage = "I am thinking of a number between 0 and 99";
  mysteryNumber = 50;

  //Initialize text fields
  output.text = startMessage
  input.text = "";

  //Add an event listener for key presses
  stage.addEventListener(KeyboardEvent.KEY_DOWN, keyPressHandler);
}
public function keyPressHandler(event:KeyboardEvent):void
{
  if (event.keyCode == Keyboard.ENTER)
  {
    trace(input.text);
  }
}
```

Enter this code carefully—you should have two more closing braces, following this new code, at the end of your program. Figure 4-10 shows what your code editor should look like when you've added this new code.

```
        //Display and position the input text field
        stage.addChild(input);
        input.x = 70;
        input.y = 150;
        stage.focus = input;
    }
    public function startGame():void
    {
        //Initialize variables
        startMessage = "I am thinking of a number between 0 and 99";
        mysteryNumber = 50;

        //Initialize text fields
        output.text = startMessage
        input.text = "";

        //Add an event listener for key presses
        stage.addEventListener(KeyboardEvent.KEY_DOWN, keyPressHandler);
    }
    public function keyPressHandler(event:KeyboardEvent):void
    {
        if (event.keyCode == Keyboard.ENTER)
        {
            trace(input.text);
        }
    }
}
}
```

Figure 4-10. Add the new code to the end of your program.

2. Compile the program. Enter some numbers in the `input` field and press the Enter key. You'll see the number you entered displayed as a trace message. Figure 4-11 illustrates this.

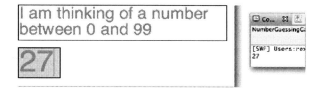

Figure 4-11. Any number you enter in the input field is displayed as a trace message.

Your code first added a listener to the stage. It works in exactly the same way as the button listeners you used in Chapter 3, except it listens for key presses.

```
stage.addEventListener(KeyboardEvent.KEY_DOWN, keyPressHandler);
```

The `KeyboardEvent` class, which you imported along with your other classes for this project, has a special `KEY_DOWN` property that you can use to detect any key pressed on the keyboard. When a key press is detected, the listener launches the `keyPressHandler` to find out what it should do.

```
public function keyPressHandler(event:KeyboardEvent):void
```

```
{
  if (event.keyCode == Keyboard.ENTER)
  {
    trace(input.text);
  }
}
```

As you learned in Chapter 3, event listeners send a lot of information to the event handler in a special event object. You can see the event object in the handler's parameters: it has the name event. Figure 4-12 highlights this for you.

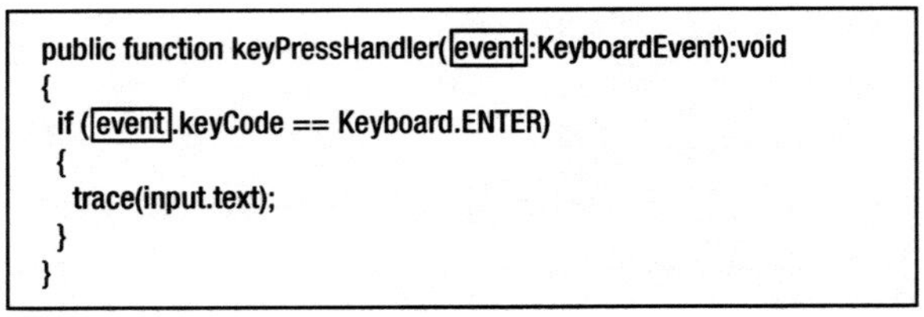

```
public function keyPressHandler(event:KeyboardEvent):void
{
  if (event.keyCode == Keyboard.ENTER)
  {
    trace(input.text);
  }
}
```

Figure 4-12. Event objects store a lot of information about the event that happened, including the key that was pressed.

All event handlers must include an event object to store this information—it's just part of the deal. Event objects that contain keyboard information are typed as **KeyboardEvent** objects, like this:

event:KeyboardEvent

They're declared directly in the event handler, as this code in bold highlights:

```
private function onKeyDown(event:KeyboardEvent):void
{...
```

You can access this event object at any time to use the information it contains. One piece of information is the key code number for the key that's being pressed. This number is stored in a property of the event variable called keyCode. You can access it like this:

event.keyCode

It contains the key code number of the key being pressed. This is important, because it means you can use this information to find out which key on the keyboard is being pressed. The key code is a number (for example, 40 or 37) that corresponds to a specific key on the keyboard. Luckily you don't need to know or remember what these key codes actually are. The Keyboard class contains convenient properties called LEFT, RIGHT, UP, DOWN and ENTER that you can use in place of the actual key code numbers.

An if statement checks whether the key pressed was the Enter key.

```
if (event.keyCode == Keyboard.ENTER)
```

```
{
  trace(input.text);
}
```

The code checks whether the event object's key code matches the value of Keyboard.ENTER. If it does, the trace directive is run. The trace directive displays the value of the input field's text property—and that will be whatever you type into it on the stage. Clever!

The key code number for the Enter key is 13. You could, in fact, have written the conditional statement like the following and it would have worked just fine:

```
if (event.keyCode == 13)
{
  trace(input.text);
}
```

And actually, if you want to write it this way, I won't stop you! But AS3.0's **Keyboard** class contains loads of predefined properties that already represent these numbers, like Keyboard.ENTER, so you don't have to memorize the number associated with each key on the keyboard. Instead, you just need to use the **Keyboard** class's easy-to-read-and-remember Keyboard properties. You'll take a look at many more of these Keyboard properties in Chapter 5.

> *In fact, the **Keyboard** class contains a property for every key on the keyboard. If you want to have a look at the whole list, point your web browser to http://help.adobe.com/en_US/FlashPlatform/reference/actionscript/3/flash/ui/Keyboard.html?filter_flash=cs5&filter_flashplayer=10.2&filter_air=2.6*

You now have a way to get information directly from the player into your program. Plug this into your game to see how it works.

Making decisions

You've done a lot of work on your program, but so far it doesn't yet do anything useful. What you need to do now is build the brains of the game so the program can figure out what number the player has entered and whether it's too high, too low, or correct.

You can do this by using an if/else statement. Note that if/else statements are very similar to the simple if statements that you looked at in Chapter 3, except that they provide an extra course of action if the condition being checked turns out to be false.

Here's an example of the basic kind of if statement that you looked at in the previous chapter:

```
if (this condition or variable is true)
{
  Perform this directive.
}
```

But what if the condition is not true? Obviously, the directive inside the if statement won't run. But what if you want *something else* to happen instead? That's where the addition of the keyword else comes in. Here's an example of a simple if/else statement:

```
if (this condition or variable is true)
{
  Perform this directive...
}
else
{
  Perform this directive if the condition or variable isn't true...
}
```

If the condition turns out to be false, the program will jump straight to the second directive enclosed inside the braces of the else block statement. This allows the program to make a choice between two alternatives, and at least one of them will be chosen.

You can take this system one step further and add a third or more possible choices by throwing an additional else if statement into the mix. Have a look at how this works:

```
if (this condition or variable is true)
{
  Perform this directive.
}
  else if (some other condition or variable is true)
{
  Perform this directive.
}
else
{
  Perform this directive if neither is true.
}
```

This if/else statement checks each of the conditions in turn. If the first is false, it skips to the second. If the second is also false, the final directive in the else block statement is run as the default value.

This format is perfect for the number guessing game because you need the program it to check for three possible conditions:

- If the player's guess is less than the mystery number.

- If the player's guess is greater than the mystery number.

- If the player correctly guesses the mystery number.

To implement this decision making in the program, you need to first find a way of getting the number from the input text field on the stage into the program so that it can be processed. This is pretty easy to do.

- You need to create a new variable called currentGuess to store the number the player enters in the input text field. You'll use this new variable to convert the text from the input text field from a string to a number so that an if/else statement can process it.

- You need to make something happen when the player presses the Enter key on the keyboard.

- You need to create a new method called `playGame`. Its job will be to analyze the player's input and determine whether the guess is too low, too high, or correct.

Let's get to work!

1. Add the following new variable, `currentGuess`, to the class definition, just after the previous two new variables you added:

```
public class NumberGuessingGame extends Sprite
{
  //Create the text objects
  public var format:TextFormat = new TextFormat();
  public var output:TextField = new TextField();
  public var input:TextField = new TextField();

  //Game variables
  public var startMessage:String;
  public var mysteryNumber:uint;
  public var currentGuess:uint;
```

2. Write the `playGame` method. Add it to your code just after the `startGame` method, but before the `keyPressHandler`. If you're unsure of where to add it, take a look at Figure 4-13.

```
public function playGame():void
{
  currentGuess = uint(input.text);

  if (currentGuess > mysteryNumber)
  {
    output.text = "That's too high.";
  }
  else if (currentGuess < mysteryNumber)
  {
    output.text = "That's too low.";
  }
  else
  {
    output.text = "You got it!";
  }
}
```

```
        //Initialize text fields
        output.text = startMessage
        input.text = "";

        //Add an event listener for key presses
        stage.addEventListener(KeyboardEvent.KEY_DOWN, keyPressHandler);
    }
    public function playGame():void
    {
        currentGuess = uint(input.text);

        if (currentGuess > mysteryNumber)
        {
            output.text = "That's too high.";
        }
        else if (currentGuess < mysteryNumber)
        {
            output.text = "That's too low.";
        }
        else
        {
            output.text = "You got it!";
        }
    }
    public function keyPressHandler(event:KeyboardEvent):void
    {
        if (event.keyCode == Keyboard.ENTER)
        {
            trace(input.text);
        }
    }
}
}
```

Figure 4-13. Add the playGame method between startGame and keyPressHandler.

It actually doesn't really matter where you add this method as long as it's part of its own block inside the class definition. However, I like to keep event handlers near the end of the program to keep them out of the way.

3. You now need to connect the keyPressHandler to the playGame method. This will make the playGame method run when the Enter key is pressed. Change the keyPressHandler so that the trace method is replaced with the playGame() method call, as shown:

```
public function keyPressHandler(event:KeyboardEvent):void
{
  if (event.keyCode == Keyboard.ENTER)
  {
    playGame();
  }
}
```

4. Compile the program. Enter a number into the input field and press the Enter key The game will now tell you whether your guess is too high, too low, or correct (see Figure 4-14).

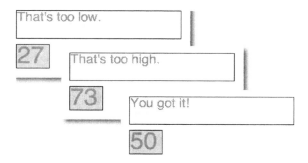

Figure 4-14. With an if/else statement, the game knows whether the player's guess is correct.

When you press the Enter key, the keyboard event listener calls the `keyPressHandler`. If the Enter key is being pressed, the `playGame` method is called. The `playGame` method analyses the player's input and displays the result. Figure 4-15 shows the route the code follows when the Enter key is pressed.

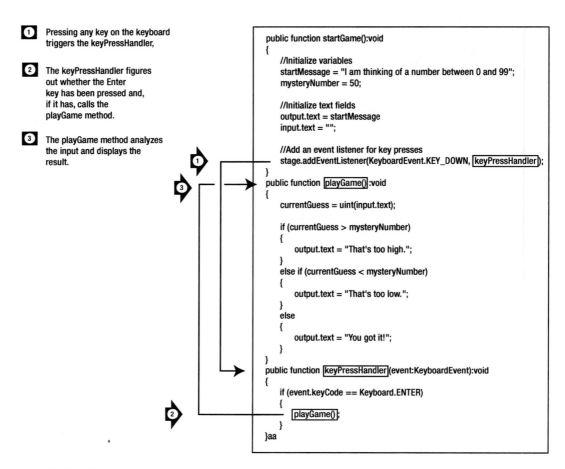

1. Pressing any key on the keyboard triggers the keyPressHandler,

2. The keyPressHandler figures out whether the Enter key has been pressed and, if it has, calls the playGame method.

3. The playGame method analyzes the input and displays the result.

```
public function startGame():void
{
    //Initialize variables
    startMessage = "I am thinking of a number between 0 and 99";
    mysteryNumber = 50;

    //Initialize text fields
    output.text = startMessage
    input.text = "";

    //Add an event listener for key presses
    stage.addEventListener(KeyboardEvent.KEY_DOWN, keyPressHandler);
}
public function playGame():void
{
    currentGuess = uint(input.text);

    if (currentGuess > mysteryNumber)
    {
        output.text = "That's too high.";
    }
    else if (currentGuess < mysteryNumber)
    {
        output.text = "That's too low.";
    }
    else
    {
        output.text = "You got it!";
    }
}
public function keyPressHandler(event:KeyboardEvent):void
{
    if (event.keyCode == Keyboard.ENTER)
    {
        playGame();
    }
}aa
```

Figure 4-15. What happens when you press the Enter key

Let's take a look at how the playGame method works.

```
public function playGame():void
{
  currentGuess = uint(input.text);

  if (currentGuess > mysteryNumber)
  {
    output.text = "That's too high.";
  }
  else if (currentGuess < mysteryNumber)
  {
    output.text = "That's too low.";
  }
  else
```

```
  {
    output.text = "You got it!";
  }
}
```

The first directive may be a little puzzling.

```
currentGuess = uint(input.text);
```

What's that all that about? It copies the text from the **input** field in to the **currentGuess** variable. But that's not all; it also converts the input data from plain text into a number.

When you enter text into an **input** text field, that text is stored in the field's built-in text property as a String object. String objects are words or letters, and you can usually spot them because they're surrounded by quotes. Even if you type in numbers, those numbers are interpreted as characters in a line of text, not something that can be processed mathematically. As far as strings are concerned, "789" is just another word like "bike" or "elephant." That's bit of a problem because the game depends on the player entering numbers that can actually be understood as numbers.

What you need to do then is convert the data from the **input** field's text property from a string to a number. Because the numbers from 0 to 99 are all positive and don't contain decimal values, it makes sense that they should be interpreted as data with a uint type.

It's very easy to convert data types in AS3.0. All you need to do is surround the data you want to convert in parentheses and then add the name of the type you want to convert it to. That's all that this bit of code in bold does:

```
currentGuess = uint(input.text);
```

It converts the string from the **input** field's text variable into a number of the uint type. This process of converting one type of data to another is called **casting**. You'll be encountering casting a lot over the course of the book. It's often necessary for you to cast data or objects as a certain type to encourage AS3.0's compiler to run the code correctly.

> *An alternative way of casting variables is to use the* **as** *keyword. You can write the previous line of code like this:*
>
> ```
> currentGuess = input.text as uint;
> ```
>
> *This line is very readable and the effect is exactly the same. It's entirely up to you which style of casting you prefer.*

Now that you have a number in the **currentGuess** variable, you can use the if/else statement to analyze it.

```
if (currentGuess > mysteryNumber)
```

```
{
  output.text = "That's too high.";
}
else if (currentGuess < mysteryNumber)
{
  output.text = "That's too low.";
}
else
{
  output.text = "You got it!";
}
```

The logic behind this is really simple. If the `currentGuess` variable is greater than the `mysteryNumber`, "That's too high" displays in the `output` text field. If it's less than the `mysteryNumber`, "That's too low" displays. If it's neither too low nor too high, there's only one alternative left: the number is correct. The `output` text field displays "You got it!"

Not so hard at all, is it? If you understand how this works, you might be pleased to know that writing if/else statements will be at the very heart of the logic in your game design projects. It really doesn't get much more difficult than this.

Displaying the game status

The logic works well enough, but you can't actually win or lose the game. The game gives you an endless number of guesses and even after you guess the mystery number correctly, you can keep playing forever! Again, a fascinating glimpse into the nature of eternity and the fleeting and ephemeral nature of life on Earth, but not at all fun to play!

To limit the number of guesses, the program needs to know a little more about the status of the game and then what to do when the conditions for winning or losing the game have been reached. You'll solve this in two parts, beginning with displaying the game status.

To know whether the player has won or lost, the game first needs to know a few more things.

- How many guesses the player has remaining before the game finishes.

- How many guesses the player has made. This is actually optional information but interesting to implement so let's give it a whirl.

When a program needs more information about something, it usually means that you need to create more variables to capture and store that information. That's exactly what you'll do in this case: create two new variables called `guessesRemaining` and `guessesMade`. You'll also create a third variable called `gameStatus` that will be used to display this new information in the `output` text field.

1. Add the following three new variables to the class definition, just below the other variables you added in previous steps:

```
public class NumberGuessingGame extends Sprite
{
  //Create the text objects
```

```
public var format:TextFormat = new TextFormat();
public var output:TextField = new TextField();
public var input:TextField = new TextField();

//Game variables
public var startMessage:String;
public var mysteryNumber:uint;
public var currentGuess:uint;
public var guessesRemaining:uint;
public var guessesMade:uint;
public var gameStatus:String;
```

2. Initialize these three new variables in the startGame method, like so:

```
public function startGame():void
{
  //Initialize variables
  startMessage = "I am thinking of a number between 0 and 99";
  mysteryNumber = 50;

  //Initialize text fields
  output.text = startMessage
  input.text = "";
  guessesRemaining = 10;
  guessesMade = 0;
  gameStatus = "";

  //Add an event listener for key presses
  stage.addEventListener(KeyboardEvent.KEY_DOWN, keyPressHandler);
}
```

3. Add the following code in bold to the playGame method:

```
public function playGame():void
{
  guessesRemaining--;
  guessesMade++;
  gameStatus
    = "Guess: " + guessesMade + ", Remaining: " + guessesRemaining;
  currentGuess = uint(input.text);

  if (currentGuess > mysteryNumber)
  {
    output.text = "That's too high." + "\n" + gameStatus;
  }
  else if (currentGuess < mysteryNumber)
  {
    output.text = "That's too low." + "\n" + gameStatus;
  }
  else
  {
```

```
    output.text = "You got it!";
  }
}
```

4. Compile the program and play the game. The `output` text field now tells you how many guesses you have remaining and how many you made. Figure 4-16 shows an example of what your game might look like.

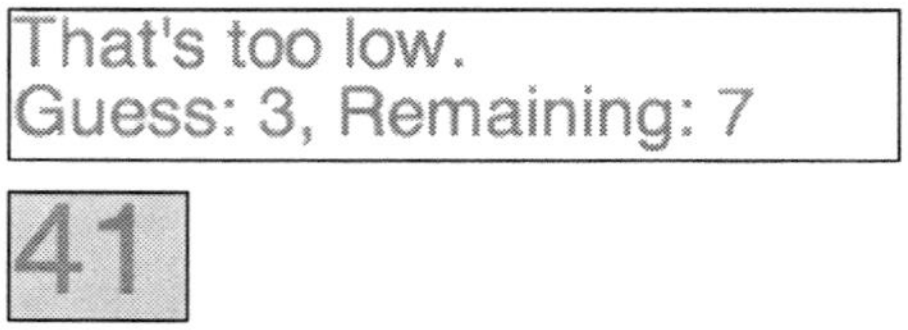

That's too low.
Guess: 3, Remaining: 7

41

Figure 4-16. The game keeps track of the number of guesses remaining and the number of guesses made.

Let's find out what this new code is doing.

Using postfix operators to change variable values by one

The new code assigns the three new variables their initial values.

```
guessesRemaining = 10;
guessesMade = 0;
gameStatus =   "";
```

The total number of guesses the player gets before the game ends is stored in the guessesRemaining variable. You gave it an initial value of 10, but you can, of course, change it to make the game easier or harder to play. You also want to count the number of guesses the player makes, so a guessesMade variable is created to store that information. When the game first starts, the player has obviously not made any guesses, so the guessesMade variable is set to 0. The gameStatus variable is a String that will be used to output this new information, and you'll see how it does this in a moment. It contains no text initially (it is assigned a pair of empty quotation marks).

Now take a look at the first two new directives in the playGame method.

```
guessesRemaining--;
guessesMade++;
```

When you play the game, you'll notice that Guesses Remaining in the output text field decreases by 1, and the Guesses Made increases by 1. That's all thanks to the two lines that use the extremely convenient **postfix operators**.

Remember the discussion of increment and decrement operators from the previous chapter? If you want to increase a value by 1, you can write some code that looks like this:

```
numberVariable += 1;
```

It turns out that increasing values by 1 is something programmers want their programs to do all the time. So frequently, in fact, that AS3.0 has special shorthand for it: a double-plus sign, which is a special kind of operator called a postfix operator. You can use it to rewrite the previous line of code like this:

```
numberVariable++;
```

It will do exactly the same thing: add 1 to the value of the variable. You can use another postfix operator, the double-minus sign, to subtract 1 from the value of a variable in exactly the same way, like this:

```
numberVariable--;
```

Postfix operators change the value of the variable by 1 each time the directive runs. The directives in the playGame event handler are run each time the Enter key is pressed, which, of course, is each time the player makes a guess. Having the guessesRemaining and guessesMade variables update with each key press is therefore a perfect way to keep track of the number of guesses the player has made.

When the game starts, the guessesRemaining variable is initialized to 10. On the first click of the guess button, this directive is run:

```
guessesRemaining--;
```

It subtracts 1, making its new value 9. On the next click, the very same directive runs again, and 1 is subtracted for the second time, leaving it with a value of 8. One will be subtracted every time the Enter key is pressed for the rest of the game.

The guessesMade variable does the same thing, but instead uses the double-plus sign to add 1 to its value. When you test the game, you can clearly see how this is working by the way the values update in the output text field.

Tying up strings

Let's create another new variable in the program called gameStatus. You declared this variable as a String, which means that it will be used to store text. The first time it makes its appearance is in this directive:

```
gameStatus
   = "Guess: " + guessesMade + ", Remaining: " + guessesRemaining;
```

(This is a very long line of code, so to allow it to print easily in this book, I've split it up over two lines by breaking it at the equal sign. In your program, you can probably keep it all together as a single unbroken line of code, as you can see in Figure 4-17.)

```
guessesRemaining--;
guessesMade++;
gameStatus = "Guess: " + guessesMade + ", Remaining: " + guessesRemaining;
currentGuess = uint(input.text);
```

Figure 4-17. Keep long bits of code together on a single line.

For the uninitiated, this is a potentially terrifying segment of code. What on earth does it do?

The first time you make a guess in the game, you'll see the following text on the second line of the output text field:

Guess: *1*, Remaining: 9

This text has to come from somewhere, and it's the preceding directive that's responsible for putting it all together.

Think about it carefully: what are the values of the guessesRemaining and guessesMade variables the first time you click the Guess button? (They're 9 and I.)

Okay then, let's imagine that you replace the variable names you used in the directive with the actual numbers they represent: 9 and 1. It will look something like this:

gameStatus = "Guess: " + 1 + ", Remaining: " + 9;

Make sense, right? Great, now let's pretend that the plus signs have disappeared and everything is inside a single set of quotes:

gameStatus = "Guess:*1*, Remaining: 9";

Aha! Can you see how it's all fitting together now? That's exactly the text that is displayed in the output text field. Figure 4-18 shows how the entire line of text is interpreted, from the initial directive to being displayed in the output text field.

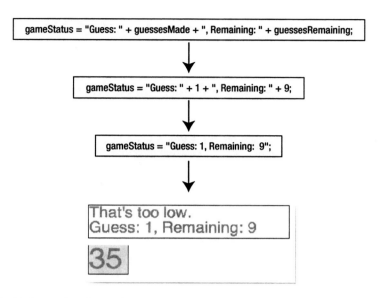

Figure 4-18. From the kitchen to the plate: string concatenation in action!

The directive uses plus signs to join all the separate elements together to make a single cohesive string of text. This is something known in computer programming as **string concatenation**. This just means "joining text together with plus signs." It's a very useful technique to use when you need to mix text that doesn't change with variables that do. Because the values of the variables change, the entire string of text updates itself accordingly. It's so simple, really, but a sort of magical thing to watch when the program runs.

When you use plus signs to concatenate strings, they don't have any mathematical meaning—they're just like stitches that are used to sew all the bits of text together into one long piece. In the program, the final result of all this stitching is copied into the gameStatus variable so you just need to use the gameStatus variable whenever you need to display this text. And that's exactly what the next bit of code does.

A small technical detail that you should be aware of is that the following directive actually mixes String and uint variables:

```
gameStatus = "Guess: " + guessesMade + ", Remaining: " +
guessesRemaining;
```

In the program, you declared the gameStatus variable to be a String type. That means it can't contain numbers, except in the form of numeric characters (which are interpreted like letters or words). However, you declared both the guessesRemaining and guessesMade variables as uint variables (which are interpreted as numbers). Both of

> *them are joined together with ordinary text and copied into the gameStatus string variable. Isn't the purpose of assigning variable types to prevent this sort of mixing and matching between strings and numbers? How is this possible?*
>
> *In fact, you can use number variables with strings by joining them together with plus signs, but when you do this, AS3.0 converts the values of the number variables into strings. The data type in the guessesRemaining and guessesMade variables remains unchanged as uint, but the values they contain are converted into a string when they're assigned to the gameStatus String variable. This is very useful for exactly the purpose you've put it to: to display text with numbers that are updated by the program. It's such a common requirement in programs that AS3.0 does this type conversion automatically.*

Now that you have the gameStatus variable packed up and ready to go, you can get lot of mileage out of it in the if/else statement. The new bits of code are highlighted in bold:

```
if (currentGuess > mysteryNumber)
{
   output.text = "That's too high." + "\n" + gameStatus;
}
else if (currentGuess < mysteryNumber)
{
   output.text = "That's too low." + "\n" + gameStatus;
}
else
{
   output.text = "You got it!";
}
```

You're using string concatenation to add the contents of the gameStatus variable to the output text field. But there's something here that you haven't seen before.

"\n"

A backslash followed by the letter n is known as a **newline character**. The newline character forces whatever text that comes after it onto a new line. That's why the game displays the game status information just below the first bit of text.

You can use the newline character in the middle of any string to break the text onto two lines or more. Here's an example:

```
"This text\nis broken in the middle."
```

It displays as follows:

```
This text
is broken in the middle.
```

In the program you added the newline character by joining it to the rest of the text using string concatenation. Here's how it looks using the example text:

```
"This text" + "\n" + "is broken in the middle."
```

The result is exactly the same, but the code is a little easier to read because it's visually very clear where the line break falls.

Hey, why use the gameStatus variable, anyway?

There's one last thing you should quickly look at, and a question that you might have had about how you've written the code in the if/else statement. You could have written the first two directives in the if/else statement without the gameStatus variable, like this:

```
if (currentGuess > mysteryNumber)
{
  output.text
    = "That's too high." + "\n" + "Guess: "
    + guessesMade + ", Remaining: " + guessesRemaining;
}
else if (currentGuess < mysteryNumber)
{
  output.text
    = "That's too low." + "\n" + "Guess: "
    + guessesMade + ", Remaining: " + guessesRemaining;
}
else
{
  output.text = "You got it!";
}
```

Why then did you go to all the trouble of creating a special gameStatus variable if you could easily have done without it? Obviously, it's a lot of code, it makes the if/else statement more difficult to read, and you'd have to write it all out twice.

The other reason might be less obvious: if you have that text neatly stored in the gameStatus variable and you need to make any changes to it, you have to change it only once. Any place you use the gameStatus variable in the program is automatically updated with the new text. This might not be such a big issue in a small program like this number guessing game, but if it were used 10 or 20 times in different places in a bigger program, it would be a lot of work to update.

Whenever you find yourself using a lot of the same text over and over again in any of your programs, try storing it in a variable. You'll save yourself a lot of typing and a lot of trouble in the long run.

Using uint vs. int variables

Did you try making more than the ten guesses the game said you had remaining? If you did, you would have noticed that the output text field displayed something like this:

Remaining: 4294967295

(You may need to scroll down the output text field to see it if the number doesn't quite fit.)

At the moment, you haven't programmed the game to end when the player has run out of guesses, so the game keeps on subtracting 1 from the `guessesRemaining` variable even after the 10 guesses are used up. After it passes 0, it suddenly jumps to this crazy long number: 4294967295. No, your program isn't about to join a secret botnet of computers plotting to overthrow the human race; there is actually very interesting logic behind it.

You declared the `guessesRemaining` variable as a uint type, which store whole numbers that are only positive. They can never be negative. When a variable that's declared as a uint type does try to become less than zero, exactly the opposite thing happens: it flips to the maximum possible number, which happens to be 4294967295.

This is very important to know because sometimes you need or want to know whether a number has run into negative territory. In those cases, make sure that you declare the variable as an int type. (As mentioned before, int stands for *integer,* which is a whole number that can be positive or negative.)

To see the effect that changing the `guessesRemaining` variable to an int type has on your program, try it and see what happens!

1. Change the line of code in the class definition that declares the `guessesRemaining` variable so that its type is set to int:

```
public var guessesRemaining:int;
```

2. Compile the program.

3. Press the Enter key more than ten times. You should see the Remaining value become negative, like this:

Remaining: -3

Keep this in mind whenever you decide what type to declare your variables.

Winning and losing

The game now has enough information about what the player is doing to figure out whether the game has been won or lost. All you need to do now is to find a way to say, "Hey, the game is over!" and tell players how well they did.

To do this, add the following to the program:

- A Boolean (true/false) variable called gameWon that is set to true if the game has been won and false if it hasn't.

- A method called `checkGameOver` that checks to see whether the player has enough guesses remaining to continue playing.

- A method called `endGame` that tells players whether they've won or lost.

An important aspect of this next bit of code is that it shows you an example of how you can use methods to modularize your code. As discussed in the beginning of this chapter, *modular programming* is a way of breaking down complex bits of code into smaller manageable pieces, or *modules*. Modules can really be any pieces of code, such as classes or methods, that perform one specific helpful function. Have a look at the two new methods added in the following code and see if you can figure out how they're used to modularize the program.

1. Add the new gameWon variable to the class definition.

```
public class NumberGuessingGame extends Sprite
{
  //Create the text objects
  public var format:TextFormat = new TextFormat();
  public var output:TextField = new TextField();
  public var input:TextField = new TextField();

  //Game variables
  public var startMessage:String;
  public var mysteryNumber:uint;
  public var currentGuess:uint;
  public var guessesRemaining:int;
  public var guessesMade:uint;
  public var gameStatus:String;
  public var gameWon:Boolean;
```

2. Give it an initial value of false in the `startGame` method.

```
public function startGame():void
{
  //Initialize variables
  startMessage = "I am thinking of a number between 0 and 99";
  mysteryNumber = 50;

  //Initialize text fields
  output.text = startMessage
  input.text = "";
  guessesRemaining = 10;
  guessesMade = 0;
  gameStatus = "";
  gameWon = false;

  //Add an event listener for key presses
  stage.addEventListener(KeyboardEvent.KEY_DOWN, keyPressHandler);
}
```

3. Add the following code in bold to the `startGame` method. Add two new methods, `checkGameOver` and `endGame`, just below it.

```
public function playGame():void
{
  guessesRemaining--;
  guessesMade++;
  gameStatus = "Guess: " + guessesMade + ", Remaining: " + guessesRemaining;
  currentGuess = uint(input.text);

  if (currentGuess > mysteryNumber)
  {
    output.text = "That's too high." + "\n" + gameStatus;
    checkGameOver();
  }
  else if (currentGuess < mysteryNumber)
  {
    output.text = "That's too low." + "\n" + gameStatus;
    checkGameOver();
  }
  else
  {
    output.text = "You got it!";
    gameWon = true;
    endGame();
  }
}
public function checkGameOver():void
{
  if (guessesRemaining < 1)
  {
    endGame();
  }
}
public function endGame():void
{
  if (gameWon)
  {
    output.text
      = "Yes, it's " + mysteryNumber + "!" + "\n"
      + "It only took you " + guessesMade + " guesses.";
  }
  else
  {
    output.text
      = "No more guesses left!" + "\n"
      + "The number was: " + mysteryNumber + ".";
  }
}
```

4. Delete the following directive from the if statement in the startGame method. This text will be replaced by the new text from the endGame method. There's actually no harm in leaving it in, but it's redundant.

```
output.text = "You got it!";
```

5. Compile the program and play the game. It now prevents you from guessing more than ten times and tells you whether you've won or lost. Figure 4-19 shows what your game might now look like if you guess correctly.

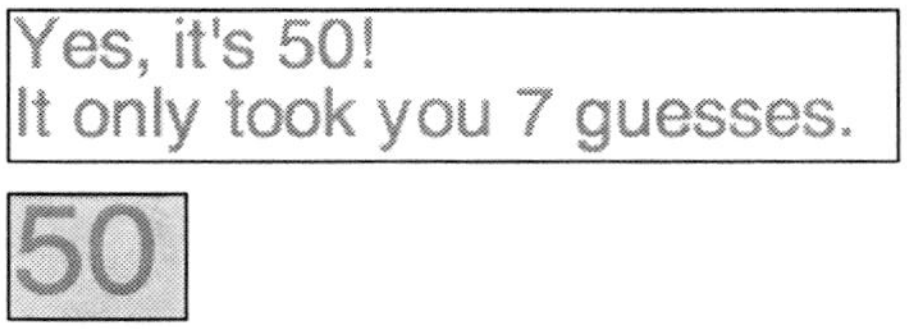

Figure 4-19. The game can now be won or lost.

The game needed to figure out whether the player used up all the guesses. Before you added the new code, you could count the guesses, but the program didn't know what to do with that information. The new code solves that.

The new methods have helped modularize the program by breaking the steps down into manageable pieces. Let's go on a little tour of how all this new code fits together.

First, you need to help the game figure out whether the player can still continue playing. You add the same checkGameOver method call to the first two blocks of the if/else statement in the startGame method, highlighted in bold:

```
public function playGame():void
{
  guessesRemaining--;
  guessesMade++;
  gameStatus = "Guess: " + guessesMade + ", Remaining: " + guessesRemaining;
  currentGuess = uint(input.text);

  if (currentGuess > mysteryNumber)
  {
    output.text = "That's too high." + "\n" + gameStatus;
    checkGameOver();
  }
  else if (currentGuess < mysteryNumber)
  {
    output.text = "That's too low." + "\n" + gameStatus;
    checkGameOver();
  }
```

```
  else
  {
    output.text = "You got it!";
    gameWon = true;
    endGame();
  }
}
```

The two new directives are method calls to the `checkGameOver` method. So as soon as the program reads one of these directives, it immediately jumps ahead to the `checkGameOver` method's function definition and runs whatever directives it contains.

This is what the `checkGameOver` function definition looks like:

```
public function checkGameOver():void
{
  if (guessesRemaining < 1)
  {
    endGame();
  }
}
```

The method checks to see how many guesses the player has remaining. If there are still enough, nothing happens and the game continues. But if `guessesRemaining` is less than 1, the game is brought to an end by calling the `endGame` method.

```
public function endGame():void
{
  if (gameWon)
  {
    output.text
      = "Yes, it's " + mysteryNumber + "!" + "\n"
      + "It only took you " + guessesMade + " guesses.";
  }
  else
  {
    output.text
      = "No more guesses left!" + "\n"
      + "The number was: " + mysteryNumber + ".";
  }
}
```

The `endGame` method looks to see whether the game has been won or lost by checking whether the `gameWon` variable is true or false. It then displays the appropriate message. (Can you figure out how string concatenation is being used to display these messages? Compare the code with what you see in the game's output text field. I'm sure you can do it!)

> *If statements work by running their directives if the condition in the parentheses is true.*
> *With Boolean variables, there are two ways to check whether they're true or false. You*
> *can use an equality operator (a double-equal sign) and compare it with a true or false*
> *value, like this:*
>
> *if(gameWon == true)*
>
> *If gameWon is false, this statement is read as being false and the directives don't run. If*
> *gameWon is true, the statement is read as being true and the directives run.*
>
> *You should be familiar with this way of checking for true or false conditions from the*
> *previous chapter. However, if the condition you're checking happens to be the value of a*
> *Boolean variable, it's much more convenient and often makes your code easier to read*
> *to use this shorthand:*
>
> *if(gameWon)*
>
> *Because the value of gameWon can be only true or false, it provides exactly the same*
> *information as the first example.*
>
> *You'll be using this as the preferred way for checking the value of Boolean variables in if*
> *statements throughout the book. if(gameWon) is very close to the English phrase "If the*
> *game is won." Choose the names of your variables carefully to help to make your*
> *programs are easier to read.*

How does the program know whether the gameWon variable is true or false?

You initialized gameWon to false in the `startGame` method. That means it will always be false unless you change it to true somewhere in the game. You would change it to true only if the player actually meets the conditions for winning the game. In this game, there is only one way the player can win: by guessing the correct number.

This makes things really easy because you know that if players still have enough guesses remaining, and they've guessed the correct number, they must have won the game. So all you need to do is set the gameWon variable to true and call the endGame method in the same if/else block that checks whether the player's guess is correct. Easy!

Don't believe me? Check out the section of the `playGame` method's if/else statement that does this (shown in bold text):

```
public function playGame():void
{
  guessesRemaining--;
  guessesMade++;
  gameStatus = "Guess: " + guessesMade + ", Remaining: " + guessesRemaining;
```

```
currentGuess = uint(input.text);

if (currentGuess > mysteryNumber)
{
  output.text = "That's too high." + "\n" + gameStatus;
  checkGameOver();
}
else if (currentGuess < mysteryNumber)
{
  output.text = "That's too low." + "\n" + gameStatus;
  checkGameOver();
}
else
{
  output.text = "You got it!";
  gameWon = true;
  endGame();
}
}
```

Think about the logic behind what the if/else statement is saying. If players still have enough guesses remaining, the game will continue. If the game is still continuing, and players have guessed the right number, they must have won the game. The gameWon variable is then set to true, and the directives in the endGame method are run. When the endGame method runs, its conditional statement notices that gameWon is true and displays the message telling the player she's won.

Modular programming with methods

Can you see how the checkGameOver and endGame methods were used to help modularize the code? In truth, you could have written this program without them by adding all the conditions they check for in one extremely long if/else statement. But if you'd done so, you'd have to write some of the same code over twice, and it would all start to become very difficult to read and debug.

Modularizing specific tasks inside self-contained methods allows you to modify or debug those bits of code in isolation without having to change (and possibly damage) other parts of the program that are working. It also means that whenever you want to perform a certain task, you don't need to duplicate any of the code you've already written; you just have to call the method you need to do the job.

Using methods to modularize your code might take a bit of practice, and you might find it a bit of a brain-twister until you've seen a few more examples and experimented with using them in your own projects. Have a look at how the game is working so far and see if you can figure out how the interrelationships between methods and method calls are working. Figure 4-20 is a map of how it all fits together. You can think of each code block as a module in the program.

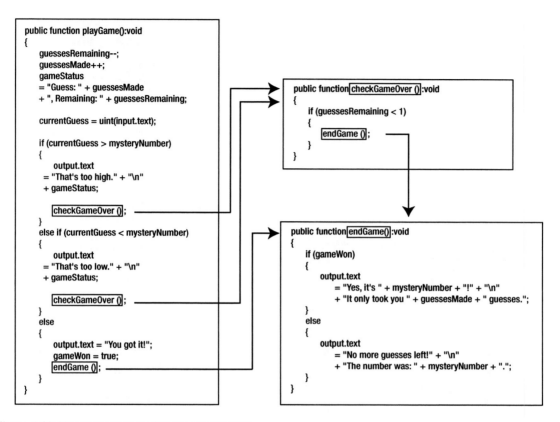

Figure 4-20. Use methods to modularize specific tasks.

Polishing up

As the saying goes, 30% of the time it takes to program a piece of software goes into making it work, and the other 70% goes into making it work well. There's no better example of this principle at work than the number guessing game. It's playable, but there's a lot lacking that most players would complain about.

Here are some things you can improve:

- The game still goes on counting guesses after the player has won the game.

- How about the mystery number? The game won't have much replay value if it's 50 every time you play it. You can solve this by randomizing the mystery number.

- It would be nice to add some buttons to play the game, including a Play again button.

Time to roll up your sleeves and see if you can fix these problems!

Tackling random numbers

You'll tackle the random number problem first because you'll almost certainly find yourself needing to use random numbers in most of your game projects. AS3.0 has a built-in class called `Math` that includes quite a few methods that are useful for manipulating numbers. One of these is the `random` method, which generates a random number between 0 and 1. Here's what it looks like:

```
Math.random()
```

You can assign this random number to a variable just as you assign other values to variables, as in this example:

```
randomVariable = Math.random();
```

The fictitious `randomVariable` is now assigned a random number between 0 and 1, with up to 16 decimal places. So it could be anything; for example, 0.3669164208535294 or 0.5185672459021346.

What use is a random number between 0 and 1 with 16 decimal places? Well, practically none whatsoever. Fortunately, you can do a bit of tweaking to get something more useful.

First, random numbers for games usually need to be integers (whole numbers). All those decimal places have got to go! Can you imagine what a nightmare the guessing game would be to play if the mystery number were something like 33.6093155708325684? If you chop off all those decimals, you'll have something useful, such as 33, which is much more user-friendly.

The `Math` class fortunately has a few built- in methods that can help you round decimals up or down:

- `Math.round` can be used to round numbers either up or down. For example, `Math.round(3.4)` returns a value of 3. `Math.round(3.8)` returns 4. `Math.round(3.5)` also returns 4.

- `Math.floor` always rounds numbers down. `Math.floor(3.2)` returns 3. `Math.floor(3.9)` also returns 3.

- `Math.ceil` always rounds numbers up. `Math.ceil(3.2)` returns 4, and `Math.ceil(3.9)` also returns 4. (What is ceil? It's short for *ceiling*. Ceilings are up; floors are down. Make sense?)

To use any of these methods along with the `Math.random` method, you need to use a format that looks like this:

```
Math.round(Math.random())
```

Think about what this is doing. `Math.random()` generates a random number between 0 and 1 with loads of decimals. So imagine that it came up with a deliciously useless number such as 0.6781340985784098. You could pretend that the preceding line of code now looks like this:

```
Math.round(0.6781340985784098)
```

How would you round that number? You'd round it up, and the result would be the following:

1

But what would happen if the random number were lower, like this?

```
Math.round(0.2459678308703125)
```

It would be rounded down to this:

0

This means that you can use the line of code, `Math.round(Math.random())`, to generate a random number that has a 50% chance of being either 0 or 1. Not yet what you're looking for in the game, but not entirely useless, either. There will be many instances where calculating a 50% chance of something happening will be really useful in your games, and you can use this little snippet of code to do exactly that.

> *In fact, you can use this bit of code to generate random Boolean (true/false) values. Let's pretend that you have a Boolean variable called* rainToday. *You could initialize it with a value of false.*
>
> ```
> rainToday = false;
> ```
>
> *Oh, if only that were true! So to make it a little more realistic, you can give it a 50% chance of being either true or false. All you need to do is use the* Math.round(Math. random()) *code snippet in an if/else statement and compare it against a value of 1. Here's what the code might look like:*
>
> ```
> if(Math.round(Math.random()) == 1)
> {
>   rainToday = true;
> }
> else
> {
>   rainToday = false;
> }
> ```
>
> Math.round(Math.random()) *has an exactly 50% chance of generating either the number 1 or 0. If it happens to be 1, the first directive runs and* rainToday *becomes true. If it's 0, no rain today!*

So a random number between 0 and 1 is slightly more useful, but it's not exactly what you're looking for in the game. How can you get a number between 0 and 99? Here's how:

```
Math.floor(Math.random() * 100)
```

The asterisk is AS3.0's **multiplication operator**. * 100 means *multiplied by 100*. This line of code multiplies the random number by 100 and then uses `Math.floor` to round it down so the lowest number it can possibly be is 0 and the highest is 99. That gives a perfect random whole number that falls within the range of 0 to 99.

Here's another way of looking at it. Let's say that the random number is 0.3378208608542148. That would mean the code will look like this:

`Math.floor(0.3378208608542148 * 100)`

Multiplied by 100, the random number will then look like this:

`Math.floor(33.78208608542148)`

The decimal point is just moved two spaces to the right, giving you a nice big number to work with. But you still have the problem of those infuriating decimals to deal with! Not to worry; `Math.floor` comes to the rescue by rounding the whole thing down. So the result is very satisfying.

33

Perfect for the number guessing game! Figure 4-21 shows an example of this process in action.

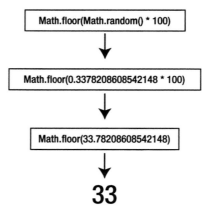

Figure 4-21. From useless to useful: using Math.random and Math.floor to generate random whole numbers within a specific range.

If you need a random number between 1 and 100, you can create it by using code that looks like this:

`Math.ceil(Math.random() * 100);`

`Math.ceil` rounds the random number up, so the lowest it can be is 1, and the highest it can be is 100.

You can use this same format for any range of numbers simply by changing the number that you multiply the random number by. Here are some examples:

- `Math.ceil(Math.random() * 10)` generates a random number between 1 and 10.

- `Math.ceil(Math.random() * 27)` generates a random number between 1 and 27.

- `Math.ceil(Math.random() * 5)` generates a random number between 1 and 5.

The reason why using `Math.ceil` starts the range of random numbers with 1 is that any number less than 1, such as 0.23, will be rounded up to 1 That saves you from having to deal with values of 0, which are often not useful for the ranges of numbers you'll be looking for in your games. If you do want 0 to be part of the range, however, use `Math.round` instead. `Math.round(Math.random() * 100)` will give you a random number between 0 and 100.

> *What if you want to generate a random number within a range of numbers that starts at something other than 1 or zero?*
>
> *Let's say you need a number between 10 and 25. That means that you have 15 possible numbers that could be chosen: 10, 11, 12 . . . up to 25. All you need to do is generate a random number between 0 and 15, and then add 10 to it push it up to within the range you need. This is what the code will look like:*
>
> *`Math.round(Math.random() * 15) + 10`*
>
> *Think about it this way. The random number is between 0 and 15. Let's say it's 8. Then you add 10 to it. You end up with 18. You've got a range of possible random numbers between 10 and 25.*

Now use what you've learned about random numbers and apply it to the game.

1. Modify the `startGame` method with the new code in bold. In addition to randomizing the `mysteryNumber` variable, you'll add a `trace` directive for testing purposes so that you can check that the number really is random. (Notice that string concatenation was used in the `trace` directive so that the message it displays is more readable.)

```
public function startGame():void
{
  //Initialize variables
  startMessage = "I am thinking of a number between 0 and 99";
  mysteryNumber = Math.floor(Math.random() * 100);

  //Initialize text fields
  output.text = startMessage
  input.text = "";
  guessesRemaining = 10;
  guessesMade = 0;
  gameStatus = "";
  gameWon = false;

  //Trace the mystery number
```

```
trace("The mystery number: " + mysteryNumber);

//Add an event listener for key presses
stage.addEventListener(KeyboardEvent.KEY_DOWN, keyPressHandler);
}
```

2. Compile the program and play the game. The mystery number is now a random number between 0 and 99. You'll also see the text, "The mystery number: ??" displayed as a trace message so that you can make sure everything is working as you expect it to. Figure 4-22 shows an example of what your game might now look like.

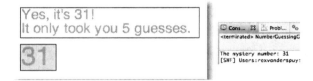

Figure 4-22. Randomizing the mystery number

Disabling the Enter key

One quirky bug in the game so far is that if the player wins the game but continues pressing the Enter key, the game still continues to count the guesses. You can see this in the output text field, as shown in Figure 4-23.

Figure 4-23. Randomizing the mystery number

If you think about how the program is working, this makes perfect sense because the Enter key itself has no way of knowing whether or not the game is over; it just keeps on dutifully doing the job you assigned to it.

To fix this, you need to do three things when the game ends.

1. Remove the keyPressHandler event listener from the stage object.

2. Disable the input text field so that you can't enter any text into it.

3. Dim the input text field so that it's obvious it's been disabled. This is optional, but it's a good visual cue for the player that the game is finished.

Two very straightforward lines of code are all you need.

1. Add the following code in bold to the endGame method:

```
public function endGame():void
{
  if (gameWon)
  {
    output.text
      = "Yes, it's " + mysteryNumber + "!" + "\n"
      + "It only took you " + guessesMade + " guesses.";
  }
  else
  {
    output.text
      = "No more guesses left!" + "\n"
      + "The number was: " + mysteryNumber + ".";
  }
  stage.removeEventListener
    (KeyboardEvent.KEY_DOWN, keyPressHandler);
  input.type = "dynamic";
  input.alpha = 0.5;
}
```

2. Compile the program and play through the game. When it's finished, you won't be able to enter any more text into the input field and the input field will be dimmed, as you can see in Figure 4-24

No more guesses left!
The number was: 57.

Figure 4-24. Disable and dim the input text field when the game is finished.

All the new code was added inside the endGame method's function definition because its directives run only when the game is finished.

The first new directive removes the event listener from the stage object:

```
stage.removeEventListener(KeyboardEvent.KEY_DOWN, keyPressHandler);
```

After you add this line of code, nothing will happen when the Enter key is pressed, but you'll still be able to enter text into the input field. To prevent this, you need to specifically disable the input text field using this line of code:

```
input.type = "dynamic";
```

TextField objects can be of two types: "input" or "dynamic". (These values are Strings, so you have to surround them with quotes.) The output text field that displays the game status is "dynamic", which means that it can display text but won't allow users to type into it. All TextField objects are "dynamic" by default when you first create them. You'll recall that when you created the input field, you set its type to "input". What this new line of code does is switch it back to "dynamic", which prevents you from typing text into it.

The last new directive dims the button on the stage. Use the input text field's alpha property and set it to 0.5, which makes it semitransparent:

```
input.alpha = 0.5;
```

To help you keep things a bit more modular, you could actually move all these directives related to disabling the game into their own method, perhaps called disableGame. In such a small program as the number guessing game, however, it would probably be more trouble than it's worth. Modularize your code wherever you can, but also use your judgment about when it's appropriate or practical.

You'll find all the code for this game that you've written up till now in the folder NumberGuessingGameFinished in the chapter's source files.

Making really nice buttons

In Chapter 3 you created buttons to control your interactive game character. The buttons worked, but they were a little limited. They didn't react or give you any feedback when you clicked on them. When you interact with buttons in most games or software, you'll notice that they behave in three important ways.

- When your mouse moves over them, there's a highlighting effect.

- When you click or hold the mouse button down, the button often darkens or changes position slightly to look as though it's being pressed.

- The button returns to normal when the mouse leaves it.

These three basic button states are called **up**, **over**, and **down**. Figure 4-25 shows a typical example of a button from the tool bar in Adobe Illustrator.

Figure 4-25. Typical example of up, over, and down buttons states

You'll see these three button states everywhere once you start looking for them. Exactly what these three different button states look like will always vary depending on the personal style of the illustrator or the design fashion of the moment, so there's no rule as to what they should look like. There are hundreds of variations on these three states.

Interactive buttons like this are easy to make but involve a bit of planning. First, you need three PNG images of each button state. The three images need to be exactly the same size. The only differences between them should be the slight change of effect for each button state.

In Chapter 2 you learned how to make many buttons of the same size, with only one change to it: the text. Instead of just changing the text, you can change the highlighting effect on the button to indicate each state. For every single button, you'll need three separate images.

To get you started, I've got a little mini-project for you to do before you get back to the number guessing game.

1. Create three PNG images, each representing one of the three button states. Name these images buttonUp.png, buttonOver.png, and buttonDown.png. Figure 4-26 shows what the sample buttons look like. (I made these quickly in Adobe Illustrator using its built-in Symbol library. I'll be introducing Adobe Illustrator in Chapter 7.) Your button states don't need to look anything like this. My button image dimensions are 50 by 57 pixels, but you can make your button any size you like. The main thing is that all three images need to be exactly the same size; otherwise the button states won't align properly when you program them.

Figure 4-26. The up, over, and down buttons states

2. In the chapter's source files you'll find a project folder called Buttons. It has a subfolder called images. You'll find my three sample PNG files there. Copy your three button PNG files into the images folder, replacing mine with yours, as shown in Figure 4-27.

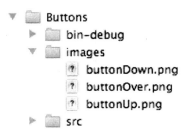

Figure 4-27. Copy your PNG button state to the Buttons project's images folder.

3. Import the Buttons project and compile the Buttons.as file. Your button will appear on the stage, roughly centered. Click on it and watch what happens. A hand icon appears over the button, and all the button states work as expected. Trace messages tell you which state is being triggered by the mouse. Figure 4-28 shows what you'll see.

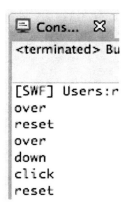

Figure 4-28. Test your button.

Understanding the concepts

Let's review what you know about how images are loaded into a program. A PNG file is loaded from the images folder into a loader object. The loader object is then added to a Sprite. The Sprite containing the loaded image is then placed on the stage. Figure 4-29 illustrates how this works for a single button image. But this is nothing new; it's what you did in the previous chapter to load all your images. Easy stuff!

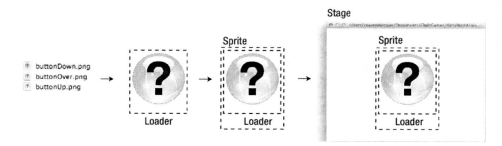

Figure 4-29. The processes of loading one image into the program

To make a button with three states, all three images are loaded into one Sprite. Yes, you heard right: three images in one Sprite! However, only one of those images is visible at any one time. The images of the button states will become visible or invisible depending on what the mouse is doing. Figure 4-30 illustrates this concept.

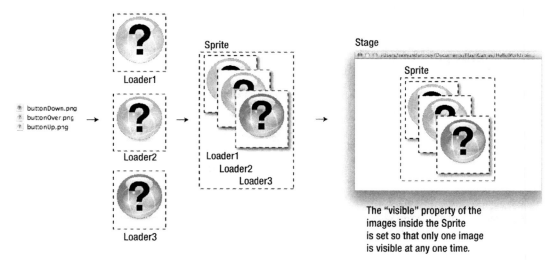

The "visible" property of the images inside the Sprite is set so that only one image is visible at any one time.

Figure 4-30. The processes of loading one image into the program

If you understand this concept, the code will be very easy to follow. Let's take a look at the code that does this in the Buttons.as file.

Loading the images and displaying the button

The Buttons.as file is surprisingly long, so you're first going to look at the specific code that loads the button images and adds the button Sprite to the stage. You'll see how all this code fits together in context with the rest of the program in the pages ahead. The highlighted comments explain what each section of code does.

This is the code in the class definition that creates the three image loaders and the single button Sprite:

```
//Create URLRequest objects to get the paths to the images
public var buttonUpURL:URLRequest
  = new URLRequest("../images/buttonUp.png");
public var buttonOverURL:URLRequest
  = new URLRequest("../images/buttonOver.png");
public var buttonDownURL:URLRequest
  = new URLRequest("../images/buttonDown.png");

//Create Loaders for the images
public var buttonUpImage:Loader = new Loader();
public var buttonOverImage:Loader = new Loader();
public var buttonDownImage:Loader = new Loader();

//Create a single Sprite to contain the images
public var button:Sprite = new Sprite();
```

There's nothing new here; you saw all this code in the previous chapter. The only slight difference is a shortcut that I took to create the URLRequest objects. AS3.0 allows you to create the URLRequest object and assign the path to the file at the same time, like this:

```
public var buttonUpURL:URLRequest
  = new URLRequest("../images/buttonUp.png");
```

You can see that the path to the image file is included in the parentheses. This saves you from having to write this line later in the program:

```
buttonUpURL.url = "../images/buttonUp.png";
```

The next step is to load the images, which happens when the program runs.

```
buttonUpImage.load(buttonUpURL);
buttonDownImage.load(buttonDownURL);
buttonOverImage.load(buttonOverURL);
```

But watch what happens next. The visible property of all the images is set to false, except for the buttonUpImage.

```
buttonUpImage.visible = true;
buttonDownImage.visible = false;
buttonOverImage.visible = false;
```

All three images are then added to the button Sprite.

```
button.addChild(buttonUpImage);
button.addChild(buttonDownImage);
button.addChild(buttonOverImage);
```

They're all aligned on the button Sprite in exactly the same way—with their registration points at the top left corner. You can think of them as three playing cards that are perfectly stacked one of top each other. But only the buttonUpImage is visible.

The button Sprite then sets a few special properties that make it behave like a proper button.

```
button.buttonMode = true;
button.mouseEnabled = true;
button.useHandCursor = true;
button.mouseChildren = false;
```

Let's take a look at what each of these properties does.

- **buttonMode** turns a Sprite object into a button. It allows a hand icon to be displayed when the mouse hovers over it. It also allows the button to accept click events using the Enter or Space key, if it's active. The buttonMode can be true or false.

- **mouseEnabled** determines whether or not the Sprite object can accept mouse events. Its default value is true, so you don't actually have to specifically write a line of code to set it to true. However, it's important to know that you can set it to false if you want to prevent the button from being clicked.

- **useHandCursor** determines whether or not the mouse arrow icon turns into a pointing hand when you move the mouse over the button. You can set this to either true or false. As soon as you set the buttonMode property to true, useHandCursor becomes true by default, so you don't specifically need to set it as such. But again, it's important to know that you can turn this off if you need to.

4. **mouseChildren** determines whether the mouse can interact with any other objects inside the Sprite. In this example, there are three objects inside the button Sprite: the three images that you've loaded into it. AS3.0 refers to these internal objects as **children**. When you create a button, you don't want the mouse to interact directly with any of these children. You just want to the mouse to interact with the parent button Sprite. This means you should always set the mouseChildren property to false. If you don't, your program will become confused about whether the mouse is intending to click the button or the images that it contains.

Lastly, the button Sprite is added to the stage and roughly centered.

```
stage.addChild(button);
button.x = 225;
button.y = 175;
```

Now that the images are loaded into the button and the button is on the stage, you can use mouse events to determine which image is displayed.

Understanding the mouse events

The code adds four listeners to the button Sprite, with matching event handlers.

```
button.addEventListener(MouseEvent.ROLL_OVER, overHandler);
button.addEventListener(MouseEvent.MOUSE_DOWN, downHandler);
button.addEventListener(MouseEvent.ROLL_OUT, resetHandler);
button.addEventListener(MouseEvent.CLICK, clickHandler);
```

Each controls the display of a different state. In the previous chapter you just used the CLICK event. These other listeners work in an identical way, except that they're triggered by different mouse actions. Let's see how they work in the context of the running program.

The ROLL_OVER event happens when the mouse rolls over the button. This creates a highlighting effect by displaying the **buttonOverImage** and hiding the other states.

```
public function overHandler(event:MouseEvent):void
{
  buttonUpImage.visible = false;
  buttonDownImage.visible = false;
  buttonOverImage.visible = true;
}
```

Figure 4-31 illustrates this.

Figure 4-31. The ROLL_OVER event

The MOUSE_DOWN event happens when the left mouse button is pressed down over the button. This is the effect of pressing the button (see Figure 4-32).

```
public function downHandler(event:MouseEvent):void
{
  buttonUpImage.visible = false;
  buttonDownImage.visible = true;
  buttonOverImage.visible = false;
}
```

```
button.addEventListener(MouseEvent.MOUSE_DOWN, downHandler);
```

```
public function downHandler(event:MouseEvent):void
{
    buttonUpImage.visible = false;
    buttonDownImage.visible = true;
    buttonOverImage.visible = false;
}
```

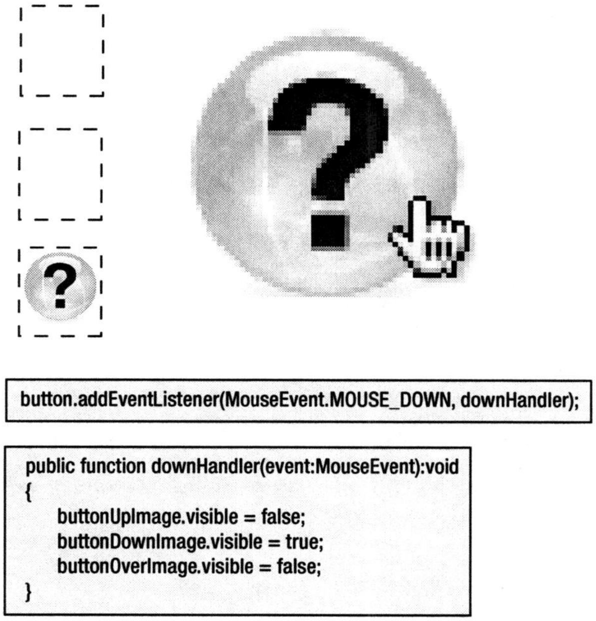

Figure 4-32. The MOUSE_DOWN event

The ROLL_OUT event happens when the left mouse leaves the button. In this case, the button is reset to its up state (see Figure 4-33).

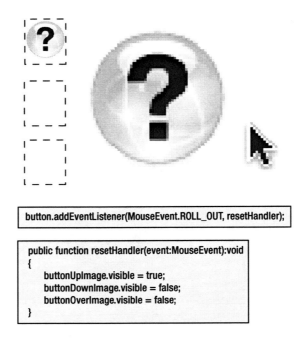

```
button.addEventListener(MouseEvent.ROLL_OUT, resetHandler);
```

```
public function resetHandler(event:MouseEvent):void
{
    buttonUpImage.visible = true;
    buttonDownImage.visible = false;
    buttonOverImage.visible = false;
}
```

Figure 4-33. The ROLL_OUT event

The CLICK event happens when the left mouse is clicked. In this example, it sets the button to its up state again. The effect is the same as the ROLL_OUT event.

```
public function clickHandler(event:MouseEvent):void
{
  buttonUpImage.visible = true;
  buttonDownImage.visible = false;
  buttonOverImage.visible = false;
}
```

And there you have all four button events that control the display of the button. Here's the entire code for the Buttons.as file so you can see it all in its proper context:

```
package
{
  import flash.net.URLRequest;
  import flash.display.Loader;
  import flash.display.Sprite;
  import flash.events.MouseEvent;

  [SWF(width="550", height="400",
  backgroundColor="#FFFFFF", frameRate="60")]

  public class Buttons extends Sprite
```

```
{
  //Create URLRequest objects to get the paths to the images
  public var buttonUpURL:URLRequest
    = new URLRequest("../images/buttonUp.png");
  public var buttonOverURL:URLRequest
    = new URLRequest("../images/buttonOver.png");
  public var buttonDownURL:URLRequest
    = new URLRequest("../images/buttonDown.png");

  //Create Loaders for the images
  public var buttonUpImage:Loader = new Loader();
  public var buttonOverImage:Loader = new Loader();
  public var buttonDownImage:Loader = new Loader();

  //Create a single Sprite to contain the images
  public var button:Sprite = new Sprite();

  public function Buttons()
  {
    makeButton();
  }
  public function makeButton():void
  {
    //Load the images
    buttonUpImage.load(buttonUpURL);
    buttonDownImage.load(buttonDownURL);
    buttonOverImage.load(buttonOverURL);

    //Make the images invisible, except
    //for the up image
    buttonUpImage.visible = true;
    buttonDownImage.visible = false;
    buttonOverImage.visible = false;

    //Add the images to the button Sprite
    button.addChild(buttonUpImage);
    button.addChild(buttonDownImage);
    button.addChild(buttonOverImage);

    //Set the Sprite's button properties
    button.buttonMode = true;
    button.mouseEnabled = true;
    button.useHandCursor = true;
    button.mouseChildren = false;

    //Add the button Sprite to the stage
    stage.addChild(button);
    button.x = 225;
    button.y = 175;

    //Add the button event listeners
    button.addEventListener(MouseEvent.ROLL_OVER, overHandler);
```

```
      button.addEventListener(MouseEvent.MOUSE_DOWN, downHandler);
      button.addEventListener(MouseEvent.ROLL_OUT, resetHandler);
      button.addEventListener(MouseEvent.CLICK, clickHandler);
    }
    public function overHandler(event:MouseEvent):void
    {
      buttonUpImage.visible = false;
      buttonDownImage.visible = false;
      buttonOverImage.visible = true;
      trace("over");
    }
    public function downHandler(event:MouseEvent):void
    {
      buttonUpImage.visible = false;
      buttonDownImage.visible = true;
      buttonOverImage.visible = false;
      trace("down");
    }
    public function clickHandler(event:MouseEvent):void
    {
      buttonUpImage.visible = true;
      buttonDownImage.visible = false;
      buttonOverImage.visible = false;
      trace("click");
    }
    public function resetHandler(event:MouseEvent):void
    {
      buttonUpImage.visible = true;
      buttonDownImage.visible = false;
      buttonOverImage.visible = false;
      trace("reset");
    }
  }
}
```

The structure of this program is identical to the other programs you've looked at in this book so far. The only anomaly to point out is that the constructor method has delegated its work of creating the button to the makeButton method.

```
public function Buttons()
{
  makeButton();
}
```

This is the same technique you used to modularize the code in the constructor method of the number guessing game.

> This is a very common way to make interactive buttons, but AS3.0 also has a
> specialized class called SimpleButton, which is a very efficient way of making
> interactive buttons. Using the SimpleButton class requires an advanced understanding
> of AS3.0 programming, but by the end of the book you should have all the skills you

need to feel comfortable using it. Using the *SimpleButton* class is covered in detail in Advanced Game Design with Flash, *and you can read more about it in Adobe's AS3.0 documentation at* `http://help.adobe.com/en_US/FlashPlatform/reference /actionscript/3/flash/display/SimpleButton.html?filter_flash=cs5&filte r_flashplayer=10.2&filter_air=2.6`

Adding the button to the number guessing game

I'm now going to give you the delicate job of merging the code from the Buttons.as file with the NumberGuessingGame.as file. The number guessing game is going to end up with a button that you can click. Clicking it should have the same effect as pressing the Enter key.

Before you panic, know that you don't need to learn any new code or techniques. As long as you understand how to add code to a program—where to put it and what effect it has—you'll be able to do this. This will be good practice to make sure you've properly absorbed all the concepts covered in the past four chapters. When you're done, you'll end up with a game that looks a bit like Figure 4-34.

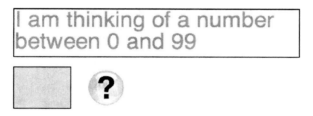

Figure 4-34. The number guessing game with an interactive button

Here are some things you'll need to do:

1. Copy your images folder from the Buttons project folder to the NumberGuessingGame folder.

2. Keep all the code that makes and sets up the button in its own `makeButton` method. You can then call that method in the number guessing game's constructor method, like this:

```
public function NumberGuessingGame()
{
  setupTextfields();
  makeButton();
  startGame();
}
```

3. Add the button event listeners to the `startGame` method. This lets you easily reinitialize the game if you want to add a Play again button in later steps. Here's where the button event listeners should be added:

```
public function startGame():void
{
  //Initialize variables
  startMessage = "I am thinking of a number between 0 and 99";
  mysteryNumber = Math.floor(Math.random() * 100);

  //Initialize text fields
  output.text = startMessage
  input.text = "";
  guessesRemaining = 10;
  guessesMade = 0;
  gameStatus = "";
  gameWon = false;

  //Trace the mystery number
  trace("The mystery number: " + mysteryNumber);

  //Add an event listener for key presses
  stage.addEventListener(KeyboardEvent.KEY_DOWN, keyPressHandler);

  //Add the button event listeners
  button.addEventListener(MouseEvent.ROLL_OVER, overHandler);
  button.addEventListener(MouseEvent.MOUSE_DOWN, downHandler);
  button.addEventListener(MouseEvent.ROLL_OUT, resetHandler);
  button.addEventListener(MouseEvent.CLICK, clickHandler);
}
```

4. When the player clicks the button, the game should read the number that's in the input field. You already have a method called playGame that analyzes the input. All you need to do is connect it to the button's CLICK event, like this:

```
public function clickHandler(event:MouseEvent):void
{
  buttonUpImage.visible = true;
  buttonDownImage.visible = false;
  buttonOverImage.visible = false;
  playGame();
}
```

Because you've modularized all your code into methods, it's very easy to connect the button to the existing playGame method. You don't need to write any new code for your game at all. The Enter key and the button call the same method when they're activated.

Disabling the button at the end of the game

When you've got the button working nicely in your game, you may want to disable it when the game is over, the same way you disable the Enter key. To do that, add the following code in bold text to the end of the endGame method:

```
public function endGame():void
{
  if (gameWon)
  {
    output.text
      = "Yes, it's " + mysteryNumber + "!" + "\n"
      + "It only took you " + guessesMade + " guesses.";
  }
  else
  {
    output.text
      = "No more guesses left!" + "\n"
      + "The number was: " + mysteryNumber + ".";
  }
  stage.removeEventListener
    (KeyboardEvent.KEY_DOWN, keyPressHandler);
  input.type = "dynamic";
  input.alpha = 0.5;

  button.removeEventListener(MouseEvent.ROLL_OVER, overHandler);
  button.removeEventListener(MouseEvent.MOUSE_DOWN, downHandler);
  button.removeEventListener(MouseEvent.ROLL_OUT, resetHandler);
  button.removeEventListener(MouseEvent.CLICK, clickHandler);
  button.alpha = 0.5;
  button.mouseEnabled = false
}
```

This new code removes all the listeners so the button has no more functionality. It also makes the button transparent as a visual cue that the button doesn't work anymore. Finally, it sets the button's mouseEnabled property to false, which prevents it from being sensitive to the mouse. Figure 4-35 shows what you'll see.

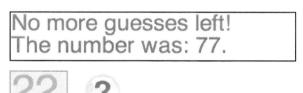

Figure 4-35. Dim and disable the button at the end of the game.

This is a lot of new code for you to write! In case you have any doubts as to how it should look, you'll find the entire project, up to this point, in the folder NumberGuessingGameWithButton, in the chapter's source files. Here's a complete listing of all the code for the game so far:

```
package
{
  import flash.net.URLRequest;
  import flash.display.Loader;
```

```
import flash.display.Sprite;
import flash.events.MouseEvent;
import flash.events.KeyboardEvent;
import flash.ui.Keyboard;
import flash.text.*;

[SWF(width="550", height="400",
backgroundColor="#FFFFFF", frameRate="60")]

public class NumberGuessingGame extends Sprite
{
  //Create the text objects
  public var format:TextFormat = new TextFormat();
  public var output:TextField = new TextField();
  public var input:TextField = new TextField();

  //Create the button objects
  public var buttonUpURL:URLRequest
    = new URLRequest("../images/buttonUp.png");
  public var buttonOverURL:URLRequest
    = new URLRequest("../images/buttonOver.png");
  public var buttonDownURL:URLRequest
    = new URLRequest("../images/buttonDown.png");
  public var buttonUpImage:Loader = new Loader();
  public var buttonOverImage:Loader = new Loader();
  public var buttonDownImage:Loader = new Loader();
  public var button:Sprite = new Sprite();

  //Game variables
  public var startMessage:String;
  public var mysteryNumber:uint;
  public var currentGuess:uint;
  public var guessesRemaining:int;
  public var guessesMade:uint;
  public var gameStatus:String;
  public var gameWon:Boolean;

  public function NumberGuessingGame()
  {
    setupTextfields();
    makeButton();
    startGame();
  }

  public function setupTextfields():void
  {
    //Set the text format object
    format.font = "Helvetica";
    format.size = 32;
    format.color = 0xFF0000;
    format.align = TextFormatAlign.LEFT;
```

```
//Configure the output text field
output.defaultTextFormat = format;
output.width = 400;
output.height = 70;
output.border = true;
output.wordWrap = true;
output.text = "This is the output text field";

//Display and position the output text field
stage.addChild(output);
output.x = 70;
output.y = 65;

//Configure the input text field
format.size = 60;
input.defaultTextFormat = format;
input.width = 80;
input.height = 60;
input.border = true;
input.type = "input";
input.maxChars = 2;
input.restrict = "0-9";
input.background = true;
input.backgroundColor = 0xCCCCCC;
input.text = "";

//Display and position the input text field
stage.addChild(input);
input.x = 70;
input.y = 150;
stage.focus = input;
}
public function makeButton():void
{
    //Load the images
    buttonUpImage.load(buttonUpURL);
    buttonDownImage.load(buttonDownURL);
    buttonOverImage.load(buttonOverURL);

    //Make the images invisible, except
    //for the up image
    buttonUpImage.visible = true;
    buttonDownImage.visible = false;
    buttonOverImage.visible = false;

    //Add the images to the button Sprite
    button.addChild(buttonUpImage);
    button.addChild(buttonDownImage);
    button.addChild(buttonOverImage);

    //Set the Sprite's button properties
    button.buttonMode = true;
```

```
    button.mouseEnabled = true;
    button.useHandCursor = true;
    button.mouseChildren = false;

    //Add the button Sprite to the stage
    stage.addChild(button);
    button.x = 175;
    button.y = 155;
}
public function startGame():void
{
    //Initialize variables
    startMessage = "I am thinking of a number between 0 and 99";
    mysteryNumber = Math.floor(Math.random() * 100);

    //Initialize text fields
    output.text = startMessage
    input.text = "";
    guessesRemaining = 10;
    guessesMade = 0;
    gameStatus = "";
    gameWon = false;

    //Trace the mystery number
    trace("The mystery number: " + mysteryNumber);

    //Add an event listener for key presses
    stage.addEventListener
      (KeyboardEvent.KEY_DOWN, keyPressHandler);

    //Add the button event listeners
    button.addEventListener(MouseEvent.ROLL_OVER, overHandler);
    button.addEventListener(MouseEvent.MOUSE_DOWN, downHandler);
    button.addEventListener(MouseEvent.ROLL_OUT, resetHandler);
    button.addEventListener(MouseEvent.CLICK, clickHandler);
}
public function playGame():void
{
    guessesRemaining--;
    guessesMade++;

    gameStatus
      = "Guess: " + guessesMade
      + ", Remaining: " + guessesRemaining;
    currentGuess = uint(input.text);

    if (currentGuess > mysteryNumber)
    {
      output.text = "That's too high." + "\n" + gameStatus;
      checkGameOver();
    }
    else if (currentGuess < mysteryNumber)
```

```
    {
      output.text = "That's too low." + "\n" + gameStatus;
      checkGameOver();
    }
    else
    {
      output.text = "You got it!";
      gameWon = true;
      endGame();
    }
  }
  public function checkGameOver():void
  {
    if (guessesRemaining < 1)
    {
      endGame();
    }
  }
  public function endGame():void
  {
    if (gameWon)
    {
      output.text
        = "Yes, it's " + mysteryNumber + "!" + "\n"
        + "It only took you " + guessesMade + " guesses.";
    }
    else
    {
      output.text
        = "No more guesses left!" + "\n"
        + "The number was: " + mysteryNumber + ".";
    }
    //Disable the Enter key
    stage.removeEventListener
      (KeyboardEvent.KEY_DOWN, keyPressHandler);
    input.type = "dynamic";
    input.alpha = 0.5;

    //Disable the button
    button.removeEventListener
      (MouseEvent.ROLL_OVER, overHandler);
    button.removeEventListener
      (MouseEvent.MOUSE_DOWN, downHandler);
    button.removeEventListener
      (MouseEvent.ROLL_OUT, resetHandler);
    button.removeEventListener
      (MouseEvent.CLICK, clickHandler);
    button.alpha = 0.5;
    button.mouseEnabled = false;
  }
  public function keyPressHandler(event:KeyboardEvent):void
  {
```

```
    if (event.keyCode == Keyboard.ENTER)
    {
      playGame();
    }
  }
  public function overHandler(event:MouseEvent):void
  {
    buttonUpImage.visible = false;
    buttonDownImage.visible = false;
    buttonOverImage.visible = true;
  }
  public function downHandler(event:MouseEvent):void
  {
    buttonUpImage.visible = false;
    buttonDownImage.visible = true;
    buttonOverImage.visible = false;
  }
  public function clickHandler(event:MouseEvent):void
  {
    buttonUpImage.visible = true;
    buttonDownImage.visible = false;
    buttonOverImage.visible = false;
    playGame();
  }
  public function resetHandler(event:MouseEvent):void
  {
    buttonUpImage.visible = true;
    buttonDownImage.visible = false;
    buttonOverImage.visible = false;
  }
  }
}
```

Managing complex code

This is a long program but notice that the bulk of the code has nothing to do with the mechanics of the game. About 70% of it has to do with setting up, displaying, and managing the text fields and buttons. In a big game project you'll find that most of your code will be about displaying graphics and managing the user interface, just like in this game.

Part of the reason why it's important to modularize your code using bite-sized methods is so that you can separate the programming of the visual elements from the programming of the game logic. Doing so makes the game much easier to write because when you finish programming one method, you don't need to look at it again. You can concentrate on the code in another method.

Still, in a complex game with hundreds of different graphic elements, this approach will only take you so far. You're going to need to learn how to modularize your code even further so that you can completely bury code that you no longer need to work on. In Chapter 7 you'll be looking at how to make games using multiple classes, which will partially solve the problem. The ultimate solution is to use a more advanced approach using a programming *design pattern* called the Model View Controller (MVC). It's beyond the scope of this book to cover the MVC, but you can find out all about it in the sequel to this book, *Advanced Game Design with Flash*.

While you're still learning, however, modularizing your code using methods will take you quite far, and you'll learn a lot in the process. Here are some ideas for making your games and programs easier to manage:

- Create very specific methods that perform one or two tasks—and no more.

- Keep all the setting up and displaying of your visual elements (like buttons, text, game characters, game objects, and backgrounds) in their own methods. This is important so that they don't clutter up the delicate logic programming that makes your game work.

- Keep all your event handlers at the end of the program. You rarely need to look at event handlers after you've written and tested then. If they're all sitting at the end of your program then they're neatly out of the way.

You'll see all these techniques at work in the code in the chapters ahead.

Project extensions

This is the first complete game in this book. But is it really done?

Game design is a funny thing. Games, even complex ones, are never really finished. Designers just stop working on them when they seem to play well enough that no one complains. There are usually many deep layers of complexity or added functionality that *could* be added to games if the designer had enough time, patience, and imagination to do so. Patience and imagination are things game designers seem to have in endless supply. It's usually *time* that throws the spanner in the works.

There's quite a bit more that you could add to this game. Here are some ideas.

Make a Play again button

Display a button at the end of the game that allows the player to play again. I'm not going to explain how to do this because you already know how! You know how to make buttons, set object properties, and create and call methods. By creating a Play again button on your own, you're going to practice all the skills you've learned over the last four chapters: everything from designing the graphics to writing the code. You'll also run into some problems you never imagined existed, eventually solve them, and feel like you're walking on clouds when everything is finally working properly.

When you're done, your number guessing game might look something like Figure 4-36.

Figure 4-36. Create a Play again button to restart the game.

Here are a few hints to help you on the way:

- The Play again button will need to be disabled and invisible when you first create and add it to the game.

- The endGame method should enable the Play again button.

- You need to disable the Play again button after it's been clicked. You can do this directly in its CLICK event handler.

- The Play again button will need to restart the game when you click it. You can do this by calling the startGame method in the play again button's CLICK event handler

- You'll need to re-enable the Enter key and guess button when the game restarts. Where will you add the code to do this?

If you get terminally stuck, you'll find the finished game with a Play again button in the PlayAgain folder in this chapter's source files.

Good luck!

Tracking guesses

You set the game up to allow ten guesses, but some players might not have the patience to remember what their previous guesses were. You can add another text field that displays all their previous guesses for them and adds the new guess when they make it.

To do this, you'll need a new text field, perhaps called guessHistory. You can create a new string variable called previousGuesses that stores all the guesses as a string of text with each number separated by a blank space. Whenever the player makes a new guess, you can add it to the previousGuesses variable and then update the guessHistory text field. Here's a sample of what the core of this code will look like:

```
previousGuesses += currentGuess + "  ";
guessHistory.text = previousGuesses;
```

This line of code will work well in the playGame method. Can you see how the code in the first directive would separate each number with a blank space?

Adding a visual display

A hangman-style visual display of how well (or poorly!) the player is doing is an interesting enhancement. You could create ten images showing ten different hangman states. Use the visible property to selectively display or hide each state depending on how the game is going. Each state can incrementally show the player how close they are to impeding peril, like the addition of limbs to the chalk figure in game of Hangman.

Turning the tables

A more advanced project that's fun to try is to change the game so that the program needs to guess a number that *you're* thinking of. This will be a completely new program, but you currently have all the skills you need to make it work.

Want to give it a try? Here's a hint: to get this game working, you'll need to use a **division operator**. You've already seen the multiplication operator.

```
*
```

You used the multiplication operator to multiply the random number by 100. The division operator looks like this:

```
/
```

It's a simple forward slash. You can use it in any directive to divide two numbers.

```
100 / 2
```

This example gives a result of 50. You can then assign this calculation to variable in a directive. Here's an example:

```
computersGuess = (100 / 2);
```

Can you see where I'm going with this? I'm not going to spoil your fun of figuring out the rest! This will be a difficult project for you, but you can do it. And what you'll learn along the way will give you an invaluable insight into your own developing skills and style as a game programmer.

A quick guide to embedding fonts

If you want the fonts in your games to display correctly on computers other than yours, you'll need to **embed** them. An embedded font is stored inside the SWF file and doesn't require the person who's playing the game to have that same font installed on his or her computer. Here are the steps you need to follow to embed a font:

1. Create a folder called fonts in your Project directory. Copy a font file into it. (Font files usually have the file extensions .ttf, .otf, or .ttc.)

2. Fonts are embedded using a metatag. Add the following code at the top of your class definition:

```
public class EmbeddedFonts extends Sprite
{
  [Embed
    (
      source="../fonts/Optima.ttc",
      embedAsCFF="false",
      fontName="embeddedFont",
      fontWeight="normal",
      advancedAntiAliasing="true",
      mimeType="application/x-font"
    )
  ]
  private var EmbeddedFontClass:Class;
```

The most important thing about this code is that the source parameter needs to provide the exact path to the font file in your project directory.

1. Set the format object's font property to "embeddedFont". This should match the name you provided in the fontName parameter in your code.

```
format.size = 32;
format.color = 0x000000;
format.font = "embeddedFont"
```

2. Set the text field's embedFonts property to true.

```
output.embedFonts = true;
```

Your published SWF will now display the font correctly on any computer.

In the chapter's source files you'll find a folder called EmbeddedFonts with a working example of this system. It displays a line of text using an embedded font. Here's the entire EmbeddedFont class:

```
package
{
  import flash.display.Sprite;
  import flash.text.*;

  public class EmbeddedFonts extends Sprite
  {
    [Embed
      (
        source = "../fonts/Optima.ttc",
        embedAsCFF = "false",
```

```
        fontName = "embeddedFont",
        fontWeight = "normal",
        advancedAntiAliasing = "true",
        mimeType = "application/x-font"
    )
]
private var EmbeddedFontClass:Class;

//Create the format and text field objects
public var format:TextFormat = new TextFormat();
public var output:TextField = new TextField();

public function EmbeddedFonts()
{
  //1. Configure the format
  format.size = 32;
  format.color = 0x000000;

  //The name of the font should match
  //the "name" parameter in the Embed tag
  format.font = "embeddedFont";

  //2. Configure the text field
  output.defaultTextFormat = format;
  output.embedFonts = true;
  output.autoSize = TextFieldAutoSize.LEFT;
  output.antiAliasType = flash.text.AntiAliasType.ADVANCED;
  output.border = false;
  output.defaultTextFormat = format;
  output.text = "The text you want to display.";
  stage.addChild(output);
  output.x = 50;
  output.y = 175;
  }
 }
}
```

> Embedded fonts can sometimes behave in quirky ways, and this often depends on the
> specific font file you're trying to embed. If you have any problems, first try removing this
> line from the Embed metatag:
>
> embedAsCFF = "false",
>
> This often does the trick.

Summary

The number guessing game that you looked at in this chapter is extremely important for a few reasons:

- It's the first complete and "real" game in the book. It's small in size, but it contains everything that a fully working game should have. Even though you can and will build more complex larger-scale games, this number guessing game is a model for the kinds of problems your games need to solve. If you understand the problems of game design and the solutions you found for them here, you'll be in a very strong position when you attempt something a bit more ambitious.

- You now understand input and output, variables, methods, if/else statements, button and keyboard events, and how to modularize a program using methods. These topics represent the core concepts of computer programming. You have a lot of programming power now at your disposal to build a wide variety of logic-based games.

- To keep things as simple as possible, the focus of this chapter has been on the internal logic and structure of games. There's no reason, however, why you shouldn't combine these techniques with the techniques you looked at in the previous chapter for controlling visual objects on the stage. In fact, you should definitely combine these techniques! With a bit of creativity, you'll be able to build complex puzzle and logic-based mystery adventure games that can be completely visual.

Before you continue in this book, take a short break to create a game of your own based on the techniques covered so far. There's no better way to learn than by trying things out in your own way, and it will give you a greater appreciation for some of the more advanced techniques you'll be looking at in the chapters ahead.

In Chapter 5, you'll take a detailed look at how to control objects on the stage with the keyboard. It will be the stepping stone you need to progress from designing *games* to designing *video games*.

Chapter 5

Controlling A Player Character

One of the first things your games should do is allow game players to move an object around the stage. A game object could be moved with either the mouse or the keyboard. In this chapter, you'll look at techniques for controlling an object with the keyboard.

This chapter covers the following topics:

- Using the KEY_DOWN, KEYUP, and ENTER_FRAME events.

- Stopping the player character at the edges of the stage and screen wrapping.

- Scrolling: vertical, horizontal, and parallax scrolling

- How to embed images into a game.

Controlling a player character with the keyboard

One of the most basic things a game should do is allow players to control a game character with a keyboard. It's not hard to do. It's a technique that makes use of two of AS3.0's built-in classes: the KeyboardEvent class and the Keyboard class. To use them, you simply import them into the top of your program, along with your other imported classes.

```
import flash.events.KeyboardEvent;
import flash.ui.Keyboard;
```

You used both of these classes in Chapter 4 to allow players to enter text into the input text field by pressing the Enter key on the keyboard. The KeyboardEvent and Keyboard classes contain methods and properties that you can use to help your players interact with your games using the keyboard. And, like the MouseEvent class properties, you'll be using all these new methods and properties with your eyes closed in no time at all.

Controlling with the keyboard—the wrong way!

There are two ways to control an object with the keyboard: the right way and the wrong way. Let's look at the wrong way of doing it first.

Why would you learn the wrong way? Well, the nice thing about doing player keyboard control incorrectly is that it's very straightforward and easy to understand. And, oh yeah, it kind of works, too. But even if you never use it to control a player character in one of your games, you'll find endless other uses for it as a general technique for figuring out which keys your players are pressing on the keyboard. It's also the basis for understanding the right way to do keyboard control, which adds a few extra layers of flexibility and polish to the same underlying system. If you understand how the wrong way works first, you'll be better able to understand and appreciate the right way to do things. But don't worry, I'll take things a step at a time. You'll be surprised at how simple the process is when you put all the pieces together.

Let's write a simple program that demonstrates this.

1. Create a new ActionScript project called SimpleKeyboardControl.

2. In the project folder, create a subfolder called images.

3. Copy the character.png file that you created in Chapter 2 into the images folder. When you're done, your project folder should look like Figure 5-1.

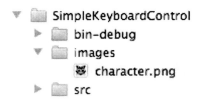

Figure 5-1. Copy the character.png file into the images folder.

4. Write the following program in the code editor window. (If you don't feel like typing it all out, you'll find the finished program in the SimpleKeyboardControl folder in the chapter's source files.)

```
package
{
  import flash.net.URLRequest;
  import flash.display.Loader;
  import flash.display.Sprite;
  import flash.events.KeyboardEvent;
  import flash.ui.Keyboard;
```

```
[SWF(width="550", height="400",
  backgroundColor="#FFFFFF", frameRate="60")]

public class SimpleKeyboardControl extends Sprite
{
  //Create the game character objects
  public var characterURL:URLRequest
    = new URLRequest("../images/character.png");
  public var characterImage:Loader = new Loader();
  public var character:Sprite = new Sprite();

  public function SimpleKeyboardControl()
  {
    //Load the image and add the character to the stage
    characterImage.load(characterURL);
    character.addChild(characterImage);
    stage.addChild(character);
    character.x = 225;
    character.y = 150;

    //Add a KeyboardEvent listener
    stage.addEventListener
      (KeyboardEvent.KEY_DOWN, keyDownHandler);
  }
  public function keyDownHandler(event:KeyboardEvent):void
  {
    if (event.keyCode == Keyboard.LEFT)
    {
      character.x -= 10;
    }
      else if (event.keyCode == Keyboard.RIGHT)
    {
      character.x += 10;
    }
    else if (event.keyCode == Keyboard.DOWN)
    {
      character.y += 10;
    }
    else if (event.keyCode == Keyboard.UP)
    {
      character.y -= 10;
    }
  }
}
}
```

5. Compile the program. Your game character will appear on the stage. You can move it around the stage using the arrow keys, as shown in Figure 5-2.

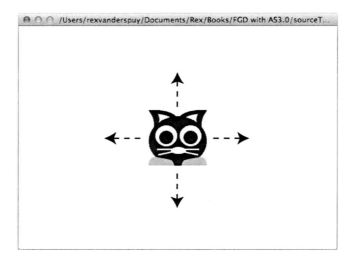

Figure 5-2. Move the game character around the stage with the keyboard arrow keys.

I'm sure you noticed some obvious problems with this player character control scheme already, but before I show you the solutions, let's have a quick look at how it works. The first thing you had to do was import the KeyboardEvent and Keyboard classes into the program.

```
import flash.events.KeyboardEvent;
import flash.ui.Keyboard;
```

The Keyboard class's primary job is to make it easier to figure out which keys the player is pressing. The KeyboardEvent class allows you to add an event listener to the stage to listen for key presses. That's exactly what this bit of code in the constructor method does:

```
stage.addEventListener(KeyboardEvent.KEY_DOWN, keyDownHandler);
```

This is the same event listener you used in Chapter 4, and it works in the same way. Its job is to detect when any keys are pressed on the keyboard. It calls the keyDownHandler, whose job is to process this event.

```
public function keyDownHandler(event:KeyboardEvent):void
{
  if (event.keyCode == Keyboard.LEFT)
  {
    character.x -= 10;
  }
  else if (event.keyCode == Keyboard.RIGHT)
  {
    character.x += 10;
  }
  else if (event.keyCode == Keyboard.DOWN)
  {
```

```
    character.y += 10;
  }
  else if (event.keyCode == Keyboard.UP)
  {
    character.y -= 10;
  }
}
```

> As you learned in Chapter 4, *Keyboard.LEFT, Keyboard.RIGHT, Keyboard.DOWN,* and *Keyboard.UP* represent numbers that AS3.0 links to keys on the keyboard. These numbers are called key codes.
>
> The key codes that AS3.0 uses are based on ASCII, which is a fixed standard for interpreting numbers as characters. For example, the ASCII number 65 refers to the uppercase letter A. However, different operating systems don't map these codes to the keyboard keys in exactly the same way. If you design and test a game using key codes on a Windows computer and then run the SWF on another operating system such as OS X, the key codes that you used might not match OS X's keyboard mapping. For this reason, it's preferable to use the *Keyboard* class's built-in key properties (such as LEFT and RIGHT,) instead of the actual key code numbers.
>
> If you need to use a key that isn't represented by these properties, you have to use a key code number. Make sure that you test these key codes carefully on each operating system your game will run on to ensure that it's mapped to the correct keys on every one.
>
> If you're building a game using Flash Professional software, some keys may not work while you're building and testing the game. Flash Professional reserves some keys for shortcuts (for example, Ctrl and S to save a file). So if you used any of these keys or key combinations in your game, you need to hold down Shift while testing the keys to override Flash Professional's own use of them. The keys will work fine in the published SWF.

Very simply, the `keyPressHandler` contains an if/else statement that figures out which key is being pressed and then moves the character left, right, down, or up by adding or subtracting 10 pixels from its x or y positions.

That's easy enough, but why is it working so badly? When you tested the program, you might have noticed a few big problems:

- The movement of the character is jittery.

- When you press one of the arrow keys, there's a slight delay before the character starts moving.

- You can move the character in only one axis (x or y) at a time. You can move the character left and right, or up and down, but not diagonally. Try pressing both the up arrow and the left arrow at the same time; it just moves the character in the direction of whichever key you pressed last. How can you move the character on the diagonal?

These problems are due to your computer keyboard's **key buffer**. When you press a key on the keyboard, the keyboard tells the computer that the key has been pressed down only once; it doesn't know if the key is being *held down*. The computer's operating system has a key repeat feature built into it that resends the KEY_DOWN event at regular intervals. The key repeat is needed for word processors, for example, so that you can hold down a key to repeat a character on the screen. You don't have any control over how the key repeat runs, and the result with a Flash game is the jittery movement you see on the stage.

To solve this problem, you need to work around the key buffer so the keys don't directly move the object. You can use the keys to determine the object's direction and speed, but you need to find another way to actually move the object.

Controlling the keyboard—the right way!

Now that you know how AS3.0 can find out which keys you're pressing, you can use this same basic system to refine the keyboard control program.

There's a lot of new stuff here, but don't panic! I'll break everything down step by step once you have the program running to show you exactly how it works. But for now, here's a quick summary of what you need to do:

- You have to import AS3.0's Event class so that you can use its ENTER_FRAME property.

- You have to create two new variables: **vx** and **vy**. These variables will store the vertical and horizontal velocities of the object.

- You have to change the keyDownHandler so that it no longer changes the position of the character. Instead, it updates the **vx** and **vy** variables with the speed and direction that the object should move in.

- You have to add an event handler called keyUpHandler. Its job is to detect when the arrow keys are released. When they are, it sets the character's speed to 0.

- You have to create a new event handler called enterFrameHandler that uses the vx and vy variables to actually move the character.

Let's write a new program to demonstrate all these features.

1. Create a new ActionScript project called KeyboardControl.

2. Create an images folder in the project directory and copy the character.png file into it.

3. Write the following program in the code editor:

```
package
{
  import flash.net.URLRequest;
  import flash.display.Loader;
```

```
import flash.display.Sprite;
import flash.events.KeyboardEvent;
import flash.ui.Keyboard;
import flash.events.Event;

[SWF(width="550", height="400",
  backgroundColor="#FFFFFF", frameRate="60")]

public class KeyboardControl extends Sprite
{
  //Create the game character objects
  public var characterURL:URLRequest
    = new URLRequest("../images/character.png");
  public var characterImage:Loader = new Loader();
  public var character:Sprite = new Sprite();

  //Create and initialize the vx and vy variable
  public var vx:int = 0;
  public var vy:int = 0;

  public function KeyboardControl()
  {
    //Load the image and add the character to the stage
    characterImage.load(characterURL);
    character.addChild(characterImage);
    stage.addChild(character);
    character.x = 225;
    character.y = 150;

    //Add event listeners
    stage.addEventListener
      (KeyboardEvent.KEY_DOWN, keyDownHandler);
    stage.addEventListener
      (KeyboardEvent.KEY_UP, keyUpHandler);
    stage.addEventListener
      (Event.ENTER_FRAME, enterFrameHandler);
  }
  public function keyDownHandler(event:KeyboardEvent):void
  {
    if (event.keyCode == Keyboard.LEFT)
    {
      vx = -5;
    }
    else if (event.keyCode == Keyboard.RIGHT)
    {
      vx = 5;
    }
    else if (event.keyCode == Keyboard.UP)
    {
      vy = -5;
    }
    else if (event.keyCode == Keyboard.DOWN)
```

```
    {
      vy = 5;
    }
  }
  public function keyUpHandler(event:KeyboardEvent):void
  {
    if (event.keyCode == Keyboard.LEFT
      || event.keyCode == Keyboard.RIGHT)
    {
      vx = 0;
    }
    else if (event.keyCode == Keyboard.DOWN
      || event.keyCode == Keyboard.UP)
    {
      vy = 0;
    }
  }
  public function enterFrameHandler(event:Event):void
  {
    //Move the player
    character.x += vx;
    character.y += vy;
  }
 }
}
```

4.   Compile the program. Use the arrow keys to move the character around the stage. The movement is now very smooth, and you can also move the character across the stage diagonally—just the kind of character control you're looking for!

You'll find the complete KeyboardControl program in the chapter's source files. Let's take a look at how this new program differs from the first one you wrote.

Moving with velocity

The first things to notice are the two new integer variables, **vx** and **vy**, which store the character's speed—how fast it's going. Actually, I need to be a little more accurate here. It's not really the *speed* of the object that you're storing, but the **velocity**.

Velocity is speed, but it's also direction. This is sometimes a confusing thing for beginners to grasp, so it's worth discussing in more detail. Have a look at this directive:

vx = -5;

vx refers to the velocity on the x (horizontal) axis. This actually tells you two things. First, 5 is the number of pixels that you want the character to move each frame. You've set the set the frame rate of the SWF file to 60 fps, which means that the object will move 5 pixels each frame, or 300 pixels each second. So that's the first thing: its speed.

Notice the negative sign.

vx = -5;

What does it tell you? Remember that the very left edge of the stage has an x value of 0. As you move to the right, the x value increases. If you move to the left, it decreases. That means that those x values that are negative are actually *pointing to the left*. Positive values *point to the right*. This directive thus tells you the speed and direction, also known as velocity.

5 pixels to the left.

Here's another example:

vy = +5;

vy refers to the velocity of the object on the y (vertical) axis. The very top of the stage has a y value of 0. As you move down the stage, the values increase. This directive says the following:

5 pixels down.

That's its velocity! Not so hard at all, is it? Figure 5-3 is a diagram of how positive and negative values can show direction.

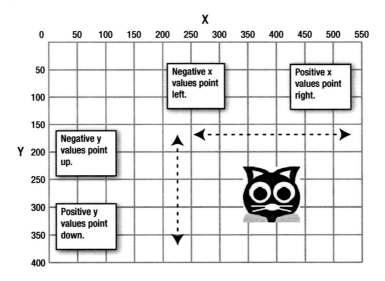

Figure 5-3. You can find the direction of movement by determining whether the x or y values are positive or negative.

If all this seems spectacularly underwhelming and blindingly obvious, good for you! It should be! Now let's see how all this talk of velocity fits in to what's going on in the program.

> *The choice of the variable names vx and vy has become a programming convention for variables that refer to horizontal and vertical velocities, so they're used in this book. Most programmers who see the variable names vx and vy immediately know what they're referring to. It's just one of those unwritten programming rules that everyone seems to follow, and no one knows why. Of course, you can give these variables any name you like, such as velocityX and velocityY (which are much more descriptive and might make your program easier to read). But, hey, conventions are sometimes a hard thing to knock, so this book sticks with vx and vy.*

Using the new keyDownHandler

The keyDownHandler has changed slightly from the first program you looked at in this chapter.

```
public function keyDownHandler(event:KeyboardEvent):void
{
  if (event.keyCode == Keyboard.LEFT)
  {
    vx = -5;
  }
  else if (event.keyCode == Keyboard.RIGHT)
  {
    vx = 5;
  }
  else if (event.keyCode == Keyboard.UP)
  {
    vy = -5;
  }
  else if (event.keyCode == Keyboard.DOWN)
  {
    vy = 5;
  }
}
```

The if/else statement is no longer changing the character's x or y properties directly. Instead, it's simply updating the vx and vy variables with the appropriate velocity. The job of actually moving the object is delegated to the enterFrameHandler. More on that in a moment, but first let's take a quick look at this other new event handler: keyUpHandler.

Using the keyUpHandler

In the first simple keyboard control program, an event handler called keyDownHandler was added to the stage. Its job was to listen for key presses. The funny thing about the keyDownHandler is that it only knows when keys are being pressed down, not when they're released. It turns out that knowing that a key is up is just as important for games as knowing that it's down. AS3.0 therefore has a handy little property of the KeyboardEvent class called KEY_UP that can tell you this information. You used the KEY_UP property in an event listener that you attached to the stage object in this directive:

```
stage.addEventListener(KeyboardEvent.KEY_UP, keyUpHandler);
```

It listens for keys that are being *released*. It sends this information to the keyUpHandler so that you can do something useful with it. But why would you want to know whether a key is no longer being pressed?

Think about it this way: you changed the keyDownHandler so that when the player of the game presses one of the arrow keys, the velocity of the character is changed by 5 pixels. That's great because when you press one of the arrow keys, you obviously want the character to move. But what about when you stop pressing one of the arrow keys? It would make sense for the character to also stop. However, unless you specifically tell the program this, it doesn't know what you intend, and the character just continues moving endlessly, forever. This wasn't a problem in the simple keyboard control program in which the keyDownHandler was changing the character's x and y properties directly, but now that you're using velocities and delegating the task of actual movement to the enterFrameHandler, it becomes a big problem.

The job of keyUpHandler is to check whether any of the arrow keys is released and then set the character's velocity to 0. That's what this code does:

```
public function keyUpHandler(event:KeyboardEvent):void
{
  if (event.keyCode == Keyboard.LEFT
    || event.keyCode == Keyboard.RIGHT)
  {
    vx = 0;
  }
  else if (event.keyCode == Keyboard.DOWN
    || event.keyCode == Keyboard.UP)
  {
    vy = 0;
  }
}
```

It should be pretty self explanatory, but there's one thing that will be new to you: the **or operator**. It looks like this:

```
||
```

It's made up of two **pipe characters**. The pipe character is a vertical line, and you'll find it somewhere on your keyboard near the brace or forward slash keys. Take a good look; it's there somewhere!

The or operator is used inside conditional statements to help you find out whether one thing *or* another thing is true.

Have a look at this line of code:
```
if (event.keyCode == Keyboard.LEFT
  || event.keyCode == Keyboard.RIGHT)
{...
```

It literally means this:

If the left arrow key is being pressed,
OR the right arrow key is being pressed,
 do the following.

Releasing either the left or right arrow key sets the horizontal velocity to 0—the character stops moving left or right. Because both conditions have exactly the same result, it makes sense to combine them into one statement with an or operator. It very efficiently saved a few extra lines of redundant code.

Using the enterFrameHandler

The enterFrameHandler is what actually makes the character move. It's triggered by an event listener that uses the ENTER_FRAME property of the Event class. To use it, you first have to import the Event class with this import directive in the class definition:

```
import flash.events.Event;
```

You then set up the event listener in the constructor method with this directive:

```
addEventListener(Event.ENTER_FRAME, onEnterFrame);
```

It follows the same format as the other two listeners, with one important difference: the listener isn't attached to the stage object. So what is it attached to? Adding an event listener without attaching it to an object means that the listener is attached *directly to the actual class it's in;* in this case, the KeyboardControl class, the actual program you're writing. This won't be of much relevance now, but it will become very important when you start looking at building games using different classes in Chapter 8.

When the event listener is triggered, it calls the enterFrameHandler.

```
public function enterFrameHandler(event:Event):void
{
  //Move the player
  character.x += vx;
  character.y += vy;
}
```

What this event handler does is very simple: it takes the horizontal and vertical velocities in the vx and vy variables and assigns them to the character's x and y properties. That makes the object move. Yay!

But wait. What is the event that calls this handler? You know that other events in the program are triggered by keys being pressed or released. KeyboardEvent.KEY_DOWN and KeyboardEvent.KEY_UP are pretty self-explanatory in that regard, but what kind of event is Event.ENTER_FRAME?

Put the kettle on and throw another log on the fire. Here's a little story that might help explain what's going on. The Flash technology was originally designed as a tool for doing animation, which is the art of creating the illusion of motion from nonmoving objects. A lot of the concepts that Flash borrowed came from the animation industry, which used celluloid film to create this illusion. Here, briefly, is how animation with film works:

Film is a long strip of celluloid (plastic) made up of a series of little squares called **frames**. Each frame contains an image, and each image in a frame is just slightly different from the image in the frame that comes before it. If enough of these slightly different images are flashed in front of a viewer's eyes fast enough, the individual nonmoving images will appear to be a single image that moves. This illusion of motion, which is the basis of all film, video, animation, and even game animation, is called **persistence of vision**.

To create a believable illusion of motion, these slightly different images need to be flashed in front of a viewer's eyes at least 12 times per second (also known as frames per second or fps.) Most cartoon animation is animated at 12 fps. For really fluid natural motion, you need to increase the frame rate to about 24 fps. The 24 fps rate is the frame rate used by films shown in a cinema and high-quality animated films. Video uses a frame rate of roughly 30 fps.

In this project, the fps is set to 60, which is a common frame rate for games. This means that all the objects on the stage are updated 60 times per second. Each time the stage does one of these updates, it "enters a frame." So the program *enters a frame* 60 times per second.

In a nutshell, that is what Event.ENTER_FRAME means. Every time the program enters a new frame, the ENTER_FRAME event is triggered. So whatever directives you put inside an event handler called by an ENTER_FRAME event runs 60 times per second. It runs for the entire duration of the program or until you remove the event listener.

In the current program, these two directives are being run 60 times per second:

```
player.x += vx;
player.y += vy;
```

It makes the object appear as though it's moving. Here's how:

Imagine that the character is at an x position of 100. If the player of the game presses the left arrow key, the vx variable is assigned the value -5. The next time the SWF enters a new frame, -5 is added to the character's x current position. The object's new position is now 95. On the next frame, -5 is added to the character's x position again, so its new position becomes 90. If the left arrow key is released, the **vx** variable is assigned a value of 0. Zero is then added to the character's x position (using the += operator), so its position remains 90 and it stops moving.

Clever, huh?

These may seem like a lot of hoops to jump through just to get the character to move on the screen. Hang on for a bit; the advantages of this approach will be very apparent a bit later in the book when you look at natural motion using physics simulations. If you can calculate the velocity first, there are all kinds of fun things you can do with it before you use it to update the position of the game character. Patience, my child; all shall be revealed!

The ENTER_FRAME event is one of the most important of AS3.0's events for game designers. It's the basis for moving objects with programming code in AS3.0 Most of the new techniques you'll be looking at will be triggered by the ENTER_FRAME event, so you'll find that the `enterFrameHandler` will become quite a busy, bustling little place from now on—soon to be full of new friends and cheerful chitchat.

Setting stage boundaries

Now that you can move the little player character around the stage, notice that you can drive it completely off the edge and keep going on forever and ever if you want to. There are three main strategies that game designers use to prevent this from happening.

- Blocking movement at the edge of the stage.

- Screen wrapping, which is what happens when the player leaves the left side of the stage and emerges from the right.

- Scrolling, which happens when the character is in a very big environment and the background moves to reveal unexplored areas.

You'll look at each of these techniques one at a time.

Blocking movement at the stage edges

Like most programming problems, if you understand the logic behind what you're trying to accomplish, all you need to do is figure out a way of representing that logic with programming code. Here's the logic behind what is accomplished with this bit of code:

If the character reaches the edge of the screen, push it back.

Hmm. Easier said than done? Let's see.

AS3.0 doesn't have any way of representing "the edge of the screen" as a whole, but you can access the built-in `stage` object. It contains `stageWidth` and `stageHeight` properties that tell you the size of the stage. Maybe you can use those properties to figure out the top, bottom, left, and right boundaries of the stage and then stop the character from moving if you discover that its x or y positions go beyond them.

Sound promising? Give it a whirl! Follow these steps:

1. Add the following code to the `enterFrameHandler`:

```
public function enterFrameHandler(event:Event):void
{
  //Move the character
  character.x += vx;
  character.y += vy;

  //Stop the character at the stage edges
  if (character.x < 0)
  {
    character.x = 0;
  }
  if (character.y < 0)
  {
    character.y = 0;
  }
  if (character.x + character.width > stage.stageWidth)
```

```
{
  character.x = stage.stageWidth - character.width;
}
if (character.y + character.height > stage.stageHeight)
{
  character.y = stage.stageHeight - character.height;
}
}
```

2. Compile the program and use the arrow keys to move the character to the edges of the stage. It will stop moving when any of its sides reach the edge, as shown in Figure 5-4

Figure 5-4. The character stops moving when it reaches the edge of the stage.

Let's take a detailed look at how this code works to prevent the character from crossing the left, top, right, and bottom edges of the stage.

You know that the very left side of the stage has an x position value of 0. And remember that your character's registration point, the point at which its x and y position is measured, is its top left corner. That means you can use the following logic to prevent the character from crossing the left side of the stage:

If the character's x position is less than zero, then set it to exactly zero.

In code, this same logic looks like this:

```
if (character.x < 0)
{
  character.x = 0;
}
```

If the character is moving from right to left, its x position value will gradually decrease. If it goes far enough, its x value will eventually reach zero, or even become negative. When this happens, the code pushes the character back so that it's at exactly position zero—the left edge of the stage. Figure 5-5 illustrates how this works.

299

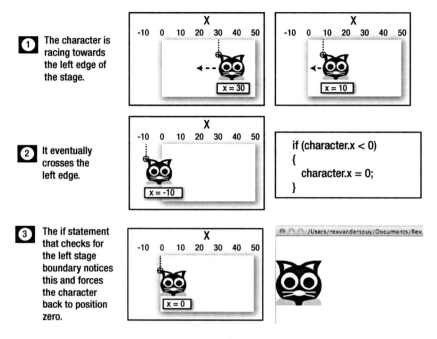

Figure 5-5. The character stops moving when it reaches the edge of the stage.

Even though the character does actually move slightly beyond the stage boundaries that you set, you don't ever see it do that; you see it only at the point at which it's been forced back.

This logic works exactly the same for code that checks the top stage boundary.

> *If the character's y position is less than zero, then set it to exactly zero.*

```
if (character.y < 0)
{
  character.y = 0;
}
```

If the character crosses the top of the stage, it's forced back to a y position of zero.

Things get a little more complicated for checking the right and bottom stage boundaries. The reason for this is because the character's x and y position is measured from its top left corner. That means you need to stop the character *before* its top left corner reaches the right and bottom boundaries. If you stopped the character when its top left corner reached the right or bottom of the stage, the character's body would already have disappeared off the edge. Figure 5-6 illustrates this problem.

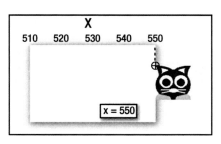
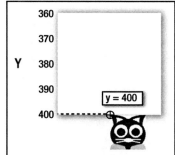

Figure 5-6. You can't directly use the character's x and y position to stop it at the right and bottom stage edges.

By how much before do you need to stop it? By exactly the amount of its width or height. Figure 5-7 shows why this works.

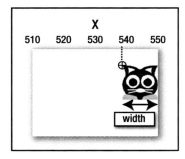
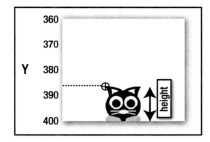

Figure 5-7. Add the character's width and height to accurately stop it at the right and bottom edges.

You can find out what the character's height and width are by using the built-in `height` and `width` properties.

```
character.height
character.width
```

You created your character object in Chapter 2 with a height and width of 100 pixels. So in this project, `character.height` and `character.width` will equal 100.

To find out the pixel values of the right edge and bottom of the stage, use the stage object's built-in `stageWidth` and `stageHeight` properties.

```
stage.stageWidth
stageHeight
```

The stage dimensions are 550 by 400 pixels. That means that the `stage.stageWidth` property has a value of 550, and the `stage.stageHeight` property has a value of 400.

Here's what you need to do to accurately stop the character at the right and bottom edge:

1.   First, *add the character's width or height to its x or y position.* This will give you the position of the character's leading edge.

2.   If that leading edge has a value that is greater than the right or bottom edge of the stage, move the character back to an x or y position that equals the stage dimensions, minus the character's height or width.

So here's the code in the if statement that checks whether the character's x and y positions have crossed the right and bottom stage boundaries:

```
if (character.x + character.width > stage.stageWidth)
{
  character.x = stage.stageWidth - character.width;
}
if (character.y + character.height > stage.stageHeight)
{
  character.y = stage.stageHeight - character.height;
}
```

It compensates for the character's height and width, and stops it exactly at the stage boundaries. Figure 5-8 illustrates this concept at work.

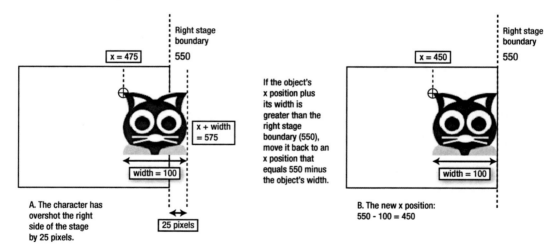

Figure 5-8. Precise screen boundaries using the object's width

The nice thing about using the built-in height and width properties for the character and the stage is that you don't have to know how big either of those things is. This code will work, unchanged, no matter the dimensions of the game character or the stage.

You can find the completed version of this code in the StageBoundaries file in this chapter's source files.

Screen wrapping

Screen wrapping happens when an object disappears from one side of the stage and then reemerges from the opposite side. This is quite a fun effect and very easy to implement. In fact, the logic that's used to accomplish it is almost exactly the *inverse* of the logic you used to block movement at the stage's edges. Let's try it out!

1. Change the conditional statements inside the `enterFrameHandler` to match the text in bold:

```
public function enterFrameHandler(event:Event):void
{
  //Move the character
  character.x += vx;
  character.y += vy;

  //Screen wrapping
  if (character.x + character.width < 0)
  {
    character.x = 550;
  }
  if (character.y + character.height < 0)
  {
    character.y = 400;
  }
  if (character.x > stage.stageWidth)
  {
    character.x = 0 - character.width;
  }
  if (character.y  > stage.stageHeight)
  {
    character.y = 0 - character.height;
  }
}
```

2. Compile the program.

3. Use the arrow keys to move the character past the edges of the stage. Peek-a-boo! It emerges from the opposite side (see Figure 5-9).

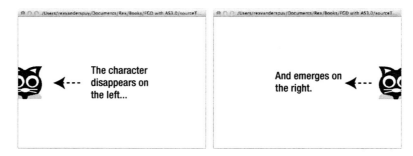

Figure 5-9. Screen wrapping

After the detailed look at how to stop an object at the stage edges, I'm sure you can figure out what's going on in this code already. It's almost exactly the same, except for being delightfully backward! It uses the object's width and height to figure out whether the object has completely disappeared off the edge of the stage. As soon as it detects that this is the case, it positions the object on the opposite side of the stage, just beyond the visible boundary. This creates the illusion that the object is trapped on the surface of some kind of cylindrical, never-ending plane. I usually complain about these sorts of things in this book, but this time, it's a blast! Have fun with it! Screen wrapping is, of course, a staple of many old skool games like PAC-MAN and Asteroids, and now you know how to do it if you ever need to.

You can find the complete code for this screen wrapping example in the ScreenWrapping folder in the chapter's source files.

Embedding images

Before you go much further, let's look at an alternate system for loading images into your games. I'm going to show you how to embed images into a program.

This is how you've been loading images into your programs up till now:

First, you created an URLRequest and Loader object.

```
public var characterURL:URLRequest
  = new URLRequest("../images/character.png");
public var characterImage:Loader = new Loader();
```

Then you loaded the image into the Loader object

```
.
characterImage.load(characterURL);
```

This system of loading images is called **runtime** loading. The images are loaded not when the program is compiled, but when the SWF file runs. It's actually the finished SWF file that is loading these images, not your program. The SWF file reads the paths to PNG files in your images folder and loads the images.

Runtime loading is useful because it means you can change any of the images in your game without having to recompile your program. Just drop different images into the images folder, and the finished SWF file will read the new ones automatically.

However, runtime loading has one fatal flaw. The images load slower than your code runs. That means that your program could start running before any of the images have loaded. This is especially true if you're running ENTER_FRAME events that update your code 60 times per second; it can lead to all sorts of problems.

AS3.0's `Loader` class has a number of built-in methods and properties that allow you to monitor the state of loaded images and initialize the program only when images have finished loaded. This requires quite a bit of additional coding to set up and manage, but, if you're working on a project that requires runtime loading for whatever reason, it may be the only solution. You can find out more about the `Loader` class's properties and methods that allow you to do this in AS3.0's documentation at `http://help.adobe.com/en_US/FlashPlatform/reference/actionscript/3/flash/display/Loader.html?filter_flash=cs5&filter_flashplayer=10.2&filter_air=2.6`

For most games you'll be working on, however, there's a more reliable, simpler, and better way. You can embed images directly into the program. This means that the images are available to the program immediately, before any of the code runs. And it also means that the finished SWF file isn't dependent on an external images folder.

Here are the steps to embedding an image into your program:

1. Import the `DisplayObject` class.

```
import flash.display.DisplayObject;
```

You add this import statement to the other import statements in your program.

2. Add these two lines to the class definition:

```
[Embed(source="../images/character.png")]
public var CharacterImage:Class;
```

The first line is an `Embed` metatag. It tells your program where to look for the image file. (When you embed an image, the path to the file is relative to the AS file, not the SWF file.)

The second line creates a `Class` variable. The image is stored directly in this variable. (Notice that its name begins with a capital letter, which indicates that it's a class.)

Very importantly, these two lines have to appear together like this, and in this order. You can't separate them or add any other code between them. This is just an odd quirk in AS3.0's syntax.

3. Create the image object from the `Class` variable you created in the previous step.

```
public var characterImage:DisplayObject = new CharacterImage();
```

This new image object has to be typed as `DisplayObject`.

4. Finally, you need add the image object to the container Sprite in exactly the same way you added your loader objects in previous examples.

```
character.addChild(characterImage);
```

Figure 5-10 illustrates how embedding images works.

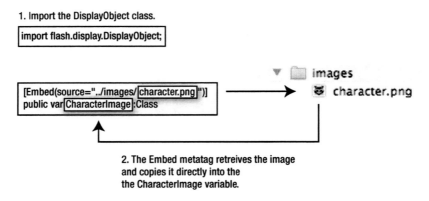

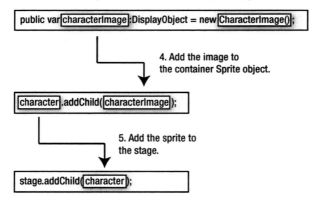

Figure 5-10. Embedding an image into a program

Because of all the problems it solves, embedding images like this is going to be the preferred system for loading images into your games for the rest of the projects in this book. You'll see a practical example of how to embed images in the next section.

You can embed any kind of file, not just image files. In Chapter 9, you'll learn how to embed sounds; in Chapter 11, you'll learn how to embed SWF files.

Scrolling

Scrolling is an effect that allows a player to move about in an environment that is much bigger than the confines of the stage. Like an ancient Chinese scroll being unrolled over a long wooden table, the background moves to allow the character to explore the space beyond the stage edges.

Although it's hard to pick favorites, there's probably very little to learn about game design that isn't in some way embodied in one or the other of the two greatest classic game series of all time: *Super Mario Bros.* and *The Legend of Zelda*. Pretty much anything game designers need to consider about good game design can be found in these two games, and scrolling is no exception.

Super Mario Bros. uses primarily what's known as **horizontal side-scrolling**. That's when the background moves left or right when the player reaches the left or right edges of the screen. The perspective in horizontal side-scrolling games is usually designed so that it looks as if you're viewing the environment from the side. *The Legend of Zelda* uses **overhead multi-axis scrolling**. In overhead scrolling, you view the environment from above, as if you were a bird flying in the sky and surveying the scene below. With multi-axis scrolling, the player character is free to move in any direction (up, down, left, or right), and the environment scrolls to keep up.

In truth, most games that use scrolling use a combination of these two systems. I'll first show you the more complex of the two, multi-axis scrolling, and finish the chapter with a quick look at horizontal side scrolling. Once you're comfortable with the scrolling techniques covered here, you'll be able to implement any combination of these two systems.

The first thing you need to implement in the scrolling system is some kind of background scene that is much bigger than the stage. In this example, you'll use a very large image.

1. Find a very large image that you think might be suitable for your scrolling system. Any picture with a width and height greater than 1,000 pixels should work well for this example. I decided to give my hard-working little cat character a holiday in space: a journey to one of Mars's moons, Phobos. Lucky for me, NASA maintains a large collection of copyright-free photos, including extremely high-resolution images of Phobos, which I was able to download. (To download your own high-resolution scenes from space, visit `http://photojournal.jpl.nasa.gov/`. Any images labeled Full Resolution are big enough.)

2. Rename your downloaded photo to background. Be careful; this is probably a JPEG image with a .jpg file extension. If that's the case, you'll need to use the file name "background.jpg" in the sample code that follows.

3. Create a new ActionScript project called BasicScrolling.

4. Create an images folder in the BackgroundScrolling project directory and copy your background and character images into it.

5. Write the following program in the code editor. (You'll find this finished code in the BasicScrolling folder in the chapter's source files.)

```
package
{
  import flash.display.Sprite;
  import flash.display.DisplayObject;
  import flash.events.KeyboardEvent;
  import flash.ui.Keyboard;
  import flash.events.Event;

  [SWF(width="550", height="400",
    backgroundColor="#FFFFFF", frameRate="60")]

  public class BasicScrolling extends Sprite
  {
    //Embed the background image
    [Embed(source="../images/background.png")]
    public var BackgroundImage:Class;
    public var backgroundImage:DisplayObject
      = new BackgroundImage();
    public var background:Sprite = new Sprite();

    //Embed the character image
    [Embed(source="../images/character.png")]
    public var CharacterImage:Class;
    public var characterImage:DisplayObject = new CharacterImage();
    public var character:Sprite = new Sprite();

    //Create and initialize the vx and vy variables
    public var vx:int = 0;
    public var vy:int = 0;

    public function BasicScrolling()
    {
      //Add the background
      background.addChild(backgroundImage);
      stage.addChild(background);
      background.x = -1325;
      background.y = -961;

      //Add the character
      character.addChild(characterImage);
      stage.addChild(character);
      character.x = 225;
      character.y = 150;

      //Add the event listeners
      stage.addEventListener
        (KeyboardEvent.KEY_DOWN, keyDownHandler);
      stage.addEventListener
        (KeyboardEvent.KEY_UP, keyUpHandler);
      stage.addEventListener
        (Event.ENTER_FRAME, enterFrameHandler);
```

```
}
public function keyDownHandler(event:KeyboardEvent):void
{
  if (event.keyCode == Keyboard.LEFT)
  {
    vx = -5;
  }
  else if (event.keyCode == Keyboard.RIGHT)
  {
    vx = 5;
  }
  else if (event.keyCode == Keyboard.UP)
  {
    vy = -5;
  }
  else if (event.keyCode == Keyboard.DOWN)
  {
    vy = 5;
  }
}
public function keyUpHandler(event:KeyboardEvent):void
{
  if (event.keyCode == Keyboard.LEFT
    || event.keyCode == Keyboard.RIGHT)
  {
    vx = 0;
  }
  else if (event.keyCode == Keyboard.DOWN
    || event.keyCode == Keyboard.UP)
  {
    vy = 0;
  }
}
public function enterFrameHandler(event:Event):void
{
  //Move the background
  background.x -= vx;
  background.y -= vy;

  //Check the stage boundaries
  if (background.x > 0)
  {
    background.x = 0;
  }
  if (background.y > 0)
  {
    background.y = 0;
  }
  if (background.x < stage.stageWidth - background.width)
  {
    background.x = stage.stageWidth - background.width;
```

```
      }
      if (background.y < stage.stageHeight - background.height)
      {
        background.y = stage.stageHeight - background.height;
      }
    }
  }
}
```

6. Remember, you may have to change "background.png" to "background.jpg" If you used a JPEG file.

```
[Embed(source="../images/background.jpg")]
```

7. Compile the program. Move the character around the stage with the arrow keys, and you'll see that you can fly across the surface of Phobos! (See Figure 5-11.)

Figure 5-11. A holiday in space!

Looking at the code

Let's take a look at some of the new code and concepts this program has introduced.

Embedding the character and background images

In order to embed images, the program first imports the DisplayObject class.
```
import flash.display.Sprite;
```

```
import flash.display.DisplayObject;
import flash.events.KeyboardEvent;
import flash.ui.Keyboard;
import flash.events.Event;
```

The images are embedded in the class definition. The code to do this is exactly the same as the example you just looked at. Keep in mind that even if you embed an image you still need to eventually copy it into a Sprite object if you want to display it on the stage. That's why the code creates accompanying Sprite objects for both the character and the background.

```
public class BasicScrolling extends Sprite
{
  //Embed the background image
  [Embed(source="../images/background.png")]
  public var BackgroundImage:Class;
  public var backgroundImage:DisplayObject = new BackgroundImage();
  public var background:Sprite = new Sprite();

  //Embed the character image
  [Embed(source="../images/character.png")]
  public var CharacterImage:Class;
  public var characterImage:DisplayObject = new CharacterImage();
  public var character:Sprite = new Sprite();

  //Create and initialize the vx and vy variables
  public var vx:int = 0;
  public var vy:int = 0;

  public function BasicScrolling()
  {...
```

The Sprites containing the images are then added to the stage in the constructor method in the same way you added them in previous programs.

```
public function BasicScrolling()
{
  //Add the background
  background.addChild(backgroundImage);
  stage.addChild(background);
  background.x = -1005;
  background.y = -761;

  //Add the character
  character.addChild(characterImage);
  stage.addChild(character);
  character.x = 225;
  character.y = 150;

  //Add the event listeners
  stage.addEventListener
    (KeyboardEvent.KEY_DOWN, keyDownHandler);
  stage.addEventListener
    (KeyboardEvent.KEY_UP, keyUpHandler);
  stage.addEventListener
```

```
    (Event.ENTER_FRAME, enterFrameHandler);
}
```

But take a look at the code that positions the background:

```
background.x = -1325;
background.y = -961;
```

This deserves some further explanation.

Positioning the background

My image of Phobos is pretty big: it's 2561 by 1922 pixels. The stage is only 550 by 400 pixels. I want to add the background to the stage so that it's centered—so that the middle point of Phobos is visible on the stage when the game first starts. That means I need to add it to the stage at a position that's the negative of half its width and half its height. Then I need to add half the stage's width to the x position, and half the stage's height to the y position. Remember that you position objects from their top left corners. And the top left corner of the stage has x and y values of 0. That means if I give my background an initial x position of -1005 and -761, it will be centered over the stage when the game starts. Figure 5-12 illustrates why this works.

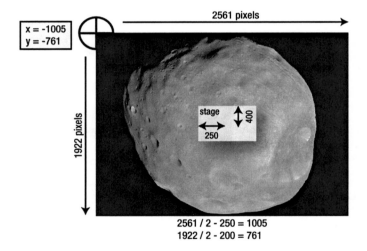

Figure 5-12. Center the background over the stage.

Of course, most of the background is hidden off stage. But it will be centered directly over the center of the stage.

To center your own background image, divide its height and width by half then subtract half the stage's width and height. Make those numbers negative by putting a minus sign in front of them, and use those negative numbers for the background's x and y position. If you don't feel like doing that math (and why would you?) just let AS3.0 do it for you automatically like this:

```
background.x = -(background.width - stage.stageWidth) / 2;
```

```
background.y = -(background.height - stage.stageHeight) / 2;
```

This code will center any large background image, no matter its size.

The character is centered on the stage. In fact, the character never moves from its position at the center of the stage the entire time. It looks like it's moving, but it isn't. That's all part of the scrolling illusion, and I'll explain how that works next.

Scrolling the background

So if the character doesn't move, what does? The background. The background object is the new center of attention in the code in the enterFrameHandler.

All you did is reverse a bit of the logic you were using to move the character. When you press the arrow keys, they move the background object in the direction *opposite* to the one you want the character to move in. That's why you should add a minus sign to the **vx** and **vy** variables with these two lines:

```
background.x += -vx;
background.y += -vy;
```

This creates the illusion that the character is moving when it's actually the background object that's moving in the opposite direction. Oh, the wily ways of the video game programmer!

The conditional statements stop the background object from moving when its edges reach the stage edges.

```
if (background.x > 0)
{
  background.x = 0;
}
if (background.y > 0)
{
  background.y = 0;
}
if (background.x < stage.stageWidth - background.width)
{
  background.x = stage.stageWidth - background.width;
}
if (background.y < stage.stageHeight - background.height)
{
  background.y = stage.stageHeight - background.height;
}
```

I'll leave the mental gymnastics up to you to figure out why it works the way it does, but it's simply one more permutation of exactly the same logic used to stop the character at the stage edges.

Better scrolling

This simple scrolling system can actually take you quite far, but there are a few problems that some fine-tuning can help solve:

- When the scrollable area reaches its limit, the character is prevented from moving all the way to the stage's edge. Try holding down the right arrow key and see how far you get. At some point, the background will stop moving, but the player won't be able to travel all the way to stage's right side. This seems to be an artificial constraint that would be a frustrating limitation for the player in many action or adventure games. Figure 5-13 illustrates this problem.

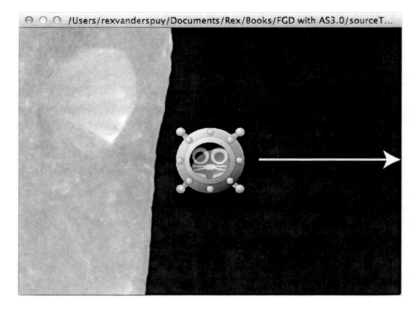

Figure 5-13. When the background has reached the limit of its scrollable area, the character can't travel all the way to the stage's edge.

- The other potential problem is that the scrolling background *always* scrolls. For many games, it might make more sense if the background scrolls only when the character is *approaching* the edge of the stage. Otherwise, the character should explore freely without the background moving.

Here's how to solve these problems. You can set up a system that figures out whether the character should move or the background object should move, depending on where each is. If the background object has reached the limit of its movement, the character should be free to travel to the edge of the stage. Also, if the player is not near any of the stage's edges, it should be free to move around without the background object moving.

The trick of making this work is to set up an imaginary **inner boundary**, which is a rectangular area inside the stage that's exactly half the stage's height and width. The character will be free to move around within the inner boundary; when it reaches the edge, it will stop moving, and the background will start to scroll. When the background reaches its scroll limit, the inner boundary that's been blocking the player from going further will extend to the limits of the stage to allow the player to move right to the edge.

The inner boundary that you'll create isn't a real object in the way that player and background are objects. Instead, it's just four numbers that define the top, bottom, left, and right of these boundaries. In fact, the logic behind finding these numbers is exactly the same as the logic used to set the real stage boundaries; you just cut them down to half the size.

You'll build this code in two stages so that you can see how it's working. (For the complete final working version of this code, see the BetterScrolling.as file in this chapter's source files.)

1. You can either create a new ActionScript project or modify the code from the previous example. The following is a listing of the entire program; all the new code has been highlighted in bold text.

```actionscript
package
{
  import flash.display.Sprite;
  import flash.display.DisplayObject;
  import flash.events.KeyboardEvent;
  import flash.ui.Keyboard;
  import flash.events.Event;

  [SWF(width="550", height="400",
    backgroundColor="#FFFFFF", frameRate="60")]

  public class BetterScrolling extends Sprite
  {
    //Embed the background image
    [Embed(source="../images/background.png")]
    public var BackgroundImage:Class;
    public var backgroundImage:DisplayObject
      = new BackgroundImage();
    public var background:Sprite = new Sprite();

    //Embed the character image
    [Embed(source="../images/character.png")]
    public var CharacterImage:Class;
    public var characterImage:DisplayObject = new CharacterImage();
    public var character:Sprite = new Sprite();

    //Create and initialize the vx and vy variables
    public var vx:int = 0;
    public var vy:int = 0;

    //Variables for the inner boundary
    public var rightInnerBoundary:uint;
    public var leftInnerBoundary:uint;
```

```
public var topInnerBoundary:uint;
public var bottomInnerBoundary:uint;

public function BetterScrolling()
{
  //Add the background
  background.addChild(backgroundImage);
  stage.addChild(background);
  background.x = -(background.width - stage.stageWidth) / 2;
  background.y = -(background.height - stage.stageHeight) / 2;
  //Add the character
  character.addChild(characterImage);
  stage.addChild(character);
  character.x = 225;
  character.y = 150;

  //Define the inner boundary variables
  rightInnerBoundary
    = (stage.stageWidth / 2) + (stage.stageWidth / 4);
  leftInnerBoundary
    = (stage.stageWidth / 2) - (stage.stageWidth / 4);
  topInnerBoundary
    = (stage.stageHeight / 2) - (stage.stageHeight / 4);
  bottomInnerBoundary
    = (stage.stageHeight / 2) + (stage.stageHeight / 4);

  //Add the event listeners
  stage.addEventListener
    (KeyboardEvent.KEY_DOWN, keyDownHandler);
  stage.addEventListener
    (KeyboardEvent.KEY_UP, keyUpHandler);
  stage.addEventListener
    (Event.ENTER_FRAME, enterFrameHandler);
}

public function keyDownHandler(event:KeyboardEvent):void
{
  if (event.keyCode == Keyboard.LEFT)
  {
    vx = -5;
  }
  else if (event.keyCode == Keyboard.RIGHT)
  {
    vx = 5;
  }
  else if (event.keyCode == Keyboard.UP)
  {
    vy = -5;
  }
  else if (event.keyCode == Keyboard.DOWN)
  {
    vy = 5;
```

```
    }
  }
  public function keyUpHandler(event:KeyboardEvent):void
  {
    if (event.keyCode == Keyboard.LEFT
      || event.keyCode == Keyboard.RIGHT)
    {
      vx = 0;
    }
    else if (event.keyCode == Keyboard.DOWN
      || event.keyCode == Keyboard.UP)
    {
      vy = 0;
    }
  }
  public function enterFrameHandler(event:Event):void
  {
    //Disable the code that moves the background
    //background.x -= vx;
    //background.y -= vy;

    //Move the player
    character.x += vx
    character.y += vy;

    //Stop character at the inner boundary edges
    if(character.x < leftInnerBoundary)
    {
      character.x = leftInnerBoundary;
      background.x -= vx;
    }
    if(character.x + character.width > rightInnerBoundary)
    {
      character.x = rightInnerBoundary - character.width
      background.x -= vx;
    }
    if(character.y < topInnerBoundary)
    {
      character.y = topInnerBoundary;
      background.y -= vy;
    }
    if(character.y + character.height  > bottomInnerBoundary)
    {
      character.y = bottomInnerBoundary - character.height;
      background.y -= vy;
    }

    //Check the stage boundaries
    if (background.x > 0)
    {
      background.x = 0;
    }
```

```
    if (background.y > 0)
    {
      background.y = 0;
    }
    if (background.x < stage.stageWidth - background.width)
    {
      background.x = stage.stageWidth - background.width;
    }
    if(background.y < stage.stageHeight - background.height)
    {
      background.y = stage.stageHeight - background.height;
    }
  }
 }
}
```

2. Compile the program and move the character with the arrow keys. You can now move it freely within the inner boundaries of the stage. When it reaches the edge of the inner boundary, the background starts scrolling. Figure 5-14 illustrates this.

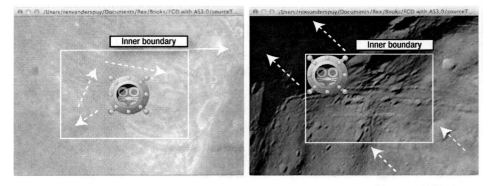

Figure 5-14. The character is free to move within the inner boundary. When it reaches one of the edges, the character stops moving and the background scrolls.

The first thing the code does is define the inner boundary with these four new variables. You first declared these new variables in the class definition.

```
public var rightInnerBoundary:uint;
public var leftInnerBoundary:uint;
public var topInnerBoundary:uint;
public var bottomInnerBoundary:uint;
```

You then set their value in the constructor method.

```
rightInnerBoundary
  = (stage.stageWidth / 2) + (stage.stageWidth / 4);
leftInnerBoundary
```

```
 = (stage.stageWidth / 2) - (stage.stageWidth / 4);
topInnerBoundary
 = (stage.stageHeight / 2) - (stage.stageHeight / 4);
bottomInnerBoundary
 = (stage.stageHeight / 2) + (stage.stageHeight / 4);
```

This is the first time you've written code that uses the division operator. It's represented by a forward slash (/) character and means "divided by."

Can you figure out how the boundaries were calculated? (Try it; it's not that hard!) What you end up with is an inner area that's half the size of the stage.

The following is the new code from the enterFrameHandler that really makes this whole system work:

```
//Move the player
character.x += vx
character.y += vy;

//Stop character at inner the boundary edges
if (character.x < leftInnerBoundary)
{
  character.x = leftInnerBoundary;
  background.x -= vx;
}
else if (character.x + character.width > rightInnerBoundary)
{
  character.x = rightInnerBoundary - character.width
  background.x -= vx;
}
if (character.y < topInnerBoundary)
{
  character.y = topInnerBoundary;
  background.y -= vy;
}
else if (character.y + character.height > bottomInnerBoundary)
{
  character.y = bottomInnerBoundary - character.height;
  background.y -= vy;
}
```

You can see that you're back to moving the character again. But it is allowed to move only while it's within the inner boundaries. Let's have a look at how the first if statement works.

```
if (character.x < leftInnerBoundary)
{
  character.x = leftInnerBoundary;
  background.x -= vx;
}
```

The conditional statement checks to see whether the left edge of the player is less than the left inner boundary. If it is, the player is forced back to that edge. This is exactly the same logic used to stop the character at the edges of the stage.

But the next line is interesting.

```
background.x -= vx;
```

The background starts moving! And that's really all there is to it. The code is quite simple, but the effect it produces seems complex when the program runs.

Even better scrolling

You still have one more problem to solve. The character still can't move all the way to the edges of the stage when the scrolling background has reached its limit. To do this, you need to temporarily extend the boundaries and then move them back if the player returns to the center of the stage again. A few lines of very simple code in the right place are all you need to achieve this.

1. Add the following lines in bold to the enterFrameHandler:

```
public function enterFrameHandler(event:Event):void
{
  //Move the player
  character.x += vx
  character.y += vy;

  //Check the inner boundaries
  if (character.x < leftInnerBoundary)
  {
    character.x = leftInnerBoundary;
    rightInnerBoundary
      = (stage.stageWidth / 2) + (stage.stageWidth / 4);
    background.x -= vx;
  }
  else if (character.x + character.width > rightInnerBoundary)
  {
    character.x = rightInnerBoundary - character.width
    leftInnerBoundary
      = (stage.stageWidth / 2) - (stage.stageWidth / 4);
    background.x -= vx;
  }
  if (character.y < topInnerBoundary)
  {
    character.y = topInnerBoundary;
    bottomInnerBoundary
      = (stage.stageHeight / 2) + (stage.stageHeight / 4);
    background.y -= vy;
  }
  else if
```

```
(character.y + character.height > bottomInnerBoundary)
{
  character.y = bottomInnerBoundary - character.height;
  topInnerBoundary
    = (stage.stageHeight / 2) - (stage.stageHeight / 4);
  background.y -= vy;
}

//Check the stage boundaries
if (background.x > 0)
{
  background.x = 0;
  leftInnerBoundary = 0;
}
else if (background.y > 0)
{
  background.y = 0;
  topInnerBoundary = 0;
}
else if
(background.x < stage.stageWidth - background.width)
{
  background.x = stage.stageWidth - background.width;
  rightInnerBoundary = stage.stageWidth;
}
else if
(background.y < stage.stageHeight - background.height)
{
  background.y = stage.stageHeight - background.height;
  bottomInnerBoundary = stage.stageHeight;
}
}
```

2. Compile the program and try it out. The character can now explore the entire area—right up to the stage edges.

This code works by extending the inner boundaries to the stage edges when the background has reached the limit of its movement. Let's look at how this works with the first if statement in the code (the new code is highlighted in bold).

```
if (background.x > 0)
{
  background.x = 0;
  leftInnerBoundary = 0;
}
```

If you press the left arrow key, the background object moves until the conditional statement detects that it has reached its limit. When that happens, it stops the background object from moving and then gives the leftInnerBoundary variable a new value that is equivalent to the x value of the left side of the stage. You know that the very left edge of the stage has an x position value of zero. That allows the character to move all the way to the stage edge. Figure 5-15 illustrates how this works.

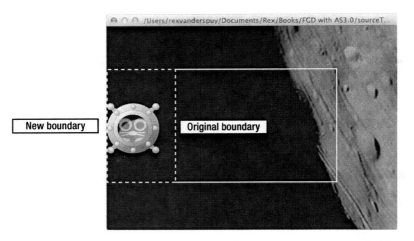

Figure 5-15. When the background object stops moving, the boundary is extended to allow the character to travel to the edge of the stage.

Problem solved! But you just created another one. How can you move the boundary back to its original position if the player moves back to the center of the stage?

Think about it this way. Imagine that the character has traveled to the leftmost edge of the stage, as shown in Figure 5-15. When it travels back to the center of the stage, you don't have to start moving the background object again until the character has reached the inner-right boundary. If it does, you know that you can safely reset the inner-left boundary to its original position. That's what this new line of code in bold does:

```
else if (character.x + character.width > rightInnerBoundary)
{
  character.x = rightInnerBoundary - character.width
  leftInnerBoundary
    = (stage.stageWidth / 2) - (stage.stageWidth / 4);
  background.x -= vx;
}
```

Figure 5-16 illustrates what is happening.

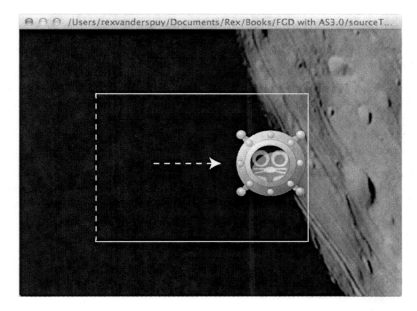

Figure 5-16. The left boundary resets to its original position when the character reaches the right boundary.

The other bits of new code that you added in this section follow exactly the same logic for each of the three other boundaries.

You can find the entire working example of this code in the EvenBetterScrolling folder in the chapter's source files.

Taking it further

You'll be able to get quite a bit of mileage out of these examples of scrolling for your games. Any type of scrolling system you can dream up will use these same techniques in some kind of combination. You've actually tackled the most difficult type of scrolling, combined vertical and horizontal scrolling, so if you need to make a game that requires only horizontal scrolling, it should be a piece of cake. The techniques are exactly the same; you just need half the amount of code because you'll only need to check boundaries on the x axis.

This is not the last word on scrolling; it's really just the beginning. Have a look at some of your favorite games and study very carefully how they've implemented scrolling. You'll notice that many of them modify how and when scrolling takes place in very subtle ways. The core of all this, however, is based on the examples you looked at in this chapter.

Things get a little more complex when you need to scroll the background and foreground game objects at the same time. You'll take a look at how to do that in Chapter 7.

Parallax scrolling

There's one additional scrolling technique that you should look at briefly because it's very widely used and extremely effective: **parallax scrolling**.

Parallax is a visual effect in which the position of an object appears to change depending on the point of view from which it's being observed. The effect of parallax scrolling in games is used to create the illusion of shallow depth. It's a simple 3D effect in which distant background objects move at a slower rate than closer foreground objects, creating the illusion that slower-moving objects are farther away. Parallax scrolling can give even simple 2D games very strong visual impact.

It's very to easy to do. First, you need split your background scene into two separate images. The first will be for things that are far away, like mountains or clouds. Perhaps you could call this the distantBackground. Make its height the same as the stage, (400 pixels), but make it really long, with a width of perhaps over 2000 pixels. Figure 5-17 illustrates what this could look like.

distantBackground (2311 x 400 pixels)

Figure 5-17. A distant background object for things that are far away

Next, you need an image for things that are closer. Perhaps you could call it the foreground. Make it exactly the same size as the distant background. Figure 5-18 shows what this might look like.

foreground (2311 x 400 pixels)

Figure 5-18. A foreground object for things that are closer

Add them to both to the stage, center them, and add your game character to create a single scene (Figure 5-19).

Figure 5-19. Add the two background components to you game, along with your game character.

Now all you need to do is move the distantBackground object at a slower rate than the foreground object. The directives you use might look like this:

```
foreground.x += -vx;
foreground.y += -vy;
distantBackground.x += -vx / 2;
distantBackground.y += -vy / 2;
```

When your game character moves, the distant background moves at half the speed of the foreground, making it look as though it's far in the distance. Try it! It's a mesmerizing effect. And there's also nothing stopping you from adding a third element as an extremely distant background object moving at an even slower rate.

To get you started on your own parallax scrolling experiments, take a look at the ParallaxScrolling program in the chapter's source files. Here's the code that makes it work:

```
package
{
  import flash.display.Sprite;
  import flash.display.DisplayObject;
  import flash.events.KeyboardEvent;
  import flash.ui.Keyboard;
  import flash.events.Event;

  [SWF(width="550", height="400",
    backgroundColor="#FFFFFF", frameRate="60")]

  public class ParallaxScrolling extends Sprite
  {
    //Embed the distant background image
    [Embed(source="../images/distantBackground.png")]
    public var DistantBackgroundImage:Class;
    public var distantBackgroundImage:DisplayObject
      = new DistantBackgroundImage();
    public var distantBackground:Sprite = new Sprite();

    //Embed the distant foreground image
    [Embed(source="../images/foreground.png")]
    public var ForegroundImage:Class;
    public var foregroundImage:DisplayObject
      = new ForegroundImage();
    public var foreground:Sprite = new Sprite();

    //Embed the character image
    [Embed(source="../images/character.png")]
    public var CharacterImage:Class;
    public var characterImage:DisplayObject = new CharacterImage();
    public var character:Sprite = new Sprite();

    //Create and initialize the vx variable
```

```
public var vx:int = 0;

//Variables for the inner boundary
public var rightInnerBoundary:uint;
public var leftInnerBoundary:uint;

public function ParallaxScrolling()
{
  //Add the distant background
  distantBackground.addChild(distantBackgroundImage);
  stage.addChild(distantBackground);
  distantBackground.x
    = -(distantBackground.width - stage.stageWidth) / 2;
  distantBackground.y = 0;

  //Add the foreground
  foreground.addChild(foregroundImage);
  stage.addChild(foreground);
  foreground.x = -(foreground.width - stage.stageWidth) / 2;
  foreground.y = 0;

  //Add the character
  character.addChild(characterImage);
  stage.addChild(character);
  character.x = 225;
  character.y = 290;

  //Define the inner boundary variables
  rightInnerBoundary
    = (stage.stageWidth / 2) + (stage.stageWidth / 4);
  leftInnerBoundary
    = (stage.stageWidth / 2) - (stage.stageWidth / 4);

  //Add the event listeners
  stage.addEventListener
    (KeyboardEvent.KEY_DOWN, keyDownHandler);
  stage.addEventListener
    (KeyboardEvent.KEY_UP, keyUpHandler);
  stage.addEventListener
    (Event.ENTER_FRAME, enterFrameHandler);
}

public function keyDownHandler(event:KeyboardEvent):void
{
  if (event.keyCode == Keyboard.LEFT)
  {
    vx = -5;
  }
  else if (event.keyCode == Keyboard.RIGHT)
  {
    vx = 5;
  }
```

```
    }
    public function keyUpHandler(event:KeyboardEvent):void
    {
      if (event.keyCode == Keyboard.LEFT
        || event.keyCode == Keyboard.RIGHT)
      {
        vx = 0;
      }
    }
    public function enterFrameHandler(event:Event):void
    {
      //Move the player
      character.x += vx

      //Check the inner boundaries
      if (character.x < leftInnerBoundary)
      {
        character.x = leftInnerBoundary;
        rightInnerBoundary
          = (stage.stageWidth / 2) + (stage.stageWidth / 4);
        distantBackground.x -= vx / 2;
        foreground.x -= vx;
      }
      if (character.x + character.width > rightInnerBoundary)
      {
        character.x = rightInnerBoundary - character.width
        leftInnerBoundary
          = (stage.stageWidth / 2) - (stage.stageWidth / 4);
        distantBackground.x -= vx / 2;
        foreground.x -= vx;
      }

      //Check the stage boundaries
      if (foreground.x > 0)
      {
        foreground.x = 0;
        distantBackground.x
          = -(distantBackground.width - stage.stageWidth) / 4;
        leftInnerBoundary = 0;
      }
      if (foreground.x < stage.stageWidth - foreground.width)
      {
        foreground.x = stage.stageWidth - foreground.width;
        distantBackground.x
          = ((distantBackground.width - stage.stageWidth) / 4) * -3;
        rightInnerBoundary = stage.stageWidth;
      }
    }
  }
}
```

This code employs all the techniques you've looked at in the chapter. However, it uses a little less code that the previous example because the scrolling just happens on the x axis.

There's a bit of this code that I need to clarify. When the scrolling reaches the limit of the foreground's left border, the foreground stops moving. This is the same effect you saw in the previous example. However, now you have to stop the distant background from moving as well. And because the distant background is moving at half the speed as the foreground, you can't stop it an x position of zero. You have to stop it at an x position that's one quarter of its width below zero, minus the stage width.

```
if (foreground.x > 0)
{
  foreground.x = 0;
  distantBackground.x
    = -(distantBackground.width - stage.stageWidth) / 4;
  leftInnerBoundary = 0;
}
```

Another brain twister for you! But perhaps Figure 5-20 will help clarify this for you.

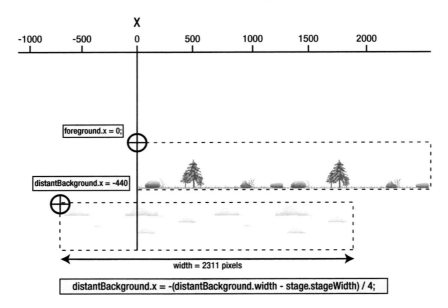

Figure 5-20. Because the distant background is moving at half the rate, you have to stop it at an x position that's one quarter of its width below zero, minus the stage width.

The left boundary needs to do the same bit of gymnastics.

```
else if (foreground.x < stage.stageWidth - foreground.width)
{
  foreground.x = stage.stageWidth - foreground.width;
```

```
distantBackground.x
    = ((distantBackground.width - stage.stageWidth) / 4) * -3;
  rightInnerBoundary = stage.stageWidth;
}
```

Don't let the math worry you. Just use it; it works!

Summary

So, is that it? No way! This chapter gave you a taste of setting up a player control scheme, but there's so much more refinement that can be done. Later in the book, you'll learn how to modify these models to incorporate acceleration, friction, and gravity into the character's movements. You'll also be looking at a player control scheme to allow the game to be played with a mouse instead of the keyboard.

In this chapter, you solved some extremely important problems central to game design that you'll see popping up again and again in different contexts in the chapters that follow. Experiment a bit with some of these techniques on your own, and I'll meet you in Chapter 6 when you're ready. I'll show you how to create an environment that your objects can interact with using collision detection.

Chapter 6

Bumping Into Things

Welcome to a fun chapter! In these pages you'll build an interactive playground of clever little game design techniques that you can expand upon to build completely interactive two-dimensional environments, better known as action and adventure games! A whole grab bag of things from collision detection, building walls, and picking up and dropping objects—they're all here. With a little imagination, you'll be able to use these very simple techniques to produce different kinds of games. Hey, congratulate yourself: you've come a long way since page 1! All your hard work is about to pay off.

At the end of the chapter, I'll introduce the Collision class, which is a custom class designed just for this book. It contains a specialized method for handling complex collisions between objects that you can use with any of your game projects.

Basic collision detection with hitTestObject

What makes most computer games fun to play is that they are, in their essence, a simplified simulation of the real world. Like the real world, they contain objects that you can interact with in some way. These objects might be walls that block your movement, friends who help you, or enemies who harm you.

To create these sorts of interactive objects, you first need a way of finding out whether one object is touching another object. In computer game programming, this is called **collision detection**. Collision detection is just game programming jargon for what happens when things bump into one another. AS3.0 has a very simple way of detecting collisions between objects: the hitTestObject method.

It's amazing what kind of power the hitTestObject method can give you. In the examples in the following pages, you'll be looking at how you can use it to do the following:

- Change text in a dynamic text field.
- Trigger a change of state.
- Reduce a health meter.
- Update a score.
- Pick up and drop an object.

With a little imagination, you'll be able to use these techniques to produce a richly varied number of games.

In this chapter's source files you'll find a project folder called BasicCollisionDetection that demonstrates how hitTestObject works. Compile the project, and you'll see a scene that looks like Figure 6-1. Move the cat character around the stage with the arrow keys and watch what happens when the cat bumps into the monster. The word "Hey!!!" is displayed in the output text field. If you move the player object away from the enemy, the text field displays "No collision..." again.

Figure 6-1. Use hitTestObject to change the words in the text field.

The code that makes all this work will be good for you to look at as a review of all the concepts and techniques you've learned so far. It embeds and displays images, uses a dynamic text field, uses keyboard control, and modularizes the constructor method's tasks into three separate methods. You should understand all this code by now, but if there's something you're a bit fuzzy on, now might be a good time to revisit the section in the book that covers it—before you get into some trickier stuff.

Out of all this code there's only one new technique you haven't seen before: the use of the hitTestObject method. It's used to change the words in the output text field when the game characters collide. I've highlighted it in the listing of the BasicCollisionDetection program next. Can you figure out how it works?

```
package
{
  import flash.display.Sprite;
  import flash.display.DisplayObject;
  import flash.events.KeyboardEvent;
  import flash.ui.Keyboard;
  import flash.events.Event;
```

```
import flash.text.*;

[SWF(width="550", height="400",
  backgroundColor="#FFFFFF", frameRate="60")]

public class BasicCollisionDetection extends Sprite
{
  //Create the text objects
  public var format:TextFormat = new TextFormat();
  public var output:TextField = new TextField();
  public var input:TextField = new TextField();

  //Embed the character image
  [Embed(source="../images/character.png")]
  public var CharacterImage:Class;
  public var characterImage:DisplayObject = new CharacterImage();
  public var character:Sprite = new Sprite();

  //Embed the monster image
  [Embed(source="../images/monsterNormal.png")]
  public var MonsterNormalImage:Class;
  public var monsterNormalImage:DisplayObject
    = new MonsterNormalImage();
  public var monster:Sprite = new Sprite();

  //Create and initialize the vx and vy variable
  public var vx:int = 0;
  public var vy:int = 0;

  public function BasicCollisionDetection()
  {
    setupTextfields();
    createGameObjects();
    setupEventListeners();
  }
  public function setupTextfields():void
  {
    //Set the text format object
    format.font = "Helvetica";
    format.size = 32;
    format.color = 0xFF0000;
    format.align = TextFormatAlign.LEFT;

    //Configure the output text field
    output.defaultTextFormat = format;
    output.width = 300;
    output.height = 36;
    output.border = true;
    output.text = "";

    //Display and position the output text field
    stage.addChild(output);
```

```
    output.x = 125;
    output.y = 65;
}
public function createGameObjects():void
{
    //Add the monster to the stage
    monster.addChild(monsterNormalImage);
    stage.addChild(monster);
    monster.x = 125;
    monster.y = 150;

    //Add the character to the stage
    character.addChild(characterImage);
    stage.addChild(character);
    character.x = 300;
    character.y = 150;
}
public function setupEventListeners():void
{
    stage.addEventListener
      (KeyboardEvent.KEY_DOWN, keyDownHandler);
    stage.addEventListener
      (KeyboardEvent.KEY_UP, keyUpHandler);
    stage.addEventListener
      (Event.ENTER_FRAME, enterFrameHandler);
}
public function keyDownHandler(event:KeyboardEvent):void
{
    if (event.keyCode == Keyboard.LEFT)
    {
      vx = -5;
    }
    else if (event.keyCode == Keyboard.RIGHT)
    {
      vx = 5;
    }
    else if (event.keyCode == Keyboard.UP)
    {
      vy = -5;
    }
    else if (event.keyCode == Keyboard.DOWN)
    {
      vy = 5;
    }
}
public function keyUpHandler(event:KeyboardEvent):void
{
    if (event.keyCode == Keyboard.LEFT
      || event.keyCode == Keyboard.RIGHT)
    {
      vx = 0;
    }
```

```
    else if (event.keyCode == Keyboard.DOWN
      || event.keyCode == Keyboard.UP)
    {
      vy = 0;
    }
  }
  public function enterFrameHandler(event:Event):void
  {
    //Move the player
    character.x += vx;
    character.y += vy;

    //Collision detection
    if (character.hitTestObject(monster))
    {
      output.text = "Hey!!!";
    }
    else
    {
      output.text = "No collision...";
    }
  }
 }
}
```

Let's find out how `hitTestObject` works.

Using hitTestObject

The `hitTestObject` method can be used to check whether any two objects have bumped into one another. Let's say that you have a Sprite object called `car` that the player can control. You also have a Sprite object called `wall`. In your game, if the player's car hits the wall, it should crash.

In plain English, you would want to write some computer code that looks something like this:

```
if (the car hits the wall)
{
  the car must crash;
}
```

Here's what this might look like in AS3.0 code:

```
if(car.hitTestObject(wall))
{
  car.crash();
}
```

The `hitTestObject` method is attached to the `car` object with dot notation. It has an argument, `(wall)`, which contains the name of the object that you want to check for a collision. Figure 6-2 shows how this all fits together.

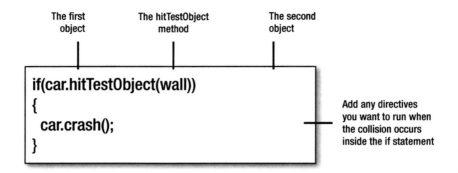

Figure 6-2. Use the hitTestObject method inside a conditional statement to check for a collision between two objects.

Usually you use the `hitTestObject` method inside the conditional statement of an if statement. If the objects are touching, the method returns a Boolean value of `true`, and the directives inside the if statement run. If it returns a value of `false` (if the objects are not touching), the directives inside the if statement don't run.

Here's the section of code in the BasicCollisionDetection program that changes the text display in the output field:

```
public function enterFrameHandler(event:Event):void
{
  //Move the player
  character.x += vx;
  character.y += vy;

  //Collision detection
  if (character.hitTestObject(monster))
  {
    output.text = "Hey!!!";
  }
  else
  {
    output.text = "No collision...";
  }
}
```

It very simply checks to see if the two objects are touching. If they are, "Hey!!!" is displayed in the `output` text field. If they aren't, the words "No collision..." are displayed.

Very importantly, notice that this `hitTestObject` if statement occurs inside the `enterFrameHandler`. That means that the program is checking for a collision 60 times per second. That's why the display changes instantly when the cat and the monster touch. And it instantly changes back again when they aren't touching. `hitTestObject` is almost always used inside the `enterFrameHandler`.

Isn't amazing what a powerful effect just a few lines of code produces? And it gets even better!

Triggering a change of state

You can put any directives you like inside the if statement that checks for a collision. In this next example, the appearance of the monster changes when the collision occurs. Let's take a look at the effect and then I'll explain how it works.

Open the StateChange project that you'll find in the chapter's source files. Compile the project and watch what happens when the objects collide: the monster opens its mouth. Figure 6-3 shows what you'll see.

Figure 6-3. The monster opens its mouth when the cat bumps into it.

Here's the program listing that makes this work. Notice that there are two different monster images that are being added to a single Sprite. Does that ring a bell? It should! (Hint: think buttons from Chapter 3!)

```
package
{
  import flash.display.Sprite;
  import flash.display.DisplayObject;
  import flash.events.KeyboardEvent;
  import flash.ui.Keyboard;
  import flash.events.Event;

  [SWF(width="550", height="400",
    backgroundColor="#FFFFFF", frameRate="60")]

  public class StateChange extends Sprite
  {
    //Embed the character image
    [Embed(source="../images/character.png")]
    public var CharacterImage:Class;
    public var characterImage:DisplayObject = new CharacterImage();
    public var character:Sprite = new Sprite();

    //Embed the monster images
    [Embed(source="../images/monsterNormal.png")]
    public var MonsterNormalImage:Class;
    public var monsterNormalImage:DisplayObject
      = new MonsterNormalImage();
    [Embed(source="../images/monsterScared.png")]
    public var MonsterScaredImage:Class;
    public var monsterScaredImage:DisplayObject
```

```
  = new MonsterScaredImage();
public var monster:Sprite = new Sprite();

//Create and initialize the vx and vy variable
public var vx:int = 0;
public var vy:int = 0;

public function StateChange()
{
  createGameObjects();
  setupEventListeners();
}
public function createGameObjects():void
{
  //Compose the monster and add it to the stage
  monster.addChild(monsterNormalImage);
  monster.addChild(monsterScaredImage);
  monsterScaredImage.visible = false;
  stage.addChild(monster);
  monster.x = 125;
  monster.y = 150;

  //Add the character to the stage
  character.addChild(characterImage);
  stage.addChild(character);
  character.x = 300;
  character.y = 150;
}
public function setupEventListeners():void
{
  stage.addEventListener
    (KeyboardEvent.KEY_DOWN, keyDownHandler);
  stage.addEventListener
    (KeyboardEvent.KEY_UP, keyUpHandler);
  stage.addEventListener
    (Event.ENTER_FRAME, enterFrameHandler);
}
public function keyDownHandler(event:KeyboardEvent):void
{
  if (event.keyCode == Keyboard.LEFT)
  {
    vx = -5;
  }
  else if (event.keyCode == Keyboard.RIGHT)
  {
    vx = 5;
  }
  else if (event.keyCode == Keyboard.UP)
  {
    vy = -5;
  }
  else if (event.keyCode == Keyboard.DOWN)
```

```
    {
      vy = 5;
    }
  }
  public function keyUpHandler(event:KeyboardEvent):void
  {
    if (event.keyCode == Keyboard.LEFT
      || event.keyCode == Keyboard.RIGHT)
    {
      vx = 0;
    }
    else if (event.keyCode == Keyboard.DOWN
      || event.keyCode == Keyboard.UP)
    {
      vy = 0;
    }
  }
  public function enterFrameHandler(event:Event):void
  {
    //Move the player
    character.x += vx;
    character.y += vy;

    //Collision detection
    if (character.hitTestObject(monster))
    {
      monsterScaredImage.visible = true;
      monsterNormalImage.visible = false;
    }
    else
    {
      monsterScaredImage.visible = false;
      monsterNormalImage.visible = true;
    }
  }
  }
}
```

The first thing that you'll notice is that two different monster images are embedded into the program: monsterNormal.png and monsterScared.png. Figure 6-4 shows what these look like. They're exactly the same size—the only diffenence between them is the monster's mouth.

monsterNormal.png   monsterScared.png

Figure 6-4. The monster's two different states

Here's the code that embeds these images and creates the monster Sprite.

```
[Embed(source="../images/monsterNormal.png")]
public var MonsterNormalImage:Class;
public var monsterNormalImage:DisplayObject
  = new MonsterNormalImage();

[Embed(source="../images/monsterScared.png")]
public var MonsterScaredImage:Class;
public var monsterScaredImage:DisplayObject
  = new MonsterScaredImage();

public var monster:Sprite = new Sprite();
```

Notice also that, even though there are two images being created, there's only one monster Sprite. The key to this system is that *both images are added to that single Sprite*. However, only the monsterNormal image is visible when the program first starts. Here's the code that composes the monster Sprite from the two images:

```
monster.addChild(monsterNormalImage);
monster.addChild(monsterScaredImage);
monsterScaredImage.visible = false;
stage.addChild(monster);
```

The monsterScared image has its visible property set to `false` so that it's hidden. This is exactly the same technique you used to create different button states in Chapter 3. The monster Sprite contains the two different images that are perfectly aligned on top of each other, like stacked playing cards. But only one of these images will be visible at any one time. By selectively displaying one image or the other, you can make the monster change its appearance.

Any condition in the game that you choose can make the monster's appearance change. In this example, it happens when the two characters collide. Here's the if statement, using `hitTestObject`, that makes this happen:

```
if (character.hitTestObject(monster))
```

```
{
  monsterScaredImage.visible = true;
  monsterNormalImage.visible = false;
}
else
{
  monsterScaredImage.visible = false;
  monsterNormalImage.visible = true;
}
```

The if statement hides one image or the other depending on whether or not the cat and monster are touching. It's an extremely simple but extremely useful effect.

You can use this same technique to make game objects with very complex states. Imagine that you have an object that contains 10 or 20 different images. You could selectively display these images depending on how events in your game are changing. This is the foundation for creating games with great complexity, and it's all based on this simple technique.

Reducing a health meter

Many games use a **health meter** to determine when the game is over. When the game characters bump into bad things like monsters, the health meter gradually shrinks in size. When the health meter disappears, the game ends.

Implementing a health meter is very easy to do. It makes clever use of the width property. You'll find an example of a health meter in action in the HealthMeter project folder in the chapter's source files. Compile the program and you'll see the effect shown in Figure 6-5. When the game characters collide, the health meter decreases. When it's completely down to zero, "Game over" is displayed as a trace message.

Figure 6-5. Reduce a health meter when the objects collide.

The health meter is composed of two separate images: meterInside.png and meterOutside.png. They're both the same size and width (200 by 28 pixels). Figure 6-6 shows what they look like.

meterInside.png   meterOutside.png

Figure 6-6. The two images that make up the health meter

Very importantly, the meterOutside PNG image is transparent on the inside. It's just a black frame. That means that whatever is behind it will show through.

The two images are combined together into one Sprite. This is the same concept you used to create the monster object with two states in the previous example. The only difference this time is that both images, the inside and outside components, are visible at the same time.

The code for most of this program is almost identical to the code for the previous two examples, so let's take a look at the differences. First, both images are embedded into the program.

```
[Embed(source="../images/meterInside.png")]
public var MeterInsideImage:Class;
public var meterInsideImage:DisplayObject
  = new MeterInsideImage();

[Embed(source="../images/meterOutside.png")]
public var MeterOutsideImage:Class;
public var meterOutsideImage:DisplayObject
  = new MeterOutsideImage();

public var meter:Sprite = new Sprite();
```

A single Sprite object, called meter, is going to be used to compose them together. This happens when the program initializes in the createGameObjects method.

```
meter.addChild(meterInsideImage);
meter.addChild(meterOutsideImage);
stage.addChild(meter);
meter.x = 125;
meter.y = 65;
```

The outside image is added after the inside image so that it will sit overtop of it, neatly framing it.

The enterFrameHandler contains the collision code and displays the "Game over" message.

```
public function enterFrameHandler(event:Event):void
{
  //Move the player
  character.x += vx;
  character.y += vy;

  //Collision detection
  if (character.hitTestObject(monster))
  {
    if(meterInsideImage.width > 0)
    {
```

```
        meterInsideImage.width--;
    }
  }
  if(meterInsideImage.width < 1)
  {
    trace("Game over");
  }
}
```

The first if statement checks for a collision. If it finds one, it reduces the meter's width by 1 pixel every frame. But it also does one additional check. It only reduces the width of the meter if the width is greater than zero. That prevents the width from ever becoming negative, which would happen without this extra check.

```
if (character.hitTestObject(monster))
{
  if(meterInsideImage.width > 0)
  {
    meterInsideImage.width--;
  }
}
```

Preventing the meter's width from becoming negative is really not necessary in this simple example. But in a complex game program where you might have other code that's dependent on the value of the meter's width, your game could develop bugs if it wasn't expecting negative values.

This is the first time you've seen an if statement being used inside another if statement. It's called a **nested if statement** and is a very common programming structure. Nested if statements allow you to fine-tune the logic a bit to check for other conditions after the first condition has passed as true. (It's called a nested if statement because it's cozily tucked inside the first one, like an egg in a nest. If you turn this page on its side, I'm sure you can imagine a crow or magpie making a perfectly comfortable nest in the indentation created by the second if statement.)

The enterFrameHandler also displays a "Game over" trace message if it finds that the meter's width is less than 1 pixel.

```
if(meterInsideImage.width < 1)
{
  trace("Game over");
}
```

In a proper game, you could instead display "Game over" in a text field. Or you could display a whole Game Over image over the stage and a button that lets the player play again.

Using scaleX to scale the meter based on a percentage

You can also use the scaleX property to change the meter's size. scaleX changes the size of an object based on its ratio. It lets you change the width of the meter based on a percentage instead of a fixed pixel amount.

This is often preferable because it means the meter is reduced at the same rate, no matter how long or short it is.

A scaleX value of 1 means the object is full size. You can reduce a meter by 1% by subtracting 0.01 from the scaleX property each frame.

Here's the code to use if you want to duplicate the health meter example using scaleX:

```
if (character.hitTestObject(monster))
{
  if(meterInsideImage.scaleX > 0)
  {
    meterInsideImage.scaleX -= 0.02;
  }
}
if(meterInsideImage.scaleX <= 0)
{
  trace("Game over");
}
```

A value of 0.02 reduces the meter by 2% each frame, so the meter will reach 0 in 50 frames.

Scaling by percentages is very useful because you can use meters to graph other data that might be using percentages in your game.

Updating a score

Most games keep track of whether a player has won or lost by updating a score based on how well the player is performing. The following example shows you how to update a score and end the game when a certain score has been reached. Open the UpdateScore project folder in the chapter's source files and try it out. Each time the cat bumps into the monster, the score is increased by 1. When the score reaches 5, a "Game over" trace message is displayed. Figure 6-7 shows what you'll see.

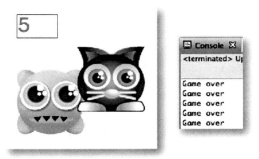

Figure 6-7. Use collision detection to increase a score.

There's a problem that this code has to solve. Remember that the collision detection code is running inside the enterFrameHandler. The enterFrameHandler is updated 60 times per second. If a collision occurs, all the collision code will also be triggered 60 times per second. And if that code has the job of updating the score when a collision occurs, the score will be updated 60 times per second until the objects are no longer touching.

What does that mean? If the collision code updates the score by 1 each frame, over 3 seconds the score will race up to 180. You could see this effect happening in the previous example where the health meter was decreased continuously each frame while the objects touched.

That's not the way the score should be updated. It should only be updated once, the first time the objects touch, and not again, even if they remain touching. You have to find a way of detecting the very first collision and then preventing it from registering a second time—until the objects separate.

You can do this with a Boolean variable that switches the collision detection on and off depending on the conditions I've just described. Here's the important code that makes this work. First, you need to create two new variables in the class definition.

```
public var score:uint = 0;
public var collisionHasOccurred:Boolean = false;
```

score is a number that tracks how many times the two objects collide. It's set to zero when the game starts. collisionHasOccurred has the job of tracking whether or not there's been a collision. It's set to false when the program starts. If there ever is a collision, it's going to be set to true to prevent a second collision being detected. This variable is extremely important for the scoring system to work properly, and you'll see why next.

The enterFrameHandler has the job of moving the character, checking for a collision, updating the score, and checking for the end of the game. Here's all the code from the enterFrameHandler:

```
public function enterFrameHandler(event:Event):void
{
  //Move the player
  character.x += vx;
  character.y += vy;

  //Collision detection
  if (character.hitTestObject(monster))
  {
    if(! collisionHasOccurred)
    {
      score++;
      output.text = String(score);
      collisionHasOccurred = true;
    }
  }
  else
  {
    collisionHasOccurred = false;
  }

  //Check for the end of the game
  if(score == 5)
```

```
    {
      trace("Game over");
    }
}
```

Let's break this down and see what's happening, and why. First, the code checks for a collision between the character and the monster.

```
if (character.hitTestObject(monster))
{...
```

If there is a collision, the next if statement checks to see if the collision between the objects *hasn't* *occurred*. That's right, you didn't misread the previous sentence; you want to check to see whether the collision *has not* already happened. That's what this line is doing:

```
if(!collisionHasOccurred)
{...
```

It checks to see if the `collisionHasOccurred` variable is `false`. Usually, conditional statements check to see whether certain conditions or variables are true, but not this time. Instead, you used the not operator to check for a `false` condition. The not operator is an exclamation mark (!). When it's used in a conditional statement in front of a Boolean variable, it allows the directives inside the if statement to run as if the Boolean value were `false`.

So, is it `false`? You initialized `collisionHasOccurred` to `false` when the program started, so the first time the collision occurs, it is `false`, and all the directives inside the if statement will run.

```
score++;
output.text = String(score);
collisionHasOccurred = true;
```

This updates the score and the dynamic text field, but it also does something very important: it sets the `collisionHasOccurred` variable to `true`.

Why is that so important? Remember, all this code is running inside the `enterFrameHandler`. That means exactly 1/60th of a second later, this same if statement will be called upon a *second time* if the objects are still touching.

```
if(!collisionHasOccurred)
{
  score++;
  output.text = String(score);
  collisionHasOccurred = true;
}
```

You don't want this code to run a second time because you only want to update the score the first time the objects touch. Fortunately the `collisionHasOccurred` variable was set to `true` the first time this code ran, so it will prevent it from running a second time. That means none of the directives run, and the score and the text field are only updated once.

Perfect—just what you wanted!

But there's another problem. You want the score to update *again* if the objects separate and happen to collide again some at future point in the game. This won't happen if `collisionHasOccurred` is still set to `true`. You have to find some way to reset it back to `false` so you can update the score for a future collision.

This is very simple; you just need to set `collisionHasOccurred` to `false` when the objects are *not colliding*. The second part of the if/else statement takes care of that, which the following code in bold shows:

```
if (character.hitTestObject(monster))
{
  if(! collisionHasOccurred)
  {
    score++;
    output.text = String(score);
    collisionHasOccurred = true;
  }
}
else
{
  collisionHasOccurred = false;
}
```

Yes, I know what you're thinking. If you're new to programming, this logic can seem a little on the mind-bending side! This is the most complex use of logical operators and if statements you've seen so far. Don't feel too discouraged if you don't understand it right away or don't think you'll be able to write similarly complex code yourself any time soon. Look it over a few times, think about it while lying in bed at night, come back to it in a few days, and try it with some of your own games. It will gradually start to make sense—trust me! Seeing how others have solved problems and then trying out those solutions in your own games is an extremely important part of learning how to program. To help you out, Figure 6-8 illustrates what's happening.

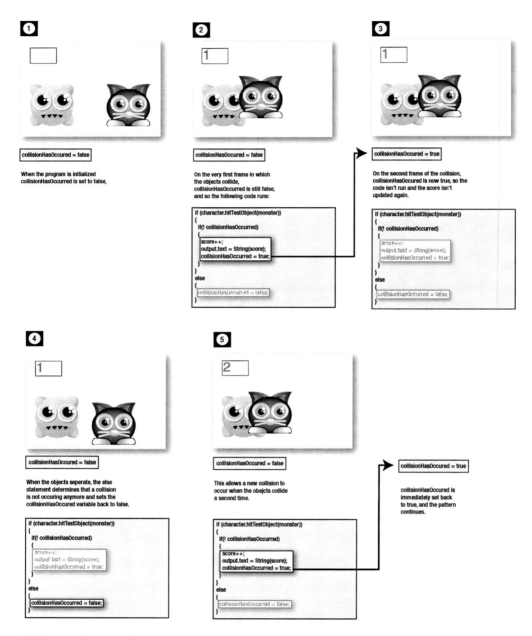

Figure 6-8. Prevent the score from updating more than once per collision.

This bit of code also demonstrates another example of casting. You'll recall that casting is the system of converting one variable type into another.

The `score` variable was declared as a uint number type.

```
public var score:uint = 0;
```

You need the `score` variable to be a number so that you can update it by adding 1 each time there's a collision, like this:

```
score++;
```

So score could be 1, 5, 14, or any number, depending on how many times the objects have collided. A problem arises when you need to display this number in a text field. TextField objects can only display information in the form of Strings (letters or words). That means you need to convert the value of the score variable in to a string of characters that the text field can display. That's where casting comes in. Your code can force the `score` variable to be read as a String like this:

```
String(score)
```

The value of `score` can now be readily displayed in the output text field, like this:

```
output.text = String(score);
```

Checking for the end of the game

The score variable is also used for figuring out when the game ends. A very simple if statement inside the `enterFrameHandler` displays a trace message when the `score` reaches 5.

```
if(score == 5)
{
  trace("Game over");
}
```

But there's a problem with this system that you'll quickly notice. The program continues to add 1 to the score and display the "Game over" message well after the score reaches 5, as you can see in Figure 6-9. To work properly, the program should stop counting collisions when the score reaches 5 and the "Game over" message should only be displayed once.

Figure 6-9. The program should stop counting collisions when the sore reaches 5, but it doesn't.

You can easily fix this by applying some simple logic.

Only check for a collision if the score is less than 5.

You know how to do this! It's just a matter of surrounding the collision code with one more if statement, like this:

```
if(score < 5)
{
  if (character.hitTestObject(monster))
  {
    if(! collisionHasOccurred)
    {
      score++;
      output.text = String(score);
      collisionHasOccurred = true;
    }
  }
  else
  {
    collisionHasOccurred = false;
  }

  //Check for the end of the game
  if(score == 5)
  {
    trace("Game over");
  }
}
```

Compile the program again with this new code, and you'll notice that the score now stops being counted at 5 and the "Game over" message is displayed only once. Figure 6-10 illustrates this.

Figure 6-10. One more simple if statement stops the game when the score reaches 5.

You'll find that many Potentially Puzzling Programming Problems you'll need to solve in your games can be solved by applying very simple logic like this.

Picking up and dropping objects

It's time for the cat and monster to put aside their differences and make peace! In the next example, you'll see how you can make the cat pick up an object and carry it to the monster. This is very easy to implement using the techniques discussed so far in this chapter.

You'll find a working example of this effect in the in PickingUpObjects folder in the chapter's source files. Move the cat character over the star. Press the space bar. The cat will pick up the star. Carry the star over to the monster and press the space bar again. The cat will drop the star and "Thanks!!" will be displayed as a trace message. Figure 6-11 illustrates this process.

1. Move to the star.

2. Press the space key to pick it up.

3. Carry it to the monster.

1. Press the space key again to drop it.

Figure 6-11. Pick up the star and carry it to the monster.

The program uses a Boolean variable called `characterHasStar` to determine whether or not the cat is carrying the star. It's initialized to `false` when it's created in the class definition.

```
public var characterHasStar:Boolean = false;
```

You might be forgiven for thinking that the `enterFrameHandler` is now the star of the show as far as making fun things happen in your games. After all, most of the new techniques shown in the last 40-odd pages involved placing directives inside it. But don't forget that you have a few other just-as-useful-if-somewhat-neglected methods waiting to do your bidding if you can find some work for them. This time, the `keyDownHandler` gets to shine in the spotlight. The text in bold below highlights the code in the `keyDownHandler` that makes this program work.

```
public function keyDownHandler(event:KeyboardEvent):void
{
  if (event.keyCode == Keyboard.LEFT)
  {
    vx = -5;
  }
  else if (event.keyCode == Keyboard.RIGHT)
  {
    vx = 5;
  }
  else if (event.keyCode == Keyboard.UP)
  {
    vy = -5;
  }
```

```
else if (event.keyCode == Keyboard.DOWN)
{
  vy = 5;
}

if (event.keyCode == Keyboard.SPACE
  && character.hitTestObject(star))
{
  if (!characterHasStar)
  {
    character.addChild(star);
    star.x = 0;
    star.y = 0;
    characterHasStar = true;
  }
  else
  {
    stage.addChild(star);
    star.x = character.x;
    star.y = character.y;
    characterHasStar = false;
    if (monster.hitTestObject(star))
    {
      trace("Thanks!!");
    }
  }
}
}
```

To understand how this works, think about what conditions need to be met before the player character can either pick up or drop the star.

- The player of the game needs to press the space key. You can check for this condition with a conditional statement that looks like this:

```
if(event.keyCode == Keyboard.SPACE)
```

- The character object needs to be touching the star. You can check for this condition using a conditional statement that looks like this:

```
if(character.hitTestObject(star))
```

If those two things happen at the same time, you know that the player is either trying to pick up or drop the star. But the important thing is that *both conditions need to be true at exactly the same time*. Why? Well, obviously it wouldn't make sense if the cat could pick up the star if it weren't touching it. And the game also needs to know that the player *wants* to pick up the object, which is what pressing the space key tells it.

To check whether two conditions are true at the same time, you can combine them into a single conditional statement using the **and operator**. You looked at the and operator briefly in Chapter 3, but you haven't really seen it in action until now. The and operator is a double ampersand (&&).

It's used in the first new if statement in this line of code:

```
if (event.keyCode == Keyboard.SPACE
&& character.hitTestObject(star))
{...
```

Great! In one line of code, you can check whether both the conditions for picking up or dropping objects have been met. But which one is it? Picking up or dropping?

That's pretty easy to figure out. If those two conditions are true, and the cat doesn't already have the star, you know that the star needs to be picked up. If the cat already has the star, you know the star should be dropped. All it requires is an additional nested if/else statement that checks whether the characterHasStar variable is false. Here's a simplified version of this logic:

```
if (the character doesn't have the star)
{
  Pick the star up...
}
else
{
  Drop the star...
}
```

Keep this in mind because this is what the actual code looks like:

```
if (!characterHasStar)
{
  character.addChild(star);
  star.x = 0;
  star.y = 0;
  characterHasStar = true;
}
else
{
  stage.addChild(star);
  star.x = character.x;
  star.y = character.y;
  characterHasStar = false;
  if (monster.hitTestObject(star))
  {
    trace("Thanks!!");
  }
}
```

Is this making a little more sense now? Figure 6-12 illustrates how the all this logic translates into code.

```
if (event.keyCode == Keyboard.SPACE
&& character.hitTestObject(star))
{
    if (!characterHasStar)
    {
        character.addChild(star);
        star.x = 0;
        star.y = 0;
        characterHasStar = true;
    }
    else
    {
        stage.addChild(star);
        star.x = character.x;
        star.y = character.y;
        characterHasStar = false;
        if (monster.hitTestObject(star))
        {
            trace("Thanks!!");
        }
    }
}
```

If the space key is pressed
and the character is touching
the star, check for these things:

If the character doesn't have the star:

Pick the star up.

If the character already has the star:

Drop it at the character's current location.

If the star is dropped and touches the monster:

Display a trace message saying "Thanks!!"

Figure 6-12. The code that picks up and drops the star

But how is the code actually picking up and dropping the object? First, let's look at the directives that pick up the star.

```
character.addChild(star);
star.x = 0;
star.y = 0;
characterHasStar = true;
```

The code uses the addChild method to make the star a **child object** of the character.

```
character.addChild(star);
```

This is the same technique you used to add multiple images to a single Sprite. In this case, you're adding the star Sprite to the character Sprite. This essentially glues the star to the character. So, like a baby duckling, wherever the cat goes, the star is sure to follow.

The code then sets the x and y position of the star to 0.

```
star.x = 0;
star.y = 0;
```

Because the star has just become a child of the character, it now uses the character Sprite's internal coordinate system, not the stage's. An x and y position of 0 means that it's positioned at the character's top left corner, inside the character Sprite. Figure 6-13 illustrates this.

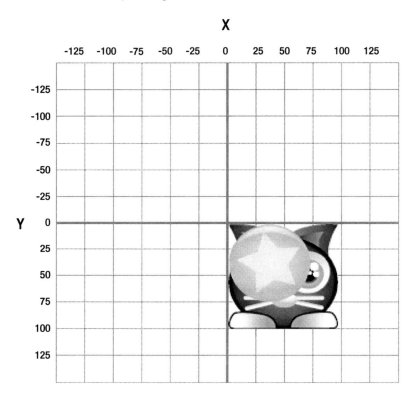

**The Sprite's internal,
local coordinates**

Figure 6-13. When the star becomes a child of the character, it becomes part of the character's local coordinate system.

Any x and y positions you now give the star will refer to these coordinates *inside* the character Sprite.

The last thing is to set the `characterHasStar` variable to `true`, which prevents the program from trying to pick the star up again if the character already has it.

```
characterHasStar = true;
```

The directives that drop the star are just as straightforward.

```
stage.addChild(star);
star.x = character.x;
star.y = character.y;
characterHasStar = false;
if (monster.hitTestObject(star))
{
   trace("Thanks!!");
}
```

The code first uses the addChild method to make the star a child of the stage again. This frees it from bondage to the cat.

```
stage.addChild(star);
```

The star is now part of the stage's coordinate system again, not the character Sprite's.

The stage object is the parent of *all* objects on the stage, including the character and monster. Objects that are children of the stage are at the top of the food chain and are footloose and fancy free. The star now no longer has to mindlessly follow the character around and can get into any of its own trouble that it wants to.

The next thing the code does is give the star the same x and y positions as the character.

```
star.x = character.x;
star.y = character.y;
```

This fixes it on the stage at its current position, which makes it look like it's being dropped.

The characterHasStar variable is set to false, which allows the character to pick the star up again later.

```
characterHasStar = false;
```

The last thing the code does is actually a bit of a bonus. It adds this if statement:

```
if (monster.hitTestObject(star))
{
   trace("Thanks!!");
}
```

It checks to see whether the monster is touching the star. If it is, "Thanks!!" is displayed as a trace message. Awww . . . friends at last! (You can find the complete code for this example in the PickingUpObjects folder in the chapter's source files.)

The bad news about hitTestObject

First, let me just say that I *love* the hitTestObject method! You can see from these examples what incredible power it can give you with just a few lines of code, a little imagination, and a bit of simple logic. I'm sure your head must be swimming with ideas for games already. If you have any doubts, let me just confirm to you right now: yes, you already have all the skills you need to start making them! I won't stop you. Go ahead; take a break from this chapter and start building them if you feel inspired. A whole universe of possibilities exists!

But before you do go much further into this book, let's take a closer look at just what makes `hitTestObject` tick. This must be said, dear reader: `hitTestObject` holds a deep, dark secret that will cripple your games if you don't understand it.

Detecting collisions with the bounding box

How does AS3.0 actually know that two objects are touching? All display objects (objects you can see on the stage) are surrounded by imaginary rectangular boxes called bounding boxes. The **bounding box** defines the area of the object that `hitTestObject` checks for a collision. The bounding box is invisible, but it's there. Figure 6-14 shows you the bounding boxes of the objects from the previous example

Figure 6-14. Bounding boxes define the areas of an object that are sensitive to a collision.

A collision is detected whenever any portion of the bounding box intersects with any portion of another object's bounding box. Figure 6-15 shows some examples.

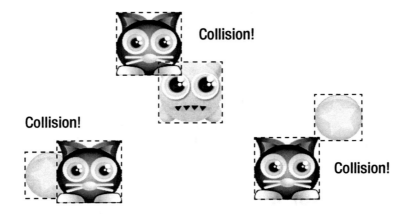

Figure 6-15. Collisions are detected when bounding boxes touch or intersect.

This is all fine if the objects are square-ish or rectangular, but what if they're not? Have a good look at Figure 6-15: one of these collisions is not like the others! The bounding boxes of the third collisions overlap, even though the actual objects themselves don't touch. You can see this clearly in Figure 6-16.

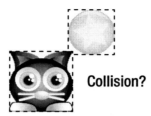

Figure 6-16. The bounding boxes determine a collision even if the images that represent the shape of the object aren't touching.

To be fair, this is not a problem with `hitTestObject`; its job is to check for collisions between the bounding boxes of two objects. That's just what it does. If it's not working for you, you need to decide whether you want to modify the structure of your game and objects so that it starts working or find another way of doing collision detection.

There are many other ways to do collision detection without using `hitTestObject`, but let's look at some of the advantages it has over more complex methods and how you can make it work in your games.

There are two great things about `hitTestObject` that make it the favored first choice for doing collision detection: it is easy to understand, easy to implement, and puts very little strain on the CPU or Flash Player. In game design, in which performance considerations can dictate many design decisions, this last reason alone is enough to spur you on to see how much mileage you can wring out of the humble `hitTestObject`.

So, can you use `hitTestObject` and still make it work reasonably well for irregularly shaped objects?

Let's take a look at a few solutions.

Learning to live with it

The first solution, which is not really a solution at all, is to design your game according to the constraints that `hitTestObject` imposes on you. Limitations can be an enormous strength in the same way that writing poetry according to the rules of a sonnet can be a strength. They can help you focus and streamline your design—just ask Shakespeare!

If you know that `hitTestObject` works best with square or rectangular objects, design your objects accordingly.

Have a look at the cat and monster game characters that are used in the examples in this chapter. They're both square shaped, but you wouldn't know that unless you actually saw a square outline traced around them. They've been designed so that most of the edges and corners meet the edges of the grid square in which they were designed. This means that there are very few places in which the shape of the character doesn't fill the bounding box, so the shapes of the objects almost always overlap when a collision occurs.

However, what do you do in the situation shown in Figure 6-16 where the corner of a square-ish object intersects the corner of a round-ish object? There are a few spots on both of these objects where a collision will be detected even if the visible shapes don't overlap.

Isn't this the fatal Achilles heel in the whole system? Not if the objects are moving fast enough, and in most games they will be. The empty gap between the edge of the round star isn't more than about 5 pixels at its maximum. Remember that the character object in these examples is moving at the rate of 5 pixels every 1/60th of a second. That's really fast. It's so fast, and the gap is so small, that no one playing the game will ever notice that the collision isn't accurate.

Of course, if the objects are moving slower, you'll have a problem. But the point of this section is this: design your game so that it's *not* a problem. Make your objects short and stout, and make them move reasonably quickly. If you can do that, `hitTestObject` will be all you'll ever need.

Have a look at some of your favorite 2D games. Isn't it funny that all the characters and objects seem to be sort of plump and square-ish? They're dealing with exactly the same constraints you're dealing with here. Welcome to the video game designer's club!

Creating subobjects

The simplest way to improve collision detection using `hitTestObject` is to create subobjects inside the main object and use them to check for a collision.

Let's stick with the problem of collision between the square-ish cat and the round star. You could greatly improve the collision detection between them if you created a smaller rectangular object *inside* the cat Sprite that defined the collision area. You could give this subobject the instance name `collisionArea`.

If you used it with `hitTestObject` in an if statement, it might look something like this:

```
if(collisionArea.hitTestObject(star))
{
  //Collision directives...
}
```

Of course, you'll have to set the visible property of the `collisionArea` subobject to `false` so it will be completely transparent. You don't want to see it; you just want to use its shape inside the main object to define the collision area.

You'll find a working example of just such a system in the SubObjects project folder in the chapter's source files. Figure 6-17 shows what you'll see when you run the SWF file. In the center of the cat is a small white square. It follows the cat everywhere it goes on the stage. When the image of the cat touches the star, there's no collision. But if the white square touches the star, a collision is registered. The white square is a child object of the cat and is the collision area that's used to determine whether a collision has occurred.

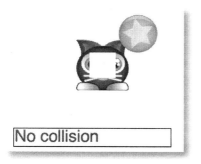

Figure 6-17. Use a subobject to create a collision area inside the main object.

You could make a PNG image file of a square, embed it into your program, and use addChild to make it a subobject of your character. That would work, and it's the same principle you used when you made the star a child object of the character in the previous example. However, for making simple shapes, AS3.0 has a better way. AS3.0 has built-in class called Shape that lets you draw basic shapes on the stage. This example uses the Shape class to draw a square using AS3.0 code and then adds that square to the character as a subobject. The collision detection code then checks for a collision between the square and the star, not the character and the star.

Here's how the code in the SubObjects example program works. First, it imports the Shape class.

```
import flash.display.Shape;
```

The code then creates a Shape object called square in the class definition.

```
public var square:Shape = new Shape();
```

The createGameObjects method has the job of drawing the white 50 by 50 pixel square and adding it to the character Sprite.

```
square.graphics.beginFill(0xFFFFFF);
square.graphics.drawRect(0, 0, 50, 50);
square.graphics.endFill();
character.addChild(square);
square.x = 25;
square.y = 25;
```

It also centers the square inside the character Sprite by giving it an x and y position of 25.

The job of drawing the square is done by AS3.0's graphics package, which can be used by any Shape or Sprite objects. The code first uses the `beginFill` method to choose a color for the square.
```
square.graphics.beginFill(0xFFFFFF);
```
You can use any hexadecimal color code in its parentheses. 0xFFFFFF is the hex code for white.

The next bit of code uses the `drawRect` method to draw the square.

```
square.graphics.drawRect(0, 0, 50, 50);
```
The first two arguments, 0 and 0, determine by how much the shape should be offset from the top left corner. You don't want any offset, so these are set to 0. The second two numbers, 50 and 50, are the width and height of the square, in pixels. This is exactly half the size of the character object, which is 100 x 100 pixels. You can use the `drawRect` method to draw any sized rectangle.

The last bit of drawing code uses the `endFill` method.

```
square.graphics.endFill();
```
It basically means, "We're done now, so stop filling the shape with color."

These three lines of code have drawn a white 50 by 50 pixel square. The next bit of code adds the square to the character Sprite and offsets its position inside the character by 25 pixels from the top left corner. That neatly centers it.

```
character.addChild(square);
square.x = 25;
square.y = 25;
```
You can see the effect of this code in Figure 6-18. Charming!

Figure 6-18. Draw a square and center it inside the character object.

> *This has been a quick introduction to AS3.0's drawing package, which allows you to draw all sorts of simple shapes with AS3.0 code. You won't be using it again in this book, but it's covered in detail in* Advanced Game Design with Flash. *You'll also find very detailed information on how to use it in Adobe's AS3.0 documentation at* `http://help.adobe.com/en_US/FlashPlatform/reference/actionscript/3/fla sh/display/Graphics.html`.

To make the white square invisible so that it's not blocking the character's face, just add this line to the last bit of code:

```
square.visible = false;
```

Now that the character is carrying around this square subobject, you can use it in the enterFrameHandler to check it for a collision with the star. The code is very straightforward.

```
if (square.hitTestObject(star))
{
    output.text = "Collision!"
}
else
{
    output.text = "No collision"
}
```

Of course, this collision detection still isn't perfect. It will avoid the problem of a collision being detected when the cat's ear intersects with the empty corner of the star's bounding box. But it's still not precise collision detection between the image of the character and the star. Is that important? In all likelihood, it won't be.

Take a good look at the collision detection going on in some of your favorite 2D games, and you'll notice that you can often touch an enemy just slightly and get away with it without a collision being registered. I can't count the number of times I've been saved by this fuzzy collision detection when jumping over barrels in *Donkey Kong* or evading Koopa shells in *Super Mario Bros.,* and it never seemed like there was something wrong with the game.

This boils down to very carefully thinking about the collision detection in your game and deciding which kinds of collisions are important and which aren't. Let's have another look at the cat and star problem. Would it really make sense to have the cat pick the star up if its ears were touching the empty corner of its bounding box? It definitely wouldn't, and if it did happen it would certainly look wrong. Is it okay for the star to overlap with the cat's body a bit and not register a collision? Probably—because as soon as the cat touches the star with the part of its body that includes its paws, the collision will occur. This would make sense to the player. The slight overlap would be accounted for as the shallow depth (or maybe the cat's fur), and the player wouldn't notice there was anything wrong with it.

However, if you tested this and discovered that it actually did look really awkward, you could start adding more rectangular subobjects in areas of the cat to improve or fine-tune the collision accuracy. You could add as many of these additional subobjects as you need. The only drawback is that you'll have to write more code to check for these collisions. And if you have a huge number of them, they might start to slow down your game. Still, it's a good solution, and there are very few collision detection problems you won't be able to solve by doing this judiciously.

All this is an art, not a science. If you get the balance right, you'll have an amazingly comfortable and natural collision detection system. Hooray for hitTestObject!

Advanced collision detection strategies

HitTestObject is going to keep you busy for most of this book, but eventually your games will need more precise ways of detecting collisions. The following are some techniques you can look into:

- hitTestPoint. This is a related method to hitTestObject. It tests whether a single point is intersecting the shape of an object. However, it only works with vector shapes, which you can make with code using AS3.0's Shape class or draw with Flash Professional software. Here's the format for using the hitTestPoint method:

```
if(vectorShape.hitTestPoint(pointX, pointY, true))
{
  //Collision directives...
}
```

If pointX and PointY are touching the vector shape, the collision will register as true, and the collision directives will run. hitTestPoint actually tells you if the point is touching the actual shape of the object, not just its bounding box.

This seems like it could be useful, but it's almost never used for games. That's not because it doesn't work well for what it does, but it turns out that there are better, more useful, and more precise ways of checking for collisions between shapes. Most game designers thus step over it on the way to greater things. Don't discount it completely, however; you may find some innovative uses for it in some of your games. You can find out more about hitTestPoint at http://help.adobe.com/en_US/FlashPlatform/ reference/actionscript/3/flash/display/DisplayObject.html?filter_flash=cs5&fi lter_flashplayer=10.2&filter_air=2.6#hitTestPoint().

- BitmapData.hitTest. This AS3.0 method, if properly used, will lead you to the holy grail of collision detection: pixel-perfect collision between shapes. It requires an advanced understanding of AS3.0 and programming to use, but you'll have all those skills by the time you've finished this book. You'll find out everything you need to use BitmapData.hitTest for very sophisticated collision detection in *Advanced Game Design with Flash*.

- Use math. Perhaps surprisingly, the best way of figuring out whether two objects are colliding is to ditch AS3.0's built-in methods like hitTestObject completely and figure it out for yourself. Not only does this give you a lot of precision, but if you use math to work out collisions, your games will run much faster. At an advanced level, you can use **vector math** to do extremely precise collision detection between objects of all shapes and sizes (you'll find all about how to do this in *Advanced Game Design with Flash*.) However, you can use much simpler math to do very precise collision detection between rectangular shapes, which is perfect for 95% of the games you're likely to write.

So let's take a look at another way of doing collision detection that you'll find great uses for in your games.

Working with vector based collision detection

So far, the collision detection code you've looked at has told you when two objects are touching, and you've been able to use that information to change the values of variables and object properties. However, for most games you need to go one step further. You need the objects to be able to react in some physical way to the collision. For example, if a game character bumps into a box, the box should block its movement. Or, if a game character finds a rock, perhaps it should be able to push that rock around stage.

There are no features built in to AS3.0 that let you do these things. You can certainly make these things happen, but you'll have to write all the code to do it from scratch. That means learning a little easy math, and taking the time to see how the code works. Don't let this put you off—the skills you'll learn along the way will be invaluable to your developing career as a game designer, and you'll be able to directly apply all these same techniques to any other game design technologies or programming languages.

Vector based collision detection is one of the great black arts of video game design. Learn how to do it and you'll have precision control over all the collision detection and reaction in your games. You're going to use it to prevent two objects from overlapping, so that one object blocks the movement of the other.

Preventing objects from overlapping

If you want a game object, like a box, to block the movement of a game character, you have to find a way of preventing the character and box from overlapping. But you can only do this if you know by how much the objects are overlapping when they collide. `hitTestObject` won't help you with this at all because it doesn't give you any information about the amount of overlap between objects in a collision. Figure 6-19 illustrates this problem.

The box should block
the character's movement
when the two objects
touch.

The code can only do that
if it knows by how much
the objects overlap
when they first collide.

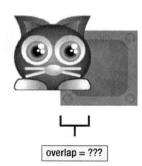

overlap = ???

Figure 6-19. You can separate objects in a collision if you know by how much they're overlapping. But how can you figure that out?

If you know the amount of overlap between the objects, then you can separate them by exactly that amount. How can you figure that out? The solution is to use **vectors**.

You can think of vectors as imaginary lines that connect objects together. By "imaginary" I mean they just exist as numbers; you can't see them on the stage. But if you draw these imaginary lines between the centers of your game objects, you can find out if the objects are touching and also by exactly how much they're overlapping. If you know by how much they overlap, you can separate them with knife-edge precision. It's all done using some simple math. Here's how it works:

First, you need to calculate a vector between the center of the first object and the center of the second object. You can describe this vector using two variables.

- vx: tells you how wide the vector is. "vx" stands for "vector along the x axis."

- vy: tells you how high the vector is. "vy" stands for "vector along the y axis."

If you have **vx** and **vy** variables that store this information, then you've created a vector that you can use in your game. Figure 6-20 shows how to use the **vx** and **vy** variables to describe the distance between two game objects.

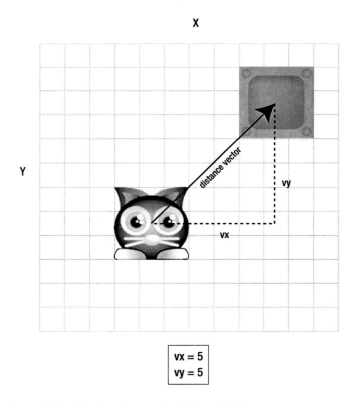

Figure 6-20. The vx and vy variables describe the vector's width and height.

The distance vector that you see in Figure 6-20 is the imaginary line I was talking about. You can't see it on the stage. It only exists because the **vx** and **vy** variables are describing its height and width.

You can easily see in Figure 6-20 that the objects are 5 units apart on the x axis and 5 units apart on the y axis. That's all the **vx** and **vy** variables are telling you. Easy stuff!

> *If you ever need to know exactly how long the distance vector is, you can use the Pythagorean theorem. The Pythagorean theorem is a very common, well-worn formula for working this out. Here's how to use it with the vx and vy variables to calculate the exact distance between the objects:*
>
> *distance = Math.sqrt(vx * vx + vy * vy);*
>
> `Math.sqrt` *is a built-in AS3.0 method that tells you the square root of whatever value is in its argument.*
>
> *In Figure 6-20, the vx and vy variables have the values 5 and 5. If you substitute these in the formula above, it will look like this:*
>
> *distance = Math.sqrt(5 * 5 + 5 * 5);*
>
> *If you run this code in AS3.0, you'll end up with the following result:*
>
> *distance = 5.9*
>
> *That's exactly the length of the distance vector between the objects that you see in Figure 6-20.*
>
> *Being able to figure out the exact distance between objects like this is extremely useful for games. If you know which objects are closer to others, your game characters could make decisions about where to go or what they should be avoiding based on how close or far they are to other objects. You don't need to use the Pythagorean theorem in this chapter, but you'll revisit it in Chapter 10.*

Now that you have a vector that tells you the distance between two objects, how can you use it to find out if they are touching? First, you have to calculate the combined half-widths and half-heights of the two objects. What do I mean by that? Take the width of the first object, and divide it by half. Then take the width of the second object, and divide it by half also. Add these two numbers together, and you end up with a number that tells you what the combined half-widths of the objects are. Here's an example:

```
combinedHalfWidths
  = (objectOne.width / 2) + (objectTwo.width / 2);
```

Then do the same thing with the objects' heights.

```
combinedHalfHeights
  = (objectOne.height / 2) + (objectTwo.height / 2);
```

Figure 6-21 shows what these numbers look like.

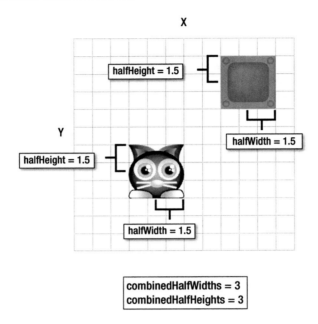

Figure 6-21. Find the combined half-heights and half-widths of the objects.

You can see that it's really simple math. But it also might seem like a lot of useless information! It's not. Here's why it's important:

> *If the combined half-widths and half-heights are less than the vx and vy variables, then the objects are touching.*

Let's go on a practical tour of why this works:

1. Imagine that the cat character is moving around the stage. You want to know whether or not it's touching the box. Check the **vx** and **vy** variables against the combined half-height and half-widths of the objects. If the **vx** and **vy** variables have a greater value than the half-widths and half-heights, then there's no collision. Figure 6-22 illustrates this.

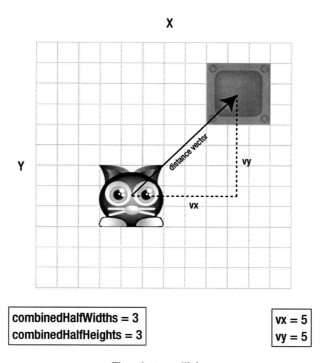

combinedHalfWidths = 3
combinedHalfHeights = 3

vx = 5
vy = 5

There's no collision.

Figure 6-22. There's no collision if the vx and vy variables are greater than the objects' combined half-widths and half-heights.

2. But what happens if the cat creeps a little closer to the right side of the stage? As soon as its **vx** value becomes less than the combined half-widths, a possible collision might be on its way. But it's not happening yet because the **vy** value is still greater than the combined half-heights. You can see this in Figure 6-23.

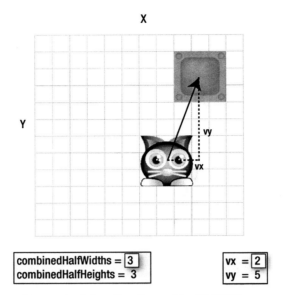

combinedHalfWidths = 3
combinedHalfHeights = 3

vx = 2
vy = 5

The vx value is less than the combinedHalfWidths.
A collision might be approaching!

Figure 6-23. *There's the potential of a collision occurring if the vx value becomes less than the combined half-widths.*

3. If the both the **vx** and **vy** values are less than the combined half-widths and half-heights, you definitely know that the objects are colliding. You can see this in Figure 6-24.

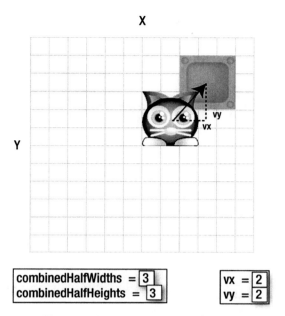

| combinedHalfWidths | = | 3 |
| combinedHalfHeights | = | 3 |

| vx | = | 2 |
| vy | = | 2 |

The vx and vy values are less than the
combinedHalfWidths and combinedHalfHeights.

A collision is definitely occuring!

Figure 6-24. A collision is definitely occurring if both the vx and vy values are less than the both half-widths and half-heights.

4. Now that you know a collision is occurring, you have to separate the objects. You can only do that if you know by how much they're overlapping. How can you figure this out? By subtracting the vx and vy values from the half-widths and half-heights, as shown in Figure 6-25.

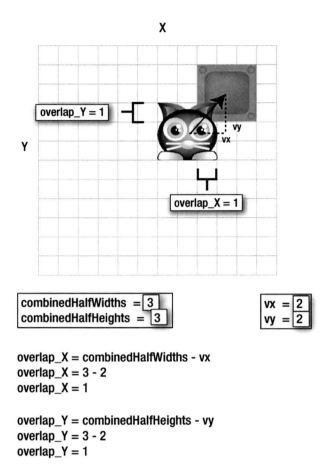

$$\text{combinedHalfWidths} = 3$$
$$\text{combinedHalfHeights} = 3$$

$$vx = 2$$
$$vy = 2$$

overlap_X = combinedHalfWidths - vx
overlap_X = 3 - 2
overlap_X = 1

overlap_Y = combinedHalfHeights - vy
overlap_Y = 3 - 2
overlap_Y = 1

Figure 6-25. Figure out the amount of overlap.

5. The last step is to separate the objects so that they're not touching. Now that you know by how much the objects are overlapping, this is easy to do. Just subtract the amount of overlap from the object's x and y positions, like this:

```
character.x = character.x - overlap_X;
character.y = character.y - overlap_Y;
```

This is the same as saying:

> *The character's new position will be the same as its old position, minus the amount of overlap.*

This will move the object out of the collision. Figure 6-26 illustrates this.

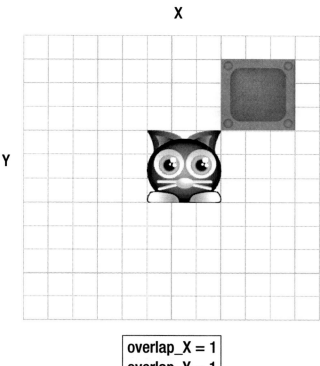

X

Y

| overlap_X = 1 |
| overlap_Y = 1 |

character.x = character.x - overlapX;
character.y = character.y - overlapY;

Figure 6-26. Subtract the amount of overlap from the character's current position to move it out of the collision.

Usually there's slightly more overlap on the x axis or the y axis. In that case, you move the object out of the collision on the axis that has the least amount of overlap.

Hey, that's the theory! But didn't I promise you that there wouldn't be much math in this book? Fortunately, you don't need to know any of this math to be able to use this in your games. I'll show you how next.

Programming with the Collision class

If you understand these basic concepts, all you need to do is figure out how to use them in a game. You'll do that in a moment, but you'll be doing it very differently than any of the other code you've written so far in this book. You'll actually use this code as part of a completely separate class. The class is called Collision, and you'll find it in the chapter's source files.

But what exactly is a class? You can think of a class as a self-contained component of a program. You can link different classes together so that they can share code and work together to make complex games and programs. How to do this will comprise much of the substance of the rest of the book, so don't panic if this seems daunting at the moment! I'll provide small, manageable steps.

Technically, every program you've written so far has been a class. I've been calling them computer programs, but you've really been writing classes. You can tell that because all of your programs have all included a program block called a class definition.

```
public class PickingUpObjects extends Sprite
{...
```

All of your programs so far have been contained inside one class. That's been great for learning purposes and the short programs you've been building, but as your games increase in complexity you'll find that it's vastly more efficient to break components of your games up into separate classes.

Let's look at a practical application of all these new concepts and theories. In the chapter's source files you'll find a project folder called BlockingMovement. Open the src folder. You'll see that it contains two AS files, as shown in Figure 6-27.

Figure 6-27. The BlockingMovement program uses two classes to do its work.

These AS files, BlockingMovement.as and Collision.as, are both classes. BlockingMovement.as is the main class. It's the class that launches the program and gets everything going. The main class of your program is called the **application class**. All the classes you've written so far in the book have been application classes.

The other class is Collision.as. This class contains specialized code that helps the application class do its work. In fact, it contains all the code that represents the collision logic you just looked at. You can use this class if you want a game object to block the movement of another game object.

There are few good reasons why all the collision code is in its own class.

- The code that the Collision class contains is very useful, and you'll want to use it in many game projects. Rather than having to write all the code from scratch for every game you want to use it in, just make a copy of the class and drop it into any project's src folder. You can then use all of the Collision class's code without having to rewrite any of it.

- You never need to look the code in the Collision class, or understand how it works, if you don't want to. It's a self-contained "black box." You can use it very easily in your main program without needing to make any sense of it .

Let's see what these two classes do. Open the BlockingMovement project and compile the program. Move the cat character up to the box. The character can't move through the box—it's a solid environmental boundary. An output text field tells you which side of the character is touching the box. Figure 6-28 shows what you'll see.

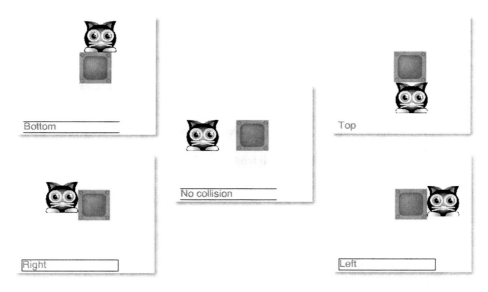

Figure 6-28. The cat is blocked by the box on all sides.

The code that makes all this work is simplicity itself. Most of it is identical to the other examples in this chapter. All the magic happens in the **enterFrameHandler**. The following bold code is what does all the work:

```
public function enterFrameHandler(event:Event):void
{
  //Move the player
  character.x += vx;
  character.y += vy;

  //Collision code
  Collision.block(character, box);

  //Display the collision side in the output text field
  output.text = Collision.collisionSide;
}
```

Yes, it's really just one line of code!

```
Collision.block(character, box);
```

It's sending the `character` and `box` objects to the `Collision` class's `block` method. The `Collision.block` method is doing all the work of preventing the objects from overlapping. You don't need to worry about how it does this; you just need to use this single line of code if you want to block movement between any two game objects. It works in this program because the `Collision` class is in the same src folder as the `BlockingMovement` class. Figure 6-29 shows how these two classes work together.

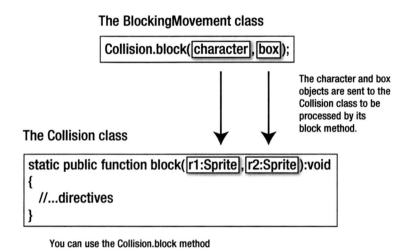

You can use the Collision.block method
without having to know how it works.

Figure 6-29. The character and box objects are sent to the Collision class's block method.

*Collision.block is a special kind of method called a **static method**. Static methods are methods that belong to external classes that you can use inside your main program.*

To use a static method in your program, simply use the name of the class that the method belongs to, followed by a dot, and then the method name with the parentheses. Here's an example:

ClassName.methodName();

You've seen static methods before; you just weren't aware of it at the time. In Chapter 4, you used one of AS3.0's special built- in methods:

Math.random()

Look familiar? Yes, it's a static method! random is a method that is part of AS3.0's Math class. It does the specialized job of giving you a random number between 0 and 1, and

> *you can use it anywhere in the program inside any other class. Static methods used like this are often called **utilities**. They do a useful little job for you in your program, and you don't need to worry about how they work as long as they provide the result you need.*
>
> *You can make any class's method static by adding the keyword **static** to the method definition, like this:*
>
> ```
> static public function block(r1:Sprite, r2:Sprite):void
> {…
> ```

The other extra feature of this code is that it tells you on which of the character's sides the collision is occurring on.

```
output.text = Collision.collisionSide;
```

This code is reading a `String` variable that's inside the `Collision` class and displaying it in the output text field.

There's one extra bonus to this code. With a tiny change, you can make the character push the box around the stage. All you need to do is switch the order of the objects in the method's arguments. Put the box first, and then the `character`, like this:

```
Collision.block(box, character);
```

Recompile the program and watch what happens. The cat can now push the box around the stage, as shown in Figure 6-30.

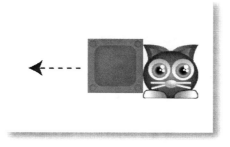

Figure 6-30. Switch the order of the arguments in the Collision.block method to let the cat push the box around the stage.

How is this possible? By changing the order of the arguments, the effect of the code is on the box, not the character. The only difference is that because the character is moving, the box has to continuously reposition itself in front of the direction the character is traveling in to prevent the two objects from overlapping.

And that's how you use the `Collision` class!

If you are just happy that the new code works and aren't really too worried about the fine details, feel free to skip to the next chapter. The main thing is that you have a great little tool you can use in any of your games. If you now have a general idea of how vector based collision detection works, why you might need to use it, and how to use a static method in a custom class, that's all you need to know. Like `Math.random`, `Collision.block` is a utility that you can use whenever you want to, and you don't need to know how it works.

But if you're a code junkie, read on!

Another look at methods, arguments, and parameters

The `Collision.block` method uses two arguments. They can be any Sprite objects in your game. In the previous example, they were the `character` and `box` objects.

```
Collision.block(character, box);
```

These arguments are sent to the method's parameters in the function definition (which you'll find in the `Collision` class, and you'll look at soon). The parameters are highlighted.

```
static public function block(r1:Sprite, r2:Sprite):void
{...
```

I discussed how to use method parameters in Chapter 3, but let's review them again before you continue.

Imagine that you want to write a method that has the task of displaying the names of fruit. Let's call the method `fruitDisplay`. You want to be able to give it the names of any fruit, and the method should then accept those names and display them as a trace message.

The method doesn't know what the names of the fruit will be; you could send it any fruit imaginable. All it knows is that you'll be giving it two names. You could write some code that looks something like this:

```
fruitDisplay("apple", "orange");
```

The names of the fruit are provided inside the parentheses that follow the name of the method, which is known as the argument. You supplied the names of the fruit as strings (words surrounded by quotes), and separated them with a comma. Now it's the job of the method's function definition to do something useful with this information.

Here's what the `fruitDisplay` method's function definition looks like:

```
public function fruitDisplay
    (parameterOne:String, parameterTwo:String):void
{
    trace(parameterOne, parameterTwo);
}
```

If you ran this code in a program, you'd see the following trace message:

apple orange

You can change the arguments in the method call at any time in the program to display different fruit. For example, you might decide that you're tired of apples and oranges, and write this line of code a little later in the program:

```
fruitDisplay("mango", "banana");
```

You'd then see the following trace message:

mango banana

You didn't change the method in any way; all you did was change the arguments in the method call. When the arguments are sent to the method's function definition, they're copied into the parameters, which are highlighted here:

```
function fruitDisplay
  (parameterOne:String,  parameterTwo:String):void
{
  trace(parameterOne,  parameterTwo);
}
```

The parameters are just variables that can be used anywhere in the function definition. Because you're expecting them to accept string values, you've set their variable type as String the same way you would for any other variables.

The values of the two parameters contain whatever values are passed to them in the method call. That means that whenever the method uses the variable names parameterOne and parameterTwo, it will replace them with the values apple and orange or mango and banana—or whatever else you choose to send it. The beauty of this system is that you can reuse the method for many different related tasks without having to know the specific values of the variables.

Here's another example. Let's create a method that adds three numbers and displays the result. Here's what it might look like:

```
public function add(one:int,  two:int, three:int):void
{
  trace(one + two + three);
}
```

You can then use this method with a method call that might look like this:
add(4,10,6);

It will display this trace message.
20

379

Any three numbers you supply will give you a different result. I'm sure you can start to see how useful this can be.

Methods that return a value

You can also create methods that return something back to the main program. Let's say you've got a method called add that adds two numbers together. It could look like this:

```
public function add(numberOne:Number, numberTwo:Number):Number
{
  var result:Number = numberOne + numberTwo;
  return result;
}
```

The method adds the two parameters together and stores the result in a variable called result. The keyword return then sends the result value back to the main program. You could use this method in your main program like this:

```
anyVariable = add(23, 13);
```

The add method's result value will be copied into anyVariable. In this case, anyVariable will now equal 36.

To use a return value in a method, the method's function definition has to specify what type of value that method will return. In this example, it returns a Number, which you can see as the last item in the function definition, highlighted here:

```
public function add(numberOne:Number, numberTwo:Number):Number
```

Methods can return any type of value back to the main program, like String or Sprite objects. Just make sure that you specify the correct return type in the function definition, just like in the previous code. (You'll find a working example of this system in the ReturningAValue project folder in the chapter's source files.)

Using the block method's arguments with the Collision class

As you've seen, if you want to stop the character object from walking through the box, you can write the method call so that it looks like this:

```
Collision.block(character, box);
```

It might work for this program, but what if you've got another game where you want to prevent a mouse from crossing a stream? Without changing anything in the method's function definition, you can just use this line of code:

```
Collision.block(mouse, stream);
```

The method is written in general way so that it doesn't need to know specifically which objects it will be asked to block, just that they'll be two Sprite objects. You can reuse exactly the same code anywhere in any context.

Taking a look at the Collision.block method

So now you have no excuse for claiming not to understand what method arguments and parameters are! Are you ready for a bigger challenge? Let's take a look at the Collision class and figure out exactly how the code is working.

> *Warning! The code is a little complex, and you almost certainly won't understand it right away. It may actually be more beneficial for you to come back to this section of the chapter when your programming skills are slightly more refined, a few chapters down the road.*

Before you do, flip back a few pages to the section called "Preventing objects from overlapping" and try to become familiar with the problem you need to solve. If you understand the problem and the logic used to solve it, all the new code does is turn that logic into AS3.0 code. Let's walk the through the Collision class and have a look at what's new and how it works.

Here's the entire Collision class. You'll see a lot of code that you won't understand, but don't worry about that yet. I'll walk you through all of it in the pages ahead. Note that r1 and r2 stand for "rectangle one" and "rectangle two." In the example you just looked at, r1 is the character and r2 is the box.

```
package
{
  import flash.display.Sprite;

  public class Collision
  {
    static public var collisionSide:String = "";

    public function Collision()
    {
    }
    static public function block(r1:Sprite, r2:Sprite):void
    {
      //Calculate the distance vector
      var vx:Number
        = (r1.x + (r1.width / 2))
        - (r2.x + (r2.width / 2));

      var vy:Number
        = (r1.y + (r1.height / 2))
        - (r2.y + (r2.height / 2));

      //Check whether vx
```

```
//is less than the combined half widths
if(Math.abs(vx) < r1.width / 2 + r2.width / 2)
{
  //A collision might be occurring! Check
  //whether vy is less than the combined half heights
  if(Math.abs(vy) < r1.height / 2 + r2.height / 2)
  {
    //A collision has occurred! This is good!
    //Find out the size of the overlap
    //on both the X and Y axes
    var overlap_X:Number
      = r1.width / 2
      + r2.width / 2
      - Math.abs(vx);

    var overlap_Y:Number
      = r1.height / 2
      + r2.height / 2
      - Math.abs(vy);

    //The collision has occurred on the axis with the
    //*smallest* amount of overlap. Let's figure out which
    //axis that is

    if(overlap_X >=  overlap_Y)
    {
      //The collision is happening on the X axis
      //But on which side? vy can tell us
      if(vy > 0)
      {
        collisionSide = "Top";

        //Move the rectangle out of the collision
        r1.y = r1.y + overlap_Y;
      }
      else
      {
        collisionSide = "Bottom";

        //Move the rectangle out of the collision
        r1.y = r1.y - overlap_Y;
      }
    }
    else
    {
      //The collision is happening on the Y axis
      //But on which side? vx can tell us
      if(vx > 0)
      {
        collisionSide = "Left";

        //Move the rectangle out of the collision
```

```
            r1.x = r1.x + overlap_X;
          }
          else
          {
            collisionSide = "Right";

            //Move the rectangle out of the collision
            r1.x = r1.x - overlap_X;
          }
        }
      }
      else
      {
        //No collision
        collisionSide = "No collision";
      }
    }
    else
    {
      //No collision
      collisionSide = "No collision";
    }
    }
  }
}
```

This is the most complex code that you've come across in the book so far, but I'll break it apart to look at one little piece at a time. The first odd thing is the Collision class's constructor method.

```
public function Collision()
{
}
```

Remember that a class *has* to have a constructor method, and the constructor method name always has to be the same name as the class name. Any directives inside the constructor method run immediately when the class is instantiated.

This constructor method is completely empty, which might seem strange. The reason is that you have no initialization directives that you want to run. It's perfectly fine to have a constructor method that's empty like this. In fact, you can even leave out the entire constructor method if you want to, although it's generally considered bad programming form to do so. (If you do leave it out, AS3.0 will add it automatically when it compiles the program.)

Next is the block method's function definition.

```
static public function block(r1:Sprite, r2:Sprite):void
{...
```

The static keyword means that you can use this method directly in any other class, using this format:

`Collision.block`

That's convenient, because if this method wasn't declared as static, you would first need to make an instance of the class with the new keyword, like this:

```
public var collision:Collision = new Collision();
```

And you'd then be able to use the block method, like this:

```
collision.block(character, box);
```

By declaring the method as static, you don't have to go to the trouble of making an instance of the class first.

The other important things about this function definition are its parameters.

```
(r1:Sprite, r2:Sprite)
```

These are local variables that are typed as Sprites. In the `BlockingMovement` application class, you used this line of code to call the method:

```
Collision.block(character, box);
```

Both `character` and `box` are Sprite objects, so it makes sense that `r1` and `r2` should be typed as Sprite objects, too. When the method is called, a reference to the `character` object is copied into the `r1` variable, and a reference to the `box` object is copied into the `r2` variable. Whenever you see `r1` and `r2` in the body of the method, you can replace them with `character` and `box` in your mind if that helps you better understand how the code is working. (The "r" is just short for "rectangle." Keeping the variable names short in this bit of code keeps it compact and makes it a little easier to read.)

The first few lines of code inside the `block` method create the `vx` and `vy` variables that define the distance vector between the objects.

```
var vx:Number
  = (r1.x + (r1.width / 2))
  - (r2.x + (r2.width / 2));

var vy:Number
  = (r1.y + (r1.height / 2))
  - (r2.y + (r2.height / 2));
```

This is the imaginary line that runs between the character and the box. The vector is being drawn from the *centers* of the objects. To find the centers, you need to add half the value of their widths and heights to their top left corner x and y positions. What you end up with is a vector that runs from the center of the character to the center of the box. Remember that a pair of `vx` and `vy` variables always describes a single vector. (Check back to Figure 6-20 to review this if you're a bit hazy as to why).

Now that you have the vector defined, the code goes through a methodical process of checking whether the **vx** and **vy** variables are less than the combined half widths. Remember, if they are, then a collision is occurring. This is all done with a series of nested if statements. Here's the first one:

```
if(Math.abs(vx) < r1.width / 2 + r2.width / 2)
{...
```

This code is not as daunting as it seems! All it means is this:

if(the vx value is less than the combined half-width of r1 and half-width of r2)
{...

Take a second look at that if statement. Do you see it now? Just like I promised, it's no more than a bit of easy math.

But one new thing is this bit of code:

```
Math.abs(vx)
```

`Math.abs` is one of AS3.0's built-in methods. (And, yes, it's a static method!) Its job is to find out the **absolute value** of a number. Absolute values can only be positive; negative numbers that are forced to be absolute have their sign dropped. Let's imagine that you use `Math.abs` in a line of code that looks like this:

```
Math.abs(-27);
```

It would return this:

```
27
```

Why is this useful for you? If the first object has a lower x position value than the second object, the value of **vx** will be negative. The negative value would overly complicate the code because you'd need an additional if statement to check for it. It's simpler for you just to deal with positive values.

So what happens if the code discovers that **vx** is less than the combined half-widths? It checks whether **vy** is less than the combined half-heights.

```
if(Math.abs(vy) < r1.height / 2 + r2.height / 2)
{...
```

If this turns out to be true, then you know that a collision absolutely must be occurring. This is the condition illustrated in Figure 6-24. The next step is to calculate the amount of overlap on the x and y axis, and then use those amounts to figure out on which side of the object the collision is happening: top, left, bottom, or right.

The amount of overlap is stored in two variables called `overlap_X` and `overlap_Y`. Here's how they're calculated:

```
var overlap_X:Number
  = r1.width / 2 + r2.width / 2 - Math.abs(vx);
var overlap_Y:Number
```

```
= r1.height / 2 + r2.height / 2 - Math.abs(vy);
```

You'll notice that these variables are declared without the keyword `public`. That's because they're variables that are only used inside the method and don't belong to the class. They can't be used outside of the `block` method. These are known as **local variables.** You'll see many more examples of local variables at work in over the rest of the book.

Now that you know the amount of overlap, you just have to compare the overlap values against the vx and vy values to find out on which side of the first object the collision is occurring. When the code knows that, it can use the correct overlap value to reposition the object so that it's no longer touching the second object.

```
if(overlap_X >=  overlap_Y)
{
  //The collision is happening on the X axis
  //But on which side? vy can tell us
  if(vy > 0)
  {
    collisionSide = "Top";

    //Move the rectangle out of the collision
    r1.y = r1.y + overlap_Y;
  }
  else
  {
    collisionSide = "Bottom";

    //Move the rectangle out of the collision
    r1.y = r1.y - overlap_Y;
  }
}
else
{
  //The collision is happening on the Y axis
  //But on which side? vx can tell us
  if(vx > 0)
  {
    collisionSide = "Left";

    //Move the rectangle out of the collision
    r1.x = r1.x + overlap_X;
  }
  else
  {
    collisionSide = "Right";

    //Move the rectangle out of the collision
    r1.x = r1.x - overlap_X;
  }
}
```

And that's really all there is to it. You can see that the logic is slightly intricate, but if you spend a few minutes carefully stepping through the code in your own mind, you'll also see that it's pretty straightforward.

As a bonus, the `Collision` class has a String variable called `collisionSide`.

```
static public var collisionSide:String = "";
```

Its job is to record the side on which the collision is occurring. It may be useful for some of your games to know this information. In fact, knowing this information is crucial to programming a platform game, as you'll see in Chapter 9.

`collisionSide` has been declared as a `static` variable. That means you can access this variable in the main application class like this:

```
Collision.collisionside
```

That will return the current text of the `collisionSide` variable. You could possibly use it in a game scenario like this:

```
if(Collision.collisionSide == "Bottom")
{
  //The character is standing on top of the box,
  //so release the swarms of killer bees!
}
```

I'll leave it up to your skill and imagination to actually program this game. (I can't wait to play it!)

Summary

Collision detection is quite a big subject in game design. Hopefully the introductory taste you've had of it here is enough whet your appetite for what's to come.

But before you jump ahead to the next chapter you might want to take short break to make a game. Hey, don't be scared; you can do it! And that's what this book is all about, after all—making your own games. If you combine the collision detection techniques from this chapter with the player control techniques from the last one (along with the logical analysis you looked at in the number guessing game), you have all the tools you need to make some pretty sophisticated games.

And that's what you're going to do in the next chapter. You're going to take all the skills you've learned so far and put them together to make your first real video game!

Chapter 7

Making Games

You've now got all the skills you need to start making real games. But how do you do that? The way to make the leap from small examples to a big, complete game may not be so obvious, but don't worry. In this chapter, I'm going to show you exactly how it's done. I'm going to take you on a step-by-step tour of how to make a video game just using the techniques you've already learned. (OK, I'll admit it; I'm going to sneak in one or two new little tricks, too!)

You're going to walk through the whole process of making the game—from the graphics to the programming. The game you're going to make is a very simple object collection game. The player needs to collect five bombs to defuse them before a 10-second timer runs out. Figure 7-1 shows what this looks like.

Figure 7-1. Defuse the bombs before time runs out!

I'm going to use this chapter as an opportunity to introduce another useful game graphics creation tool: Adobe Illustrator. If you're curious about how Illustrator works but have been daunted by its apparent complexity, this chapter will teach you everything you need to know to start working with it. But you don't need to use Illustrator to make any of these graphics; feel free to make them using Photoshop or any other graphic design or illustration software that produces PNG files.

You're also going to learn a fun new programming technique: how to make a timer. And I'll show you how to turn each game object into its own class so that you can greatly reduce the amount of code you need in your main application class.

It's time to make your first real game!

Making the game graphics

You need five PNG images for your game. Here are their names and dimensions:

- character.png (width: 50px, height: 50px)
- box.png (width: 50px, height: 50px)
- bomb.png (width: 40px, height: 30px)
- background.png (width: 550px, height: 400px)
- gameOver.png (width: 300px, height: 150px)

Figure 7-2 shows how I've designed them for this project. You can design these PNG files however you like. As long as they have these same names and dimensions they'll work with the game program.

character.png

gameOver.png

box.png

background.png

bomb.png

Figure 7-2. The game graphics you'll make

I've made all these graphics using Adobe Illustrator CS5.0, and I'll show you how in the step-by-step instructions that follow. I'll start with the easiest graphic and end with the most complex. By the time you're done, you'll have all the skills you need to start making your own game graphics with Illustrator.

This chapter assumes that you've worked through Chapter 2 or already know how to use Photoshop.

Making the textured box

The first graphic you're going to make is the textured game box shown in Figure 7-3. These kinds of all-purpose boxes are a video game staple, and I'll use it as an opportunity to show you some of the most useful basic Illustrator drawing techniques.

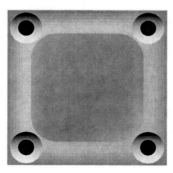

Figure 7-3. The textured game box

Getting accustomed to Adobe Illustrator

When you first launch Adobe Illustrator, you'll notice that the tools and the workspace look comfortingly similar to Photoshop. But as you start playing with it, you'll soon discover that, although it does indeed look similar, there are some radical differences. Panels are in different places, many of the concepts it uses are different, and some of the keyboard shortcuts are different as well. There's quite a bit of overlap between Photoshop and Illustrator, and that's just what can make it so confusing at first. Just when you think you know how to do something, Illustrator changes the rules of the game and you hit a brick wall. But there's a solution! Don't think of it as similar to Photoshop at all—think of it as a completely different program. Set aside any expectations you may have and make a commitment to learning it from scratch. It will be well worth the effort because, in truth, it's actually *easier* to make game graphics with Illustrator than Photoshop, once you get the hang of it. Illustrator is a bit more lenient, not quite as finicky, and a lot more flexible. Like Photoshop, learning to use Illustrator is a good long-term investment. It's one of the most widely used and powerful graphic design packages out there, and the time you spend learning it properly now will put you in good stead for years to come.

But, just like Photoshop, Illustrator is a wildly complex piece of software. It can be customized in a gazillion different configurations, and there are often 10 ways or more to achieve any particular effect. I'm going to take you on quite a narrow tour of Illustrator in this chapter; I'll only cover about 5% of its actual functionality. However, like the tour of Photoshop, you'll be happy to know that the 5% that you learn are the techniques that you'll be using 95% of the time for game graphics. Once you've worked through this chapter, you'll be fluent enough using Illustrator to create a vast range of graphics for games, and these skills will be an important stepping stone to learning more advanced techniques if you feel inspired…and you should!

One of the most important differences between Illustrator and Photoshop is that Illustrator is primarily a tool for making **vector graphics**. Vector graphics are pictures made with lines, not pixels. Photoshop is all about pixels. Drawing with vectors is actually a great feature of Illustrator because it means that you can scale your images to any size and they won't lose resolution quality. Also, when your drawings are finished, you can choose whether you want to use them in your game as PNG files (which use pixels) or SWF files (which use vectors). You can use either type in your Flash games.

> *All the Flash games in this book use PNG files, but you can use SWF files just as easily. You can save any graphics you make in Illustrator by selecting File ↗ Export and then choosing the Flash (swf) format.*
>
> *Whether you choose to use SWF or PNG files is really a matter of style and personal choice. PNG graphics tend to put a little less strain on the processor in the Flash Player. That's good for games, which tend to be very processor-heavy. On the other hand, you can scale games that use SWF graphics to any size and you won't lose resolution quality. Which do you prefer? Try both and decide!*

You're going to be working with pixels for this project, so the first thing you should do is tell Illustrator to use pixels as its general unit of measure. Open the Preferences menu by selecting Edit ↗ Preferences ~Units (Windows) or Illustrator ↗ Preferences (OS X). Select Units and change the General option to Pixels.

Now you'll create your first Illustrator file and start drawing!

Setting up the workspace

Launch Illustrator and create a new document called box.

Select File ↗ New from Illustrator's main menu. The New Document dialogue box opens. Change the parameters in this widow so that they match the following (Figure 7-4 shows what your New Document window should look like):

- Name: box

- Width: 50 px

- Height: 50 px

- Units: Pixels

- Color Model: RGB (Click the Advanced button to make this option visible if you can't see it.)

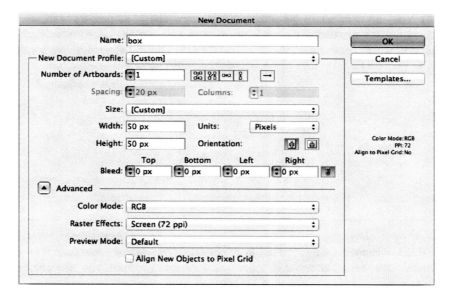

Figure 7-4. Parameters for the new document

The width and height are specified in pixels, but those are really just numbers that apply to your finished PNG file. All your drawing will be done using vectors, which means that your illustrations can be scaled to any size if you later change your mind about how large you want your finished image to be. Illustrator has a Pixel Preview view that shows how vector drawings will look as pixels, and you'll see how to use that soon.

Also, very importantly, the Color Model needs to be RGB. RGB stands for Red, Green, and Blue, which refers to the visible light spectrum. It's a way of interpreting colors that's used on any media that projects light, like computer monitors or TV screens. It's what you should always use for games. The other color system in wide use is CMYK which stands for Cyan, Magenta, Yellow, and Key ("Key" refers to black). It's used with printed images like books and magazines, and describes the underlying process in which inks are applied to paper.

You'll notice that the very last option is called Align New Objects to Pixel Grid. This is actually a very useful feature because it nudges your drawings into positions that exactly correspond to the underlying pixel grid. For very small images, like the ones you're making, it can sometimes be a bit frustrating to work like this because the pixels are relatively large, and your lines and shapes will be nudged around by large amounts. But for true pixel-perfect precision it's essential, so consider choosing this option at some point.

Click the OK button and you'll see a blank drawing surface called an **artboard**. Artboards are the same as the canvas in Photoshop—it's where are all your drawing happens. You can draw in the gray area around the artboard, but anything you draw there won't appear in your finished image. The gray area surrounding the artboard is a good place to experiment with techniques or drawing elements. You can copy or drag them into your finished work if you find you can use them.

If you need to make any changes to the artboard, like changing its size, click the Artboard Tool in the Tools bar (Figure 7-5). You can then resize the artboard or change any of its properties in the Control Panel, which runs across the top of Illustrator's workspace. (You can actually have multiple artboards in one Illustrator document, which could be useful if you're creating lots of different game graphics that share certain elements. You could copy and paste between different artboards rather than between different documents.)

Figure 7-5. Change the size and properties of the drawing area with the Artboard Tool.

As with Photoshop, Illustrator lets you choose different workspaces, which are customized arrangements of tools and panels. The default workspace is called Essentials, and that's the one I suggest you stick with for now. You can change the workspace by selecting Window ↗ Workspace from Illustrator's main menu, or by clicking the Essentials button at the top right corner of the Control Panel. If you've a made mess of the panels by dragging them around, re-docking them in strange places, or opening and closing them, just re-select the Essentials workspace from either of these two menus and everything will reset to their original positions.

Choosing the colors

I always struggle to choose appropriate colors for my games. Happily, you can simplify your color choices by letting Illustrator choose for you from a pre-set selection of color swatches. You'll find the Swatches panel in the Panel bar on the right side of the workspace.

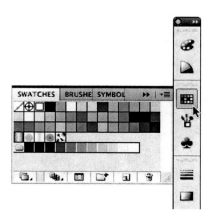

Figure 7-6. Open the Swatches panel.

You'll see a basic selection of swatches when you open the panel, shown in Figure 7-6, but Illustrator actually has many other color swatch collections that are hidden away in the Swatches panel's menu.

1. Click the Swatches panel's menu button at the very top right of the panel. Select Open Swatch Library. A whole list of different swatch color combinations appears. Choose any of these you like. I've chosen Kids Stuff for this project because it's a nice selection of bright, happy colors that are good for video games. Figure 7-7 shows where to find the swatch library. The new swatches will open in their own panel.

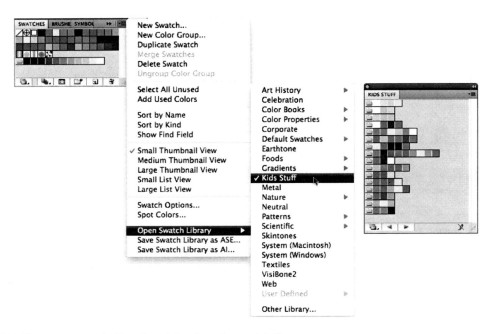

Figure 7-7. Choose a new selection of swatches from the swatch library.

You now have a nice selection of bright saturated and pastel colors to choose from.

Drawing the outside shape

You're first going to draw the box's outside shape. It's a green rectangle that has an inner glow effect applied to it.

    1.   Select the Rectangle Tool from the Tools bar (Figure 7-8).

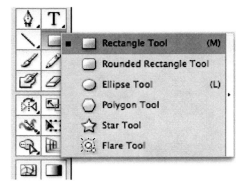

Figure 7-8. Select the Rectangle Tool.

2. Click the foreground color selector in the Tools bar and then click a green swatch. Set the stroke (outline) color to none. (Do this by selecting the stroke color selector in the Tools panel and then clicking the small button with a red stripe through it. The stroke color should have a matching red stripe through it if you've done this successfully.) Figure 7-9 shows what the foreground and stroke colors in the Tools bar should look like.

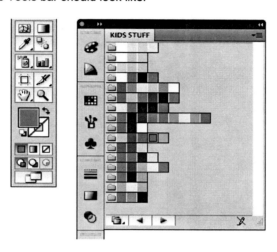

Figure 7-9. Choose a green foreground color and set the stroke color to none.

3. Hold down the left mouse button and Shift key simultaneously and drag from the very top left corner of the artboard to the very bottom right corner. A solid green square will fill the entire artboard, as shown in Figure 7-10. Holding down the Shift key while dragging with the Rectangle Tool lets you make perfect squares.

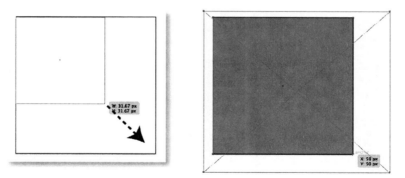

Figure 7-10. Click and drag to draw a green rectangle.

4. Make sure the rectangle is still selected. (If it isn't, re-select it with the black arrow tool.) Select Effect ↗ Stylize ↗ Inner Glow. The Inner Glow window will open to let you configure the effect. Make sure the Preview option is selected and configure the effect with the following settings:

- Mode: Normal
- Opacity: 80
- Blur: 9px
- Center

The final effect will look like Figure 7-11. There are no rules on how to go about choosing these settings—just play around with them until you're happy with the way the effect looks.

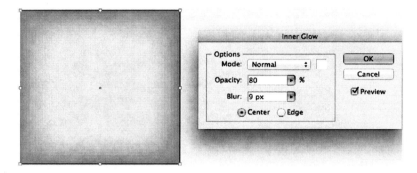

Figure 7-11. Give the rectangle an inner glow.

If you need to change this effect, or any others you might add to a drawing object, make sure the object is selected and open the Appearance panel (Figure 7-12). Click the effect name to modify it. You can modify all the other visual properties of the object from the Appearance panel as well.

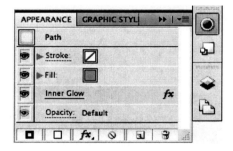

Figure 7-12. The Appearance panel lets you modify all of an object's visual properties, such as the effects, colors, and opacity.

Drawing the inside shape

Next you're going to draw an inner square with rounded corners. You'll fill it with a semi-transparent gradient and add a drop-shadow effect to make it look like it's floating above the outside square.

1. Choose the Rounded Rectangle Tool from the Tools bar (Figure 7-13). The Rounded Rectangle Tool lets you make squares and rectangles with round corners.

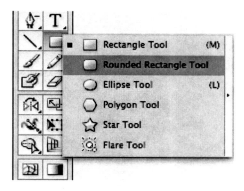

Figure 7-13. Select the Rounded Rectangle Tool.

2. Click the Preferences button in the Control Panel at the top of the workspace. Set the Corner Radius to 8px and click the OK button, as shown in Figure 7-14. The corner radius determines by how much to round the corners of the rectangle. (You can also change the corner radius interactively while you draw the rectangle by pressing the up or down arrows on the keyboard.)

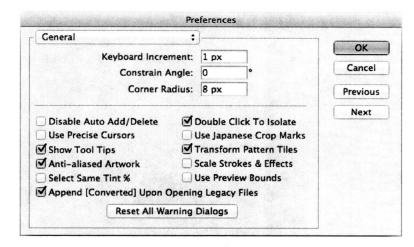

Figure 7-14. Set the rounded rectangle's corner radius in the Preferences window.

3. Draw a rounded rectangle of any size over the first rectangle you drew, as shown in Figure 7-15. It doesn't matter what the fill color is, but it shouldn't have a stroke color.

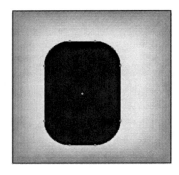

Figure 7-15. Make sure the new rounded rectangle doesn't have a stroke color.

4. Make sure that this new rectangle is still selected, and enter the follow values in the X, Y, W (width) and H (height) fields in the Control Panel:

    ▪ X: 25

    ▪ Y: 25

    ▪ W: 35

    ▪ H: 35

    This gives the square an exact height and width and centers it, as shown in Figure 7-16.

Figure 7-16. Enter the exact dimensions and position in the Control Panel.

> *You now have two drawing objects on the artboard. If you double-click on either of them with the black arrow, Illustrator will switch to **isolation mode**. This dims and disables all the other objects on the artboard except the selected object so that it's easier for you to work on the selected item. To exit isolation mode, double-click away from the selected object.*

Next, you're going to fill this new square with a semi-transparent gradient fill.

1. Open the Gradient panel. Drag a light blue swatch from the Swatches panel into the gradient color stop on the very left side of the gradient preview. Drag a black swatch from the Swatches panel into the very right color stop in the gradient preview. Move the gradient midpoint slider about 75% to the right. Figure 7-17 illustrates this.

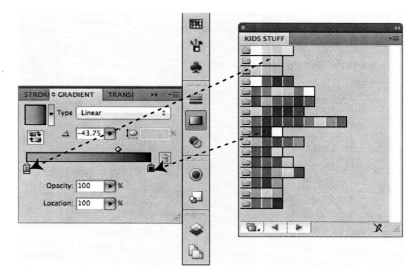

Figure 7-17. Create the gradient by dragging swatches into the color stops.

2. Select the right-most color stop, which should now be black, and change the Opacity value to 0. You should now see this gradient fill being applied to the new square you've drawn.

3. Select the Gradient Tool in the Tools bar. You'll see a long bar appear across the square. This is called the **gradient annotator**. It's a really useful tool that lets you interactively change the rotation, size, and position of the gradient by moving it around the artboard. Figure 7-18 shows what you'll see. You can drag, rotate, resize, and deform the gradient with this tool; you can also change the gradient's colors and color distribution.

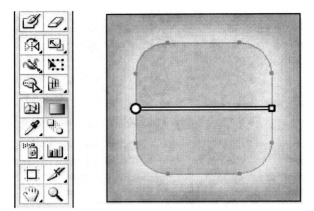

Figure 7-18. Select the gradient tool to display the gradient annotator.

4. Rotate and position the gradient annotator so that gradient runs diagonally across the square, from the top left to the bottom right, as shown in Figure 7-19.

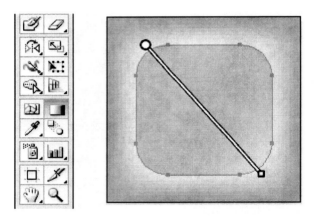

Figure 7-19. Rotate and reposition the gradient.

Now add a shallow drop-shadow effect to give the inner square a bit more depth.

1. Make sure that the inner square is still selected and choose Effect ↗ Stylize ↗ Drop Shadow from Illustrator's main menu. The Drop Shadow window will open (see Figure 7-20). Enter the following values:

   - Mode: Normal
   - Opacity: 30
   - X Offset: 1px
   - Y Offset: 1px

- Blur: 2px

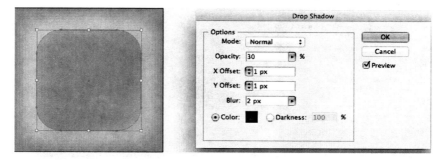

Figure 7-20. Add a drop shadow to the inner square.

> Make sure that the Preview option is selected so that you can see the changes in the square while you're setting these values. Again, it's simply a question of choosing settings that seem to have a nice effect.

Now add some rivets in the box's corners.

1. Select the Ellipse Tool from the Tools bar. It's part of the same button set as the Rectangle Tool. Give it a dark green fill color.

2. While holding down the Shift key, click and drag to draw a small circle in the outer square's top left corner. Figure 2-21 illustrates this. Holding down Shift while drawing with the Ellipse Tool lets you makes perfect circles.

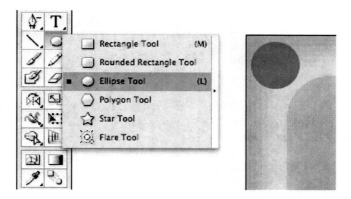

Figure 7-21. Draw a circle in the top left corner.

3. Use your newly acquired gradient skills to fill the dark green circle with a linear gradient. It should be dark at the top and light at the bottom. Your final result should look something like Figure 7-22.

Figure 7-22. Draw a circle in the top left corner.

   4.   Draw a smaller dark green circle inside the first circle, as shown in Figure 7-23.

Figure 7-23. Add a smaller circle.

> *If you ever need to perfectly align two or more objects, you can use Illustrator's Alignment buttons. To use them, hold down Shift and click on all the objects you want to align with the black arrow. Alignment buttons will appear in the Control Panel at the top of the workspace. Click any of the buttons, and you'll see your objects magically align in the proper positions.*
>
> *If you need to center a smaller object inside a bigger object, as you do to make these rivets, make sure both circles are selected and click the Horizontal Align Center button and then the Vertical Align Center button.*

Make a few more copies of this rivet for the other three corners.

   1.   Holding down the Shift key while clicking with the black arrow lets you select multiple objects. Select both the inner circle and the outer circle together. You'll know that you've done this correctly if you see blue bounding boxes appear around both circles, as shown in Figure 7-24.

Figure 7-24. Hold down the Shift key and click to select multiple objects.

2. Select Object ↗ Group from the main menu. Grouping objects lets you treat multiple objects as one. It means that you can move, copy, and paste a group of objects around the artboard, and they'll stay together as a single unit. You can edit individual units in the group by double-clicking on them. You can ungroup objects by selecting Object ↗ Ungroup.

3. Now that the two circles are grouped as one unit, select Edit ↗ Copy (or use the keyboard shortcuts: Ctrl+C for Windows, Command+C for OSX). Select Edit ↗ Paste in Front (or the shortcuts: Ctrl+F for Windows, Command+F for OSX). This makes a duplicate of the group and pastes it directly on top of the original.

4. Move the duplicated group to the square's top right corner, as shown in Figure 7-25.

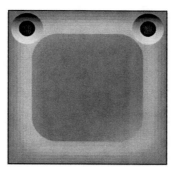

Figure 7-25. Duplicate the grouped circles with the Copy/Paste In Front command and move the new copy to the square's top right corner.

5. Use Paste In Front two more times, and move the duplicated rivets to the square's bottom corners, as shown in Figure 7-26.

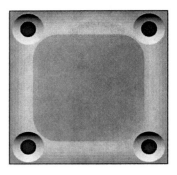

Figure 7-26. Make two more copies of the rivets and move them into position.

Your all-purpose video game box is now finished!

However, you've been doing all your drawing using vectors. The final PNG image that you're going to use in the game will be made out of pixels. What will this look like? To find out, select View ↗ Pixel Preview from Illustrator's main menu. You'll see exactly what the pixels in your 50 by 50 pixel game box will look like, as you can see in Figure 7-27.

Figure 7-27. Pixel Preview lets you see what your drawing will look like in pixels.

This perfectly demonstrates the differences between vector and bitmap artwork: lines vs. dots. You can actually do all your drawing with Pixel Preview switched on the whole time if you want to. Sometimes this is necessary to make sure fine, detailed work aligns properly, especially for small graphics. You'll see how useful this can be when you design the bomb graphic in the next section. (Uncheck Pixel Preview from the View menu to switch it off.)

The last step is to save your work.

1. Select File ↗ Save As from the main menu. Choose a location on your computer to save the Illustrator document and click the Save button. (Illustrator documents have an .ai file extension.)

2. Now you need to make the PNG version. Select File ⌐ Save For Web and Devices from the main menu. Select PNG-24 from the Preset menu. Click the Save button and choose a save location for the finished PNG image.

This has been quite a grab bag of different Illustrator techniques. Let's pick up the pace a bit and design the bomb graphic.

Making the bomb

Making the bomb graphic gives you a chance to use Illustrator's Pen Tool and Star Shape Tool, and it shows you how you can merge two or more shapes into one.

1. Create a new Illustrator document called bomb. Keep all the new document settings the same as for the box, but change the width to 40 and the height to 30.

2. Select the Ellipse Tool. Hold down Shift and drag to create a perfect circle that's the height of the artboard. (If you want to draw a circle from its center, hold down the Alt (Windows) or Option (OSX) key.)

3. Fill the circle with a very dark, almost black, radial gradient, as shown in Figure 7-28. Position the circle on the left side of the artboard.

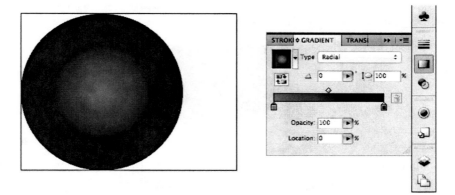

Figure 7-28. Draw a circle with a dark radial gradient.

4. Select the Gradient Tool. Use the gradient annotator to reposition the center of the gradient so that its lightest area is near the top left of the circle (Figure 7-29). This creates a highlighting effect and gives the circle a sense of depth, as though it were a sphere.

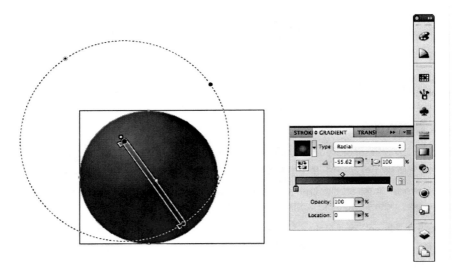

Figure 7-29. Rotate and move the gradient to create a spherical highlight effect.

5. Draw a black rectangle about a fifth the size of the circle. Use the white arrow tool to taper the left and right corners. The arrow tools in Illustrator work exactly as they do in Photoshop You'll end up with a shape that looks like Figure 7-30.

Figure 7-30. Draw a black tapered rectangle.

6. Rotate and move this new shape to the top left edge of the circle. Let it slightly overlap the circle, as shown in Figure 7-31.

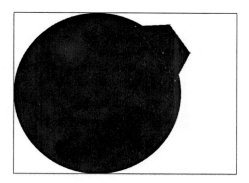

Figure 7-31. Move the new shape over the circle.

The next trick is to move the new shape to a position behind the circle. In Photoshop, you would do this by moving the new shape's layer below the circle layer. Illustrator has layers, just like Photoshop, but you often don't need to use them. Shapes are usually layered by adjusting their stacking order on a single layer. Let's see how.

    7.   Make sure that the new shape is still selected. Choose Object ↗ Arrange ↗ Send Backward from the main menu. The new shape will position itself below the circle, as shown in Figure 7-32.

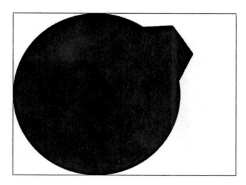

Figure 7-32. Move the new shape behind the circle.

Moving shapes in front of or behind other shapes like this is such a common task in Illustrator that you'll want to learn the keyboard shortcuts for doing this. First, hold down CTRL (Windows) or the Command key (OSX). Then press either of the square bracket keys, [and], to bring objects forwards or backwards in the stacking order. If you hold down the Shift key as well, the selected shape will jump to the very top or bottom of the stack. This works really well, and you'll often find you'll only need to use layers for very complex shapes.

Now merge the two shapes together.

    8.   Open the Pathfinder panel by selecting Window ↗ Pathfinder from the main menu. The Pathfinder panel has numerous buttons that let you combine or subtract shapes from each other.

9. Select both shapes by holding down the Shift key and clicking both of them with the black arrow. You can also select all the shapes by choosing Select ↗ All from the main menu. Or you can use the useful keyboard shortcut for this: Ctrl+A (Windows) or Command+A (OSX). You'll know that both shapes are selected together because they'll both be surrounded by blue bounding boxes. Figure 7-33 shows what this should look like.

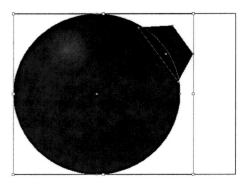

Figure 7-33. Select both shapes together.

10. Click the Unite button in the Pathfinder panel, as shown in Figure 7-34. The two shapes have now merged together.

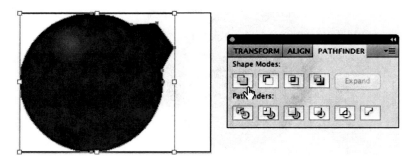

Figure 7-34. Unite the shapes using the pathfinder panel.

When you unite shapes like this, the bottom shape takes on the shading quality of the top shape. You'll notice that the tapered rectangle now blends seamlessly with the black radial gradient of the circle that was covering it. You can use the Pathfinder menu to subtract a shape from another as well. Do some experimenting with it when you have some time and you'll see how useful it can be for making complex compound shapes.

The next step is to make the bomb's fuse. You're going to do this by drawing a path with the Pen Tool. Illustrator's Pen Tool works exactly like the one in Photoshop, so review that section in Chapter 2 if you're unsure of how to use it. You'll be switching between the black arrow, white arrow, and Convert Anchor Point Tool constantly while drawing and reshaping paths, so it's really useful to use the following keyboard shortcuts:

- Black arrow (Selection Tool): V

- White arrow (Direct Selection Tool): A

- Convert Anchor point: Shift+C

- And, while you're at it, you might as well learn the shortcut for the Pen Tool itself: P

(The shortcut keys for the black and white arrows are easy to remember because the letters A and V look a bit like arrows.)

Use these tools to draw the bomb's fuse.

1. Draw a curved path that looks something like Figure 7-35. (Make sure that you don't have a fill or stroke color selected while you do this so that it will be easier to concentrate on drawing the path precisely.)

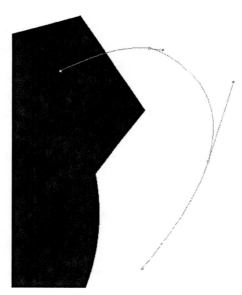

Figure 7-35. Use the Pen and Arrow Tools to draw a path for the fuse.

2. Select a dark brown stroke color.

3. Open the Stroke panel. Set the weight to 0.25. This would normally be an impossibly narrow width for a line, but because your bomb graphic is so small you'll see that it's going to be quite appropriate. (Normally you would set a line weight between 1 and 5 pixels.) The Stroke panel lets you set all the properties of lines and outlines, and it lets you do useful things with your lines like add arrowheads or change the line style. Figure 7-36 shows where to find the Stroke panel and what it looks like.

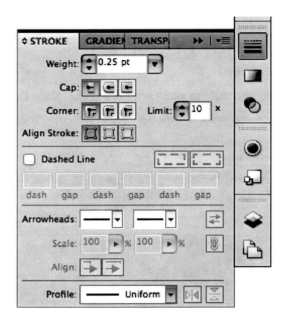

Figure 7-36. The Stroke panel lets you change all of a line's properties.

You're now going to add an artistic brush stroke to the path you've made.

    4.   Open the Brushes panel, as shown in Figure 7-37.

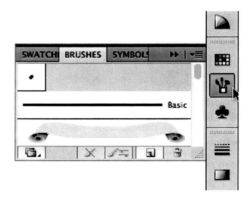

Figure 7-37. The Brushes panel lets you choose a brush style for your lines.

    5.   You're going to load the Artistic Ink brush set, which is hidden away in the Brushes menu. Click the menu button at the very top right corner of the Brushes panel. Select Open Brush Library ↗ Artistic ↗ Artistic Ink. This will open the Artistic Ink brush set as a new panel.

6. Choose the Tapered Round brush from the Artistic Ink set, as shown in Figure 7-38. You'll see the brush style applied to the path you drew, and you should end up with an image that looks a bit like Figure 7-39.

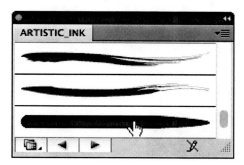

Figure 7-38. Choose an artistic brush style for the bomb's fuse.

Figure 7-39. The brush style is applied to the path.

7. You need to move the fuse behind the bomb shape. Make sure the fuse is still selected and choose Object ↗ Arrange ↗ Send to Back from the main menu. (You can also right-click on it and choose Arrange ↗ Send to Back from the option menu or hold down Shift+Ctrl+[in Windows or Shift+Command+[in OSX.) The fuse will now be positioned behind the bomb, as shown in Figure 7-40.

Figure 7-40. Use the Send To Back command to position the fuse behind the bomb shape.

The last step is to add a spark to the end of the fuse. You'll use the Star Tool to do this.

8. Select the Star Tool from the Tools bar (Figure 7-41). You'll find it in the same button set as the Rectangle and Ellipse tools.

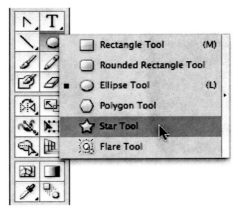

Figure 7-41. The Star Tool lets you draw stars.

9. The Star Tool does what it says on the tin: you can draw stars with it! Click and drag to draw a star shape, but before you release the left mouse button, press the up and down arrow keys on the keyboard. This adds or removes points on the star. Release the left mouse button when you're happy with the number of points.

10. Give the star a radial gradient fill. Make the center of the gradient yellow and the outside red. Position the star over the end of the fuse and scale it so that the size looks right. Figure 7-42 shows what you might come up with.

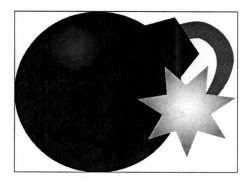

Figure 7-42. Add a spark to the fuse with the Star Tool.

You could improve this effect by adding a Gaussian Blur from the Effects ↗ Blur menu, but in this case the graphic is going to be so small it won't make any difference in the way that it appears on the stage in the final game.

Because it is such a small image, you need to make sure that that all the pixels are staying within the artboard's borders and that everything is properly aligned. Select View ↗ Pixel Preview to see what the actual pixels of your image will look like. Illustrator does a decent job translating vectors into pixels, but it won't ever be as good as your own eye. You might find that bits of the image are sticking over the edge of the artboard, like the spark in Figure 4-43. If they are, nudge them back in. (You can use the arrow keys on the keyboard to do this very precisely. If you hold down Shift while pressing the arrow keys, you can move the object in larger increments.) Use Pixel Preview as an opportunity to reposition or reshape anything else that doesn't look quite right. When you're working with small graphics, which most game graphics will be, it's a good idea to switch on Pixel Preview intermittently during the design process to catch small issues like this quickly.

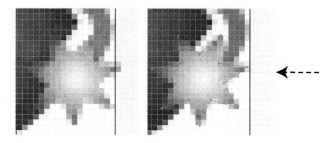

Figure 7-43. Use Pixel Preview to reposition, realign, or reshape any odd looking shapes.

Lastly, save the file and create the PNG image.

1. Select File ↗ Save As and find an appropriate spot on your computer to save the file.

2. Select File ↗ Save For Web and Devices. Save the file as a PNG file.

Let's learn a few more useful Illustrator techniques by creating a simple game character.

Making a game character

The game character is made out of a few basic shapes, and you'll be able to use it as a starting point for your own ideas about how to make characters for your games.

Setting up the document and drawing the body

1. Create a new Illustrator document with a width and height of 50 by 50 pixels. Give it the document the name of character.

2. Use the Ellipse Tool to draw a slightly flattened ellipse. Give it a light-blue-to-dark-gray radial gradient. Move the gradient's midpoint so that it's about 85% to the left. This ellipse is going to be the character's body. Position it so that its bottom edge is at the bottom of the artboard. Give it a black stroke color of 1pt. Figure 7-44 shows what this should look like.

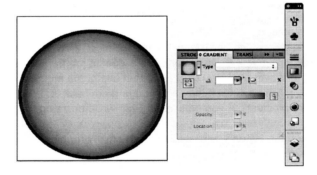

Figure 7-44. Draw the character's body with the Ellipse tool.

Drawing the antenna

The game character needs a pair of shiny metallic antennae. In the next few steps, you're going to make the first antenna out of two components, group the components together, and attach it to the body.

1. First, draw a small, elongated oval. You can draw this in the gray drawing area beyond the edge of the artboard so you have some space to work.

   In the Swatches panel, click the menu button in the panel's top right corner. Select Open Swatch Library ↗ Gradients ↗ Metals. This opens a panel of gradients that simulates the way light reflects off of different types of metals. Choose the Steel Radial gradient as a fill color for the oval. Set its stroke color to none. Figure 7-45 illustrates what the oval shape should now look like.

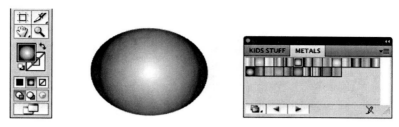

Figure 7-45. Draw an oval and fill it with a metallic gradient.

The Swatches Library has a wide range of different gradient pre-sets like this that you'll certainly find lots of use for when coloring your game objects. Spend some time exploring it when you have a chance.

2. Select the Gradient Tool. Use the gradient annotator to move the gradient so that the white highlight is in the oval's top left corner. Flatten the gradient so that it's the same shape as the oval, but just slightly smaller. Do this by dragging the small black circle that's on the dotted line that defines the gradient's area. You can see this in Figure 7-46.

Figure 7-46. Distort the gradient so that it's about the same shape as the oval.

Draw a slightly angled tapered rectangle. Use the Convert Path Tool to curve its base. It should look a bit like Figure 7-47. This will become the antenna's base.

Figure 7-47. Draw the antenna's base.

Set the new tapered rectangle's stroke color to none. Select the Eyedropper Tool and click the center of the oval you made in step 5. The tapered rectangle will now be filled with the same gradient as the oval, as you can see in Figure 7-48.

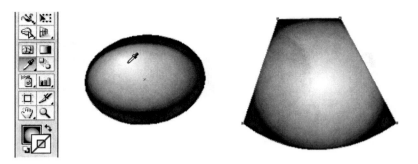

Figure 7-48. Use the Eyedropper Tool to fill the base of the antenna with the same gradient as the oval.

3. Select the Gradient Tool and reposition the gradient on the tapered rectangle so that its center is just above its base. Make it slightly wider and longer as well. You can see the result in Figure 7-49.

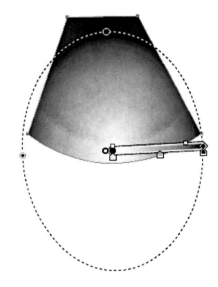

Figure 7-49. Reposition the gradient on the antenna's base.

Move the oval above the rectangle's tapered end and bring it to the front with the Object ↗ Arrange ↗ Bring to Front command. Select both shapes and group them together (Select Object ↗ Group from the main menu.) Figure 7-50 shows the result.

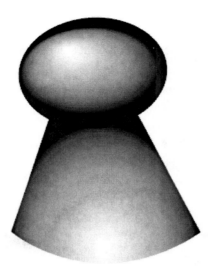

Figure 7-50. Group the two components of the antenna together so that you can move them as a single unit.

You now have a nice metallic antenna you can stick onto your character's body.

4.   Position and rotate the grouped antenna so that it's angled away from the body at the top left corner of the artboard. You may want to switch on Pixel Preview while you're positioning it to make sure that no stray pixels cross the artboard's boundary. Tweak the size and scale of the antenna until you're happy with the way it looks attached to the body. Remember, you can edit any of the grouped shapes individually if you need to by double-clicking them and entering isolation mode. Figure 7-51 shows the end result.

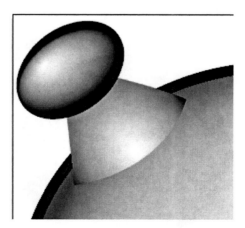

Figure 7-51. Attach the antenna to the body.

Make the second antenna

You'll make the second antenna by duplicating the first one and then using the Reflect command to invert it.

1. Make sure that the grouped antenna is still selected. Select Edit ↗ Copy and then Edit ↗ Paste In Front. This makes an exact duplicate of the antenna and pastes it directly above the original.

2. Select Object ↗ Transform ↗ Reflect from the main menu. The Reflect window will open. Select the type as Vertical and set the Angle to 90 degrees. Click the OK button, and you'll see that the new, duplicated antenna has flipped over (Figure 7-52).

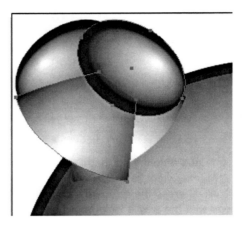

Figure 7-52. Reflect the duplicated antenna.

3. Move the new antenna to the body's left side, as shown in Figure 7-53.

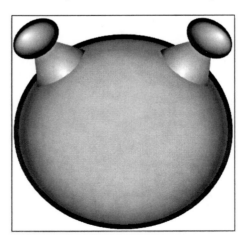

Figure 7-53. The body and two antennae

The last thing you need to do is reposition the gradient on the second antenna so that it appears that the light is catching it from the same angle as the first antenna.

4. Double-click the oval in the new antenna to enter isolation mode. Select the Gradient Tool and use it to rotate the gradient and shift its center to the top left. It should look something like Figure 7-54.

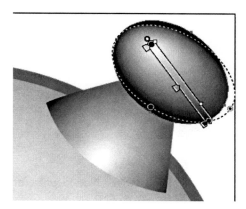

Figure 7-54. Correct the position of the highlight on the second antenna.

The body and antenna are finished; you'll work on the character's eyes next.

Making the character's eyes

The character's eyes are very simply made with three circles.

1. Draw a white circle under the left antenna (Figure 7-55).

Figure 7-55. The eye's first circle

Draw a smaller circle inside the first. Fill it with a blue-to-white radial gradient (Figure 7-56).

Figure 7-56. Fill the second circle with a radial gradient.

2. Add a smaller black circle inside the second. Fill it with a black-to-dark-gray radial gradient (Figure 7-57). This is the eye's pupil.

Figure 7-57. Fill the third circle with a dark radial gradient.

    3.   Draw three white circles of differing sizes and position them as shown in Figure 7-58. These are known as specular highlights. They simulate ambient light reflections and add life and vibrancy to the character's eyes.

Figure 7-58. Add three specular highlights.

    4.   Group all the circles together. Duplicate them to make the second eye. Position the second eye to the right side of the body.

Figure 7-59 shows what the character looks like with its new pair of eyes.

Figure 7-59. The character's eyes

Adding the smile

At the moment the character looks a bit too serious. You should give it something to smile about.

1. Draw an elongated ellipse centered just below the eyes. Give it a 1 pt black stroke outline and a pink fill color, as shown in Figure 7-60.

Figure 7-60. Draw a pink ellipse with a black outline.

2. Make sure it's selected, and choose Effect ↗ Warp ↗ Arc from the main menu. The Warp Options window will open. Set the following options:

    ▪ Style: Arc

    ▪ Horizontal

    ▪ Blend: -17%

Click the OK button when you're done and the ellipse will be distorted into the shape of a smile, as you can see in Figure 7-61.

Figure 7-61. Use the Arc Warp effect to make the character smile.

Illustrator has a large number of warp effects and you can use them to transform simple shapes into very complex ones very quickly and easily.

Bring in the stylist!

Give your character some hair by very simple adding three triangles between the antennae.

1. Select the Polygon Tool from the Tools bar. The Polygon Tool occupies the same button set as the Rectangle and Ellipse tools. You can use it to make polygons with any number of sides by pressing the up or down arrow keys. Click and drag to create a polygon, but before you release the mouse button, press the down arrow key. Release the mouse button when the polygon becomes a triangle.

2. Give the triangle a black fill color, and position it between the two antennae and behind the body, as shown in Figure 7-62. Size it so that it fits neatly.

Figure 7-62. Use the Polygon Tool to draw a black triangle.

3. Copy this triangle and use the Edit ↗ Paste in Back command to paste the duplicate behind the original. Move it to the left of the first triangle and rotate it so that it's properly aligned with the curvature of the body. Make another copy of the triangle and position it to the right of the first. Your character will end up with a spikey haircut, like that in Figure 7-63. Switch on Pixel Preview to make sure that any of the triangle points aren't overlapping the artboard.

Figure 7-63. Your character's new haircut

You're almost done! You just need to give your character some feet.

Drawing the shoes

You'll draw the shoes with the Pen Tool and give them a simple dark-to-light linear gradient.

1.   Use the Pen Tool to draw to roughly define the shape of the left shoe (Figure 7-64).

Figure 7-64. Draw a basic path.

2.   Use the Convert Anchor Point Tool to round the edges (Figure 7-65).

Figure 7-65. Round the edges.

3. Give the shoe a white-to-gray linear gradient fill.

4. Use the black arrow to resize, scale, or reposition the shoe so that it fits neatly inside the left half of the artboard. Confirm this using Pixel Preview (Figure 7-66).

Figure 7-66. Fine-tune the size and position of the shoe using the black arrow in Pixel Preview mode.

5. If everything looks good, make another copy of the shoe. Then select Object ↗ Transform ↗ Reflect from the main menu to flip over the new copy of the shoe. Move it to the character's right side.

The character is almost finished! Figure 7-67 shows what it now looks like.

Figure 7-67. The almost-finished game character

You could leave your character like this and it would be just fine for your game. But let's take it one small step further.

Add some extra cuteness

The finishing touch is to give the character some rosy cheeks.

1. Add two circles below the character's eyes. Fill them with a transparent-to-light-pink radial gradient. The effect is subtle, but adds a little something to the depth and liveliness of the character. You're aiming for a final image that looks like Figure 7-68.

Figure 7-68. Add some rosy cheeks.

2. Finally, save your work and create the character.png file.

The next step is to design the background game screen.

Designing the playing field

Rather than take you on a step-by-step tour on how to make the game background, I'll explain how it was made. There are no new techniques here, and your Illustrator skills should now be good enough that you will easily be able to create something similar.

I first created a 550 by 400 pixel document. To make my job easier, I made Illustrator's grid visible and set the grid cell size to 50 by 50 pixels. None of the objects in the game are larger than 50 pixels square, so it makes sense to use that as a base size for planning the layout of the game playing field.

To set the grid size, select Edit ↗ Preferences ↗ Guides and Grid (Windows) or Illustrator ↗ Preferences ↗ Guides and Grid (OSX). Set the Gridline every: option to 50px.

With the grid cell size defined, you can make it visible by selecting View ↗ Show Grid. Then select the View ↗ Snap to Grid option so that objects will neatly align themselves to the grid squares.

With that done, I made a copy of my box graphic. I removed the corner rivets, and made a copy of it into each grid square. I then grouped all the squares and set their opacity to 40% in the Transparency panel. Figure 7-69 shows what this looks like.

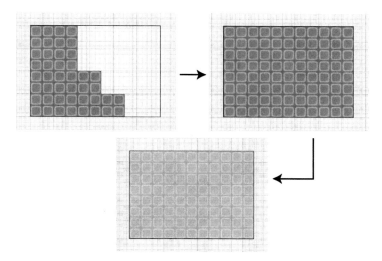

Figure 7-69. The process of creating the game background

To make the border, I first created a new layer. I made copies of the box graphic around the perimeter. I grouped them together and added a drop shadow effect to make it look as though the border is floating slightly above the main playing field. I then drew a black rounded rectangle with a white stroke color on the top border. This is where the game's timer will be displayed. You can see the end result in Figure 7-70.

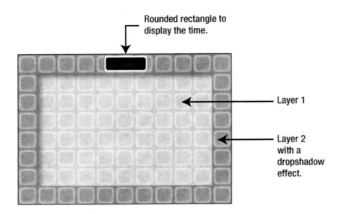

Rounded rectangle to display the time.

Layer 1

Layer 2 with a dropshadow effect.

Figure 7-70. The finished background graphic

The Game Over graphic was just as easy to make.

Making the Game Over graphic

To make the explosion for the Game Over graphic, I started with a simple star shape and filled it with a red-to-yellow radial gradient. I then added a Fisheye Warp effect from the Effects menu, just to puff it out a bit. I then added a Pucker and Bloat effect from the Effects menu. A simple drop shadow finished it off, and you can see the final effect in Figure 7-71. It took less than 30 seconds to make.

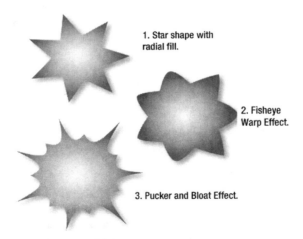

1. Star shape with radial fill.

2. Fisheye Warp Effect.

3. Pucker and Bloat Effect.

Figure 7-71. Effects applied to the star shape to create a cartoon explosion.

It was really just a matter of playing around with the parameters in those effect menus until I liked the result I saw on the artboard

The 3D text was just as easy to make. I typed out the words "GAME OVER" with the Emulogic font. I gave the text a bright green fill and white outline color. I then applied an Extrude and Bevel effect from the Effects ↗ 3D menu. Again, it was just a matter of fiddling with the effect parameters until the result seemed to look good. Lastly, I rotated the text slightly. Figure 7-72 shows the end result. Another 30 seconds of work well spent!

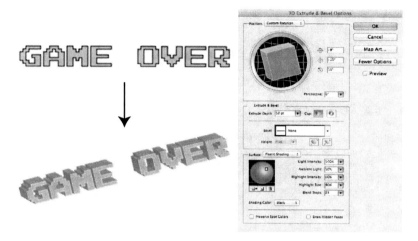

Figure 7-72. Create 3D text with the Extrude and Bevel effect.

Figure 7-73 shows the final Game Over graphic. When this graphic is displayed in the game, the words "You Won!" or "You Lost!" will be displayed just below the "GAME OVER" text.

Figure 7-73. The finished Game Over graphic

All the graphics are finished, so copy the PNG files into the game project's images folder. Now let's look at how to program the game.

You now know more than enough about Adobe Illustrator to start making sophisticated game graphics. However, you'll certainly want to learn more about Illustrator and the first place to look is Illustrator's own help menu. Select Help ↗ Illustrator Help and the Adobe Help application will open with a chapter-by-chapter description of Illustrator's features and how to use them.

Adobe also maintains an excellent tutorial site featuring many videos on how to use basic features and achieve special effects. You can find out more at Adobe's support web site at www.adobe.com/support/illustrator/.

Programming the game

Time Bomb Panic combines all the programming techniques you've learned in the book so far. When you take a look at the code, you'll see that 90% of it is more or less identical to the code you were using in the previous chapters. That's good, because it shows that you can use all the code you've been learning in the context of a real game. There's not much new to learn.

What about the 10% that you haven't seen before? Here are the new things you'll learn:

- How to create and use a `Timer` object. Like random numbers, timers are essential to most types of video games.

- How to create individual classes for all your game objects.

- How to use a custom method to simplify and reduce repetitive code.

You'll go on a tour of all these new features as well as the specific way in which the game handles a few techniques you've looked at before, such as:

- Collision detection between the boxes and bombs.

- Stage boundaries.

- Checking for the end of the game.

- Displaying the Game Over image.

By the time you're done, you should have all the confidence you need to make a game of similar complexity.

Dealing with many objects

Before you look at the code of the main application class, you must overcome a big problem: there are many objects in this game. If you don't find a way to manage them before you start programming the game, you drown in hundreds of lines of repetitive code.

How many objects are there? You've created five game graphics, so you've got at least five. But many of those images, like the boxes and bombs, are used multiple times in the game. Take a good look at Figure

7-74. Knowing what you now about game programming, how many objects do you think you'll have to deal with?

Figure 7-74. How do you make code manageable if you have a game with lots of objects?

You've got 14 boxes, five bombs, one character, one background, one visible text field, and the Game Over graphic that appears at the end of the game. This Game Over graphic also contains another text field. That's a total of 24 objects. At most, the example programs in previous chapters have had five.

Why is this a problem? Think about how much code you have to write to create and add just one object to a game. First, you have to embed the image, create the DisplayObject container, and create the containing Sprite, like this:

```
[Embed(source="../images/character.png")]
public var CharacterImage:Class;
public var characterImage:DisplayObject = new CharacterImage();
public var character:Sprite = new Sprite();
```

Then you have to add the image to the Sprite, add the Sprite to the stage, and position it, like this:

```
character.addChild(characterImage);
stage.addChild(character);
character.x = 300;
character.y = 150;
```

That's eight lines of code—for just one object. With the 24 objects you have in this game you'd need to duplicate this same code 24 times. You'd end up with 192 lines of repetitive code just to add all the objects to the game.

It's just not manageable, so let's learn a better way. You're going to keep all of your objects inside their own individual classes and then use a custom method to add and position them on the stage.

What is a class, really?

I've talked a lot about classes already, but don't worry if you didn't understand too much about what I tried to explain. Unless you've got a real, living, breathing class in front of you, it can be a very abstract concept to understand. So let's look at some living, breathing classes!

You've seen many classes already in this book.

- AS3.0's built-in classes like `Sprite`, `TextField`, and `Event` that you import into your programs.

- The application classes in which you wrote our main programs, like `PickingUpObjects`, `KeyboardControl`, or `NumberGuessingGame`. I've been calling them "programs" up till now, but they are really "application classes."

- The `Collision` class, a specialized class in Chapter 6 that helped you create a collision boundary between game objects.

Fine, but what is a class exactly? In short, it's just a "thing" in your game. You can make a class for any object you want to use in your game. Those objects can be abstract bits of code, like the `Collision` class, or they can be the real game objects you see on the stage.

So if a "class" is just a "thing," doesn't that mean you should be able to make a class for each of the things in your game? It absolutely does! To prove it, open the TimeBombPanic project folder and peer into the src folder. You'll see these files (also shown in Figure 7-75):

- TimeBombPanic.as

- Collision.as

- Character.as

- Box.as

- Bomb.as

- Background.as

- GameOver.as

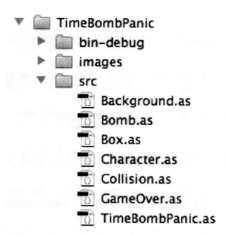

Figure 7-75. The classes used in Time Bomb Panic. There's one for each game object.

You know now that `TimeBombPanic.as` is the application class—the main program. And you know that `Collision.as` is the specialized class you wrote in Chapter 6. But you can clearly see that there is now also a class for each and every one of the five game objects you drew with Illustrator in the first part of the chapter.

What do those classes do? It's very easy. All they do is load the embedded images into themselves. To prove this, have a look at the `Character` class.

```
package
{
  import flash.display.DisplayObject;
  import flash.display.Sprite;

  public class Character extends Sprite
  {
    //Embed the image
    [Embed(source="../images/character.png")]
    public var GameObjectImage:Class;
    public var gameObjectImage:DisplayObject
      = new GameObjectImage();

    public function Character()
    {
      this.addChild(gameObjectImage);
    }
  }
}
```

The job of the `Character` class is just to display the `character.png` image. That's all! And you've seen all this code before—it's six of those eight lines of rather tedious code you always use to embed and display an image.

Why is this useful? It means that because you've written this code in the class, you never have to write it out again, and you can reuse it in any other game you write. You'll see this at work soon.

There are two details I need to point out. First, the `Character` class is extending the `Sprite` class.

```
public class Character extends Sprite
```

This means that any game objects you make using the `Character` class are actually `Sprite` objects under their skin. The `extends` keyword means that the `Character` class has *inherited* all the properties and methods of the `Sprite` class. It means that you can use all the same properties and methods that you usually use with `Sprite` objects. Properties like x, y, visible, alpha, or methods like `addChild` will all work with any objects that you make with this new `Character` class.

> *This is an important programming concept called* inheritance. *When you use the* extends *keyword, the new class you're making "inherits" all of the properties and methods of the class you're extending. Inheritance is a key feature of a programming style called Object Orient Programming (OOP). AS3.0 is an OOP language, as is Java, C++, C #, and Objective C.*

It also means that you don't have to create a separate `Sprite` object and add the image to it. The image is already wrapped inside a `Sprite` because the `Character` extends the `Sprite` class.

All of this means that `Character` objects will be able do everything that `Sprite` objects can, with the bonus that they display the image of the game character.

But where is the character.png actually being displayed? It's not being displayed on the stage. It's being displayed inside *this* class. That's what this line does:

```
this.addChild(gameObjectImage);
```

The keyword `this` means "this class." This line of code means that you're adding the gameObjectImage to *this*, `Character`, class. The result is that whenever you use a `Character` class object in a game, the character.png image will automatically be displayed. It's part of the class.

Why didn't you use `stage.addChild()` like you've done in other programs? That's because only the application class can add things directly to the stage. The application class, in this case, is `TimeBombPanic.as`. You'll see how it will add a `Character` class object to the stage very soon.

So now you know that the `Character` class just has the job of displaying the character.png image. But what do the `Bomb`, `Box`, `Background`, and `GameOver` classes do? Exactly the same thing: they display the images you designed in the first part of the chapter. In fact, the code in each is almost identical. Take a look at the `Box` class.

```
package
{
  import flash.display.DisplayObject;
  import flash.display.Sprite;

  public class Box extends Sprite
  {
    //Embed the image
    [Embed(source="../images/box.png")]
    public var GameObjectImage:Class;
    public var gameObjectImage:DisplayObject
      = new GameObjectImage();

    public function Box()
    {
      this.addChild(gameObjectImage);
    }
  }
}
```

The only difference between the Box class and the Character class is the name and the PNG file that it's embedding. Browse through the other classes and you'll see that they all follow this identical format.

So now that you've got these classes and stuffed your game graphics inside them, how do you use them? You first have to make objects from them, and you can do this in the application class.

Of course you already know how to make objects: with the new keyword. You can make an object from the Character class like this:

```
public var character:Character = new Character();
```

You can then add it to the stage like this:

```
stage.addChild(character);
```

You can now use the character object anywhere you like in your game, and it will work like any other Sprite object you've ever created. But the one bonus is that it will already contain the character.png image.

Where this saves you a lot of work is if you have to make multiple copies of an object. There are 14 boxes in Time Bomb Panic. You don't need to make 14 separate classes for each box. You just need one parent Box class and you can make 14 instances (copies) of it. Each of those instances will automatically contain the embedded box.png image. This saves you having to type out dozens of lines of repetitive code.

Here's how you can make multiple box instances using just one Box class. First, make a few box objects in the application class.

```
public var box1:Box = new Box();
public var box2:Box = new Box();
```

```
public var box3:Box = new Box();
```

You can add them to the stage like this:

```
stage.addChild(box1);
stage.addChild(box2);
stage.addChild(box3);
```

There's not a single Embed metatag in sight! box1, box2, and box3 will all contain the box.png image that was embedded into their parent Box class.

Do you see now how classes are just "things" in your game?

These five simple classes have just contained images, but you can put anything you like into a class. In the next chapter, you'll see how to put logic code inside them so that you can create objects with very complex, autonomous behavior.

Figure 7-76 illustrates how these object classes work with the application class to produce the images that you can see on the stage.

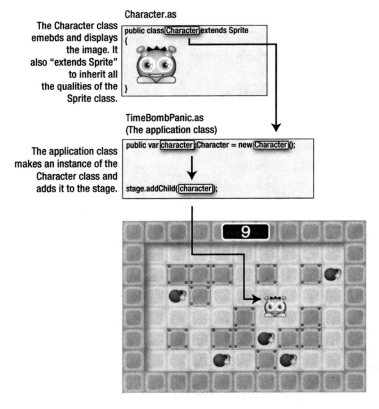

Figure 7-76. The application class makes game objects from the game object classes.

Now that you know your five game objects are self-contained classes, let's take a look at the entire TimeBombPanic application class, and I'll show you how they've been used in the game.

Looking at the TimeBombPanic application class

I'm going to list the entire TimeBombPanic application here so that you have a reference to it for the rest of the chapter. You'll recognize some very familiar code, but a few new things as well. I'll walk you through exactly how all of it works.

```
package
{
  import flash.display.DisplayObject;
  import flash.display.Sprite;
  import flash.events.Event;
  import flash.events.KeyboardEvent;
  import flash.text.*;
  import flash.ui.Keyboard;
  import flash.events.TimerEvent;
  import flash.utils.Timer;

  [SWF(width="550", height="400",
    backgroundColor="#FFFFFF", frameRate="60")]
  public class TimeBombPanic extends Sprite
  {
    //Create the text objects
    public var format:TextFormat = new TextFormat();
    public var output:TextField = new TextField();
    public var input:TextField = new TextField();
    public var gameResult:TextField = new TextField();

    //Create the game objects
    public var character:Character = new Character();
    public var background:Background = new Background();
    public var gameOver:GameOver = new GameOver();

    //The bombs
    public var bomb1:Bomb = new Bomb();
    public var bomb2:Bomb = new Bomb();
    public var bomb3:Bomb = new Bomb();
    public var bomb4:Bomb = new Bomb();
    public var bomb5:Bomb = new Bomb();

    //The boxes
    public var box1:Box = new Box();
    public var box2:Box = new Box();
    public var box3:Box = new Box();
    public var box4:Box = new Box();
    public var box5:Box = new Box();
    public var box6:Box = new Box();
    public var box7:Box = new Box();
```

```
public var box8:Box = new Box();
public var box9:Box = new Box();
public var box10:Box = new Box();
public var box11:Box = new Box();
public var box12:Box = new Box();
public var box13:Box = new Box();
public var box14:Box = new Box();

//Create the timer
public var timer:Timer;

//Create and initialize the vx and vy variables
public var vx:int = 0;
public var vy:int = 0;

//The bombsDefused variable that counts
//the number of bombs collected
public var bombsDefused:uint = 0;

public function TimeBombPanic()
{
  createGameObjects();
  setupTextfields()
  setupEventListeners();
}
public function createGameObjects():void
{
  //Add the background
  addGameObjectToStage(background, 0, 0);

  //Add the character
  addGameObjectToStage(character, 50, 50);

  //Add the boxes
  addGameObjectToStage(box1, 100, 100);
  addGameObjectToStage(box2, 150, 100);
  addGameObjectToStage(box3, 200, 100);
  addGameObjectToStage(box4, 150, 150);
  addGameObjectToStage(box5, 100, 250);
  addGameObjectToStage(box6, 200, 250);
  addGameObjectToStage(box7, 250, 250);
  addGameObjectToStage(box8, 250, 200);
  addGameObjectToStage(box9, 300, 100);
  addGameObjectToStage(box10, 300, 300);
  addGameObjectToStage(box11, 350, 250);
  addGameObjectToStage(box12, 400, 100);
  addGameObjectToStage(box13, 400, 200);
  addGameObjectToStage(box14, 400, 250);

  //The bombs
  addGameObjectToStage(bomb1, 105, 160);
  addGameObjectToStage(bomb2, 205, 310);
```

```
    addGameObjectToStage(bomb3, 305, 260);
    addGameObjectToStage(bomb4, 355, 310);
    addGameObjectToStage(bomb5, 455, 110);

    //Add the gameOver image and
    //make it invisible when the game starts
    addGameObjectToStage(gameOver, 125, 50);
    gameOver.visible = false;

    //Initialize the timer
    timer = new Timer(1000);
    timer.addEventListener(TimerEvent.TIMER, updateTimeHandler);
    timer.start();
}
public function setupTextfields():void
{
    //Set the text format object
    format.font = "Helvetica";
    format.size = 38;
    format.color = 0xFFFFFF;
    format.align = TextFormatAlign.CENTER;

    //Configure the output text field
    output.defaultTextFormat = format;
    output.autoSize = TextFieldAutoSize.CENTER;
    output.border = false;
    output.text = "0";

    //Display and position the output text field
    stage.addChild(output);
    output.x = 265;
    output.y = 7;

    //Configure and display the gameResult Textfield
    format.color = 0x000000;
    format.size = 32;
    gameResult.defaultTextFormat = format;
    gameResult.autoSize = TextFieldAutoSize.CENTER;
    gameResult.text = "You Won!";
    gameOver.addChild(gameResult);
    gameResult.x = 145;
    gameResult.y = 160;
}
public function setupEventListeners():void
{
    stage.addEventListener
      (KeyboardEvent.KEY_DOWN, keyDownHandler);
    stage.addEventListener
      (KeyboardEvent.KEY_UP, keyUpHandler);
    stage.addEventListener
      (Event.ENTER_FRAME, enterFrameHandler);
}
```

```
public function updateTimeHandler(event:TimerEvent):void
{
  output.text = String(timer.currentCount);

  //Stop the timer when it reaches 10
  if(timer.currentCount == 10)
  {
    checkGameOver();
  }
}
public function enterFrameHandler(event:Event):void
{
  //Move the player
  character.x += vx;
  character.y += vy;

  //Stage boundaries
  if (character.x < 50)
  {
    character.x = 50;
  }
  if (character.y < 50)
  {
    character.y = 50;
  }
  if (character.x + character.width > stage.stageWidth - 50)
  {
    character.x = stage.stageWidth - character.width - 50;
  }
  if (character.y + character.height > stage.stageHeight -50)
  {
    character.y = stage.stageHeight - character.height - 50;
  }

  //Box Collision code
  Collision.block(character, box1);
  Collision.block(character, box2);
  Collision.block(character, box3);
  Collision.block(character, box4);
  Collision.block(character, box5);
  Collision.block(character, box6);
  Collision.block(character, box7);
  Collision.block(character, box8);
  Collision.block(character, box9);
  Collision.block(character, box10);
  Collision.block(character, box11);
  Collision.block(character, box12);
  Collision.block(character, box13);
  Collision.block(character, box14);

  //Bomb collision code
  if(character.hitTestObject(bomb1) && bomb1.visible == true)
```

```
    {
      bomb1.visible = false;
      bombsDefused++;
      checkGameOver();
    }
    if(character.hitTestObject(bomb2) && bomb2.visible == true)
    {
      bomb2.visible = false;
      bombsDefused++;
      checkGameOver();
    }
    if(character.hitTestObject(bomb3) && bomb3.visible == true)
    {
      bomb3.visible = false;
      bombsDefused++;
      checkGameOver();
    }
    if(character.hitTestObject(bomb4) && bomb4.visible == true)
    {
      bomb4.visible = false;
      bombsDefused++;
      checkGameOver();
    }
    if(character.hitTestObject(bomb5) && bomb5.visible == true)
    {
      bomb5.visible = false;
      bombsDefused++;
      checkGameOver();
    }
  }
  public function checkGameOver():void
  {
    if(bombsDefused == 5)
    {
      gameOver.visible = true;
      gameResult.text = "You Won!";
      character.alpha = 0.5;
      background.alpha = 0.5;
      timer.removeEventListener
        (TimerEvent.TIMER, updateTimeHandler);
      stage.removeEventListener
        (Event.ENTER_FRAME, enterFrameHandler);
    }
    else if(timer.currentCount == 10)
    {
      gameOver.visible = true;
      gameResult.text = "You Lost!";
      character.alpha = 0.5;
      background.alpha = 0.5;
      timer.removeEventListener
        (TimerEvent.TIMER, updateTimeHandler);
      stage.removeEventListener
```

```
        (Event.ENTER_FRAME, enterFrameHandler);
    }
}
public function addGameObjectToStage
  (gameObject:Sprite, xPos:int, yPos:int):void
{
    stage.addChild(gameObject);
        gameObject.x = xPos;
    gameObject.y = yPos;
}
public function keyDownHandler(event:KeyboardEvent):void
{
    if (event.keyCode == Keyboard.LEFT)
    {
      vx = -5;
    }
    else if (event.keyCode == Keyboard.RIGHT)
    {
      vx = 5;
    }
    else if (event.keyCode == Keyboard.UP)
    {
      vy = -5;
    }
    else if (event.keyCode == Keyboard.DOWN)
    {
      vy = 5;
    }
}
public function keyUpHandler(event:KeyboardEvent):void
{
    if (event.keyCode == Keyboard.LEFT
      || event.keyCode == Keyboard.RIGHT)
    {
      vx = 0;
    }
    else if (event.keyCode == Keyboard.DOWN
      || event.keyCode == Keyboard.UP)
    {
      vy = 0;
    }
  }
 }
}
```

Adding objects to the game

You know that all the game objects are classes. To use them in the game you need to make an object from the class and add it to the stage. The character, background, and gameOver objects are made like this:

```
public var character:Character = new Character();
public var background:Background = new Background();
public var gameOver:GameOver = new GameOver();
```

Five objects are made from the Bomb class and 14 are made from the Box classes. Here's the abbreviated code:

```
public var bomb1:Bomb = new Bomb();
...
public var bomb5:Bomb = new Bomb();

public var box1:Box = new Box();
...
public var box14:Box = new Box();
```

Yes, it's a long list of code, but almost four times less to write than if you weren't using classes. In future chapters you'll see how to make this code much more compact.

You now have to use addChild() to add the objects to the stage, and then set their x and y positions. To do this you would usually write something like this:

```
stage.addChild(character);
character.x = 225;
character.y = 150;
```

That would work just fine in this game, except that this time around you've got 22 objects, not just three or four. You don't want to have to write 66 lines of code to do this—what a boring chore that would be! It would be much better if you could reduce it down to one line per object. Of course you can!

I've created a custom method for this game called addGameObjectToStage. Here's how to use it to add one of the game objects to the stage:

```
addGameObjectToStage(character, 50, 50);
```

The method takes three parameters: the name of the object, the x position, and the y position.

You'll find the method's function definition about three quarters of the way down the program listing in the TimeBombPanic application class.

```
public function addGameObjectToStage
   (gameObject:Sprite, xPos:int, yPos:int):void
{
  stage.addChild(gameObject);
  gameObject.x = xPos;
  gameObject.y = yPos;
}
```

It adds the objects to the stage and assigns them the x and y positions that you gave them in the method arguments.

> *A small technical detail that you should notice is that the method's function definition types the incoming gameObject in its parameter as a Sprite.*
>
> *gameObject:Sprite*
>
> *However, all the game objects in this game are typed as Character, Background, Box, GameOver, and Bomb. None of them are typed as Sprite. But remember that when you created the game object classes, they all extended the Sprite class, like this:*
>
> *public class Character extends Sprite*
>
> *This means that Sprite is the parent class. By typing objects to their parent class in method parameters, you can make the method very general so that it works for all objects that share the same parent class.*

Think carefully about any bits or repetitive code you might have in your game programs and you'll often find you can write a custom method like this to do the grunt work for you.

Stage boundaries

In this game you'll notice that the character can't cross the border of squares around the playing field's perimeter, as illustrated in Figure 7-77.

Figure 7-77. The character can't cross the playing field border.

Because you designed the background graphic yourself, you know that there's nothing physically blocking the character from crossing this border—it's just an image. But it definitely looks like a solid border. This illusion was very easy to create. All the code did was reduce the stage boundary code by 50 pixels on each axis, in effect making the stage 50 pixels smaller on each side. Here's the if statement from the enterFrameHandler that does this, with the modified stage boundaries highlighted:

```
if (character.x < 50)
{
  character.x = 50;
}
if (character.y < 50)
{
  character.y = 50;
}
if (character.x + character.width > stage.stageWidth - 50)
{
  character.x = stage.stageWidth - character.width - 50;
}
if (character.y + character.height > stage.stageHeight -50)
{
  character.y = stage.stageHeight - character.height - 50;
}
```

The playing field's border width is 50 pixels, so all the code needed to do was compensate for this in both the x and y axes.

Collisions between the character and the boxes

Time Bomb Panic uses the same Collision class that I introduced in Chapter 6. The only difference in this game is that the Collision.block method is called 14 times in the enterFrameHandler—once for each box. Here's the abbreviated code that does this:

```
Collision.block(character, box1);
...
Collision.block(character, box14);
```

It couldn't be easier. It works well, but in Chapter 10 you'll look at a more efficient way of handling collisions between multiple objects using a **for loop** so that you don't have to type out the same line of code 14 times.

Defusing the bombs

It's the job of the bombsDefused variable to count the number of bombs the character has collected. It's created and initialized to 0 in the class definition at the start of the game.

```
public var bombsDefused:uint = 0;
```

The enterFrameHandler checks for collisions between the character and the bombs. There's one if statement for each of the five bomb objects. When the character collides with a bomb, the bomb's visible property is set to false. That's what essentially removes the bomb from the game. The bombsDefused variable is then increased by 1, and another line of code checks if the game has ended. Here's the if statement that checks for a collision with the first bomb:

```
if(character.hitTestObject(bomb1) && bomb1.visible == true)
{
  bomb1.visible = false;
  bombsDefused++;
  checkGameOver();
}
```

There are many ways to remove an object from a game, but making it invisible is the simplest. However, you should be aware that even though you can't see an object on the stage anymore, it's still there. That means that if the character collides with a bomb, and the bomb's visible property is set to false, that won't prevent the character from colliding with it again. It just means that the character would be colliding with an invisible bomb rather than a visible one.

You can't allow this, so you need an extra check in the if statement to make sure that the character only collides with visible bombs.

```
if(character.hitTestObject(bomb1) && bomb1.visible == true)
{...
```

If any bomb is not visible, it means that it's already been defused, and this if statement is ignored.

After updating the bombsDefused variable, the last thing these if statements do is call the checkGameOver method:

```
checkGameOver();
```

This method's job is to find out if the game is finished, and you'll soon see how it works.

Using a timer

A brand new feature of this game is that it uses a timer to count the number of seconds that have elapsed from the start. If ten seconds pass and the player hasn't defused all the bombs, the player loses the game.

Let's first look at how a timer works in a very focused example program, and I'll then show you how a timer is used in Time Bomb Panic.

Understanding timers

In the chapter's source files you'll find a project folder called UsingATimer. Open and compile it. It counts seconds from 0 to 10. When it reaches 10, the counting starts again. Figure 7-78 shows what you'll see.

Figure 7-78. Counting seconds from 0 to 10

The UsingATimer application class uses a timer to update a text field. Here's the entire program. I've highlighted all the code that specifically relates to making and using a Timer object.

```
package
{
  import flash.display.Sprite;
  import flash.text.*;
  import flash.events.TimerEvent;
  import flash.utils.Timer;

  public class UsingATimer extends Sprite
  {
    //The Timer object
    public var timer:Timer;

    //The Text objects
    public var output:TextField = new TextField();
    public var format:TextFormat = new TextFormat();

    public function UsingATimer()
    {
      //Initialize the timer
      timer = new Timer(1000);
      timer.addEventListener(TimerEvent.TIMER, updateTimeHandler);
      timer.start();

      //Set the text format object
      format.font = "Helvetica";
      format.size = 200;
      format.color = 0x000000;
      format.align = TextFormatAlign.CENTER;

      //Configure the output text field
      output.defaultTextFormat = format;
      output.autoSize = TextFieldAutoSize.CENTER;
      output.border = true;
      output.text = "0";
```

```
        //Display and position the output text field
        stage.addChild(output);
        output.x = 200;
        output.y = 100;
    }
    public function updateTimeHandler(event:TimerEvent):void
    {
        output.text = String(timer.currentCount);

        //Reset and restart the timer when it reaches 10
        if(timer.currentCount == 10)
        {
            timer.reset();
            timer.start();
        }
    }
  }
}
```

To use timers in your programs, you first need to import the Timer and TimerEvent classes.

```
import flash.events.TimerEvent;
import flash.utils.Timer;
```

Timers are objects, so you need to create them in the same way you create other objects. First, declare the timer variable in the class definition.

```
public var timer:Timer;
```

Then turn it into a Timer object in the constructor method by using the new keyword.

```
timer = new Timer(1000);
```

The Timer class requires one argument, which is a number that represents milliseconds. (One millisecond represents 1/1000th of a second. One thousand milliseconds, as in this example, equal one second.)

Timers in AS3.0 work by triggering an event at regular intervals. In this example, you want to trigger an event to fire every second. The event's job is to update the output text field on the stage by one. To set this in place, however, you need to add a TimerEvent event listener to the new timer object that you just created.

```
timer.addEventListener(TimerEvent.TIMER, updateTimeHandler);
```

Next, you need to use the Timer class's start method to actually start the timer working.

```
timer.start();
```

The timer object now triggers the updateTimeHandler event handler every second.

```
public function updateTimeHandler(event:TimerEvent):void
{
  output.text = String(timer.currentCount);

  //Reset and restart the timer when it reaches 10
  if(timer.currentCount == 10)
  {
    timer.reset();
    timer.start();
  }
}
```

Timer objects have a property called currentCount that tells you how many times the timer event has fired since it started. The updateTimeHandler copies the value of currentCount to the output text field on the stage.

```
output.text = String(timer.currentCount);
```

You can use currentCount as done here: to display the number of times the event has been triggered. The if statement uses currentCount to check whether ten seconds have elapsed; if they have, it calls the Timer class's reset and start methods:

```
timer.reset();
timer.start();
```

reset stops the timer and also resets currentCount to zero. To start the timer again, you need to use the start method once more. (If you need to stop the timer completely in any of your games, you can use the stop method, which stops the timer without resetting currentCount.)

When you create a Timer object, you can add a second argument, which is known as repeatCount. This is a number that tells the timer how many times it should repeat. You can see the effect of using repeatCount by updating the directive that creates the timer object so that it looks like this:

```
timer = new Timer(1000, 5);
```

If you recompile the program, you'll see that the numbers count up to five. After that, the handler is no longer called.

There are a few more Timer class properties that you should know about. If you need to change the interval between events, you can use the delay property. For example, if you want the timer event to be triggered every one-half second, you can set the delay to 500 milliseconds, like this:

```
timer.delay = 500;
```

If you need to know whether a timer is currently running, you can use the running property, which returns true when the timer is running and is false when it isn't.

Finally, you can use the `TimerEvent` class's `TIMER_COMPLETE` property to trigger an event when the timer finishes.

```
timer.addEventListener
  (TimerEvent.TIMER_COMPLETE, timerCompleteHandler);
```

This is a very basic introduction to how timers work. You can use a `Timer` object to create a countdown timer, make an object move intermittently, or calculate a player's score based on how long it takes to complete a task.

> *Another feature of this example program, and of Time Bomb Panic, is that the text fields set their height and width automatically. This is done with the TextFieldAutoSize class, like this:*
>
> *output.autoSize = TextFieldAutoSize.CENTER;*

Using a timer in Time Bomb Panic

The timer in Time Bomb Panic is created and used in exactly the same way as the example program. Every second it fires the `updateTimeHandler`, which looks like this:

```
public function updateTimeHandler(event:TimerEvent):void
{
  output.text = String(timer.currentCount);

  //Stop the timer when it reaches 10
  if(timer.currentCount == 10)
  {
    checkGameOver();
  }
}
```

It just does two things. First, it updates the output text field with the time.

```
output.text = String(timer.currentCount);
```

This is what displays the current time on the stage, as shown in Figure 7-79.

Figure 7-79. The output text field displays the timer's currentCount property.

The second thing that updateTimerEvent does is check for the end of the game.

```
if(timer.currentCount == 10)
{
  checkGameOver();
}
```

It only checks for the end of the game if the timer reaches 10. So what does that mysterious checkGameOver method actually do?

Ending the game

There are two ways the game can end: if the player defuses five bombs or if the timer reaches 10. Each time the player collides with a bomb, the checkGameOver method is called. And, as you've just seen, it's also called when the value of timer.currentCount equals 10. Here's the checkGameOver method:

```
public function checkGameOver():void
{
  if(bombsDefused == 5)
  {
    gameOver.visible = true;
    gameResult.text = "You Won!";
    character.alpha = 0.5;
    background.alpha = 0.5;
    timer.removeEventListener(TimerEvent.TIMER, updateTimeHandler);
    stage.removeEventListener(Event.ENTER_FRAME, enterFrameHandler);
  }
  else if(timer.currentCount == 10)
  {
    gameOver.visible = true;
    gameResult.text = "You Lost!";
    character.alpha = 0.5;
```

```
        background.alpha = 0.5;
        timer.removeEventListener(TimerEvent.TIMER, updateTimeHandler);
        stage.removeEventListener(Event.ENTER_FRAME, enterFrameHandler);
    }
}
```

You can see that it very simply checks for these two conditions. If the player defused five bombs, the game is won. If, on the other hand, the timer reaches 10, the game is lost.

If the player wins the game, these directives are displayed:

```
gameOver.visible = true;
gameResult.text = "You Won!";
character.alpha = 0.5;
background.alpha = 0.5;
timer.removeEventListener(TimerEvent.TIMER, updateTimeHandler);
stage.removeEventListener(Event.ENTER_FRAME, enterFrameHandler);
```

You can see the result of this in Figure 7-80.

Figure 7-80. The gameOver object is displayed when the player wins the game.

The first thing that happens is that the gameOver object is displayed.

```
gameOver.visible = true;
```

When the game was initialized in the constructor method, the gameOver object's visible property was set to false. When the game ends, it's set to true, and that's what makes it visible on the stage.

The code then displays "You Won!" in the gameResult text field.

```
gameResult.text = "You Won!";
```

The gameResult text field is actually a child of the gameOver object. When it was created in the constructor method, it wasn't made a child of the stage. Instead, it was added directly to gameOver, like this:

```
gameOver.addChild(gameResult);
gameResult.x = 145;
gameResult.y = 160;
```

This means it's part of the gameOver object. The x and y position that it's been given are the local coordinates *inside* the gameOver object. This is the same technique you used in Chapter 6 to make subobjects inside a single Sprite. It's useful to do here because it means that the gameResult text field's visibility and its position will be determined by its parent, the gameOver object. They're a single unit.

The directives in the checkGameOver method also dim the background and character when the game is over with these two lines:

```
character.alpha = 0.5;
background.alpha = 0.5;
```

This is a visual cue to the player that the game is no longer active.

Finally, the code disables the enterFrameHandler and removes the updateTimerHandler from the timer.

```
timer.removeEventListener(TimerEvent.TIMER, updateTimeHandler);
stage.removeEventListener(Event.ENTER_FRAME, enterFrameHandler);
```

Removing the enterFrameHandler essentially freezes the game, because the game character stops moving and the collision code stops running. Removing the updateTimerEvent from the timer also stops the timer from counting.

The only difference between the code that displays the winning or losing result is that when the player loses, "You Lost!" is displayed in the gameResult text field, as shown in Figure 7-81.

```
gameResult.text = "You Lost!";
```

Figure 7-81. "You Lost!" is displayed in the gameResult text field if the player looses.

And that's really all there is to it. Game over!

Creating a scrolling game environment

With your first real game in the bag, there's lots of fine-tuning you could do to make it better. You could add a Play Again button. You could make the game easier or harder by adjusting the timer. As a bigger challenge, you could even design and program new levels for the game that increase the difficulty. (You'll look at how to make games with more than one level in the next chapter.)

One obvious modification is that you could make a much bigger, scrolling game environment. In fact, you'll almost certainly want to; the ability to make a potentially huge game world is just too compelling. You learned how to make a scrolling game world in Chapter 5. But in that example, only the background scrolled. Things get a little more involved when you have other objects in your world, like boxes and bombs. That's because every time the background scrolls, the foreground game objects have to adjust their positions to compensate for this. This isn't difficult to do; you just have to get the object position numbers right. I'll show you how to do that next.

In the chapter's source files you'll find the TimeBombScroll project folder. Open and compile the application class (`TimeBombScroll.as`). You see that the game now occupies a playing field four times bigger than the original. Only a quarter of the playing field is visible at any one time. As the character moves around the game world, it scrolls to keep up with it. Figure 7-82 shows what this looks like.

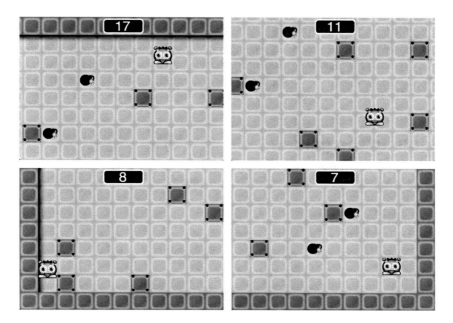

Figure 7-82. A large scrolling game world

Let's see how this is done.

Preparing your artwork for scrolling

The first thing you need to do is make a big background image. The background image in this example is four times the size of the original: 1100 pixels by 800 pixels. I named it bigBackground.png, and you can see it in Figure 7-83.

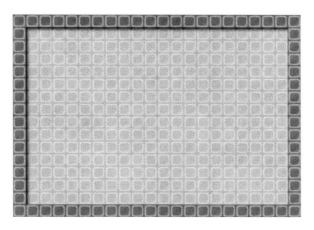

Figure 7-83. Make a big background image.

I made a class for this new background image called BigBackground.

I also needed to separate the black rounded rectangle that frames the time display from the border. That's because the black rectangle should stay fixed in one position on the stage, not scroll with the background. I called this black rectangle image timeDisplay.png and created a class for it called TimeDisplay. The TimeDisplay and BigBackground classes are identical to the other game object classes that you looked at in this chapter.

Adding objects to the game

I created the BigBackground and TimeDisplay objects using the BigBackground and TimeDisplay classes like this:

```
public var background:BigBackground = new BigBackground();
public var timeDisplay:TimeDisplay = new TimeDisplay();
```

I then added them to the stage and positioned them like this:

```
addGameObjectToStage
  (
    background,
    -(background.width - stage.stageWidth) / 2,
    -(background.height - stage.stageHeight) / 2
  );
addGameObjectToStage(timeDisplay, 200, 5);
```

The background is centered using the same formula you used in Chapter 6.

Make sure that you add the timeDisplay object *after you add all the other objects to the stage*. That will ensure that it floats above them when the game scrolls.

With the background's position in place, you can start to add the game objects. However, now that you're dealing with a huge space, you can't position them using simple stage coordinates. You need to provide coordinates relative to where you want them to be placed on the background. Most of these objects will be off-stage when the game starts.

This is luckily very easy to do. Just add the game objects' x and y coordinates to the background's x and y coordinates. Here's how the fist box is positioned:

```
addGameObjectToStage(box1, background.x + 100, background.y + 100);
```

This places it 100 pixels to the right and 100 pixels below wherever the background's top left corner happens to be. You can see this in Figure 7-84.

Figure 7-84. The game objects are positioned relative to the background object's x and y position.

This is really convenient because if you ever change the initial start position of the background, the box's position will automatically adjust its own position to compensate.

All the game objects are positioned like this, relative to the background's position:

```
//The boxes
addGameObjectToStage(box1, background.x + 100, background.y + 100);
addGameObjectToStage(box2, background.x + 200, background.y + 300);
addGameObjectToStage(box3, background.x + 400, background.y + 450);
addGameObjectToStage(box4, background.x + 100, background.y + 600);
addGameObjectToStage(box5, background.x + 300, background.y + 700);
addGameObjectToStage(box6, background.x + 500, background.y + 200);
addGameObjectToStage(box7, background.x + 600, background.y + 600);
addGameObjectToStage(box8, background.x + 500, background.y + 500);
addGameObjectToStage(box9, background.x + 700, background.y + 200);
addGameObjectToStage(box10, background.x + 700, background.y + 400);
addGameObjectToStage(box11, background.x + 800, background.y + 500);
addGameObjectToStage(box12, background.x + 100, background.y + 700);
addGameObjectToStage(box13, background.x + 900, background.y + 300);
addGameObjectToStage(box14, background.x + 800, background.y + 200);

//The bombs
addGameObjectToStage(bomb1, background.x + 55, background.y + 710);
addGameObjectToStage(bomb2, background.x + 255, background.y + 310);
addGameObjectToStage(bomb3, background.x + 355, background.y + 160);
addGameObjectToStage(bomb4, background.x + 855, background.y + 510);
addGameObjectToStage(bomb5, background.x + 755, background.y + 610);
```

For this to work, you have to make sure that you set the x and y position of the background first, before you set those of the game objects.

Scrolling and stage boundaries

Here's all the code from the enterFrameHandler that scrolls the background and game objects. It uses a custom method called scroll to do the actual work of scrolling the game objects. I'll explain how all this works in the pages ahead.

```
//Calculate the scroll velocity
var temporaryX:int = background.x;
var temporaryY:int = background.y;

//Check the stage boundaries
//1. Check the inner boundaries
if (character.x < leftInnerBoundary)
{
  character.x = leftInnerBoundary;
  rightInnerBoundary
    = (stage.stageWidth / 2) + (stage.stageWidth / 4);
  background.x -= vx;
}
else if (character.x + character.width > rightInnerBoundary)
{
  character.x = rightInnerBoundary - character.width
  leftInnerBoundary
    = (stage.stageWidth / 2) - (stage.stageWidth / 4);

  background.x -= vx;
}
if (character.y < topInnerBoundary)
{
  character.y = topInnerBoundary;
  bottomInnerBoundary
    = (stage.stageHeight / 2) + (stage.stageHeight / 4);
  background.y -= vy;
}
else if (character.y + character.height > bottomInnerBoundary)
{
  character.y = bottomInnerBoundary - character.height;
  topInnerBoundary
    = (stage.stageHeight / 2) - (stage.stageHeight / 4);
  background.y -= vy;
}

//2. Background stage boundaries
if (background.x > 0)
{
  background.x = 0;
  leftInnerBoundary = 0;
}
if (background.y > 0)
{
  background.y = 0;
```

```
  topInnerBoundary = 0;
}
if (background.x < stage.stageWidth - background.width)
{
  background.x = stage.stageWidth - background.width;
  rightInnerBoundary = stage.stageWidth;
}
if (background.y < stage.stageHeight - background.height)
{
  background.y = stage.stageHeight - background.height;
  bottomInnerBoundary = stage.stageHeight;
}

//3. Character stage boundaries
if (character.x < 50)
{
  character.x = 50;
}
if (character.y < 50)
{
  character.y = 50;
}
if (character.x + character.width > stage.stageWidth - 50)
{
  character.x = stage.stageWidth - character.width - 50;
}
if (character.y + character.height > stage.stageHeight -50)
{
  character.y = stage.stageHeight - character.height - 50;
}

//Calculate the scroll velocity
var scroll_Vx:int = background.x - temporaryX;
var scroll_Vy:int = background.y - temporaryY;

//Use the scroll velocity to move the game objects
scroll(box1, scroll_Vx, scroll_Vy);
scroll(box2, scroll_Vx, scroll_Vy);
scroll(box3, scroll_Vx, scroll_Vy);
scroll(box4, scroll_Vx, scroll_Vy);
scroll(box5, scroll_Vx, scroll_Vy);
scroll(box6, scroll_Vx, scroll_Vy);
scroll(box7, scroll_Vx, scroll_Vy);
scroll(box8, scroll_Vx, scroll_Vy);
scroll(box9, scroll_Vx, scroll_Vy);
scroll(box10, scroll_Vx, scroll_Vy);
scroll(box11, scroll_Vx, scroll_Vy);
scroll(box12, scroll_Vx, scroll_Vy);
scroll(box13, scroll_Vx, scroll_Vy);
scroll(box14, scroll_Vx, scroll_Vy);
scroll(bomb1, scroll_Vx, scroll_Vy);
scroll(bomb2, scroll_Vx, scroll_Vy);
```

```
scroll(bomb3, scroll_Vx, scroll_Vy);
scroll(bomb4, scroll_Vx, scroll_Vy);
scroll(bomb5, scroll_Vx, scroll_Vy);
```

Here's the scroll method used by the code above:

```
public function scroll
  (gameObject:Sprite, scroll_Vx:int, scroll_Vy:int):void
{
  gameObject.x += scroll_Vx;
  gameObject.y += scroll_Vy;
}
```

Most of this code is used to scroll the background and set the stage boundaries for both the character and the background. You've see all of it before—it's a combination of the scrolling code from Chapter 5, along with the extra modification you made in this chapter to prevent the character from crossing the playing field's 50 pixel wide borders. Review Chapter 5 and the earlier section in this chapter if you're unsure about how any of the code works.

What's new here is that the code is making all the game objects move relative to the background. That makes them look as if they're fixed in position to the background. Of course, it's just an illusion, but a brilliant one. Let's see how it works.

First, you have to create two variables to temporarily capture the current x and y position of the background. You have to do this *before* you scroll the background. These variables are called temporaryX and temporaryY.

```
var temporaryX:int = background.x;
var temporaryY:int = background.y;
```

All they do is record the background's position before it moves.

After the background is moved with the scrolling code, you use these variables to calculate something called the **scroll velocity**. This tells you the difference between the background's previous position and its current position. The scroll_Vx and scroll_Vy variables calculate this.

```
var scroll_Vx:int = background.x - temporaryX;
var scroll_Vy:int = background.y - temporaryY;
```

Now that you know the difference, you can use it to correctly reposition the game objects. All you need to do is apply the scroll_Vx and scroll_Vy values to the objects' x and y positions, like this:
```
box1.x += scroll_Vx;
box1.y += scroll_Vy;
```

That's all you need to do. The objects will now remain fixed in place relative to the background, no matter how it scrolls.

However, the code in TimeBombScroll goes one step further. Rather than meticulously setting the x and y positions of 14 boxes and five bombs, it delegates this work to a method called scroll.

```
scroll(box1, scroll_Vx, scroll_Vy);
```

The `scroll` method's function definition then takes care of the repetitive work of setting the objects' x and y properties, like this:

```
public function scroll
  (gameObject:Sprite, scroll_Vx:int, scroll_Vy:int):void
{
  gameObject.x += scroll_Vx;
  gameObject.y += scroll_Vy;
}
```

It just saves you a bit of tedious typing. And this is really all there is to it. Here's the procedure you have to follow to make sure this works:

1. Copy the background's x and y positions into the `temporaryX` and `temporaryY` variables.

2. Scroll the background

3. Calculate the `scroll_Vx` and `scroll_Vy` values to find out by how much the background has moved.

4. Apply the `scroll_Vx` and `scroll_Vy` values to the game objects that you want to scroll along with the background.

You have to add the code in *exactly* this order for this to work. And, of course, all this code is running inside the `enterFrameHandler`.

> *This is actually an easy introduction to a very precise game animation technique called* Verlet integration. *Verlet integration isn't covered in this book, but you can read all about it in* Advanced Game Design with Flash. *The basic process of capturing an object's position in temporary variables, moving the object, and then calculating the difference is what Verlet integration is all about.*

The rest of the code in TimeBombScroll.as is identical to TimeBombPanic.as, except for two small changes: the character is centered when the game starts and the time limit has been increased to 20 seconds. (But, come on, you should still be able to beat it in 10!) Take a look the full code in the source files so that you can see it all in context.

Summary

You now know how to make a complete game from beginning to end. This chapter showed you how to make game graphics, control them with code, and turn them into a real working game.

But there are still a lot of things you'll want your games to do that you haven't learned yet. How do you make enemy game objects that move by themselves? How can you switch game levels? And how can you fire bullets? Chapter 8, coming up next, will explain all this and more.

Chapter 8

Making Bigger Games

Time Bomb Panic is a good model of a small, one level game. It's a simple concept, takes only ten seconds to play, and you still have enough time in the day to play with your cats or go surfing. But it's probably not the kind of game you want to make. Those game ideas that keep you lying awaking at night planning no doubt involve hundreds of levels; take 50 hours or more to play; and contain dozens of different game objects, puzzles, and interesting scenarios. They're big games. In this chapter you'll learn how to make them.

The game you're going to look at this chapter is called Monster Mayhem. It's a two level game with just a few objects, but you can use the same structure to make games with any number of levels and objects and still keep your programming code under control. It's a good model for a big game—and for most of the smaller ones you'll make as well.

You'll find the game in the MonsterMayhem project folder in this chapter's source files. Play through it a few times to get a sense of what it's all about. In the first level, you need to kill the two monsters wandering around the stage. Press the space bar to launch a star projectile upwards; if the star hits the monsters three times they explode. The game ends if any of the monsters touch the character. If you kill them both, the second level loads. There are four monsters in level two, and they move much faster, but this time you can fire the star in four directions. Can you kill all four to beat the game? It's harder than it looks! Figure 8-1 shows how the game plays.

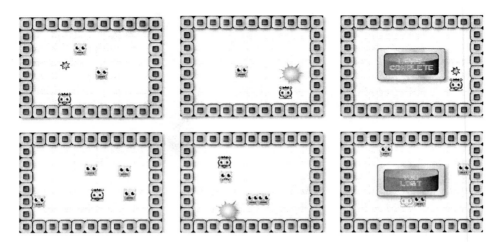

Figure 8-1. Monster Mayhem

Understanding the game structure

The structure of the code in Monster Mayhem game is radically different from any previous games you've made in the book so far. Each level of the game is contained entirely inside a single Sprite. When a level is complete, the main application class removes the current level Sprite from the stage and adds a new one. That means that none of the game objects, like the character or the monsters, are added to the main stage. They're all first added to a containing Sprite. And it's that containing Sprite that's added to the stage by the application class.

To get a clearer idea of how this works, let's compare the structure of Monster Mayhem with Time Bomb Panic. In Time Bomb Panic, all the game objects are created as separate classes. Those classes are then added directly to the stage in the main application class. Figure 8-2 illustrates this structure at work.

TimeBombPanic.as
(The application class)

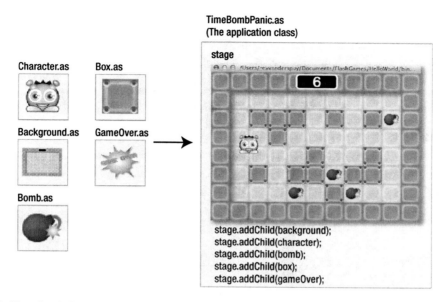

Character.as   Box.as

Background.as   GameOver.as

Bomb.as

```
stage.addChild(background);
stage.addChild(character);
stage.addChild(bomb);
stage.addChild(box);
stage.addChild(gameOver);
```

Figure 8-2. In Time Bomb Panic all the objects are added to the stage in the main application class.

In Monster Mayhem, all the game objects are first added to a class called LevelOne. An object called _levelOne is then added to the stage by the MonsterMayhem application class. Figure 8-3 Illustrates this.

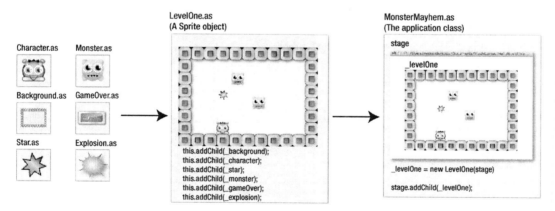

LevelOne.as
(A Sprite object)

MonsterMayhem.as
(The application class)

Character.as   Monster.as

Background.as   GameOver.as

Star.as   Explosion.as

```
this.addChild(_background);
this.addChild(_character);
this.addChild(_star);
this.addChild(_monster);
this.addChild(_gameOver);
this.addChild(_explosion);
```

```
_levelOne = new LevelOne(stage)

stage.addChild(_levelOne);
```

Figure 8-3. In Monster Mayhem all the objects are first added to the LevelOne class. The main application class then adds a _levelOne object and adds it to the stage.

LevelOne is a Sprite. That means that all the action in the game, and all the game logic, is taking place inside the LevelOne Sprite, not the application class. All the application class does is to add the level to the stage so that you can see it. The reason for containing the entire game level in a Sprite is so that the application class can easily switch levels by adding or removing them from the stage.

And here's something really important to know: *only the application class has access to the stage*. That means it's the only class that can make objects visible by displaying them on the stage. Infuse this into your memory cells because it's really important in understanding some technical details of the code you'll need to know soon. The application class is the only class that can use a line of code like this:

```
stage.addChild(gameObject);
```

Other classes can display objects inside themselves *but not directly on the stage*. They can only add objects to themselves by referring to this, which means "this class."

```
this.addChild(gameObject);
```

You can see from Figure 8-3 that the LevelOne class is adding objects to itself using code like the following:

```
this.addChild(_character);
this.addChild(_monster);
this.addChild(_star);
```

This means that these objects are being added to the LevelOne class. That's just fine, but you won't be able to actually see any of these objects until the LevelOne class that's containing them is visible on the stage itself. That's why it's the job of the application class to create a _levelOne object from the LevelOne class and add it to the stage, like this:

```
stage.addChild(_levelOne);
```

Let's take a look at the application class, MonsterMayhem.as, and see how it adds levelOne to the stage. Here's the entire class:

```
package
{
  import flash.display.Sprite;
  import flash.events.Event;

  [SWF(width="550", height="400",
  backgroundColor="#FFFFFF", frameRate="60")]

  public class MonsterMayhem extends Sprite
  {
    private var _levelOne:LevelOne;
    private var _levelTwo:LevelTwo;

    public function MonsterMayhem()
    {
      _levelOne = new LevelOne(stage);
      _levelTwo = new LevelTwo(stage);
      stage.addChild(_levelOne)
```

```
    stage.addEventListener("levelOneComplete", switchLevelHandler)
  }
  private function switchLevelHandler(event:Event):void
  {
    trace("Hello from the application class! Switch levels!");
    stage.removeChild(_levelOne);
    _levelOne = null;
    stage.addChild(_levelTwo);
  }
}
}
```

The application class has these jobs:

- It sets up the Flash Player's parameters with the SWF metatag.

- It creates two objects called _levelOne and _levelTwo. These are the game levels. Both of these objects are passed a reference to the stage in their arguments when they're created, like this:

```
_levelOne = new LevelOne(stage);
```

I'll explain how this works and why this is important soon.

- It adds the _levelOne object to the stage.

- When the player has completed level one, it removes the _levelOne object from the stage and adds _levelTwo. Don't worry about this bit of code in the switchLevelHander yet—you'll look at it in detail later in the chapter.

Notice also that the application class only imports two classes: Sprite and Event—nothing else. That's because it doesn't need any other classes to do the simple jobs it does.

Using private variables and methods

There's something new in MonsterMayhem.as that you haven't seen yet. The two level objects, _levelOne and _levelTwo, are declared as private.

```
private var _levelOne:LevelOne;
private var _levelTwo:LevelTwo;
```

The switchLevelHandler is also declared as private.

```
private function switchLevelHandler(event:Event):void
{...
```

Note that private means that those variables and methods can be used only within the class they're defined. They can only be used in the MonsterMayhem class and nowhere else.

If you don't use the private keyword when you declare a property or method, AS3.0 assumes that they're public. Public properties can be accessed freely by any other classes. You can use the public keyword to make this explicit in your code if necessary.

Why should you declare a variable or method as private? Imagine that your house is a class and your oven is one of the class's variables. Your oven is having trouble switching on, so you call a repairman to take a look at it. But you're really busy and can't be home when the repairman comes, so you leave the door unlocked and trust that all will be well. Best-case scenario: you come home to find that your oven works, but a vase is lying broken on the floor, an empty pizza box is on the sofa, and a bill arrives at the end of the month for all kinds of pay-per-view movies you know you never watched. Worst-case scenario: you come home to find your house a smoldering ruin and all the other houses in the neighborhood up in flames. If only you could have been there to tell the repairman (who was standing ready with his 10,000-volt charge-jumper), "It's a gas stove, not electric!" Because your stove was public, any other class that doesn't know what it's doing, such as the repairman, can make any changes it wants to and cause havoc with your game. If the stove were declared as private, the clueless repairman would be locked out.

In a very small game with only a few classes, you could certainly get away with keeping all of your variables and methods public, and everything would be just fine. In a larger game, however, you'd be opening yourself up to a potential debugging nightmare scenario. So, in the interest of helping you develop good long-term programming habits, all the code in this book will keep a class's variables and methods private, unless another class needs to access them.

*Using private properties to lock down a class in this way is an aspect of object-oriented programming called **encapsulation**. Encapsulation means that your class is completely sealed off from tampering by other classes and is as self-contained as possible. If other classes want to access or modify any properties in an encapsulated class, they have to follow very strict rules about doing so.*

AS3.0 also has two special accessor methods called get and set that let classes use another class's private properties in a controlled way. They're not used in this book but you can read more about them in the chapter "Methods" from Adobe's online document Programming ActionScript 3.0 for Flash at http://help.adobe.com/ en_US/ActionScript/3.0_ProgrammingAS3/.

You'll also notice that the names of both the private _levelOne and _levelTwo objects begin with an underscore character (_). This is a naming convention that is entirely optional, but one that I'll be using in this book. Preceding the names of private variables with underscore characters helps you tell at a glance which properties are private. It can help you to easily distinguish which variables are accessible throughout the whole class and which variables are only accessible inside a method. You'll see how this will be helpful in some of the code examples ahead.

Now that you know the MonsterMayhem application class does almost nothing except create and display a _levelOne object, where is all the code for the game? Most of it is in the LevelOne and LevelTwo classes.

Programming the game

These are the classes that MonsterMayhem uses:

```
MonsterMayhem.as
LevelOne.as
LevelTwo.as
Background.as
Character.as
Explosion.as
GameOver.as
Monster.as
Star.as
```

MonsterMayhem is the application class and adds the levels to the game, as you've just seen. LevelOne and LevelTwo contain all the game programming. All the other classes are game object classes. You'll first take a look at how LevelOne is added to the stage and then at how all the specific features of the game are programmed.

Giving LevelOne access to the stage

You've just seen that when the application class creates the _levelOne object, it passes it a reference to the stage as an argument, like this:

```
_levelOne = new LevelOne(stage);
```

Remember that the application class, MonsterMayhem, is the only class that has direct access to the stage object. If any other objects need to access the stage for some reason, the application class has to pass that class a reference to the stage when it creates an object. The reference to the stage gets passed to an object through its constructor method. LevelOne needs to know about the stage because one of the things is has to do is attach keyboard event listeners to the stage so that players can move the character with the arrow keys. To keep a reference to the stage inside itself, LevelOne also needs a variable to store it. Here's the code for the LevelOne constructor and its variable called _stage that it uses to store the stage reference (the highlighted code is the important stuff):

```
private var _stage:Object;
public function LevelOne(stage:Object)
{
  _stage = stage;
  this.addEventListener(Event.ADDED_TO_STAGE, addedToStageHandler);
}
```

When the application class creates the _levelOne object, it sends it a reference to the stage. The _levelOne object then stores that reference in its own variable called _stage. This means that whenever the code in the LevelOne class uses the variable _stage, it can access the main stage in the MonsterMayhem application class. Figure 8-4 illustrates how the reference to the stage gets passed from the MonsterMayhem application class to the _levelOne object.

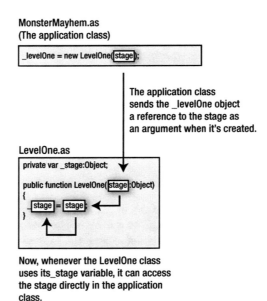

MonsterMayhem.as
(The application class)

_levelOne = new LevelOne(stage);

The application class
sends the _levelOne object
a reference to the stage as
an argument when it's created.

LevelOne.as

private var _stage:Object;

public function LevelOne(stage:Object)
{
    _stage = stage;
}

Now, whenever the LevelOne class
uses its_stage variable, it can access
the stage directly in the application
class.

Figure 8-4. The application class sends LevelOne a reference to the stage.

LevelOne needs this reference to the stage because it has to attach the keyDownHandler and KeyUpHandler to it. Here's how it does this using its new _stage variable:

```
_stage.addEventListener(KeyboardEvent.KEY_DOWN, keyDownHandler);
_stage.addEventListener(KeyboardEvent.KEY_UP, keyUpHandler);
```

You'll see this in the context of the full class soon.

Making sure that LevelOne is actually on the stage

There's one additional technical problem that comes up if you give classes access to the stage like you've just done. You have to make sure that those objects are actually on the stage before you try to access the stage object. If you create an object with the new keyword and that object tries to access the stage before it's been added to the stage by the application class with the stage.addChild() method, you'll see this error message:

```
Error #1009:  Cannot access a property or
method of a null object reference
```

If you're adding objects to the game, there's a good chance that many of those objects will need to access the stage as soon as they're created. They might need to do this to set stage boundaries or access the properties of other objects that are also on the stage. If they can't find the stage object because they haven't been added to the stage yet, AS3.0's compiler will "throw its hands in the air" and you'll see the preceding error message.

To solve this problem, you need to initialize objects only when they've been added to the stage, not before. There's a special event listener called ADDED_TO_STAGE that does just that. It waits for the object to be added to the stage and runs any code that you need it to.

The LevelOne class needs access to the stage to attach the keyboard event listeners that move the game character, so it needs to wait until it's been added to the stage before trying to do that. Here's how it uses the ADDED_TO_STAGE event listener (the important code is highlighted):

```
public function LevelOne(stage:Object)
{
  _stage = stage;
  this.addEventListener(Event.ADDED_TO_STAGE, addedToStageHandler);
}
private function addedToStageHandler(event:Event):void
{
  startGame();
  this.removeEventListener
    (Event.ADDED_TO_STAGE, addedToStageHandler);
}
private function startGame():void
{
  //All the directives that setup and
  //initialize the game
}
```

As soon as a LevelOne object is created by the application class, the constructor method sets up the ADDED_TO_STAGE listener.

```
this.addEventListener(Event.ADDED_TO_STAGE, addedToStageHandler);
```

It waits until the object appears on the stage. As soon as it does, it runs the addedToStageHandler. This has the job of calling the startGame method and also of removing the listener, like this:

```
private function addedToStageHandler(event:Event):void
{
  startGame();
  this.removeEventListener
    (Event.ADDED_TO_STAGE, addedToStageHandler);
}
```

The startGame method then runs all the directives that create the game objects and initializes the game variables.

This is a bit of a technical hurdle to have to jump through. Yes, it's a full-blown drag! But it's unfortunately essential if any class that isn't the application class needs to refer to or use the stage object. Figure 8-5 illustrates how the ADDED_TO_STAGE listener jumpstarts the class's code. And luckily, this is all very routine code that you don't really waste any excess brainpower thinking too much about. Just blindly follow this example as-is to use it in your own games and don't fret about it too much.

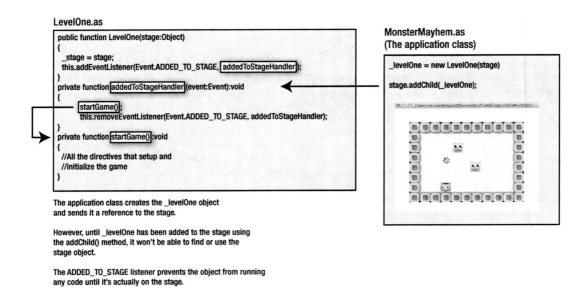

LevelOne.as

```
public function LevelOne(stage:Object)
{
    _stage = stage;
    this.addEventListener(Event.ADDED_TO_STAGE, addedToStageHandler );
}
private function addedToStageHandler (event:Event):void
{
    startGame();
    this.removeEventListener(Event.ADDED_TO_STAGE, addedToStageHandler);
}
private function startGame():void
{
    //All the directives that setup and
    //initialize the game
}
```

MonsterMayhem.as
(The application class)

```
_levelOne = new LevelOne(stage)

stage.addChild(_levelOne);
```

The application class creates the _levelOne object
and sends it a reference to the stage.

However, until _levelOne has been added to the stage using
the addChild() method, it won't be able to find or use the
stage object.

The ADDED_TO_STAGE listener prevents the object from running
any code until it's actually on the stage.

Figure 8-5. Wait until an object is on the stage before it's initialized.

The ADDED_TO_STAGE listener has a companion called REMOVED_FROM_STAGE. The REMOVED_FROM_STAGE event listener fires when an object is removed from the stage. Very importantly, REMOVED_FROM_STAGE allows you to remove any other event listeners that might be running on an object. This is particularly important for ENTER_FRAME or timer events. One of AS3.0's little quirks is that even after objects are taken off the stage using removeChild, their ENTER_FRAME events will still run silently in the background. If an ENTER_FRAME event is running and trying to reference objects that no longer exist, it will generate a torrent of error messages. To prevent this, you can use the REMOVED_FROM_STAGE event to remove the object's enterFrameHandler event listener when the object itself is removed, if your code doesn't remove it in any other way.

Here's the format for using a REMOVED_FROM_STAGE event listener. First, add it in the class's constructor method:

```
public function ClassConstructorMethod()
{
    //... any class initialization code
    //or other listeners...
    this.addEventListener
        (Event.REMOVED_FROM_STAGE, removedFromStageHandler);
}
```

Next, use the removedFromStageHandler to run any code that should be run when the object is removed from the stage. Very importantly, you also need to remove the removedFromStageHandler itself.

```
private function removedFromStageHandler(event:Event):void
```

```
{
  //... any directives you want to run when the
  //object is removed from the stage
  this.removeEventListener
    (Event.ENTER_FRAME, enterFrameHandler);
  this.removeEventListener
    (Event.REMOVED_FROM_STAGE, removedFromStageHandler);
}
```

> *Although manually removing ENTER_FRAME events is required, removing other event listeners manually is optional. Flash still deletes objects even if they have listeners on them in most cases. However, just to make sure, it's considered best practice to manually remove them so you know with absolute certainty that that there won't be any lingering code running in the background after the object is gone.*

The LevelOne class

All the game logic for the first level is in the LevelOne class. It does what the application classes were doing in previous chapters. So, except for some of the new technical details that were just covered, much of the code will be very familiar. But the code is doing a lot of new things as well:

- Letting the character fire star projectiles.

- Making the monsters open their mouths when they're hit.

- Adding explosions to the stage when the monsters are killed.

- Displaying the "Level Complete" or "Game Over, You Lost" messages at the end of the level.

- Generating a levelComplete event when the level is finished so that the application class knows it has to load level two.

You'll look at each of these new features in detail, one at a time. But just so that you have all the code in one place as a reference, here's the entire code listing for LevelOne:

```
package
{
  import flash.display.Sprite;
  import flash.events.Event;
  import flash.events.KeyboardEvent;
  import flash.events.TimerEvent;
  import flash.ui.Keyboard;
  import flash.utils.Timer;

  public class LevelOne extends Sprite
  {
    //Declare the variables to hold
    //the game objects
    private var _character:Character;
    private var _background:Background;
```

```
private var _gameOver:GameOver;
private var _monster1:Monster;
private var _monster2:Monster;
private var _star:Star;
private var _levelWinner:String;

//The timers
private var _monsterTimer:Timer;
private var _gameOverTimer:Timer;

//A variable to store the reference
//to the stage from the application class
private var _stage:Object;

public function LevelOne(stage:Object)
{
  _stage = stage;
  this.addEventListener
    (Event.ADDED_TO_STAGE, addedToStageHandler);
}
private function addedToStageHandler(event:Event):void
{
  startGame();
  this.removeEventListener
    (Event.ADDED_TO_STAGE, addedToStageHandler);
}
private function startGame():void
{
  //Create the game objects
  _character = new Character();
  _star = new Star();
  _background = new Background();
  _monster1 = new Monster();
  _monster2 = new Monster();
  _gameOver = new GameOver();

  //Add the game objects to the stage
  addGameObjectToLevel(_background, 0, 0);
  addGameObjectToLevel(_monster1, 400, 150);
  addGameObjectToLevel(_monster2, 150, 150);
  addGameObjectToLevel(_character, 250, 300);
  addGameObjectToLevel(_star, 250, 300);
  _star.visible = false;
  addGameObjectToLevel(_gameOver, 140, 130);

  //Initialize the monster timer
  _monsterTimer = new Timer(1000);
  _monsterTimer.addEventListener
    (TimerEvent.TIMER, monsterTimerHandler);
  _monsterTimer.start();

  //Event listeners
```

```
  _stage.addEventListener
    (KeyboardEvent.KEY_DOWN, keyDownHandler);
  _stage.addEventListener
    (KeyboardEvent.KEY_UP, keyUpHandler);
  this.addEventListener
    (Event.ENTER_FRAME, enterFrameHandler);
}
private function enterFrameHandler(event:Event):void
{
  //Move the game character and
  //check its stage boundaries
  _character.x += _character.vx;
  _character.y += _character.vy;
  checkStageBoundaries(_character);

  //Move the monsters and
  //check their stage boundaries
  if(_monster1.visible)
  {
    _monster1.x += _monster1.vx;
    _monster1.y += _monster1.vy;
    checkStageBoundaries(_monster1);
  }

  if(_monster2.visible)
  {
    _monster2.x += _monster2.vx;
    _monster2.y += _monster2.vy;
    checkStageBoundaries(_monster2);
  }

  //If the star has been launched,
  //move it, check its stage
  //boundaries and collisions
  //with the monsters
  if(_star.launched)
  {
    //If it has been launched,
    //make it visible
    _star.visible = true;

    //Move it
    _star.y -= 3;
    _star.rotation += 5;

    //Check its stage boundaries
    checkStarStageBoundaries(_star);

    //Check for collisions with the monsters
    starVsMonsterCollision(_star, _monster1);
    starVsMonsterCollision(_star, _monster2);
  }
```

```
      else
      {
        _star.visible = false;
      }
      //Collision detection between the
      //character and  monsters
      characterVsMonsterCollision(_character, _monster1);
      characterVsMonsterCollision(_character, _monster2);
    }
    private function characterVsMonsterCollision
      (character:Character, monster:Monster):void
    {
      if(monster.visible
      && character.hitTestObject(monster))
      {
        character.timesHit++;
        checkGameOver();
      }
    }
    private function starVsMonsterCollision
      (star:Star, monster:Monster):void
    {
      if(monster.visible
      && star.hitTestObject(monster))
      {
        //Call the monster's openMouth
        //method to make it open its mouth
        monster.openMouth();

        //Deactivate the star
        star.launched = false;

        //Add 1 to the monster's timesHit variable
        monster.timesHit++;

        //Has the monster been hit 3 times?
        if(monster.timesHit == 3)
        {
          //call the killMonster
          //method
          killMonster(monster);

          //Check to see if the
          //game is over
          checkGameOver();
        }
      }
    }
    private function killMonster(monster:Monster):void
    {
      //Make the monster invisible
      monster.visible = false;
```

```
    //Create a new explosion object
    //and add it to the stage
    var explosion:Explosion = new Explosion();
    this.addChild(explosion);

    //Center the explosion over
    //the monster
    explosion.x = monster.x -21;
    explosion.y = monster.y -18;

    //Call the explosion's
    //explode method
    explosion.explode();
}
private function checkGameOver():void
{
    if(_monster1.timesHit == 3
    && _monster2.timesHit == 3)
    {
        _levelWinner = "character"
        _gameOverTimer = new Timer(2000);
        _gameOverTimer.addEventListener
            (TimerEvent.TIMER, gameOverTimerHandler);
        _gameOverTimer.start();
        _monsterTimer.removeEventListener
            (TimerEvent.TIMER, monsterTimerHandler);
        this.removeEventListener
            (Event.ENTER_FRAME, enterFrameHandler);
    }
    if(_character.timesHit == 1)
    {
        _levelWinner = "monsters"
        _character.alpha = 0.5;
        _gameOverTimer = new Timer(2000);
        _gameOverTimer.addEventListener
            (TimerEvent.TIMER, gameOverTimerHandler);
        _gameOverTimer.start();
        _monsterTimer.removeEventListener
            (TimerEvent.TIMER, monsterTimerHandler);

        this.removeEventListener
        (Event.ENTER_FRAME, enterFrameHandler);
    }
}
private function checkStageBoundaries(gameObject:Sprite):void
{
    if (gameObject.x < 50)
    {
        gameObject.x = 50;
    }
    if (gameObject.y < 50)
```

```
    {
      gameObject.y = 50;
    }
    if (gameObject.x + gameObject.width > _stage.stageWidth - 50)
    {
      gameObject.x = _stage.stageWidth - gameObject.width - 50;
    }
    if (gameObject.y + gameObject.height
    > _stage.stageHeight - 50)
    {
      gameObject.y = _stage.stageHeight - gameObject.height - 50;
    }
  }
  private function checkStarStageBoundaries(star:Star):void
  {
    if (star.y < 50)
    {
      star.launched = false;
    }
  }
  private function monsterTimerHandler(event:TimerEvent):void
  {
    changeMonsterDirection(_monster1);
    changeMonsterDirection(_monster2);
  }
  private function changeMonsterDirection(monster:Monster):void
  {
    var randomNumber:int = Math.ceil(Math.random() * 4);
    if(randomNumber == 1)
    {
      //Right
      monster.vx = 1;
      monster.vy = 0;
    }
    else if (randomNumber == 2)
    {
      //Left
      monster.vx = -1;
      monster.vy = 0;
    }
    else if(randomNumber == 3)
    {
      //Up
      monster.vx = 0;
      monster.vy = -1;
    }
    else
    {
      //Down
      monster.vx = 0;
      monster.vy = 1;
    }
```

```
    }
    private function gameOverTimerHandler(event:TimerEvent):void
    {
      if(_levelWinner == "character")
      {
        if(_gameOverTimer.currentCount == 1)
        {
          _gameOver.levelComplete.visible = true;
        }
        if(_gameOverTimer.currentCount == 2)
        {
          _gameOverTimer.reset();
          _gameOverTimer.removeEventListener
            (TimerEvent.TIMER, gameOverTimerHandler);
          dispatchEvent(new Event("levelOneComplete", true));
        }
      }
      if(_levelWinner == "monsters")
      {
        _gameOver.youLost.visible = true;
        _gameOverTimer.removeEventListener
          (TimerEvent.TIMER, gameOverTimerHandler);
      }
    }
    private function keyDownHandler(event:KeyboardEvent):void
    {
      if (event.keyCode == Keyboard.LEFT)
      {
        _character.vx = -5;
      }
      else if (event.keyCode == Keyboard.RIGHT)
      {
        _character.vx = 5;
      }
      else if (event.keyCode == Keyboard.UP)
      {
        _character.vy = -5;
      }
      else if (event.keyCode == Keyboard.DOWN)
      {
        _character.vy = 5;
      }
      if(event.keyCode == Keyboard.SPACE)
      {
        if(!_star.launched)
        {
          _star.x = _character.x + _character.width / 2;
          _star.y = _character.y + _character.width / 2;
          _star.launched = true;
        }
      }
    }
```

```
    private function keyUpHandler(event:KeyboardEvent):void
    {
      if (event.keyCode == Keyboard.LEFT
      || event.keyCode == Keyboard.RIGHT)
      {
        _character.vx = 0;
      }
      else if (event.keyCode == Keyboard.DOWN
      || event.keyCode == Keyboard.UP)
      {
        _character.vy = 0;
      }
    }
    private function addGameObjectToLevel
      (gameObject:Sprite, xPos:int, yPos:int):void
    {
      this.addChild(gameObject);
      gameObject.x = xPos;
      gameObject.y = yPos;
    }
  }
}
```

Programming the game character

In the previous chapter you saw how each object in the game was its own separate class. Those game object class were very simple. All they did was load and display the PNG file. In Monster Mayhem, the game object classes are more complex. Not only do they display the object's image, but they also perform these two additional functions.

- They store data about the objects in variables, known as **properties**.

- They let the objects perform actions using methods. These actions change the way the object appears.

Let's find out a little more about class properties and methods, and then see how they're used in the game

Understanding properties and methods

A class is essentially a description of an object. A class describes an object in these two ways:

- **Properties**: The things that it is.

- **Methods**: The things that it does.

To get an idea of what properties and methods are, let's take a look at an imaginary class called Giraffe:

```
package
{
  import flash.display.Sprite;

  public class Giraffe extends Sprite
```

```
    {
      //Properties
      private var _isHungry:Boolean;
      private var _favoriteActivity:String;

      public function Giraffe()
      {
        _isHungry = true;
        _favoriteActivity = "eating";
      }
      //Methods
      private function eatLeaves():void
      {
        //... directives
      }
      private function wanderAimlessly():void
      {
        //... directives
      }
    }
}
```

I'm sure you can get a pretty good idea of what the life of the poor giraffe is like by looking at the preceding class!

Properties is just another name for *variables* such as these:

```
_hungry
_favoriteActivity
```

Yes, they're just plain old variables—as simple as that! Variables that describe features of an object, like they do in this giraffe, are called properties. That's just a bit of terminology you'll have to learn. Properties also refer to all the built-in Sprite properties (such as x, y, rotation, and visible) that you've been using all along.

Methods? Of course you know what methods are by now! Here are the giraffe's methods:

```
eatLeaves
wanderAimlessly
```

> *By using properties and methods together, you can create a **model** of an object. All game object classes in your game are really just models that are described by their properties and methods.*

The `Character.as` class is one of the simplest in the game. It doesn't have any methods, just properties. Here's the entire class:

```
package
{
```

```
import flash.display.DisplayObject;
import flash.display.Sprite;

public class Character extends Sprite
{
  //Embed the image
  [Embed(source="../images/character.png")]
  private var CharacterImage:Class;

  //Private properties
  private var _character:DisplayObject = new CharacterImage();

  //Public properties
  public var vx:int = 0;
  public var vy:int = 0;
  public var timesHit:int = 0;

  public function Character()
  {
    //Display the image in this class
    this.addChild(_character);
  }
}
}
```

The Character class has three public properties.

- vx: The character's horizontal velocity.

- vy: The character's vertical velocity.

- timesHit: The number of times the character has been hit by the monsters.

These are all the important bits of information the game needs about the character. Figure 8-6 illustrates this.

Figure 8-6. The Character class's public properties

Notice that all these properties are declared as public. That's because other classes must be able to access them. You'll see how next. The other private variable, `_character`, is also a property, but it's just used internally by the class itself to display the PNG image.

Moving the character

In previous examples, the application class contained vx and vy variables that you used to move the character around the stage. In this game those variables are actually part of the character class itself. You can access them inside the _character object from the LevelOne class using dot notation, like this:

```
_character.vx
_character.vy
```

Because those properties have been declared as public, the application class can easily access and change them. When the player presses arrow keys on the keyboard, the code in the keyDownHandler directly changes the vx and vy properties inside the _character object. (The bold code below highlights this):

```
if (event.keyCode == Keyboard.LEFT)
{
  _character.vx = -5;
}
else if (event.keyCode == Keyboard.RIGHT)
{
  _character.vx = 5;
}
else if (event.keyCode == Keyboard.UP)
{
  _character.vy = -5;
}
else if (event.keyCode == Keyboard.DOWN)
{
  _character.vy = 5;
}
```

Figure 8-7 illustrates that this code is directly changing the vx and vy properties inside the _character object.

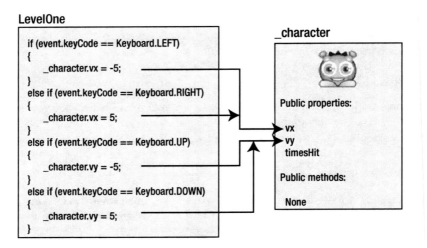

LevelOne

```
if (event.keyCode == Keyboard.LEFT)
{
    _character.vx = -5;
}
else if (event.keyCode == Keyboard.RIGHT)
{
    _character.vx = 5;
}
else if (event.keyCode == Keyboard.UP)
{
    _character.vy = -5;
}
else if (event.keyCode == Keyboard.DOWN)
{
    _character.vy = 5;
}
```

_character

Public properties:

vx
vy
timesHit

Public methods:

None

Figure 8-7. The LevelOne class can directly change an object's public properties

The code in the `enterFrameHandler` can then use the character's changed vx and vy properties to move it on the stage, like this:

```
_character.x += _character.vx;
_character.y += _character.vy;
```

Checking for stage boundaries

After the character is moved, the `checkStageBoundaries` method prevents it from moving outside the area of the stage.

```
checkStageBoundaries(_character);
```

Here's the method's function definition that does all the hard work:

```
private function checkStageBoundaries(gameObject:Sprite):void
{
  if (gameObject.x < 50)
  {
    gameObject.x = 50;
  }
  if (gameObject.y < 50)
  {
    gameObject.y = 50;
  }
  if (gameObject.x + gameObject.width >_stage.stageWidth- 50)
  {
    gameObject.x = _stage. stageWidth- gameObject.width - 50;
  }
  if (gameObject.y + gameObject.height >_stage.stageHeight - 50)
  {
```

```
    gameObject.y = _stage.stageHeight - gameObject.height - 50;
  }
}
```

This method is also used to check the stage boundaries of the _monster1 and _monster2 objects. Notice that it uses the LevelOne class's private _stage variable to find the height and width of the stage.

Checking for collisions between the character and the monster

The enterFrameHandler uses the characterVsMonsterCollision method to check for collisions between the character and monsters. There are two monster collisions to check for, so the method is called twice—once for each monster.

```
characterVsMonsterCollision(_character, _monster1);
characterVsMonsterCollision(_character, _monster2);
```

Here's the method's function definition:

```
private function characterVsMonsterCollision
  (character:Character, monster:Monster):void
{
  if(monster.visible
  && character.hitTestObject(monster))
  {
    character.timesHit++;
    checkGameOver();
  }
}
```

Notice that the method only checks for a collision if the monster is visible.

```
if(monster.visible&&character.hitTestObject(monster))
{...
```

This is because when the star hits any of the monsters, their visible property is set to false. The code only needs to check for collisions between the character and monsters if the monster in question is actually visible and thus still in the game.

If there is a collision, the character's timesHit property is increased by one, and the checkGameOver method is called.

```
character.timesHit++;
checkGameOver();
```

The character's timesHit property is initialized to 0 in the Character class. It becomes 1 after the first collision. Unfortunately for the player, the character only needs to be hit once to lose the game. I'll explain how this happens in the checkGameOver method in the pages ahead.

The order of the code in the enterFrameHandler

Take a look at the entire enterFrameHandler in the complete LevelOne code listing once again. Notice that the characterVsMonsterCollision method is the very last bit of code it runs. That's because the game should only check for collisions *after* the game objects have been moved. The reason for this is to make sure that you're checking collisions and boundaries based on the objects' current new positions—and not the positions they had in the previous frame.

Here's the order in which you should run the code in the enterFrameHandler:

1. First, move the game objects.

2. After they've been moved, check stage boundaries and collisions with other objects.

3. Make sure that you check for collisions between pairs of game objects after you've moved both of them. For example, first move the character, then move the monsters, and only after that check for collisions between them.

If you check for collisions and boundaries before you move the objects, the collisions won't be based on their current positions. They'll be based on the positions the objects had *in the previous frame*. All of your collisions will look slightly off.

You can test this yourself by running the character's checkStageBoundaries method before changing its position on the stage, like this:

```
checkStageBoundaries(_character);
_character.x += _character.vx;
_character.y += _character.vy;
```

Recompile the code, and move the character to one of the stage boundaries. You'll see that the character will overlap with the boundaries by 5 pixels, as you can see in Figure 8-8. That's because the character hasn't yet been updated to its new, current position.

Figure 8-8. If you don't move game objects before you check for collisions or boundaries, the collisions will be off by one frame.

This is a very common problem in game design but, as you can see, it's easy to fix. Remember this if you ever notice that collisions in your own games are slightly imprecise.

Programming the monsters

LevelOne creates the monster objects using the same Monster class, like this:

```
_monster1 = new Monster();
_monster2 = new Monster();
```

Both monsters behave in exactly the same way so they can both use exactly the same class. Two for the price of one! This is one great thing about using classes: you only need to write a class once. As long as it's general enough, you can reuse it over and over again for as many objects of the same type as you need.

The monsters have a charming quality. When they're hit by the star, they open their mouths, as you can see in Figure 8-9.

Figure 8-9. The monster opens its mouth when it's hit by a star. Poor thing!

The monster's mouth stays open for two seconds and then closes again.

You saw this in Chapter 6 when you looked at how to change an object's image state when it collides with something. So you already know that this trick is done by making one image visible and the other invisible. What's new here is that the switching of images all happens *inside* the Monster class. The class uses a timer to keep the monster's mouth open for two seconds and then closes it again.

Here's the Monster class that makes this work:

```
package
{
  import flash.display.DisplayObject;
  import flash.display.Sprite;
  import flash.events.TimerEvent;
  import flash.utils.Timer;

  public class Monster extends Sprite
  {
    //Embed the monster images
    [Embed(source="../images/monsterMouthClosed.png")]
    private var MonsterMouthClosedImage:Class;
    [Embed(source="../images/monsterMouthOpen.png")]
    private var MonsterMouthOpenImage:Class;

    //Private properties
    private var _monsterMouthClosed:DisplayObject
      = new MonsterMouthClosedImage();
    private var _monsterMouthOpen:DisplayObject
      = new MonsterMouthOpenImage();
    private var _timer:Timer;

    //Public properties
    public var vx:int = 0;
```

```
public var vy:int = 0;
public var timesHit:int = 0;

public function Monster()
{
  this.addChild(_monsterMouthClosed);
  this.addChild(_monsterMouthOpen);
  _monsterMouthOpen.visible = false;

  //The mouth timer
  _timer = new Timer(2000);
}

//Public methods
public function openMouth():void
{
  _monsterMouthOpen.visible = true;
  _monsterMouthClosed.visible = false;
  _timer.addEventListener(TimerEvent.TIMER, mouthTimeHandler);
  _timer.start();
}

//Private methods
private function mouthTimeHandler(event:TimerEvent):void
{
  _monsterMouthOpen.visible = false;
  _monsterMouthClosed.visible = true;
  _timer.reset();
  _timer.removeEventListener
    (TimerEvent.TIMER, mouthTimeHandler);
  }
 }
}
```

The monsters have the same public properties as the character: vx, vy, and timesHit. But they also have a public method: openMouth. Figure 8-10 illustrates this.

Monster

Public properties:

vx
vy
timesHit

Public methods:

openMouth

Figure 8-10. The Monster class's public properties and methods

The LevelOne class can make a monster open its mouth at any time by calling the monster's openMouth method, like this:

```
_monster1.openMouth();
_monster2.openMouth();
```

The Monster class has a timer that is set to fire every two seconds (2000 milliseconds).

```
_timer = new Timer(2000);
```

When the monster's openMouth method is called, the image of it with an open mouth is made visible, and the image of it with a closed mouth is made invisible. The timer is then started.

```
public function openMouth():void
{
  _monsterMouthOpen.visible = true;
  _monsterMouthClosed.visible = false;
  _timer.addEventListener(TimerEvent.TIMER, mouthTimeHandler);
  _timer.start();
}
```

When the timer counts two seconds, it calls the mouthTimeHandler. This method makes the image of the monster with the closed mouth visible again and makes the open mouth image invisible. It then resets the timer so that it will start counting from zero the next time it's used. Finally, the timer's event listener is removed.

```
private function mouthTimeHandler(event:TimerEvent):void
{
  _monsterMouthOpen.visible = false;
  _monsterMouthClosed.visible = true;
  _timer.reset();
  _timer.removeEventListener
    (TimerEvent.TIMER, mouthTimeHandler);
}
```

What's important to notice is that the `Monster` class doesn't do anything that affects the logic of the game. All it does is handle the monster's change of state: it opens and closes its mouth. It's the `LevelOne` class that decides when this should happen based on what's happening in the game. It's important to design your game object classes like this so that you can reuse them in other games or levels without having to rewrite the class.

For example, maybe later you decide that the monster should also open its mouth when it bumps into a wall. You won't need to make any changes to the `Monster` class to do this. All you would need to do is write `_monster1.openMouth()` in the `LevelOne` class when the monster bumps into a wall.

Moving the monsters

Monster Mayhem is the first game you've seen where objects other than the game character move around the stage. The monsters randomly change their direction every second—either up, down, left, or right, as illustrated in Figure 8-11.

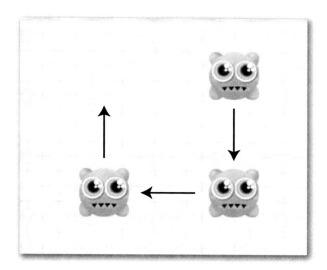

Figure 8-11. The monster chooses a random direction every second.

The `levelOne` class uses a timer to trigger the `monsterTimerHandler` every second.

```
_monsterTimer = new Timer(1000);
_monsterTimer.addEventListener
(TimerEvent.TIMER, monsterTimerHandler);
_monsterTimer.start();
```

The `monsterTimerHandler` sends the `_monster1` and `_monster2` objects to the `changeMonsterDirection` method.

```
private function monsterTimerHandler(event:TimerEvent):void
{
```

```
  changeMonsterDirection(_monster1);
  changeMonsterDirection(_monster2);
}
```

The changeMonsterDirection method generates a random number between 1 and 4. It uses that random number to assign the monsters different vx and vy values, which will move the monsters either right, left, up, or down.

```
private function changeMonsterDirection(monster:Monster):void
{
  var randomNumber:int = Math.ceil(Math.random() * 4);
  if(randomNumber == 1)
  {
    //Right
    monster.vx = 1;
    monster.vy = 0;
  }
  else if (randomNumber == 2)
  {
    //Left
    monster.vx = -1;
    monster.vy = 0;
  }
  else if(randomNumber == 3)
  {
    //Up
    monster.vx = 0;
    monster.vy = -1;
  }
  else
  {
    //Down
    monster.vx = 0;
    monster.vy = 1;
  }
}
```

Figure 8-12 shows how this system works.

The _monsterTimer calls the
monsterTimerHandler every second.

LevelOne

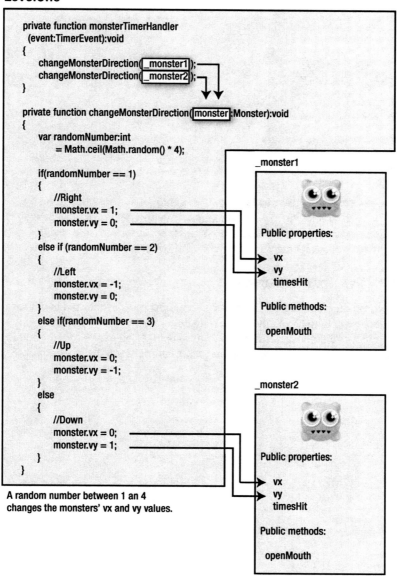

```
private function monsterTimerHandler
  (event:TimerEvent):void
{
    changeMonsterDirection(_monster1);
    changeMonsterDirection(_monster2);
}

private function changeMonsterDirection(monster:Monster):void
{
    var randomNumber:int
      = Math.ceil(Math.random() * 4);

    if(randomNumber == 1)
    {
        //Right
        monster.vx = 1;
        monster.vy = 0;
    }
    else if (randomNumber == 2)
    {
        //Left
        monster.vx = -1;
        monster.vy = 0;
    }
    else if(randomNumber == 3)
    {
        //Up
        monster.vx = 0;
        monster.vy = -1;
    }
    else
    {
        //Down
        monster.vx = 0;
        monster.vy = 1;
    }
}
```

A random number between 1 an 4
changes the monsters' vx and vy values.

_monster1

Public properties:

vx
vy
timesHit

Public methods:

openMouth

_monster2

Public properties:

vx
vy
timesHit

Public methods:

openMouth

Figure 8-12. The monsters are assigned a random direction.

The enterFrameHandler then uses these new vx and vy values to make the monsters move. It also uses the same checkStageBoundaries method used by the character to keep them within the playing field. However, all this code will only run if the monsters are visible.

```
if(_monster1.visible)
{
  _monster1.x += _monster1.vx;
  _monster1.y += _monster1.vy;
  checkStageBoundaries(_monster1);
}

if(_monster2.visible)
{
  _monster2.x += _monster2.vx;
  _monster2.y += _monster2.vy;
  checkStageBoundaries(_monster2);
}
```

In this game, the monsters have their visible properties set to false when they're hit by the star three times. Making them invisible is a simple way of removing them from the game. However, even if the monsters are invisible, they'll still be on the stage and can still be moved around by the enterFrameHandler. The if statement makes sure that the monsters aren't moved if they're invisible.

Programming the star weapon

When the player presses the space key, the star weapon becomes visible and is launched from the center of the character. It spins and moves up the stage. If it hits the playing field border or a monster, it becomes invisible again. The first two times it hits a monster, the monster opens its mouth, but on the third time an explosion graphic is displayed and the monster disappears. Figure 8-13 illustrates how the star weapon works.

Figure 8-13. Fire the star weapon to vanquish the monsters.

The Star class shares the same vx and vy properties as the other game objects, but includes a new one called launched. This is a Boolean variable that tells the game whether or not the player has launched the star by pressing the space key. You'll see how important this property will become in controlling the behavior of the star. Here's the entire Star class:

```
package
{
  import flash.display.DisplayObject;
  import flash.display.Sprite;

  public class Star extends Sprite
  {
    //Embed the image
    [Embed(source="../images/star.png")]
    private var StarImage:Class;

    //Private properties
    private var _star:DisplayObject = new StarImage();

    //Public properties
    public var vx:int = 0;
    public var vy:int = 3;
    public var launched:Boolean = false;

    public function Star()
    {
      this.addChild(_star);

      //Center the star image
      _star.x = -(_star.width / 2);
```

```
    _star.y = -(_star.height / 2);
  }
 }
}
```

Figure 8-14 illustrates the Star class's public properties and methods.

Figure 8-14. The star's public properties

But because the star needs to spin around its center, the _starImage needs to be centered. This is easily done with two lines of code that subtract half the star images' height and width from its x and y position. This neatly centers the image.

```
_star.x = -(_star.width / 2);
_star.y = -(_star.height / 2);
```

Because the star image is now centered, its spin axis will be its center point. If the star image isn't centered like this, the spin axis will be its top left corner and the spin effect will be lopsided.

Launching the star

When the player presses the space key on the keyboard, the onKeyDownHandler sets the star's launched property to true. It does this only if launched isn't already true so that the star isn't launched more than once while it's on the stage.

```
if(event.keyCode == Keyboard.SPACE)
{
  if(!_star.launched)
  {
    _star.x = _character.x + _character.width / 2;
    _star.y = _character.y + _character.width / 2;
    _star.launched = true;
  }
}
```

This code also centers the star on the character.

If the star has been launched, the enterFrameHandler then runs this code:

```
if(_star.launched)
{
  //If it has been launched, make it visible
  _star.visible = true;

  //Move it
  _star.y -= 3;
  _star.rotation += 5;

  //Check its stage boundaries
  checkStarStageBoundaries(_star);

  //Check for collisions with the monsters
  starVsMonsterCollision(_star, _monster1);
  starVsMonsterCollision(_star, _monster2);
}
else
{
  _star.visible = false;
}
```

This code makes the star visible, moves it, rotates it, checks its stage boundaries, and checks for collisions with the monsters. If the launched property is false, this code also makes the star invisible. As you'll soon see, the launched property is set to false when the star hits the stage boundary or any of the monsters.

Checking the star's collisions

Because the star only moves upwards, the code that checks its stage boundaries only needs to check for a collision with the top of the stage. The checkStarStageBoundaries method does this:

```
private function checkStarStageBoundaries(star:Star):void
{
  if (star.y < 50)
  {
    star.launched = false;
  }
}
```

It sets the star's launched property to false if it hits the top playing field boundary.

The starVsMonsterCollision method checks for collisions between the star and the monsters. It takes two arguments: the star and the monster that you want to check for a collision against.

```
starVsMonsterCollision(_star, _monster1);
starVsMonsterCollision(_star, _monster2);
```

The method's function definition will only check for a collision if the monster being checked is visible. (If it's invisible, it means it's already been hit three times and has been removed from the game.) If the monster is visible, the code does the following things:

- Opens the monsters mouth.

- Adds 1 to the monster's timesHit property.

- Sets the star's launched property to false.

- Checks whether the monster has been hit three times; if it has, it calls the killMonster method.

- If the monster has been hit three times, it also calls the checkGameOver method to find out if the game is possibly finished.

Here's the starVsMonsterCollision method that does all this work:

```
private function starVsMonsterCollision
  (star:Star, monster:Monster):void
{
  if(monster.visible
  &&star.hitTestObject(monster))
  {
    //Call the monster's openMouth
    //method to make it open its mouth
    monster.openMouth();

    //Deactivate the star
    star.launched = false;

    //Add 1 to the monster's
    //timesHit variable
    monster.timesHit++;

    //Has the monster been hit
    //3 times?
    if(monster.timesHit == 3)
    {
      //call the killMonster
      //method
      killMonster(monster);

      //Check to see if the
      //game is over
      checkGameOver();
    }
  }
}
```

This is an interesting bit of code because it changes one property in the star, two properties in the monsters, and calls two methods in the LevelOne class. Figure 8-15 shows how all these connections fit together.

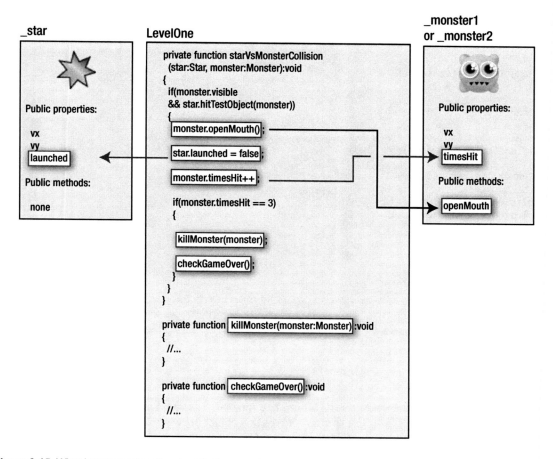

Figure 8-15. What happens when the star hits the monster

You'll look at the checkGameOver method in detail soon, but first take a look at what happens when one of the monsters is hit three times.

Vanquishing the monsters and creating an explosion

If the star hits one of the monsters three times, the killMonster method is called. It performs the following tasks:

- Makes the monster invisible.

- Creates an explosion object from the Explosion class and adds it to the stage.

- Centers the explosion over the monster's current position.

- Calls the explosion object's explode method. This makes the explosion image appear and then disappear again after two seconds.

Here's the `killMonster` method that does all this:

```
private function killMonster(monster:Monster):void
{
  //Make the monster invisible
  monster.visible = false;

  //Create a new explosion object
  //and add it to the stage
  var explosion:Explosion = new Explosion();
  this.addChild(explosion);

  //Center the explosion over
  //the monster
  explosion.x = monster.x -21;
  explosion.y = monster.y -18;

  //Call the exlposion's
  //explode method
  explosion.explode();
}
```

This is the first time you've seen how you can create an object while the game is in progress. All the other game objects, like `_star`, `_character`, `_monster1`, and `_monster2`, were created when the game was initialized. The explosion objects are created by the `killMonster` method whenever they're needed, like this:

```
var explosion:Explosion = new Explosion();
this.addChild(explosion);
```

This new explosion object is *local* to the `killMonster` method. That means that you can only access it inside this method. You can't refer to this new `explosion` object anywhere else in the class. That's just fine because it's just a simple visual effect that you don't need to use anywhere else. You also don't know how many explosion objects you'll need before the game starts, so this method will make a new one whenever you need it, whether that's 1 or 100. You don't need to plan this in advance by creating all the explosion objects when you initialize the game.

> *Local variables* and objects can only be used inside the method that creates them. You can make a local variable inside a method like this:
>
> *var localVariable:VariableType = new ClassName();*
>
> Notice that "var" is not preceded by "public" or "private".
>
> *Instance variables* and objects can be used in all the code, anywhere in the class. Instance variables are created in the class definition, like this:
>
> *private var _instanceVariable:VariableType = new ClassName();*

> *public var instanceVariable:VariableType = new ClassName();*
>
> *These variables can be used anywhere in the class, all the time and by any method. If they're declared as public, other classes can access them too. Most of the variables and game objects you've been working with have been instance variables.*
>
> *Because local variables have a more limited scope, they occupy slightly less space in the Flash Player's memory.*

After this new explosion object is created, it's centered over the monster's current position.

```
explosion.x = monster.x -21;
explosion.y = monster.y -18;
```

Finally, the explosion object's explode method is called.

```
explosion.explode();
```

This makes the explosion image visible for two seconds and then makes it invisible again. All this is done with a timer in the Explosion class, and it uses exactly the same technique you used to make the monster open and close its mouth.

Here's the entire Explosion class with its public explode method that starts the timer that makes the image visible:

```
package
{
  import flash.display.DisplayObject;
  import flash.display.Sprite;
  import flash.events.TimerEvent;
  import flash.utils.Timer;

  public class Explosion extends Sprite
  {
    //Embed the image
    [Embed(source="../images/explosion.png")]
    private var ExplosionImage:Class;

    //Private properties
    private var _explosion:DisplayObject = new ExplosionImage();
    private var _timer:Timer;

    public function Explosion()
    {
      this.addChild(_explosion);
      _explosion.visible = false;

      _timer = new Timer(2000);
    }
```

```
    //Public methods
    public function explode():void
    {
      _explosion.visible = true;
      _timer.addEventListener
        (TimerEvent.TIMER, explosionTimeHandler);
      _timer.start();
    }

    //Private methods
    private function explosionTimeHandler(event:TimerEvent):void
    {
      _explosion.visible = false;
      _timer.reset();
      _timer.removeEventListener
        (TimerEvent.TIMER, explosionTimeHandler);
    }
  }
}
```

Figure 8-16 illustrates the Explosion class's properties and methods.

Now that you know how all the objects in the game work, let's see how the code determines whether or not the level has been finished.

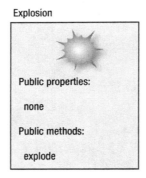

Explosion

Public properties:

Public methods:

explode

Figure 8-16. The Explosion class

Checking for the end of the level

The level is completed when the character has been hit once by the monsters or each of the monsters has been hit three times by the player's star. As you saw in the previous example, when this happens, the code calls the checkGameOver method.

```
private function checkGameOver():void
{
  if(_monster1.timesHit == 3
  && _monster2.timesHit == 3)
  {
```

```
      _levelWinner = "character"
      _gameOverTimer = new Timer(2000);
      _gameOverTimer.addEventListener
        (TimerEvent.TIMER, gameOverTimerHandler);
      _gameOverTimer.start();
      _monsterTimer.removeEventListener
        (TimerEvent.TIMER, monsterTimerHandler);
      this.removeEventListener
        (Event.ENTER_FRAME, enterFrameHandler);
    }
    if(_character.timesHit == 1)
    {
      _levelWinner = "monsters"
      _character.alpha = 0.5;
      _gameOverTimer = new Timer(2000);
      gameOverTimer.addEventListener
        (TimerEvent.TIMER, gameOverTimerHandler);
      _gameOverTimer.start();
      monsterTimer.removeEventListener
        (TimerEvent.TIMER, _monsterTimerHandler);
      this.removeEventListener(Event.ENTER_FRAME, enterFrameHandler);
    }
}
```

Here's how checkGameOver works:

- It finds out who won the game: the monsters or the character. It assigns this to a variable called _levelWinner.

```
if(_monster1.timesHit == 3
&& _monster2.timesHit == 3)
{
  _levelWinner = "character"
  //...
}
if(_character.timesHit == 1)
{
  _levelWinner = "monsters"
  //...
}
```

- It removes the enterFrameHandler, which freezes all the action on the stage. If the character has lost, the code sets the character's alpha to 0.5, which makes it semitransparent.

```
this.removeEventListener(Event.ENTER_FRAME, enterFrameHandler);
_character.alpha = 0.5;
```

- It removes the monster timer's TIMER event handler so that you stop assigning random directions to the monsters. It's important do this because the monster timer won't quit automatically when the level is finished. You don't want to waste precious CPU power running the timer if you don't need to.

```
_monsterTimer.removeEventListener(TimerEvent.TIMER, monsterTimerHandler);
```

- It starts the _gameOverTimer, which calls gameOverTimerHandler.

```
_gameOverTimer = new Timer(2000);
_gameOverTimer.addEventListener
  (TimerEvent.TIMER, gameOverTimerHandler);
_gameOverTimer.start();
```

It's the gameOverTimerHandler that does the work of displaying the "Level Complete" message or "Game Over" message and informing the application class that the level has been finished. Let's see how this works next.

Ending the level

The gameOverTimerHandler introduces some new techniques.

- It uses the timer's currentCount property to perform a new action every two seconds.

- It announces that the level is complete so that the application class can load the second level.

Here's the gameOverTimerHandler that does this, and I'll explain how it works in detail next.

```
private function gameOverTimerHandler(event:TimerEvent):void
{
  if(_levelWinner == "character")
  {
    if(_gameOverTimer.currentCount == 1)
    {
      _gameOver.levelComplete.visible = true;
    }
    if(_gameOverTimer.currentCount == 2)
    {
      _gameOverTimer.reset();
      _gameOverTimer.removeEventListener
        (TimerEvent.TIMER, gameOverTimerHandler);
      dispatchEvent(new Event("levelOneComplete", true));
    }
  }
  if(_levelWinner == "monsters")
  {
    _gameOver.youLost.visible = true;
    _gameOverTimer.removeEventListener
      (TimerEvent.TIMER, gameOverTimerHandler);
  }
}
```

If the monsters win...

Let's first take a look at what happens when the monsters win the game because the code is very simple. The _gameOverTimer removes the gameOverTimerHandler so that all this code isn't called a second time.

```
_gameOverTimer.removeEventListener(TimerEvent.TIMER, gameOverTimerHandler);
```

The code also makes _gameOver object's youLost subobject visible.

```
_gameOver.youLost.visible = true;
```

The _gameOver object was added to the game by the LevelOne class when the class was initialized.

```
private var _gameOver:GameOver;
//...
addGameObjectToLevel(_gameOver, 140, 130);
```

It's been sitting on the stage the whole time, but you couldn't see it because the subobjects that it contains have been invisible. The GameOver class contains two subobjects: youLost and levelComplete. Their visible properties are both set to false when they're added to their parent class. Here's the complete GameOver class that does this:

```
package
{
  import flash.display.DisplayObject;
  import flash.display.Sprite;

  public class GameOver extends Sprite
  {
    //Embed the images
    [Embed(source="../images/levelComplete.png")]
    private var LevelCompleteImage:Class;
    [Embed(source="../images/youLost.png")]
    private var YouLostImage:Class;

    //Private properties
    public var levelComplete:DisplayObject
      = new LevelCompleteImage();
    public var youLost:DisplayObject = new YouLostImage();

    public function GameOver()
    {
      //Add the images to this class
      //and make them invisible
      this.addChild(levelComplete);
      levelComplete.visible = false;

      this.addChild(youLost);
      youLost.visible = false;
    }
  }
}
```

Figure 8-17 shows the effect that making the _gameOver object's youLost subobject visible has when the monsters win the game.

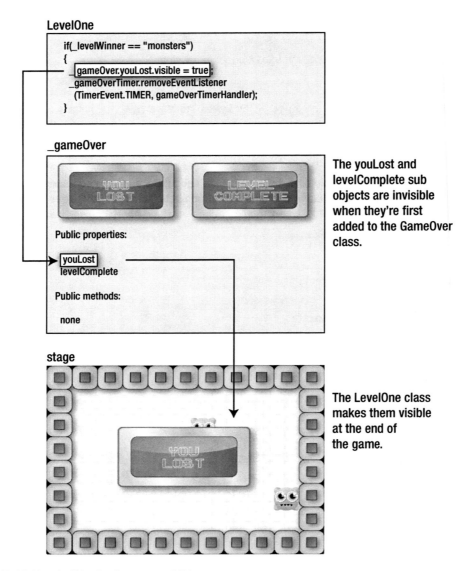

Figure 8-17. Making the "You lost" message visible

So, if the monsters win, that's the end of the game and nothing else happens. Things get a lot more interesting if the character wins.

If the character wins...

When the `_gameOverTimer` is created, it's initialized so that it calls the `gameOverTimerHandler` every two seconds.

```
_gameOverTimer = new Timer(2000);
_gameOverTimer.addEventListener
  (TimerEvent.TIMER, gameOverTimerHandler);
_gameOverTimer.start();
```

As mentioned in Chapter 7, timers have a property called currentCount that counts the number of times the timer has run. In this example, the _gameOverTimer will increase its currentCount property by 1 every two seconds. The game uses this feature to manage displaying the "Level Complete" message and to load level two.

Then currentCount starts counting from 0 and the timer fires once every 2,000 milliseconds. That means that when it becomes 1, two seconds have already passed. When currentCount becomes 2, four seconds have passed. Here's how it's used to manage the transition from level one to level two:

- currentCount = 0: There's a two second pause at the end game when the enterFrameHandler is removed by the checkGameOver method. The checkGameOver method also starts the _gameOverTimer.

- currentCount = 1: The "Level Complete" message is displayed.

- currentCount = 2: Two seconds later, the code announces that the level is complete. The application class hears this and loads the game's second level. (The _gameOverTimer is also reset.)

Figure 8-18 illustrates how the _gameOverTimer.currentCount property is managing the last four seconds of the game.

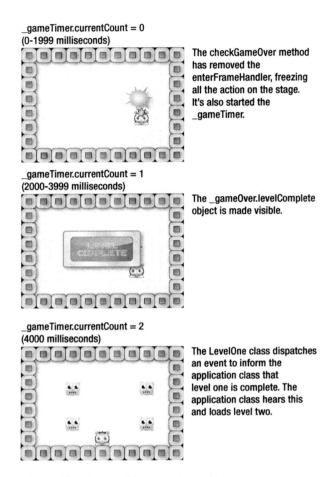

_gameTimer.currentCount = 0
(0-1999 milliseconds)

The checkGameOver method has removed the enterFrameHandler, freezing all the action on the stage. It's also started the _gameTimer.

_gameTimer.currentCount = 1
(2000-3999 milliseconds)

The _gameOver.levelComplete object is made visible.

_gameTimer.currentCount = 2
(4000 milliseconds)

The LevelOne class dispatches an event to inform the application class that level one is complete. The application class hears this and loads level two.

Figure 8-18. The timer is used to end level one and transition to level two.

Here's the code in the gameOverTimerHandler method that actually does this:

```
if(_levelWinner == "character")
{
  if(_gameOverTimer.currentCount == 1)
  {
    _gameOver.levelComplete.visible = true;
  }
  if(_gameOverTimer.currentCount == 2)
  {
    _gameOverTimer.reset();
    _gameOverTimer.removeEventListener
      (TimerEvent.TIMER, gameOverTimerHandler);
    dispatchEvent(new Event("levelOneComplete", true));
  }
```

```
}
```

You should now understand what this code is doing, except for this one very important line:

```
dispatchEvent(new Event("levelOneComplete", true));
```

This bit of code is *dispatching an event* called `levelOneComplete`. It's broadcasting this message to the rest of the game that level one is finished. Any objects who are interested in this message can listen for it and perform some kind of action when they hear this event being broadcast.

The `MonsterMayhem` application class is extremely interested in this event because it needs to know when level one is finished. Let's take a look at the `MonsterMayhem` class again. I've highlighted all the code that adds a listener for the `levelOneComplete` event and the `switchLevelHandler` that takes some action when it hears it.

```
package
{
  import flash.display.Sprite;
  import flash.events.Event;

  [SWF(width="550", height="400",
  backgroundColor="#FFFFFF", frameRate="60")]

  public class MonsterMayhem extends Sprite
  {
    private var _levelOne:LevelOne;
    private var _levelTwo:LevelTwo;

    public function MonsterMayhem()
    {
      _levelOne = new LevelOne(stage);
      _levelTwo = new LevelTwo(stage);
      stage.addChild(_levelOne);

      stage.addEventListener
        ("levelOneComplete", switchLevelHandler);
    }
    private function switchLevelHandler(event:Event):void
    {
      trace("Hello from the application class! Switch levels!");
      stage.removeChild(_levelOne);
      _levelOne = null;
      stage.addChild(_levelTwo);
    }
  }
}
```

The `MonsterMayhem` application class listens for the `levelOneComplete` event by attaching an event listener to the stage.

```
stage.addEventListener("levelOneComplete", switchLevelHandler);
```

The listener waits until this line of code is run by any object on the stage:

```
dispatchEvent(new Event("levelOneComplete", true));
```

As soon as it hears this event, the application class runs its `switchLevelHandler`.

```
private function switchLevelHandler(event:Event):void
{
  trace("Hello from the application class! Switch levels!");
  stage.removeChild(_levelOne);
  _levelOne = null;
  stage.addChild(_levelTwo);
}
```

The `switchLevelHandler` does these things:

- It generates a trace message to let you know that this event is working. This is optional and just used for testing.

```
trace("Hello from the application class! Switch levels!");
```

- It uses the `removeChild` method to remove the `_levelOne` object from the stage. It also gives the `_levelOne` object a value of null, which clears it from the Flash Player's memory.

```
stage.removeChild(_levelOne);
_levelOne = null;
```

- It adds the `_levelTwo` object to the stage.

```
stage.addChild(_levelTwo);
```

Figure 8-19 shows how the `MonsterMayhem` application class can "hear" when `_levelOne` dispatches an event.

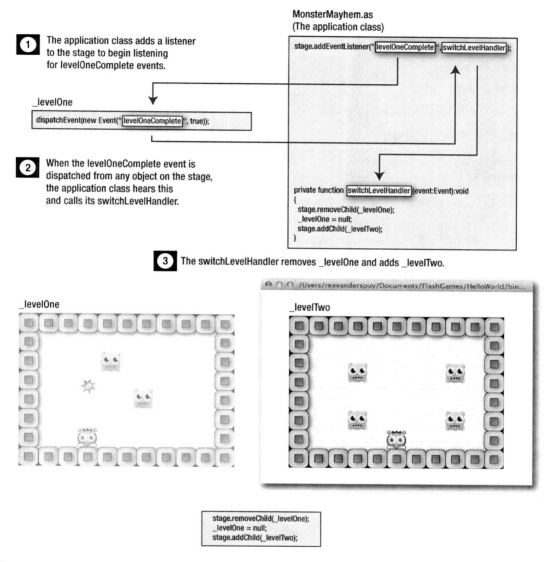

Figure 8-19. Using events to switch levels

This is the first time you've seen how `removeChild` is used, and it's also the first time you've seen how a class can listen for an event being broadcast by another class. Let's take a slightly deeper look at these two new features.

Using removeChild to completely get rid of objects

In all the game examples so far, you've removed objects from the game by setting their visible properties to false, like this:

```
_monster1.visible = false;
```

You can then check whether the object is still in the game or not with a simple if/else statement, like this:

```
if(_monster1.visible)
{
  //The monster is active, so keep
  //it moving and check for collisions
}
else
{
  //The monster isn't in the game anymore
}
```

This is an easy way of removing game objects, and it's often the best. The nice thing about this technique is that the objects still actually exist on the stage the entire time. If you have a game in which you hide and show the same objects over and over again, this is the way to do it. It's easy to reset games or game levels just by making objects visible again.

The only problem with this is that the game object still actually exists and is occupying memory space in the Flash Player. This could become a problem if you have hundreds of invisible objects on the stage that might still be running internal events, like timers or enterFrameHandlers. In that case, it's best to get rid of them completely with removeChild. Here's how:

```
removeChild(objectName);
```

If the object you want to remove is on the stage, remove it like this:

```
stage.removeChild(objectName);
```

If it's inside another class, like LevelOne, remove it like this:

```
this.removeChild(objectName);
```

To completely clear the object from memory, give any variables that refer to the object a null value, like this:

```
objectName = null;
```

What actually happens to the object when it's removed? AS3.0 has a **garbage collector** to do the job. You can think of the garbage collector as a little software robot that runs around your game looking for objects and properties that aren't being used or don't have any value and deletes them for good. This saves memory and processing power, and AS3.0 does this for you automatically. One of the jobs of the garbage collector is to find objects that have been removed with removeChild and wipe them from the Flash Player's memory. However, the garbage collector is a bit of a finicky fellow, so it's very picky about what it chooses to completely delete.

- The garbage collector doesn't delete objects that have an ENTER_FRAME event running. These objects make the garbage collector a bit squeamish, so you have to manually remove the ENTER_FRAME event with removeListener, as you did in the removedFromStage event handlers. Although objects do remove their own event listeners (such as ADDED_TO_STAGE and REMOVED_FROM_STAGE) it's considered good programming form to also remove them manually.

- The garbage collector doesn't like MovieClip objects that are animated using a timeline. It doesn't touch them unless the animation is stopped by using the stop method.

- If any objects have timers running using the Timer class, the garbage collector doesn't delete them.

- The garbage collector doesn't delete an object if there are one or more variables in the game that make a reference to it.

Usually, however, AS3.0's garbage collector is pretty efficient about these sorts of things. As long as you keep these guidelines in mind, your game won't be unexpectedly slowed down by objects running in the background that you thought you deleted completely but hadn't.

If you've removed an object from a game with removeChild, you can test whether or not it exists by using an if statement that looks like this:

```
if(gameObject == null)
{
  //The object is no longer in the game
}
```

Remember also that when you remove an object from the stage, the object's REMOVED_FROM_STAGE event handler will be run, if you've created one for the object. That's a good place to remove timers or the object's enterFrameHandler to prevent them from secretly running in the background after the object has been removed.

Communicating between classes by dispatching events

The coolest bit of new programming voodoo you've used is the dispatchEvent method.

```
dispatchEvent(new Event("levelOneComplete", true));
```

This broadcasts an event called "levelOneComplete" to any other class that might be interested in listening for it. You can give this event any name you please, and you can dispatch as many events as you think your game will need.

Dispatching events is one of most useful things you can learn how to do as a game programmer. You've seen events used in almost every chapter in this book. Button clicks, timers, frames—almost every important thing in an AS3.0 program seems to happen because of an event. But so far, all the events that you've used have been built into AS3.0. By using the dispatchEvent method, you can create your own events and then trigger them whenever anything important happens in your game.

For example, imagine that you're making an adventure game in which the hero or heroine needs to steal a magical gingerbread cookie from a sleeping witch. As soon as the cookie has been stolen, it might be very useful for other objects in the game to know that this has happened. You could inform the application class to update a score, you could inform the character to update its inventory, and you could even inform the sleeping witch who may well wake up if the player isn't tip-toeing quietly enough. Instead of informing each of these objects individually, however, the magical gingerbread cookie needs to broadcast only one event to the entire game: "I've been picked up!" This is known as *dispatching an event*. Other objects can then choose whether they want to listen to this event or take any action if it concerns them.

The elegance of this system is that the event isn't dispatched to a specific object, and the objects that are listening for the event don't need to know anything about the object that broadcast the event.

Here's a quick-start guide to dispatching events:

1. Import the **Event** class.

```
import flash.events.Event;
```

2. When something happens that any objects in your game might be interested in, create an event for it using the `dispatchEvent` method. The basic format for creating an event looks like this:

```
dispatchEvent(new Event("eventName", true));
```

This directive broadcasts to the rest of your program that an event has occurred. You can give the event any name you like, such as **"eventName"**, as in this example.

3. Any other class can now listen to this event by adding an event listener, like this:

```
stage.addEventListener("eventName",eventNameHandler);
```

In your games, you'll probably want to add the event listener to the stage for reasons I'll explain ahead. You can attach event listeners to any object, however.

4. You then need to create the event handler to make something happen when the event occurs.

```
private function eventNameHandler(event:Event)
{
  trace(event.target);
}
```

In the event handler, you can use the event object's `target` property to access the object that called the event and all its properties. (If you want to access the object with which the event was registered, such as the stage in this example, use the currentTarget property.)

5. Wait for the event to occur.

You can create events for anything in your game that you think other objects should know about, such as a door opening, an enemy being destroyed, or a variable changing its value. Any objects can then choose to listen to those events if they want to and take actions based on them.

By using events, objects can communicate with each other without having to depend on other classes to function properly. They can listen for events that interest them and change their own private properties internally.

Event bubbling

When events are dispatched, they travel through three different states: **capture**, **target**, and **bubbling**. The only one you're interested in is the *bubbling* state, which is most useful in the kinds of game design scenarios that you've seen at work in this book.

When an object dispatches an event, the object broadcasts the event like a radio station broadcasts a news item. Other objects can then "tune in" to the event if they want to listen to it.

Events aren't broadcast to every object in the program at the same time, however. They either travel up or down through the hierarchy of objects. You can listen to events at any point in this journey.

If an event is set to bubble, it means that the event travels up through the hierarchy. It starts with the child object and then informs the parent object. That parent object can then perform any action it needs to. Figure 8-20 illustrates this.

Any application class

```
stage.addChild(_character);
stage.addEventListener("hello", helloHandler);

private function helloHandler(event:Event):void
{
  //Do something interesting when an object
  //dispatches a "hello" event
}
```

3 The object's parent listens for the "hello" event and does something interesting when it hears it.

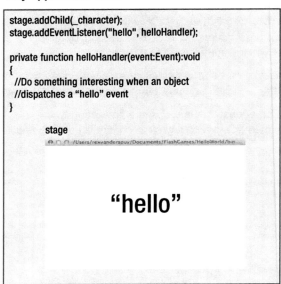

2 The event "bubbles" up to the character's container, which in this example happens to be stage.

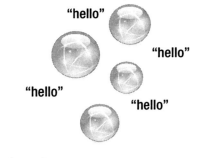

1 The _character object dispatches a "hello" event.

Figure 8-20. Events bubble up from the child to the parent object.

The dispatchEvent method has one argument, which is called the **event constructor**. It's highlighted here in bold:

```
dispatchEvent(new Event("eventName", true));
```

The event constructor creates the event. Events can be made to bubble by setting the second argument in the event constructor to true:

```
new Event("eventName",true)
```

If you change it to false or leave it out entirely, the event doesn't bubble.

> *If other classes or objects want to listen to an event, they have to do it by attaching their event listeners to the parent object. Often, that object will be the stage, which is the common parent of all display objects. However, your games will be much easier to manage if you only have one class that's listening for events from all objects. That might be the application class or an intermediary class, like LevelOne in this chapter's example. That way the control of the game is centralized, and you'll know where in your code to look to change what your game objects should do if an event is triggered.*

And that's really all you need to know about how to dispatch and listen for events in games.

Finishing off level one

You're just about finished with the first level of Monster Mayhem. The only class you haven't looked at is the Background class. All it does is display the background image—nothing special! Just for completeness, here's the entire Background class:

```
package
{
  import flash.display.DisplayObject;
  import flash.display.Sprite;

  public class Background extends Sprite
  {
    //Embed the image
    [Embed(source="../images/background.png")]
    private var BackgroundImage:Class;
    private var _background:DisplayObject
      = new BackgroundImage();

    public function Background()
    {
      this.addChild(_background);
    }
  }
}
```

Firing stars in four directions in level two

Level two introduces a few new twists to the game. There are now four monsters on the stage, and they move much faster. This was easy to implement by increasing their velocities from 1 pixel per frame to 2. Most of the rest of the code in LevelTwo is identical to LevelOne, but make sure that you take a look at all the code in its proper context in the LevelTwo.as file in the chapter's source files.

The biggest change in level two is that the game character can fire stars in all four directions, as illustrated in Figure 8-21.

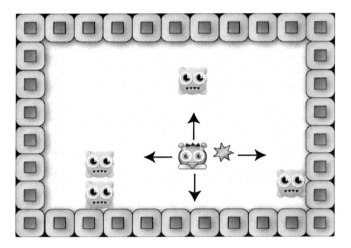

Figure 8-21. In level two, the character can fire stars in four directions.

This feature is very easy to implement by keeping track of which of the four arrow keys the player is pressing, and then changing the star's vx and vy properties based on that direction.

First, LevelTwo uses a new String variable called _starDirection to track which direction the star should move in. Note that _starDirection is changed to "left", "right", "up", or "down" depending on which key is pressed and it's only changed if the star hasn't already been launched. This prevents the star from changing direction in mid-flight if the player presses the arrow keys after the star has been launched.

```
private function keyDownHandler(event:KeyboardEvent):void
{
  if (event.keyCode == Keyboard.LEFT)
  {
    _character.vx = -5;
    if(!_star.launched)
    {
      _starDirection = "left";
    }
  }
  else if (event.keyCode == Keyboard.RIGHT)
  {
```

```
      _character.vx = 5;
      if(!_star.launched)
      {
        _starDirection = "right";
      }
    }
    else if (event.keyCode == Keyboard.UP)
    {
      _character.vy = -5;
      if(!_star.launched)
      {
        _starDirection = "up";
      }
    }
    else if (event.keyCode == Keyboard.DOWN)
    {
      _character.vy = 5;
      if(!_star.launched)
      {
        _starDirection = "down";
      }
    }
    if(event.keyCode == Keyboard.SPACE)
    {
      if(!_star.launched)
      {
        _star.x = _character.x + _character.width / 2;
        _star.y = _character.y + _character.width / 2;
        _star.launched = true;
      }
    }
  }
}
```

The `enterFrameHandler` then sets the star's velocity to move it in any of those four directions depending on what `_starDirection` is set to.

```
if(_star.launched)
{
  _star.visible = true;

  //Set the star's velocity based on the
  //_starDirection variable set in the
  //keyDownHandler
  if(_starDirection == "up")
  {
    _star.vy = -3;
    _star.vx = 0;
  }
  else if(_starDirection == "down")
  {
    _star.vy = 3;
    _star.vx = 0;
```

```
    }
    else if(_starDirection == "left")
    {
      _star.vy = 0;
      _star.vx = -3;
    }
    else if(_starDirection == "right")
    {
      _star.vy = 0;
      _star.vx = 3;
    }

    //Move and rotate the star
    _star.x += _star.vx;
    _star.y += _star.vy;
    _star.rotation += 5;

    //Check its stage boundaries
    checkStarStageBoundaries(_star);

    //Check for collisions with the monsters
    starVsMonsterCollision(_star, _monster1);
    starVsMonsterCollision(_star, _monster2);
    starVsMonsterCollision(_star, _monster3);
    starVsMonsterCollision(_star, _monster4);
}
else
{
  _star.visible = false;
}
```

Those are the only changes that need to be made.

Optionally you could create a property called direction inside the Star *class itself. You could then change this direction property like this:*

```
_star.direction = "up"
```

You could then use it to check in which direction the star should move like this:

```
if(_star.Direction == "up")
{...
```

The style you use to track the star's direction is entirely up to you.

In Monster Mayhem the character can't fire another star while the first one is still on the stage. In many games, however, characters can fire limitless numbers of projectiles, no matter how many are on the stage. To implement this, you need to know about **arrays** and **loops**. You'll learn about arrays and loops in Chapter 9, and you'll learn how to use them to fire multiple projectiles in Chapter 10.

Level two ends in the same way as level one. The code checks to see whether the monsters or the character has won and displays the appropriate message.

More Monster Mayhem!

Monster Mayhem is a great model for a game project, but if you're making a similar type of game, there are probably a few more advanced things you'll want it to do.

- **A scrolling background**: You'll want to make a big environment larger than the borders of the stage and have the character and monsters move through it.

- **Intelligent monsters**: The monsters in Monster Mayhem move randomly around the stage. Wouldn't it be fun if they could figure out where the character is and move towards it?

You can implement both these features. Let's find out how.

Moving objects in a scrolling game world

In Chapter 7 I showed you how to make a game with a large scrolling background. The trick to making this work is to calculate the **scroll velocity** and apply it to game objects. This keeps their positions synchronized with the scrolling background. You're going to use exactly the same technique to make the objects in Monster Mayhem scroll so make sure that you fully understand the code from Chapter 7 before you work through this next section.

In Monster Mayhem, the monsters and the star weapon are moving across the stage. This means that they have to adjust their velocities to account for the moving background. This is, fortunately, very easy to do but requires a bit of thought and planning, so I'm going to walk you through the details of this code so you'll be more easily able to implement scrolling in your own games.

You'll find a scrolling version of Monster Mayhem in the ScrollingMonsters project folder. It only has one level with four monsters, and the collision detection has been disabled so that it's easier to test how the scrolling works. Run the SWF file and you'll see that the monsters can now meander freely all over the game world (Figure 8-22).

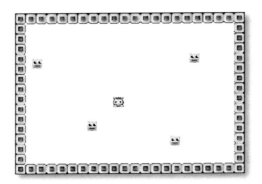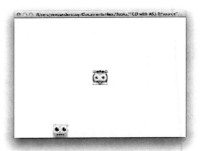

Figure 8-22. Moving objects in a large scrolling game world

The scrolling game code

I've structured this example in exactly the same way as the original Monster Mayhem so that you can see another, simplified version of your game structure system at work. The application class, ScrollingMonsters, creates an object called _scrollingLevel and adds it to the stage. All of the game logic is in the ScrollingLevel class. Here's the ScrollingMonsters application class that loads the game level:

```
package
{
  import flash.display.Sprite;
  import flash.events.Event;

  [SWF(width="550", height="400",
  backgroundColor="#FFFFFF", frameRate="60")]

  public class ScrollingMonsters extends Sprite
  {
    private var _scrollingLevel:ScrollingLevel;

    public function ScrollingMonsters()
    {
      _scrollingLevel = new ScrollingLevel(stage);
      stage.addChild(_scrollingLevel);
    }
  }
}
```

So that you can see all the code in context, here's the entire ScrollingLevel class that contains all the game logic. Most of it is identical to the code in the LevelOne and LevelTwo classes that you looked at earlier in the chapter. I've highlighted all the new code that's relevant to scrolling, and I'll explain all in detail ahead.

```
package
{
  import flash.display.Sprite;
  import flash.events.Event;
  import flash.events.KeyboardEvent;
  import flash.events.TimerEvent;
  import flash.ui.Keyboard;
  import flash.utils.Timer;

  public class ScrollingLevel extends Sprite
  {
    //Declare the variables to hold
    //the game objects
    private var _character:Character;
    private var _background:BigBackground;
    private var _gameOver:GameOver;
    private var _monster1:Monster;
    private var _monster2:Monster;
    private var _monster3:Monster;
    private var _monster4:Monster;
    private var _star:Star;
    private var _levelWinner:String;
    private var _stage:Object;
    private var _starDirection:String;

    //The timers
    private var _monsterTimer:Timer;
    private var _gameOverTimer:Timer;

    //Variables needed for scrolling
    private var _temporaryX:int;
    private var _temporaryY:int;
    private var _scroll_Vx:int;
    private var _scroll_Vy:int;
    private var _rightInnerBoundary:uint;
    private var _leftInnerBoundary:uint;
    private var _topInnerBoundary:uint;
    private var _bottomInnerBoundary:uint;
    private var _currentExplosion:Sprite = null;

    public function ScrollingLevel(stage:Object)
    {
      _stage = stage;
      this.addEventListener
        (Event.ADDED_TO_STAGE, addedToStageHandler);
    }
    private function addedToStageHandler(event:Event):void
    {
      startGame();
      this.removeEventListener
        (Event.ADDED_TO_STAGE, addedToStageHandler);
    }
```

```
private function startGame():void
{
  //Create the game objects
  _character = new Character();
  _star = new Star();
  _background = new BigBackground();
  _monster1 = new Monster();
  _monster2 = new Monster();
  _monster3 = new Monster();
  _monster4 = new Monster();
  _gameOver = new GameOver();

  //Add the game objects to the stage
  addGameObjectToLevel
    (
      _background,
      -(_background.width - stage.stageWidth) / 2,
      -(_background.height - stage.stageHeight) / 2
    );
  addGameObjectToLevel(_monster1, 400, 125);
  addGameObjectToLevel(_monster2, 150, 125);
  addGameObjectToLevel(_monster3, 400, 250);
  addGameObjectToLevel(_monster4, 150, 250);
  addGameObjectToLevel(_character, 250, 175);
  addGameObjectToLevel(_star, 250, 300);
  _star.visible = false;
  addGameObjectToLevel(_gameOver, 140, 130);

  //Initialize the monster timer
  _monsterTimer = new Timer(1000);
  _monsterTimer.addEventListener
    (TimerEvent.TIMER, monsterTimerHandler);
  _monsterTimer.start();

  //Event listeners
  _stage.addEventListener
    (KeyboardEvent.KEY_DOWN, keyDownHandler);
  _stage.addEventListener
    (KeyboardEvent.KEY_UP, keyUpHandler);
  this.addEventListener(Event.ENTER_FRAME, enterFrameHandler);

  //Define the inner boundary variables
  _rightInnerBoundary
    = (_stage.stageWidth / 2) + (_stage.stageWidth / 4);
  _leftInnerBoundary
    = (_stage.stageWidth / 2) - (_stage.stageWidth / 4);
  _topInnerBoundary
    = (_stage.stageHeight / 2) - (_stage.stageHeight / 4);
  _bottomInnerBoundary
    = (_stage.stageHeight / 2) + (_stage.stageHeight / 4);
}
private function enterFrameHandler(event:Event):void
```

```
{
  //Move the game character
  _character.x += _character.vx;
  _character.y += _character.vy;

  //Move the monsters and
  //check their stage boundaries
  if(_monster1.visible)
  {
    _monster1.x += _monster1.vx;
    _monster1.y += _monster1.vy;
    checkStageBoundaries(_monster1);
  }
  if(_monster2.visible)
  {
    _monster2.x += _monster2.vx;
    _monster2.y += _monster2.vy;
    checkStageBoundaries(_monster2);
  }
  if(_monster3.visible)
  {
    _monster3.x += _monster3.vx;
    _monster3.y += _monster3.vy;
    checkStageBoundaries(_monster3);
  }
  if(_monster4.visible)
  {
    _monster4.x += _monster4.vx;
    _monster4.y += _monster4.vy;
    checkStageBoundaries(_monster4);
  }
  //Has the star been launched?
  if(_star.launched)
  {
    //If it has, make it visible
    _star.visible = true;

    //Set the star's velocity based on the
    //_starDirection variable set in the
    //keyDownHandler
    if(_starDirection == "up")
    {
      _star.vy = -3;
      _star.vx = 0;
    }
    else if(_starDirection == "down")
    {
      _star.vy = 3;
      _star.vx = 0;
    }
    else if(_starDirection == "left")
    {
```

```
      _star.vy = 0;
          _star.vx = -3;
    }
    else if(_starDirection == "right")
    {
      _star.vy = 0;
      _star.vx = 3;
    }

  //Move and rotate the star
  _star.x += _star.vx;
  _star.y += _star.vy;
  _star.rotation += 5;

  //Check its stage boundaries
  checkStarStageBoundaries(_star);

  //Check for collisions with the monsters
  starVsMonsterCollision(_star, _monster1);
  starVsMonsterCollision(_star, _monster2);
  starVsMonsterCollision(_star, _monster3);
  starVsMonsterCollision(_star, _monster4);
}
else
{
  _star.visible = false;
}

//Collision detection between the
//character and  monsters
//Uncomment this code to re-enable the collisions
/*
characterVsMonsterCollision(_character, _monster1);
characterVsMonsterCollision(_character, _monster2);
characterVsMonsterCollision(_character, _monster3);
characterVsMonsterCollision(_character, _monster4);
*/

//Scroll the background
 //Calculate the scroll velocity
 _temporaryX = _background.x;
 _temporaryY = _background.y;

//Check the inner boundaries
if (_character.x < _leftInnerBoundary)
{
  _character.x = _leftInnerBoundary;
  _rightInnerBoundary
  = (_stage.stageWidth / 2) + (_stage.stageWidth / 4);
  _background.x -= _character.vx;
}
else if
```

```
  (_character.x + _character.width > _rightInnerBoundary)
{
  character.x
   = _rightInnerBoundary - _character.width
  _leftInnerBoundary
        = (_stage.stageWidth / 2) - (_stage.stageWidth / 4);
  _background.x -= _character.vx;
}
if (_character.y < _topInnerBoundary)
{
  _character.y = _topInnerBoundary;
  _bottomInnerBoundary
        = (_stage.stageHeight / 2) + (_stage.stageHeight / 4);
  _background.y -= _character.vy;
}
else if
  (_character.y + _character.height > _bottomInnerBoundary)
{
  _character.y = _bottomInnerBoundary - _character.height;
  _topInnerBoundary
        = (_stage.stageHeight / 2) - (_stage.stageHeight / 4);
  _background.y -= _character.vy;
}

//Background stage boundaries
if (_background.x > 0)
{
  _background.x = 0;
  _leftInnerBoundary = 0;
}
else if (_background.y > 0)
{
  _background.y = 0;
  _topInnerBoundary = 0;
}
else if
  (_background.x < _stage.stageWidth - _background.width)
{
  _background.x = _stage.stageWidth - _background.width;
  _rightInnerBoundary = _stage.stageWidth;
}
else if
  (_background.y < _stage.stageHeight - _background.height)
{
  _background.y = _stage.stageHeight - _background.height;
  _bottomInnerBoundary = _stage.stageHeight;
}

//Character stage boundaries
if (_character.x < 50)
{
  _character.x = 50;
```

```
    }
    if (_character.y < 50)
    {
      _character.y = 50;
    }
    if(_character.x + _character.width > _stage.stageWidth - 50)
    {
      _character.x = _stage.stageWidth - _character.width - 50;
    }
    if(_character.y + _character.height > _stage.stageHeight -50)
    {
      _character.y = _stage.stageHeight - _character.height - 50;
    }

    //Calculate the scroll velocity
    _scroll_Vx = _background.x - _temporaryX;
    _scroll_Vy = _background.y - _temporaryY;

    //1. Scroll the moving objects
    //Scroll the monsters
    scroll(_monster1);
    scroll(_monster2);
    scroll(_monster3);
    scroll(_monster4);

    //2. Scroll the star
    if(_star.launched)
    {
      scroll(_star);
    }

    //3. Scroll the current explosion
    if(_currentExplosion != null)
    {
      scroll(_currentExplosion);
    }
  }
  public function scroll(gameObject:Sprite):void
  {
    gameObject.x += _scroll_Vx;
    gameObject.y += _scroll_Vy;
  }
  private function characterVsMonsterCollision
    (character:Character, monster:Monster):void
  {
    if(monster.visible
    && character.hitTestObject(monster))
    {
      character.timesHit++;
      checkGameOver();
    }
  }
```

```
private function starVsMonsterCollision
  (star:Star, monster:Monster):void
{
  if(monster.visible
  && star.hitTestObject(monster))
  {
    //Call the monster's "openMouth"
    //method to make it open its mouth
    monster.openMouth();

    //Deactivate the star
    star.launched = false;

    //Add 1 to the monster's
    //timesHit variable
    monster.timesHit++;

    //Has the monster been hit
    //3 times?
    if(monster.timesHit == 3)
    {
      //call the "killMonster"
      //method
      killMonster(monster);

      //Check to see if the
      //game is over
      checkGameOver();
    }
  }
}
private function killMonster(monster:Monster):void
{
  //Make the monster invisible
  monster.visible = false;

  //Create a new explosion object
  //and add it to the stage
  var explosion:Explosion = new Explosion();
  this.addChild(explosion);
  _currentExplosion = explosion;

  //Center the explosion over
  //the monster
  explosion.x = monster.x -21;
  explosion.y = monster.y -18;

  //Call the explosion's
  //"explode" method
  explosion.explode();
}
private function checkGameOver():void
```

```
{
  if(_monster1.timesHit == 3
  && _monster2.timesHit == 3
  && _monster3.timesHit == 3
  && _monster4.timesHit == 3)
  {
    _levelWinner = "character"
    _gameOverTimer = new Timer(2000);
    _gameOverTimer.addEventListener
      (TimerEvent.TIMER, gameOverTimerHandler);
    _gameOverTimer.start();
    _monsterTimer.removeEventListener
      (TimerEvent.TIMER, monsterTimerHandler);
    this.removeEventListener
      (Event.ENTER_FRAME, enterFrameHandler);
  }
  if(_character.timesHit == 1)
  {
    _levelWinner = "monsters"
    _character.alpha = 0.5;
    _gameOverTimer = new Timer(2000);
    _gameOverTimer.addEventListener
      (TimerEvent.TIMER, gameOverTimerHandler);
    _gameOverTimer.start();
    _monsterTimer.removeEventListener
      (TimerEvent.TIMER, monsterTimerHandler);
    this.removeEventListener
      (Event.ENTER_FRAME, enterFrameHandler);
  }
}
private function checkStageBoundaries(gameObject:Sprite):void
{
  if (gameObject.x < _background.x + 50)
  {
    gameObject.x = _background.x + 50;
  }
  if (gameObject.y < _background.y + 50)
  {
    gameObject.y = _background.y + 50;
  }
  if (gameObject.x + gameObject.width
  > _background.x + _background.width - 50)
  {
    gameObject.x
      = _background.x + _background.width
      - gameObject.width - 50;
  }
  if (gameObject.y + gameObject.height
  > _background.y + _background.height - 50)
  {
    gameObject.y
      = _background.y + _background.height
```

```
      - gameObject.height - 50;
    }
  }
  private function checkStarStageBoundaries(star:Star):void
  {
    if (star.y < 0
    || star.x < 0
    || star.x > _stage.stageWidth
    || star.y > _stage.stageHeight)
    {
      _star.launched = false;
    }
  }
private function monsterTimerHandler(event:TimerEvent):void
{
  changeMonsterDirection(_monster1);
  changeMonsterDirection(_monster2);
  changeMonsterDirection(_monster3);
  changeMonsterDirection(_monster4);
}
private function changeMonsterDirection(monster:Monster):void
{
  var randomNumber:int = Math.ceil(Math.random() * 4);
  if(randomNumber == 1)
  {
    //Right
    monster.vx = 2;
    monster.vy = 0;
  }
  else if (randomNumber == 2)
  {
    //Left
    monster.vx = -2;
    monster.vy = 0;
  }
  else if(randomNumber == 3)
  {
    //Up
    monster.vx = 0;
    monster.vy = -2;
  }
  else
  {
    //Down
    monster.vx = 0;
    monster.vy = 2;
  }
}
private function gameOverTimerHandler(event:TimerEvent):void
{
  if(_levelWinner == "character")
  {
```

```
    if(_gameOverTimer.currentCount == 1)
    {
      _gameOver.levelComplete.visible = true;
    }
     if(_gameOverTimer.currentCount == 2)
     {
      _gameOverTimer.reset();
      gameOverTimer.removeEventListener
        (TimerEvent.TIMER, gameOverTimerHandler);
      //dispatchEvent(new Event("levelOneComplete", true));
     }
  }
  if(_levelWinner == "monsters")
  {
    _gameOver.youLost.visible = true;
    gameOverTimer.removeEventListener
      (TimerEvent.TIMER, gameOverTimerHandler);
  }
}
private function keyDownHandler(event:KeyboardEvent):void
{
  if (event.keyCode == Keyboard.LEFT)
  {
    _character.vx = -5;
    if(!_star.launched)
    {
      _starDirection = "left";
    }
  }
  else if (event.keyCode == Keyboard.RIGHT)
  {
    _character.vx = 5;
    if(!_star.launched)
    {
      _starDirection = "right";
    }
  }
  else if (event.keyCode == Keyboard.UP)
  {
    _character.vy = -5;
    if(!_star.launched)
    {
      _starDirection = "up";
    }
  }
  else if (event.keyCode == Keyboard.DOWN)
  {
    _character.vy = 5;
    if(!_star.launched)
    {
      _starDirection = "down";
    }
```

```
      }
      if(event.keyCode == Keyboard.SPACE)
      {
        if(!_star.launched)
        {
          _star.x = _character.x + _character.width / 2;
          _star.y = _character.y + _character.width / 2;
          _star.launched = true;
        }
      }
    }
    private function keyUpHandler(event:KeyboardEvent):void
    {
      if (event.keyCode == Keyboard.LEFT
      || event.keyCode == Keyboard.RIGHT)
      {
        _character.vx = 0;
      }
      else if (event.keyCode == Keyboard.DOWN
      || event.keyCode == Keyboard.UP)
      {
        _character.vy = 0;
      }
    }
    private function addGameObjectToLevel
      (gameObject:Sprite, xPos:int, yPos:int):void
    {
      this.addChild(gameObject);
      gameObject.x = xPos;
      gameObject.y = yPos;
    }
  }
}
```

How the scrolling code works

To simplify the code a bit, I've declared all the variables and objects you need for scrolling as instance variables in the class definition. This means they can be accessed anywhere in the class by any method or object whenever they're needed.

```
private var _temporaryX:int;
private var _temporaryY:int;
private var _scroll_Vx:int;
private var _scroll_Vy:int;
private var _rightInnerBoundary:uint;
private var _leftInnerBoundary:uint;
private var _topInnerBoundary:uint;
private var _bottomInnerBoundary:uint;
private var _currentExplosion:Sprite = null;
```

The startGame method then initializes the inner boundary variables.

```
_rightInnerBoundary
  = (_stage.stageWidth / 2) + (_stage.stageWidth / 4);
_leftInnerBoundary
  = (_stage.stageWidth / 2) - (_stage.stageWidth / 4);
_topInnerBoundary
  = (_stage.stageHeight / 2) - (_stage.stageHeight / 4);
_bottomInnerBoundary
  = (_stage.stageHeight / 2) + (_stage.stageHeight / 4);
```

The enterFrameHandler calculates the scroll velocity by first capturing the background's position in temporary variables, moving the background, and then calculating the scroll velocity.

```
_temporaryX = _background.x;
_temporaryY = _background.y;

//...scroll the background...

_scroll_Vx = _background.x - _temporaryX;
_scroll_Vy = _background.y - _temporaryY;
```

With the _scroll_Vx and _scroll_Vy variables now in the bag, you can scroll the game objects using the scroll method.

```
//Scroll the monsters
scroll(_monster1);
scroll(_monster2);
scroll(_monster3);
scroll(_monster4);

//Scroll the star
if(_star.launched)
{
  scroll(_star);
}
```

Here's the scroll method that does this work:

```
public function scroll(gameObject:Sprite):void
{
  gameObject.x += _scroll_Vx;
  gameObject.y += _scroll_Vy;
}
```

Because the game world is now so much bigger, the checkStageBoundaries method needs to compensate for this. Here's the updated checkStageBoundaries method that makes sure the game objects don't cross the edges of the playing field:

```
private function checkStageBoundaries(gameObject:Sprite):void
{
  if (gameObject.x < _background.x + 50)
  {
    gameObject.x = _background.x + 50;
```

```
    }
    if (gameObject.y < _background.y + 50)
    {
        gameObject.y = _background.y + 50;
    }
    if (gameObject.x + gameObject.width
    > _background.x + _background.width - 50)
    {
        gameObject.x
            = _background.x + _background.width - gameObject.width - 50;
    }
    if (gameObject.y + gameObject.height
    > _background.y + _background.height - 50)
    {
        gameObject.y
        = _background.y + _background.height - gameObject.height - 50;
    }
}
```

The `checkStarStageBoundaries` method is also modified to let the star move to the edge of the stage boundaries.

```
private function checkStarStageBoundaries(star:Star):void
{
    if (star.y < 0
    || star.x < 0
    || star.x > _stage.stageWidth
    || star.y > _stage.stageHeight)
    {
        _star.launched = false;
    }
}
```

As you can see, all this code just compensates for the larger game world and adds the scroll velocity to the game objects' velocities.

There's one exception that you need to take a special look at: how to scroll the explosions.

Scrolling the explosions

All the explosion objects are created locally in the `killMonster` method, like this:

```
var explosion:Explosion = new Explosion();
this.addChild(explosion);
```

That means they can't be accessed outside the `killMonster` method. This is a problem because the `enterFrameHandler` needs some sort of access to them so that they can be scrolled after they're added to the stage.

A simple solution to this is to create an instance variable that stores a reference to the current explosion. You'll recall that instance variables are any variables declared in the class definition. They're available to all objects and all methods anywhere in the class. I created an instance variable called _currentExplosion in the class definition and gave it an initial value of null.

```
private var _currentExplosion:Sprite = null;
```

It's a Sprite, so it can contain any objects that extend the Sprite class, just as the explosion objects do.

When the killMonster class creates a temporary explosion object, all you need to do is copy it into the _currentExplosion variable, like this:

```
var explosion:Explosion = new Explosion();
this.addChild(explosion);
_currentExplosion = explosion;
```

This lets you hold a reference to the temporary explosion that can be used in other methods in the class. The enterFrameHandler can use this _currentExplosion object to scroll the explosion, like this:

```
if(_currentExplosion != null)
{
   scroll(_currentExplosion);
}
```

This technique is a quick and easy way to reference temporary objects and use them outside of the method where they were created. But it might not be the best way. It starts to become complicated to track and control temporary objects, especially if you need to access more than one at a time. In Chapter 10 you'll learn how to use loops and arrays to precisely add, remove, and control temporary objects in a game.

Intelligent monsters

It's very easy to make the monsters actively hunt the character. All the code needs to do is figure out whether a monster is above, below, to the left, or to the right of the character. Once you know that, just change the monster's velocity so that it moves towards the player. The code you need to write follows this logic.

```
if(the character is to the left of the monster)
{
   move the monster to the left
}
```

Here's what the actual code could look like in Monster Mayhem:

```
if(_character.x < monster.x)
{
  monster.vx = -2;
  monster.vy = 0;
}
```

As you can see, it's just a simple matter of comparing the x position of the character to the x position of the monster and then moving the monster to the left.

You can see all this code in action in the IntelligentMonsters example in the project's source files. Run the SWF and you'll notice that the monsters chase the character around the stage. Every second they decide whether they should move closer to the character by going left or right, or by going up or down. If you stop moving the character, you'll notice the monsters swarm around it. Figure 8-23 illustrates the monsters' behavior.

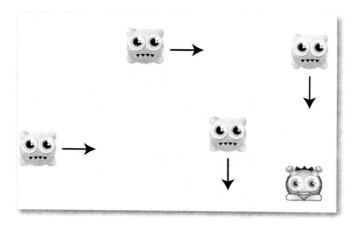

Figure 8-23. Monsters that chase the player

The code that does this is extremely simple. All it requires is a small change to the changeMonsterDirection method. Here's the updated method:

```
private function changeMonsterDirection(monster:Monster):void
{
  //Choose a random number between 1 and 2
  var randomNumber:int = Math.ceil(Math.random() * 2);

  //If the number is 1, move closer to the character
  //on the horizontal axis
  if(randomNumber == 1)
  {
    if(_character.x > monster.x)
    {
      //Right
      monster.vx = 2;
      monster.vy = 0;
    }
    if(_character.x < monster.x)
    {
      //Left
      monster.vx = -2;
      monster.vy = 0;
    }
  }
```

```
//If the number is 2, move closer to the character
//on the vertical axis
if(randomNumber == 2)
{
  if(_character.y < monster.y)
  {
    //Up
    monster.vx = 0;
    monster.vy = -2;
  }
  if(_character.y > monster.y)
  {
    //Down
    monster.vx = 0;
    monster.vy = 2;
  }
}
}
```

The code first chooses a random number between 1 and 2.

```
var randomNumber:int = Math.ceil(Math.random() * 2);
```

If the number is 1, the monster decides to move closer to the character on the x axis.

```
if(randomNumber == 1)
{
    //Move left or right...
}
```

If the random number is 2, the monster moves closer to the character on the y axis.

```
if(randomNumber == 2)
{
    //Move up or down...
}
```

I've added this bit of randomness to make the game slightly easier to play. You could easily make the monsters very precise in their direction choices by making them move only in the direction that is closest to the character. To do this, compare the distance between the x and y positions and have the monster choose whichever distance is the longest. Use the `Math.abs` method to find out what the distances are without having to worry about whether the x and y positions of the objects are positive or negative.

```
//Find out whether the monster is closer to the
//character on the x axis or the y axis

var vx:Number = Math.abs(_character.x - monster.x);
var vy:Number = Math.abs(_character.y - monster.y);

//Move the character right or left if it's
//already closer on the y axis
```

```
if(vx>vy)
{
  if(_character.x > monster.x)
  {
    //Right
    monster.vx = 2;
    monster.vy = 0;
  }
  else
  {
    //Left
    monster.vx = -2;
    monster.vy = 0;
  }
}

//Move the character up or down if it's
//already closer on the x axis
else
{
  if(_character.y < monster.y)
  {
    //Up
    monster.vx = 0;
    monster.vy = -2;
  }
  else
  {
    //Down
    monster.vx = 0;
    monster.vy = 2;
  }
}
```

This modification lets the monsters zero in on the character with surgical precision. It would make for a very difficult game, but by experimenting with a bit of extra added randomness you'll be able find a good balance that will make for a fun and challenging game. You'll find all this working code in the comments of changeMonsterDirection method in the IntelligentMonsters class.

Obstacles and pathfinding

This has been your first introduction to area of game design called Artificial Intelligence (usually referred to as AI). It's a big topic, and if you're serious about game design (which you are!) you'll want to explore it in much more depth.

A further modification that you'll want to make to Monster Mayhem is to add obstacles, like a maze for the monsters to navigate around. You could do this by using the Collision.block method that you used in the previous two chapters and make the monsters change their directions when they hit a section of the wall. But because each monster will be checking for collisions between each and every section of the wall, you'd have to manage a huge amount of repetitive code. In Chapter 10 you'll learn how to handle multiple object collisions and I'll revisit this problem with a slice of very efficient and compact code.

> *You may also want to make your monsters find their way intelligently around a maze, possibly by the shortest path. To do this, you'll need to look at the **tile-based** approach to building games and implement a famous piece of code called **A-Star**. You can find out how to do all of this in Advanced Game Design with Flash.*

A little more about game structure

The structure for building games that you've used in this chapter will likely become the model for all the games you build from now on. Here's a quick view of how it works:

- The application class loads the level classes and switches levels when a level dispatches an event that informs the game that the level is complete.

- The level classes contain all the game logic and controls the game objects.

- Each object in the game is made from its own class. The game objects have properties that contain important data about those objects and manage their changes of state. They don't contain any code that's specific to the logic of the game. This makes it easy to reuse the same game object classes in other games.

This structure is an extremely simplified version of a well-know software **design pattern** called the Model View Controller (MVC). A design pattern is a structure for organizing computer code across multiple classes so that they're easy to manage. I've cut a few corners so that the structure is much easier to understand and work with than a true MVC pattern. Let's call this the LMVC pattern (Lazy Model View Controller). It's great for understanding how classes work together and will hold you in good stead for many, many game projects, especially while you're learning to program. In fact, it might be the only pattern you ever need to use.

The essential thing to understand with this structure is that one class is entirely responsible for the game logic and controlling the objects on the stage. This is known as the **View/Controller** class. In Monster Mayhem, the LevelOne and LevelTwo classes are the View/Controller classes. The game object classes are the **Model** classes. The Model classes just contain data about the objects and manage their own internal changes of state. The data they contain is in their properties. The View/Controller classes control these Model classes like a puppet master pulling all their strings. If you understand this structure and can be disciplined about sticking to it in your own games, you'll find your games easy to build, manage, and debug. Figure 8-24 illustrates this structure.

The View/Controller classes

The Model classes

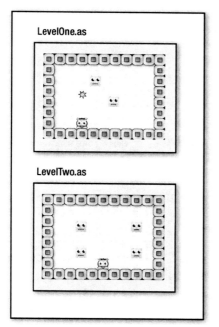

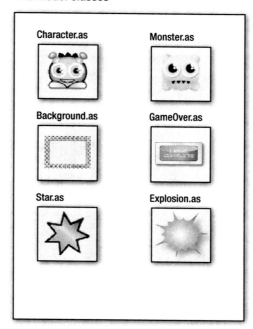

View/Controller classes display and control the game objects and handle all the game logic.

The Model classes contain data about themselves as properties and manage their own internal changes of stage when a View/Controller tells them to.

Figure 8-24. View/Controller classes control the game logic and Model classes.

You're going to use this same structure for the rest of the examples in this book, so make sure you fully understand it before going much further. To simplify the code examples, however, and because they won't contain more than one game level, all the logic will be in the application class, as it has been in the previous chapters. (That means the application class will become the game's View/Controller.) But if you ever design a game with more than one level or you have lots of different game screens you need to switch between, come back to this chapter and use the structure of Monster Mayhem for planning your game.

> When you gain more experience as a programmer and your games start to become much more complex, you're going to need to learn the true Model View Controller pattern. It's a very efficient way of managing complex games and can save you from writing a lot of repetitive code. You can find out all about how to structure a Model View Controller system in Advanced Game Design with Flash.

Summary

This was a big chapter! There was a lot of code and many new concepts to absorb. Everything covered here, however, is absolutely essential to gaining a solid foundation in AS3.0 game design. You'll have to deal with all these issues sooner or later in your game design career. If you didn't understand everything the first time, break the chapter down into smaller chunks and work through each section carefully until it makes sense. Compare what you see happening while you play the game with the code that makes it work. The best way to understand this chapter is to create your own version of Monster Mayhem from scratch. You definitely have the skills to do it, and the steps you go through will reinforce all the concepts covered here.

I hope this chapter got you thinking about how to start using classes to help build games. The structure you used here can take you quite far if you use it carefully.

Until then, have fun with some of the new techniques you looked at in this chapter. How about coming up with a game that combines them with some of the other techniques you learned in earlier chapters? For example, what about a dungeon or space game with huge scrolling levels? That would be amazing! And how about incorporating some puzzle solving using text input, such as the number guessing game from Chapter 4? Perhaps combine Monster Mayhem and Time Bomb Panic into a hybrid game with increasing difficulty at each new level? Even at this stage in the book, you have some real game-coding power at your fingertips. The best way to learn is to dive in and start making a game.

In the next chapter, you'll look at a completely different game genre: a platform game. You'll learn how to make objects move using physics simulations, how to store and analyze data using arrays, and add sounds and music to your games.

Have fun designing your next great game! I'll meet you in Chapter 9 when you're done!

Chapter 9

Physics, Loops, Arrays, and Sounds

One of the most popular genres of video game is the **platform game**, which also poses some very interesting programming and design challenges. From a programming point of view, if you can program a platform game, you've reached a benchmark in your development as a game designer.

In this chapter, I'm going to show you all the skills you need to make your own platform game. You'll take a detailed look at core video game design techniques such as

- Natural motion using physics and thermodynamics simulations.
- Complex player character behavior.
- Collisions with accurate bounce and friction.
- Embedding sound and music.
- Using arrays.

You'll look at these techniques within a practical, real-world context so that you'll have a clear idea of how to apply them to your own games. But first, let's take a detailed look at the techniques you need to know to use physics in your own games.

Natural motion using physics

When you bump into a wall, what happens? If you are a character in Monster Mayhem from the previous chapter, absolutely nothing—you just stop moving and that's the end of the story. In real life, things are much more complicated. A bouncy rubber ball traveling at high speed bounces back at an angle. Something heavier, such as a rock, falls with a thud. Here's another example: when you step on a car's accelerator, the car gradually increases in speed and takes a bit of time to slow down after you hit the brakes. These sorts of physical reactions are part of what makes real-world games such as tennis and car racing so much fun.

Over the next few pages you'll see how to create a moving game character that simulates real-world physics and thermodynamics using the following techniques:

- **Acceleration**: Gradually speeding up.

- **Friction**: Gradually slowing down.

- **Bouncing**: Changing the direction of motion when the object hits the edge of the stage.

- **Gravity**: Adding a force that pulls the object to the bottom of the stage.

- **Jumping**: One of the most required abilities for video game characters.

Applying physics to games is easy to do. Most of the techniques boil down to a simple calculation that's applied to the vx and vy properties. Although the calculations are simple, it's sometimes far from obvious how they can be used in a practical way. It's exactly this practical application that you'll examine.

> In this book, most of the physics calculations that you'll apply are based on a system called **Euler integration** (its popular name is "easy video game physics"). Video game physics appear to be absolutely precise in the context of a video game but are actually only approximations of the real thing. Games use approximated physics because the CPU power required to process them is far, far less than if you used calculations from a physics textbook. If you need to perform text-book–level physical simulations of the real world, Keith Peters' ActionScript 3.0 Animation: Making Things Move and AdvanceED ActionScript 3.0 Animation go into detail on this subject.

To start experimenting with physics, you first need to create a game object class with properties that you can use to apply some physics formulas.

A game object class for playing with physics

In the chapter's source files you'll find a folder called Acceleration. Open the src subfolder and find the **Character** class. It embeds an image of the cat game character using code that should be very familiar to you by now. It also includes some special public properties that you're going to need for the examples in this chapter. Here's the **Character** class with the special physics properties highlighted:

```
package
{
  import flash.display.DisplayObject;
  import flash.display.Sprite;
```

```
public class Character extends Sprite
{
  //Embed the image
  [Embed(source="../images/character.png")]
  private var CharacterImage:Class;

  //Private properties
  private var _character:DisplayObject = new CharacterImage();

  //Public properties
  public var vx:Number = 0;
  public var vy:Number = 0;
  public var accelerationX:Number = 0;
  public var accelerationY:Number = 0;
  public var speedLimit:Number = 5;
  public var friction:Number = 0.96;
  public var bounce:Number = -0.7;
  public var gravity:Number = 0.3;
  public var isOnGround:Boolean = undefined;
  public var jumpForce:Number = -10;

  public function Character()
  {
    //Display the image in this class
    this.addChild(_character);
  }
}
}
```

You'll recognize the vx and vy properties, but the others will be new. You'll see how each of these new properties works in the examples ahead. Figure 9-1 illustrates the **Character** class's public properties with their initial values.

Character

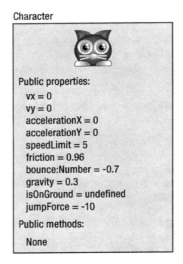

Public properties:
  vx = 0
  vy = 0
  accelerationX = 0
  accelerationY = 0
  speedLimit = 5
  friction = 0.96
  bounce:Number = -0.7
  gravity = 0.3
  isOnGround = undefined
  jumpForce = -10

Public methods:

  None

Figure 9-1. The Character class contains properties needed for physics.

Notice that most of the properties are typed as Number. This is because they need to store decimal values. You can't type properties as int or uint if you need them to store physics values because physics values will always be fractional.

The isOnGround property is a Boolean variable. It's been initialized as undefined. If you don't know whether a Boolean variable should be true or false, assigning it a value of undefined means "I don't know yet." This is the same as assigning a number variable a value of 0 or a string value a pair of empty quotes.

The simplest type of physics motion is acceleration, so let's see how to make it work with the new character object.

Acceleration

Acceleration means to gradually increase velocity. This is what your bicycle does when you start pedaling faster. To gradually speed up game objects, you need to add a value to your object's vx or vy properties in the **enterFrameHandler**. You might recall from Chapter 5 that vx refers to velocity on the x axis and vy refers to velocity on the y axis. In a nutshell, these properties represent an object's speed travelling either horizontally or vertically.

In AS3.0, if you gradually want to increase an object's velocity on the x axis, you need to use an addition assignment operator (+=) to add the value of the acceleration to the vx property. Your code might look something like this:

```
vx += 0.2;
```

On the y axis, your code might look like this:

vy += 0.2;

Where did 0.2 come from? That's the value of acceleration. The exact number depends entirely on you and how quickly or slowly you want the object to speed up. A larger number such as 0.6 makes the object accelerate faster, and a lower number such as 0.I makes it accelerate much more slowly. Choosing the right number is just a matter of trial and error, and observing the effect it has on the object.

Let's see this effect on the cat character on the stage. Run the **Acceleration** application class and move the cat object around the stage with the arrow keys. It gradually speeds up before reaching its maximum speed of 5 pixels per frame, as illustrated in Figure 9-2.

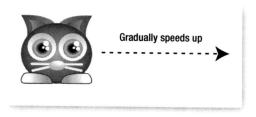

Figure 9-2. Gradually increase an object's speed with acceleration.

The Acceleration class

Here's the **Acceleration** application class. I've highlighted all the code involved in applying acceleration and moving the character.

```
package
{
  import flash.display.Sprite;
  import flash.events.Event;
  import flash.events.KeyboardEvent;
  import flash.ui.Keyboard;

  [SWF(width="550", height="400",
    backgroundColor="#FFFFFF", frameRate="60")]

  public class Acceleration extends Sprite
  {
    private var _character:Character = new Character();;

    public function Acceleration()
    {
      //Add the character to the stage
      stage.addChild(_character);
      _character.x = 250;
      _character.y = 175;

      //Add the event listeners
```

```
    stage.addEventListener
      (KeyboardEvent.KEY_DOWN, keyDownHandler);
    stage.addEventListener
      (KeyboardEvent.KEY_UP, keyUpHandler);
    stage.addEventListener
      (Event.ENTER_FRAME, enterFrameHandler);
  }
  public function keyDownHandler(event:KeyboardEvent):void
  {
    if (event.keyCode == Keyboard.LEFT)
    {
      _character.accelerationX = -0.2;
    }
    else if (event.keyCode == Keyboard.RIGHT)
    {
      _character.accelerationX = 0.2;
      }
    else if (event.keyCode == Keyboard.UP)
    {
      _character.accelerationY = -0.2;
    }
    else if (event.keyCode == Keyboard.DOWN)
    {
      _character.accelerationY = 0.2;
    }
  }
  public function keyUpHandler(event:KeyboardEvent):void
  {
    if (event.keyCode == Keyboard.LEFT
    || event.keyCode == Keyboard.RIGHT)
    {
      _character.accelerationX = 0;
      _character.vx = 0;
    }
    else if (event.keyCode == Keyboard.DOWN
    || event.keyCode == Keyboard.UP)
    {
      _character.accelerationY = 0;
      _character.vy = 0;
    }
  }
  public function enterFrameHandler(event:Event):void
  {
    //Apply acceleration
    _character.vx += _character.accelerationX;
    _character.vy += _character.accelerationY;

    //Limit the speed
    if (_character.vx > _character.speedLimit)
    {
      _character.vx = _character.speedLimit;
    }
```

```
    if (_character.vx < -_character.speedLimit)
    {
        _character.vx = -_character.speedLimit;
    }
    if (_character.vy > _character.speedLimit)
    {
        _character.vy = _character.speedLimit;
    }
    if (_character.vy < -_character.speedLimit)
    {
        _character.vy = -_character.speedLimit;
    }

    //Move the character
    _character.x += _character.vx;
    _character.y += _character.vy;

    //Check stage boundaries
    if (_character.x < 0)
    {
        _character.x = 0;
    }
    if (_character.y < 0)
    {
        _character.y = 0;
    }
    if (_character.x + _character.width > stage.stageWidth)
    {
        _character.x = stage.stageWidth - _character.width;
    }
    if (_character.y + _character.height > stage.stageHeight)
    {
        _character.y = stage.stageHeight - _character.height;
    }

    //Trace the result
    trace("_character.vx:  " + _character.vx);
    trace("_character.x:  " + _character.x);
    trace("    ----------");
    }
  }
}
```

Despite the length of the code, it's nothing more than a slight modification of the run-of-the mill code you've been using since Chapter 5. I'm sure you recognize most of it. Let's look at what's new and see how acceleration works.

The **_character** object has three properties to store the new acceleration data. They're given their initial values in the **Character** class definition.

```
public var accelerationX:Number = 0;
```

```
public var accelerationY:Number = 0;
public var speedLimit:Number = 5;
```

The accelerationX and accelerationY properties store the values that determine by how much the object accelerates. Because you don't want the object to move when it first appears on the stage, accelerationX and accelerationY are initialized to zero. Lastly, speedLimit is the maximum speed that you want the object to travel. A value of 5 means that the object will travel a maximum of no more than 5 pixels per frame.

The work of assigning a value to the character's accelerationX and accelerationY properties is done by the **keyDownHandler**.

```
public function keyDownHandler(event:KeyboardEvent):void
{
  if (event.keyCode == Keyboard.LEFT)
  {
    _character.accelerationX = -0.2;
  }
  else if (event.keyCode == Keyboard.RIGHT)
  {
    _character.accelerationX = 0.2;
  }
  else if (event.keyCode == Keyboard.UP)
  {
    _character.accelerationY = -0.2;
  }
  else if (event.keyCode == Keyboard.DOWN)
  {
    _character.accelerationY = 0.2;
  }
}
```

If accelerationX has a positive value, the object moves to the right. A negative value makes it move left. A positive accelerationY value makes the object move down, and a negative value makes it move up. When any of the arrow keys are pressed, these new values are assigned. All you need to do to make the character move is to assign these values to its vx and vy properties. You can do this easily enough with two lines of code.

```
_character.vx += _character.accelerationX;
_character.vy += _character.accelerationY;
```

However, if you leave things as is, the acceleration values are added to the object's velocity on every frame—without any limit on how fast the object can go. This means that the object eventually moves so fast that it will be nothing more than a blur on the stage. This won't be of much use in most games, so it's usually a good idea to assign a speed limit, which is what this section of code does:

```
if (_character.vx > _character.speedLimit)
{
  _character.vx = _character.speedLimit;
}
```

```
if (_character.vx < -_character.speedLimit)
{
  _character.vx = -_character.speedLimit;
}
if (_character.vy > _character.speedLimit)
{
  _character.vy = _character.speedLimit;
}
if (_character.vy < -_character.speedLimit)
{
  _character.vy = -_character.speedLimit;
}
```

The acceleration values are added to the character's velocity only if the vx and vx properties are within its speed limit, which is 5 in this case. This means that the character will accelerate up to 5 pixels per frame and then travel at a constant rate. The logic behind this is exactly the same logic used to set stage boundaries.

The next step is to add these new velocity values to the object's x and y positions. This is done with some venerable old friends—essentially the same directives you've been using since Chapter 5.

```
_character.x += _character.vx;
_character.y += _character.vy;
```

In fact, these two directives are all you will *ever* need to move the character, even though the physics involved in making them move become quite complex. All the physics calculations are applied to the vx and vy properties; they are then simply assigned to the character's x and y properties to make it move.

So how does this actually work to accelerate the object? The trace output at the end of the **enterFrameHandler** gives you a clue.

```
trace("_character.vx: " + _character.vx);
trace("_character.x: " + _character.x);
trace("----------");
```

Compile the project, press the right arrow key, and watch the trace output. When the character starts moving, you'll see output that looks like this:

```
----------
_character.vx:  0
_character.x:  250
----------
_character.vx:  0.2
_character.x:  250.2
----------
_character.vx:  0.4
_character.x:  250.6
----------
_character.vx:  0.6000000000000001
_character.x:  251.2
```

```
----------
_character.vx:  0.8
_character.x:   252
----------
_character.vx:  1
_character.x:   253
----------
_character.vx:  1.2
_character.x:   254.2
----------
```

These are the first seven frames of movement, but this pattern continues until vx reaches a maximum value of 5, which is what the speedLimit property is set to. The numbers with the large number of decimal places are a byproduct of the way the CPU's binary number system stores fractions.
0.6000000000000001

For all practical purposes, you can ignore the strings of zeros and round off to two decimal places.

> *The smallest unit into which AS3.0 can divide a pixel is 0.05. This unit is known by the whimsical name **twip** (20 twips equal 1 pixel). That's why all the x and y values you see in the trace output are multiples of 0.05.*

On the second frame, accelerationX has an initial value of 0.2, which is added to the character's current x position. This results in a new x value of 250.2. Because the right arrow key is still being held down, this code is then run:

```
else if (event.keyCode == Keyboard.RIGHT)
{
  _character.accelerationX = 0.2;
}
```

It adds an *additional* 0.2 to the vx value, giving it a new value of 0.4. You can see this new value reflected in the third trace.

```
_character.vx:  0.4
_character.x:   250.6
```

Then 0.4 is added to the object's x position, resulting in a new position of 250.6. You can see from the trace output that the accelerationX value continues to compound by adding 0.2 to its value each frame until it finally reaches 5, and the object is clipping along at quite a quick pace. All this adds up to a very neat illusion that the object is accelerating.

The last thing that the code does is stop the object, which is handled by the **keyUpHandler**.

```
public function keyUpHandler(event:KeyboardEvent):void
{
  if (event.keyCode == Keyboard.LEFT
    || event.keyCode == Keyboard.RIGHT)
```

```
{
  _character.accelerationX = 0;
  _character.vx = 0;
}
else if (event.keyCode == Keyboard.DOWN
  || event.keyCode == Keyboard.UP)
{
  _character.accelerationY = 0;
  _character.vy = 0;
}
}
```

This sets the object's acceleration and velocity to zero when the appropriate keys are released.

Friction

Friction is the exact opposite of acceleration: it causes the object to gradually slow down. Figure 9-3 illustrates this.

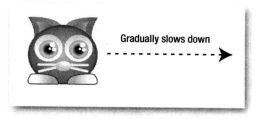

Figure 9-3. Friction makes an object gradually slow down.

Let's see how friction works with the cat character. You'll find the **Friction** project folder in the chapter's source files. Run the SWF and move the character around the stage with the arrow keys. You'll notice that the cat gradually speeds up and then gradually slows down when you release the keys. It appears to float around the stage.

The code in the **Friction** application class is almost identical to the code you just looked at in the **Acceleration** class, except for a few small additions. Open it in your code editor and take a look. The biggest change is in the **enterFrameHandler**. Two new lines of code multiply the character's vx and vy properties by its **friction** value. This happens just below the lines that add acceleration, and I've highlighted them here:

```
//Apply acceleration
_character.vx += _character.accelerationX;
_character.vy += _character.accelerationY;

//Apply friction
_character.vx *= _character.friction;
_character.vy *= _character.friction;
```

Remember that the value of the character's friction value is 0.96. A friction value of 1 amounts to no friction, so anything less than 1 gradually slows the object down. Values from 0.94 to 0.98 apply friction very gradually for very fluid movement. Values such as 0.7 or 0.6 slow the object very quickly.

The two lines of code that apply friction multiply the character's velocities by a number less than 1, which gradually reduces them. It's very simple and very effective.

There's one technical detail you have to fix, however. Here's the scenario: imagine that the object's velocity is 5. Its friction is 0.6. The object needs a velocity of zero to stop completely. You apply some friction every frame, multiplying the velocity by 0.6, hoping to finally reach zero. Here's what the first five frames might look like:

5 * 0.6 = 3

3 * 0.6 = 1.8

1.8 * 0.6 = 1.08

1.08 * 0.6 = 0.648

0.648 * 0.6 = 0.3888

But you're not at zero yet. How long do you think it will take before you get there? Well, you can keep going all day—you never will!

This is an effect known as **Xeno's paradox**. It goes something like this: let's say you have a slice of cake, which you cut in half. You cut one of those slices in half once more. Then you do the same to the third slice. The pieces of cake keep getting thinner and thinner. How many times can you slice them until there's nothing left to slice? Xeno's paradox is that you never reach an end—the pieces of cake just become infinitely thin, and you can go on slicing them forever. Crazy as it sounds, the math actually backs this up, and even more crazily, you have to deal with this in AS3.0!

This means that when you apply friction, vx and vy never reach zero. The object will never stop completely. What you need to do then is *force a value of zero* when vx and vy fall below a certain threshold. This is what this next bit of new code in the **enterFrameHandler** does:

```
if (Math.abs(_character.vx) < 0.1)
{
  _character.vx = 0;
}
if (Math.abs(_character.vy) < 0.1)
{
  _character.vy = 0;
}
```

If vx and vy fall below an absolute value of 0.1, it forces them to a value of 0, thus halting Xeno in his tracks. 0.1 is low enough that it won't have any observable effect on the motion of the object and the object appears to stop very naturally, even at low friction values such as 0.99. Without this code, your objects will creep slightly up and to the left on the stage—and never actually stop.

This bit of code is in the **enterFrameHandler**, just below the block of code that checks the character's speed limit.

> As a quick refresher, Math.abs forces the value in its argument to be positive ("absolute"). It simplifies the code because you don't have to check for negative values.

One final small change to the code is that the **keyUpHandler** now no longer sets the character's vx and vy properties to zero. That job is left for the friction calculation to do. All the **keyUpHandler** needs to do is stop the object's acceleration.

```
public function keyUpHandler(event:KeyboardEvent):void
{
  if (event.keyCode == Keyboard.LEFT
    || event.keyCode == Keyboard.RIGHT)
  {
    _character.accelerationX = 0;
  }
  else if (event.keyCode == Keyboard.DOWN
    || event.keyCode == Keyboard.UP)
  {
    _character.accelerationY = 0;
  }
}
```

And that's it for friction!

Bouncing

After acceleration and friction, bouncing is a piece of cake (the un-infinite kind!). Open the Bounce project folder in the chapter's source files and run the SWF. Move the cat around the stage with the arrow keys and you'll notice that you can bounce it off the stage edges, as shown in Figure 9-4.

Figure 9-4. Bounce the cat off the edges of the stage.

The **Character** class has a property called bounce that's initialized to -0.7.

```
public var bounce:Number = -0.7;
```

The bounce value has to be negative because bouncing works by *reversing* the object's velocity. You'll see how this happens in a moment. A value of -0.7 creates the effect of a moderate bounce. A value of -1 makes the object super bouncy. A value of 1 makes the object completely bounce-less. Any value less than -1 makes the object look like it's hitting an extremely springy surface, such as a trampoline. This is important to keep in mind if you want to make a springing platform in a game.

The bounce property doesn't make a further appearance until the section of code that handles stage boundaries. I've highlighted the relevant code here:

```
//Check stage boundaries
if (_character.x < 0)
{
  _character.vx *= _character.bounce;
  _character.x = 0;
}
if (_character.y < 0)
{
  _character.vy *= _character.bounce;
  _character.y = 0;
}
if (_character.x + _character.width > stage.stageWidth)
{
  _character.vx *= _character.bounce;
```

```
    _character.x = stage.stageWidth - _character.width;
}
if (_character.y + _character.height > stage.stageHeight)
{
    _character.vy *= _character.bounce;
    _character.y = stage.stageHeight - _character.height;
}
```

All that's happening is that the object's velocity is being multiplied by the bounce value, which is negative. If you reverse an object's velocity, it looks as if it is bouncing. No, I'm not hiding anything from you here—this remarkable effect is achieved with only four lines of dead-simple code. Who said physics was difficult?

Gravity

Gravity is just as easy to implement as the other physical forces. All you need to do is create one more value and add it to the object's vy property.

To see gravity at work, open the Gravity project and run the SWF. The cat drops to the bottom of the stage. If you press the up arrow key, the cat moves up. When the up arrow is released again, the cat falls downward until you press the up arrow key again. If it hits the ground, it bounces. Figure 9-5 illustrates what you'll see.

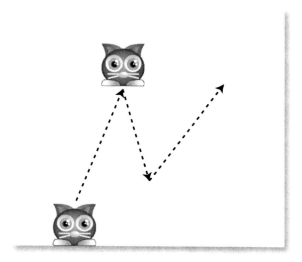

Figure 9-5. Use the arrow keys to make the cat fly.

Even though the code is very simple, the result is a very convincing simulation of the real world. In fact, it's almost scarily realistic! Let's see how it works.

The Character class has a property called gravity, which is initialized to 0.3.

```
public var gravity:Number = 0.3;
```

Like the other values, 0.3 is just one that came about through trial and error, and it looks natural in this context. A higher number increases gravity, and a lower number decreases it.

Applying gravity to the character is simply a matter of adding it to the character's vy property in the **enterFrameHandler**.

```
_character.vy += _character.gravity;
```

That's it! That's all you need to do to implement gravity. Here's how this line of code fits into the other code in the **enterFrameHandler**:

```
//Apply acceleration
_character.vx += _character.accelerationX;
_character.vy += _character.accelerationY;

//Apply friction
_character.vx *= _character.friction;

//Apply gravity
_character.vy += _character.gravity;
```

(The other small change to this code from the previous examples is that friction isn't added to the vy property. It doesn't need to be because gravity takes care of that.)

The **Gravity** class goes a little bit further, however. You want to allow the player to make the cat move up when the up arrow is pressed. There is actually more than one way to do this, and this class implements the slightly more complex way.

The way this works is that when the player presses the up arrow key, **gravity** is set to 0 in the **keyDownHandler** (highlighted here):

```
public function keyDownHandler(event:KeyboardEvent):void
{
  if (event.keyCode == Keyboard.LEFT)
  {
    _character.accelerationX = -0.2;
  }
  else if (event.keyCode == Keyboard.RIGHT)
  {
    _character.accelerationX = 0.2;
  }
  else if (event.keyCode == Keyboard.UP)
  {
    _character.accelerationY = -0.2;
    _character.gravity = 0;
  }
}
```

This allows the cat to move up the stage freely. Notice that there's also no code for the down arrow key. You don't need it—gravity takes care of moving the object down.

When the keys are released, the gravity property is set back to its original value of 0.3.

```
public function keyUpHandler(event:KeyboardEvent):void
{
  _character.accelerationX = 0;
  _character.accelerationY = 0;
  _character.gravity = 0.3;
}
```

You can create this same gravity effect by just giving accelerationY a positive value when you need gravity applied. (A positive y value pulls the object to the bottom of the stage.) It means that you could dispense with having to create the gravity property in the character altogether. However, an advantage to using a separate gravity value is that it makes the code easier to understand, and it keeps your options open for mixing and matching the gravity force with other physical forces that you might add later.

There are two other bits of fine-tuning done to this code. I want the object to fall at a faster rate than it ascends. I modified the speed limit in the if statement that checks to see how fast the object is moving down the stage, like so:

```
//Limit the speed
if (_character.vx > _character.speedLimit)
{
  _character.vx = _character.speedLimit;
}
if (_character.vx < -_character.speedLimit)
{
  _character.vx = -_character.speedLimit;
}
if (_character.vy > _character.speedLimit * 2)
{
  _character.vy = _character.speedLimit * 2;
  trace("Terminal velocity!");
}
if (_character.vy < -_character.speedLimit)
{
  _character.vy = -_character.speedLimit;
}
```

Multiplying the speedLimit by 2 allows it fall twice as fast as it climbs. It also displays a "Terminal velocity!" trace message when it reaches its maximum speed. You could use this in a Lunar Lander-type game to figure out whether the spacecraft is going too fast when it hits the planet surface.

Jumping

Probably half of all video games ever made use jumping as a primary character action. All it boils down to is a temporary increase in the object's y velocity. Once you understand how acceleration, friction, and gravity work, jumping is not at all difficult to implement. However, there are a few additional things to keep in mind that make it a little more complex.

- You want your object to be able to jump when it's on the ground—and only on the ground. But how will your object know that it's on the ground? And what is the ground, anyway? The code has to be able to figure these things out.

- You need to prevent the jump keys from triggering a jump more than once if they're held down.

Let's look at an example of jumping in action and how to solve these problems. Open the Jumping project folder and run the SWF. Use the left and right arrow keys to move the cat horizontally, and press the up arrow key or the spacebar to make it jump. Figure 9-6 illustrates this.

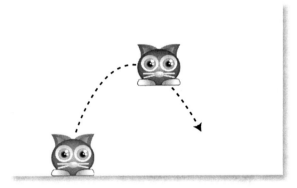

Figure 9-6. Press the spacebar or up arrow key to make the cat jump.

To implement jumping you need to use these two properties in the **Character** class:

```
public var isOnGround:Boolean = undefined;
public var jumpForce:Number = -10;
```

isOnGround is a Boolean value that tells the class whether the object is on the ground. It's initialized as undefined because you might not always know whether the object will be on the ground when the game starts.

jumpForce is the force with which the character will jump. It needs to move upward toward the top of the stage, so it has a negative value. The actual value that you give it is again a matter of trial and error. You'll need to make sure that its value is enough to counteract gravity and any other forces that might be acting on the object.

How does the object know whether it's on the ground? This is something that could become quite complex depending on the game you're designing, so you'll need to think about this carefully when you start any project that uses jumping. In this simple example, the cat is "on the ground" when it's at the bottom of the stage. So all you need to do is set isOnGround to true in the same section of code that checks for the bottom stage boundary.

```
//Check stage boundaries
if (_character.x < 0)
{
  _character.vx = 0;
  _character.x = 0;
}
if (_character.y < 0)
{
  _character.vy = 0;
  _character.y = 0;
}
if (_character.x + _character.width > stage.stageWidth)
{
  _character.vx = 0;
  _character.x = stage.stageWidth - _character.width;
}
if (_character.y + _character.height > stage.stageHeight)
{
  _character.vy = 0;
  _character.y = stage.stageHeight - _character.height;
  _character.isOnGround = true;
}
```

That's pretty straightforward. In most games that use jumping, game characters also need to know when they're standing on platforms. That makes detecting the ground a little more complex, but you'll be looking at a solution later in the chapter. Telling the object to jump happens in the **onKeyDown** event handler.

```
public function keyDownHandler(event:KeyboardEvent):void
{
  if (event.keyCode == Keyboard.LEFT)
  {
    _character.accelerationX = -0.2;
  }
  else if (event.keyCode == Keyboard.RIGHT)
  {
    _character.accelerationX = 0.2;
  }
  else if (event.keyCode == Keyboard.UP
    || event.keyCode == Keyboard.SPACE)
  {
    if(_character.isOnGround)
    {
      _character.vy += _character.jumpForce;
      _character.isOnGround = false;
    }
  }
}
```

If the spacebar or up arrow key is pressed, the code checks to see whether the object is on the ground. If it is, it adds the jump force value to the vertical acceleration. It also sets isOnGround to false.

If you're using if statements to enforce a speed limit on your object, don't check for this while the jumping object is moving upwards. It could put an unnatural choke on the jump effect.

And that's really all there is to it. Figure 9-7 illustrates how this system works.

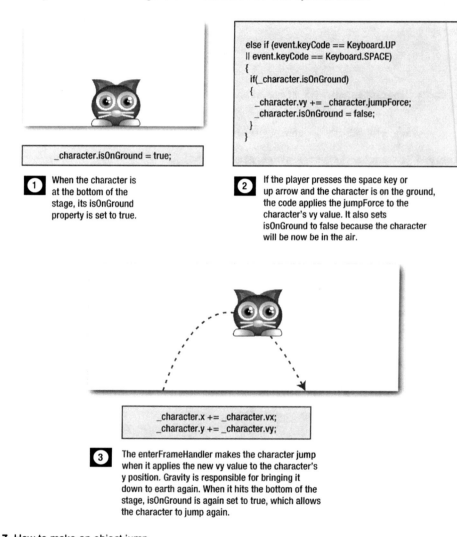

Figure 9-7. How to make an object jump.

This is a delicate tangle of interrelated code to work through, so here's the entire **Jumping** application class so that you can see it all in context. I've highlighted all the code related to the jump effect.

package

```
{
  import flash.display.Sprite;
  import flash.events.Event;
  import flash.events.KeyboardEvent;
  import flash.ui.Keyboard;

  [SWF(width="550", height="400",
    backgroundColor="#FFFFFF", frameRate="60")]

  public class Jumping extends Sprite
  {
    private var _character:Character = new Character();;

    public function Jumping()
    {
      //Add the character to the stage
      stage.addChild(_character);
      _character.x = 250;
      _character.y = 175;

      //Add the event listeners
      stage.addEventListener
        (KeyboardEvent.KEY_DOWN, keyDownHandler);
      stage.addEventListener
        (KeyboardEvent.KEY_UP, keyUpHandler);
      stage.addEventListener
        (Event.ENTER_FRAME, enterFrameHandler);
    }
    public function keyDownHandler(event:KeyboardEvent):void
    {
      if (event.keyCode == Keyboard.LEFT)
      {
        _character.accelerationX = -0.2;
      }
      else if (event.keyCode == Keyboard.RIGHT)
      {
        _character.accelerationX = 0.2;
      }
      else if (event.keyCode == Keyboard.UP
        || event.keyCode == Keyboard.SPACE)
      {
        if(_character.isOnGround)
        {
          _character.vy += _character.jumpForce;
          _character.isOnGround = false;
        }
      }
    }
    public function keyUpHandler(event:KeyboardEvent):void
    {
      if (event.keyCode == Keyboard.LEFT
        || event.keyCode == Keyboard.RIGHT)
```

```
    {
      _character.accelerationX = 0;
    }
  }
  public function enterFrameHandler(event:Event):void
  {
    //Apply acceleration
    _character.vx += _character.accelerationX;

    //Apply friction
    _character.vx *= _character.friction;

    //Apply gravity
    _character.vy += _character.gravity;

    //Limit the speed, except when the character
    //is moving upwards
    if (_character.vx > _character.speedLimit)
    {
      _character.vx = _character.speedLimit;
    }
    if (_character.vx < -_character.speedLimit)
    {
      _character.vx = -_character.speedLimit;
    }
    if (_character.vy > _character.speedLimit * 2)
    {
      _character.vy = _character.speedLimit * 2;
    }

    //Force the velocity to zero
    //after it falls below 0.1
    if (Math.abs(_character.vx) < 0.1)
    {
      _character.vx = 0;
    }
    if (Math.abs(_character.vy) < 0.1)
    {
      _character.vy = 0;
    }

    //Move the character
    _character.x += _character.vx;
    _character.y += _character.vy;

    //Check stage boundaries
    if (_character.x < 0)
    {
      _character.vx = 0;
      _character.x = 0;
    }
    if (_character.y < 0)
```

```
  {
    _character.vy = 0;
    _character.y = 0;
  }
  if (_character.x + _character.width > stage.stageWidth)
  {
    _character.vx = 0;
    _character.x = stage.stageWidth - _character.width;
  }
  if (_character.y + _character.height > stage.stageHeight)
  {
    _character.vy = 0;
    _character.y = stage.stageHeight - _character.height;
    _character.isOnGround = true;
  }
    }
  }
    }
}
```

Adding sounds to games

You now have a nice, bouncing, jumping game character. Wouldn't it be great to add a sound effect each time it jumps? Playing sounds in game is not difficult at all, and I'll show you how in this section.

Open the PlayingSounds project folder in the chapter's source file. Along with the usual folders, you'll find a new folder called sounds. It contains an MP3 file called bounce.mp3 (Figure 9-8). This MP3 file is going to be embedded into the application class in exactly the same way you've been embedding images.

Figure 9-8. Keep your game sounds in a sounds folder with the rest of the project files.

Run the SWF file and press the space key. You'll hear a "bounce" sound, typical of the kind made by jumping game characters

Here's the entire PlayingSounds class. I've highlighted all the code that embeds the sound, creates the sound objects, and plays the sound.

```
package
{
  import flash.display.Sprite;
  import flash.events.Event;
```

```
import flash.events.KeyboardEvent;
import flash.ui.Keyboard;

//Classes needed to play sounds
import flash.media.Sound;
import flash.media.SoundChannel;

[SWF(width="550", height="400",
  backgroundColor="#FFFFFF", frameRate="60")]

public class PlayingSounds extends Sprite
{
  //Embed the sound
  [Embed(source="../sounds/bounce.mp3")]
  private var Bounce:Class;

  //Create the Sound and Sound channel
  //objects for the sound
  private var _bounce:Sound = new Bounce();
  private var _bounceChannel:SoundChannel = new SoundChannel();

  public function PlayingSounds()
  {
    stage.addEventListener
      (KeyboardEvent.KEY_DOWN, keyDownHandler);
  }
  public function keyDownHandler(event:KeyboardEvent):void
  {
    if (event.keyCode == Keyboard.SPACE)
    {
      //Tell the bounce sound channel
      //to play the bounce sound
      _bounceChannel = _bounce.play();
    }
  }
}
}
```

To use sounds in a game, you need to import two classes: **Sound** and **SoundChannel**.

```
import flash.media.Sound;
import flash.media.SoundChannel;
```

You then embed the MP3 file in the class definition in exactly the same way that you embed an image.

```
[Embed(source="../sounds/bounce.mp3")]
private var Bounce:Class;
```

You then need to create two objects to help you play the sound.

- **The Sound object**: This is the actual sound that you want to play.

```
private var _bounce:Sound = new Bounce();
```

- **The SoundChannel object**: This is an object that plays the sound for you.

```
private var _bounceChannel:SoundChannel = new SoundChannel();
```

You need to use both objects together to play sounds. You can think of the **Sound** class as a CD and a **SoundChannel** as the CD player that actually loads and plays it.

The **SoundChannel** object can then play the **Sound** whenever it's called on to do so. In this case, it happens when you press the space key.

```
_bounceChannel = _bounce.play();
```

And that's really all there is to it. Keep this format in mind and you can't go wrong.

Integrating sound effects in a game

To see how to integrate sound effects into the context of a real game, open the JumpingWithSounds projects folder. Run the SWF, turn up the sound on your computer, and you'll now hear a bounce sound each time the character jumps. This is accomplished by playing the bounce sound each time the player presses the up or space key, which happens by running this directive:

```
_bounceChannel = _bounce.play();
```

There's a sounds folder in the project folder that contains the bounce.mp3 file. Here's the new code in the **JumpingWithSounds** application class that embeds and plays the sound. First, the **Sound** and **SoundChannel** classes are imported along with all the other classes needed in this example.

```
import flash.display.Sprite;
import flash.events.Event;
import flash.events.KeyboardEvent;
import flash.ui.Keyboard;

//Classes needed to play sounds
import flash.media.Sound;
import flash.media.SoundChannel;
```

Next, the MP3 file is embedded and the sound objects are created in the class definition.

```
public class JumpingWithSound extends Sprite
{
  //Embed the sound
  [Embed(source="../sounds/bounce.mp3")]
  private var Bounce:Class;

  //Create the Sound and Sound channel
  //objects for the sound
```

```
private var _bounce:Sound = new Bounce();
private var _bounceChannel:SoundChannel = new SoundChannel();

private var _character:Character = new Character();
```

Finally, the sound is played by the **keyDownHandler** when the player presses the up or space keys.

```
else if (event.keyCode == Keyboard.UP
  || event.keyCode == Keyboard.SPACE)
{
  if(_character.isOnGround)
  {
    _bounceChannel = _bounce.play();
    _character.vy += _character.jumpForce;
    _character.isOnGround = false;
  }
}
```

Adding sound effects to games like this is just a matter of choosing the right place to call the sound's **play** method. Most of your game sound effects will be short like this, but if you ever need to stop any of them, call the sound object's **stop** method, like this:

```
_bounceChannel = _bounce.stop();
```

If you're using longer sounds that you need to loop, the next section will show you how to do this.

Looping music and setting volume and pan levels

You'll likely have music in your games that you'll need to loop over and over again during the course of the game. And you might also need to control the volume levels of sounds and balance sounds between the left and right speakers. The next sections cover some simple techniques to help you do this.

Looping sounds

Here's the format you need to use to loop a sound when you play it:

```
_soundChannel = _sound.play(startPosition, timesToPlay);
```

The **startPosition** is a number in milliseconds. Note that 0 is the very start of the sound and 1000 would be one second into the start of the sound. **timesToPlay** is the number of times you want a sound to play. So if you want to start a sound from the beginning and repeat it ten times, your code could look like this:

```
_soundChannel = _sound.play(0, 10);
```

If you want sound to repeat from the 5 second mark very time it repeats, use 5000 as the first argument:

```
_soundChannel = _sound.play(5000, 10);
```

To make a sound repeat infinitely (or almost infinitely) you need to use a little trick. Set the second argument, the times to loop, to the maximum possible number that AS3.0 knows. That's actually stored as a property of the integer class that you can access like this:

```
int.MAX_VALUE
```

`int.MAX_VALUE` is the highest possible value that an integer can be: 2,147,483,647. It means the sound won't loop forever, but it will loop long enough for the player to finish the game—and possibly even continue to loop a few decades well beyond that. Here's how you can use it to make a sound loop "forever":

```
_soundChannel = _sound.play(0, int.MAX_VALUE);
```

> If you loop continuous sounds that don't have a discernible start or end, you might hear a moment of silence before the sound plays again. This is because some MP3 formats store the ID3 tag information (the name of the song, name of the artist, and so on) at the beginning or end of the file. That's the silence you hear. If this proves to be a problem, make sure that you export the MP3 file from your audio software without the ID3 information. Most sound editors have this as an option. If you don't have access to the original uncompressed sound file, use a dedicated audio editor, like Audacity, to trim the few milliseconds of silence from the beginning or end of the file. You can download Audacity from
>
> *http://audacity.sourceforge.net/download/*
>
> You'll also need to download and install the LAME MP3 encoder so that Audacity can export the finished MP3 file. You can find a link to the LAME download site at
>
> *http://audacity.sourceforge.net/help/faq?s=install&item=lame-mp3*
>
> You can also sometimes get around the few milliseconds delay between loops by starting the sound at a start position other than zero. You'll need to experiment a bit to find the right amount, but 30 is often a good place to start.
>
> *_soundChannel = _sound.play(30, int.MAX_VALUE);*
>
> This will skip the first 30 milliseconds, which is roughly where the sound gap ends.

On occasions where you need a bit more flexibility and control, you can create a loop using a **SOUND_COMPLETE** event. First, add a **SOUND_COMPLETE** event handler to the **SoundChannel** object when you play the sound.

```
_soundChannel = _sound.play(0);
```

```
_soundChannel.addEventListener
  (Event.SOUND_COMPLETE, loopSoundHandler);
```

Next, create a **loopSoundHandler** that plays the sound again and then adds another new **SOUND_COMPLETE** listener.

```
public function loopSoundHandler(event:Event):void
{
  if (_soundChannel != null)
  {
    //Play the sound
    _soundChannel = _sound.play(0);

    //Add a new listener
    _soundChannel.addEventListener
      (Event.SOUND_COMPLETE, loopSoundHandler);
  }
}
```

Very importantly, this code first checks whether the sound channel actually exists by only running the directives if the **_soundChannel** object isn't null.

You also need to remove the listener anywhere in your program whenever the music stops.

```
_soundChannel.stop();
_soundChannel.removeEventListener
  (Event.SOUND_COMPLETE, loopSoundHandler);
```

Volume and pan setting

The **volume** of a sound is how loud or soft it is. The **pan** determines how much of the sound comes through the left or right speaker. To control these properties, you first need to import the **SoundTransform** class.

```
import flash.media.SoundTransform;
```

You then need two **Number** variables to store the volume and pan settings.
```
private var _volume:Number = 1;
private var _pan:Number = 0;
```

If the volume has a value of 1, it means it's at normal volume. If it's 0, the sound is completely silent. If it's 2, the sound is double the original volume.

The pan values have a range between -1 and 1. Note that -1 means the sound is coming completely from the left speaker, 1 means the sound is coming completely from the right speaker, and 0 means that the sound is balanced equally between both speakers. You can set the pan value to any number within this range. If you set it to 0.5, the sound will be come mainly from the right speaker, but you'll also hear it, although less audibly, in the left speaker.

Once you've chosen values for the volume and pan, you use them to create a **SoundTransform** object, like this:

```
var transform:SoundTransform = new SoundTransform(_volume, _pan);
```

The last step is to apply this **SoundTransform** object to your **SoundChannel** object, like this:
```
_soundChannel.soundTransform = transform;
```

SoundChannel objects have a property called soundTransform. You add the **SoundTransform** object to this property, as this code shows. Yes, I know, these are a few irritating and confusing little hoops to have to jump though. And the only difference between the soundTransform property and the **SoundTransform** class is the capitalization of the first letter! But courage! You can do it, and it's not hard once you actually see it in practice. To help you out, take a look in the LoopingMusic project folder and open the application class. Run the SWF or compile it, and you'll hear some looping game background music. Here's the application class:

```
package
{
  import flash.display.Sprite;
  import flash.events.Event;

  //Classes needed to play sounds
  import flash.media.Sound;
  import flash.media.SoundChannel;
  import flash.media.SoundTransform;

  [SWF(width="550", height="400",
    backgroundColor="#FFFFFF", frameRate="60")]

  public class LoopingMusic extends Sprite
  {
    //Embed the sound
    [Embed(source="../sounds/music.mp3")]
    private var Music:Class;

    //Create the Sound and Sound channel
    //objects for the sound
    private var _music:Sound = new Music();
    private var _musicChannel:SoundChannel = new SoundChannel();

    //Variables needed to set volume and panning
    private var _volume:Number = 1;
    private var _pan:Number = 0;

    public function LoopingMusic()
    {
      _musicChannel = _music.play(30, int.MAX_VALUE);

      //Change the volume and pan settings
      _volume = 0.5;
```

```
        _pan = 0;

        //Create the SoundTransform object
        var transform:SoundTransform
          = new SoundTransform(_volume, _pan);

        //Add the SoundTransform object to the
        //musicChannel's soundTransform property
        _musicChannel.soundTransform = transform;
      }
    }
}
```

The music is set to loop when the program starts, skipping the first 30 milliseconds to avoid the short gap at the start of the music.

```
_musicChannel = _music.play(30, int.MAX_VALUE);
```

Next, the volume and speaker pan values are set.

```
_volume = 0.5;
_pan = 0;
```

The volume is set to half its loudness. Because the pan has a value of zero, the music is equally balanced through both speakers. Try setting the pan value to 1 or -1, then recompile the program and listen to how the speaker panning changes.

The **SoundTransform** object is then created using the volume and pan values as arguments.

```
var transform:SoundTransform
  = new SoundTransform(_volume, _pan);
```

It's created as a local object, which is how sound transform objects are usually created. The reason for this is because you only ever need to create a SoundTransform object when you're changing pan and volume settings like this, and you'll probably never need to use it anywhere else in the class. The last step is to apply this new **transform** object to the **musicChannel** object's soundTransform property.
```
_musicChannel.soundTransform = transform;
```

This sets the new volume and pan settings. Every time you make changes to the volume and pan settings, you need to create another temporary **SoundTransform** object and re-apply it to the **SoundChannel** object.

You've only just scratched the surface of using sound with AS3.0, but it's plenty to get you started using sound in your own games. You'll also find a comprehensive look at sound in games in *Advanced Game Design with Flash*.

Working with many objects

You now have a character that can bounce and jump around the stage, but the stage itself is pretty empty. The cat needs some boxes to jump on. Wouldn't it be great if you could make an interactive game world that looks like Figure 9-9?

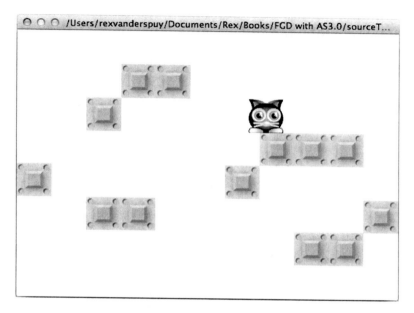

Figure 9-9. The beginnings of a platform game, with boxes to jump on.

You could easily create 13 boxes and check them for collisions with the character using the **Collision.block** method, like this:

```
Collision.block(_character, _box1);
Collision.block(_character, _box2);
Collision.block(_character, _box3);
Collision.block(_character, _box4);
Collision.block(_character, _box5);
Collision.block(_character, _box6);
Collision.block(_character, _box7);
Collision.block(_character, _box8);
Collision.block(_character, _box9);
Collision.block(_character, _box10);
Collision.block(_character, _box11);
Collision.block(_character, _box12);
Collision.block(_character, _box13);
```

These 13 lines of code will work just fine. But who really wants to write so much repetitive code?

Before you go any further in your game design career, you need to learn a pair of programming techniques that go hand in hand: **loops** and **arrays**. You're going to use them together to build a system for managing interactivity between lots of objects on the stage. This includes making lots of objects, changing properties on lots of objects, and checking for collisions between lots of objects. Over the next few pages you're going to learn some staple tricks of the trade that will vastly expand what your games are capable of doing.

Using for loops

If you're like me, you'd probably find writing out or copying/pasting those thirteen lines of repetitive code a terrible chore. Aren't computers supposed to be miraculous time-saving devices designed to spare you this sort of drudge work? Yes, they are, and yes, there is a better way.

Those 13 directives are exactly the same in every way, except for one thing: the number of the box object name. Could you make some kind of basic template to tell AS3.0 to repeat it 13 times and just insert the correct number? Yes, you can! It's a programming device called a **loop**.

Loops are used to repeat a section of code a specific number of times. There are quite a few different kinds of loops you can create in AS3.0, and even though they all do almost the same thing, some are slightly more appropriate in different situations than others. Far and away the most commonly used loop is the for loop, which is a block statement that begins with the keyword **for** (meaning *for* this many number of times). Any directives inside the for loop are repeated as many times as the loop specifies—from once to hundreds or thousands of times.

The structure of the for loop might look weird and confusing at first because its arguments actually contain three separate statements.

- A variable that's used to track the number of times the loop has repeated. This is known as the **loop index variable**, which is usually represented by the letter *i* (it stands for *index*).

- A conditional statement that tells the loop when it should stop.

- A statement that adds 1 to the index variable every time the for loop repeats. (Although 1 is usually added each time the loop repeats, you can add or subtract numbers in many different ways to fine-tune the loop if necessary.) Each of these statements is separated by a semicolon.

Here's an example of a for loop that displays the numbers from 0 to 4:

```
for(var i:int = 0;  i < 5;  i++)
{
  trace(i);
}
```

If you use this code in the class's constructor method, you'll see this trace message when you run the program:

```
0
1
2
```

3
4

In the chapter's source files you'll find a project folder called ForLoop. Here's the **ForLoop** application class that implements exactly this system:

```
package
{
  import flash.display.Sprite;

  public class ForLoop extends Sprite
  {
    public function ForLoop()
    {
      for(var i:int = 0;  i < 5;  i++)
      {
        trace(i);
      }
    }
  }
}
```

When you compile it, you'll see the numbers from 0 to 4 displayed as trace output.

It's easy to understand how a for loop works if you break down what it does into smaller parts. The first thing it does is declare the variable that will be used to count the number of loops.

```
for(var i:int = 0; i < 5;  i++)
```

This creates a local integer variable called **i**, which is initialized to 0. The next statement tells the loop how many times it should repeat.

```
for(var i:int = 0; i < 5;  i++)
```

This is a conditional statement. It tells the loop to repeat while the index variable is less than 5. In this example, the index variable is initialized to zero, so the loop will repeat until it reaches 4. You can use any kind of conditional statement you want here.

The last statement increases the index variable by 1 each time the directives in the loop are run.

```
for(var i:int = 0;  i < 5;  i++)
```

The first time the loop runs, **i** starts with its initialized value, which is zero. The next time it repeats, the ++ operator adds a value of 1. That means that **i** then equals 1 (because 0 plus 1 equals 1, of course). The next time the loop repeats, 1 is added to **i** again, which results in a value of 2. This repeats while **i** is less than 5. As soon as it gets a value of 5, the loop stops dead in its tracks.

Although i++ is the most common way to increase the value of the index variable, you can use any statement you like to increase or decrease it. For example, i += 2 will increase the index variable by 2 each time the loop repeats and i-- will decrease it by 1 if you want your loop to count backward.

If you opened the ForLoop project, experiment with a few different values and conditional statements and see what the output looks like when you test it. You can initialize i to any number you like and use any condition to quit the loop. Here's another example where i is initialized to I and the loop repeats until it becomes 5:

```
for(var i:int = 1;  i <= 5;  i++)
{
  trace(i);
}
```

This produces the following trace output:

```
1
2
3
4
5
```

Initializing the index variable to 1 and quitting the loop on 5 is particularly useful because it makes it very clear where the loop starts and ends. It counts from one to five, like a normal human being!

You'll look at a few different ways to use for loops over the course of this chapter. Figure 9-10 is a quick-reference diagram of the way for loops work.

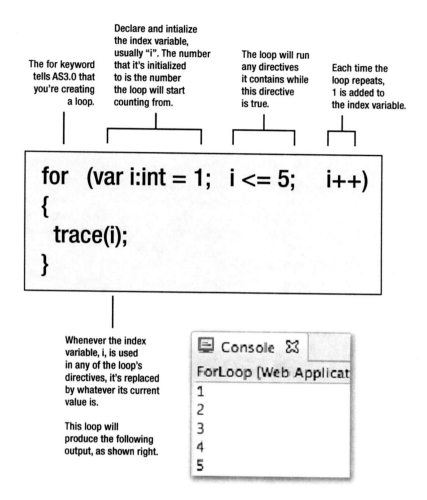

Figure 9-10. How for loops work

Although the for loop is a perennial favorite, AS3.0 allows you to create loops in a few other ways as well. You can also create a while loop or a do-while loop. They all do the same things as the for loop, although they have nuances that might be useful in certain situations.

The while loop can be particularly useful for games. It looks like this:

```
while(a certain condition is true)
{
```

```
    //...do this
}
```

While loops don't run for a set number of times; they run as many times as necessary until the condition becomes false. When you use while loops in your programs, you have to make sure that the condition eventually will become false. If it doesn't, the loop will run "forever" and the Flash Player might hang. The Flash Player usually quits the loop automatically if it runs for 15 seconds without ending, but sometimes it doesn't! Use while loops with caution and always save your work before you test them.

I won't be covering while and do-while loops in detail in this book, but it's worth doing a bit of further research into them just to see their capabilities. For more information, see the section titled "Looping" in the chapter "ActionScript Language and Syntax" from Adobe's online document, Programming Adobe ActionScript 3.0 for Adobe Flash.

Using arrays

If you understand how **for** loops work, you're half way to writing code that can check for collisions with multiple objects. The next piece in the puzzle is arrays. You can think of arrays big cupboards for storing many objects in one place.

Arrays can actually be used to store anything: variables, numbers, strings, objects, methods, or even other arrays. Everything inside the array is indexed with a number. You'll take a look at some practical examples of how you can use the index number of array objects to access and modify them.

In the book's download package you'll find a case study of a platform game called Bug Catcher where the player has to collect flying bugs in a jar. Let's get into the mood of the game and create an array called **collectionJar**. Before you can use an array, you need to instantiate it using the **new** keyword. If you want to create an empty collection jar to collect bugs with, you can create one like this:

```
var collectionJar:Array = new Array();
collectionJar = [];
```

Arrays contain their objects inside square brackets, like this:

```
[anything between these square brackets is part of the array]
```

A pair of empty brackets means that the array is empty, which is how you've initialized the **collectionJar** array. But an array doesn't need to start out empty. You can initialize the array so that it's already filled with objects.

```
collectionJar = [fly, mosquito, bee];
```

All objects in an array are numbered sequentially, starting with zero. These numbers are called **index numbers**. In this example, fly has an index number of 0, mosquito has an index number of 1, and bee has an index number of 2. You can find out which object is at which index number using the array access operator. Here's an example:

collectionJar[1]

This has the value of **mosquito** because **mosquito** has an index number of I. It's really very simple. An array is just a numbered list of things known as **elements**. Figure 9-11 illustrates an empty array compared with an array with three elements.

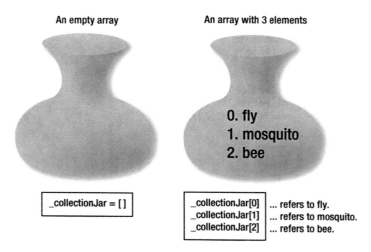

Figure 9-11. Arrays and array elements

There are several ways to put elements into arrays. In the previous example, the three elements were added to the array when it was initialized. You'll usually start with an empty array and add elements to it as necessary.

One way to put elements into an array is to assign elements directly to a position in the array's index.

collectionJar[2] = fly;

So whenever your code sees **collectionJar[2]** it returns the value of **fly**.

Let's look at a slightly more concrete example. The chapter source files include a folder called BasicArray. Open it and take a look at the application class.

```
package
{
  import flash.display.Sprite;

  public class BasicArray extends Sprite
  {
    //Declare the array
```

```
    private var _collectionJar:Array;

    public function BasicArray()
    {
      //Instantiate the array
      _collectionJar = new Array();

      //Add elements to the array
      _collectionJar[0] =  "fly";
      _collectionJar[1] =  "mosquito";
      _collectionJar[2] =  "bee";

      //Trace the entire array contents
      trace("Entire Array: " + _collectionJar);

      //Trace individual elements
      trace("Element 0: " + _collectionJar[0]);
      trace("Element 1: " + _collectionJar[1]);
      trace("Element 2: " + _collectionJar[2]);
    }
  }
}
```

If you test this, the trace displays this:

```
Entire Array: fly,mosquito,bee
Element 0: fly
Element 1: mosquito
Element 2: bee
```

It's easy to see from this example that arrays are just storage containers.

Pushing elements into an array

Another very common way to get elements into an array is to use an array's built-in **push** method. You can use push to literally push an element into an array by using this format:
`arrayName.push(elementName);`

When you push an object into an array, it gets an index number that's one higher than the last element added. This means that if the last element has an index number of [2], the object that you push into it will have an index number of [3].

Using **push** is really helpful because you don't need to worry about which index number to add the element to. The array figures this out for you.

The chapter source files include a folder called ArrayPush. Open it as a project and have a look at the application class. It's identical to the first example, except that it uses **push** to add the elements to the array.

```
_collectionJar.push("fly");
_collectionJar.push("mosquito");
_collectionJar.push("bee");
```

The trace output is exactly the same as the first example. The fact that you don't need to worry about the index numbers is very convenient.

To remove an element from an array, you can use the array's **pop** *method. The following code uses* **pop** *to remove the last element from an array and assign it to a variable:*

removedElement = _collectionJar.pop();

If the last element was "bee", **removedElement** *has the value of "bee". It also means that _collectionJar now contains only two elements: "fly" and "mosquito".*

You can also add and remove elements to an array using the **splice** *method. I'll explain how to use* **splice** *in detail in the next chapter.*

Looping arrays

Arrays become extraordinarily useful when they're used along with a loop. You can use a for loop to loop through every element in array, even if you have hundreds of elements, with just one line of code. Arrays and loops are almost always used together like this. Let's find out how you can use a loop to read all the elements of an array.

Arrays have a built-in property called length, which tells you how many elements the array has. You can access an array's length property like this:

`arrayName.length`

The numbering of the length property starts at 0. That means if you have an array with ten elements, the length property will be **9**.

To find the index number of the last element in an array, you could use some code that looks like this:

arraryName.length - 1

You can use an array's length property to control the number of times a for loop repeats. Here's a basic example of the format you can use:

```
for (var i:int = 0;  i < arrayName.length;  i++)
{
```

```
    trace(arrayName[i]);
}
```

This code displays all the elements in the array, starting with element 0 and running through all the way to the end of the array, however long it happens to be.

The chapter's source files include a folder called ArrayLoop. It contains an example of how to use a for loop to list the contents of an array. Open the application class and compile it to see the effect.

```
package
{
    import flash.display.Sprite;

    public class ArrayLoop extends Sprite
    {
        //Declare the array
        private var _collectionJar:Array;

        public function ArrayLoop()
        {
            //Instantiate the array
            _collectionJar = new Array();

            //Add elements to the array
            _collectionJar.push("fly");
            _collectionJar.push("mosquito");
            _collectionJar.push("bee");

            for (var i:int = 0; i < _collectionJar.length; i++)
            {
                trace("Element " + i + ": " + _collectionJar[i]);
            }
        }
    }
}
```

This displays the following trace output:

```
Element 0:  fly
Element 1:  mosquito
Element 2:  bee
```

This little bit of code is one of the most common and useful for game design. You'll be using variations of it hundreds or thousands of times in slightly different contexts to do everything from making objects, moving them, changing their properties, and checking for collisions.

Searching arrays

Another interesting feature of this system is that you can create basic search functionality by throwing an if statement into the mix. It's really simple: just check to see whether an array element in the loop matches a certain search term. If you have a match, the element you're looking for has been found.

Here's the basic format for searching an array:

```
for (var i:int = 0;  i < arrayName.length;  i++)
{
  if(arrayName[i] == "searchTerm")
  {
    trace("Search term found.");
    break;
  }
}
```

One new thing here is the keyword **break**, which is used to stop a loop immediately without waiting for it to complete. When you use loops to search through arrays, you're often looking for only one item. Once that item has been found, it doesn't make sense to continue the loop, so you can use **break** to stop it early. Because your program doesn't have to do any unnecessary checking, your game will run faster.

You'll find a project folder called ArraySearch in the chapter's source files. Open it and take a look at the application class. It uses an if statement inside a loop to check whether the array contains an element called "mosquito". Once the if statement finds the correct element, a **break** directive runs to stop the loop from continuing.

```
package
{
  import flash.display.Sprite;

  public class ArraySearch extends Sprite
  {
    //Declare the array
    private var _collectionJar:Array;

    public function ArraySearch()
    {
      //Instantiate the array
      _collectionJar = new Array();

      //Add elements to the array
      _collectionJar.push("fly");
      _collectionJar.push("mosquito");
      _collectionJar.push("bee");

      for (var i:int = 0; i < _collectionJar.length; i++)
      {
        if(_collectionJar[i] == "mosquito")
        {
```

```
            trace("Mosquito found at position " + i);
            break;
         }
      }
    }
  }
}
```

If you test it, you'll see this output:

Mosquito found at position 1

Because you included a **break** directive, the loop stops at that point. It never checks element [2], which is a good thing. The loop has found what it's looking for so it doesn't need to check any further. Using for loops to search arrays is a basic programming technique that you'll be using frequently from now on.

Arrays inside arrays

You can store anything you like inside arrays, including other arrays. You know that a single, empty array looks like this:

[ ]

It's just a pair of square brackets. Let's say you want to put three new arrays inside that first empty array. You can do it like this:

[[ ],[ ],[ ]]

The first array now contains three new empty arrays. But it's confusing to look at it like this, so here's an easier way to visualize this:

```
[
  [ ],
  [ ],
  [ ]
]
```

It's now very clear to see that the surrounding array contains three new arrays inside it. This is called a **two-dimensional** array, or 2D array. They're arrays inside of arrays.

Let's imagine that your hobby as a bug collector has now expanded to include not only flying insects but also birds and slow crawling things. You'll need a bigger collection jar! You don't want your slugs and worms to get mixed up with your birds because they might get eaten. So you need a new jar that has internal compartments that separate the different types of creatures you're collecting. You could put the flying insects in one section, the birds in another, and the slow crawling things in the third. A 2D array is perfect for this, and here's what it would look like:

```
_collectionJar
  = [
      ["mosquito", "bee", "fly"],
      ["lark", "magpie", "albatross"],
      ["snail", "slug", "worm"]
    ];
```

You now have one array that contains three internal arrays—one for each type of creature. (Note that there's no comma after the last array. Also note that there's a semicolon after the last square bracket.)

Each of the internal arrays is no more than simple elements of the containing array. This means if you want to access the array that contains the slow crawling things, you can do it like this:

```
_collectionJar[2]
```

This would give you **snail, slug**, and **worm**.

If you wanted to find out what the second element of that array was, you could do it like this:

```
_collectionJar[2][1]
```

This would give you **slug**.

Here's another example. If you want to find the third element of the second array, you could find it like this:

```
_collectionJar[1][2]
```

This would give you **magpie**.

In the chapter's source file you'll find a project folder called ArraysInsideArrays with a working example of this new collection jar. Here's the application class:

```
package
{
  import flash.display.Sprite;

  public class ArraysInsideArrays extends Sprite
  {
    //Declare the array
    private var _collectionJar:Array;

    public function ArraysInsideArrays()
    {
      //Initialize the 2 dimensional array
      _collectionJar
        = [
            ["mosquito", "bee", "fly"],
            ["lark", "magpie", "albatross"],
            ["snail", "slug", "worm"]
          ];
```

```
    //View the entire first array
    //mosquito, bee, fly
    trace("Array 0: " + _collectionJar[0]);

    //View the entire second array
    //lark, magpie, albatross
    trace("Array 1: " + _collectionJar[1]);

    //View the first element in the second array
    //lark
    trace("First element of the second array: "
      + _collectionJar[1][0]);

    //View the third element in the third array
    //worm
    trace("Third element of the third array: "
      + _collectionJar[2][2]);

    //View the second element in the first array
    //bee
    trace("Second element of the first array: "
      + _collectionJar[0][1]);

    //View the contents of the entire 2 dimensional array
    //mosquito, bee, fly, lark, magpie,
    //albatross, snail, slug, worm
    trace("Entire collection jar: " + _collectionJar);
    }
  }
}
```

Here's the trace output from this code:

```
Array 0: mosquito,bee,fly
Array 1: lark,magpie,albatross
First element of the second array: lark
Third element of the third array: worm
Second element of the first array: bee
Entire collection jar:
mosquito,bee,fly,lark,magpie,albatross,snail,slug,worm
```

Figure 9-12 illustrates how this two-dimensional array works.

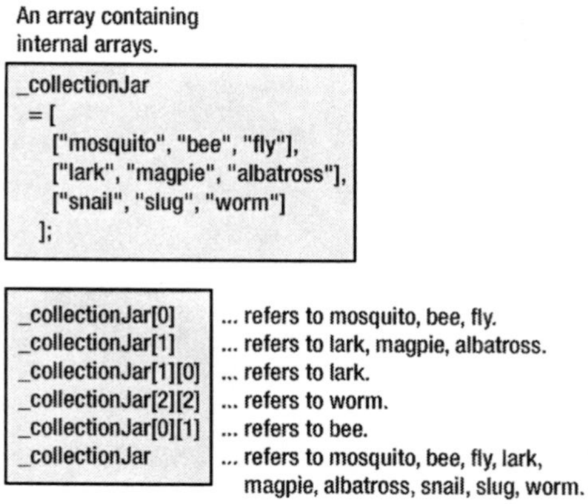

An array containing
internal arrays.

```
_collectionJar
= [
   ["mosquito", "bee", "fly"],
   ["lark", "magpie", "albatross"],
   ["snail", "slug", "worm"]
];
```

_collectionJar[0]	... refers to mosquito, bee, fly.
_collectionJar[1]	... refers to lark, magpie, albatross.
_collectionJar[1][0]	... refers to lark.
_collectionJar[2][2]	... refers to worm.
_collectionJar[0][1]	... refers to bee.
_collectionJar	... refers to mosquito, bee, fly, lark, magpie, albatross, snail, slug, worm.

Figure 9-12. Understanding two-dimensional arrays

2D arrays are a very efficient way of organizing complex information, and you can see that it's very easy to find what you're looking for if you understand the system. In the next section you'll see how to use a 2D array to store the x and y positions of boxes so that you can easily add them to their correct positions on the stage.

You'll need a bit of practice with arrays before you start to feel comfortable using them in your own code. Spend a bit of time with these example files, make some changes, and observe the way your changes affect the output. These examples are the key to understanding the rest of the chapter, so make sure you understand them before continuing further.

Making many boxes

I've decided that I want my platform game to contain 13 boxes, positioned on the stage as shown in Figure 9-13.

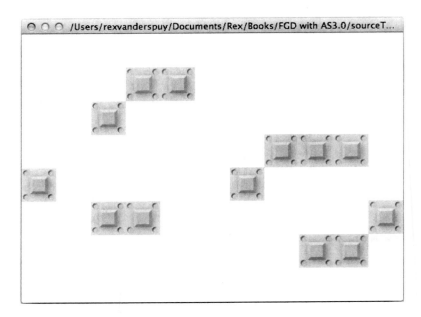

Figure 9-13. Adding lots of boxes to the stage

The first thing I did was plan this in Illustrator, which is a good way of sketching out level ideas. I made the grid visible (View   Show Grid) and choose the Snap to Grid option, which makes it easier to position objects precisely on the grid (View   Snap to Grid). (My boxes are 50 pixels wide and high, so I made sure that the gridlines were set to display every 50 pixels in Preferences   Guides & Grid). Figure 9-14 shows my level plan in Illustrator. You don't have to use Illustrator, of course; a pencil and graph paper works just as well. (Yes, a pencil and paper. Try it!)

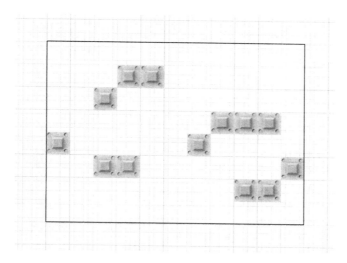

Figure 9-14. Using Illustrator to plan the positions of the game boxes

I then noted the x and y positions of each of the boxes, like this:

```
box1: x = 0, y  = 200
box2: x = 100, y = 100
box3: x =100, y = 250
...
```

I did this for all 13 boxes. I then had all the information I needed to use loops and arrays to create and add these boxes to the stage.

You'll find a project folder called MakingBoxes in the chapter's source files. The images folder contains a 50 by 50 PNG graphic of a box. The src folder contains the same **Box** class you used in Time Bomb Panic from Chapter 7. You need both these elements in the project folder for the code to work. Figure 9-15 shows what the MakingBoxes project folder looks like.

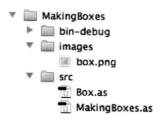

Figure 9-15. The project folder contains a PNG image of the box and a Box class which embeds the image.

Here's the entire **MakingBoxes** application class and the result is what you can see in Figure 9-13.

```
package
{
  import flash.display.Sprite;

  [SWF(width="550", height="400",
  backgroundColor="#FFFFFF", frameRate="60")]

  public class MakingBoxes extends Sprite
  {
    //An array to store the boxes
    private var _boxes:Array = new Array();

    //A 2D array to store the box x and y positions
    private var _boxPositions:Array = new Array();

    public function MakingBoxes()
    {
      //Set the box x and y positions
      _boxPositions
        = [
            [0, 200],
            [100, 100],
            [100, 250],
            [150, 50],
            [150, 250],
            [200, 50],
            [300, 200],
            [350, 150],
            [400, 150],
            [400, 300],
            [450, 150],
            [450, 300],
            [500, 250]
          ];

      //Make the boxes
      for(var i:int = 0; i < _boxPositions.length; i++)
      {
        //Create a box object
        var box:Box = new Box();

        //Add the box to the stage
        addChild(box);
        box.x = _boxPositions[i][0];
        box.y = _boxPositions[i][1];

        //Add it to the boxes array for future use
        _boxes.push(box);
      }
    }
  }
}
```

```
}
```

You need two arrays to make this code work.

```
private var _boxes:Array = new Array();
private var _boxPositions:Array = new Array();
```

The **_boxes** array is a storage container for all thirteen boxes. The **_boxPositions** array will be a 2D array that stores the x and y positions of each box.

```
_boxPositions
    = [
        [0, 200],
        [100, 100],
        [100, 250],
        [150, 50],
        [150, 250],
        [200, 50],
        [300, 200],
        [350, 150],
        [400, 150],
        [400, 300],
        [450, 150],
        [450, 300],
        [500, 250]
    ];
```

_boxPositions contains 13 arrays. Each array contains two elements: the first element is the box's x position and the second element is the box's y position.

```
[xPosition, yPosition]
```

These are the same numbers I scribbled down with my pencil when I was planning the level. There are 13 boxes, so there's one pair of x and y coordinates for each box.

The **for** loop does the work of creating a box object, pushing it into the **_boxes** array, adding it to the stage, and positioning it with the help of the **_boxPositions** 2D array.

```
for(var i:int = 0; i < _boxPositions.length; i++)
{
  //Create a box object
  var box:Box = new Box();

  //Add the box to the stage
  addChild(box);
  box.x = _boxPositions[i][0];
  box.y = _boxPositions[i][1];

  //Add it to the boxes array
```

```
//for future use
_boxes.push(box);
}
```

The for loop uses the **_boxPosition** array's length property to repeat for however many box positions coordinates there are. The **_boxPositions array** has 13 elements, so the loop repeats for 13 times.

```
for(var i:int = 0; i < _boxPositions.length; i++)
{...
```

Using the length property like this to determine the number of times to loop is really useful. It means that if you ever decide to add or remove boxes to the game, you just need to add or remove a pair of x and y coordinates in the **_boxPositions** array. The for loop will automatically adjust to the number of coordinates you have so you don't have to change the loop code at all.

The first thing that loop does is make a single box object.

```
var box:Box = new Box();
```

Next, the code adds this box to the stage.

```
addChild(box);
```

And then the cleverest trick of all: it gives the box x and y coordinates based on the coordinates you entered in the **_boxPositions** array.

```
box.x = _boxPositions[i][0];
box.y = _boxPositions[i][1];
```

How does this work? If you're new to loops and arrays, it's a bit of a mind-bender, so let's take a closer look. The first time the loop runs, the value of **i** is zero. That means the previous code will actually look like this:

```
box.x = _boxPositions[0][0];
box.y = _boxPositions[0][1];
```

First of all, what is **_boxPositions[0]**? It refers to the first element in the **_boxPositionsArray**. It's the first x and y coordinate you noted down.

```
[0, 200]
```

In this little array, element 0 is the x position and element 1 is the y position.

```
_boxPositions[0][0] = 0
_boxPositions[0][1] = 200
```

Refer to the earlier section on 2D arrays if you're confused about this. It's exactly the same way you referenced the birds and insects in those examples. All this means is that the x and y positions of the first box are being copied from the **_boxPositions** array to the box object's x and y properties. You could interpret the code in the for loop to look like this:

```
box.x = 0;
box.y = 200;
```

The second time the loop runs, **i** will have a value of 1. That means the code that positions the boxes will look like this:

```
box.x = _boxPositions[1][0];
box.y = _boxPositions[1][1];
```

_boxPositions[1] refers to **_boxPositions'** second element, which is the array that stores the coordinates of the second box.

```
[100, 100]
```

That means that you can find the second set of x and y coordinates by referring to them like this:

```
_boxPositions[1][0] = 100
_boxPositions[1][1] = 100
```

And finally, it means that the second time the loop runs, it interprets the two lines that position the box like this:

```
box.x = 100;
box.y = 100;
```

The loop runs for as many times as you have coordinates. That means it will create one box for one set of coordinates and assign one set of coordinates to each box.

The **box** object created by the **for** loop is *local*. That means that it only exists for a single iteration of the loop. The loop is going to make 13 of these box objects in total but each of these box objects will be replaced by a new one each time the loop repeats. So, before you lose it, you need to push it into the **_boxes** array so that you can store it for future use.

```
_boxes.push(box);
```

Now that the box object is safely stored in an array, you can access it at any time in the game to check for collisions—or even reposition or animate it! When the loop finishes running, all 13 box objects will be stored in the **_boxes** array.

This is a wonderfully efficient little system, and once you have it set up and running, it pretty much takes care of itself. You don't even need to think about it too much; just copy and paste this basic code whenever you need to make lots of objects and position them on the stage. You'll be able to use this basic format, unchanged except for the names of your objects, for countless game projects.

The next step in all of this is to add some collision detection so that your running, jumping game character can interact with the boxes. The hard part is now over, and you'll be surprised to see how easy it is to add collision detection.

Collisions with many objects

Open the LoopingThroughBoxes project folder and run the SWF file. You'll find a working system of exactly what I just discussed. The cat character can now explore the game world by running and jumping on the boxes on the stage, as illustrated in Figure 9-16. It's a lot of fun to play, and you now have all the skills you need to make something like this yourself and turn it into a game.

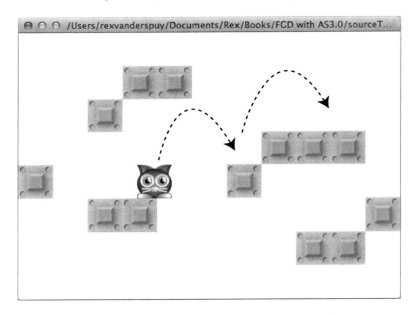

Figure 9-16. Combine physics and collision detection to build the beginnings of a platform game.

Don't panic! There's nothing new to learn! This sophisticated effect is achieved with only a few additional short lines of code, all of which you've already seen before. Let's take a look at how it works.

Take a look inside the LoopingThroughBoxes project folder, shown in Figure 9-17. In the images folder you'll find 50 by 50 pixel PNG images of the character and the box. The sound folder contains the bounce.mp3 sound file. In the src folder you'll find the application class, the **Character** class, the **Box** class, and very importantly, the **Collision** class.

Figure 9-17. The files used in the LoopingThroughBoxes project

Do you remember the **Collision** class from Chapters 6 and 7? You used it to block two objects, like this:

```
Collision.block(_character, _box);
```

It's this bit of code that you're going to use for the collision detection in this example.

The **LoopingThroughBoxes** application class combines all the techniques you've used in this chapter so far: sound, jump physics, and adding objects to a game with arrays and loops. You should recognize all of it! The only new section is the for loop in the **enterFrameHandler** that handles the collision detection between the character and the boxes. Here's the entire application class, and I'll explain how the collision detection works in the pages ahead.

```
package
{
  import flash.display.Sprite;
  import flash.events.Event;
  import flash.events.KeyboardEvent;
  import flash.media.Sound;
  import flash.media.SoundChannel;
  import flash.ui.Keyboard;

  [SWF(width="550", height="400",
    backgroundColor="#FFFFFF", frameRate="60")]

  public class LoopingThroughBoxes extends Sprite
  {
    //Embed the sound
    [Embed(source="../sounds/bounce.mp3")]
    private var Bounce:Class;

    //Create the Sound and Sound channel
    //objects for the sound
```

```
private var _bounce:Sound = new Bounce();
private var _bounceChannel:SoundChannel = new SoundChannel();

private var _character:Character = new Character();
private var _boxes:Array = new Array();
private var _boxPositions:Array = new Array();

public function LoopingThroughBoxes()
{
  //Set the box x and y positions
  _boxPositions
    = [
        [0, 200],
        [100, 100],
        [100, 250],
        [150, 50],
        [150, 250],
        [200, 50],
        [300, 200],
        [350, 150],
        [400, 150],
        [400, 300],
        [450, 150],
        [450, 300],
        [500, 250]
      ];

  //Make the boxes
  for(var i:int = 0; i < _boxPositions.length; i++)
  {
    //Create a box object
    var box:Box = new Box();

    //Add the box to the stage
    addChild(box);
    box.x = _boxPositions[i][0];
    box.y = _boxPositions[i][1];

    //Add it to the boxes array
    //for future use
    _boxes.push(box);
  }

  //Add the character
  addChild(_character);
  _character.x = 150;
  _character.y = 300

  //Add the event listeners
  stage.addEventListener
    (KeyboardEvent.KEY_DOWN, keyDownHandler);
  stage.addEventListener
```

```
      (KeyboardEvent.KEY_UP, keyUpHandler);
    stage.addEventListener
      (Event.ENTER_FRAME, enterFrameHandler);
}
public function enterFrameHandler(event:Event):void
{
    //Apply acceleration
    _character.vx += _character.accelerationX;

    //Apply friction
    _character.vx *= _character.friction;

    //Apply gravity
    _character.vy += _character.gravity;

    //Limit the speed, except when the character
    //is moving upwards
    if (_character.vx > _character.speedLimit)
    {
      _character.vx = _character.speedLimit;
    }
    if (_character.vx < -_character.speedLimit)
    {
      _character.vx = -_character.speedLimit;
    }
    if (_character.vy > _character.speedLimit * 2)
    {
      _character.vy = _character.speedLimit * 2;
    }

    //Force the velocity to zero
    //after it falls below 0.1
    if (Math.abs(_character.vx) < 0.1)
    {
      _character.vx = 0;
    }
    if (Math.abs(_character.vy) < 0.1)
    {
      _character.vy = 0;
    }

    //Move the character
    _character.x += _character.vx;
    _character.y += _character.vy;

    //Check stage boundaries
    if (_character.x < 0)
    {
      _character.vx = 0;
      _character.x = 0;
    }
    if (_character.y < 0)
```

```
      {
        _character.vy = 0;
        _character.y = 0;
      }
      if (_character.x + _character.width > stage.stageWidth)
      {
        _character.vx = 0;
        _character.x = stage.stageWidth - _character.width;
      }
      if (_character.y + _character.height > stage.stageHeight)
      {
        _character.vy = 0;
        _character.y = stage.stageHeight - _character.height;
        _character.isOnGround = true;
      }

      for(var i:int = 0; i < _boxes.length; i++)
      {
        Collision.block(_character, _boxes[i]);

        if(Collision.collisionSide == "Bottom")
        {
          //Tell the character that it's on the
          //ground if it's standing on top of
          //a platform
          _character.isOnGround = true;

          //Neutralize gravity by applying its
          //exact opposite force to the character's vy
          _character.vy = -_character.gravity;
        }
        else if(Collision.collisionSide == "Top")
        {
          _character.vy = 0;
        }
        else if(Collision.collisionSide == "Right"
          || Collision.collisionSide == "Left")
        {
          _character.vx = 0;
        }
      }
    }
    public function keyDownHandler(event:KeyboardEvent):void
    {
      if (event.keyCode == Keyboard.LEFT)
      {
        _character.accelerationX = -0.2;
      }
      else if (event.keyCode == Keyboard.RIGHT)
      {
        _character.accelerationX = 0.2;
      }
```

```
        else if (event.keyCode == Keyboard.UP
         || event.keyCode == Keyboard.SPACE)
        {
          if(_character.isOnGround)
          {
            _bounceChannel = _bounce.play();
            _character.vy += _character.jumpForce;
            _character.gravity = 0.3;
            _character.isOnGround = false;
          }
        }
        }
        public function keyUpHandler(event:KeyboardEvent):void
        {
          if (event.keyCode == Keyboard.LEFT
           || event.keyCode == Keyboard.RIGHT)
    {
      _character.accelerationX = 0;
    }
      }
    }
  }
}
```

The only bit of new code is the for loop in the **enterFrameHandler.**

```
for(var i:int = 0; i < _boxes.length; i++)
{
  Collision.block(_character, _boxes[i]);

  if(Collision.collisionSide == "Bottom")
  {
    //Tell the character that it's on the
    //ground if it's standing on top of
    //a platform
    _character.isOnGround = true;

    //Neutralize gravity by applying its
    //exact opposite force to the character's vy
    _character.vy = -_character.gravity;
  }
  else if(Collision.collisionSide == "Top")
  {
    _character.vy = 0;
  }
  else if(Collision.collisionSide == "Right"
    || Collision.collisionSide == "Left")
  {
    _character.vx = 0;
  }
}
```

It loops through all of the boxes in the **_boxes** array and checks them for a collision against the character.

```
for(var i:int = 0; i < _boxes.length; i++)
{
  Collision.block(_character, _boxes[i]);
```

The collision class contains a static String property called collisionSide that tells you on which side of the character the collision is occurring. You can access the collisionSide property like this:

```
Collision.collisionSide
```

If there's no collision, collisionSide will be "No collision". But if there is a collision, it will have the value of either "Top", "Bottom", "Left", or "Right". You can use collisionSide in an if statement to make specific changes to the collision based on the side of the character that the collision is occurring on. Figure 9-18 illustrates this.

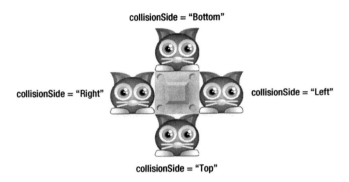

collisionSide = "Bottom"

collisionSide = "Right"   collisionSide = "Left"

collisionSide = "Top"

Figure 9-18. Use the Collision class's collisionSide property to find out which side of the character is hitting the box.

The reason you need to know this is so that you can set the character's velocity to zero when it hits the one of these sides. This creates the effect of the box absorbing the character's force, which results in a very natural looking effect. If the character collides on its top, left, or right side, this is just a simple matter of setting the vy or vx to zero, like this:

```
else if(Collision.collisionSide == "Top")
{
        _character.vy = 0;
}
else if(Collision.collisionSide == "Right"
  || Collision.collisionSide == "Left")
{
        _character.vx = 0;
}
```

But if the character hits the box on its bottom side, there's a little technical detail you must resolve. Gravity is constantly pulling the character down the stage, so you can't simply stop the character by giving it a zero vy value. You must actively counteract the force of gravity by assigning the character's vy a negative gravity value, like this:

```
if(Collision.collisionSide == "Bottom")
{
        _character.isOnGround = true;
        _character.vy = -_character.gravity;
}
```

If you don't do this, gravity will keep trying to pull the character down into the box, and this can sometimes result in it getting stuck in corners where two boxes meet. Neutralizing the force of gravity completely prevents this.

Here's a fun little modification. You can make the boxes bouncy by replacing the previous bit of code with this one:

```
_character.vy = -_character.vy / 2;
```

With this line of code, the character will bounce bit before settling on the top of the platform. If you want to make very springy kind of platform, like a trampoline, you could instead reverse the character's velocity like this:

```
_character.vy = -_character.vy;
```

Or, for a super-bounce, multiply it, like this:

```
_character.vy = -_character.vy * 1.5;
```

The other thing that happens when the bottom of the character hits the top of a platform is that its isOnGround property is set to true.

```
_character.isOnGround = true;
```

This is exactly what happens when the character hits the bottom of the stage and re-enables its jump ability.

And this is the only new code you need to know! You now have a fun little toy to play with. How will you use it to make a game? Think about the skills you learned in Chapters 6, 7, and 8, and you'll realize that you already know how.

Case studies

You now have some great new game design techniques you can use to make many different types of games. But how do you actually use them in the context of real games? In the book's download package you'll find a bonus chapter called *Case Studies: Maze and Platform Games*. It contains a detailed look at two games.

- A-MAZE-ing Monster Mayhem: A maze game featuring monsters that can move through a complex maze environment.

- Bug Catcher: A platform game featuring new enemy, AI techniques, a game state manager, detailed information about how to rotate objects toward other objects, and an explanation of how to change the stacking order of objects on the stage.

Figure 9-19 shows what these two games look like.

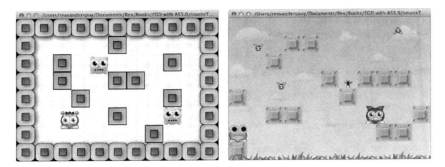

Figure 9-19. A-MAZE-ing Monster Mayhem and Bug Catcher case studies in the book's download package

Summary

I covered a number of new techniques in this chapter, all of which you'll find a use for in your own game projects. The specific game logic that you use to solve the conditions for winning and losing, as well as artificial intelligence for your game characters, will be different with every project. But hopefully this chapter has shown you some approaches to tackling these issues and some of the things that you'll need to think about in order to solve these problems in your own games.

This has been a basic introduction to platform games, physics, and managing lots of game objects, but you'll find all the building blocks here to start you off building a game that could become quite complex with a bit of planning and imagination. Add a bit of the puzzle solving and task completion, and maybe a few animated enemies, and you'll be well on your way to building a really fun game. You could also add a weapon and even some scrolling so that the player could explore a large area. What about items that give the player some special abilities, or maybe some vehicles to drive?

One bonus of the collision code that you're using is that it tells you which side of the platform the player is hitting. You can adapt it for enemy collisions to find out whether the player is jumping on an enemy's head, which is the classic way of vanquishing enemies in platform games. You can also adapt the physics code to create a flight-based action game, such as Joust, or a flight rescue or exploration game, such as Lunar Lander, Choplifter, or Defender. Actually, just about any 2D platform game is within your reach. And what about moving platforms? It could be interesting!

In the next chapter, you'll take a closer look at enemy artificial intelligence and scripted motion. I'll show you player control schemes that use the mouse. I'll also show you how to move objects and fire bullets in 360 degrees.

Chapter 10

Advanced Object And Character Control

You now have all the skills you need to build a wide variety of games, but there's still much more you'll want to learn. In this chapter, we'll take a look at the following useful techniques you'll need to know to get started on your own professional-level game design projects:

- Using easing for smooth motion

- Controlling game characters with the mouse

- Moving objects in the direction of their rotation

- Firing bullets in all directions

- Learning basic enemy artificial intelligence (AI): following, running away, and firing bullets in the direction of the player

- Complex player-controlled objects: a spaceship, a mouse-controlled platform character, a car, and a tank

This is quite a big and dense chapter, so don't feel you need to absorb all these techniques at one sitting. I've designed this chapter as a toolbox for you to delve into when you're trying to solve a particular problem in your own game design projects. Take it one small bite at a time and try to apply the techniques to your projects as much as possible.

So, without further ado, on with the game!

Moving objects with the mouse

If you start designing games professionally, your clients will probably expect that the game controls rely on the mouse instead of the keyboard. And if you can design game controls using the mouse exclusively, you're only a small step away from designing games for touch screen interface devices, such as the iPhone, iPad, or Android phones and tablets.

So, let's take a step-by-step look at how to control objects with the mouse.

Fixing an object to the mouse's position

Let's first start by fixing an object to the mouse's x and y positions using the Mouse class. In the chapter's source files, you'll find a project folder called MousePointer. Run the SWF and you'll find that you can control the up-and-coming star of this chapter, Button Fairy, just by moving the mouse around the stage. Figure 10-1 illustrates what you will see.

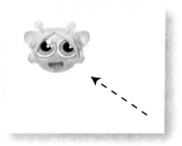

Figure 10-1. Move the mouse to make Button Fairy fly around the stage.

When you move the mouse, the mouse pointer disappears, but the object remains fixed to the exact position where it would be. This is a technique that you can use to create a custom mouse pointer for any of your games.

All the code is in the MousePointer application class, as follows:

```
package
{
  import flash.display.Sprite;
  import flash.events.Event;
  import flash.ui.Mouse;
  import flash.events.MouseEvent;

  [SWF(width="550", height="400",
  backgroundColor="#FFFFFF", frameRate="60")]

  public class MousePointer extends Sprite
  {
```

```
  private var _fairy:Fairy = new Fairy();

  public function MousePointer()
  {
    stage.addChild(_fairy);

      //Hide the mouse
    Mouse.hide();

    stage.addEventListener(Event.ENTER_FRAME, enterFrameHandler);
  }
  private function enterFrameHandler(event:Event):void
  {
    //Center the fairy over the mouse
    _fairy.x = mouseX - (_fairy.width / 2);
    _fairy.y = mouseY - (_fairy.height / 2);
  }
 }
}
```

This code relies on the use of the Mouse class, so the first thing you need to do is import it.

```
import flash.ui.Mouse;
```

The constructor method hides the mouse using the Mouse class's hide method.

```
Mouse.hide();
```

Finally, it fixes and centers the fairy's position to the now invisible mouse by using the stage's mouseX and mouseY properties.

```
_fairy.x = stage.mouseX - (_fairy.width / 2);
_fairy.y = stage.mouseY - (_fairy.height / 2);
```

And there you have a custom mouse pointer!

Moving an object with easing

It's likely that in a game scenario you will want your character to move with a little more grace than simply staying fixed to the mouse position exactly. You can use a simple technique called *easing* that gradually slows an object to a stop, and you can use it to create some very elegant systems to move objects.

In this chapter's source files, you'll find a folder called EasingWithMouse. Run the SWF to see the effect. Move the mouse, and Button Fairy will chase it around the stage and gracefully ease into position under it. You can see this illustrated in Figure 10-2.

Figure 10-2. Button Fairy follows the mouse with a bit of delay.

Here's the application class that achieves this effect. There's one new feature you haven't seen before: the value EASING, which is a special kind of value called a *constant*. I'll explain how constants work in a moment.

```
package
{
  import flash.display.Sprite;
  import flash.events.Event;
  import flash.events.MouseEvent;
  import flash.ui.Mouse;

  [SWF(width="550", height="400",
  backgroundColor="#FFFFFF", frameRate="60")]

  public class EasingWithMouse extends Sprite
  {
    private var _fairy:Fairy = new Fairy();
    private const EASING:Number = 0.1

    public function EasingWithMouse()
    {
      stage.addChild(_fairy);
      stage.addEventListener(Event.ENTER_FRAME, enterFrameHandler);
    }
    private function enterFrameHandler(event:Event):void
    {
      //Figure out the distance between the
      //mouse and the center of the fairy
      var vx:Number
        = stage.mouseX - (_fairy.x + _fairy.width / 2);
      var vy:Number
        = stage.mouseY - (_fairy.y + _fairy.height / 2);
      var distance:Number = Math.sqrt(vx * vx + vy * vy);
```

```
    //Move the fairy if it's more than 1 pixel away from the mouse
    if (distance>= 1)
    {
      _fairy.x += vx * EASING;
      _fairy.y += vy * EASING;
    }
  }
 }
}
```

The code needs to know how far away the fairy is from the mouse. It first calculates a distance vector, using some familiar code.

```
var vx:Number
  = stage.mouseX - (_fairy.x + _fairy.width / 2);
var vy:Number
  = stage.mouseY - (_fairy.y + _fairy.height / 2);
```

It then applies a simple formula, the Pythagorean Theorem, and copies the result into a variable called `distance`.

```
var distance:Number = Math.sqrt(vx * vx + vy * vy);
```

The Pythagorean Theorem states that "the square of the hypotenuse of a right triangle is equal to the sum of the squares on the other two sides." Translated into practical AS3.0 code, this means you need to use the built-in `Math.sqrt` function to find the square root of the sum of the vx and vy values, which are then multiplied by each other. Luckily for you, Pythagoras was right! Whenever you need to find the distance between two points, use his formula. It will become a regular in your arsenal of game design tricks, and you'll be using it quite frequently in this chapter.

> One pitfall of using Math.sqrt is that it's one of the most CPU-intensive math functions you can call. If you can avoid using it, you'll save a great deal of processing power.
>
> How can you avoid it? Try exchanging CPU power for brain power: use a handheld calculator and precalculate the value yourself!
>
> As an example, let's say you want to run some code if an object comes within 75 pixels of another object. First, calculate the distance squared, like this:
>
> ```
> var distanceSquared:Number =   (vx * vx + vy * vy);
> ```
>
> Then run some code if that distance is less than 75 pixels, like so:
>
> ```
> if (distanceSquared < 5625)
> {
>     //Directives to run if object is within range...
> ```

> }
>
> *Where does 5625 come from? It's 75 × 75 (or 75^2). By calculating the value yourself, you can drop Math.sqrt, and the effect will be exactly the same, except that you'll probably notice that your object moves a little more smoothly across the stage.*
>
> *Of course, 5625 is not really a very understandable number to work with, especially while you're designing and testing a game. However, you should always consider optimizing any code that uses Math.sqrt like this in the final stages of polishing up.*

Now that the program knows what the distance is between the two points, the code uses an `if` statement to move the object if the distance between the mouse and the fairy is greater than 1 pixel.

```
if (Math.abs(distance) >= 1)
{
  _fairy.x += vx * EASING;
  _fairy.y += vy * EASING;
}
```

Easing

Easing is the effect that you can see as Button Fairy gently "eases" into place over the mouse. Here are the two lines of code that achieve this effect:

```
_fairy.x += vx * EASING;
_fairy.y += vy * EASING;
```

Easing is very easy to implement using a simple formula inside an `ENTER_FRAME` event, like so:

```
(origin - destination) * easingValue;
```

You can make the animation happen faster or slower by changing the easing value. In the following example, this value is stored in a constant called `EASING` and has a value of `0.3`.

```
private const EASING:Number = 0.3;
```

Changing it to a higher number, such as 0.5, makes the easing effect happen much more quickly. Changing it to a lower number, such as 0.1, creates a much slower effect.

This is the first time we've used a constant in an example. Constants are just like variables, except their values never change. They're "constant." You declare a constant with the keyword `const`. By convention, constants are always written in uppercase letters. Programmers use constants to ensure that they don't accidentally over-write a value that should never change in a program. AS3.0 won't let you change the value of a constant after you've assigned one to it. If you know you're going to be using values that won't or shouldn't change, try and get into the habit of using a constant rather than a variable.

Click to move an object

With a small modification, you can make Button Fairy fly to any point on the stage where you click. Open the ClickToMove project folder and run the SWF file. Click anywhere on the stage and Button Fairy serenely flutters to that spot. You can see this illustrated in Figure 10-3.

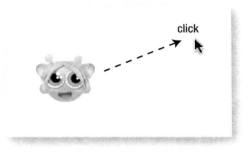

Figure 10-3. Click the stage to make Button Fairy fly to that spot.

Here's the code that makes this happen:

```
package
{
  import flash.display.Sprite;
  import flash.events.Event;
  import flash.events.MouseEvent;
  import flash.ui.Mouse;

  [SWF(width="550", height="400",
  backgroundColor="#FFFFFF", frameRate="60")]

  public class ClickToMove extends Sprite
  {
    private const EASING:Number = 0.1
    private var _fairy:Fairy = new Fairy();

    //Variables to capture the point that
    //the mouse clicks
    private var _target_X:Number;
    private var _target_Y:Number;

    public function ClickToMove()
    {
      stage.addChild(_fairy);
      stage.addEventListener
        (Event.ENTER_FRAME, enterFrameHandler);
      stage.addEventListener
        (MouseEvent.MOUSE_DOWN, mouseDownHandler)
    }
    private function mouseDownHandler(event:MouseEvent):void
```

```
  {
    _target_X = stage.mouseX;
    _target_Y = stage.mouseY;
  }
  private function enterFrameHandler(event:Event):void
  {
    //Figure out the distance between the
    //target position and the center of the fairy
    var vx:Number
      = _target_X - (_fairy.x + _fairy.width / 2);
    var vy:Number
      = _target_Y - (_fairy.y + _fairy.height / 2);
    var distance:Number = Math.sqrt(vx * vx + vy * vy);

    //Move the fairy if it's more than 1 pixel
    //away from the target position
    if (distance >= 1)
    {
      _fairy.x += vx * EASING;
      _fairy.y += vy * EASING;
    }
  }
 }
}
```

When the player clicks anywhere on the stage with the mouse, the mouseDownHandler is called. It stores the mouse's position in two variables: _target_X and _target_Y. Those two numbers are then used as the point to move the fairy to. Those values are changed only when the player clicks the mouse. The rest of the code is identical to the previous example.

Easy easing!

Our little easing formula is a wonderfully flexible bit of code, but if you want to use some more advanced easing effects in your game, consider installing and using a custom tween engine. Tween engines are specialized classes written by helpful programmers that you can add to your AS3.0 code library to animate your objects in all sorts of interesting ways. There are too many tween engines available to recommend one over another, and they're all really good, so you'll need to do a bit of research on your own to find out which of them might be best to use with your game. Here are the best known AS3.0 tween engines available at the time of writing: Tweener, TweenLite, GTween, Twease and Tweensy.

A web search will turn up the current download sites and installation instructions.

But, better yet, make your own tween engine! It's not hard to do at all, and Keith Peter's superb books, Foundation ActionScript 3.0 Animation *and* AdvancED ActionScript 3.0 Animation *(both available from Apress), will show you how.*

Case study: Firing projectiles in all directions

To round off this discussion of mouse-driven player control systems, let's look at a real-world example that takes into account the kind of complexity that some of your games will demand. We're going to use this as the model for the player control scheme that we're going to use in the demo game, Killer Bee Pandemonium!, at the end of the chapter.

You'll find this example in the ButtonFairy project folder in the chapter's source files. Run the SWF and you'll see that you can fly Button Fairy around the stage by dragging the mouse, much like you could in the example from the previous section "Moving an object with easing." In this version, an orange circle, the fairy's "wand," rotates around the fairy and angles itself toward the mouse cursor. Click the left mouse button and you can fire stars in all directions. The stars are removed when they hit the stage boundaries. Figure 10-4 shows what you'll see.

Figure 10-4. Button Fairy flies in the direction her wand is pointing, and she can fire stars in all directions.

This is an important example that demonstrates the following key game design techniques:

- How to rotate an object around another object

- How to fire projectiles in all directions

- How to use composition to make all the game objects using a single GameObject class

Figure 10-5 illustrates how the project is structured.

ButtonFairy
(The View/Controller
application class)

The project files

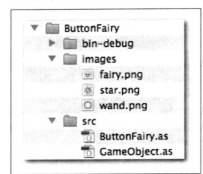

GameObject
(The model class)

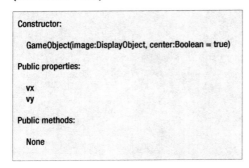

Figure 10-5. The project classes and files

The code that moves Button Fairy around the stage is identical to the code we looked at in the section "Moving an object with easing." The new code that moves the wand and fires the stars has been added to it, and you'll find out exactly how it works in the following pages. Here's the entire application class that makes all this work:

```
package
{
  import flash.display.DisplayObject;
  import flash.display.Sprite;
  import flash.events.Event;
  import flash.events.MouseEvent;
  import flash.ui.Mouse;

  [SWF(width="550", height="400",
  backgroundColor="#FFFFFF", frameRate="60")]

  public class ButtonFairy extends Sprite
  {
```

```
//Embed the images
[Embed(source="../images/fairy.png")]
private var FairyImage:Class;
[Embed(source="../images/wand.png")]
private var WandImage:Class;
[Embed(source="../images/star.png")]
private var StarImage:Class;

//Private properties
private const EASING:Number = 0.1;
private var _fairyImage:DisplayObject = new FairyImage();
private var _wandImage:DisplayObject = new WandImage();

//Create the fairy and wand game objects
//(The images will be centered by the GameObject class)
private var _fairy:GameObject = new GameObject(_fairyImage);
private var _wand:GameObject = new GameObject(_wandImage);

//A variable to store the angle between
//the mouse and the center of the fairy
private var _angle:Number;

//An array to store the stars
private var _stars:Array = new Array();

public function ButtonFairy()
{
  //Add the fairy and the wand to the stage
  stage.addChild(_fairy);
  stage.addChild(_wand);

  //Hide the mouse
  Mouse.hide();

  //Add the event listeners
  stage.addEventListener
    (Event.ENTER_FRAME, enterFrameHandler);
  stage.addEventListener
    (MouseEvent.MOUSE_DOWN, mouseDownHandler);
}
private function enterFrameHandler(event:Event):void
{
  //Find the angle between the center of the
  //fairy and the mouse
  _angle
    = Math.atan2
    (
      _fairy.y - stage.mouseY,
      _fairy.x - stage.mouseX
    );

  //Move the wand around the fairy
```

```
var radius:int = -50;
_wand.x = _fairy.x + (radius * Math.cos(_angle));
_wand.y = _fairy.y + (radius * Math.sin(_angle));

//Figure out the distance between the
//mouse and the center of the fairy
var vx:Number = stage.mouseX - _fairy.x;
var vy:Number = stage.mouseY - _fairy.y;
var distance:Number = Math.sqrt(vx * vx + vy * vy);

//Move the fairy if it's more than 1 pixel away from the mouse
if (distance >= 1)
{
  _fairy.x += vx * EASING;
  _fairy.y += vy * EASING;
}

//Move the stars
for(var i:int = 0; i < _stars.length; i++)
{
  var star:GameObject = _stars[i];
  star.x += star.vx;
  star.y += star.vy;

  //check the star's stage boundaries
  if (star.y < 0
  || star.x < 0
  || star.x > stage.stageWidth
  || star.y > stage.stageHeight)
  {
    //Remove the star from the stage
    stage.removeChild(star);
    star = null;

    //Remove the star from the _stars array
    _stars.splice(i,1);

    //Reduce the loop counter
    //by one to compensate
    //for the removed star
    i--;
  }
}
}
private function mouseDownHandler(event:MouseEvent):void
{
  //Create a star and add it to the stage
  var starImage:DisplayObject = new StarImage();
  var star:GameObject = new GameObject(starImage);
  stage.addChild(star);

  //Set the star's starting position
```

```
    //to the wand's position
    star.x = _wand.x;
    star.y = _wand.y;

    //Set the star's velocity based
    //on the angle between the center of
    //the fairy and the mouse
    star.vx = Math.cos(_angle) * -7;
    star.vy = Math.sin(_angle) * -7;

    //Push the star into the _stars array
    _stars.push(star);
    }
  }
}
```

Making the game objects

The images of all the objects are embedded into the application class. Each individual object is made using composition by sending the image to the GameObject class, like this:

```
private var _fairy:GameObject = new GameObject(_fairyImage);
private var _wand:GameObject = new GameObject(_wandImage);
```

The GameObject class contains the vx and vy properties that all the objects need to move. When it receives an image through its constructor method, it displays it and centers it within its containing sprite. Here's the entire GameObject class that does this:

```
package
{
  import flash.display.DisplayObject;
  import flash.display.Sprite;
  {
    public class GameObject extends Sprite
    {
      //Public properties
      public var vx:Number = 0;
      public var vy:Number = 0;

      public function GameObject
        (image:DisplayObject, center:Boolean = true)
      {
        //Add the image
        this.addChild(image);

        //Center the image if the "center" option is true
        if(center)
        {
          image.x -= image.width / 2;
          image.y -= image.height / 2;
        }
```

```
      }
    }
  }
}
```

The center parameter is set to true by default. This means that the object's x and y positions will refer to its center point. This is very useful in this game example because we want the fairy to be centered over the mouse, the wand to rotate around the fairy's center, and the stars to be added to the stage at the wand's center point. Centering all the objects will simplify the code in the application class.

If you want to use this class to create a game object, but you don't want the image to be centered, include false as the second argument, like this:

```
private var _fairy:GameObject = new GameObject(_fairyImage, false);
```

Now the object's x and y registration point will be its top-left corner, as it has been for most of the examples in this book.

Creating all the game objects from this one class is a powerful programming technique called *composition*. It saves you the trouble of having to make a unique class for each object. If all your game objects share the same properties, it's a great solution.

> For many more examples of composition, and a detailed explanation of exactly how it works, see the bonus chapter "Drag-and-Drop Games" in the book's download package.

Rotating the wand around the fairy

Button Fairy's wand is the yellow dot that fires stars in all directions. It rotates around the center of the fairy, and always points toward the mouse, as shown in Figure 10-6.

Figure 10-6. The wand rotates around the center of the fairy and always points in the direction of the mouse.

To make this work, you first have to find the angle between the mouse and the center of the fairy. The code does this using the `Math.atan2` function. Here's the code that works out the angle between the mouse and the fairy:

```
_angle
  = Math.atan2
  (
    _fairy.y - stage.mouseY,
    _fairy.x - stage.mouseX
  );
```

AS3.0 has a specialized function called `Math.atan2` function that tells you the angle of rotation of an object. You use it by supplying it with any vx or vy values that describe a distance vector between two objects. (Refer back to Chapter 6 for a refresher on what a distance vector is and how to find it.) In this example, the distance vector is described by the difference between the fairy and the mouse's position on the stage:

```
    _fairy.y - stage.mouseY,
    _fairy.x - stage.mouseX
```

Very importantly, when you use `Math.atan2`, make sure that vy value is the first argument, and the vx value the second, like so:

```
Math.atan2(vy, vx)
```

`Math.atan2` returns a number in *radians.* Unfortunately, this is not useful for rotating sprite objects. You need to convert this number to *degrees,* which is the type of value expected by the rotation property.

To convert radians to degrees, you can use a simple calculation: multiply the value in radians by 180 divided by pi (3.14). AS3.0 has a built-in function called `Math.PI` that returns the value of pi, just to make things easier for you. Here's what the final line of code might look like:

```
Math.atan2(vy, -vx) * (180/Math.PI)
```

This gives you a rounded-off value in degrees that you can apply to the `rotation` property of any sprite.

> For a detailed explanation of how rotation and Math.atan2 works, see the bonus chapter "Case Studies: Maze and Platform Games" in the book's download package.

I decided that I wanted the wand to rotate around the fairy within a 50-pixel radius. A variable called `radius` defines this distance.

```
var radius:int = -50;
```

A negative value pushes the wand away from the center of the fairy, which happens to be the direction in which the mouse will be pointing.

The wand's x and y position is found by multiplying the radius by angle ratios obtained using two specialized functions: `Math.cos` and `Math.sin`. They both take the _angle value as arguments. The result is then added to the fairy's x and y position so that the wand moves with the fairy.

```
_wand.x = _fairy.x + (radius * Math.cos(_angle));
_wand.y = _fairy.y + (radius * Math.sin(_angle));
```

`Math.cos` and `Math.sin` functions are two specialized trigonometry functions that return the ratio of two sides of the triangle formed by the measurement of the angle. The result is exactly as you see it on the stage.

Firing stars in 360 degrees

Each time you click the left mouse button, the code calls the `mouseDownHandler` that creates and fires stars in whatever direction the fairy's wand is pointing.

```
private function mouseDownHandler(event:MouseEvent):void
{
  //Create a star and add it to the stage
  var starImage:DisplayObject = new StarImage();
  var star:GameObject = new GameObject(starImage);
  stage.addChild(star);

  //Set the star's starting position
  //to the wand's position
  star.x = _wand.x;
  star.y = _wand.y;

  //Set the star's velocity based
  //on the angle between the center of
  //the fairy and the mouse
  star.vx = Math.cos(_angle) * -7;
  star.vy = Math.sin(_angle) * -7;

  //Push the star into the _stars array
  _stars.push(star);
}
```

Each star is created and added to the stage using the `GameObject`, class, in exactly the same way that the code created the _fairy and _wand objects.

```
var starImage:DisplayObject = new StarImage();
var star:GameObject = new GameObject(starImage);
stage.addChild(star);
```

When it's created, the star's x and y positions are the same as the wand's.

```
star.x = _wand.x;
star.y = _wand.y;
```

Each star then needs a unique velocity that will make it move away from the fairy in the direction that the mouse is pointing. To find this, we can use the same _angle value we're using to rotate the wand and feed it to the Math.cos and Math.sin values. If we multiply those results by −7, it will make the star move away from the center of the fairy at seven pixels per frame.

```
star.vx = Math.cos(_angle) * -7;
star.vy = Math.sin(_angle) * -7;
```

The star is then pushed into the _stars array so that we can move and manage it along with all the other stars in the game.

```
_stars.push(star);
```

A for loop in the enterFrameHandler is what makes the stars move and checks the stage boundaries.

```
for(var i:int = 0; i < _stars.length; i++)
{
  var star:GameObject = _stars[i];
  star.x += star.vx;
  star.y += star.vy;

  //check the star's stage boundaries
  if (star.y < 0
  || star.x < 0
  || star.x > stage.stageWidth
  || star.y > stage.stageHeight)
  {
    //Remove the star from the stage
    stage.removeChild(star);
    star = null;

    //Remove the star from the _stars
    //array
    _stars.splice(i,1);

    //Reduce the loop counter
    //by one to compensate
    //for the removed star
    i--;
  }
}
```

The loop first makes each star in the _stars array move in the correct direction by adding its vx and vy values that we calculated in the mouseDownHandler to its x and y positions.

```
var star:GameObject = _stars[i];
star.x += star.vx;
star.y += star.vy;
```

It then checks to see whether the star has crossed the stage boundaries.

```
if (star.y < 0
```

```
|| star.x < 0
|| star.x > stage.stageWidth
|| star.y > stage.stageHeight)
{…
```

If it has, it removes the star. First, it removes it from the stage and sets its value to null.

```
stage.removeChild(star);
star = null;
```

It then uses the splice method to delete the star from the _stars array.

```
_stars.splice(i,1);
```

The code then has to reduce the loop counter by one to compensate for the star that was just cut out of the array.

```
i--;
```

If you don't do this, it throws the counter off by one, and the loop will skip the next item.

What's new here is using splice to remove an element from an array. splice uses two arguments: the first is the index number of the element to remove, and the second is the number of elements it should remove from that point onward.

```
splice(whereToRemoveTheElement, numberOfElementsToRemove);
```

In this case, you want to remove the current star, which is at index number i. If the loop is in its third repetition, that would be element number 2. (Remember, array elements are numbered starting at zero.)

In the second argument, 1 is the number of elements to remove. In this case, you want to remove only one element.

What splice does in this program is to remove the star from the array so the program no longer has to move it or check it for stage boundaries. If you don't splice it out of the array, the array will just get bigger and bigger, and the program will start to generate errors because it would contain references to star objects that have already been removed from the stage with removeChild.

You can also use splice to insert elements into an array. For example, if you want to add an object called box into an array as the third element, you can use a line of code that looks like this:

```
array.splice(2, 0,  box);
```

This adds the box object at index position 2. 0 means that you didn't delete the element that was originally at position 2. That object will be pushed up to position 3, and any objects that come after it would also be renumbered.

> *If you want to insert an object into an array and replace the existing element, you can use the following format:*
>
> ```
> array.splice(2, 1, box);
> ```
>
> *The box object will now be inserted at position 2, but it also indicates that one element should be deleted from the array. That would be the original element at position number 2. It's now gone for good, replaced by box, and the rest of the elements in the array won't be renumbered.*

`splice` is a very versatile method to use with arrays, and you'll certainly find many occasions when it will help you manage game objects.

This little bit of code for firing projectiles is one of the most important you need to know as a game designer. If any of your game objects need to fire bullets, come back to this section in the chapter and adapt this code to your game. It's a game programming classic.

Advanced player control systems

We've taken a detailed look at many different types of player control systems in this book, but it hasn't been exhaustive. To make the widest variety of games possible, there are a few more player control schemes that you'll likely want to implement, such as the following:

- A mouse-controlled platform game character
- A keyboard-controlled spaceship
- A car for an overhead driving game
- A tank that can rotate and fire bullets from a turret

You'll find working examples and detailed explanations of how all these systems work in the bonus chapter "Advanced Player Control Systems," which you'll find in the book's download package. Figure 10-7 shows the kinds of game objects you'll learn how to make.

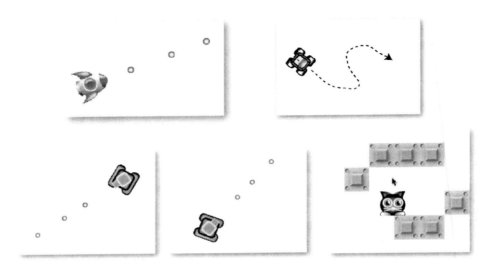

Figure 10-7. Advanced player control systems

Enemy AI systems

We've taken a good look at player control systems, but what about your game enemies? They're fun to make and easy to program. As you'll see in this next section, just a few simple techniques and a bit of run-of-the-mill logic is all you need to build some surprisingly sophisticated enemy artificial intelligence (AI) systems.

You already know how to make an object follow the mouse, and that basic skill is at the heart of an AI system that you can modify for use in a wide variety of game situations. All you need to do is mix and match some of the techniques you already know, and you can design enemies that do the following:

- Follow the player
- Run away from the player
- Aim and fire bullets at the player

Let's find out how.

Following another object

Open the `Follow` project folder and run the SWF. You'll see that Killer Bee follows and rotates toward the mouse if it's within a 200-pixel range. Figure 10-8 illustrates what you will see. After it reaches the mouse, it circles around it with very bee-like persistence.

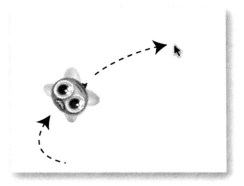

Figure 10-8. The bee rotates toward the mouse and follows it around the stage.

The bee is created using the general `GameObject` class we used in the ButtonFairy project. Here's the `Follow` application class that creates the effect:

```
package
{
  import flash.display.DisplayObject;
  import flash.display.Sprite;
  import flash.events.Event;
  import flash.events.MouseEvent;
  import flash.ui.Mouse;

  [SWF(width="550", height="400",
  backgroundColor="#FFFFFF", frameRate="60")]

  public class Follow extends Sprite
  {
    //Embed the image
    [Embed(source="../images/bee.png")]
    private var BeeImage:Class;

    //Properties
    private const SPEED:Number = 3;
    private const TURN_SPEED:Number = 0.3;
    private const RANGE:Number = 200;
    private const FRICTION:Number = 0.96;
    private var _beeImage:DisplayObject = new BeeImage();
    private var _bee:GameObject = new GameObject(_beeImage);

    //The bee's angle of rotation
    private var _beeAngle:Number;

    public function Follow()
    {
      stage.addChild(_bee);
```

```
      _bee.x = 275;
      _bee.y = 175;

      //Add the event listeners
      stage.addEventListener(Event.ENTER_FRAME, enterFrameHandler);
   }
   private function enterFrameHandler(event:Event):void
   {
      //Get the target object
      var target_X:Number = stage.mouseX;
      var target_Y:Number = stage.mouseY;

      //Calculate the distance between the target and the bee
      var vx:Number = target_X - _bee.x;
      var vy:Number = target_Y - _bee.y;

      var distance:Number = Math.sqrt(vx * vx + vy * vy);
      if (distance <= RANGE)
      {
         //Find out how much to move
         var move_X:Number = TURN_SPEED * vx / distance;
         var move_Y:Number = TURN_SPEED * vy / distance;

         //Increase the bee's velocity
         _bee.vx += move_X;
         _bee.vy += move_Y;

          //Find total distance to move
         var moveDistance:Number
           = Math.sqrt(_bee.vx * _bee.vx + _bee.vy * _bee.vy);

         //Apply easing
         _bee.vx = SPEED * _bee.vx / moveDistance;
         _bee.vy = SPEED * _bee.vy / moveDistance;

         //Rotate the bee towards the target
          //Find the angle in radians
         _beeAngle = Math.atan2(_bee.vy, _bee.vx);

         //Convert the radians to degrees to rotate the bee correctly
         _bee.rotation = _beeAngle * 180 / Math.PI + 90;
      }
      //Apply friction
      _bee.vx *= FRICTION;
      _bee.vy *= FRICTION;

      //Move the bee
      _bee.x += _bee.vx;
      _bee.y += _bee.vy;
   }
  }
}
```

After the bee knows what its target is (the mouse), it calculates the distance between itself and the target. If the distance is less than the RANGE value (which is 200), the bee moves.

It moves using a variation of the easing formula we looked at earlier in the chapter. It's a little more complex, however, because you want to limit the bee's speed and the rate at which it turns. Here are the steps the code takes and the formulas it uses to accomplish each task:

1. The code finds out how far to move the object and assigns these values to move_X and move_Y variables:

```
var move_X:Number = TURN_SPEED * vx / distance;
var move_Y:Number = TURN_SPEED * vy / distance;
```

2. The values of these new variables are used to modify the velocity:

```
_bee.vx += move_X;
_bee.vy += move_Y;
```

3. The bee's new vx and vy properties are used to help it find the total distance required to move:

```
var moveDistance:Number
  = Math.sqrt(_bee.vx * _bee.vx + _bee.vy * _bee.vy);
```

4. The code then uses this new distance value along with the SPEED constant to find the correct velocity:

```
_bee.vx = SPEED * _bee.vx / moveDistance;
_bee.vy = SPEED * _bee.vy / moveDistance;
```

This is a variation of our easing formula, with SPEED representing the easing value.

5. Finally, the code rotates the bee toward the target. This is the same formula we've been using for rotation throughout the book. The addition of + 90 is there to offset the rotation of the bee object by 90 degrees. Without that, the leading edge of the bee would be its right side. (That's because of the way the object was drawn with its "front" being the stinger on the bee's head.) Any objects you use with this code might be oriented differently, so you'll probably want to adjust 90 to another number that you can figure out by trial and error when you see the direction toward which your object rotates:

```
_bee.rotation = Math.atan2(_bee.vy, _bee.vx) * 180 / Math.PI + 90;
```

If the target is *not* within the bee's range, the following directives kick in, which gradually slow the bee down by using friction:

```
//Apply friction
_bee.vx *= FRICTION;
_bee.vy *= FRICTION;

//Move the bee
_bee.x += _bee.vx;
```

```
_bee.y += _bee.vy;
```

A bit of simple logic, a few careful adjustments to the easing formula, and you have a very effective following behavior.

Running away from the player

It's very easy to create the exact opposite behavior to make the bee run away from the mouse. To see this at work, open the RunAway project folder and run the SWF. You'll see the bee flee from the mouse, as illustrated in Figure 10-9.

When I say that this is the opposite behavior, I mean that in the most literal sense imaginable. The application class is exactly the same as the in the previous case, except that the three plus signs have been made negative.

The bee's rotation is negative so that it points in the opposite direction, like so:

```
_bee.rotation
  = 180 * Math.atan2(_bee.vy, _bee.vx) / Math.PI - 90;
```

The velocity is also negative, as you can see here:

```
_bee.x -= _bee.vx;
_bee.y -= _bee.vy;
```

That's it!

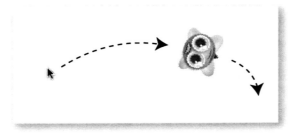

Figure 10-9. Get too close and the bee flies away.

Rotating and shooting toward the mouse

In the final AI system, the bee turns and fires bullets toward the mouse if the mouse is within range. You'll find this example in the RotateAndShoot project folder, and Figure 10-10 shows what you'll see when you run the SWF file.

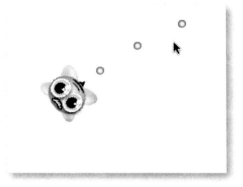

Figure 10-10. The bee flies toward the mouse and fires bullets at it.

The code that does this is a fusion of the Follow example, with the addition of a bullet-firing system. The bullets are fired using a timer that's started when the mouse comes within range of the bee. Here's the application class that makes this work:

```
package
{
  import flash.display.DisplayObject;
  import flash.display.Sprite;
  import flash.events.Event;
  import flash.events.MouseEvent;
  import flash.ui.Mouse;
  import flash.events.TimerEvent;
  import flash.utils.Timer;

  [SWF(width="550", height="400",
  backgroundColor="#FFFFFF", frameRate="60")]

  public class RotateAndShoot extends Sprite
  {
    //Embed the images
    [Embed(source="../images/bee.png")]
    private var BeeImage:Class;
    [Embed(source="../images/bullet.png")]
    private var BulletImage:Class;

    //Properties
    private const SPEED:Number = 3;
    private const TURN_SPEED:Number = 0.3;
    private const RANGE:Number = 200;
    private const FRICTION:Number = 0.96;
    private var _beeImage:DisplayObject = new BeeImage();
    private var _bee:GameObject = new GameObject(_beeImage);

    //The bee's angle of rotation
    private var _beeAngle:Number;
```

```
//A timer to fire bullets
private var _bulletTimer:Timer;

//An array to store the bullets
private var _bullets:Array = new Array();

public function RotateAndShoot()
{
  //Add the bee to the stage
  stage.addChild(_bee);
  _bee.x = 275;
  _bee.y = 175;

  //Initialize the timer
  _bulletTimer = new Timer(1000);
  _bulletTimer.addEventListener
    (TimerEvent.TIMER, bulletTimerHandler);

  //Add the event listeners
  stage.addEventListener
    (Event.ENTER_FRAME, enterFrameHandler);
}
private function bulletTimerHandler(event:TimerEvent):void
{
  //Create a bullet and add it to the stage
  var bulletImage:DisplayObject = new BulletImage();
  var bullet:GameObject = new GameObject(bulletImage);
  stage.addChild(bullet);

  //Set the bullet's starting position
  var radius:int = 30;
  bullet.x = _bee.x + (radius * Math.cos(_beeAngle));
  bullet.y = _bee.y + (radius * Math.sin(_beeAngle));

  //Set the bullet's velocity based the angle
  bullet.vx = Math.cos(_beeAngle) * 2 + _bee.vx;
  bullet.vy = Math.sin(_beeAngle) * 2 + _bee.vy;

  //Push the bullet into the _bullets array
  _bullets.push(bullet);
}
private function enterFrameHandler(event:Event):void
{
  //Get the target object
  var target_X:Number = stage.mouseX;
  var target_Y:Number = stage.mouseY;

  //Calculate the distance between the target and the bee
  var vx:Number = target_X - _bee.x;
  var vy:Number = target_Y - _bee.y;
```

```
var distance:Number = Math.sqrt(vx * vx + vy * vy);
if (distance <= RANGE)
{
  //Find out how much to move
  var move_X:Number = TURN_SPEED * vx / distance;
  var move_Y:Number = TURN_SPEED * vy / distance;

  //Increase the bee's velocity
  _bee.vx += move_X;
  _bee.vy += move_Y;

  //Find the total distance to move
  var moveDistance:Number
    = Math.sqrt(_bee.vx * _bee.vx + _bee.vy * _bee.vy);

  //Apply easing
  _bee.vx = SPEED * _bee.vx / moveDistance;
  _bee.vy = SPEED * _bee.vy / moveDistance;

  //Rotate towards the bee towards the target
  //Find the angle in radians
  _beeAngle = Math.atan2(_bee.vy, _bee.vx);

  //Convert the radians to degrees to rotate the bee correctly
  _bee.rotation = _beeAngle * 180 / Math.PI + 90;

  //Start the bullet timer
  _bulletTimer.start();
}
else
{
  _bulletTimer.stop();
}

//Apply friction
_bee.vx *= FRICTION;
_bee.vy *= FRICTION;

//Move the bee
_bee.x += _bee.vx;
_bee.y += _bee.vy;

//Move the bullets
for(var i:int = 0; i < _bullets.length; i++)
{
  var bullet:GameObject = _bullets[i];
  bullet.x += bullet.vx;
  bullet.y += bullet.vy;

  //check the bullet's stage boundaries
  if (bullet.y < 0
  || bullet.x < 0
```

```
        || bullet.x > stage.stageWidth
        || bullet.y > stage.stageHeight)
        {
          //Remove the bullet from the stage
          stage.removeChild(bullet);
          bullet = null;
          _bullets.splice(i,1);
          i--;
        }
      }
    }
  }
}
```

Using a timer to fire bullets

A timer is set up to fire bullets every second if the mouse is within range of the bee. The timer is started if it's within range, and stopped if it's out of range, as you can see in the following abridged code from the enterFrameHandler:

```
if (distance <= RANGE)
{
  //...
  _bulletTimer.start();
}
else
{
  _bulletTimer.stop();
}
```

The enterFrameHandler then loops through all the bullets in the _bullets array to move them, and removes them from the game if they cross the stage boundaries.

Shooting at random intervals

There's one small modification you can make that will make the bee's shooting behavior much more realistic. As it's been coded, the bee shoots right on cue every 1,000 milliseconds. You can use the Timer class's delay property to randomize this. Add the following highlighted code to the bulletTimerHandler event handler to see the effect:

```
private function bulletTimerHandler(event:TimerEvent):void
{
  var bulletImage:DisplayObject = new BulletImage();
  var bullet:GameObject = new GameObject(bulletImage);
  stage.addChild(bullet);
  var radius:int = 30;
  bullet.x = _bee.x + (radius * Math.cos(_beeAngle));
  bullet.y = _bee.y + (radius * Math.sin(_beeAngle));
  bullet.vx = Math.cos(_beeAngle) * 2 + _bee.vx;
  bullet.vy = Math.sin(_beeAngle) * 2 + _bee.vy;
  _bullets.push(bullet);
```

```
//Find a random start time for the next bullet
var randomFireTime:Number
  = Math.round(Math.random() * 1000) + 200;
_bulletTimer.delay = randomFireTime;
}
```

The bee now fires randomly between 200 and 1,200 milliseconds.

This AI system is at the heart of what you need to know if you want to create any kind of rotating enemy gun turret for your games. Just substitute another game object for the mouse, and the bee will chase and fire at the object, as we'll see in the next example.

Case study: Killer Bee Pandemonium!

We've made a lot of fun little toys in this chapter, and it doesn't take much work to turn them into a real game. What would happen if we put Button Fairy in the same environment as Killer Bee? We'd get an all-out power shootout between two arch enemies in Killer Bee Pandemonium!, which you'll find in the source files. Run the SWF file and play the game, which you can see in Figure 10-11.

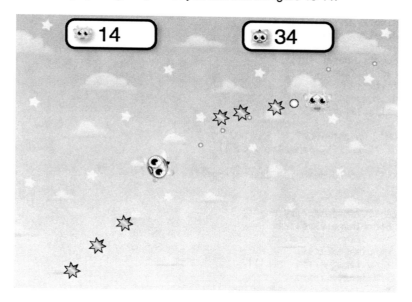

Figure 10-11. Can Button Fairy save the woodland creatures from the grumpy Killer Bee?

Button Fairy can fly around the screen and shoot the bee. The Killer Bee flies toward her and fires bullets if she's within range. The scoreboards at the top of the stage keep track of the number of hits each has achieved.

All the objects in the game are made using the general GameObject class, so there are no custom classes to keep track of. That keeps the game structure and code really simple, and you can find out everything you need to know about how the game works just by looking at the application class. The application class doesn't contain any new code at all; it's just an everything-but-the-kitchen-sink example using most of the code we've already covered in this chapter. The one thing to keep an eye on, however, is the loops that move the star and bullet projectiles and check them for collisions. The loops have to make sure that they don't check for collisions with projectiles that they've already removed. We'll take a closer look at how this works ahead.

Here's the KillerBeePandemonium application class. You'll see that all the sections of code that move the different kinds of objects are in their own methods. Each of these methods is being called by the enterFrameHandler. This is just to help organize the code so that it's easier to find and work with these different sections.

```
package
{
    import flash.display.DisplayObject;
    import flash.display.Sprite;
    import flash.events.Event;
    import flash.events.MouseEvent;
    import flash.events.TimerEvent;
    import flash.text.*;
    import flash.ui.Mouse;
    import flash.utils.Timer;

    [SWF(width="800", height="600",
    backgroundColor="#FFFFFF", frameRate="60")]

    public class KillerBeePandemonium extends Sprite
    {
        //The images
        [Embed(source="../images/fairy.png")]
        private var FairyImage:Class;
        [Embed(source="../images/wand.png")]
        private var WandImage:Class;
        [Embed(source="../images/star.png")]
        private var StarImage:Class;
        [Embed(source="../images/background.png")]
        private var BackgroundImage:Class;
        [Embed(source="../images/bee.png")]
        private var BeeImage:Class;
        [Embed(source="../images/bullet.png")]
        private var BulletImage:Class;

        //Properties
        private const SPEED:Number = 3;
```

```
private const TURN_SPEED:Number = 0.3;
private const RANGE:Number = 500;
private const FRICTION:Number = 0.96;
private const EASING:Number = 0.1;
private var _fairyImage:DisplayObject = new FairyImage();
private var _wandImage:DisplayObject = new WandImage();
private var _backgroundImage:DisplayObject
  = new BackgroundImage();
private var _beeImage:DisplayObject = new BeeImage();
private var _fairy:GameObject = new GameObject(_fairyImage);
private var _wand:GameObject = new GameObject(_wandImage);
private var _bee:GameObject = new GameObject(_beeImage);
private var _background:GameObject
  = new GameObject(_backgroundImage, false);
private var _angle:Number;
private var _beeAngle:Number;
private var _stars:Array = new Array();
private var _bullets:Array = new Array();
private var _bulletTimer:Timer;
private var _format:TextFormat = new TextFormat();
private var _fairyScoreDisplay:TextField = new TextField();
private var _beeScoreDisplay:TextField = new TextField();
private var _fairyScore:int;
private var _beeScore:int;

public function KillerBeePandemonium()
{
  //Add game the objects
  stage.addChild(_background);
  setupTextFields();
  stage.addChild(_fairy);
  stage.addChild(_wand);
  stage.addChild(_bee);
  _bee.x = 275;
  _bee.y = 175;

  //Initialize the timer
  _bulletTimer = new Timer(500);
  _bulletTimer.addEventListener
    (TimerEvent.TIMER, bulletTimerHandler);

  //Hide the mouse
  Mouse.hide();

  //Add the event listeners
  stage.addEventListener
   (Event.ENTER_FRAME, enterFrameHandler);
  stage.addEventListener
   (MouseEvent.MOUSE_DOWN, mouseDownHandler);
}
private function setupTextFields():void
{
```

```
          //Set the text format object
          _format.font = "Helvetica";
          _format.size = 44;
          _format.color = 0x000000;
          _format.align = TextFormatAlign.CENTER;

          //Configure the fairy's score  text field
          _fairyScoreDisplay.defaultTextFormat = _format;
          _fairyScoreDisplay.autoSize = TextFieldAutoSize.CENTER;
          _fairyScoreDisplay.border = false;
          _fairyScoreDisplay.text = "0";

          //Display and position the fairy's score text field
          stage.addChild(_fairyScoreDisplay);
          _fairyScoreDisplay.x = 180;
          _fairyScoreDisplay.y = 21;

          //Configure the bee's score  text field
          _beeScoreDisplay.defaultTextFormat = _format;
          _beeScoreDisplay.autoSize = TextFieldAutoSize.CENTER;
          _beeScoreDisplay.border = false;
          _beeScoreDisplay.text = "0";

          //Display and position the bee's score text field
          stage.addChild(_beeScoreDisplay);
          _beeScoreDisplay.x = 550;
          _beeScoreDisplay.y = 21;
      }
      private function enterFrameHandler(event:Event):void
      {
        moveFairy();
        moveBee();
        moveStars();
        moveBullets();
      }
      private function moveBullets():void
      {
        //Move the bullets
        for(var i:int = 0; i < _bullets.length; i++)
        {
          var bullet:GameObject = _bullets[i];
          bullet.x += bullet.vx;
          bullet.y += bullet.vy;

          //check the bullet's stage boundaries
          if (bullet.y < 0
          || bullet.x < 0
          || bullet.x > stage.stageWidth
          || bullet.y > stage.stageHeight)
          {
            //Remove the bullet from the stage
            stage.removeChild(bullet);
```

```
      bullet = null;
      _bullets.splice(i,1);
      i--;
    }
    //Check for a collision with the fairy
    if(bullet != null
    && bullet.hitTestObject(_fairy))
    {
      //Update the score, the score display
      //and remove the bullet
      _beeScore++;
      _beeScoreDisplay.text = String(_beeScore);
      stage.removeChild(bullet);
      bullet = null;
      _bullets.splice(i,1);
      i--;
    }
  }
}
private function moveStars():void
{
  //Move the stars
  for(var i:int = 0; i < _stars.length; i++)
  {
    var star:GameObject = _stars[i];
    star.x += star.vx;
    star.y += star.vy;

    //check the star's stage boundaries
    if (star.y < 0
    || star.x < 0
    || star.x > stage.stageWidth
    || star.y > stage.stageHeight)
    {
      //Remove the star from the stage
      stage.removeChild(star);
      star = null;
      _stars.splice(i,1);
      i--;
    }
    //Check for a collision with the bee
    if(star != null
    && star.hitTestObject(_bee))
    {
      //Update the score, the score display
      //and remove the bullet
      _fairyScore++;
      _fairyScoreDisplay.text = String(_fairyScore);
      stage.removeChild(star);
      star = null;
      _stars.splice(i,1);
      i--;
```

```
      }
    }
  }
  private function moveBee():void
  {
    //Get the target object
    var target_X:Number = _fairy.x;
    var target_Y:Number = _fairy.y;

    //Calculate the distance between the target and the bee
    var vx:Number = target_X - _bee.x;
    var vy:Number = target_Y - _bee.y;

    var distance:Number = Math.sqrt(vx * vx + vy * vy);
    if (distance <= RANGE)
    {
      //Find out how much to move
      var move_X:Number = TURN_SPEED * vx / distance;
      var move_Y:Number = TURN_SPEED * vy / distance;

      //Increase the bee's velocity
      _bee.vx += move_X;
      _bee.vy += move_Y;

      //Find the total distance to move
      var moveDistance:Number
        = Math.sqrt(_bee.vx * _bee.vx + _bee.vy * _bee.vy);

      //Apply easing
      _bee.vx = SPEED * _bee.vx / moveDistance;
      _bee.vy = SPEED * _bee.vy / moveDistance;

      //Rotate towards the bee towards the target
      //Find the angle in radians
      _beeAngle = Math.atan2(_bee.vy, _bee.vx);

      //Convert the radians to degrees to rotate
      //the bee correctly
      _bee.rotation = _beeAngle * 180 / Math.PI + 90;

      //Start the bullet timer
      _bulletTimer.start();
    }
    else
    {
      _bulletTimer.stop();
    }

    //Apply friction
    _bee.vx *= FRICTION;
    _bee.vy *= FRICTION;
```

```
  //Move the bee
  _bee.x += _bee.vx;
  _bee.y += _bee.vy;
}
private function moveFairy():void
{
  //Find the angle between the center of the
  //fairy and the mouse
  _angle
  = Math.atan2
    (
       _fairy.y - stage.mouseY,
       _fairy.x - stage.mouseX
     );

  //Move the wand around the fairy
  var radius:int = -50;
  _wand.x = _fairy.x + (radius * Math.cos(_angle));
  _wand.y = _fairy.y + (radius * Math.sin(_angle));

  //Figure out the distance between the
  //mouse and the center of the fairy
  var vx:Number = stage.mouseX - _fairy.x;
  var vy:Number = stage.mouseY - _fairy.y;
  var distance:Number = Math.sqrt(vx * vx + vy * vy);

  //Move the fairy if it's more than 1 pixel away from the mouse
  if (distance >= 1)
  {
    _fairy.x += vx * EASING;
    _fairy.y += vy * EASING;
  }
}

//Let the bee fire bullets using a timer
private function bulletTimerHandler(event:TimerEvent):void
{
  //Create a bullet and add it to the stage
  var bulletImage:DisplayObject = new BulletImage();
  var bullet:GameObject = new GameObject(bulletImage);
  stage.addChild(bullet);

  //Set the bullet's starting position
  var radius:int = 30;
  bullet.x = _bee.x + (radius * Math.cos(_beeAngle));
  bullet.y = _bee.y + (radius * Math.sin(_beeAngle));

  //Set the bullet's velocity based on the angle
  bullet.vx = Math.cos(_beeAngle) * 5 + _bee.vx;
  bullet.vy = Math.sin(_beeAngle) * 5 + _bee.vy;

  //Push the bullet into the _bullets array
```

```
      _bullets.push(bullet);

      //Find a random start time for the next bullet
      var randomFireTime:Number
        = Math.round(Math.random() * 1000) + 200;
      _bulletTimer.delay = randomFireTime;
    }

    //Let Button Fairy fire stars when the mouse is clicked
    private function mouseDownHandler(event:MouseEvent):void
    {
      //Create a star and add it to the stage
      var starImage:DisplayObject = new StarImage();
      var star:GameObject = new GameObject(starImage);
      stage.addChild(star);

      //Set the star's starting position
      //to the wand's position
      star.x = _wand.x;
      star.y = _wand.y;

      //Set the star's velocity based
      //on the angle between the center of
      //the fairy and the mouse
      star.vx = Math.cos(_angle) * -7;
      star.vy = Math.sin(_angle) * -7;

      //Push the star into the _stars array
      _stars.push(star);
    }
  }
}
```

As I mentioned, the important thing to keep aware of in this code is that the loops that check for collisions between the projectiles and the game objects have to make sure that the projectile hasn't already been removed from the game earlier, if it had crossed a stage boundary. That's why the `if` statement that checks for a collision also has to make sure that the object isn't `null`.

```
if(bullet != null
&& bullet.hitTestObject(_fairy))
{…
```

This is just a small technical detail to take care of, but will ensure that your game doesn't generate any runtime errors while it's playing.

Flash animation and publishing your game

Most of this book has been about writing the computer code you need to know to make video games. That's been the hardest part, but there's much more that you can and should do with your games besides just program them. How can you easily create animated objects for your games, and how can you publish your game after you've created it? You'll find out how to do both these things in the bonus chapter "Flash

Animation and Publishing Your Game" that you'll find in the book's download package. You'll learn how to use Flash Professional software to quickly make game animations that you can control using AS3.0 code. In addition, if you want to make games for mobile phones and tablets, you'll find out how to use Flash Builder to publish your games to those platforms.

Summary

Hey, is the book finished already? It is, but it seemed like all the fun was only just starting! If you've reached this last section in the book, congratulate yourself: You're a game designer! With the skills you've acquired throughout this book, there are few game design scenarios that you won't be able to approach with confidence.

However, if you're like everyone else who's ever started learning game design, you'll find that the desire to learn more is insatiable. Although you've accomplished so much already, there's a great universe of learning ahead of you. Here's a quick roundup of some of the areas you might want to explore:

- *Adobe's online help documentation:* Adobe maintains excellent online documents detailing most aspects of AS3.0 programming. You can access these documents by pointing your web browser to Adobe's ActionScript Technology Center: `www.adobe.com/devnet/actionscript.html`. There you'll find links to the ActionScript 3 Developer's Guide and ActionScript 3 Reference for the Flash Platform. I've made numerous references to sections of these documents throughout this book, and they remain the most comprehensive primary source for all things Flash and AS3.0. Although many of the topics they deal with and the approaches they take are reasonably advanced, they should match your current level of ability. Spend some time going through some of the hundreds of articles and you're sure to find great food to fuel your developing programming skills.

- *3D:* With the release of Flash Player 11 and Stage 3D, Flash has become a superb platform for building interactive 3D worlds and games. You can find out how to program 3D games with AS3.0 at Adobe's Stage 3D web site here: `www.adobe.com/devnet/flashplayer/stage3d.html`. There are some 3D game engines you can use to help you create 3D games with AS3.0 and Flash: Alternativa, Flare3D, Away 3D, and Adobe's own Proscenium. You can also use Stage 3D to make 2D games with full access to the computer or mobile devices Graphics Processing Unit (GPU) for great performance. The easy-to-use Starling framework can help you do this, as well as ND2D.

- *Physics:* There are some excellent packages of classes available for doing precise physics simulations with AS3.0. They include Box2D, Motor2, APE, Foam, Flave, World Construction Kit, JigLib, and Glaze.

- *Tile-based games:* In this style of game design, all objects on the stage are assigned to squares in a grid. The code then creates an abstract model of the game behind the scenes in arrays, and that model is used to update the objects on the stage. Board games, strategy games, and certain puzzle games really benefit from the tile-based approach. Tile-based games run very efficiently, use relatively little CPU power and memory, and are easy to extend if you want to add new game levels. Because of this, the tile-based approach also works well for platform and adventure games.

- *Vector math and geometry:* If you want to create games that involve some degree of physics simulation, it is really beneficial to spend a bit of time learning some vector math and 2D geometry. Even if you don't think you're good at math, give it a try—you might just surprise yourself. You can immediately apply what you learn to your games.

- *Saving game data:* If you want to save some data in your game (such as a score or a game level) so the player can quit the game and continue it later, you need to create a *shared object*. This is covered in detail in the section "Storing local data" in the chapter "Networking and Communication" from Adobe's online document *Programming ActionScript 3.0 for Flash*.

- *Multiplayer games:* It's always more fun to play games with friends. To make multiplayer games, you need to store game data on a server on the Web so that other players can access that data to update their own game screens. There are quite a few ways you can do this, but all require some research into additional "server- side technologies." Your Flash games will be able to communicate with these server-side technologies, but to implement most of them you'll need to learn new programming languages such as PHP or Java. Do a bit of research into Java socket servers such as SmartFoxServer, ElectroServer, and Pulse, among many others. (Java is very closely related to AS3.0, so you won't find it completely unfamiliar.) You can create a high-score list for your games using PHP, and you can store game data using a MySQL database. You can avoid Java and PHP directly by storing game data in a content management system (CMS) and accessing the data in Flash using XML. Adobe also provides its own Flash Media Servers. The Media Development Server is free, and although limited, is a great way to get your feet wet with multiplayer technologies in a familiar environment. As you can see, there's a lot to learn! But it's all well worth the time you'll put into it.

But of course, this book isn't really finished—you're only halfway through. *Advanced Game Design with Flash* picks up where this book leaves off, and covers all the advanced techniques you'll need take your skills to a truly professional level.

As every game designer knows, making games is much more fun than playing them. Like an artist who's just learned how to mix paints and sketch out a few simple scenes, a bit of practice is all you'll need, and you'll be well on your way to creating that masterpiece. You've now got a solid foundation in game design with Flash and AS3.0—go and make some great games!

Index

L

M

CPSIA information can be obtained at www.ICGtesting.com
Printed in the USA
LVOW110846210112

264944LV00005BA/1/P